Globalization and the Challenges of a New Century

A READER

Edited by **Patrick O'Meara,
Howard D. Mehlinger,
and Matthew Krain**

Roxana Ma Newman, Managing Editor

INDIANA UNIVERSITY PRESS

BLOOMINGTON AND INDIANAPOLIS

This book is a publication of
Indiana University Press
601 North Morton Street
Bloomington, IN 47404-3797 USA

http://www.indiana.edu/~iupress
Telephone orders 800-842-6796
Fax orders 812-855-7931
Orders by e-mail iuporder@indiana.edu

The paper used in this publication meets the minimum requirements
of American National Standard for Information Sciences—
Permanence of Paper for Printed Library Materials, ANSI
Z39.48-1984.

MANUFACTURED IN THE UNITED STATES OF AMERICA

Library of Congress Cataloging-in-Publication Data

Globalization and the challenges of a new century : a reader / edited by Patrick
    O'Meara, Howard D. Mehlinger, and Matthew Krain.
        p.   cm.
    Includes bibliographical references and index.
    ISBN 0-253-33658-9 (cloth : alk. paper). — ISBN 0-253-21355-X (pbk. :
alk. paper)
    1. World politics—1989– I. O'Meara, Patrick. II. Mehlinger, Howard
D.   III. Krain, Matthew.
    D860.G654   2000
    909.82'9—dc21   99-37634

    1 2 3 4 5   05 04 03 02 01 00

CONTENTS

PREFACE / vii
ACKNOWLEDGMENTS / ix
INTRODUCTION / xiii

Part 1. Global Order and Disorder: Speculations   1

The Clash of Civilizations?   *Samuel P. Huntington*   3
Jihad vs. McWorld   *Benjamin R. Barber*   23
The Coming Anarchy   *Robert D. Kaplan*   34

Part 2. Global Order and Disorder: Rejoinders   61

The Summoning   *Fouad Ajami*   63
The End of Progressivism: A Search for New Goals   *Eisuke Sakakibara*   71
The Myth of Global Ethnic Conflict   *John R. Bowen*   79

Part 3. Redrawing the Map?
The New Nature of National Borders   91

The Rise of the Region State   *Kenichi Ohmae*   93
Has Globalization Created a Borderless World?   *Janet Ceglowski*   101
The Real New World Order   *Anne-Marie Slaughter*   112

Part 4. Conflict and Security in a New World Order   123

The Politics of Globalization   *Kofi Annan*   125
Redefining Security: The New Global Schisms   *Michael T. Klare*   131
Organised Chaos: Not the New World We Ordered   *David Keen*   140
Postmodern Terrorism   *Walter Laqueur*   149

Part 5. Globalization and the Evolution of Democracy   159

The End of History?   *Francis Fukuyama*   161
The Rise of Illiberal Democracy   *Fareed Zakaria*   181
Was Democracy Just a Moment?   *Robert D. Kaplan*   196

Part 6. The New Global Economy   215

International Economics: Unlocking the Mysteries of Globalization
  Jeffrey Sachs   217
Sense and Nonsense in the Globalization Debate   *Dani Rodrik*   227
The Nuke of the 90's   *Roger C. Altman*   240
New Rules: The American Economy in the Next Century
  Lester C. Thurow   244
The Gender and Labor Politics of Postmodernity   *Aihwa Ong*   253
Neo-Liberalism and Globalization
  Tupac Amaru Revolutionary Movement   282

Part 7. Doing Business in the Information Age   287

The Dawn of the E-Lance Economy
  Thomas W. Malone and Robert J. Laubacher   289
Electronic Cash and the End of National Markets   *Stephen J. Kobrin*   300
Local Memoirs of a Global Manager   *Gurcharan Das*   309

Part 8. Forecasting the Future:
Innovations, Technology, Winners, and Losers   321

Preparing for the 21st Century: Winners and Losers   *Paul Kennedy*   323
Emerging Technologies: What's Ahead for 2001–2030
  William E. Halal, Michael D. Kull, and Ann Leffmann   355
The Promise of Genetics
  Joseph F. Coates, John B. Mahaffie, and Andy Hines   368

Part 9. "Think Global, Act Local": The Environment   375

Growth and the Environment: Allies or Foes?
  Vinod Thomas and Tamara Belt   377
A Special Moment in History   *Bill McKibben*   383
The Exploding Cities of the Developing World   *Eugene Linden*   406

Part 10. An Emerging Global Culture?   417

Four Faces of Global Culture   *Peter L. Berger*   419
English Rules   *Madelaine Drohan and Alan Freeman*   428
The New Linguistic Order   *Joshua A. Fishman*   435
In Praise of Cultural Imperialism?   *David Rothkopf*   443
Culture Wars   *The Economist*   454

Resource Bibliography   *Robert Goehlert and Anthony Stamatoplos*   461

CONTRIBUTORS / 483
INDEX / 487

PREFACE

This book is one of two volumes resulting from a national conference, "International Education in American Colleges and Universities: Prospect and Retrospect," held in Washington, D.C. in April
1998 to celebrate the 40th Anniversary of Title VI of the Higher
Education Act (formerly Title VI of the National Defense Education Act). In a special message read at the opening of the conference, President Bill Clinton recognized the important contribution
of Title VI in encouraging the free exchange of ideas and knowledge and in promoting international understanding and world
peace. United States Secretary of Education Richard Riley's letter
addressed to the conference participants praised Title VI's successful partnership between the federal government and American
colleges and universities.

Indiana University received support from the United States
Department of Education, International Education and Graduate
Program Service, to conduct the conference and to publish related
materials. This first volume, *Globalization and the Challenges of a
New Century: A Reader,* is intended for university classroom use.
A companion volume, *Changing Perspectives on International
Education* (Indiana University Press, in press), edited by Patrick
O'Meara, Howard D. Mehlinger, and Roxana Ma Newman, is
aimed at key university administrators and planners concerned
with new directions affecting the future of international studies.

ACKNOWLEDGMENTS

Grateful acknowledgment is made to the following authors and sources for permission to reprint material in this anthology:

"The Summoning," by Fouad Ajami, from *Foreign Affairs*, vol. 72, no. 4 (1993). Copyright © 1993 by the Council on Foreign Relations, Inc. Reprinted with the permission of the publisher.

"The Nuke of the 90's," by Roger C. Altman, from the *New York Times Magazine*, March 1, 1998. Copyright © 1998 by Roger C. Altman. Reprinted with the permission of the author.

"The Politics of Globalization," by the Hon. Kofi Annan. Address delivered to Harvard University, sponsored by the Harvard Academy for International and Area Studies, Cambridge, Massachusetts, 17 September 1998. The speech appears on the Web site http://data.fas.harvard.edu/cfia/annan.htm.

"Jihad vs. McWorld," by Benjamin R. Barber. Published originally in the March 1992 issue of *The Atlantic Monthly*. Revised as the introduction to *Jihad vs. McWorld* (Ballantine Paperback, 1996), a volume that discusses and extends the themes of the original article. Copyright © 1992 by Benjamin R. Barber. Reprinted with the permission of the author.

"Four Faces of Global Culture," by Peter L. Berger, from *The National Interest*, no. 49 (Fall 1997), Washington, D.C. Copyright © 1997 by *The National Interest*. Reprinted with the permission of the publisher.

"The Myth of Global Ethnic Conflict," by John R. Bowen, from *Journal of Democracy*, vol. 7, no. 4 (1996), pp. 3–14. Copyright © 1996 by The Johns Hopkins University Press and National Endowment for Democracy. Reprinted with the permission of the publisher.

"Has Globalization Created a Borderless World?" by Janet Ceglowski, from *Business Review*, March/April (1998). Copyright © 1998 by the Federal Reserve Bank of Philadelphia. Reprinted with the permission of the publisher.

"The Promise of Genetics," by Joseph F. Coates, John B. Mahaffie, and Andy Hines, from *The Futurist* (September-October 1997). Copyright © 1997 by the

World Future Society. Reprinted with permission of the publisher. This article draws upon the authors' book, *2025: Scenarios of U.S. and Global Society Reshaped by Science and Technology* (Oakhill Press, 1997).

"Local Memoirs of a Global Manager," by Gurcharan Das, from *Harvard Business Review* (March/April 1993). Copyright © 1993 by the President and Fellows of Harvard College, all rights reserved. Reprinted with the permission of the publisher.

"English Rules," by Madelaine Drohan and Alan Freeman, from *The Globe and Mail* (Toronto), 27 July 1997. Copyright © 1997 by *The Globe and Mail*. Reprinted with the permission of the publisher.

"The New Linguistic Order," by Joshua A. Fishman, from *Foreign Policy* 113 (Winter 1998/99). Copyright © 1998 by the Carnegie Endowment for International Peace. Reprinted with the permission of the publisher.

"The End of History?" by Francis Fukuyama, from *The National Interest* (Summer 1989). Copyright © 1989 by Francis Fukuyama. Reprinted with the permission of International Creative Management Inc. and the author.

"Culture Wars," editorial from *The Economist,* September 12, 1998, pp. 97–99. Copyright © 1998 by The Economist Newspaper Group, Inc. Reprinted with permission. Further reproduction prohibited. www.economist.com

"Resource Bibliography," by Robert Goehlert and Anthony Stamatoplos. This bibliography is an abridged and revised version of *International and Area Studies Resources: A Selected Guide,* prepared for the Title VI 40th Anniversary Conference, "International Education in American Colleges and Universities," April 16–17, 1998, Washington, D.C. Copyright © 1998 by Indiana University. Reproduced with the permission of the Office of International Programs, Indiana University.

"Emerging Technologies: What's Ahead for 2001–2030," by William E. Halal, Michael D. Kull, and Ann Leffmann, from *The Futurist* (November-December 1997). Copyright © 1997 by the World Future Society. Reprinted with permission of the publisher.

"The Clash of Civilizations?" by Samuel P. Huntington, from *Foreign Affairs,* vol. 72, no. 3 (1993). Copyright © 1993 by the Council on Foreign Relations, Inc. Reprinted with the permission of the publisher.

"The Coming Anarchy," by Robert D. Kaplan, from *The Atlantic Monthly* (February 1994). Copyright © 1994 by Robert D. Kaplan. Reprinted with the permission of the author.

"Was Democracy Just a Moment?" by Robert D. Kaplan, from *The Atlantic Monthly* (December 1997). Copyright © 1997 by Robert D. Kaplan. Reprinted with the permission of the author.

"Organised Chaos: Not the New World We Ordered," by David Keen, from *The*

World Today (January 1996), pp. 14–17. Copyright © 1996 by *The World Today,* a publication of the Royal Institute of International Affairs. Reprinted with the permission of the publisher.

"Preparing for the 21st Century: Winners and Losers," by Paul Kennedy, from *The New York Review of Books,* February 11, 1993, pp. 32–44. Copyright © 1993 by Paul Kennedy. The article was drawn from *Preparing for the 21st Century* by Paul Kennedy (Random House, 1993). Reprinted by permission of Random House, Inc.

"Redefining Security: The New Global Schisms," by Michael T. Klare, from *Current History* (November 1996). Copyright © 1996 by Current History, Inc. Reprinted with the permission of the publisher.

"Electronic Cash and the End of National Markets," by Stephen J. Kobrin, from *Foreign Policy* 107 (Summer 1997). Copyright © 1997 by the Carnegie Endowment for International Peace. Reprinted with the permission of the publisher.

"Postmodern Terrorism," by Walter Laqueur, from *Foreign Affairs,* vol. 75, no. 5 (1996). Copyright © 1996 by the Council on Foreign Relations, Inc. Reprinted with the permission of the publisher.

"The Exploding Cities of the Developing World," by Eugene Linden, from *Foreign Affairs,* vol. 75, no. 1 (1996). Copyright © 1996 by the Council on Foreign Relations, Inc. Reprinted with the permission of the publisher.

"The Dawn of the E-Lance Economy," by Thomas W. Malone and Robert J. Laubacher, from *Harvard Business Review* (September/October 1998). Copyright © 1998 by the President and Fellows of Harvard College, all rights reserved. Reprinted with the permission of the publisher.

"A Special Moment in History," by Bill McKibben, from *The Atlantic Monthly* (May 1998). Copyright © 1998 by Bill McKibben. Reprinted with the permission of the author.

"The Rise of the Region State," by Kenichi Ohmae, from *Foreign Affairs,* vol. 72, no. 2 (1993). Copyright © 1993 by the Council on Foreign Relations, Inc. Reprinted with the permission of the publisher.

"The Gender and Labor Politics of Postmodernity," by Aihwa Ong, from the *Annual Review of Anthropology,* vol. 20 (1991). Copyright © 1991 by Annual Reviews. Reprinted with the permission of the publisher.

"Sense and Nonsense in the Globalization Debate," by Dani Rodrik, from *Foreign Policy* 107 (Summer 1997). Copyright © 1997 by the Carnegie Endowment for International Peace. Reprinted with the permission of the publisher.

"In Praise of Cultural Imperialism?" by David Rothkopf, from *Foreign Policy* 107 (Summer 1997). Copyright © 1997 by the Carnegie Endowment for International Peace. Reprinted with the permission of the publisher.

"International Economics: Unlocking the Mysteries of Globalization," by Jeffrey Sachs, from *Foreign Policy* 110 (Spring 1998). Copyright © 1998 by the Carnegie Endowment for International Peace. Reprinted with the permission of the publisher.

"The End of Progressivism: A Search for New Goals," by Eisuke Sakakibara, from *Foreign Affairs,* vol. 74, no. 5 (1995). Copyright © 1995 by the Council on Foreign Relations, Inc. Reprinted with the permission of the publisher.

"The Real New World Order," by Anne-Marie Slaughter, from *Foreign Affairs,* vol. 76, no. 5 (1997). Copyright © 1997 by the Council on Foreign Relations, Inc. Reprinted with the permission of the publisher.

"Growth and the Environment: Allies or Foes?" by Vinod Thomas and Tamara Belt, from *Finance & Development* (June 1997). Copyright © 1997 by the International Monetary Fund and the International Bank for Reconstruction and Development/The World Bank. Reprinted with permission of the publisher.

"New Rules: The American Economy in the Next Century," by Lester C. Thurow, from the *Harvard International Review* (Winter 1997/98). Copyright © 1997 by the *Harvard International Review.* Reprinted with the permission of the publisher.

"Neo-Liberalism and Globalization," by the Tupac Amaru Revolutionary Movement. Originally appeared on the Web site http://burn.ucsd.edu/~ats/MRTA/neo-lib.htm.

"The Rise of Illiberal Democracy," by Fareed Zakaria, from *Foreign Affairs,* vol. 76, no. 6 (1997). Copyright © 1997 by the Council on Foreign Relations, Inc. Reprinted with the permission of the publisher.

INTRODUCTION

In April 1998, the 40th Anniversary of Title VI of the Higher Education Act was celebrated with a national conference in Washington, D.C. Participants acknowledged the significant contributions Title VI has made to the development of American-based human and material resources in international education, particularly those that focus on foreign areas and the languages spoken in those world areas. That these federally supported and locally developed resources were and continue to be important to meeting the nation's needs for expertise and the public's understanding of world issues and problems was well documented. The conference struck a sound balance between those who reaffirmed the centrality of the area concept to the study of international affairs and those who emphasized approaches encompassed by the term "globalization." Both approaches to the study of international affairs are reflected in the projects funded by the U.S. Department of Education's Title VI programs.

Without the solid foundation of area studies, global analysis would be difficult if not impossible. This book focuses on globalization while at the same time reaffirming the importance of the area concept. There has been considerable discussion over the use of the term "globalization," but few attempts have been made to synthesize it. Ironically, different approaches to globalization are frequently confined to a given field or discipline. Thus, for example, those concerned with the effects of economic globalization, while aware of the social or cultural implications, view it as inherently economic. A partial explanation for this might be the enormity of the topic itself. To move from the assurance and familiarity of working within a particular discipline to a more integrated approach often proves daunting.

By its very nature, globalization implies both broadening and deepening. Phenomena that once affected a particular country or region now have broader implications, and, of necessity, must include a larger set of nations or actors. What were previously considered discrete problems can now no longer be understood in isolation. Additionally, there is now great overlap between the local and the global. What happens in one particular sphere inevitably spills over into another.

The fact that we live in a globally interconnected world has become a cliché. Scholars, business leaders, and policymakers are increasingly addressing globalization in their writings and actions, yet as a field of study it is still in its infancy. Numerous conferences and a limited number of publications have begun to address its multiple implications. There is little consensus on how to approach this new field or on its guiding principles.

By bringing together a number of different perspectives, this book attempts to demonstrate the richness of the ongoing debate. The book broadens the scope of the discussion and lays the groundwork for a more interdisciplinary and collaborative dialogue. It is readily apparent from the writings included in this book that a global approach is not only timely, but mandatory.

For us the term "global" implies overarching studies that are international, inter-area, and interdisciplinary. Politics, culture, business, trade, the environment, population, conflict, and many other pressing issues and concerns are global in nature and should not be looked at through a single disciplinary lens.

Among the articles included in this reader are some of the most controversial of the past decade. In attempting to demarcate and explain the post–cold war world, the authors survey the dramatic changes in human organization, thought, and behavior that are taking place daily all over the world. Their strong convictions have often led them to take polarized stances.

In an attempt to present various perspectives on globalization, we have brought together in one place articles that have appeared in a broad range of publications. Some of them are seminal works that subsequently appeared in book form. Others were addressed to a more general audience, but we believe that they present some of the leading ideas in the field. We might have included different writings, but, in our judgment, the ones we have chosen best reflect the current thinking on globalization. In addition, while the book as a whole provides a useful guide to current thinking, the articles also stand alone and can be read individually. Because the field is so diverse, we have grouped related articles into ten parts that we believe address important aspects of the globalization debate. We hope that this juxtaposition will highlight the fundamentally different perspectives that particular authors bring to common problems.

This book is intended for a general audience interested in world affairs. Teachers and students at different levels in higher education will also find it useful. For example, the text might be equally effective as an introduction as well as in a capstone course in the field of international studies. The ten sections into which we have arranged the articles are suggestive rather than fixed. Instructors will have the flexibility to choose from among different articles in teaching their own courses. In particular, we hope that linkages will be made between the global and the local. The study of globalization may appear to be challenging and daunting. By infusing the effects of globalization into a local context, teachers and students can bring immediacy to some of the most challenging issues of our time.

The articles and the bibliography should stimulate many discussions among readers. World Wide Web and Internet sites have also been included to enable students and teachers to have better access to the vast resources now available on line. By including these sites, we hope readers will begin to harness the power of globalization.

Patrick O'Meara, Indiana University
Howard D. Mehlinger, Indiana University
Matthew Krain, The College of Wooster

Global Order and Disorder: Speculations

Three of the most controversial contemporary writers on global issues, Samuel P. Huntington, Benjamin R. Barber, and Robert D. Kaplan, present contrasting views of the future. Each essay outlines different expectations of future power distributions and relationships between state and society. These articles were selected because they are the most widely read and have stirred up worldwide debate with their statements, and because they resonate with many of the issues that trouble scholars and concerned citizens all over the world. Huntington believes that world politics is entering a new era in which the source of conflict will be based on cultural divisions rather than on ideology or economic forces. He emphasizes that conflict will occur along fault lines that divide civilizations. Barber sees the simultaneous forces of global disintegration and global homogenization as the primary sources of future conflict. What he refers to as the forces of "Jihad and McWorld" operate with equal strength in opposite directions, and ultimately, his guess is that "globalization will vanquish retribalization." He charts a middle course between the "dull realities" of McWorld and the brutalities of jihad in the form of regional economic communities. For Kaplan, the disintegration of the state in Africa is a metaphor for what is likely to happen in the rest of the world. Scarcity, crime, ethnic conflict, overpopulation, and disease are destroying what he refers to as the "social fabric of our planet."

The Clash of Civilizations?

Samuel P. Huntington

The Next Pattern of Conflict

World politics is entering a new phase, and intellectuals have not hesitated to proliferate visions of what it will be—the end of history, the return of traditional rivalries between nation states, and the decline of the nation state from the conflicting pulls of tribalism and globalism, among others. Each of these visions catches aspects of the emerging reality. Yet they all miss a crucial, indeed a central, aspect of what global politics is likely to be in the coming years.

It is my hypothesis that the fundamental source of conflict in this new world will not be primarily ideological or primarily economic. The great divisions among humankind and the dominating source of conflict will be cultural. Nation states will remain the most powerful actors in world affairs, but the principal conflicts of global politics will occur between nations and groups of different civilizations. The clash of civilizations will dominate global politics. The fault lines between civilizations will be the battle lines of the future.

Conflict between civilizations will be the latest phase in the evolution of conflict in the modern world. For a century and a half after the emergence of the modern international system with the Peace of Westphalia, the conflicts of the Western world were largely among princes—emperors, absolute monarchs and constitutional monarchs attempting to expand their bureaucracies, their armies,

Reprinted with permission from *Foreign Affairs,* Vol. 72, No. 3, 1993. © 1993 by the Council on Foreign Relations, Inc.

their mercantilist economic strength and, most important, the territory they ruled. In the process they created nation states, and beginning with the French Revolution the principal lines of conflict were between nations rather than princes. In 1793, as R. R. Palmer put it, "The wars of kings were over; the wars of peoples had begun." This nineteenth-century pattern lasted until the end of World War I. Then, as a result of the Russian Revolution and the reaction against it, the conflict of nations yielded to the conflict of ideologies, first among communism, fascism-Nazism and liberal democracy, and then between communism and liberal democracy. During the Cold War, this latter conflict became embodied in the struggle between the two superpowers, neither of which was a nation state in the classical European sense and each of which defined its identity in terms of its ideology.

These conflicts between princes, nation states and ideologies were primarily conflicts within Western civilization, "Western civil wars," as William Lind has labeled them. This was as true of the Cold War as it was of the world wars and the earlier wars of the seventeenth, eighteenth and nineteenth centuries. With the end of the Cold War, international politics moves out of its Western phase, and its centerpiece becomes the interaction between the West and non-Western civilizations and among non-Western civilizations. In the politics of civilizations, the peoples and governments of non-Western civilizations no longer remain the objects of history as targets of Western colonialism but join the West as movers and shapers of history.

The Nature of Civilizations

During the Cold War the world was divided into the First, Second and Third Worlds. Those divisions are no longer relevant. It is far more meaningful now to group countries not in terms of their political or economic systems or in terms of their level of economic development but rather in terms of their culture and civilization.

What do we mean when we talk of a civilization? A civilization is a cultural entity. Villages, regions, ethnic groups, nationalities, religious groups, all have distinct cultures at different levels of cultural heterogeneity. The culture of a village in southern Italy may be different from that of a village in northern Italy, but both will share in a common Italian culture that distinguishes them from German villages. European communities, in turn, will share cultural features that distinguish them from Arab or Chinese communities. Arabs, Chinese and Westerners, however, are not part of any broader cultural entity. They constitute civilizations. A civilization is thus the highest cultural grouping of people and the broadest level of cultural identity people have short of that which distinguishes humans from other species. It is defined both by common objective elements, such as language, history, religion, customs, institutions, and by the subjective self-identification of people. People have levels of identity: a resident of Rome may define himself with varying degrees of intensity as a Roman, an Italian, a Catholic, a Christian, a European, a Westerner. The civilization to which he belongs is the broadest level of identification with which he intensely identifies. People can and do redefine their identities and, as a result, the composition and boundaries of civilizations change.

Civilizations may involve a large number of people, as with China ("a civilization pretending to be a state," as Lucian Pye put it), or a very small number of people, such as the Anglophone Caribbean. A civilization may include several nation states, as is the case with Western, Latin American and Arab civilizations, or only one, as is the case with Japanese civilization. Civilizations obviously blend and overlap, and may include subcivilizations. Western civilization has two major variants, European and North American, and Islam has its Arab, Turkic and Malay subdivisions. Civilizations are nonetheless meaningful entities, and while the lines between them are seldom sharp, they are real. Civilizations are dynamic; they rise and fall; they divide and merge. And, as any student of history knows, civilizations disappear and are buried in the sands of time.

Westerners tend to think of nation states as the principal actors in global affairs. They have been that, however, for only a few centuries. The broader reaches of human history have been the history of civilizations. In *A Study of History,* Arnold Toynbee identified 21 major civilizations; only six of them exist in the contemporary world.

Why Civilizations Will Clash

Civilization identity will be increasingly important in the future, and the world will be shaped in large measure by the interactions among seven or eight major civilizations. These include Western, Confucian, Japanese, Islamic, Hindu, Slavic-Orthodox, Latin American and possibly African civilization. The most important conflicts of the future will occur along the cultural fault lines separating these civilizations from one another.

Why will this be the case?

First, differences among civilizations are not only real; they are basic. Civilizations are differentiated from each other by history, language, culture, tradition and, most important, religion. The people of different civilizations have different views on the relations between God and man, the individual and the group, the citizen and the state, parents and children, husband and wife, as well as differing views of the relative importance of rights and responsibilities, liberty and authority, equality and hierarchy. These differences are the product of centuries. They will not soon disappear. They are far more fundamental than differences among political ideologies and political regimes. Differences do not necessarily mean conflict, and conflict does not necessarily mean violence. Over the centuries, however, differences among civilizations have generated the most prolonged and the most violent conflicts.

Second, the world is becoming a smaller place. The interactions between peoples of different civilizations are increasing; these increasing interactions intensify civilization consciousness and awareness of differences between civilizations and commonalities within civilizations. North African immigration to France generates hostility among Frenchmen and at the same time increased receptivity to immigration by "good" European Catholic Poles. Americans react far more negatively to Japanese investment than to larger investments from Canada and European countries. Similarly, as Donald Horowitz has pointed out, "An Ibo may be . . . an Owerri Ibo or an Onitsha Ibo in what was the Eastern region of Nigeria. In Lagos, he is simply an Ibo. In London, he is a Nigerian. In New York, he is an African." The interactions among peoples of different civilizations enhance the civilization-consciousness of people that, in turn, invigorates differences and animosities stretching or thought to stretch back deep into history.

Third, the processes of economic modernization and social change throughout the world are separating people from longstanding local identities. They also weaken the nation state as a source of identity. In much of the world religion has moved in to fill this gap, often in the form of movements that are labeled "fundamentalist." Such movements are found in Western Christianity, Judaism, Buddhism and Hinduism, as well as in Islam. In most countries and most religions the people active in fundamentalist movements are young, college-educated, middle-class technicians, professionals and business persons. The "unsecularization of the world," George Weigel has remarked, "is one of the dominant social facts of life in the late twentieth century." The revival of religion, "la revanche de Dieu," as Gilles Kepel labeled it, provides a basis for identity and commitment that transcends national boundaries and unites civilizations.

Fourth, the growth of civilization-consciousness is enhanced by the dual role of the West. On the one hand, the West is at a peak of power. At the same time, however, and perhaps as a result, a return to the roots phenomenon is occurring among non-Western civilizations. Increasingly one hears references to trends toward a turning inward and "Asianization" in Japan, the end of the Nehru legacy and the "Hinduization" of India, the failure of Western ideas of socialism and nationalism and hence "re-Islamization" of the Middle East, and now a debate over Westernization versus Russianization in Boris Yeltsin's country. A West at the peak of its power confronts non-Wests that increasingly have the desire, the will and the resources to shape the world in non-Western ways.

In the past, the elites of non-Western societies were usually the people who were most involved with the West, had been educated at Oxford, the Sorbonne or Sandhurst, and had absorbed Western attitudes and values. At the same time, the populace in non-Western countries often remained deeply imbued with the indigenous culture. Now, however, these relationships are being reversed. A de-Westernization and indigenization of elites is occurring in many non-Western countries at the same time that Western, usually American, cultures, styles and habits become more popular among the mass of the people.

Fifth, cultural characteristics and differences are less mutable and hence less easily compromised and resolved than political and economic ones. In the former Soviet Union, communists can become democrats, the rich can become poor and the poor rich, but Russians cannot become Estonians and Azeris cannot become Armenians. In class and ideological conflicts, the key question was "Which side are you on?" and people could and did choose sides and change sides. In conflicts between civilizations, the question is "What are you?" That is a given that cannot be changed. And as we know, from Bosnia to the Caucasus to the Sudan, the wrong answer to that question can mean a bullet in the head. Even more than ethnicity, religion discriminates sharply and exclusively among people. A person can be half-French and half-Arab and simultaneously even a citizen of two countries. It is more difficult to be half-Catholic and half-Muslim.

Finally, economic regionalism is increasing. The proportions of total trade that were intraregional rose between 1980 and 1989 from 51 percent to 59 percent in Europe, 33 percent to 37 percent in East Asia, and 32 percent to 36 percent in North America. The importance of regional economic blocs is likely to continue to increase in the future. On the one hand, successful economic regionalism will reinforce civilization-consciousness. On the other hand, economic regionalism may succeed only when it is rooted in a common civilization. The European Community rests on the shared foundation of European culture and Western Christianity. The success of the North American Free Trade Area depends on the convergence now underway of Mexican, Canadian and American cultures. Japan, in contrast, faces difficulties in creating a comparable economic entity in East Asia because Japan is a society and civilization unique to itself. However strong the trade and investment links Japan may develop with other East Asian countries, its cultural differences with those countries inhibit and perhaps preclude its promoting regional economic integration like that in Europe and North America.

Common culture, in contrast, is clearly facilitating the rapid expansion of the economic relations between the People's Republic of China and Hong Kong, Taiwan, Singapore and the overseas Chinese communities in other Asian countries. With the Cold War over, cultural commonalities increasingly overcome ideological differences, and mainland China and Taiwan move closer together. If cultural commonality is a prerequisite for economic integration, the principal East Asian economic bloc of the future is likely to be centered on China. This bloc is, in fact, already coming into existence. As Murray Weidenbaum has observed,

> Despite the current Japanese dominance of the region, the Chinese-based economy of Asia is rapidly emerging as a new epicenter for industry, commerce and finance. This strategic area contains substantial amounts of technology and manufacturing capability (Taiwan), outstanding entrepreneurial, marketing and services acumen (Hong Kong), a fine communications network (Singapore), a tremendous pool of financial capital (all three), and very large endowments of land, resources and labor (mainland China). . . . From Guangzhou to Singapore, from Kuala Lumpur to Manila, this influential network—often based on extensions of the traditional clans—has been described as the backbone of the East Asian economy.[1]

Culture and religion also form the basis of the Economic Cooperation Organization, which brings together ten non-Arab Muslim countries: Iran, Pakistan, Turkey, Azerbaijan, Kazakhstan, Kyrgyzstan, Turkmenistan, Tadjikistan, Uzbekistan and Afghanistan. One impetus to the revival and expansion of this organization, founded originally in the 1960s by Turkey, Pakistan and Iran, is the realization by the leaders of several of these countries that they had no chance of admission to the European Community. Similarly, Caricom, the Central American Common Market and Mercosur rest on common cultural foundations. Efforts to build a broader Caribbean-Central American economic entity bridging the Anglo-Latin divide, however, have to date failed.

As people define their identity in ethnic and religious terms, they are likely to see an "us" versus "them" relation existing between themselves and people of different ethnicity or religion. The end of ideologically defined states in Eastern Europe and the former Soviet Union permits traditional ethnic identities and animosities to come to the fore. Differences in culture and religion create differences over policy issues, ranging from human rights to immigration to trade and commerce to the environment. Geographical propinquity gives rise to conflicting territorial claims from Bosnia to Mindanao. Most important, the efforts of the West to promote its values of democracy and liberalism as universal values, to maintain its military predominance and to advance its economic interests engender countering responses from other civilizations. Decreasingly able to mobilize support and form coalitions on the basis of ideology, governments and groups will increasingly attempt to mobilize support by appealing to common religion and civilization identity.

The clash of civilizations thus occurs at two levels. At the micro-level, adjacent groups along the fault lines between civilizations struggle, often violently, over the control of territory and each other. At the macro-level, states from different civilizations compete for relative military and economic power, struggle over the control of international institutions and third parties, and competitively promote their particular political and religious values.

The Fault Lines between Civilizations

The fault lines between civilizations are replacing the political and ideological boundaries of the Cold War as the flash points for crisis and bloodshed. The Cold War began when the Iron Curtain divided Europe politically and ideologically. The Cold War ended with the end of the Iron Curtain. As the ideological division of Europe has disappeared, the cultural division of Europe between Western Christianity, on the one hand, and Orthodox Christianity and Islam, on the other, has reemerged. The most significant dividing line in Europe, as William Wallace has suggested, may well be the eastern boundary of Western Christianity in the year 1500. This line runs along what are now the boundaries between Finland and Russia and between the Baltic states and Russia, cuts through Belarus and Ukraine separating the more Catholic western Ukraine from Orthodox eastern Ukraine, swings westward separating Transylvania from the rest of Romania, and then goes through Yugoslavia almost exactly along the line now separating Croatia and Slovenia from the rest of Yugoslavia. In the Balkans this line, of course, coincides with the historic boundary between the Hapsburg and Ottoman empires. The peoples to the north and west of this line are Protestant or Catholic; they shared the common experiences of European history—feudalism, the Renaissance, the Reformation, the Enlightenment, the French Revolution, the Industrial Revolution; they are generally economically better off than the peoples to the east; and they may now look forward to increasing involvement in a common European economy and to the consolidation of democratic political systems. The peoples to the east and south of this line are Orthodox or Muslim; they historically belonged to the Ottoman or Tsarist empires and were only lightly touched by the shaping events in the rest of Europe; they are generally less advanced economically; they seem much less likely to develop stable democratic political systems. The Velvet Curtain of culture has replaced the Iron Curtain of ideology as the most significant dividing line in Europe. As the events in Yugoslavia show, it is not only a line of difference; it is also at times a line of bloody conflict.

Conflict along the fault line between Western and Islamic civilizations has been going on for 1,300 years. After the founding of Islam, the Arab and Moorish surge west and north only ended at Tours in 732. From the eleventh to the thirteenth century the Crusaders attempted with temporary success to bring Christianity and Christian rule to the Holy Land. From the fourteenth to the seventeenth century, the Ottoman Turks reversed the balance, extended their sway over the Middle East and the Balkans, captured Constantinople, and twice laid siege to Vienna. In the nineteenth and early twentieth centuries as Ottoman power declined Britain, France, and Italy established Western control over most of North Africa and the Middle East.

After World War II, the West, in turn, began to retreat; the colonial empires disappeared; first Arab nationalism and then Islamic fundamentalism manifested themselves; the West became heavily dependent on the Persian Gulf countries for its energy; the oil-rich Muslim countries became money-rich and, when they wished to, weapons-rich.

Source: W. Wallace, The Transformation of Western Europe. London: Pinter, 1990. Map by Ib Ohlsson for Foreign Affairs.

Several wars occurred between Arabs and Israel (created by the West). France fought a bloody and ruthless war in Algeria for most of the 1950s; British and French forces invaded Egypt in 1956; American forces went into Lebanon in 1958; subsequently American forces returned to Lebanon, attacked Libya, and engaged in various military encounters with Iran; Arab and Islamic terrorists, supported by at least three Middle Eastern governments, employed the weapon of the weak and bombed Western planes and installations and seized Western hostages. This warfare between Arabs and the West culminated in 1990, when the United States sent a massive army to the Persian Gulf to defend some Arab countries against aggression by another. In its aftermath NATO planning is increasingly directed to potential threats and instability along its "southern tier."

This centuries-old military interaction between the West and Islam is unlikely to decline. It could become more virulent. The Gulf War left some Arabs feeling proud that Saddam Hussein had attacked Israel and stood up to the West. It also left many feeling humiliated and resentful of the West's military presence in the Persian Gulf, the West's overwhelming military dominance, and their apparent inability to shape their own destiny. Many Arab countries, in addition to the oil exporters, are reaching levels of economic and social development where autocratic forms of government become inappropriate and efforts to introduce democracy become stronger. Some openings in Arab political systems have already occurred. The principal beneficiaries of these openings have been Islamist movements. In the Arab world, in short, Western democracy strengthens anti-Western political forces. This may be a passing phenomenon, but it surely complicates relations between Islamic countries and the West.

Those relations are also complicated by demography. The spectacular population growth in Arab countries, particularly in North Africa, has led to increased migration to Western Europe. The movement within Western Europe toward minimizing internal boundaries has sharpened political sensitivities with respect to this development. In Italy, France and Germany, racism is increasingly open, and political reactions and violence against Arab and Turkish migrants have become more intense and more widespread since 1990.

On both sides the interaction between Islam and the West is seen as a clash of civilizations. The West's "next confrontation," observes M. J. Akbar, an Indian Muslim author, "is definitely going to come from the Muslim world. It is in the sweep of the Islamic nations from the Maghreb to Pakistan that the struggle for a new world order will begin." Bernard Lewis comes to a similar conclusion:

> We are facing a mood and a movement far transcending the level of issues and policies and the governments that pursue them. This is no less than a clash of civilizations—the perhaps irrational but surely historic reaction of an ancient rival against our Judeo-Christian heritage, our secular present, and the worldwide expansion of both.[2]

Historically, the other great antagonistic interaction of Arab Islamic civilization has been with the pagan, animist, and now increasingly Christian black peoples to the south. In the past, this antagonism was epitomized in the image of Arab slave dealers and black slaves. It has been reflected in the on-going civil war in the Sudan between Arabs and blacks, the fighting in Chad between Libyan-supported insurgents and the government, the tensions between Orthodox Christians and Muslims in the Horn of Africa, and the political conflicts, recurring riots and communal violence between Muslims and Christians in Nigeria. The modernization of

Africa and the spread of Christianity are likely to enhance the probability of violence along this fault line. Symptomatic of the intensification of this conflict was the Pope John Paul II's speech in Khartoum in February 1993 attacking the actions of the Sudan's Islamist government against the Christian minority there.

On the northern border of Islam, conflict has increasingly erupted between Orthodox and Muslim peoples, including the carnage of Bosnia and Sarajevo, the simmering violence between Serb and Albanian, the tenuous relations between Bulgarians and their Turkish minority, the violence between Ossetians and In-gush, the unremitting slaughter of each other by Armenians and Azeris, the tense relations between Russians and Muslims in Central Asia, and the deployment of Russian troops to protect Russian interests in the Caucasus and Central Asia. Religion reinforces the revival of ethnic identities and restimulates Russian fears about the security of their southern borders. This concern is well captured by Archie Roosevelt:

> Much of Russian history concerns the struggle between the Slavs and the Turkic peoples on their borders, which dates back to the foundation of the Russian state more than a thousand years ago. In the Slavs' millennium-long confrontation with their eastern neighbors lies the key to an under-standing not only of Russian history, but Russian character. To understand Russian realities today one has to have a concept of the great Turkic ethnic group that has preoccupied Russians through the centuries.[3]

The conflict of civilizations is deeply rooted elsewhere in Asia. The historic clash between Muslim and Hindu in the subcontinent manifests itself now not only in the rivalry between Pakistan and India but also in intensifying religious strife within India between increasingly militant Hindu groups and India's substantial Muslim minority. The destruction of the Ayodhya mosque in December 1992 brought to the fore the issue of whether India will remain a secular democratic state or become a Hindu one. In East Asia, China has outstanding territorial disputes with most of its neighbors. It has pursued a ruthless policy toward the Buddhist people of Tibet, and it is pursuing an increasingly ruthless policy toward its Turkic-Muslim minority. With the Cold War over, the underlying differences between China and the United States have reasserted themselves in areas such as human rights, trade and weapons proliferation. These differences are unlikely to moderate. A "new cold war," Deng Xaioping reportedly asserted in 1991, is under way between China and America.

The same phrase has been applied to the increasingly difficult relations between Japan and the United States. Here cultural difference exacerbates economic conflict. People on each side allege racism on the other, but at least on the American side the antipathies are not racial but cultural. The basic values, attitudes, behavioral patterns of the two societies could hardly be more different. The economic issues between the United States and Europe are no less serious than those between the United States and Japan, but they do not have the same political salience and emotional intensity because the differences between American culture and European culture are so much less than those between American civilization and Japanese civilization.

The interactions between civilizations vary greatly in the extent to which they are likely to be characterized by violence. Economic competition clearly predominates between the American and European subcivilizations of the West and between both of them and Japan. On the Eurasian continent, however, the proliferation of ethnic conflict, epitomized at the extreme in "ethnic cleansing," has not been totally random. It has been most frequent and most violent between groups belonging to different civilizations. In Eurasia the great historic fault lines between civilizations are once more aflame. This is particularly true along the boundaries of the crescent-shaped Islamic bloc of nations from the bulge of Africa to central Asia. Violence also occurs between Muslims, on the one hand, and Orthodox Serbs in the Balkans, Jews in Israel, Hindus in India, Buddhists in Burma and Catholics in the Philippines. Islam has bloody borders.

Civilization Rallying: The Kin-Country Syndrome

Groups or states belonging to one civilization that become involved in war with people from a different civilization naturally try to rally support from other members of their own civilization. As the post-Cold War world evolves, civilization commonality, what H. D. S. Greenway has termed the "kin-country" syndrome, is replacing political ideology and traditional balance of power considerations as the principal basis for cooperation and coalitions. It can be seen gradually emerging in the post-Cold War conflicts in the Persian Gulf, the Caucasus and Bosnia. None of these was a full-scale war between civilizations, but each involved some elements of civilizational rallying, which seemed to become more important as the conflict continued and which may provide a foretaste of the future.

First, in the Gulf War one Arab state invaded another and then fought a coalition of Arab, Western and other states. While only a few Muslim governments overtly supported Saddam Hussein, many Arab elites privately cheered him on, and he was highly popular among large sections of the Arab publics. Islamic fundamentalist movements universally supported Iraq rather than the Western-backed governments of Kuwait and Saudi Arabia. Forswearing Arab nationalism, Saddam Hussein explicitly invoked an Islamic appeal. He and his supporters attempted to define the war as a war between civilizations. "It is not the world against Iraq," as Safar Al-Hawali, dean of Islamic Studies at the Umm Al-Qura University in Mecca, put it in a widely circulated tape. "It is the West against Islam." Ignoring the rivalry between Iran and Iraq, the chief Iranian religious leader, Ayatollah Ali Khamenei, called for a holy war against the West: "The struggle against American aggression, greed, plans and policies will be counted as a jihad, and anybody who is killed on that path is a martyr." "This is a war," King Hussein of Jordan argued, "against all Arabs and all Muslims and not against Iraq alone."

The rallying of substantial sections of Arab elites and publics behind Saddam Hussein caused those Arab governments in the anti-Iraq coalition to moderate their activities and temper their public statements. Arab governments opposed or distanced themselves from subsequent Western efforts to apply pressure on Iraq, including enforcement of a no-fly zone in the summer of 1992 and the bombing of Iraq in January 1993. The Western-Soviet-Turkish-Arab anti-Iraq coalition of 1990 had by 1993 become a coalition of almost only the West and Kuwait against Iraq.

Muslims contrasted Western actions against Iraq with the West's failure to protect Bosnians against Serbs and to impose sanctions on Israel for violating U.N. resolutions. The West, they alleged, was using a double standard. A world of clashing civilizations, however, is inevitably a world of double standards: people apply one standard to their kin-countries and a different standard to others.

Second, the kin-country syndrome also appeared in conflicts in the former Soviet Union. Armenian military successes in 1992 and 1993 stimulated Turkey to become increasingly supportive of its religious, ethnic and linguistic brethren in Azerbaijan. "We have a Turkish nation feeling the same sentiments as the Azerbaijanis," said one Turkish official in 1992. "We are under pressure. Our newspapers are full of the photos of atrocities and are asking us if we are still serious about pursuing our neutral policy. Maybe we should show Armenia that there's a big Turkey in the region." President Turgut Özal agreed, remarking that Turkey should at least "scare the Armenians a little bit." Turkey, Özal threatened again in 1993, would "show its fangs." Turkish Air Force jets flew reconnaissance flights along the Armenian border; Turkey suspended food shipments and air flights to Armenia; and Turkey and Iran announced they would not accept dismemberment of Azerbaijan. In the last years of its existence, the Soviet government supported Azerbaijan because its government was dominated by former communists. With the end of the Soviet Union, however, political considerations gave way to religious ones. Russian troops fought on the side of the Armenians, and Azerbaijan accused the "Russian government of turning 180 degrees" toward support for Christian Armenia.

Third, with respect to the fighting in the former Yugoslavia, Western publics manifested sympathy and support for the Bosnian Muslims and the horrors they suffered at the hands of the Serbs. Relatively little concern was expressed, however, over Croatian attacks on Muslims and participation in the dismemberment of Bosnia-Herzegovina. In the early stages of the Yugoslav breakup, Germany, in an unusual display of diplomatic initiative and muscle, induced the other 11 members of the European Community to follow its lead in recognizing Slovenia and Croatia. As a result of the pope's determination to provide strong backing to the two Catholic countries, the Vatican extended recognition even before the Community did. The United States followed the European lead. Thus the leading actors in Western civilization rallied behind their coreligionists. Subsequently Croatia was reported to be receiving substantial quantities of arms from Central European and other Western countries. Boris Yeltsin's government, on the other hand, attempted to pursue a middle course that would be sympathetic to the Orthodox Serbs but not alienate Russia from the West. Russian conservative and nationalist groups, however, including many legislators, attacked the government

for not being more forthcoming in its support for the Serbs. By early 1993 several hundred Russians apparently were serving with the Serbian forces, and reports circulated of Russian arms being supplied to Serbia.

Islamic governments and groups, on the other hand, castigated the West for not coming to the defense of the Bosnians. Iranian leaders urged Muslims from all countries to provide help to Bosnia; in violation of the U.N. arms embargo, Iran supplied weapons and men for the Bosnians; Iranian-supported Lebanese groups sent guerrillas to train and organize the Bosnian forces. In 1993 up to 4,000 Muslims from over two dozen Islamic countries were reported to be fighting in Bosnia. The governments of Saudi Arabia and other countries felt under increasing pressure from fundamentalist groups in their own societies to provide more vigorous support for the Bosnians. By the end of 1992, Saudi Arabia had reportedly supplied substantial funding for weapons and supplies for the Bosnians, which significantly increased their military capabilities vis-à-vis the Serbs.

In the 1930s the Spanish Civil War provoked intervention from countries that politically were fascist, communist and democratic. In the 1990s the Yugoslav conflict is provoking intervention from countries that are Muslim, Orthodox and Western Christian. The parallel has not gone unnoticed. "The war in Bosnia-Herzegovina has become the emotional equivalent of the fight against fascism in the Spanish Civil War," one Saudi editor observed. "Those who died there are regarded as martyrs who tried to save their fellow Muslims."

Conflicts and violence will also occur between states and groups within the same civilization. Such conflicts, however, are likely to be less intense and less likely to expand than conflicts between civilizations. Common membership in a civilization reduces the probability of violence in situations where it might otherwise occur. In 1991 and 1992 many people were alarmed by the possibility of violent conflict between Russia and Ukraine over territory, particularly Crimea, the Black Sea fleet, nuclear weapons and economic issues. If civilization is what counts, however, the likelihood of violence between Ukrainians and Russians should be low. They are two Slavic, primarily Orthodox peoples who have had close relationships with each other for centuries. As of early 1993, despite all the reasons for conflict, the leaders of the two countries were effectively negotiating and defusing the issues between the two countries. While there has been serious fighting between Muslims and Christians elsewhere in the former Soviet Union and much tension and some fighting between Western and Orthodox Christians in the Baltic states, there has been virtually no violence between Russians and Ukrainians.

Civilization rallying to date has been limited, but it has been growing, and it clearly has the potential to spread much further. As the conflicts in the Persian Gulf, the Caucasus and Bosnia continued, the positions of nations and the cleavages between them increasingly were along civilizational lines. Populist politicians, religious leaders and the media have found it a potent means of arousing mass support and of pressuring hesitant governments. In the coming years, the local conflicts most likely to escalate into major wars will be those, as in Bosnia and the Caucasus, along the fault lines between civilizations. The next world war, if there is one, will be a war between civilizations.

The West versus the Rest

The West is now at an extraordinary peak of power in relation to other civilizations. Its superpower opponent has disappeared from the map. Military conflict among Western states is unthinkable, and Western military power is unrivaled. Apart from Japan, the West faces no economic challenge. It dominates international political and security institutions and with Japan international economic institutions. Global political and security issues are effectively settled by a directorate of the United States, Britain and France, world economic issues by a directorate of the United States, Germany and Japan, all of which maintain extraordinarily close relations with each other to the exclusion of lesser and largely non-Western countries. Decisions made at the U.N. Security Council or in the International Monetary Fund that reflect the interests of the West are presented to the world as reflecting the desires of the world community. The very phrase "the world community" has become the euphemistic collective noun (replacing "the Free World") to give global legitimacy to actions reflecting the interests of the United States and other Western powers.[1] Through the IMF and other international economic institutions, the West promotes its economic interests and imposes on other nations the economic policies it thinks appropriate. In any poll of non-Western peoples, the IMF undoubtedly would win the support of finance ministers and a few others, but get an overwhelmingly unfavorable rating from just about everyone else, who would agree with Georgy Arbatov's characterization of IMF officials as "neo-Bolsheviks who love expropriating other people's money, imposing undemocratic and alien rules of economic and political conduct and stifling economic freedom."

Western domination of the U.N. Security Council and its decisions, tempered only by occasional abstention by China, produced U.N. legitimation of the West's use of force to drive Iraq out of Kuwait and its elimination of Iraq's sophisticated weapons and capacity to produce such weapons. It also produced the quite unprecedented action by the United States, Britain and France in getting the Security Council to demand that Libya hand over the Pan Am 103 bombing suspects and then to impose sanctions when Libya refused. After defeating the largest Arab army, the West did not hesitate to throw its weight around in the Arab world. The West in effect is using international institutions, military power and economic resources to run the world in ways that will maintain Western predominance, protect Western interests and promote Western political and economic values.

That at least is the way in which non-Westerners see the new world, and there is a significant element of truth in their view. Differences in power and struggles for military, economic and institutional power are thus one source of conflict between the West and other civilizations. Differences in culture, that is basic values and beliefs, are a second source of conflict. V. S. Naipaul has argued that Western civilization is the "universal civilization" that "fits all men." At a superficial level much of Western culture has indeed permeated the rest of the world. At a more basic level, however, Western concepts differ fundamentally from those prevalent in other civilizations. Western ideas of individualism, liberalism, constitutionalism, human rights, equality, liberty, the rule of law, democracy, free markets, the separation of church and state, often have little resonance in Islamic, Confucian, Japanese, Hindu, Buddhist or Orthodox cultures. Western efforts to propagate such ideas produce instead a reaction against "human rights imperialism" and a reaffirmation of indigenous values, as can be seen in the support for religious fundamentalism by the younger generation in non-Western cultures. The very notion that there could be a "universal civilization" is a Western idea, directly at odds with the particularism of most Asian societies and their emphasis on what distinguishes one people from another. Indeed, the author of a review of 100 comparative studies of values in different societies concluded that "the values that are most important in the West are least important worldwide."[5] In the political realm, of course, these differences are most manifest in the efforts of the United States and other Western powers to induce other peoples to adopt Western ideas concerning democracy and human rights. Modern democratic government originated in the West. When it has developed in non-Western societies it has usually been the product of Western colonialism or imposition.

The central axis of world politics in the future is likely to be, in Kishore Mahbubani's phrase, the conflict between "the West and the Rest" and the responses of non-Western civilizations to Western power and values.[6] Those responses generally take one or a combination of three forms. At one extreme, non-Western states can, like Burma and North Korea, attempt to pursue a course of isolation, to insulate their societies from penetration or "corruption" by the West, and, in effect, to opt out of participation in the Western-dominated global community. The costs of this course, however, are high, and few states have pursued it exclusively. A second alternative, the equivalent of "band-wagoning" in international relations theory, is to attempt to join the West and accept its values and institutions. The third alternative is to attempt to "balance" the West by developing economic and military power and cooperating with other non-Western societies against the West, while preserving indigenous values and institutions; in short, to modernize but not to Westernize.

The Torn Countries

In the future, as people differentiate themselves by civilization, countries with large numbers of peoples of different civilizations, such as the Soviet Union and Yugoslavia, are candidates for dismemberment. Some other countries have a fair degree of cultural homogeneity but are divided over whether their society belongs to one civilization or another. These are torn countries. Their leaders typically wish to pursue a bandwagoning strategy and to make their countries members of the West, but the history, culture and traditions of their countries are non-Western. The most obvious and prototypical torn country is Turkey. The late twentieth-century leaders of Turkey have followed in the Attatürk tradition and defined Turkey as a modern, secular, Western nation state. They allied Turkey with the West in NATO and in the Gulf War; they applied for membership in the European Community. At the same time, however, elements in Turkish society have supported an Islamic revival and have argued that Turkey is basically a Middle

Eastern Muslim society. In addition, while the elite of Turkey has defined Turkey as a Western society, the elite of the West refuses to accept Turkey as such. Turkey will not become a member of the European Community, and the real reason, as President Özal said, "is that we are Muslim and they are Christian and they don't say that." Having rejected Mecca, and then being rejected by Brussels, where does Turkey look? Tashkent may be the answer. The end of the Soviet Union gives Turkey the opportunity to become the leader of a revived Turkic civilization involving seven countries from the borders of Greece to those of China. Encouraged by the West, Turkey is making strenuous efforts to carve out this new identity for itself.

During the past decade Mexico has assumed a position somewhat similar to that of Turkey. Just as Turkey abandoned its historic opposition to Europe and attempted to join Europe, Mexico has stopped defining itself by its opposition to the United States and is instead attempting to imitate the United States and to join it in the North American Free Trade Area. Mexican leaders are engaged in the great task of redefining Mexican identity and have introduced fundamental economic reforms that eventually will lead to fundamental political change. In 1991 a top adviser to President Carlos Salinas de Gortari described at length to me all the changes the Salinas government was making. When he finished, I remarked: "That's most impressive. It seems to me that basically you want to change Mexico from a Latin American country into a North American country." He looked at me with surprise and exclaimed: "Exactly! That's precisely what we are trying to do, but of course we could never say so publicly." As his remark indicates, in Mexico as in Turkey, significant elements in society resist the redefinition of their country's identity. In Turkey, European-oriented leaders have to make gestures to Islam (Özal's pilgrimage to Mecca); so also Mexico's North American-oriented leaders have to make gestures to those who hold Mexico to be a Latin American country (Salinas' Ibero-American Guadalajara summit).

Historically Turkey has been the most profoundly torn country. For the United States, Mexico is the most immediate torn country. Globally the most important torn country is Russia. The question of whether Russia is part of the West or the leader of a distinct Slavic-Orthodox civilization has been a recurring one in Russian history. That issue was obscured by the communist victory in Russia, which imported a Western ideology, adapted it to Russian conditions and then challenged the West in the name of that ideology. The dominance of communism shut off the historic debate over Westernization versus Russification. With communism discredited Russians once again face that question.

President Yeltsin is adopting Western principles and goals and seeking to make Russia a "normal" country and a part of the West. Yet both the Russian elite and the Russian public are divided on this issue. Among the more moderate dissenters, Sergei Stankevich argues that Russia should reject the "Atlanticist" course, which would lead it "to become European, to become a part of the world economy in rapid and organized fashion, to become the eighth member of the Seven, and to put particular emphasis on Germany and the United States as the two dominant members of the Atlantic alliance." While also rejecting an exclusively

Eurasian policy, Stankevich nonetheless argues that Russia should give priority to the protection of Russians in other countries, emphasize its Turkic and Muslim connections, and promote "an appreciable redistribution of our resources, our options, our ties, and our interests in favor of Asia, of the eastern direction." People of this persuasion criticize Yeltsin for subordinating Russia's interests to those of the West, for reducing Russian military strength, for failing to support traditional friends such as Serbia, and for pushing economic and political reform in ways injurious to the Russian people. Indicative of this trend is the new popularity of the ideas of Petr Savitsky, who in the 1920s argued that Russia was a unique Eurasian civilization.[7] More extreme dissidents voice much more blatantly nationalist, anti-Western and anti-Semitic views, and urge Russia to redevelop its military strength and to establish closer ties with China and Muslim countries. The people of Russia are as divided as the elite. An opinion survey in European Russia in the spring of 1992 revealed that 40 percent of the public had positive attitudes toward the West and 36 percent had negative attitudes. As it has been for much of its history, Russia in the early 1990s is truly a torn country.

To redefine its civilization identity, a torn country must meet three requirements. First, its political and economic elite has to be generally supportive of and enthusiastic about this move. Second, its public has to be willing to acquiesce in the redefinition. Third, the dominant groups in the recipient civilization have to be willing to embrace the convert. All three requirements in large part exist with respect to Mexico. The first two in large part exist with respect to Turkey. It is not clear that any of them exist with respect to Russia's joining the West. The conflict between liberal democracy and Marxism-Leninism was between ideologies which, despite their major differences, ostensibly shared ultimate goals of freedom, equality and prosperity. A traditional, authoritarian, nationalist Russia could have quite different goals. A Western democrat could carry on an intellectual debate with a Soviet Marxist. It would be virtually impossible for him to do that with a Russian traditionalist. If, as the Russians stop behaving like Marxists, they reject liberal democracy and begin behaving like Russians but not like Westerners, the relations between Russia and the West could again become distant and conflictual.[8]

The Confucian-Islamic Connection

The obstacles to non-Western countries joining the West vary considerably. They are least for Latin American and East European countries. They are greater for the Orthodox countries of the former Soviet Union. They are still greater for Muslim, Confucian, Hindu and Buddhist societies. Japan has established a unique position for itself as an associate member of the West: it is in the West in some respects but clearly not of the West in important dimensions. Those countries that for reason of culture and power do not wish to, or cannot, join the West compete with the West by developing their own economic, military and political power. They do this by promoting their internal development and by cooperating with other non-Western countries. The most prominent form of this cooperation is the Confucian-Islamic connection that has emerged to challenge Western interests, values and power.

Almost without exception, Western countries are reducing their military power; under Yeltsin's leadership so also is Russia. China, North Korea and several Middle Eastern states, however, are significantly expanding their military capabilities. They are doing this by the import of arms from Western and non-Western sources and by the development of indigenous arms industries. One result is the emergence of what Charles Krauthammer has called "Weapon States," and the Weapon States are not Western states. Another result is the redefinition of arms control, which is a Western concept and a Western goal. During the Cold War the primary purpose of arms control was to establish a stable military balance between the United States and its allies and the Soviet Union and its allies. In the post-Cold War world the primary objective of arms control is to prevent the development by non-Western societies of military capabilities that could threaten Western interests. The West attempts to do this through international agreements, economic pressure and controls on the transfer of arms and weapons technologies.

The conflict between the West and the Confucian-Islamic states focuses largely, although not exclusively, on nuclear, chemical and biological weapons, ballistic missiles and other sophisticated means for delivering them, and the guidance, intelligence and other electronic capabilities for achieving that goal. The West promotes nonproliferation as a universal norm and nonproliferation treaties and inspections as means of realizing that norm. It also threatens a variety of sanctions against those who promote the spread of sophisticated weapons and proposes some benefits for those who do not. The attention of the West focuses, naturally, on nations that are actually or potentially hostile to the West.

The non-Western nations, on the other hand, assert their right to acquire and to deploy whatever weapons they think necessary for their security. They also have absorbed, to the full, the truth of the response of the Indian defense minister when asked what lesson he learned from the Gulf War: "Don't fight the United States unless you have nuclear weapons." Nuclear weapons, chemical weapons and missiles are viewed, probably erroneously, as the potential equalizer of superior Western conventional power. China, of course, already has nuclear weapons; Pakistan and India have the capability to deploy them. North Korea, Iran, Iraq, Libya and Algeria appear to be attempting to acquire them. A top Iranian official has declared that all Muslim states should acquire nuclear weapons, and in 1988 the president of Iran reportedly issued a directive calling for development of "offensive and defensive chemical, biological and radiological weapons."

Centrally important to the development of counter-West military capabilities is the sustained expansion of China's military power and its means to create military power. Buoyed by spectacular economic development, China is rapidly increasing its military spending and vigorously moving forward with the modernization of its armed forces. It is purchasing weapons from the former Soviet states; it is developing long-range missiles; in 1992 it tested a one-megaton nuclear device. It is developing power-projection capabilities, acquiring aerial refueling

technology, and trying to purchase an aircraft carrier. Its military buildup and assertion of sovereignty over the South China Sea are provoking a multilateral regional arms race in East Asia. China is also a major exporter of arms and weapons technology. It has exported materials to Libya and Iraq that could be used to
manufacture nuclear weapons and nerve gas. It has helped Algeria build a reactor
suitable for nuclear weapons research and production. China has sold to Iran
nuclear technology that American officials believe could only be used to create
weapons and apparently has shipped components of 300-mile-range missiles to
Pakistan. North Korea has had a nuclear weapons program under way for some
while and has sold advanced missiles and missile technology to Syria and Iran.
The flow of weapons and weapons technology is generally from East Asia to the
Middle East. There is, however, some movement in the reverse direction; China
has received Stinger missiles from Pakistan.

A Confucian-Islamic military connection has thus come into being, designed
to promote acquisition by its members of the weapons and weapons technologies needed to counter the military power of the West. It may or may not last. At
present, however, it is, as Dave McCurdy has said, "a renegades' mutual support
pact, run by the proliferators and their backers." A new form of arms competition
is thus occurring between Islamic-Confucian states and the West. In an old-fash-
ioned arms race, each side developed its own arms to balance or to achieve superiority against the other side. In this new form of arms competition, one side is
developing its arms and the other side is attempting not to balance but to limit and
prevent that arms build-up while at the same time reducing its own military capabilities.

Implications for the West

This article does not argue that civilization identities will replace all other identities, that nation states will disappear, that each civilization will become a single
coherent political entity, that groups within a civilization will not conflict with
and even fight each other. This paper does set forth the hypotheses that differences between civilizations are real and important; civilization-consciousness is
increasing; conflict between civilizations will supplant ideological and other
forms of conflict as the dominant global form of conflict; international relations,
historically a game played out within Western civilization, will increasingly be
de-Westernized and become a game in which non-Western civilizations are actors
and not simply objects; successful political, security and economic international
institutions are more likely to develop within civilizations than across civilizations; conflicts between groups in different civilizations will be more frequent,
more sustained and more violent than conflicts between groups in the same civilization; violent conflicts between groups in different civilizations are the most
likely and most dangerous source of escalation that could lead to global wars; the
paramount axis of world politics will be the relations between "the West and the
Rest"; the elites in some torn non-Western countries will try to make their countries part of the West, but in most cases face major obstacles to accomplishing this;

a central focus of conflict for the immediate future will be between the West and several Islamic-Confucian states.

This is not to advocate the desirability of conflicts between civilizations. It is to set forth descriptive hypotheses as to what the future may be like. If these are plausible hypotheses, however, it is necessary to consider their implications for Western policy. These implications should be divided between short-term advantage and long-term accommodation. In the short term it is clearly in the interest of the West to promote greater cooperation and unity within its own civilization, particularly between its European and North American components; to incorporate into the West societies in Eastern Europe and Latin America whose cultures are close to those of the West; to promote and maintain cooperative relations with Russia and Japan; to prevent escalation of local inter-civilization conflicts into major inter-civilization wars; to limit the expansion of the military strength of Confucian and Islamic states; to moderate the reduction of Western military capabilities and maintain military superiority in East and Southwest Asia; to exploit differences and conflicts among Confucian and Islamic states; to support in other civilizations groups sympathetic to Western values and interests; to strengthen international institutions that reflect and legitimate Western interests and values and to promote the involvement of non-Western states in those institutions.

In the longer term other measures would be called for. Western civilization is both Western and modern. Non-Western civilizations have attempted to become modern without becoming Western. To date only Japan has fully succeeded in this quest. Non-Western civilizations will continue to attempt to acquire the wealth, technology, skills, machines and weapons that are part of being modern. They will also attempt to reconcile this modernity with their traditional culture and values. Their economic and military strength relative to the West will increase. Hence the West will increasingly have to accommodate these non-Western modern civilizations whose power approaches that of the West but whose values and interests differ significantly from those of the West. This will require the West to maintain the economic and military power necessary to protect its interests in relation to these civilizations. It will also, however, require the West to develop a more profound understanding of the basic religious and philosophical assumptions underlying other civilizations and the ways in which people in those civilizations see their interests. It will require an effort to identify elements of commonality between Western and other civilizations. For the relevant future, there will be no universal civilization, but instead a world of different civilizations, each of which will have to learn to coexist with the others.

NOTES

1. Murray Weidenbaum, *Greater China: The Next Economic Superpower?*, St. Louis: Washington University Center for the Study of American Business, Contemporary Issues, Series 57, February 1993, pp. 2–3.

2. Bernard Lewis, "The Roots of Muslim Rage," *The Atlantic Monthly,* vol. 266, September 1990, p. 60; *Time,* June 15, 1992, pp. 24–28.

3. Archie Roosevelt, *For Lust of Knowing,* Boston: Little, Brown, 1988, pp. 332–333.

4. Almost invariably Western leaders claim they are acting on behalf of "the world community." One minor lapse occurred during the run-up to the Gulf War. In an interview on "Good Morning America," Dec. 21, 1990, British Prime Minister John Major referred to the actions "the West" was taking against Saddam Hussein. He quickly corrected himself and subsequently referred to "the world community." He was, however, right when he erred.

5. Harry C. Triandis, *The New York Times,* Dec. 25, 1990, p. 41, and "Cross-Cultural Studies of Individualism and Collectivism," Nebraska Symposium on Motivation, vol. 37, 1989, pp. 41–133.

6. Kishore Mahbubani, "The West and the Rest," *The National Interest,* Summer 1992, pp. 3–13.

7. Sergei Stankevich, "Russia in Search of Itself," *The National Interest,* Summer 1992, pp. 47–51; Daniel Schneider, "A Russian Movement Rejects Western Tilt," *Christian Science Monitor,* Feb. 5, 1993, pp. 5–7.

8. Owen Harries has pointed out that Australia is trying (unwisely in his view) to become a torn country in reverse. Although it has been a full member not only of the West but also of the ABCA military and intelligence core of the West, its current leaders are in effect proposing that it defect from the West, redefine itself as an Asian country and cultivate close ties with its neighbors. Australia's future, they argue, is with the dynamic economies of East Asia. But, as I have suggested, close economic cooperation normally requires a common cultural base. In addition, none of the three conditions necessary for a torn country to join another civilization is likely to exist in Australia's case.

Jihad vs. McWorld

Benjamin R. Barber

Just beyond the horizon of current events lie two possible political futures—both bleak, neither democratic. The first is a retribalization of large swaths of humankind by war and bloodshed: a threatened Lebanonization of national states in which culture is pitted against culture, people against people, tribe against tribe —a Jihad in the name of a hundred narrowly conceived faiths against every kind of interdependence, every kind of artificial social cooperation and civic mutual ity. The second is being borne in on us by the onrush of economic and ecological forces that demand integration and uniformity and that mesmerize the world with fast music, fast computers, and fast food—with MTV, Macintosh, and McDonald's, pressing nations into one commercially homogenous global network: one McWorld tied together by technology, ecology, communications, and commerce. The planet is falling precipitantly apart *and* coming reluctantly together at the very same moment.

These two tendencies are sometimes visible in the same countries at the same instant: thus Yugoslavia, clamoring just recently to join the New Europe, is exploding into fragments; India is trying to live up to its reputation as the world's largest integral democracy while powerful new fundamentalist parties like the Hindu nationalist Bharatiya Janata Party, along with nationalist assassins, are imperiling its hard-won unity. States are breaking up or joining up: the Soviet Union has disappeared almost overnight, its parts forming new unions with one another

Published originally in the March 1992 issue of *The Atlantic Monthly*. Reprinted by permission of the author.

with like-minded nationalities in neighboring states. The old interwar national state based on territory and political sovereignty looks to be a mere transitional development.

The tendencies of what I am here calling the forces of Jihad and the forces of McWorld operate with equal strength in opposite directions, the one driven by parochial hatreds, the other by universalizing markets, the one re-creating ancient subnational and ethnic borders from within, the other making national borders porous from without. They have one thing in common: neither offers much hope to citizens looking for practical ways to govern themselves democratically. If the global future is to pit Jihad's centrifugal whirlwind against McWorld's centripetal black hole, the outcome is unlikely to be democratic—or so I will argue.

McWorld, or the Globalization of Politics

Four imperatives make up the dynamic of McWorld: a market imperative, a resource imperative, an information-technology imperative, and an ecological imperative. By shrinking the world and diminishing the salience of national borders, these imperatives have in combination achieved a considerable victory over factiousness and particularism, and not least of all over their most virulent traditional form—nationalism. It is the realists who are now Europeans, the utopians who dream nostalgically of a resurgent England or Germany, perhaps even a resurgent Wales or Saxony. Yesterday's wishful cry for one world has yielded to the reality of McWorld.

The market imperative. Marxist and Leninist theories of imperialism assumed that the quest for ever-expanding markets would in time compel nation-based capitalist economies to push against national boundaries in search of an international economic imperium. Whatever else has happened to the scientist predictions of Marxism, in this domain they have proved farsighted. All national economies are now vulnerable to the inroads of larger, transnational markets within which trade is free, currencies are convertible, access to banking is open, and contracts are enforceable under law. In Europe, Asia, Africa, the South Pacific, and the Americas such markets are eroding national sovereignty and giving rise to entities—international banks, trade associations, transnational lobbies like OPEC and Greenpeace, world news services like CNN and the BBC, and multinational corporations that increasingly lack a meaningful national identity—that neither reflect nor respect nationhood as an organizing or regulative principle.

The market imperative has also reinforced the quest for international peace and stability, requisites of an efficient international economy. Markets are enemies of parochialism, isolation, fractiousness, war. Market psychology attenuates the psychology of ideological and religious cleavages and assumes a concord among producers and consumers—categories that ill fit narrowly conceived national or religious cultures. Shopping has little tolerance for blue laws, whether dictated by pub-closing British paternalism, Sabbath-observing Jewish Orthodox fundamentalism, or no-Sunday-liquor-sales Massachusetts puritanism. In the context of common markets, international law ceases to be a vision of justice and becomes a workaday framework for getting things done—enforcing contracts, ensuring that governments abide by deals, regulating trade and currency relations, and so forth.

Common markets demand a common language, as well as a common currency, and they produce common behaviors of the kind bred by cosmopolitan city life everywhere. Commercial pilots, computer programmers, international bankers, media specialists, oil riggers, entertainment celebrities, ecology experts, demographers, accountants, professors, athletes—these compose a new breed of men and women for whom religion, culture, and nationality can seem only marginal elements in a working identity. Although sociologists of everyday life will no doubt continue to distinguish a Japanese from an American mode, shopping has a common signature throughout the world. Cynics might even say that some of the recent revolutions in Eastern Europe have had as their true goal not liberty and the right to vote but well-paying jobs and the right to shop (although the vote is proving easier to acquire than consumer goods). The market imperative is, then, plenty powerful; but, notwithstanding some of the claims made for "democratic capitalism," it is not identical with the democratic imperative.

The resource imperative. Democrats once dreamed of societies whose political autonomy rested firmly on economic independence. The Athenians idealized what they called autarky, and tried for a while to create a way of life simple and austere enough to make the polis genuinely self-sufficient. To be free meant to be independent of any other community or polis. Not even the Athenians were able to achieve autarky, however: human nature, it turns out, is dependency. By the time of Pericles, Athenian politics was inextricably bound up with a flowering empire held together by naval power and commerce—an empire that, even as it appeared to enhance Athenian might, ate away at Athenian independence and autarky. Master and slave, it turned out, were bound together by mutual insufficiency.

The dream of autarky briefly engrossed nineteenth-century America as well, for the underpopulated, endlessly bountiful land, the cornucopia of natural resources, and the natural barriers of a continent walled in by two great seas led many to believe that America could be a world unto itself. Given this past, it has been harder for Americans than for most to accept the inevitability of interdependence. But the rapid depletion of resources even in a country like ours, where they once seemed inexhaustible, and the maldistribution of arable soil and mineral resources on the planet, leave even the wealthiest societies ever more resource-dependent and many other nations in permanently desperate straits.

Every nation, it turns out, needs something another nation has; some nations have almost nothing they need.

The information-technology imperative. Enlightenment science and the technologies derived from it are inherently universalizing. They entail a quest for descriptive principles of general application, a search for universal solutions to particular problems, and an unswerving embrace of objectivity and impartiality.

Scientific progress embodies and depends on open communication, a common discourse rooted in rationality, collaboration, and an easy and regular flow and exchange of information. Such ideals can be hypocritical covers for power-mongering by elites, and they may be shown to be wanting in many other ways, but they are entailed by the very idea of science and they make science and globalization practical allies.

Business, banking, and commerce all depend on information flow and are facilitated by new communication technologies. The hardware of these technologies tends to be systemic and integrated—computer, television, cable, satellite, laser, fiber-optic, and microchip technologies combining to create a vast interactive communications and information network that can potentially give every person on earth access to every other person, and make every datum, every byte, available to every set of eyes. If the automobile was, as George Ball once said (when he gave his blessing to a Fiat factory in the Soviet Union during the Cold War), "an ideology on four wheels," then electronic telecommunication and information systems are an ideology at 186,000 miles per second—which makes for a very small planet in a very big hurry. Individual cultures speak particular languages; commerce and science increasingly speak English; the whole world speaks logarithms and binary mathematics.

Moreover, the pursuit of science and technology asks for, even compels, open societies. Satellite footprints do not respect national borders; telephone wires penetrate the most closed societies. With photocopying and then fax machines having infiltrated Soviet universities and *samizdat* literary circles in the eighties, and computer modems having multiplied like rabbits in communism's bureaucratic warrens thereafter, *glasnost* could not be far behind. In their social requisites, secrecy and science are enemies.

The new technology's software is perhaps even more globalizing than its hardware. The information arm of international commerce's sprawling body reaches out and touches distinct nations and parochial cultures, and gives them a common face chiseled in Hollywood, on Madison Avenue, and in Silicon Valley. Throughout the 1980s one of the most-watched television programs in South Africa was *The Cosby Show*. The demise of apartheid was already in production. Exhibitors at the 1991 Cannes film festival expressed growing anxiety over the "homogenization" and "Americanization" of the global film industry when, for the third year running, American films dominated the awards ceremonies. America has dominated the world's popular culture for much longer, and much more decisively. In November of 1991 Switzerland's once insular culture boasted best-seller lists featuring *Terminator 2* as the No. 1 movie, *Scarlett* as the No. 1 book, and Prince's *Diamonds and Pearls* as the No. 1 record album. No wonder the Japanese are buying Hollywood film studios even faster than Americans are buying Japanese television sets. This kind of software supremacy may in the long term be far more important than hardware superiority, because culture has become more potent than armaments. What is the power of the Pentagon compared with Disneyland? Can the Sixth Fleet keep up with CNN? McDonald's in Moscow and Coke in China will do more to create a global culture than military colonization ever could. It is less the goods than the brand names that do the work, for they convey life-style images that alter perception and challenge behavior. They make up the seductive software of McWorld's common (at times much too common) soul.

Yet in all this high-tech commercial world there is nothing that looks particularly democratic. It lends itself to surveillance as well as liberty, to new forms of manipulation and covert control as well as new kinds of participation, to skewed, unjust market outcomes as well as greater productivity. The consumer society and the open society are not quite synonymous. Capitalism and democracy have a relationship, but it is something less than a marriage. An efficient free market after all requires that consumers be free to vote their dollars on competing goods, not that citizens be free to vote their values and beliefs on competing political candidates and programs. The free market flourished in junta-run Chile, in military-governed Taiwan and Korea, and, earlier, in a variety of autocratic European empires as well as their colonial possessions.

The ecological imperative. The impact of globalization on ecology is a cliché even to world leaders who ignore it. We know well enough that the German forests can be destroyed by Swiss and Italians driving gas-guzzlers fueled by leaded gas. We also know that the planet can be asphyxiated by greenhouse gases because Brazilian farmers want to be part of the twentieth century and are burning down tropical rain forests to clear a little land to plough, and because Indonesians make a living out of converting their lush jungle into toothpicks for fastidious Japanese diners, upsetting the delicate oxygen balance and in effect puncturing our global lungs. Yet this ecological consciousness has meant not only greater awareness but also greater inequality, as modernized nations try to slam the door behind them, saying to developing nations, "The world cannot afford *your* modernization; ours has wrung it dry!"

Each of the four imperatives just cited is transnational, transideological, and transcultural. Each applies impartially to Catholics, Jews, Muslims, Hindus, and Buddhists; to democrats and totalitarians; to capitalists and socialists. The Enlightenment dream of a universal rational society has to a remarkable degree been realized—but in a form that is commercialized, homogenized, depoliticized, bureaucratized, and, of course, radically incomplete, for the movement toward McWorld is in competition with forces of global breakdown, national dissolution, and centrifugal corruption. These forces, working in the opposite direction, are the essence of what I call Jihad.

Jihad, or the Lebanonization of the World

OPEC, the World Bank, the United Nations, the International Red Cross, the multinational corporation . . . there are scores of institutions that reflect globalization. But they often appear as ineffective reactors to the world's real actors: national states and, to an ever greater degree, subnational factions in permanent rebellion against uniformity and integration—even the kind represented by universal law and justice. The headlines feature these players regularly: they are cultures, not countries; parts, not wholes; sects, not religions; rebellious factions and dissenting minorities at war not just with globalism but with the traditional nation-state. Kurds, Basques, Puerto Ricans, Ossetians, East Timoreans, Quebecois, the Catholics of Northern Ireland, Abkhasians, Kurile Islander Japanese, the Zulus of Inkatha, Catalonians, Tamils, and, of course, Palestinians—people without countries, inhabiting nations not their own, seeking smaller worlds within borders that will seal them off from modernity.

A powerful irony is at work here. Nationalism was once a force of integration and unification, a movement aimed at bringing together disparate clans, tribes, and cultural fragments under new, assimilationist flags. But as Ortega y Gasset noted more than sixty years ago, having won its victories, nationalism changed its strategy. In the 1920s, and again today, it is more often a reactionary and divisive force, pulverizing the very nations it once helped cement together. The force that creates nations is "inclusive," Ortega wrote in *The Revolt of the Masses*. "In periods of consolidation, nationalism has a positive value, and is a lofty standard. But in Europe everything is more than consolidated, and nationalism is nothing but a mania. . . ."

This mania has left the post–Cold War world smoldering with hot wars; the international scene is little more unified than it was at the end of the Great War, in Ortega's own time. There were more than thirty wars in progress last year, most of them ethnic, racial, tribal, or religious in character, and the list of unsafe regions doesn't seem to be getting any shorter. Some new world order!

The aim of many of these small-scale wars is to redraw boundaries, to implode states and resecure parochial identities: to escape McWorld's dully insistent imperatives. The mood is that of Jihad: war not as an instrument of policy but as an emblem of identity, an expression of community, an end in itself. Even where there is no shooting war, there is fractiousness, secession, and the quest for ever smaller communities. Add to the list of dangerous countries those at risk: In Switzerland and Spain, Jurassian and Basque separatists still argue the virtues of ancient identities, sometimes in the language of bombs. Hyperdisintegration in the former Soviet Union may well continue unabated—not just a Ukraine independent from the Soviet Union but a Bessarabian Ukraine independent from the Ukrainian republic; not just Russia severed from the defunct union but Tatarstan severed from Russia. Yugoslavia makes even the disunited, ex-Soviet, nonsocialist republics that were once the Soviet Union look integrated, its sectarian fatherlands springing up within factional motherlands like weeds within weeds within weeds. Kurdish independence would threaten the territorial integrity of four Middle Eastern nations. Well before the current cataclysm Soviet Georgia made a claim for autonomy from the Soviet Union, only to be faced with its Ossetians (164,000 in a republic of 5.5 million) demanding their own self-determination within Georgia. The Abkhasian minority in Georgia has followed suit. Even the good will established by Canada's once promising Meech Lake protocols is in danger, with Francophone Quebec again threatening the dissolution of the federation. In South Africa the emergence from apartheid was hardly achieved when friction between

Inkatha's Zulus and the African National Congress's tribally identified members threatened to replace Europeans' racism with an indigenous tribal war. After thirty years of attempted integration using the colonial language (English) as a unifier, Nigeria is now playing with the idea of linguistic multiculturalism—which could mean the cultural breakup of the nation into hundreds of tribal fragments. Even Saddam Hussein has benefited from the threat of internal Jihad, having used renewed tribal and religious warfare to turn last season's mortal enemies into reluctant allies of an Iraqi nationhood that he nearly destroyed.

The passing of communism has torn away the thin veneer of internationalism (workers of the world unite!) to reveal ethnic prejudices that are not only ugly and deep-seated but increasingly murderous. Europe's old scourge, anti-Semitism, is back with a vengeance, but it is only one of many antagonisms. It appears all too easy to throw the historical gears into reverse and pass from a Communist dictatorship back into a tribal state.

Among the tribes, religion is also a battlefield. ("Jihad" is a rich word whose generic meaning is "struggle"—usually the struggle of the soul to avert evil. Strictly applied to religious war, it is used only in reference to battles where the faith is under assault, or battles against a government that denies the practice of Islam. My use here is rhetorical, but does follow both journalistic practice and history.) Remember the Thirty Years War? Whatever forms of Enlightenment universalism might once have come to grace such historically related forms of monotheism as Judaism, Christianity, and Islam, in many of their modern incarnations they are parochial rather than cosmopolitan, angry rather than loving, proselytizing rather than ecumenical, zealous rather than rationalist, sectarian rather than deistic, ethnocentric rather than universalizing. As a result, like the new forms of hypernationalism, the new expressions of religious fundamentalism are fractious and pulverizing, never integrating. This is religion as the Crusaders knew it: a battle to the death for souls that if not saved will be forever lost.

The atmospherics of Jihad have resulted in a breakdown of civility in the name of identity, of comity in the name of community. International relations have sometimes taken on the aspect of gang war—cultural turf battles featuring tribal factions that were supposed to be sublimated as integral parts of large national, economic, postcolonial, and constitutional entities.

The Darkening Future of Democracy

These rather melodramatic tableaux vivants do not tell the whole story, however. For all their defects, Jihad and McWorld have their attractions. Yet, to repeat and insist, the attractions are unrelated to democracy. Neither McWorld nor Jihad is remotely democratic in impulse. Neither needs democracy; neither promotes democracy.

McWorld does manage to look pretty seductive in a world obsessed with Jihad. It delivers peace, prosperity, and relative unity—if at the cost of independence, community, and identity (which is generally based on difference). The primary political values required by the global market are order and tranquillity, and freedom—as in the phrases "free trade," "free press," and "free love." Human rights are needed to a degree, but not citizenship or participation—and no more social justice and equality than are necessary to promote efficient economic production and consumption. Multinational corporations sometimes seem to prefer doing business with local oligarchs, inasmuch as they can take confidence from dealing with the boss on all crucial matters. Despots who slaughter their own populations are no problem, so long as they leave markets in place and refrain from making war on their neighbors (Saddam Hussein's fatal mistake). In trading partners, predictability is of more value than justice.

The Eastern European revolutions that seemed to arise out of concern for global democratic values quickly deteriorated into a stampede in the general direction of free markets and their ubiquitous, television-promoted shopping malls. East Germany's Neues Forum, that courageous gathering of intellectuals, students, and workers which overturned the Stalinist regime in Berlin in 1989, lasted only six months in Germany's mini-version of McWorld. Then it gave way to money and markets and monopolies from the West. By the time of the first all-German elections, it could scarcely manage to secure three percent of the vote. Elsewhere there is growing evidence that *glasnost* will go and *perestroika*— defined as privatization and an opening of markets to Western bidders—will stay. So understandably anxious are the new rulers of Eastern Europe and whatever entities are forced from the residues of the Soviet Union to gain access to credit and markets and technology—McWorld's flourishing new currencies—that they have shown themselves willing to trade away democratic prospects in pursuit of them: not just old totalitarian ideologies and command-economy production models but some possible indigenous experiments with a third way between capitalism and socialism, such as economic cooperatives and employee stock-ownership plans, both of which have their ardent supporters in the East.

Jihad delivers a different set of virtues: a vibrant local identity, a sense of community, solidarity among kinsmen, neighbors, and countrymen, narrowly conceived. But it also guarantees parochialism and is grounded in exclusion. Solidarity is secured through war against outsiders. And solidarity often means obedience to a hierarchy in governance, fanaticism in beliefs, and the obliteration of individual selves in the name of the group. Deference to leaders and intolerance toward outsiders (and toward "enemies within") are hallmarks of tribalism— hardly the attitudes required for the cultivation of new democratic women and men capable of governing themselves. Where new democratic experiments have been conducted in retribalizing societies, in both Europe and the Third World, the result has often been anarchy, repression, persecution, and the coming of new, noncommunist forms of very old kinds of despotism. During the past year, Havel's velvet revolution in Czechoslovakia was imperiled by partisans of "Czechland" and of Slovakia as independent entities. India seemed little less rent by Sikh, Hindu, Muslim, and Tamil infighting than it was immediately after the British pulled out, more than forty years ago.

To the extent that either McWorld or Jihad has a *natural* politics, it has turned out to be more of an antipolitics. For McWorld, it is the antipolitics of global-ism: bureaucratic, technocratic, and meritocratic, focused (as Marx predicted it would be) on the administration of things—with people, however, among the chief things to be administered. In its politico-economic imperatives McWorld has been guided by laissez-faire market principles that privilege efficiency, productivity, and beneficence at the expense of civic liberty and self-government.

For Jihad, the antipolitics of tribalization has been explicitly antidemocratic: one-party dictatorship, government by military junta, theocratic fundamentalism —often associated with a version of the *Führerprinzip* that empowers an indi-vidual to rule on behalf of a people. Even the government of India, struggling for decades to model democracy for a people who will soon number a billion, longs for great leaders; and for every Mahatma Gandhi, Indira Gandhi, or Rajiv Gandhi taken from them by zealous assassins, the Indians appear to seek a replacement who will deliver them from the lengthy travail of their freedom.

The Confederal Option

How can democracy be secured and spread in a world whose primary tendencies are at best indifferent to it (McWorld) and at worst deeply antithetical to it (Jihad)? My guess is that globalization will eventually vanquish retribalization. The ethos of material "civilization" has not yet encountered an obstacle it has been unable to thrust aside. Ortega may have grasped in the 1920s a clue to our own future in the coming millennium.

> Everyone sees the need of a new principle of life. But as always happens in similar crises—some people attempt to save the situation by an artificial intensification of the very principle which has led to decay. This is the meaning of the "nationalist" outburst of recent years. . . . things have always gone that way. The last flare, the longest; the last sigh, the deep-est. On the very eve of their disappearance there is an intensification of frontiers—military and economic.

Jihad may be a last deep sigh before the eternal yawn of McWorld. On the other hand, Ortega was not exactly prescient; his prophecy of peace and inter-nationalism came just before blitzkrieg, world war, and the Holocaust tore the old order to bits. Yet democracy is how we remonstrate with reality, the rebuke our aspirations offer to history. And if retribalization is inhospitable to democra-cy, there is nonetheless a form of democratic government that can accommodate parochialism and communitarianism, one that can even save them from their de-fects and make them more tolerant and participatory: decentralized participatory democracy. And if McWorld is indifferent to democracy, there is nonetheless a form of democratic government that suits global markets passably well—repre-sentative government in its federal or, better still, confederal variation.

With its concern for accountability, the protection of minorities, and the uni-versal rule of law, a confederalized representative system would serve the politi-cal needs of McWorld as well as oligarchic bureaucratism or meritocratic elitism is currently doing. As we are already beginning to see, many nations may survive in the long term only as confederations that afford local regions smaller than "nations" extensive jurisdiction. Recommended reading for democrats of the twenty-first century is not the U.S. Constitution or the French Declaration of Rights of Man and Citizen but the Articles of Confederation, that suddenly pertinent document that stitched together the thirteen American colonies into what then seemed a too loose confederation of independent states but now appears a new form of political realism, as veterans of Yeltsin's new Russia and the new Europe created at Maastricht will attest.

By the same token, the participatory and direct form of democracy that engages citizens in civic activity and civic judgment and goes well beyond just voting and accountability—the system I have called "strong democracy"—suits the political needs of decentralized communities as well as theocratic and nationalist party dictatorships have done. Local neighborhoods need not be democratic, but they can be. Real democracy has flourished in diminutive settings: the spirit of liberty, Tocqueville said, is local. Participatory democracy, if not naturally apposite to tribalism, has an undeniable attractiveness under conditions of parochialism.

Democracy in any of these variations will, however, continue to be obstructed by the undemocratic and antidemocratic trends toward uniformitarian globalism and intolerant retribalization which I have portrayed here. For democracy to persist in our brave new McWorld, we will have to commit acts of conscious political will—a possibility, but hardly a probability, under these conditions. Political will requires much more than the quick fix of the transfer of institutions. Like technology transfer, institution transfer rests on foolish assumptions about a uniform world of the kind that once fired the imagination of colonial administrators. Spread English justice to the colonies by exporting wigs. Let an East Indian trading company act as the vanguard to Britain's free parliamentary institutions. Today's well-intentioned quick-fixers in the National Endowment for Democracy and the Kennedy School of Government, in the unions and foundations and universities zealously nurturing contacts in Eastern Europe and the Third World, are hoping to democratize by long distance. Post Bulgaria a parliament by first-class mail. Fed Ex the Bill of Rights to Sri Lanka. Cable Cambodia some common law.

Yet Eastern Europe has already demonstrated that importing free political parties, parliaments, and presses cannot establish a democratic civil society; imposing a free market may even have the opposite effect. Democracy grows from the bottom up and cannot be imposed from the top down. Civil society has to be built from the inside out. The institutional superstructure comes last. Poland may become democratic, but then again it may heed the Pope, and prefer to found its politics on its Catholicism, with uncertain consequences for democracy. Bulgaria may become democratic, but it may prefer tribal war. The former Soviet Union may become a democratic confederation, or it may just grow into an anarchic and weak conglomeration of markets for other nations' goods and services.

Democrats need to seek out indigenous democratic impulses. There is always a desire for self-government, always some expression of participation, accountability, consent, and representation, even in traditional hierarchical societies. These need to be identified, tapped, modified, and incorporated into new democratic practices with an indigenous flavor. The tortoises among the democratizers may ultimately outlive or outpace the hares, for they will have the time and patience to explore conditions along the way, and to adapt their gait to changing circumstances. Tragically, democracy in a hurry often looks something like France in 1794 or China in 1989.

It certainly seems possible that the most attractive democratic ideal in the face of the brutal realities of Jihad and the dull realities of McWorld will be a confederal union of semi-autonomous communities smaller than nation-states, tied together into regional economic associations and markets larger than nation-states —participatory and self-determining in local matters at the bottom, representative and accountable at the top. The nation-state would play a diminished role, and sovereignty would lose some of its political potency. The Green movement adage "Think globally, act locally" would actually come to describe the conduct of politics.

This vision reflects only an ideal, however—one that is not terribly likely to be realized. Freedom, Jean-Jacques Rousseau once wrote, is a food easy to eat but hard to digest. Still, democracy has always played itself out against the odds. And democracy remains both a form of coherence as binding as McWorld and a secular faith potentially as inspiriting as Jihad.

The Coming Anarchy

Robert D. Kaplan

The Minister's eyes were like egg yolks, an aftereffect of some of the many ill-nesses, malaria especially, endemic in his country. There was also an irrefutable sadness in his eyes. He spoke in a slow and creaking voice, the voice of hope about to expire. Flame trees, coconut palms, and a ballpoint-blue Atlantic composed the background. None of it seemed beautiful, though. "In forty-five years I have never seen things so bad. We did not manage ourselves well after the British departed. But what we have now is something worse—the revenge of the poor, of the social failures, of the people least able to bring up children in a modern society." Then he referred to the recent coup in the West African country Sierra Leone. "The boys who took power in Sierra Leone come from houses like this." The Minister jabbed his finger at a corrugated metal shack teeming with children. "In three months these boys confiscated all the official Mercedes, Volvos, and BMWs and willfully wrecked them on the road." The Minister mentioned one of the coup's leaders, Solomon Anthony Joseph Musa, who shot the people who had paid for his school-ing, "in order to erase the humiliation and mitigate the power his middle-class sponsors held over him."

Tyranny is nothing new in Sierra Leone or in the rest of West Africa. But it is now part and parcel of an increasing lawlessness that is far more significant than any coup, rebel incursion, or episodic experiment in democracy. Crime was what my friend—a top-ranking African official whose life would be threatened were I

Article originally appeared in *The Atlantic Monthly* (February 1994). Reprinted by permission of the author.

to identify him more precisely—really wanted to talk about. Crime is what makes West Africa a natural point of departure for my report on what the political character of our planet is likely to be in the twenty-first century.

The cities of West Africa at night are some of the unsafest places in the world. Streets are unlit; the police often lack gasoline for their vehicles; armed burglars, carjackers, and muggers proliferate. "The government in Sierra Leone has no writ after dark," says a foreign resident, shrugging. When I was in the capital, Freetown, last September, eight men armed with AK-47s broke into the house of an American man. They tied him up and stole everything of value. Forget Miami: direct flights between the United States and the Murtala Muhammed Airport, in neighboring Nigeria's largest city, Lagos, have been suspended by order of the U.S. Secretary of Transportation because of ineffective security at the terminal and its environs. A State Department report cited the airport for "extortion by law-enforcement and immigration officials." This is one of the few times that the U.S. government has embargoed a foreign airport for reasons that are linked purely to crime. In Abidjan, effectively the capital of the Côte d'Ivoire, or Ivory Coast, restaurants have stick- and gun-wielding guards who walk you the fifteen feet or so between your car and the entrance, giving you an eerie taste of what American cities might be like in the future. An Italian ambassador was killed by gunfire when robbers invaded an Abidjan restaurant. The family of the Nigerian ambassador was tied up and robbed at gunpoint in the ambassador's residence. After university students in the Ivory Coast caught bandits who had been plaguing their dorms, they executed them by hanging tires around their necks and setting the tires on fire. In one instance Ivorian policemen stood by and watched the "necklacings," afraid to intervene. Each time I went to the Abidjan bus terminal, groups of young men with restless, scanning eyes surrounded my taxi, putting their hands all over the windows, demanding "tips" for carrying my luggage even though I had only a rucksack. In cities in six West African countries I saw similar young men every where—hordes of them. They were like loose molecules in a very unstable social fluid, a fluid that was clearly on the verge of igniting.

"You see," my friend the Minister told me, "in the villages of Africa it is perfectly natural to feed at any table and lodge in any hut. But in the cities this communal existence no longer holds. You must pay for lodging and be invited for food. When young men find out that their relations cannot put them up, they become lost. They join other migrants and slip gradually into the criminal process."

"In the poor quarters of Arab North Africa," he continued, "there is much less crime, because Islam provides a social anchor: of education and indoctrination. Here in West Africa we have a lot of superficial Islam and superficial Christianity. Western religion is undermined by animist beliefs not suitable to a moral society, because they are based on irrational spirit power. Here spirits are used to wreak vengeance by one person against another, or one group against another." Many of the atrocities in the Liberian civil war have been tied to belief in *juju* spirits, and the BBC has reported, in its magazine *Focus on Africa,* that in the civil fighting in adjacent Sierra Leone, rebels were said to have "a young woman with them who would go to the front naked, always walking backwards and looking in a mirror to see where she was going. This made her invisible, so that she could cross to the army's positions and there bury charms . . . to improve the rebels' chances of success."

Finally my friend the Minister mentioned polygamy. Designed for a pastoral way of life, polygamy continues to thrive in sub-Saharan Africa even though it is increasingly uncommon in Arab North Africa. Most youths I met on the road in West Africa told me that they were from "extended" families, with a mother in one place and a father in another. Translated to an urban environment, loose family structures are largely responsible for the world's highest birth rates and the explosion of the HIV virus on the continent. Like the communalism and animism, they provide a weak shield against the corrosive social effects of life in cities. In those cities African culture is being redefined while desertification and deforestation— also tied to overpopulation—drive more and more African peasants out of the countryside.

A Premonition of the Future

West Africa is becoming *the* symbol of worldwide demographic, environmental, and societal stress, in which criminal anarchy emerges as the real "strategic" danger. Disease, overpopulation, unprovoked crime, scarcity of resources, refugee migrations, the increasing erosion of nation-states and international borders, and the empowerment of private armies, security firms, and international drug cartels are now most tellingly demonstrated through a West African prism. West Africa provides an appropriate introduction to the issues, often extremely unpleasant to discuss, that will soon confront our civilization. To remap the political earth the way it will be a few decades hence—as I intend to do in this article—I find I must begin with West Africa.

There is no other place on the planet where political maps are so deceptive —where, in fact, they tell such lies—as in West Africa. Start with Sierra Leone. According to the map, it is a nation-state of defined borders, with a government in control of its territory. In truth the Sierra Leonian government, run by a twenty-seven-year-old army captain, Valentine Strasser, controls Freetown by day and by day also controls part of the rural interior. In the government's territory the national army is an unruly rabble threatening drivers and passengers at most checkpoints. In the other part of the country units of two separate armies from the war in Liberia have taken up residence, as has an army of Sierra Leonian rebels. The government force fighting the rebels is full of renegade commanders who have aligned themselves with disaffected village chiefs. A premodern formlessness governs the battlefield, evoking the wars in medieval Europe prior to the 1648 Peace of Westphalia, which ushered in the era of organized nation-states.

As a consequence, roughly 400,000 Sierra Leonians are internally displaced, 280,000 more have fled to neighboring Guinea, and another 100,000 have fled to Liberia, even as 400,000 Liberians have fled to Sierra Leone. The third largest city in Sierra Leone, Gondama, is a displaced-persons camp. With an additional 600,000 Liberians in Guinea and 250,000 in the Ivory Coast, the borders dividing these four countries have become largely meaningless. Even in quiet zones none of the governments except the Ivory Coast's maintains the schools, bridges, roads, and police forces in a manner necessary for functional sovereignty. The Koranko ethnic group in northeastern Sierra Leone does all its trading in Guinea. Sierra Leonian diamonds are more likely to be sold in Liberia than in Freetown. In the eastern provinces of Sierra Leone you can buy Liberian beer but not the local brand.

In Sierra Leone, as in Guinea, as in the Ivory Coast, as in Ghana, most of the primary rain forest and the secondary bush is being destroyed at an alarming rate. I saw convoys of trucks bearing majestic hardwood trunks to coastal ports. When Sierra Leone achieved its independence, in 1961, as much as 60 percent of the country was primary rain forest. Now six percent is. In the Ivory Coast the proportion has fallen from 38 percent to eight percent. The deforestation has led to soil erosion, which has led to more flooding and more mosquitoes. Virtually everyone in the West African interior has some form of malaria.

Sierra Leone is a microcosm of what is occurring, albeit in a more tempered and gradual manner, throughout West Africa and much of the underdeveloped world: the withering away of central governments, the rise of tribal and regional domains, the unchecked spread of disease, and the growing pervasiveness of war. West Africa is reverting to the Africa of the Victorian atlas. It consists now of a series of coastal trading posts, such as Freetown and Conakry, and an interior that, owing to violence, volatility, and disease, is again becoming, as Graham Greene once observed, "blank" and "unexplored." However, whereas Greene's vision implies a certain romance, as in the somnolent and charmingly seedy Freetown of his celebrated novel *The Heart of the Matter*, it is Thomas Malthus, the philosopher of demographic doomsday, who is now the prophet of West Africa's future. And West Africa's future, eventually, will also be that of most of the rest of the world.

Consider "Chicago." I refer not to Chicago, Illinois, but to a slum district of Abidjan, which the young toughs in the area have named after the American city. ("Washington" is another poor section of Abidjan.) Although Sierra Leone is widely regarded as beyond salvage, the Ivory Coast has been considered an African success story, and Abidjan has been called "the Paris of West Africa." Success, however, was built on two artificial factors: the high price of cocoa, of which the Ivory Coast is the world's leading producer, and the talents of a French expatriate community, whose members have helped run the government and the private sector. The expanding cocoa economy made the Ivory Coast a magnet for migrant workers from all over West Africa: between a third and a half of the country's population is now non-Ivorian, and the figure could be as high as 75 percent in Abidjan. During the 1980s cocoa prices fell and the French began to leave. The skyscrapers of the Paris of West Africa are a façade. Perhaps 15 percent of Abidjan's population of three million people live in shantytowns like Chicago and Washington, and the vast majority live in places that are not much better. Not all of these places appear on any of the readily available maps. This is another indication of how political maps are the products of tired conventional wisdom and, in the Ivory Coast's case, of an elite that will ultimately be forced to relinquish power.

Chicago, like more and more of Abidjan, is a slum in the bush: a checkerwork of corrugated zinc roofs and walls made of cardboard and black plastic wrap. It is located in a gully teeming with coconut palms and oil palms, and is ravaged by flooding. Few residents have easy access to electricity, a sewage system, or a clean water supply. The crumbly red laterite earth crawls with foot-long lizards both inside and outside the shacks. Children defecate in a stream filled with garbage and pigs, droning with malarial mosquitoes. In this stream women do the washing. Young unemployed men spend their time drinking beer, palm wine, and gin while gambling on pinball games constructed out of rotting wood and rusty nails. These are the same youths who rob houses in more prosperous Ivorian neighborhoods at night. One man I met, Damba Tesele, came to Chicago from Burkina Faso in 1963. A cook by profession, he has four wives and thirty-two children, not one of whom has made it to high school. He has seen his shanty community destroyed by municipal authorities seven times since coming to the area. Each time he and his neighbors rebuild. Chicago is the latest incarnation.

Fifty-five percent of the Ivory Coast's population is urban, and the proportion is expected to reach 62 percent by 2000. The yearly net population growth is 3.6 percent. This means that the Ivory Coast's 13.5 million people will become 39 million by 2025, when much of the population will consist of urbanized peasants like those of Chicago. But don't count on the Ivory Coast's still existing then. Chicago, which is more indicative of Africa's and the Third World's demographic present—and even more of the future—than any idyllic junglescape of women balancing earthen jugs on their heads, illustrates why the Ivory Coast, once a model of Third World success, is becoming a case study in Third World catastrophe.

President Félix Houphouët-Boigny, who died last December at the age of about ninety, left behind a weak cluster of political parties and a leaden bureaucracy that discourages foreign investment. Because the military is small and the non-Ivorian population large, there is neither an obvious force to maintain order nor a sense of nationhood that would lessen the need for such enforcement. The economy has been shrinking since the mid-1980s. Though the French are working assiduously to preserve stability, the Ivory Coast faces a possibility worse than a coup: an anarchic implosion of criminal violence—an urbanized version of what has already happened in Somalia. Or it may become an African Yugoslavia, but one without mini-states to replace the whole.

Because the demographic reality of West Africa is a countryside draining into dense slums by the coast, ultimately the region's rulers will come to reflect the values of these shanty-towns. There are signs of this already in Sierra Leone—and in Togo, where the dictator Etienne Eyadema, in power since 1967, was nearly toppled in 1991, not by democrats but by thousands of youths whom the London-based magazine *West Africa* described as "Soweto-like stone-throwing adolescents." Their behavior may herald a regime more brutal than Eyadema's repressive one.

The fragility of these West African "countries" impressed itself on me when I took a series of bush taxis along the Gulf of Guinea, from the Togolese capital of Lomé, across Ghana, to Abidjan. The 400-mile journey required two full days of driving, because of stops at two border crossings and an additional eleven customs stations, at each of which my fellow passengers had their bags searched. I had to change money twice and repeatedly fill in currency-declaration forms. I had to bribe a Togolese immigration official with the equivalent of eighteen dollars before he would agree to put an exit stamp on my passport. Nevertheless, smuggling across these borders is rampant. *The London Observer* has reported that in 1992 the equivalent of $856 million left West Africa for Europe in the form of "hot cash" assumed to be laundered drug money. International cartels have discovered the utility of weak, financially strapped West African regimes.

The more fictitious the actual sovereignty, the more severe border authorities seem to be in trying to prove otherwise. Getting visas for these states can be as hard as crossing their borders. The Washington embassies of Sierra Leone and Guinea —the two poorest nations on earth, according to a 1993 United Nations report on "human development"—asked for letters from my bank (in lieu of prepaid round-trip tickets) and also personal references, in order to prove that I had sufficient means to sustain myself during my visits. I was reminded of my visa and currency hassles while traveling to the communist states of Eastern Europe, particularly East Germany and Czechoslovakia, before those states collapsed.

Ali A. Mazrui, the director of the Institute of Global Cultural Studies at the State University of New York at Binghamton, predicts that West Africa—indeed, the whole continent—is on the verge of large-scale border upheaval. Mazrui writes,

> In the 21st century France will be withdrawing from West Africa as she gets increasingly involved in the affairs [of Europe]. France's West African sphere of influence will be filled by Nigeria—a more natural hegemonic power. . . . It will be under those circumstances that Nigeria's own boundaries are likely to expand to incorporate the Republic of Niger (the Hausa link), the Republic of Benin (the Yoruba link) and conceivably Cameroon.

The future could be more tumultuous, and bloodier, than Mazrui dares to say. France *will* withdraw from former colonies like Benin, Togo, Niger, and the Ivory Coast, where it has been propping up local currencies. It will do so not only because its attention will be diverted to new challenges in Europe and Russia but also because younger French officials lack the older generation's emotional ties to the ex-colonies. However, even as Nigeria attempts to expand, it, too, is likely to split into several pieces. The State Department's Bureau of Intelligence and Research recently made the following points in an analysis of Nigeria:

> Prospects for a transition to civilian rule and democratization are slim. . . . The repressive apparatus of the state security service . . . will be difficult for any future civilian government to control. . . . The country is

becoming increasingly ungovernable. . . . Ethnic and regional splits are deepening, a situation made worse by an increase in the number of states from 19 to 30 and a doubling in the number of local governing authorities; religious cleavages are more serious; Muslim fundamentalism and evangelical Christian militancy are on the rise; and northern Muslim anxiety over southern [Christian] control of the economy is intense . . . the will to keep Nigeria together is now very weak.

Given that oil-rich Nigeria is a bellwether for the region—its population of roughly 90 million equals the populations of all the other West African states combined—it is apparent that Africa faces cataclysms that could make the Ethiopian and Somalian famines pale in comparison. This is especially so because Nigeria's population, including that of its largest city, Lagos, whose crime, pollution, and overcrowding make it the cliché par excellence of Third World urban dysfunction, is set to double during the next twenty-five years, while the country continues to deplete its natural resources.

Part of West Africa's quandary is that although its population belts are horizontal, with habitation densities increasing as one travels south away from the Sahara and toward the tropical abundance of the Atlantic littoral, the borders erected by European colonialists are vertical, and therefore at cross-purposes with demography and topography. Satellite photos depict the same reality I experienced in the bush taxi: the Lomé-Abidjan coastal corridor—indeed, the entire stretch of coast from Abidjan eastward to Lagos—is one burgeoning megalopolis that by any rational economic and geographical standard should constitute a single sovereignty, rather than the five (the Ivory Coast, Ghana, Togo, Benin, and Nigeria) into which it is currently divided.

As many internal African borders begin to crumble, a more impenetrable boundary is being erected that threatens to isolate the continent as a whole: the wall of disease. Merely to visit West Africa in some degree of safety, I spent about $500 for a hepatitis B vaccination series and other disease prophylaxis. Africa may today be more dangerous in this regard than it was in 1862, before antibiotics, when the explorer Sir Richard Francis Burton described the health situation on the continent as "deadly, a Golgotha, a Jehannum." Of the approximately 12 million people worldwide whose blood is HIV-positive, 8 million are in Africa. In the capital of the Ivory Coast, whose modern road system only helps to spread the disease, 10 percent of the population is HIV-positive. And war and refugee movements help the virus break through to more-remote areas of Africa. Alan Greenberg, M.D., a representative of the Centers for Disease Control in Abidjan, explains that in Africa the HIV virus and tuberculosis are now "fast-forwarding each other." Of the approximately 4,000 newly diagnosed tuberculosis patients in Abidjan, 45 percent were also found to be HIV-positive. As African birth rates soar and slums proliferate, some experts worry that viral mutations and hybridizations might, just conceivably, result in a form of the AIDS virus that is easier to catch than the present strain.

It is malaria that is most responsible for the disease wall that threatens to separate Africa and other parts of the Third World from more-developed regions of the planet in the twenty-first century. Carried by mosquitoes, malaria, unlike AIDS, is easy to catch. Most people in sub-Saharan Africa have recurring bouts of the disease throughout their entire lives, and it is mutating into increasingly deadly forms. "The great gift of Malaria is utter apathy," wrote Sir Richard Burton, accurately portraying the situation in much of the Third World today. Visitors to malaria-afflicted parts of the planet are protected by a new drug, mefloquine, a side effect of which is vivid, even violent, dreams. But a strain of cerebral malaria resistant to mefloquine is now on the offensive. Consequently, defending oneself against malaria in Africa is becoming more and more like defending oneself against violent crime. You engage in "behavior modification": not going out at dusk, wearing mosquito repellent all the time.

And the cities keep growing. I got a general sense of the future while driving from the airport to downtown Conakry, the capital of Guinea. The forty-five-minute journey in heavy traffic was through one never-ending shanty-town: a nightmarish Dickensian spectacle to which Dickens himself would never have given credence. The corrugated metal shacks and scabrous walls were coated with black slime. Stores were built out of rusted shipping containers, junked cars, and jumbles of wire mesh. The streets were one long puddle of floating garbage. Mosquitoes and flies were everywhere. Children, many of whom had protruding bellies, seemed as numerous as ants. When the tide went out, dead rats and the skeletons of cars were exposed on the mucky beach. In twenty-eight years Guinea's population will double if growth goes on at current rates. Hardwood logging continues at a madcap speed, and people flee the Guinean countryside for Conakry. It seemed to me that here, as elsewhere in Africa and the Third World, man is challenging nature far beyond its limits, and nature is now beginning to take its revenge.

Africa may be as relevant to the future character of world politics as the Balkans were a hundred years ago, prior to the two Balkan wars and the First World War. Then the threat was the collapse of empires and the birth of nations based solely on tribe. Now the threat is more elemental: *nature unchecked*. Africa's immediate future could be very bad. The coming upheaval, in which foreign embassies are shut down, states collapse, and contact with the outside world takes place through dangerous, disease-ridden coastal trading posts, will loom large in the century we are entering. (Nine of twenty-one U.S. foreign-aid missions to be closed over the next three years are in Africa—a prologue to a consolidation of U.S. embassies themselves.) Precisely because much of Africa is set to go over the edge at a time when the Cold War has ended, when environmental and demographic stress in other parts of the globe is becoming critical, and when the post–First World War system of nation-states—not just in the Balkans but perhaps also in the Middle East—is about to be toppled, Africa suggests what war, borders, and ethnic politics will be like a few decades hence.

To understand the events of the next fifty years, then, one must understand environmental scarcity, cultural and racial clash, geographic destiny, and the transformation of war. The order in which I have named these is not accidental. Each concept except the first relies partly on the one or ones before it, meaning that the last two—new approaches to mapmaking and to warfare—are the most important. They are also the least understood. I will now look at each idea, drawing upon the work of specialists and also my own travel experiences in various parts of the globe besides Africa, in order to fill in the blanks of a new political atlas.

The Environment as a Hostile Power

For a while the media will continue to ascribe riots and other violent upheavals abroad mainly to ethnic and religious conflict. But as these conflicts multiply, it will become apparent that something else is afoot, making more and more places like Nigeria, India, and Brazil ungovernable.

Mention "the environment" or "diminishing natural resources" in foreign-policy circles and you meet a brick wall of skepticism or boredom. To conservatives especially, the very terms seem flaky. Public-policy foundations have contributed to the lack of interest, by funding narrowly focused environmental studies replete with technical jargon which foreign-affairs experts just let pile up on their desks.

It is time to understand "the environment" for what it is: *the* national-security issue of the early twenty-first century. The political and strategic impact of surging populations, spreading disease, deforestation and soil erosion, water depletion, air pollution, and, possibly, rising sea levels in critical, overcrowded regions like the Nile Delta and Bangladesh—developments that will prompt mass migrations and, in turn, incite group conflicts—will be the core foreign-policy challenge from which most others will ultimately emanate, arousing the public and uniting assorted interests left over from the Cold War. In the twenty-first century water will be in dangerously short supply in such diverse locales as Saudi Arabia, Central Asia, and the southwestern United States. A war could erupt between Egypt and Ethiopia over Nile River water. Even in Europe tensions have arisen between Hungary and Slovakia over the damming of the Danube, a classic case of how environmental disputes fuse with ethnic and historical ones. The political scientist and erstwhile Clinton adviser Michael Mandelbaum has said, "We have a foreign policy today in the shape of a doughnut—lots of peripheral interests but nothing at the center." The environment, I will argue, is part of a terrifying array of problems that will define a new threat to our security, filling the hole in Mandelbaum's doughnut and allowing a post–Cold War foreign policy to emerge inexorably by need rather than by design.

Our Cold War foreign policy truly began with George F. Kennan's famous article, signed "X," published in *Foreign Affairs* in July of 1947, in which Kennan argued for a "firm and vigilant containment" of a Soviet Union that was imperially, rather than ideologically, motivated. It may be that our post–Cold War foreign policy will one day be seen to have had its beginnings in an even bolder and more detailed piece of written analysis: one that appeared in the journal *International Security*. The article, published in the fall of 1991 by Thomas Fraser Homer-Dixon, who is the head of the Peace and Conflict Studies Program at the University of Toronto, was titled "On the Threshold: Environmental Changes as Causes of Acute Conflict." Homer-Dixon has, more successfully than other analysts, integrated two hitherto separate fields—military-conflict studies and the study of the physical environment.

In Homer-Dixon's view, future wars and civil violence will often arise from scarcities of resources such as water, cropland, forests, and fish. Just as there will be environmentally driven wars and refugee flows, there will be environmentally induced praetorian regimes—or, as he puts it, "hard regimes." Countries with the highest probability of acquiring hard regimes, according to Homer-Dixon, are those that are threatened by a declining resource base yet also have "a history of state [read 'military'] strength." Candidates include Indonesia, Brazil, and, of course, Nigeria. Though each of these nations has exhibited democratizing tendencies of late, Homer-Dixon argues that such tendencies are likely to be superficial "epiphenomena" having nothing to do with long-term processes that include soaring populations and shrinking raw materials. Democracy is problematic; scarcity is more certain.

Indeed, the Saddam Husseins of the future will have more, not fewer, opportunities. In addition to engendering tribal strife, scarcer resources will place a great strain on many peoples who never had much of a democratic or institutional tradition to begin with. Over the next fifty years the earth's population will soar from 5.5 billion to more than nine billion. Though optimists have hopes for new resource technologies and free-market development in the global village, they fail to note that, as the National Academy of Sciences has pointed out, 95 percent of the population increase will be in the poorest regions of the world, where governments now—just look at Africa—show little ability to function, let alone to implement even marginal improvements. Homer-Dixon writes, ominously, "Neo-Malthusians may underestimate human adaptability in *today's* environmental-social system, but as time passes their analysis may become ever more compelling."

While a minority of the human population will be, as Francis Fukuyama would put it, sufficiently sheltered so as to enter a "post-historical" realm, living in cities and suburbs in which the environment has been mastered and ethnic animosities have been quelled by bourgeois prosperity, an increasingly large number of people will be stuck in history, living in shantytowns where attempts to rise above poverty, cultural dysfunction, and ethnic strife will be doomed by a lack of water to drink, soil to till, and space to survive in. In the developing world environmental stress will present people with a choice that is increasingly among totalitarianism (as in Iraq), fascist-tending mini-states (as in Serb-held Bosnia), and road-warrior cultures (as in Somalia). Homer-Dixon concludes that "as environmental degradation proceeds, the size of the potential social disruption will increase."

Tad Homer-Dixon is an unlikely Jeremiah. Today a boyish thirty-seven, he grew up amid the sylvan majesty of Vancouver Island, attending private day schools. His speech is calm, perfectly even, and crisply enunciated. There is nothing in his background or manner that would indicate a bent toward pessimism. A Canadian Anglican who spends his summers canoeing on the lakes of northern Ontario, and who talks about the benign mountains, black bears, and Douglas firs of his youth, he is the opposite of the intellectually severe neoconservative, the kind at home with conflict scenarios. Nor is he an environmentalist who opposes development. "My father was a logger who thought about ecologically safe forestry before others," he says. "He logged, planted, logged, and planted. He got out of the business just as the issue was being polarized by environmentalists. They hate changed ecosystems. But human beings, just by carrying seeds around, change the natural world." As an only child whose playground was a virtually untouched wilderness and seacoast, Homer-Dixon has a familiarity with the natural world that permits him to see a reality that most policy analysts—children of suburbia and city streets—are blind to.

"We need to bring nature back in," he argues. "We have to stop separating politics from the physical world—the climate, public health, and the environment." Quoting Daniel Deudney, another pioneering expert on the security aspects of the environment, Homer-Dixon says that "for too long we've been prisoners of 'social-social' theory, which assumes there are only social causes for social and political changes, rather than natural causes, too. This social-social mentality emerged with the Industrial Revolution, which separated us from nature. But nature is coming back with a vengeance, tied to population growth. It will have incredible security implications.

"Think of a stretch limo in the potholed streets of New York City, where homeless beggars live. Inside the limo are the air-conditioned post-industrial regions of North America, Europe, the emerging Pacific Rim, and a few other isolated places, with their trade summitry and computer-information highways. Outside is the rest of mankind, going in a completely different direction."

We are entering a bifurcated world. Part of the globe is inhabited by Hegel's and Fukuyama's Last Man, healthy, well fed, and pampered by technology. The other, larger, part is inhabited by Hobbes's First Man, condemned to a life that is "poor, nasty, brutish, and short." Although both parts will be threatened by environmental stress, the Last Man will be able to master it; the First Man will not.

The Last Man will adjust to the loss of underground water tables in the western United States. He will build dikes to save Cape Hatteras and the Chesapeake beaches from rising sea levels, even as the Maldive Islands, off the coast of India, sink into oblivion, and the shorelines of Egypt, Bangladesh, and Southeast Asia recede, driving tens of millions of people inland where there is no room for them, and thus sharpening ethnic divisions.

Homer-Dixon points to a world map of soil degradation in his Toronto office. "The darker the map color, the worse the degradation," he explains. The West African coast, the Middle East, the Indian subcontinent, China, and Central

America have the darkest shades, signifying all manner of degradation, related to winds, chemicals, and water problems. "The worst degradation is generally where the population is highest. The population is generally highest where the soil is the best. So we're degrading earth's best soil."

China, in Homer-Dixon's view, is the quintessential example of environmental degradation. Its current economic "success" masks deeper problems. "China's fourteen percent growth rate does not mean it's going to be a world power. It means that coastal China, where the economic growth is taking place, is joining the rest of the Pacific Rim. The disparity with inland China is intensifying." Referring to the environmental research of his colleague, the Czech-born ecologist Vaclav Smil, Homer-Dixon explains how the per capita availability of arable land in interior China has rapidly declined at the same time that the quality of that land has been destroyed by deforestation, loss of topsoil, and salinization. He mentions the loss and contamination of water supplies, the exhaustion of wells, the plugging of irrigation systems and reservoirs with eroded silt, and a population of 1.54 billion by the year 2025: it is a misconception that China has gotten its population under control. Large-scale population movements are under way, from inland China to coastal China and from villages to cities, leading to a crime surge like the one in Africa and to growing regional disparities and conflicts in a land with a strong tradition of warlordism and a weak tradition of central government—again as in Africa. "We will probably see the center challenged and fractured, and China will not remain the same on the map," Homer-Dixon says.

Environmental scarcity will inflame existing hatreds and affect power relationships, at which we now look.

Skinhead Cossacks, Juju Warriors

In the summer, 1993, issue of *Foreign Affairs*, Samuel P. Huntington, of Harvard's Olin Institute for Strategic Studies, published a thought-provoking article called "The Clash of Civilizations?" [p. 3, this volume]. The world, he argues, has been moving during the course of this century from nation-state conflict to ideological conflict to, finally, cultural conflict. I would add that as refugee flows increase and as peasants continue migrating to cities around the world—turning them into sprawling villages—national borders will mean less, even as more power will fall into the hands of less educated, less sophisticated groups. In the eyes of these uneducated but newly empowered millions, the real borders are the most tangible and intractable ones: those of culture and tribe. Huntington writes, "First, differences among civilizations are not only real; they are basic," involving, among other things, history, language, and religion. "Second . . . interactions between peoples of different civilizations are increasing; these increasing interactions intensify civilization consciousness." Economic modernization is not necessarily a panacea, since it fuels individual and group ambitions while weakening traditional loyalties to the state. It is worth noting, for example, that it is precisely the wealthiest and fastest-developing city in India, Bombay, that has seen the worst intercommunal violence between Hindus and Muslims. Consider that Indian cities, like African and Chinese ones, are ecological time bombs—Delhi and Calcutta, and also Beijing, suffer the worst air quality of any cities in the world—and it is apparent how surging populations, environmental degradation, and ethnic conflict are deeply related.

Huntington points to interlocking conflicts among Hindu, Muslim, Slavic Orthodox, Western, Japanese, Confucian, Latin American, and possibly African civilizations: for instance, Hindus clashing with Muslims in India, Turkic Muslims clashing with Slavic Orthodox Russians in Central Asian cities, the West clashing with Asia. (Even in the United States, African-Americans find themselves besieged by an influx of competing Latinos.) Whatever the laws, refugees find a way to crash official borders, bringing their passions with them, meaning that Europe and the United States will be weakened by cultural disputes.

Because Huntington's brush is broad, his specifics are vulnerable to attack. In a rebuttal of Huntington's argument the Johns Hopkins professor Fouad Ajami, a Lebanese-born Shi'ite who certainly knows the world beyond suburbia, writes in the September-October, 1993, issue of *Foreign Affairs* [p. 63, this volume],

> The world of Islam divides and subdivides. The battle lines in the Caucasus . . . are not coextensive with civilizational fault lines. The lines follow the interests of states. Where Huntington sees a civilizational duel between Armenia and Azerbaijan, the Iranian state has cast religious zeal . . . to the wind . . . in that battle the Iranians have tilted toward Christian Armenia.

True, Huntington's hypothesized war between Islam and Orthodox Christianity is not borne out by the alliance network in the Caucasus. But that is only because he has misidentified *which* cultural war is occurring there. A recent visit to Azerbaijan made clear to me that Azeri Turks, the world's most secular Shi'ite Muslims, see their cultural identity in terms not of religion but of their Turkic race. The Armenians, likewise, fight the Azeris not because the latter are Muslims but because they are Turks, related to the same Turks who massacred Armenians in 1915. Turkic culture (secular and based on languages employing a Latin script) is battling Iranian culture (religiously militant as defined by Tehran, and wedded to an Arabic script) across the whole swath of Central Asia and the Caucasus. The Armenians are, therefore, natural allies of their fellow Indo-Europeans the Iranians.

Huntington is correct that the Caucasus is a flashpoint of cultural and racial war. But, as Ajami observes, Huntington's plate tectonics are too simple. Two months of recent travel throughout Turkey revealed to me that although the Turks are developing a deep distrust, bordering on hatred, of fellow-Muslim Iran, they are also, especially in the shantytowns that are coming to dominate Turkish public opinion, revising their group identity, increasingly seeing themselves as Muslims being deserted by a West that does little to help besieged Muslims in Bosnia and that attacks Turkish Muslims in the streets of Germany.

In other words, the Balkans, a powder keg for nation-state war at the beginning of the twentieth century, could be a powder keg for cultural war at the turn of the twenty-first: between Orthodox Christianity (represented by the Serbs and a classic Byzantine configuration of Greeks, Russians, and Romanians) and the House of Islam. Yet in the Caucasus that House of Islam is falling into a clash between Turkic and Iranian civilizations. Ajami asserts that this very subdivision, not to mention all the divisions within the Arab world, indicates that the West, including the United States, is not threatened by Huntington's scenario. As the Gulf War demonstrated, the West has proved capable of playing one part of the House of Islam against another.

True. However, whether he is aware of it or not, Ajami is describing a world even more dangerous than the one Huntington envisions, especially when one takes into account Homer-Dixon's research on environmental scarcity. Outside the stretch limo would be a rundown, crowded planet of skinhead Cossacks and *juju* warriors, influenced by the worst refuse of Western pop culture and ancient tribal hatreds, and battling over scraps of overused earth in guerrilla conflicts that ripple across continents and intersect in no discernible pattern—meaning there's no easy-to-define threat. Kennan's world of one adversary seems as distant as the world of Herodotus.

Most people believe that the political earth since 1989 has undergone immense change. But it is minor compared with what is yet to come. The breaking apart and remaking of the atlas is only now beginning. The crack-up of the Soviet empire and the coming end of Arab-Israeli military confrontation are merely prologues to the really big changes that lie ahead. Michael Vlahos, a long-range thinker for the U.S. Navy, warns, "We are not in charge of the environment and the world is not following us. It is going in many directions. Do not assume that democratic capitalism is the last word in human social evolution."

Before addressing the questions of maps and of warfare, I want to take a closer look at the interaction of religion, culture, demographic shifts, and the distribution of natural resources in a specific area of the world: the Middle East.

The Past Is Dead

Built on steep, muddy hills, the shantytowns of Ankara, the Turkish capital, exude visual drama. Altindag, or "Golden Mountain," is a pyramid of dreams, fashioned from cinder blocks and corrugated iron, rising as though each shack were built on top of another, all reaching awkwardly and painfully toward heaven —the heaven of wealthier Turks who live elsewhere in the city. Nowhere else on the planet have I found such a poignant architectural symbol of man's striving, with gaps in house walls plugged with rusted cans, and leeks and onions growing on verandas assembled from planks of rotting wood. For reasons that I will explain, the Turkish shacktown is a psychological universe away from the African one.

To see the twenty-first century truly, one's eyes must learn a different set of aesthetics. One must reject the overly stylized images of travel magazines, with their inviting photographs of exotic villages and glamorous downtowns. There are far too many millions whose dreams are more vulgar, more real—whose raw energies and desires will overwhelm the visions of the elites, remaking the future into something frighteningly new. But in Turkey I learned that shantytowns are not all bad.

Slum quarters in Abidjan terrify and repel the outsider. In Turkey it is the opposite. The closer I got to Golden Mountain the better it looked, and the safer I felt. I had $1,500 worth of Turkish lira in one pocket and $1,000 in traveler's checks in the other, yet I felt no fear. Golden Mountain was a real neighborhood. The inside of one house told the story: The architectural bedlam of cinder block and sheet metal and cardboard walls was deceiving. Inside was a *home*—order, that is, bespeaking dignity. I saw a working refrigerator, a television, a wall cabinet with a few books and lots of family pictures, a few plants by a window, and a stove. Though the streets become rivers of mud when it rains, the floors inside this house were spotless.

Other houses were like this too. Schoolchildren ran along with briefcases strapped to their backs, trucks delivered cooking gas, a few men sat inside a café sipping tea. One man sipped beer. Alcohol is easy to obtain in Turkey, a secular state where 99 percent of the population is Muslim. Yet there is little problem of alcoholism. Crime against persons is infinitesimal. Poverty and illiteracy are watered-down versions of what obtains in Algeria and Egypt (to say nothing of West Africa), making it that much harder for religious extremists to gain a foothold.

My point in bringing up a rather wholesome, crime-free slum is this: its existence demonstrates how formidable is the fabric of which Turkish Muslim culture is made. A culture this strong has the potential to dominate the Middle East once again. Slums are litmus tests for innate cultural strengths and weaknesses. Those peoples whose cultures can harbor extensive slum life without decomposing will be, relatively speaking, the future's winners. Those whose cultures cannot will be the future's victims. Slums—in the sociological sense—do not exist in Turkish cities. The mortar between people and family groups is stronger here than in Africa. Resurgent Islam and Turkic cultural identity have produced a civilization with natural muscle tone. Turks, history's perennial nomads, take disruption in stride.

The future of the Middle East is quietly being written inside the heads of Golden Mountain's inhabitants. Think of an Ottoman military encampment on the eve of the destruction of Greek Constantinople in 1453. That is Golden Mountain. "We brought the village here. But in the village we worked harder—in the field, all day. So we couldn't fast during [the holy month of] Ramadan. Here we fast. Here we are more religious." Aishe Tanrikulu, along with half a dozen other women, was stuffing rice into vine leaves from a crude plastic bowl. She asked me to join her under the shade of a piece of sheet metal. Each of these women had her hair covered by a kerchief. In the city they were encountering television for the first time. "We are traditional, religious people. The programs offend us," Aishe said. Another woman complained about the schools. Though her children had educational options unavailable in the village, they had to compete with wealthier, secular Turks. "The kids from rich families with connections—they get all the places." More opportunities, more tensions, in other words.

My guidebook to Golden Mountain was an untypical one: *Tales From the Garbage Hills,* a brutally realistic novel by a Turkish writer, Latife Tekin, about life in the shantytowns, which in Turkey are called *gecekondus* ("built in a night"). "He listened to the earth and wept unceasingly for water, for work and for the cure of the illnesses spread by the garbage and the factory waste," Tekin writes. In the most revealing passage of *Tales From the Garbage Hills* the squatters are told "about a certain 'Ottoman Empire' . . . that where they now lived there had once been an empire of this name." This history "confounded" the squatters. It was the first they had heard of it. Though one of them knew "that his grandfather and his dog died fighting the Greeks," nationalism and an encompassing sense of Turkish history are the province of the Turkish middle and upper classes, and of foreigners like me who feel required to have a notion of "Turkey."

But what did the Golden Mountain squatters know about the armies of Turkish migrants that had come before their own—namely, Seljuks and Ottomans? For these recently urbanized peasants, and their counterparts in Africa, the Arab world, India, and so many other places, the world is new, to adapt V. S. Naipaul's phrase. As Naipaul wrote of urban refugees in *India: A Wounded Civilization,* "They saw themselves at the beginning of things: unaccommodated men making a claim on their land for the first time, and out of chaos evolving their own philosophy of community and self-help. For them the past was dead; they had left it behind in the villages."

Everywhere in the developing world at the turn of the twenty-first century these new men and women, rushing into the cities, are remaking civilizations and redefining their identities in terms of religion and tribal ethnicity which do not coincide with the borders of existing states.

In Turkey several things are happening at once. In 1980, 44 percent of Turks lived in cities; in 1990 it was 61 percent. By the year 2000 the figure is expected to be 67 percent. Villages are emptying out as concentric rings of *gecekondu* developments grow around Turkish cities. This is the real political and demographic revolution in Turkey and elsewhere, and foreign correspondents usually don't write about it.

Whereas rural poverty is age-old and almost a "normal" part of the social fabric, urban poverty is socially destabilizing. As Iran has shown, Islamic extremism is the psychological defense mechanism of many urbanized peasants threatened with the loss of traditions in pseudo-modern cities where their values are under attack, where basic services like water and electricity are unavailable, and where they are assaulted by a physically unhealthy environment. The American ethnologist and orientalist Carleton Stevens Coon wrote in 1951 that Islam "has made possible the optimum survival and happiness of millions of human beings in an increasingly impoverished environment over a fourteen-hundred-year period." Beyond its stark, clearly articulated message, Islam's very militancy makes it attractive to the downtrodden. It is the one religion that is prepared to *fight*. A political era driven by environmental stress, increased cultural sensitivity, unregulated urbanization, and refugee migrations is an era divinely created for the spread and intensification of Islam, already the world's fastest-growing religion. (Though Islam is spreading in West Africa, it is being hobbled by syncretization with animism: this makes new converts less apt to become anti-Western extremists, but it also makes for a weakened version of the faith, which is less effective as an antidote to crime.)

In Turkey, however, Islam is painfully and awkwardly forging a consensus with modernization, a trend that is less apparent in the Arab and Persian worlds (and virtually invisible in Africa). In Iran the oil boom—because it put development and urbanization on a fast track, making the culture shock more intense—fueled the 1978 Islamic Revolution. But Turkey, unlike Iran and the Arab world, has little oil. Therefore its development and urbanization have been more gradual. Islamists have been integrated into the parliamentary system for decades. The tensions I noticed in Golden Mountain are natural, creative ones: the kind immigrants face the world over. While the world has focused on religious perversity in Algeria, a nation rich in natural gas, and in Egypt, parts of whose capital city, Cairo, evince worse crowding than I have seen even in Calcutta, Turkey has been living through the Muslim equivalent of the Protestant Reformation.

Resource distribution is strengthening Turks in another way vis-à-vis Arabs and Persians. Turks may have little oil, but their Anatolian heartland has lots of water—the most important fluid of the twenty-first century. Turkey's Southeast Anatolia Project, involving twenty-two major dams and irrigation systems, is impounding the waters of the Tigris and Euphrates rivers. Much of the water that Arabs and perhaps Israelis will need to drink in the future is controlled by Turks. The project's centerpiece is the mile-wide, sixteen-story Atatürk Dam, upon which are emblazoned the words of modern Turkey's founder: "*Ne Mutlu Turkum Diyene*" ("Lucky is the one who is a Turk").

Unlike Egypt's Aswan High Dam, on the Nile, and Syria's Revolution Dam, on the Euphrates, both of which were built largely by Russians, the Atatürk Dam is a predominantly Turkish affair, with Turkish engineers and companies in charge. On a recent visit my eyes took in the immaculate offices and their gardens, the high-voltage electric grids and phone switching stations, the dizzying sweep of giant humming transformers, the poured-concrete spillways, and the prim unfolding suburbia, complete with schools, for dam employees. The emerging power of the Turks was palpable.

Erduhan Bayindir, the site manager at the dam, told me that "while oil can be shipped abroad to enrich only elites, water has to be spread more evenly within the society. . . . It is true, we can stop the flow of water into Syria and Iraq for up to eight months without the same water overflowing our dams, in order to regulate their political behavior."

Power is certainly moving north in the Middle East, from the oil fields of

Dhahran, on the Persian Gulf, to the water plain of Harran, in southern Anatolia
—near the site of the Atatürk Dam. But will the nation-state of Turkey, as presently constituted, be the inheritor of this wealth?

I very much doubt it.

The Lies of Mapmakers

Whereas West Africa represents the least stable part of political reality outside
Homer-Dixon's stretch limo, Turkey, an organic outgrowth of two Turkish empires that ruled Anatolia for 850 years, has been among the most stable. Turkey's
borders were established not by colonial powers but in a war of independence, in
the early 1920s. Kemal Atatürk provided Turkey with a secular nation-building
myth that most Arab and African states, burdened by artificially drawn borders,
lack. That lack will leave many Arab states defenseless against a wave of Islam
that will eat away at their legitimacy and frontiers in coming years. Yet even as
regards Turkey, maps deceive.

It is not only African shantytowns that don't appear on urban maps. Many
shantytowns in Turkey and elsewhere are also missing—as are the considerable
territories controlled by guerrilla armies and urban mafias. Traveling with Eritrean guerrillas in what, according to the map, was northern Ethiopia, traveling in
"northern Iraq" with Kurdish guerrillas, and staying in a hotel in the Caucasus
controlled by a local mafia—to say nothing of my experiences in West Africa—
led me to develop a healthy skepticism toward maps, which, I began to realize,
create a conceptual barrier that prevents us from comprehending the political
crack-up just beginning to occur worldwide.

Consider the map of the world, with its 190 or so countries, each signified by
a bold and uniform color: this map, with which all of us have grown up, is generally an invention of modernism, specifically of European colonialism. Modernism, in the sense of which I speak, began with the rise of nation-states in Europe
and was confirmed by the death of feudalism at the end of the Thirty Years' War
—an event that was interposed between the Renaissance and the Enlightenment,
which together gave birth to modern science. People were suddenly flush with
an enthusiasm to categorize, to define. The map, based on scientific techniques of
measurement, offered a way to classify new national organisms, making a jigsaw
puzzle of neat pieces without transition zones between them. "Frontier" is itself
a modern concept that didn't exist in the feudal mind. And as European nations
carved out far-flung domains at the same time that print technology was making
the reproduction of maps cheaper, cartography came into its own as a way of
creating facts by ordering the way we look at the world.

In his book *Imagined Communities: Reflections on the Origin and Spread of
Nationalism,* Benedict Anderson, of Cornell University, demonstrates that the
map enabled colonialists to think about their holdings in terms of a "totalizing
classificatory grid. . . . It was bounded, determinate, and therefore—in principle
—countable." To the colonialist, country maps were the equivalent of an accoun-

tant's ledger books. Maps, Anderson explains, "shaped the grammar" that would make possible such questionable concepts as Iraq, Indonesia, Sierra Leone, and Nigeria. The state, recall, is a purely Western notion, one that until the twentieth century applied to countries covering only three percent of the earth's land area. Nor is the evidence compelling that the state, as a governing ideal, can be successfully transported to areas outside the industrialized world. Even the United States of America, in the words of one of our best living poets, Gary Snyder, consists of "arbitrary and inaccurate impositions on what is really here."

Yet this inflexible, artificial reality staggers on, not only in the United Nations but in various geographic and travel publications (themselves by-products of an age of elite touring which colonialism made possible) that still report on and photograph the world according to "country." Newspapers, this magazine, and this writer are not innocent of the tendency.

According to the map, the great hydropower complex emblemized by the Atatürk Dam is situated in Turkey. Forget the map. This southeastern region of Turkey is populated almost completely by Kurds. About half of the world's 20 million Kurds live in "Turkey." The Kurds are predominant in an ellipse of territory that overlaps not only with Turkey but also with Iraq, Iran, Syria, and the former Soviet Union. The Western-enforced Kurdish enclave in northern Iraq, a consequence of the 1991 Gulf War, has already exposed the fictitious nature of that supposed nation-state.

On a recent visit to the Turkish-Iranian border, it occurred to me what a risky idea the nation-state is. Here I was on the legal fault line between two clashing civilizations, Turkic and Iranian. Yet the reality was more subtle: as in West Africa, the border was porous and smuggling abounded, but here the people doing the smuggling, on both sides of the border, were Kurds. In such a moonscape, over which peoples have migrated and settled in patterns that obliterate borders, the end of the Cold War will bring on a cruel process of natural selection among existing states. No longer will these states be so firmly propped up by the West or the Soviet Union. Because the Kurds overlap with nearly everybody in the Middle East, on account of their being cheated out of a state in the post–First World War peace treaties, they are emerging, in effect, as *the* natural selector—the ultimate reality check. They have destabilized Iraq and may continue to disrupt states that do not offer them adequate breathing space, while strengthening states that do.

Because the Turks, owing to their water resources, their growing economy, and the social cohesion evinced by the most crime-free slums I have encountered, are on the verge of big-power status, and because the 10 million Kurds within Turkey threaten that status, the outcome of the Turkish-Kurdish dispute will be more critical to the future of the Middle East than the eventual outcome of the recent Israeli-Palestinian agreement.

America's fascination with the Israeli-Palestinian issue, coupled with its lack of interest in the Turkish-Kurdish one, is a function of its own domestic and ethnic obsessions, not of the cartographic reality that is about to transform the Middle

East. The diplomatic process involving Israelis and Palestinians will, I believe, have little effect on the early- and mid-twenty-first-century map of the region. Israel, with a 6.6 percent economic growth rate based increasingly on high-tech exports, is about to enter Homer-Dixon's stretch limo, fortified by a well-defined political community that is an organic outgrowth of history and ethnicity. Like prosperous and peaceful Japan on the one hand, and war-torn and poverty-wracked Armenia on the other, Israel is a classic national-ethnic organism. Much of the Arab world, however, will undergo alteration, as Islam spreads across artificial frontiers, fueled by mass migrations into the cities and a soaring birth rate of more than 3.2 percent. Seventy percent of the Arab population has been born since 1970—youths with little historical memory of anticolonial independence struggles, postcolonial attempts at nation-building, or any of the Arab-Israeli wars. The most distant recollection of these youths will be the West's humiliation of colonially invented Iraq in 1991. Today seventeen out of twenty-two Arab states have a declining gross national product; in the next twenty years, at current growth rates, the population of many Arab countries will double. These states, like most African ones, will be ungovernable through conventional secular ideologies. The Middle East analyst Christine M. Helms explains,

> Declaring Arab nationalism "bankrupt," the political "disinherited" are not rationalizing the failure of Arabism . . . or reformulating it. Alternative solutions are not contemplated. They have simply opted for the political paradigm at the other end of the political spectrum with which they are familiar—Islam.

Like the borders of West Africa, the colonial borders of Syria, Iraq, Jordan, Algeria, and other Arab states are often contrary to cultural and political reality. As state control mechanisms wither in the face of environmental and demographic stress, "hard" Islamic city-states or shantytown-states are likely to emerge. The fiction that the impoverished city of Algiers, on the Mediterranean, controls Tamanrasset, deep in the Algerian Sahara, cannot obtain forever. Whatever the outcome of the peace process, Israel is destined to be a Jewish ethnic fortress amid a vast and volatile realm of Islam. In that realm, the violent youth culture of the Gaza shantytowns may be indicative of the coming era.

The destiny of Turks and Kurds is far less certain, but far more relevant to the kind of map that will explain our future world. The Kurds suggest a geographic reality that cannot be shown in two-dimensional space. The issue in Turkey is not simply a matter of giving autonomy or even independence to Kurds in the southeast. This isn't the Balkans or the Caucasus, where regions are merely subdividing into smaller units, Abkhazia breaking off from Georgia, and so on. Federalism is not the answer. Kurds are found everywhere in Turkey, including the shanty districts of Istanbul and Ankara. Turkey's problem is that its Anatolian land mass is the home of two cultures and languages, Turkish and Kurdish. Identity in Turkey, as in India, Africa, and elsewhere, is more complex and subtle than conventional cartography can display.

A New Kind of War

To appreciate fully the political and cartographic implications of postmodernism
—an epoch of themeless juxtapositions, in which the classificatory grid of nation-
states is going to be replaced by a jagged-glass pattern of city-states, shanty-states,
nebulous and anarchic regionalisms—it is necessary to consider, finally, the whole
question of war.

"Oh, what a relief to fight, to fight enemies who defend themselves, enemies
who are awake!" André Malraux wrote in *Man's Fate*. I cannot think of a more
suitable battle cry for many combatants in the early decades of the twenty-first
century. The intense savagery of the fighting in such diverse cultural settings as
Liberia, Bosnia, the Caucasus, and Sri Lanka—to say nothing of what obtains in
American inner cities—indicates something very troubling that those of us inside the stretch limo, concerned with issues like middleclass entitlements and the
future of interactive cable television, lack the stomach to contemplate. It is this: a
large number of people on this planet, to whom the comfort and stability of a
middle-class life is utterly unknown, find war and a barracks existence a step up
rather than a step down.

"Just as it makes no sense to ask 'why people eat' or 'what they sleep for,'"
writes Martin van Creveld, a military historian at the Hebrew University in Jerusalem, in *The Transformation of War*, "so fighting in many ways is not a means
but an end. Throughout history, for every person who has expressed his horror
of war there is another who found in it the most marvelous of all the experiences
that are vouchsafed to man, even to the point that he later spent a lifetime bor-
ing his descendants by recounting his exploits." When I asked Pentagon officials
about the nature of war in the twenty-first century, the answer I frequently got was
"Read Van Creveld." The top brass are enamored of this historian not because
his writings justify their existence but, rather, the opposite: Van Creveld warns
them that huge state military machines like the Pentagon's are dinosaurs about to
go extinct, and that something far more terrible awaits us.

The degree to which Van Creveld's *Transformation of War* complements
Homer-Dixon's work on the environment, Huntington's thoughts on cultural
clash, my own realizations in traveling by foot, bus, and bush taxi in more than
sixty countries, and America's sobering comeuppances in intractable-culture
zones like Haiti and Somalia is startling. The book begins by demolishing the notion that men don't like to fight. "By compelling the senses to focus themselves
on the here and now," Van Creveld writes, war "can cause a man to take his leave
of them." As anybody who has had experience with Chetniks in Serbia, "tech-
nicals" in Somalia, Tontons Macoutes in Haiti, or soldiers in Sierra Leone can tell
you, in places where the Western Enlightenment has not penetrated and where
there has always been mass poverty, people find liberation in violence. In Afghanistan and elsewhere, I vicariously experienced this phenomenon: worrying about
mines and ambushes frees you from worrying about mundane details of daily existence. If my own experience is too subjective, there is a wealth of data showing

the sheer frequency of war, especially in the developing world since the Second World War. Physical aggression is a part of being human. Only when people attain a certain economic, educational, and cultural standard is this trait tranquilized. In light of the fact that 95 percent of the earth's population growth will be in the poorest areas of the globe, the question is not whether there will be war (there will be a lot of it) but what kind of war. And who will fight whom?

Debunking the great military strategist Carl von Clausewitz, Van Creveld, who may be the most original thinker on war since that early-nineteenth-century Prussian, writes, "Clausewitz's ideas . . . were wholly rooted in the fact that, ever since 1648, war had been waged overwhelmingly by states." But, as Van Creveld explains, the period of nation-states and, therefore, of state conflict is now ending, and with it the clear "threefold division into government, army, and people" which state-directed wars enforce. Thus, to see the future, the first step is to look back to the past immediately prior to the birth of modernism—the wars in medieval Europe which began during the Reformation and reached their culmination in the Thirty Years' War.

Van Creveld writes,

> In all these struggles political, social, economic, and religious motives were hopelessly entangled. Since this was an age when armies consisted of mercenaries, all were also attended by swarms of military entrepreneurs. . . . Many of them paid little but lip service to the organizations for whom they had contracted to fight. Instead, they robbed the countryside on their own behalf. . . .
>
> Given such conditions, any fine distinctions . . . between armies on the one hand and peoples on the other were bound to break down. Engulfed by war, civilians suffered terrible atrocities.

Back then, in other words, there was no "politics" as we have come to understand the term, just as there is less and less "politics" today in Liberia, Sierra Leone, Somalia, Sri Lanka, the Balkans, and the Caucasus, among other places.

Because, as Van Creveld notes, the radius of trust within tribal societies is narrowed to one's immediate family and guerrilla comrades, truces arranged with one Bosnian commander, say, may be broken immediately by another Bosnian commander. The plethora of short-lived ceasefires in the Balkans and the Caucasus constitute proof that we are no longer in a world where the old rules of state warfare apply. More evidence is provided by the destruction of medieval monuments in the Croatian port of Dubrovnik: when cultures, rather than states, fight, then cultural and religious monuments are weapons of war, making them fair game.

Also, war-making entities will no longer be restricted to a specific territory. Loose and shadowy organisms such as Islamic terrorist organizations suggest why borders will mean increasingly little and sedimentary layers of tribalistic identity and control will mean more. "From the vantage point of the present, there appears every prospect that religious . . . fanaticisms will play a larger role in the motivation of armed conflict" in the West than at any time "for the last 300 years," Van Creveld writes. This is why analysts like Michael Vlahos are closely monitoring religious cults. Vlahos says, "An ideology that challenges us may not take familiar form, like the old Nazis or Commies. It may not even engage us initially in ways that fit old threat markings." Van Creveld concludes, "Armed conflict will be waged by men on earth, not robots in space. It will have more in common with the struggles of primitive tribes than with large-scale conventional war." While another military historian, John Keegan, in his new book *A History of Warfare,* draws a more benign portrait of primitive man, it is important to point out that what Van Creveld really means is *re-primitivized* man: warrior societies operating at a time of unprecedented resource scarcity and planetary overcrowding.

Van Creveld's pre-Westphalian vision of worldwide low-intensity conflict is not a superficial "back to the future" scenario. First of all, technology will be used toward primitive ends. In Liberia the guerrilla leader Prince Johnson didn't just cut off the ears of President Samuel Doe before Doe was tortured to death in 1990—Johnson made a video of it, which has circulated throughout West Africa. In December of 1992, when plotters of a failed coup against the Strasser regime in Sierra Leone had their ears cut off at Freetown's Hamilton Beach prior to being killed, it was seen by many to be a copycat execution. Considering, as I've explained earlier, that the Strasser regime is not really a government and that Sierra Leone is not really a nation-state, listen closely to Van Creveld: "Once the legal monopoly of armed force, long claimed by the state, is wrested out of its hands, existing distinctions between war and crime will break down much as is already the case today in . . . Lebanon, Sri Lanka, El Salvador, Peru, or Colombia."

If crime and war become indistinguishable, then "national defense" may in the future be viewed as a local concept. As crime continues to grow in our cities and the ability of state governments and criminal-justice systems to protect their citizens diminishes, urban crime may, according to Van Creveld, "develop into low-intensity conflict by coalescing along racial, religious, social, and political lines." As small-scale violence multiplies at home and abroad, state armies will continue to shrink, being gradually replaced by a booming private security business, as in West Africa, and by urban mafias, especially in the former communist world, who may be better equipped than municipal police forces to grant physical protection to local inhabitants.

Future wars will be those of communal survival, aggravated or, in many cases, caused by environmental scarcity. These wars will be subnational, meaning that it will be hard for states and local governments to protect their own citizens physically. This is how many states will ultimately die. As state power fades—and with it the state's ability to help weaker groups within society, not to mention other states—peoples and cultures around the world will be thrown back upon their own strengths and weaknesses, with fewer equalizing mechanisms to protect them. Whereas the distant future will probably see the emergence of a racially hybrid, globalized man, the coming decades will see us more aware of our differences than of our similarities. To the average person, political values will mean less, personal security more. The belief that we are all equal is liable to be replaced by the overriding obsession of the ancient Greek travelers: Why the differences between peoples?

The Last Map

In *Geography and the Human Spirit,* Anne Buttimer, a professor at University College, Dublin, recalls the work of an early-nineteenth-century German geographer, Carl Ritter, whose work implied "a divine plan for humanity" based on regionalism and a constant, living flow of forms. The map of the future, to the extent that a map is even possible, will represent a perverse twisting of Ritter's vision. Imagine cartography in three dimensions, as if in a hologram. In this hologram would be the overlapping sediments of group and other identities atop the merely two-dimensional color markings of city-states and the remaining nations, themselves confused in places by shadowy tentacles, hovering overhead, indicating the power of drug cartels, mafias, and private security agencies. Instead of borders, there would be moving "centers" of power, as in the Middle Ages. Many of these layers would be in motion. Replacing fixed and abrupt lines on a flat space would be a shifting pattern of buffer entities, like the Kurdish and Azeri buffer entities between Turkey and Iran, the Turkic Uighur buffer entity between Central Asia and Inner China (itself distinct from coastal China), and the Latino buffer entity replacing a precise U.S.-Mexican border. To this protean cartographic hologram one must add other factors, such as migrations of populations, explosions of birth rates, vectors of disease. Henceforward the map of the world will never be static. This future map—in a sense, the "Last Map"—will be an ever-mutating representation of chaos.

The Indian subcontinent offers examples of what is happening. For different reasons, both India and Pakistan are increasingly dysfunctional. The argument over democracy in these places is less and less relevant to the larger issue of governability. In India's case the question arises, Is one unwieldy bureaucracy in New Delhi the best available mechanism for promoting the lives of 866 million people of diverse languages, religions, and ethnic groups? In 1950, when the Indian population was much less than half as large and nation-building idealism was still strong, the argument for democracy was more impressive than it is now. Given that in 2025 India's population could be close to 1.5 billion, that much of its economy rests on a shrinking natural-resource base, including dramatically declining water levels, and that communal violence and urbanization are spiraling upward, it is difficult to imagine that the Indian state will survive the next century. India's oft-trumpeted Green Revolution has been achieved by overworking its croplands and depleting its watershed. Norman Myers, a British development consultant, worries that Indians have "been feeding themselves today by borrowing against their children's food sources."

Pakistan's problem is more basic still: like much of Africa, the country makes no geographic or demographic sense. It was founded as a homeland for the Muslims of the subcontinent, yet there are more subcontinental Muslims outside Pakistan than within it. Like Yugoslavia, Pakistan is a patchwork of ethnic groups, increasingly in violent conflict with one another. While the Western media gushes over the fact that the country has a woman Prime Minister, Benazir Bhutto, Karachi is becoming a subcontinental version of Lagos. In eight visits to Pakistan, I have never gotten a sense of a cohesive national identity. With as much as 65 percent of its land dependent on intensive irrigation, with wide-scale deforestation, and with a yearly population growth of 2.7 percent (which ensures that the amount of cultivated land per rural inhabitant will plummet), Pakistan is becoming a more and more desperate place. As irrigation in the Indus River basin intensifies to serve two growing populations, Muslim-Hindu strife over falling water tables may be unavoidable.

"India and Pakistan will probably fall apart," Homer-Dixon predicts. "Their secular governments have less and less legitimacy as well as less management ability over people and resources." Rather than one bold line dividing the subcontinent into two parts, the future will likely see a lot of thinner lines and smaller parts, with the ethnic entities of Pakhtunistan and Punjab gradually replacing Pakistan in the space between the Central Asian plateau and the heart of the subcontinent.

None of this even takes into account climatic change, which, if it occurs in the next century, will further erode the capacity of existing states to cope. India, for instance, receives 70 percent of its precipitation from the monsoon cycle, which planetary warming could disrupt.

Not only will the three-dimensional aspects of the Last Map be in constant motion, but its two-dimensional base may change too. The National Academy of Sciences reports that

> as many as one billion people, or 20 per cent of the world's population, live on lands likely to be inundated or dramatically changed by rising waters. . . . Low-lying countries in the developing world such as Egypt and Bangladesh, where rivers are large and the deltas extensive and densely populated, will be hardest hit. . . . Where the rivers are dammed, as in the case of the Nile, the effects . . . will be especially severe.

Egypt could be where climatic upheaval—to say nothing of the more immediate threat of increasing population—will incite religious upheaval in truly biblical fashion. Natural catastrophes, such as the October, 1992, Cairo earthquake, in which the government failed to deliver relief aid and slum residents were in many instances helped by their local mosques, can only strengthen the position of Islamic factions. In a statement about greenhouse warming which could refer to any of a variety of natural catastrophes, the environmental expert Jessica Tuchman Matthews warns that many of us underestimate the extent to which political systems, in affluent societies as well as in places like Egypt, "depend on the underpinning of natural systems." She adds, "The fact that one can move with ease from Vermont to Miami has nothing to say about the consequences of Vermont acquiring Miami's climate."

Indeed, it is not clear that the United States will survive the next century in exactly its present form. Because America is a multi-ethnic society, the nation-state has always been more fragile here than it is in more homogeneous societies like Germany and Japan. James Kurth, in an article published in *The National Interest* in 1992, explains that whereas nation-state societies tend to be built around a mass-conscription army and a standardized public school system, "multicultural regimes" feature a high-tech, all-volunteer army (and, I would add, private schools that teach competing values), operating in a culture in which the international media and entertainment industry has more influence than the "national political class." In other words, a nation-state is a place where everyone has been educated along similar lines, where people take their cue from national leaders, and where everyone (every male, at least) has gone through the crucible of military service, making patriotism a simpler issue. Writing about his immigrant family in turn-of-the-century Chicago, Saul Bellow states, "The country took us over. It *was* a country then, not a collection of 'cultures.'"

During the Second World War and the decade following it, the United States reached its apogee as a classic nation-state. During the 1960s, as is now clear, America began a slow but unmistakable process of transformation. The signs hardly need belaboring: racial polarity, educational dysfunction, social fragmentation of many and various kinds. William Irwin Thompson, in *Passages About Earth: An Exploration of the New Planetary Culture,* writes, "The educational system that had worked on the Jews or the Irish could no longer work on the blacks; and when Jewish teachers in New York tried to take black children away from their parents exactly in the way they had been taken from theirs, they were shocked to encounter a violent affirmation of negritude."

Issues like West Africa could yet emerge as a new kind of foreign-policy issue, further eroding America's domestic peace. The spectacle of several West African nations collapsing at once could reinforce the worst racial stereotypes here at home. That is another reason why Africa matters. We must not kid ourselves: the sensitivity factor is higher than ever. The Washington, D.C., public school system is already experimenting with an Afrocentric curriculum. Summits between African leaders and prominent African-Americans are becoming frequent, as are Pollyanna-ish prognostications about multiparty elections in Africa that do not factor in crime, surging birth rates, and resource depletion. The Congressional Black Caucus was among those urging U.S. involvement in Somalia and in Haiti. At the *Los Angeles Times* minority staffers have protested against, among other things, what they allege to be the racist tone of the newspaper's Africa coverage, allegations that the editor of the "World Report" section, Dan Fisher, denies, saying essentially that Africa should be viewed through the same rigorous analytical lens as other parts of the world.

Africa may be marginal in terms of conventional late-twentieth-century conceptions of strategy, but in an age of cultural and racial clash, when national defense is increasingly local, Africa's distress will exert a destabilizing influence on the United States.

This and many other factors will make the United States less of a nation than it is today, even as it gains territory following the peaceful dissolution of Canada. Quebec, based on the bedrock of Roman Catholicism and Francophone ethnicity, could yet turn out to be North America's most cohesive and crime-free nation-state. (It may be a smaller Quebec, though, since aboriginal peoples may lop off northern parts of the province.) "Patriotism" will become increasingly regional as people in Alberta and Montana discover that they have far more in common with each other than they do with Ottawa or Washington, and Spanish-speakers in the Southwest discover a greater commonality with Mexico City. (*The Nine Nations of North America,* by Joel Garreau, a book about the continent's regionalization, is more relevant now than when it was published, in 1981.) As Washington's influence wanes, and with it the traditional symbols of American patriotism, North Americans will take psychological refuge in their insulated communities and cultures.

Returning from West Africa last fall was an illuminating ordeal. After leaving Abidjan, my Air Afrique flight landed in Dakar, Senegal, where all passengers had to disembark in order to go through another security check, this one demanded by U.S. authorities before they would permit the flight to set out for New York. Once we were in New York, despite the midnight hour, immigration officials at Kennedy Airport held up disembarkation by conducting quick interrogations of the aircraft's passengers—this was in addition to all the normal immigration and customs procedures. It was apparent that drug smuggling, disease, and other factors had contributed to the toughest security procedures I have ever encountered when returning from overseas.

Then, for the first time in over a month, I spotted businesspeople with attaché cases and laptop computers. When I had left New York for Abidjan, all the businesspeople were boarding planes for Seoul and Tokyo, which departed from gates near Air Afrique's. The only non-Africans off to West Africa had been relief workers in T-shirts and khakis. Although the borders within West Africa are increasingly unreal, those separating West Africa from the outside world are in various ways becoming more impenetrable.

But Afrocentrists are right in one respect: we ignore this dying region at our own risk. When the Berlin Wall was falling, in November of 1989, I happened to be in Kosovo, covering a riot between Serbs and Albanians. The future was in Kosovo, I told myself that night, not in Berlin. The same day that Yitzhak Rabin and Yasser Arafat clasped hands on the White House lawn, my Air Afrique plane was approaching Bamako, Mali, revealing corrugated-zinc shacks at the edge of an expanding desert. The real news wasn't at the White House, I realized. It was right below.

Part

2 Global Order and Disorder: Rejoinders

In Part 1, Samuel Huntington, Benjamin Barber, and Robert Kaplan presented three different scenarios of the world's future: a clash of civilizations, a clash between "tribalism" and globalism, and the threat of anarchy and disintegration. Essays by Fouad Ajami, Eisuke Sakakibara, and John R. Bowen were selected for this next part because they vigorously challenge these controversial perspectives. Ajami believes that Huntington has misread the situation: states control civilizations, not the reverse. Additionally, he argues that Huntington's concept of culture is generalized, and presented in rigid and static terms. Sakakibara draws attention to the flaws in Barber's vision of a modern world, and Bowen argues that we typically make three erroneous assumptions about ethnic conflict, casting doubts on key points made by Huntington, Barber, and Kaplan.

Parts 1 and 2 are both directed at helping the reader grasp the "big picture" about what is happening in the world today. While Huntington, Barber, and Kaplan render a service by providing this overview, Ajami, Sakakibara, and Bowen make clear that these broad visions miss crucial details, thereby oversimplifying and distorting reality.

The Summoning

Fouad Ajami

'But They Said, We Will Not Hearken.'
JEREMIAH 6:17

In Joseph Conrad's *Youth,* a novella published at the turn of the century, Marlowe, the narrator, remembers when he first encountered "the East":

> And then, before I could open my lips, the East spoke to me, but it was in a Western voice. A torrent of words was poured into the enigmatical, the fateful silence; outlandish, angry words mixed with words and even whole sentences of good English, less strange but even more surprising. The voice swore and cursed violently; it riddled the solemn peace of the bay by a volley of abuse. It began by calling me Pig, and from that went crescendo into unmentionable adjectives—in English.

The young Marlowe knew that even the most remote civilization had been made and remade by the West, and taught new ways.

Not so Samuel P. Huntington. In a curious essay, "The Clash of Civilizations?" [p. 3, this volume], Huntington has found his civilizations whole and intact, watertight under an eternal sky. Buried alive, as it were, during the years of the Cold War, these civilizations (Islamic, Slavic-Orthodox, Western, Confucian, Japanese, Hindu, etc.) rose as soon as the stone was rolled off, dusted themselves off, and proceeded to claim the loyalty of their adherents. For this student of history and culture, civilizations have always seemed messy creatures. Furrows

Reprinted with permission from *Foreign Affairs*, Vol. 72, No. 4, 1993. © 1993 by the Council on Foreign Relations, Inc.

run across whole civilizations, across individuals themselves—that was modernity's verdict. But Huntington looks past all that. The crooked and meandering alleyways of the world are straightened out. With a sharp pencil and a steady hand Huntington marks out where one civilization ends and the wilderness of "the other" begins.

More surprising still is Huntington's attitude toward states, and their place in his scheme of things. From one of the most influential and brilliant students of the state and its national interest there now comes an essay that misses the slyness of states, the unsentimental and cold-blooded nature of so much of what they do as they pick their way through chaos. Despite the obligatory passage that states will remain "the most powerful actors in world affairs," states are written off, their place given over to clashing civilizations. In Huntington's words, "The next world war, if there is one, will be a war between civilizations."

The Power of Modernity

Huntington's meditation is occasioned by his concern about the state of the West, its power and the terms of its engagement with "the rest."[1] "He who gives, dominates," the great historian Fernand Braudel observed of the traffic of civilizations. In making itself over the centuries, the West helped make the others as well. We have come to the end of this trail, Huntington is sure. He is impressed by the "de-Westernization" of societies, their "indigenization" and apparent willingness to go their own way. In his view of things such phenomena as the "Hinduization" of India and Islamic fundamentalism are ascendant. To these detours into "tradition" Huntington has assigned great force and power.

But Huntington is wrong. He has underestimated the tenacity of modernity and secularism in places that acquired these ways against great odds, always perilously close to the abyss, the darkness never far. India will not become a Hindu state. The inheritance of Indian secularism will hold. The vast middle class will defend it, keep the order intact to maintain India's—and its own—place in the modern world of nations. There exists in that anarchic polity an instinctive dread of playing with fires that might consume it. Hindu chauvinism may coarsen the public life of the country, but the state and the middle class that sustains it know that a detour into religious fanaticism is a fling with ruin. A resourceful middle class partakes of global culture and norms. A century has passed since the Indian bourgeoisie, through its political vehicle the Indian National Congress, set out to claim for itself and India a place among nations. Out of that long struggle to overturn British rule and the parallel struggle against "communalism," the advocates of the national idea built a large and durable state. They will not cede all this for a political kingdom of Hindu purity.

We have been hearing from the traditionalists, but we should not exaggerate their power, for traditions are often most insistent and loud when they rupture, when people no longer really believe and when age-old customs lose their ability to keep men and women at home. The phenomenon we have dubbed as Islamic fundamentalism is less a sign of resurgence than of panic and bewilderment and guilt that the border with "the other" has been crossed. Those young urban poor, half-educated in the cities of the Arab world, and their Sorbonne-educated lay preachers, can they be evidence of a genuine return to tradition? They crash Europe's and America's gates in search of liberty and work, and they rail against the sins of the West. It is easy to understand Huntington's frustration with this kind of complexity, with the strange mixture of attraction and repulsion that the West breeds, and his need to simplify matters, to mark out the borders of civilizations.

Tradition-mongering is no proof, though, that these civilizations outside the West are intact, or that their thrashing about is an indication of their vitality, or that they present a conventional threat of arms. Even so thorough and far-reaching an attack against Western hegemony as Iran's theocratic revolution could yet fail to wean that society from the culture of the West. That country's cruel revolution was born of the realization of the "armed Imam" that his people were being seduced by America's ways. The gates had been thrown wide open in the 1970s, and the high walls Ayatollah Khomeini built around his polity were a response to that cultural seduction. Swamped, Iran was "rescued" by men claiming authenticity as their banner. One extreme led to another.

"We prayed for the rain of mercy and received floods," was the way Mehdi Bazargan, the decent modernist who was Khomeini's first prime minister, put it. But the millennium has been brought down to earth, and the dream of a pan-Islamic revolt in Iran's image has vanished into the wind. The terror and the shabbiness have caught up with the utopia. Sudan could emulate the Iranian "revolutionary example." But this will only mean the further pauperization and ruin of a desperate land. There is no rehabilitation of the Iranian example.

A battle rages in Algeria, a society of the Mediterranean, close to Europe—a wine-producing country for that matter—and in Egypt between the secular powers that be and an Islamic alternative. But we should not rush to print with obituaries of these states. In Algeria the nomenklatura of the National Liberation Front failed and triggered a revolt of the young, the underclass and the excluded. The revolt raised an Islamic banner. Caught between a regime they despised and a reign of virtue they feared, the professionals and the women and the modernists of the middle class threw their support to the forces of "order." They hailed the army's crackdown on the Islamicists; they allowed the interruption of a democratic process sure to bring the Islamicists to power; they accepted the "liberties" protected by the repression, the devil you know rather than the one you don't.

The Algerian themes repeat in the Egyptian case, although Egypt's dilemma over its Islamicist opposition is not as acute. The Islamicists continue to hound the state, but they cannot bring it down. There is no likelihood that the Egyptian state —now riddled with enough complacency and corruption to try the celebrated patience and good humor of the Egyptians—will go under. This is an old and skeptical country. It knows better than to trust its fate to enforcers of radical religious dogma. These are not deep and secure structures of order that the national middle classes have put in place. But they will not be blown away overnight.

Nor will Turkey lose its way, turn its back on Europe and chase after some imperial temptation in the scorched domains of Central Asia. Huntington sells that country's modernity and secularism short when he writes that the Turks—rejecting Mecca and rejected by Brussels—are likely to head to Tashkent in search of a Pan-Turkic role. There is no journey to that imperial past. Ataturk severed that link with fury, pointed his country westward, embraced the civilization of Europe and did it without qualms or second thoughts. It is on Frankfurt and Bonn —and Washington—not on Baku and Tashkent that the attention of the Turks is fixed. The inheritors of Ataturk's legacy are too shrewd to go chasing after imperial glory, gathering about them the scattered domains of the Turkish peoples. After their European possessions were lost, the Turks clung to Thrace and to all that this link to Europe represents.

Huntington would have nations battle for civilizational ties and fidelities when they would rather scramble for their market shares, learn how to compete in a merciless world economy, provide jobs, move out of poverty. For their part, the "management gurus" and those who believe that the interests have vanquished the passions in today's world tell us that men want Sony, not soil.[2] There is a good deal of truth in what they say, a terrible exhaustion with utopias, a reluctance to set out on expeditions of principle or belief. It is hard to think of Russia, ravaged as it is by inflation, taking up the grand cause of a "second Byzantium," the bearer of the orthodox-Slavic torch.

And where is the Confucian world Huntington speaks of? In the busy and booming lands of the Pacific Rim, so much of politics and ideology has been sublimated into finance that the nations of East Asia have turned into veritable workshops. The civilization of Cathay is dead; the Indonesian archipelago is deaf to the call of the religious radicals in Tehran as it tries to catch up with Malaysia and Singapore. A different wind blows in the lands of the Pacific. In that world economics, not politics, is in command. The world is far less antiseptic than Lee Kuan Yew, the sage of Singapore, would want it to be. A nemesis could lie in wait for all the prosperity that the 1980s brought to the Pacific. But the lands of the Pacific Rim—protected, to be sure, by an American security umbrella—are not ready for a great falling out among the nations. And were troubles to visit that world they would erupt within its boundaries, not across civilizational lines.

The things and ways that the West took to "the rest"—those whole sentences of good English that Marlowe heard a century ago—have become the ways of the world. The secular idea, the state system and the balance of power, pop culture jumping tariff walls and barriers, the state as an instrument of welfare, all these have been internalized in the remotest places. We have stirred up the very storms into which we now ride.

The Weakness of Tradition

Nations "cheat": they juggle identities and interests. Their ways meander. One would think that the traffic of arms from North Korea and China to Libya and Iran and Syria shows this—that states will consort with any civilization, however alien, as long as the price is right and the goods are ready. Huntington turns this routine act of selfishness into a sinister "Confucian-Islamic connection." There are better explanations: the commerce of renegades, plain piracy, an "underground economy" that picks up the slack left by the great arms suppliers (the United States, Russia, Britain and France).

Contrast the way Huntington sees things with Braudel's depiction of the traffic between Christendom and Islam across the Mediterranean in the sixteenth century—and this was in a religious age, after the fall of Constantinople to the Turks and of Granada to the Spanish: "Men passed to and fro, indifferent to frontiers, states and creeds. They were more aware of the necessities for shipping and trade, the hazards of war and piracy, the opportunities for complicity or betrayal provided by circumstances."[3]

Those kinds of "complicities" and ambiguities are missing in Huntington's analysis. Civilizations are crammed into the nooks and crannies—and checkpoints—of the Balkans. Huntington goes where only the brave would venture, into that belt of mixed populations stretching from the Adriatic to the Baltic. Countless nationalisms make their home there, all aggrieved, all possessed of memories of a fabled past and equally ready for the demagogues vowing to straighten a messy map. In the thicket of these pan-movements he finds the line that marked "the eastern boundary of Western Christianity in the year 1500." The scramble for turf between Croatian nationalism and its Serbian counterpart, their "joint venture" in carving up Bosnia, are made into a fight of the inheritors of Rome, Byzantium and Islam.

But why should we fall for this kind of determinism? "An outsider who travels the highway between Zagreb and Belgrade is struck not by the decisive historical fault line which falls across the lush Slavonian plain but by the opposite. Serbs and Croats speak the same language, give or take a few hundred words, have shared the same village way of life for centuries."[4] The cruel genius of Slobodan Milosevic and Franjo Tudjman, men on horseback familiar in lands and situations of distress, was to make their bids for power into grand civilizational undertakings—the ramparts of the Enlightenment defended against Islam or, in Tudjman's case, against the heirs of the Slavic-Orthodox faith. Differences had to be magnified. Once Tito, an equal opportunity oppressor, had passed from the scene, the balancing act among the nationalities was bound to come apart. Serbia had had a measure of hegemony in the old system. But of the world that loomed over the horizon—privatization and economic reform—the Serbs were less confident. The citizens of Sarajevo and the Croats and the Slovenes had a head start on the rural Serbs. And so the Serbs hacked at the new order of things with desperate abandon.

Some Muslim volunteers came to Bosnia, driven by faith and zeal. Huntington sees in these few stragglers the sweeping power of "civilizational rallying," proof of the hold of what he calls the "kin-country syndrome." This is delusion. No Muslim cavalry was ever going to ride to the rescue. The Iranians may have railed about holy warfare, but the Chetniks went on with their work. The work of order and mercy would have had to be done by the United States if the cruel utopia of the Serbs was to be contested.

It should have taken no powers of prophecy to foretell where the fight in the Balkans would end. The abandonment of Bosnia was of a piece with the ways of the world. No one wanted to die for Srebrenica. The Europeans averted their gaze, as has been their habit. The Americans hesitated for a moment as the urge to stay out of the Balkans did battle with the scenes of horror. Then "prudence" won out. Milosevic and Tudjman may need civilizational legends, but there is no need to invest their projects of conquest with this kind of meaning.

In his urge to find that relentless war across Islam's "bloody borders," Huntington buys Saddam Hussein's interpretation of the Gulf War. It was, for Saddam and Huntington, a civilizational battle. But the Gulf War's verdict was entirely different. For if there was a campaign that laid bare the interests of states, the lengths to which they will go to restore a tolerable balance of power in a place that matters, this was it. A local despot had risen close to the wealth of the Persian Gulf, and a Great Power from afar had come to the rescue. The posse assembled by the Americans had Saudi, Turkish, Egyptian, Syrian, French, British and other riders.

True enough, when Saddam Hussein's dream of hegemony was shattered, the avowed secularist who had devastated the *ulama,* the men of religion in his country, fell back on Ayatollah Khomeini's language of fire and brimstone and borrowed the symbolism and battle cry of his old Iranian nemesis. But few, if any, were fooled by this sudden conversion to the faith. They knew the predator for what he was: he had a Christian foreign minister (Tariq Aziz); he had warred against the Iranian revolution for nearly a decade and had prided himself on the secularism of his regime. Prudent men of the social and political order, the *ulama* got out of the way and gave their state the room it needed to check the predator at the Saudi/Kuwaiti border.[5] They knew this was one of those moments when purity bows to necessity. Ten days after Saddam swept into Kuwait, Saudi Arabia's most authoritative religious body, the Council of Higher Ulama, issued a *fatwa,* or a ruling opinion, supporting the presence of Arab and Islamic and "other friendly forces." All means of defense, the ulama ruled, were legitimate to guarantee the people "the safety of their religion, their wealth, and their honor and their blood, to protect what they enjoy of safety and stability." At some remove, in Egypt, that country's leading religious figure, the Shaykh of Al Ashar, Shaykh Jadd at Haqq, denounced Saddam as a tyrant and brushed aside his Islamic pretensions as a cover for tyranny.

Nor can the chief Iranian religious leader Ayatollah Ali Khamenei's rhetoric against the Americans during the Gulf War be taken as evidence of Iran's disposition toward that campaign. Crafty men, Iran's rulers sat out that war. They stood to emerge as the principal beneficiaries of Iraq's defeat. The American-led campaign against Iraq held out the promise of tilting the regional balance in their favor. No tears were shed in Iran for what befell Saddam Hussein's regime.

It is the mixed gift of living in hard places that men and women know how to distinguish between what they hear and what there is: no illusions were thus entertained in vast stretches of the Arab Muslim world about Saddam, or about the campaign to thwart him for that matter. The fight in the gulf was seen for what it was: a bid for primacy met by an imperial expedition that laid it to waste. A circle was closed in the gulf: where once the order in the region "east of Suez" had been the work of the British, it was now provided by Pax Americana. The new power standing sentry in the gulf belonged to the civilization of the West, as did the prior one. But the American presence had the anxious consent of the Arab lands of the Persian Gulf. The stranger coming in to check the kinsmen.

The world of Islam divides and subdivides. The battle lines in the Caucasus, too, are not coextensive with civilizational fault lines. The lines follow the interests of states. Where Huntington sees a civilizational duel between Armenia and Azerbaijan, the Iranian state has cast religious zeal and fidelity to the wind. Indeed, in that battle the Iranians have tilted toward Christian Armenia.

The Writ of States

We have been delivered into a new world, to be sure. But it is not a world where the writ of civilizations runs. Civilizations and civilizational fidelities remain. There is to them an astonishing measure of permanence. But let us be clear: civilizations do not control states, states control civilizations. States avert their gaze from blood ties when they need to; they see brotherhood and faith and kin when it is in their interest to do so.

We remain in a world of self-help. The solitude of states continues; the disorder in the contemporary world has rendered that solitude more pronounced. No way has yet been found to reconcile France to Pax Americana's hegemony, or to convince it to trust its security or cede its judgment to the preeminent Western power. And no Azeri has come up with a way the lands of Islam could be rallied to the fight over Nagorno Karabakh. The sky has not fallen in Kuala Lumpur or in Tunis over the setbacks of Azerbaijan in its fight with Armenia.

The lesson bequeathed us by Thucydides in his celebrated dialogue between the Melians and the Athenians remains. The Melians, it will be recalled, were a colony of the Lacedaemonians. Besieged by Athens, they held out and were sure that the Lacedaemonians were "bound, if only for very shame, to come to the aid of their kindred." The Melians never wavered in their confidence in their "civilizational" allies: "Our common blood insures our fidelity."[6] We know what became of the Melians. Their allies did not turn up, their island was sacked, their world laid to waste.

NOTES

1. The West itself is unexamined in Huntington's essay. No fissures run through it. No multiculturalists are heard from. It is orderly within its ramparts. What doubts Huntington has about the will within the walls, he has kept within himself. He has assumed that his call to unity will be answered, for outside flutter the banners of the Saracens and the Confucians.

2. Kenichi Ohmae, "Global Consumers Want Sony, Not Soil," *New Perspectives Quarterly,* Fall 1991.

3. Ferdinand Braudel, *The Mediterranean and the Mediterranean World in the Age of Philip II,* Vol. II, New York: Harper & Row, 1976, p. 759.

4. Michael Ignatieff, "The Balkan Tragedy," *New York Review of Books,* May 13, 1993.

5. Huntington quotes one Safar al Hawali, a religious radical at Umm al Qura University in Mecca, to the effect that the campaign against Iraq was another Western campaign against Islam. But this can't do as evidence. Safar al Hawali was a crank. Among the *ulama* class and the religious scholars in Saudi Arabia he was, for all practical purposes, a loner.

6. Thucydides, *The Peloponnesian War,* New York: The Modern American Library, 1951, pp. 334–335.

The End of Progressivism
A SEARCH FOR NEW GOALS

Eisuke Sakakibara

The Cold War was nothing but a conflict between two extreme versions of progressivism—socialism and neoclassical capitalism. Both ideologies set a rapid increase and fair distribution of material welfare as their goal. According to socialists, the way to achieve such a goal is state planning; according to neoclassicists, the market.

In 1989, after the fall of the Berlin Wall, RAND analyst Francis Fukuyama and economic historian Robert L. Heilbroner separately pronounced the end of history and the victory of capitalism. But history has not quite ended. With the demise of socialism and the end of the Cold War, this rosy neoclassical dream has been tarnished. The reasons are primarily twofold: globalization and environmental constraints. Instead, what we seem to be witnessing today is the end not of history, but progressivism, the belief that there is only one ideal end, the unique path to which human beings can recognize.

The former Soviet Union and the United States could be classified together as experimental states, which provided the world with clear-cut alternative ideologies for progress. The dominance and severe military confrontation of these ideologies during the Cold War relegated cultural and historical diversities in all countries to a relatively secondary position and transformed almost all major political problems of the world into ideological confrontations. As political scientist Samuel Huntington appropriately pointed out in the Summer 1993 issue of

Reprinted with permission from *Foreign Affairs*, Vol. 74, No. 5, 1995. © 1995 by the Council on Foreign Relations, Inc.

Foreign Affairs [p. 3, this volume], "The conflicts between princes, nation-states and ideologies were primarily conflicts within Western civilization, 'Western civil wars' as William Lind has labeled them. This was as true of the Cold War as it was of the world wars and the earlier wars of the seventeenth, eighteenth, and nineteenth centuries." The Cold War was nothing but another civil war within the West or, more precisely, within the Western ideology of progressivism. The demise of socialism and the end of the Cold War released the world from a Western civil war over differing versions of progressivism to confront the more fundamental issues of environmental pollution and the peaceful coexistence of different civilizations.

The 21st century will be an age in which multiple civilizations compete, interact, coexist, and confront the need to admit the rights of nature. Indeed, clashes will be possible if the principles of tolerance and moderation are not practiced by civilizations. And cohabitation of human beings with nature becomes possible only when tolerance rather than impetuous belief, balance rather than progress, are respected. In this regard, progressivism, which has been the dominant ideology for the past 200-odd years and particularly the past 50 years, has to be and is, in fact, ending. In premodern times, when progressivism was not the dominant ideology, the coexistence of vastly diverse civilizations was the norm, and the destruction of nature by human beings was relatively limited. This does not, of course, imply that we should go back to the premodern age. Universal modern technologies, institutions, and organizations should be retained and fully utilized. Civilizations of the postmodern age can and should share these neutral technologies and institutions while retaining diverse cultures and traditions.

The Crises of Capitalism

The events unfolding in the 1990s do not bear out the end of history. Modern Western civilization, with the explosive increase in productive capacity accompanying the Industrial Revolution, has succeeded over the past century in radically transforming social and economic systems in both developed and developing countries, but it has also seriously affected global ecological systems.

With such material and political success, progressivism, particularly neoclassical capitalism, seemed to have become the dominant world ideology. But leading democratic capitalist countries of Europe, the United States, and Japan have experienced prolonged economic slumps and political instability. These issues seem chronic, and recent economic recoveries in some countries are not likely to solve structural problems. Income and wealth are polarizing as the rich get richer and the average family loses ground. Even the remarkable comeback staged by corporate America has only been possible at the expense of household America. European unemployment, despite some improvement, still hovers between 8 and 12 percent. Japan, muddling its way out of asset deflation, is now confronted by potential and hidden unemployment.

Moreover, various forms of political corruption plague these countries. Money scandals have toppled Japanese and Italian governments, while scandal-triggered resignations by key cabinet members are an almost everyday occurrence in most of the Group of Seven. Journalist Kevin Phillips proposes a fundamental overhaul of the present American political system, and French Ambassador to the Western European Union Jean-Marie Guéhenno has declared that the nation-state in this global and borderless networking age has become so powerless that democracy is obsolete, and some imperial arrangement is needed to replace it. Moreover, events in the former Soviet Union seem to have shattered the extreme optimism of 1989. Russia's experiment in shock therapy, which was aimed at swiftly establishing democracy and neoclassical capitalism, has been an utter failure.

Paths to democracy and neoclassical capitalism are not necessarily unique and depend upon the historical phase that the particular economy happens to be in. As such, policies may be modified and, for example, a more gradualist approach adopted. However, a more fundamental issue is whether or not democracy and neoclassical capitalism are the only or ultimate goals, or even whether any goal needs to be established. China has set its sights on establishing a socialist market economy and, relative to Russia, has so far succeeded in introducing many facets of market mechanisms without major economic or political upheaval. While it may still be too early to pass final judgment on the recent Chinese experiment, it does at least provide a realistic alternative goal and methodology. Vietnam, India, Myanmar, and Central Asian countries following in China's wake seem to be searching for such alternative goals and paths that fit their own historical and cultural backgrounds.

The Neoclassical Paradigm

Many Western philosophers and historians have subscribed to the belief that there has been only one civilization, namely the Western civilization, because of its dominant position in modern history. Other civilizations have either disappeared in the sand or flowed into the mainstream of modern Western civilization.

The advent of the Cold War and the relatively smooth economic performance of the developed countries of the West and Japan seemed to have rendered non-progressivist thinking out of fashion. What emerged in its place were the neoclassical theories of capitalism that made over the classical model with esoteric sophistication in mathematics and statistics. On the surface, this face-lift looked scientific, mimicking the methodology of natural science. The United States played the leading intellectual role in this process of reformulating the neoclassical paradigm in economics and related social sciences. U.S. dominance in both politics and economics contributed to this intellectual leadership, and the singular nature of the United States as a relatively new country of immigrants made it possible to experiment somewhat freely in abstract and simple principles of progressivism.

The neoclassical paradigm postulated as the antithesis of socialism after World War II had some obvious attractions and was thought by many to have solved the problems of classical capitalism. Through the mass production of such consumer goods as automobiles, appliances, and electronics and turning workers into consumers, mass consumption markets were created. The emergence of consumers at the center of the socioeconomic system laid the basis for a middle-class society, providing the necessary stability for society as a whole. Neoclassical capitalist economics emphasized consumer sovereignty as the basis of democratic choice of the mix and quantity of economic goods against the bureaucratic economic decision-making under socialism. The same consumers constituted the centerpiece of democracy, casting votes to ensure their political sovereignty.

In the United States, luxuries that had once been available only to European aristocrats were now within the reach of many Americans. A pleasant suburban house with a car and a garden were now feasible for a vast number of consumers. This American dream quickly spread throughout the noncommunist developed countries of Europe as well as Japan. Although Europe retained some aspects of its elitist tradition, mass consumption and mass democracy made it possible to construct welfare states to the satisfaction of the general public. Japan too very quickly Americanized its economic and political systems and became, in some ways, more American than the Americans in creating a mass-consumption, mass democracy, middle-class society, while at the same time retaining some elements of traditional culture.

The Shortcomings

Economic prosperity seemed everlasting, and human progress toward equitable material welfare seemed feasible. Economics, dedicated to the efficient allocation of resources or the optimization of material welfare, has come to occupy a central position in the various disciplines of the social sciences. Mechanical and electronic engineering have also significantly improved their relative status among disciplines of the natural sciences. Technological innovation and economic growth became the key concepts in this neoclassical mass consumption world. National income statistics centering on the flow of goods from production to consumption have been compiled in all the major developed countries, and economic policies have focused their attention on GNP and its components. As long as engineers and corporations continuously churned out technological innovations, and policy authorities properly managed macroeconomic matters, the everlasting progress of the neoclassical capitalist regime was thought to be guaranteed.

But this model has two major shortcomings. First, the notion that essentially laissez-faire economic management leads to consumer sovereignty is based on various assumptions, the most important of which is that factors of production, labor and capital, do not move across borders. The globalization of financial capital as well as the relatively free movement of what Secretary of Labor Robert Reich has called "symbolic analysts" directly violate this assumption. This globalization with economies of scale leads to oligopolization of the world market, inviting strategic trade rather than free trade. More important, the interests of multinational corporations and those of workers and consumers start to diverge, and the cohesion of the nation-state as an economic unit disintegrates.

In a regime where movements of factors of production are relatively scarce, gains obtained by trading corporations are distributed to a certain degree to workers and consumers. Even under globalization, oligopolistic competition takes place despite some economic concentration, and one can argue that consumer benefit remains. However, the outcome is uncertain, and even with consumer benefit, the new polarization is a major blow to the stability of mass consumption societies. Consumers essentially have to earn income by working, and the loss of income by some workers divides consumers into two categories, the affluent and the poor, thus undermining middle-class society. According to the 1994 Organization for Economic Cooperation and Development jobs study, unemployment in OECD countries was below 10 million in the 1950s and 1960s but started to climb in the mid-1970s, reaching 25 million in 1990. By 1995, unemployment is expected to reach 35 million. In the mid-1970s, the share of wages in GNP in Europe, the United States, and Japan started to decline. The European Union share in 1995 is projected to stand at 62 percent as opposed to 75 percent in 1975. Wage discrepancies between skilled and unskilled laborers has widened in the United States, Canada, and Australia, and real wages for unskilled workers in the United States declined more than one percent between 1980 and 1989.

The second problem is that environmental constraints have become visibly binding, and a further explosion in population and geometric increase in energy consumption seems unsustainable. Although environmental damage is said to have started approximately 10,000 years ago with ancient agricultural civilizations, the speed and extent of the damage accelerated geometrically after the Industrial Revolution, particularly in the twentieth century. World population was only 500 million in 1650, and its annual rate of growth was 0.3 percent, reaching 800 million in the eighteenth century before the Industrial Revolution. With Western industrial civilization this number doubled in the following 100 years to 1.6 billion and tripled in less than 100 years in the twentieth century to 5.5 billion. World population is now expected to reach 10 billion by the middle of the 21st century. When world population tripled during the twentieth century, world production jumped from $0.6 trillion in 1900 to $15 trillion in 1990, a 25-fold increase. Consumption of fossil fuels also surged 11-fold from 0.7 billion tons in 1900 to 7.8 billion tons in 1990. This precipitous quantitative increase in resource consumption has been matched by the adverse impact of technological innovation and new materials such as plastics and fluorocarbon gases, which are destroying the ozone layer.

Optimists argue that the causality between greater human activity and environmental destruction is not well established, and that environmentally friendly technological innovation will eventually solve these problems. This is a typically arrogant progressivist view. The knowledge that humans have accumulated about nature and human beings themselves is quite limited. Because natural science tries to understand vast systems from only minute observations, it will never be able to assess accurately the impact of human activity on the environment, much less solve environmental problems through technological innovation. Technological progress may, in a small way, compensate for some human impact on nature or, at best, delay the destruction for a very short time.

The Alternatives

The progressivists' confidence in human competence and technology could properly be termed a myth because there is no logical reason to believe such path-breaking technological change will occur. It is akin to believing that someday the savior will come down to earth in the form of technological innovation and for some reason reverse all the problems that past progress has wrought. This myth of technological innovation parallels unswerving faith in economic growth. Despite the structural nature of the problems of inequality and pollution at hand, many economists and politicians paradoxically believe or try to convince themselves that economic growth can solve them. But is this really a logical proposition? It is precisely because of economic growth that the population explosion, rapacious energy consumption, and environmental destruction have proceeded so rapidly and that polarization of the world population into the affluent, poor, and abjectly deprived seems to be reaching its limit. Rather than relying on myths and blind faith, it is time to face up to the reality of the situation and reexamine environmental problems in a more diffident and logical manner.

The rapid erosion of the neoclassical paradigm throws us back to the pre–World War II situation where people and nations tried to identify themselves with civilizations rather than progress. Huntington is right when he says that "civilization identity will be increasingly important in the future, and the world will be shaped in large measure by the interaction among seven or eight civilizations." But the reemergence of civilization consciousness is directly related to deep disillusionment with the ideology of progressivism.

Civilizations do indeed rise and fall and often clash with each other, but more important, they have interacted and coexisted throughout most of history. The universality of technology is often seen as the universality of Western civilization. But it is now well known that black gunpowder, the compass, and typeset printing, which were thought of as inventions of the Western Renaissance, originated in Sung China. This view that Western culture is singular while some technologies are universal was widely adhered to by Japanese intellectuals in the late nineteenth and early twentieth century who advocated modernization through "Western technology and Oriental philosophy." It should also be noted that a modern standing army and well-organized bureaucracy existed in the eighth-century Abbasid Islamic empire.

Not universality but domination has produced the ascendance of the West. The clash of civilizations is not the unavoidable result of coexisting civilizations, but rather the result of contact with Western progressivism. In the past, civilizations have peacefully coexisted. The Abbasid and following Islamic empires were relatively tolerant regarding the cultures and religions of the peripheral parts of their empires: for example in India, Hinduism and the caste system were retained to avoid confrontation with Indian tradition. Muslim merchants engaged in global trade from Africa to China. The Abbasid and following Islamic empires were probably the first civilizations where the commercial activities of merchants occupied a central place in society, along with the wide use of money and joint-venture corporate organizations. The Asian continent was therefore characterized for a period of more than 1,000 years by the interaction and coexistence of various civilizations. The major dominance-subjugation relationship emerged only when these Asian civilizations encountered modern Western civilization.

Similarly, the progressivist dominance of nature, or anthropocentrism, must be confronted head-on. Given the severity of environmental constraints, harmony and cohabitation with nature rather than conquest and development should be respected. The urbanization that started with the rise of civilization created an artificial environment detached from nature and encouraged an anthropocentric attitude. The large-scale destruction of nature started with the advent of agricultural civilization and urbanization. Destructive activities accelerated dramatically after the Industrial Revolution and the emergence of modern Western civilization. Cartesian rationalism reemphasized human beings as the center of nature, culminating in Marx's extreme anthropocentric belief in natural science and everlasting progress.

By contrast, premodern philosophies and religions, particularly Eastern ones, respect nature and the environment. In Japanese Shintoism there is no clear-cut demarcation between nature and human beings. In certain sects of Buddhism, forests and woods are considered sacred places, and many temples are built deep in the forests where monks undergo spiritual training.

The premodern Asian experience of relatively peaceful coexistence between civilizations as well as with the environment should be remembered. Moreover, conflicts or clashes between various civilizations must be avoided in view of the detrimental impact of modern wars, possibly including nuclear and chemical weapons, on the environment. In view of this more than 1,000-year experience, it seems possible that diverse civilizations can coexist peacefully if tolerance and moderation are practiced.

The Prospects for Success

Asia, which has the oldest and most diverse civilizations in the world, will probably become the main stage for action in the 21st century. It is well suited for this experiment because it has the longest history of such competition and interaction. The coexistence of diverse civilizations before the eighteenth century was possible due to the global networking of Islamic, Indian, and Chinese merchants—in other words, a system of exchange akin to global capitalism encompassed a large number of very diverse civilizations. In this sense, globalization amid diversity is nothing new, and the prospects for success are not unduly small.

However, civilizations such as the West and Islam must practice tolerance. In particular, the West must abandon sectarian progressivism in favor of respect for the environment and tolerance for other civilizations. Today's ongoing globalization is quite different from past versions in that, as a result of revolutionary technological progress in information and communications, it involves simultaneous or real-time transfers of information and technology. This contributes to the acceleration of changes due to globalization and may cause substantial difficulties for the adaptation of cultures to technology. Compared to past periods of globalization with cultural diversities, environmental constraints are more absolutely binding.

These constraints will make mutual accommodations between civilizations more difficult, particularly between the affluent and less affluent. To the extent that these new conditions exist, this is a new experiment in again making globalization compatible with cultural diversity. During the Cold War, two versions of progressivism suppressed the most important process of history, interaction and accommodation between diverse civilizations. After some 50 years, the normal process of history has started to move again. What we are witnessing is not the end of history but a fresh start.

The Myth of Global Ethnic Conflict

John R. Bowen

Much recent discussion of international affairs has been based on the misleading assumption that the world is fraught with primordial ethnic conflict. According to this notion, ethnic groups lie in wait for one another, nourishing age-old hatreds and restrained only by powerful states. Remove the lid, and the cauldron boils over. Analysts who advance this idea differ in their predictions for the future: some see the fragmentation of the world into small tribal groups; others, a face-off among several vast civilizational coalitions. They all share, however, the idea that the world's current conflicts are fueled by age-old ethnic loyalties and cultural differences.[1]

This notion misrepresents the genesis of conflict and ignores the ability of diverse people to coexist. The very phrase "ethnic conflict" misguides us. It has become a shorthand way to speak about any and all violent confrontations between groups of people living in the same country. Some of these conflicts involve ethnic or cultural identity, but most are about getting more power, land, or other resources. They do not result from ethnic diversity; thinking that they do sends us off in pursuit of the wrong policies, tolerating rulers who incite riots and suppress ethnic differences.

In speaking about local group conflicts we tend to make three assumptions: first, that ethnic identities are ancient and unchanging; second, that these identities

Bowen, John. The Myth of Global Ethnic Conflict. *Journal of Democracy*, Vol. 7, No. 4 (1996): pp. 3–14. © 1996 The Johns Hopkins University Press and National Endowment for Democracy. Reprinted by permission.

motivate people to persecute and kill; and third, that ethnic diversity itself inevitably leads to violence. All three are mistaken.

Contrary to the first assumption, ethnicity is a product of modern politics. Although people have had identities—deriving from religion, birthplace, language, and so on—for as long as humans have had culture, they have begun to see themselves as members of vast ethnic groups, opposed to other such groups, only during the modern period of colonization and state-building.

The view that ethnicity is ancient and unchanging emerges these days in the potent images of the cauldron and the tribe. Out of the violence in Eastern Europe came images of the region as a bubbling cauldron of ethnonationalist sentiments that were sure to boil over unless suppressed by strong states. The cauldron image contrasts with the American "melting pot," suggesting that Western ethnicities may melt, but Eastern ones must be suppressed by the region's unlikable, but perhaps necessary, Titos and Stalins.

Nowhere does this notion seem more apt than in the former Yugoslavia. Surely the Serbs, Croats, and Bosnians are distinct ethnic groups destined to clash throughout history, are they not? Yet it is often forgotten how small the differences are among the currently warring factions in the Balkans. Serbs, Croats, and Bosnians all speak the same language (Italy has greater linguistic diversity) and have lived side by side, most often in peace, for centuries. Although it is common to say that they are separated by religion—Croats being Roman Catholic, Serbs Orthodox Christian, and Bosnians Muslim—in fact each population includes sizeable numbers of the other two religions. The three religions have indeed become symbols of group differences, but religious differences have not, by themselves, caused intergroup conflict. Rising rates of intermarriage (as high as 30 percent in Bosnia) would have led to the gradual blurring of contrasts across these lines.

As knowledgeable long-term observers such as Misha Glenny have pointed out, the roots of the current Balkan violence lie not in primordial ethnic and religious differences but rather in modern attempts to rally people around nationalist ideas. "Ethnicity" becomes "nationalism" when it includes aspirations to gain a monopoly of land, resources, and power. But nationalism, too, is a learned and frequently manipulated set of ideas, and not a primordial sentiment. In the nineteenth century, Serb and Croat intellectuals joined other Europeans in championing the rights of peoples to rule themselves in "nation-states": states to be composed of one nationality. For their part, Serbs drew on memories of short-lived Serb national states to claim their right to expand outward to encompass other peoples, just as other countries in Europe (most notably France) had done earlier. That Balkan peoples spoke the same language made these expansionist claims all the more plausible to many Serbs.[2]

At the same time, Croats were developing their own nationalist ideology, with a twist: rather than claiming the right to overrun non-Croats, it promised to exclude them. Nationalism among the Croats naturally was directed against their strong Serb neighbors. When Serbs dominated the state of Yugoslavia that was created after the First World War, Croat resentment of Serbs grew. The most militant of Croat nationalists formed an underground organization called Ustashe

("Uprising"), and it was this group, to which the Nazis gave control of Croatia, that carried out the forced conversions, expulsions, and massacres of Serbs during the Second World War. The later calls to war of the Serb leader Slobodan Milošević worked upon the still fresh memories of these tragedies.

But the events of the Second World War did not automatically lead to the slaughters of the 1990s; wartime memories could have been overcome had Yugoslavia's new leaders set out to create the social basis for a multiethnic society. But Marshal Tito chose to preserve his rule by forbidding Yugoslavs from forming independent civic groups and developing a sense of shared political values. Political opposition, whether in Croatia, Serbia, or Slovenia, coalesced instead around the only available symbols, the nationalisms of each region. Tito further fanned nationalist flames by giving Serbs and Croats privileges in each other's territories—Serbs held positions of power in Croatia, and Croats in Belgrade. In the countryside these minority presences added to nationalist resentments. Tito's short-term political cleverness—nostalgically remembered by some in the West—in fact set the stage for later slaughter. Resentments and fears generated by modern state warfare and the absence of a civil society—not ethnic differences— made possible the murders of the nationalist politicians Milošević and Franjo Tudjman.

The Legacy of Colonialism

But what about Africa? Surely there we find raw ethnic conflict, do we not? Our understandings of African violence have been clouded by visions, not of boiling cauldrons, but of ancient tribal warfare. I recall a National Public Radio reporter interviewing an African UN official about Rwanda. Throughout the discussion the reporter pressed the official to discuss the "ancient tribal hatreds" that were fueling the slaughter. The official ever so politely demurred, repeatedly reminding the reporter that mass conflict began when Belgian colonial rulers gave Tutsis a monopoly of state power. But, as happens so often, the image of ancient tribalism was too deeply ingrained in the reporter's mind for him to hear the UN official's message.

What the African official had to say was right: ethnic thinking in political life is a product of modern conflicts over power and resources, and not an ancient impediment to political modernity. True, before the modern era some Africans did consider themselves Hutu or Tutsi, Nuer or Zande, but these labels were not the main sources of everyday identity. A woman living in central Africa drew her identity from where she was born, from her lineage and in-laws, and from her wealth. Tribal or ethnic identity was rarely important in everyday life and could change as people moved over vast areas in pursuit of trade or new lands. Conflicts were more often within tribal categories than between them, as people fought over sources of water, farmland, or grazing rights.

It was the colonial powers, and the independent states succeeding them, which declared that each and every person had an "ethnic identity" that determined his or her place within the colony or the postcolonial system. Even such a seemingly small event as the taking of a census created the idea of a colony-wide ethnic category to which one belonged and had loyalties. (And this was not the case just in Africa: some historians of India attribute the birth of Hindu nationalism to the first British census, when people began to think of themselves as members of Hindu, Muslim, or Sikh populations.) The colonial powers—Belgians, Germans, French, British, and Dutch—also realized that, given their small numbers in their dominions, they could effectively govern and exploit only by seeking out "partners" from among local people, sometimes from minority or Christianized groups. But then the state had to separate its partners from all others, thereby creating firmly bounded "ethnic groups."

In Rwanda and Burundi, German and Belgian colonizers admired the taller people called Tutsis, who formed a small minority in both colonies. The Belgians gave the Tutsis privileged access to education and jobs, and even instituted a minimum height requirement for entrance to college. So that colonial officials could tell who was Tutsi, they required everyone to carry identity cards with tribal labels.

But people cannot be forced into the neat compartments that this requirement suggests. Many Tutsis are tall and many Hutus short, but Hutus and Tutsis had intermarried to a such an extent that they were not easily distinguished physically (nor are they today). They spoke the same language and carried out the same religious practices. In most regions of the colonies the categories became economic labels: poor Tutsis became Hutus, and economically successful Hutus became Tutsis. Where the labels "Hutu" and "Tutsi" had not been much used, lineages with lots of cattle were simply labeled Tutsi; poorer lineages, Hutu. Colonial discrimination against Hutus created what had not existed before: a sense of collective Hutu identity, a Hutu cause. In the late 1950s Hutus began to rebel against Tutsi rule (encouraged by Europeans on their way out) and then created an independent and Hutu-dominated state in Rwanda; this state then gave rise to Tutsi resentments and to the creation of a Tutsi rebel army, the Rwandan Patriotic Front.

The logic of rule through ethnic division worked elsewhere, too. The case of Sri Lanka (formerly Ceylon) shows how, even when colonizers did not favor a single group, colonial rule could foster interethnic violence. The Sinhalese and Tamils of Sri Lanka have a common origin and, contrary to stereotypes of dark Tamils and light-skinned Sinhalese, they cannot easily be distinguished by their physical characteristics. The distinction between them is based mainly on the language spoken. Before this century there was little conflict between them; indeed, they did not think of themselves as two distinct kinds of people. Then came British rule. As they did throughout their empire, the British ruled Ceylon by creating an English-speaking elite, and, here as elsewhere, their favoritism engendered an opposition. In Ceylon this opposition took on racial and religious overtones. The majority of those who had been left out of the elite spoke Sinhalese and were Buddhists, and they began to promote a racist notion of Sinhalese superiority as an "Aryan race." After independence it was this Sinhalese-speaking group that gained control of the new state of Sri Lanka, and began to exclude Tamils from the best schools and jobs, mainly by requiring competence in Sinhalese. Not surprisingly, Tamils resented this discrimination, and some—initially only a few—

launched violent protests in the 1970s. These riots led to massive state repression and, by a logic similar to that shaping Tutsi rebellions in Rwanda, to the creation of the Tamil Tigers (the Liberation Tigers of Tamil Eelam) and their demands for an autonomous Tamil region. As the anthropologist Stanley Tambiah has argued, the island's violence is a late-twentieth-century response to colonial and postcolonial policies that relied on a hardened and artificial notion of ethnic boundaries.[3]

In these cases and many others—Sikhs in India, Maronites in Lebanon, Copts in Egypt, Moluccans in the Dutch East Indies, Karens in Burma—colonial and postcolonial states created new social groups and identified them by ethnic, religious, or regional categories. Only in living memory have the people who were sorted into these categories begun to act in concert, as political groups with common interests. Moreover, their shared interests have been those of political autonomy, access to education and jobs, and control of local resources. Far from reflecting ancient ethnic or tribal loyalties, their cohesion and action are products of the modern state's demand that people make themselves heard as powerful groups, or else risk suffering severe disadvantages.

Fear from the Top

A reader might say at this point: Fine, ethnic identities are modern and created, but today people surely do target members of other ethnic groups for violence, do they not? The answer is: Less than we usually think, and when they do, it is only after a long period of being prepared, pushed, and threatened by leaders who control the army and the airwaves. It is fear and hate generated from the top, and not ethnic differences, that finally push people to commit acts of violence. People may come to fear or resent another group for a variety of reasons, especially when social and economic change seems to favor the other group. And yet such competition and resentment "at the ground level" usually does not lead to intergroup violence without an intervening push from the top.

Let us return to those two most unsettling cases, Rwanda and the Balkans. In Rwanda the continuing slaughter of the past few years stemmed from efforts by the dictator-president Juvenal Habyarimana to wipe out his political opposition, Hutu as well as Tutsi. In 1990–91 Habyarimana began to assemble armed gangs into a militia called Interahamwe. This militia carried out its first massacre of a village in March 1992, and in 1993 began systematically to kill Hutu moderates and Tutsis. Throughout 1993 the country's three major radio stations were broadcasting messages of hate against Tutsis, against the opposition parties, and against specific politicians, setting the stage for what followed. Immediately after the still unexplained plane crash that killed President Habyarimana in April 1994, the presidential guard began killing Hutu opposition leaders, human rights activists, journalists, and others critical of the state, most of them Hutus. Only then, after the first wave of killings, were the militia and soldiers sent out to organize mass killings in the countryside, focusing on Tutsis.

Why did people obey the orders to kill? Incessant radio broadcasts over the previous year had surely prepared them for it; the broadcasts portrayed the Tutsi-led Rwandan Patriotic Front as bloodthirsty killers. During the massacres, radio broadcasts promised the land of the dead to the killers. Town mayors, the militia, the regular army, and the police organized Hutus into killing squads, and killed those Hutus who would not join in. The acting president toured the country to thank those villagers who had taken part in the massacres. Some people settled personal scores under cover of the massacre, and many were carried away with what observers have described as a "killing frenzy." The killings of 1994 were not random mob violence, although they were influenced by mob psychology.[4]

In reading accounts of the Rwanda killings, I was struck by how closely they matched, point by point, the ways Indonesians have described to me their participation in the mass slaughters of 1965–66. In Indonesia the supposed target was "communists," but there, too, it was a desire to settle personal scores, greed, willingness to follow the army's orders, and fear of retaliation that drove people to do things they can even now barely admit to themselves, even though many of them, like many Hutus, were convinced that the killings stopped the takeover of the country by an evil power. In both countries, people were told to kill the children and not to spare pregnant women, lest children grow up to take revenge on their killers. Americans continue to refer to those massacres in Indonesia as an instance of "ethnic violence" and to assume that Chinese residents were major targets, but they were not: the killings by and large pitted Javanese against Javanese, Acehnese against Acehnese, and so forth.

The two massacres have their differences: Rwanda in 1993–94 was a one-party state that had carried out mass indoctrination through absolute control of the mass media; Indonesia in 1965–66 was a politically fragmented state in which certain factions of the armed forces only gradually took control. But in both cases leaders were able to carry out a plan, conceived at the top, to wipe out an opposition group. They succeeded because they persuaded people that they could survive only by killing those who were, or could become, their killers.

The same task of persuasion faced Serb and Croat nationalist politicians, in particular Croatia's Franjo Tudjman and Serbia's Slobodan Milošević, who warned their ethnic brethren elsewhere—Serbs in Croatia, Croats in Bosnia—that their rights were about to be trampled unless they rebelled. Milošević played on the modern Serb nationalist rhetoric of expansion, claiming the right of Serbs everywhere to be united. Tudjman, for his part, used modern Croat rhetoric of exclusionary nationalism to build his following. Once in power in Croatia, he moved quickly to define Serbs as second-class citizens, fired Serbs from the police and military, and placed the red-and-white "checkerboard" of the Nazi-era Ustashe flag in the new Croatian banner.

Both leaders used historical memories for their own purposes, but they also had to erase recent memories of new Yugoslav identities, tentatively forged by men and women who married across ethnic boundaries or who lived in the cosmopolitan cities. The new constitutions recognized only ethnic identity, not civil identity, and people were forced, sometimes at gunpoint, to choose who they "really" were.[5]

Contrary to the "explanations" of the war frequently offered by Western journalists, ordinary Serbs do not live in the fourteenth century, fuming over the Battle of Kosovo; nor is the current fighting merely a playing out of some kind of inevitable logic of the past, as some have written. It took hard work by unscrupulous politicians to convince ordinary people that the other side consisted not of the friends and neighbors they had known for years but of genocidal people who would kill them if they were not killed first. For Milošević this meant persuading Serbs that Croats were all crypto-Nazi Ustashe; for Tudjman it meant convincing Croats that Serbs were all Chetnik assassins. Both, but particularly Milošević, declared Bosnian Muslims to be the front wave of a new Islamic threat. Each government indirectly helped the other: Milošević's expansionist talk confirmed Croat fears that Serbs intended to control the Balkans; Tudjman's politics revived Serbs' still remembered fears of the Ustashe. Serb media played up these fears, giving extensive coverage in 1990–91 to the exhumation of mass graves from the Second World War and to stories of Ustashe terror. This "nationalism from the top down," as Warren Zimmerman, the last U.S. ambassador to Yugoslavia, has characterized it, was also a battle of nationalisms, with each side's actions confirming the other's fears.

If Rwanda and the Balkans do not conform to the images of bubbling cauldrons and ancient tribal hatreds, even less do other ongoing local-level conflicts. Most are drives for political autonomy, most spectacularly in the former Soviet Union, where the collapse of Soviet power allowed long-suppressed peoples to reassert their claims to practice their own languages and religions, and to control their own territory and resources—a rejection of foreign rule much like anti-imperial rebellions in the Americas, Europe, Asia, and Africa. Elsewhere various rebellions each with its own history and motivations, have typically—and erroneously—been lumped together as "ethnic conflict." Resistance in East Timor to Indonesian control is a 20-year struggle against invasion by a foreign power, not an expression of ethnic or cultural identity. People fighting in the southern Philippines under the banner of a "Moro nation" by and large joined up to regain control of their homelands from Manila-appointed politicians. Zapatista rebels in Chiapas demand jobs, political reform, and, above all, land. They do not mention issues of ethnic or cultural identity in their statements—indeed, their leader is from northern Mexico and until recently spoke no Mayan. Other current conflicts are raw struggles for power among rival factions, particularly in several African countries (Liberia, Somalia, Angola) where rival forces often recruit heavily from one region or clan (giving rise to the notion that these are "ethnic conflicts") in order to make use of local leaders and loyalties to control their followers.[6]

Ethnic Diversity and Social Conflict

This brings us to the third mistaken assumption: that ethnic diversity brings with it political instability and the likelihood of violence. To the contrary, greater ethnic diversity is not associated with greater interethnic conflict. Some of the world's most ethnically diverse states, such as Indonesia, Malaysia, and Pakistan, though not without internal conflict and political repression, have suffered little interethnic violence, while countries with very slight differences in language or culture (the former Yugoslavia, Somalia, Rwanda) have had the bloodiest such conflicts. It is the number of ethnic groups and their relationships to power, not diversity per se, that strongly affect political stability. As shown in recent studies by political scientist Ted Gurr, and contrary to popular thinking, local conflicts have not sharply increased in frequency or severity during the last ten years. The greatest increase in local conflicts occurred during the Cold War, and resulted from the superpowers' efforts to arm their client states. (The sense that everything exploded after 1989, Gurr argues, comes from the reassertions of national identity in Eastern Europe and the former Soviet Union.)[7]

By and large, the news media focus on countries racked by violence and ignore the many more cases of peaceful relations among different peoples. Take Indonesia, where I have carried out fieldwork since the late 1970s. If people know of Indonesia, it is probably because of its occupation of East Timor and its suppression of political freedoms. But these are not matters of ethnic conflict, of which there is remarkably little in a country composed of more than three hundred peoples, each with its own distinct language and culture. Although throughout the 1950s and 1960s there were rebellions against Jakarta in many parts of the country, these concerned control over local resources, schooling, and religion. An on-again, off-again rebellion where I work, on the northern tip of Sumatra, has been about control over the region's vast oil and gas resources (although the Western press continues to stereotype it as "ethnic conflict").

Cultural diversity does, of course, present challenges to national integration and social peace. Why do some countries succeed at meeting those challenges while others fail? Two sets of reasons seem most important, and they swamp the mere fact of ethnic and cultural diversity.

First there are the "raw materials" for social peace that countries possess at the time of independence. Countries in which one group has been exploiting all others (such as Rwanda and Burundi) start off with scores to settle, while countries with no such clearly dominating group (such as Indonesia) have an initial advantage in building political consensus. So-called centralized polities, with two or three large groups that continually polarize national politics, are less stable than "dispersed" systems, in which each of many smaller groups is forced to seek out allies to achieve its goals. And if the major ethnic groups share a language or religion, or if they have worked together in a revolutionary struggle, they have a bridge already in place that they can use to build political cooperation.[8]

Take, again, the case of Indonesia. In colonial Indonesia (the Dutch East Indies) the Javanese were, as they are today, the most numerous people. But they were concentrated on Java and held positions of power only there. Peoples of Java, Sumatra, and the eastern islands, along with Malays and many in the southern Philippines, had used Malay as a *lingua franca* for centuries, and Malay became the basis for the language of independent Indonesia. Islam also cut across regions and ethnicities, uniting people on Sumatra, Java, and Sulawesi. Dominance was "dispersed," in that prominent figures in literature, religion, and the nationalist movement tended as often as not to be from someplace other than Java, notably Sumatra. Moreover, people from throughout the country had spent five years fighting Dutch efforts to regain control after the Second World War, and could draw on the shared experience of that common struggle.[9]

One can see the difference each of these features makes by looking next door at culturally similar Malaysia. Malays and Chinese, the largest ethnic groups, shared neither language nor religion, and had no shared memory of struggle to draw on. Malays had held all political power during British rule. On the eve of independence there was a clear fault line running between the Malay and Chinese communities.

The Importance of Political Choices

But these initial conditions do not tell the whole story, and here enters the second set of reasons for social peace or social conflict. States do make choices, particularly about political processes, that ease or exacerbate intergroup tensions. As political scientist Donald Horowitz has pointed out, if we consider only their starting conditions, Malaysia ought to have experienced considerable interethnic violence (for the reasons given above), whereas Sri Lanka, where Tamils and Sinhalese had mingled in the British-trained elite, should have been spared such violence. And yet Malaysia has largely managed to avoid it while Sri Lanka has not. The crucial difference, writes Horowitz, was in the emerging political systems in the two countries. Malaysian politicians constructed a multiethnic political coalition, which fostered ties between Chinese and Malay leaders and forced political candidates to seek the large middle electoral ground. In Sri Lanka, as we saw earlier, Sinhalese-speakers formed a chauvinist nationalist movement, and after early cooperation Tamils and Sinhalese split apart to form ethnically based political parties. Extreme factions appeared on the wings of each party, forcing party leaders to drift in their directions.

But political systems can be changed. Nigeria is a good example. Prior to 1967 it consisted of three regions—North, South, and East—each with its own party supported by ethnic allegiances. The intensity of this three-way division drove the southeast region of Biafra to attempt to break away from Nigeria in 1967, and the trauma of the civil war that followed led politicians to try a new system. They carved the country into 19 states, the boundaries of which cut through the territories of the three largest ethnic groups (Hausa, Yoruba, and Igbo), encouraging a new federalist politics based on multiethnic coalitions. The new system, for all its other problems, prevented another Biafra. Subsequent leaders, however, continued to add to the number of states for their own political reasons. The current leader, General Sani Abacha, is now adding to an already expanded list of 30 states; this excessive fragmentation has broken up the multiethnic coalitions and encouraged ethnic politics anew. A similar direction has been pursued by Kenya's Daniel arap Moi, who has created an ethnic electoral base that excludes most Kikuyus, increasing the relevance of ethnicity in politics and therefore the level of intergroup tensions.

What the myth of ethnic conflict would say are ever-present tensions are in fact the products of political choices. Negative stereotyping, fear of another group, killing lest one be killed—these are the doings of so-called leaders, and can be undone by them as well. Believing otherwise, and assuming that such conflicts are the natural consequences of human depravity in some quarters of the world, leads to perverse thinking and perverse policy. It makes violence seem characteristic of a people or region, rather than the consequence of specific political acts. Thinking this way excuses inaction, as when U.S. president Bill Clinton, seeking to retreat from the hard-line Balkan policy of candidate Clinton, began to claim that Bosnians and Serbs were killing each other because of their ethnic and religious differences. Because it paints all sides as less rational and less modern (more tribal, more ethnic) than "we" are, it makes it easier to tolerate their suffering. Because it assumes that "those people" would naturally follow their leaders' call to kill, it distracts us from the central and difficult question of just how and why people are sometimes led to commit such horrifying deeds.

NOTES

1. Two of the most widely read proponents of the view I am contesting are Robert Kaplan, in his dispatches for *The Atlantic* [p. 34, this volume] and in his *Balkan Ghosts: A Journey Through History* (New York: St. Martin's, 1993), and (writing mainly on large-scale conflict) Samuel P. Huntington, in "The Clash of Civilizations?" *Foreign Affairs* 72 (Summer 1993): 22–49 [p. 3, this volume]. My concern is less with the particular difficulties of these writers' arguments, about which others have written, than with the general notion, which, as with all myths, survives the death of any one of its versions.

2. See Misha Glenny, *The Fall of Yugoslavia* (New York: Penguin, 1992), for a balanced and ethnographically rich account of the Balkan wars. On recent tendencies in European nationalisms, see especially Rogers Brubaker, *Nationalism Reframed: Nationhood and the National Question in the New Europe* (Cambridge: Cambridge University Press, 1996). Brubaker makes the important point that "nationalism" should be treated as a category of social and political ideology, and not a pre-ideological "thing."

3. S.J. Tambiah, *Sri Lanka: Ethnic Fratricide and the Dismantling of Democracy* (Chicago: University of Chicago Press, 1986). For a different view on the culture of violence in Sri Lanka, see Bruce Kapferer, *Legends of People, Myths of State* (Washington, D.C.: Smithsonian Institution Press, 1988).

4. Among recent overviews of massacres in Rwanda and Burundi, see Philip Gourevitch, "The Poisoned Country," *New York Review of Books,* 6 June 1996, 58–64, and René Lemarchand, *Burundi: Ethnic Conflict and Genocide* (Cambridge: Cambridge University Press, 1995).

5. That there were memories, fears, and hatreds to exploit is important to bear in mind, lest we go to the other extreme and argue that these conflicts are entirely produced from the top, an extreme toward which an overreliance on rational-choice models may lead some analysts. Russell Hardin's otherwise excellent *One for All: The Logic of Group Conflict* (Princeton: Princeton University Press, 1995) errs, I believe, in attributing nothing but rational, self-aggrandizing motives to those leaders who stir up ethnic passions, ignoring that they, too, can be caught up in these passions. The cold rationality of leaders is itself a variable: probably Milošević fits Hardin's rational-actor model better than Tudjman, and Suharto better than Sukarno. In each case, it is an empirical question.

6. The same points could be made concerning the religious version of "ancient hatreds," such as Muslim-Hindu relations in India. However peaceful or conflictual "ancient" relations may have been (and on this issue there continues to be a great deal of controversy among historians of South Asia), the often bloody conflicts of the past ten years in India have been fueled by ambitious politicians who have seen boundless electoral opportunity in middle-class Hindu resentment toward 1) lower castes' claims that they deserve employment and education quotas, and 2) the recent prosperity of some middleclass Muslims. See the penetrating political analyses by Susanne Hoeber Rudolph and Lloyd I. Rudolph in the *New Republic,* 22 March 1993 and 14 February 1994, and a historical and ethnographic study by Peter van der Veer, *Religious Nationalism: Hindus and Muslims in India* (Berkeley: University of California Press, 1994).

7. See Ted Gurr, *Ethnic Conflict in World Politics* (Boulder, Colo.: Westview, 1994).

8. See Donald L. Horowitz, *Ethnic Groups in Conflict* (Berkeley: University of California Press, 1985), 291–364.

9. I would propose "dispersed dominance" (a situation in which each of several groups considers itself to dominate on some social or political dimension) as a second important mechanism for reducing intergroup conflict alongside the well-known "crosscutting cleavages" (a situation in which one or more important dimensions of diversity cut across others, as religion cuts across ethnicity in many countries). "Dispersed dominance" takes into account social and cultural dimensions, such as literary preeminence or a sense of social worth stemming from putative indigenous status. It is thus broader than, but similar to, political mechanisms such as federalism, when these mechanisms are aimed at (in Donald Horowitz's phrase) "proliferating the points of power." It is the empirical correlate to the normative position articulated by Michael Walzer in *Spheres of Justice* (New York: Basic Books, 1983) that dominance in one sphere (or dimension) ought not to automatically confer dominance in others.

Part

3

Redrawing the Map? The New Nature of National Borders

In the global context, the idea of the nation-state with carefully defined boundaries has diminished in importance. Global and economic power arrangements call for more flexible and porous relationships. Kenichi Ohmae argues that the nation-state has become "unnatural, even dysfunctional," for organizing activity and managing economic interests. For him the confines of state boundaries often overlook the linkages and synergies between different populations. Indeed, the linkages between "region states" tend to be part of the global economy. Foreign policy, security and defense, taxation, public investment, and education remain within the nation-state; "region states" are not the enemies of central governments. Leaders must come to terms with regional economic realities. Janet Ceglowski recognizes the concept of a borderless economy cutting across national economies. However, in looking at Mexico's and Canada's borders with the United States, Ceglowski finds that they continue to have an impact on bilateral trade flows and on relative prices. She concludes that borders still matter. Anne-Marie Slaughter sees a different world order emerging. For her the state is not disappearing but rather disaggregating into its functionally distinct parts. These parts can then network across states, resulting in a "web" that constitutes a new transgovernmental order to deal with such problems as crime, terrorism, and environmental degradation. Judges, for example, are building global communities of law, and national regulators are cooperating with their counterparts in other countries. Slaughter sees these globe-spanning networks as strengthening the state. Transgovernmentalism thus offers the world a "blueprint for the international architecture of the 21st century."

The Rise of the Region State

Kenichi Ohmae

The Nation State Is Dysfunctional

The nation state has become an unnatural, even dysfunctional, unit for organizing human activity and managing economic endeavor in a borderless world. It represents no genuine, shared community of economic interests; it defines no meaningful flows of economic activity. In fact, it overlooks the true linkages and synergies that exist among often disparate populations by combining important measures of human activity at the wrong level of analysis.

For example, to think of Italy as a single economic entity ignores the reality of an industrial north and a rural south, each vastly different in its ability to contribute and in its need to receive. Treating Italy as a single economic unit forces one—as a private sector manager or a public sector official—to operate on the basis of false, implausible and nonexistent averages. Italy is a country with great disparities in industry and income across regions.

On the global economic map the lines that now matter are those defining what may be called "region states." The boundaries of the region state are not imposed by political fiat. They are drawn by the deft but invisible hand of the global market for goods and services. They follow, rather than precede, real flows of human activity, creating nothing new but ratifying existing patterns manifest in countless individual decisions. They represent no threat to the political borders of any na-

Reprinted with permission from *Foreign Affairs*, Vol. 72, No. 2, 1993. © 1993 by the Council on Foreign Relations, Inc.

tion, and they have no call on any taxpayer's money to finance military forces to defend such borders.

Region states are natural economic zones. They may or may not fall within the geographic limits of a particular nation—whether they do is an accident of history. Sometimes these distinct economic units are formed by parts of states, such as those in northern Italy, Wales, Catalonia, Alsace-Lorraine or Baden-Württemberg. At other times they may be formed by economic patterns that overlap existing national boundaries, such as those between San Diego and Tijuana, Hong Kong and southern China, or the "growth triangle" of Singapore and its neighboring Indonesian islands. In today's borderless world these are natural economic zones and what matters is that each possesses, in one or another combination, the key ingredients for successful participation in the global economy.

Look, for example, at what is happening in Southeast Asia. The Hong Kong economy has gradually extended its influence throughout the Pearl River Delta. The radiating effect of these linkages has made Hong Kong, where GNP per capita is $12,000, the driving force of economic life in Shenzhen, boosting the per capita GNP of that city's residents to $5,695, as compared to $317 for China as a whole. These links extend to Zhuhai, Amoy and Guangzhou as well. By the year 2000 this cross-border region state will have raised the living standard of more than 11 million people over the $5,000 level. Meanwhile, Guangdong province, with a population of more than 65 million and its capital at Hong Kong, will emerge as a newly industrialized economy in its own right, even though China's per capita GNP may still hover at about $1,000. Unlike in Eastern Europe, where nations try to convert entire socialist economies over to the market, the Asian model is first to convert limited economic zones—the region states—into free enterprise havens. So far the results have been reassuring.

These developments and others like them are coming just in time for Asia. As Europe perfects its single market and as the United States, Canada and Mexico begin to explore the benefits of the North American Free Trade Agreement (NAFTA), the combined economies of Asia and Japan lag behind those of the other parts of the globe's economic triad by about $2 trillion—roughly the aggregate size of some 20 additional region states. In other words, for Asia to keep pace existing regions must continue to grow at current rates throughout the next decade, giving birth to 20 additional Singapores.

Many of these new region states are already beginning to emerge. China has expanded to 14 other areas—many of them inland—the special economic zones that have worked so well for Shenzhen and Shanghai. One such project at Yunnan will become a cross-border economic zone encompassing parts of Laos and Vietnam. In Vietnam itself Ho Chi Minh City (Saigon) has launched a similar "sepzone" to attract foreign capital. Inspired in part by Singapore's "growth triangle," the governments of Indonesia, Malaysia and Thailand in 1992 unveiled a larger triangle across the Strait of Malacca to link Medan, Penang and Phuket. These developments are not, of course, limited to the developing economies in Asia. In economic terms the United States has never been a single nation. It is a collection of region states: northern and southern California, the "power corridor" along the East Coast between Boston and Washington, the Northeast, the Midwest, the Sun Belt, and so on.

What Makes a Region State

The primary linkages of region states tend to be with the global economy and not with their host nations. Region states make such effective points of entry into the global economy because the very characteristics that define them are shaped by the demands of that economy. Region states tend to have between five million and 20 million people. The range is broad, but the extremes are clear: not half a million, not 50 or 100 million. A region state must be small enough for its citizens to share certain economic and consumer interests but of adequate size to justify the infrastructure—communication and transportation links and quality professional services—necessary to participate economically on a global scale.

It must, for example, have at least one international airport and, more than likely, one good harbor with international-class freight-handling facilities. A region state must also be large enough to provide an attractive market for the brand development of leading consumer products. In other words, region states are not defined by their economies of scale in production (which, after all, can be leveraged from a base of any size through exports to the rest of the world) but rather by their having reached efficient economies of scale in their consumption, infrastructure and professional services.

For example, as the reach of television networks expands, advertising becomes more efficient. Although trying to introduce a consumer brand throughout all of Japan or Indonesia may still prove prohibitively expensive, establishing it firmly in the Osaka or Jakarta region is far more affordable—and far more likely to generate handsome returns. Much the same is true with sales and service networks, customer satisfaction programs, market surveys and management information systems: efficient scale is at the regional, not national, level. This fact matters because, on balance, modern marketing techniques and technologies shape the economies of region states.

Where true economies of service exist, religious, ethnic and racial distinctions are not important—or, at least, only as important as human nature requires. Singapore is 70 percent ethnic Chinese, but its 30 percent minority is not much of a problem because commercial prosperity creates sufficient affluence for all. Nor are ethnic differences a source of concern for potential investors looking for consumers.

Indonesia—an archipelago with 500 or so different tribal groups, 18,000 islands and 170 million people—would logically seem to defy effective organization within a single mode of political government. Yet Jakarta has traditionally attempted to impose just such a central control by applying fictional averages to the entire nation. They do not work. If, however, economies of service allowed two or three Singapore-sized region states to be created within Indonesia, they could be managed. And they would ameliorate, rather than exacerbate, the country's internal social divisions. This holds as well for India and Brazil.

The New Multinational Corporation

When viewing the globe through the lens of the region state, senior corporate managers think differently about the geographical expansion of their businesses. In the past the primary aspiration of multinational corporations was to create, in effect, clones of the parent organization in each of the dozens of countries in which they operated. The goal of this system was to stick yet another pin in the global map to mark an increasing number of subsidiaries around the world.

More recently, however, when Nestlé and Procter & Gamble wanted to expand their business in Japan from an already strong position, they did not view the effort as just another pin-sticking exercise. Nor did they treat the country as a single coherent market to be gained at once, or try as most Western companies do to establish a foothold first in the Tokyo area, Japan's most tumultuous and overcrowded market. Instead, they wisely focused on the Kansai region around Osaka and Kobe, whose 22 million residents are nearly as affluent as those in Tokyo but where competition is far less intense. Once they had on-the-ground experience on how best to reach the Japanese consumer, they branched out into other regions of the country.

Much of the difficulty Western companies face in trying to enter Japan stems directly from trying to shoulder their way in through Tokyo. This instinct often proves difficult and costly. Even if it works, it may also prove a trap; it is hard to "see" Japan once one is bottled up in the particular dynamics of the Tokyo marketplace. Moreover, entering the country through a different regional doorway has great economic appeal. Measured by aggregate GNP the Kansai region is the seventh-largest economy in the world, just behind the United Kingdom.

Given the variations among local markets and the value of learning through real-world experimentation, an incremental region-based approach to market entry makes excellent sense. And not just in Japan. Building an effective presence across a landmass the size of China is of course a daunting prospect. Serving the people in and around Nagoya City, however, is not.

If one wants a presence in Thailand, why start by building a network over the entire extended landmass? Instead focus, at least initially, on the region around Bangkok, which represents the lion's share of the total potential market. The same strategy applies to the United States. To introduce a new top-of-the-line car into the U.S. market, why replicate up front an exhaustive coast-to-coast dealership network? Of the country's 3,000 statistical metropolitan areas, 80 percent of luxury car buyers can be reached by establishing a presence in only 125 of these.

The Challenges for Government

Traditional issues of foreign policy, security and defense remain the province of nation states. So, too, are macroeconomic and monetary policies—the taxation and public investment needed to provide the necessary infrastructure and incentives for region-based activities. The government will also remain responsible for the broad requirements of educating and training citizens so that they can participate fully in the global economy.

Governments are likely to resist giving up the power to intervene in the economic realm or to relinquish their impulses for protectionism. The illusion of control is soothing. Yet hard evidence proves the contrary. No manipulation of exchange rates by central bankers or political appointees has ever "corrected" the trade imbalances between the United States and Japan. Nor has any trade talk between the two governments. Whatever cosmetic actions these negotiations may have prompted, they rescued no industry and revived no economic sector. Textiles, semiconductors, autos, consumer electronics—the competitive situation in these industries did not develop according to the whims of policymakers but only in response to the deeper logic of the competitive marketplace. If U.S. market share has dwindled, it is not because government policy failed but because individual consumers decided to buy elsewhere. If U.S. capacity has migrated to Mexico or Asia, it is only because individual managers made decisions about cost and efficiency.

The implications of region states are not welcome news to established seats of political power, be they politicians or lobbyists. Nation states by definition require a domestic political focus, while region states are ensconced in the global economy. Region states that sit within the frontiers of a particular nation share its political goals and aspirations. However, region states welcome foreign investment and ownership—whatever allows them to employ people productively or to improve the quality of life. They want their people to have access to the best and cheapest products. And they want whatever surplus accrues from these activities to ratchet up the local quality of life still further and not to support distant regions or to prop up distressed industries elsewhere in the name of national interest or sovereignty.

When a region prospers, that prosperity spills over into the adjacent regions within the same political confederation. Industry in the area immediately in and around Bangkok has prompted investors to explore options elsewhere in Thailand. Much the same is true of Kuala Lumpur in Malaysia, Jakarta in Indonesia, or Singapore, which is rapidly becoming the unofficial capital of the Association of Southeast Asian Nations. São Paulo, too, could well emerge as a genuine region state, someday entering the ranks of the Organization of Economic Cooperation and Development. Yet if Brazil's central government does not allow the São Paulo region state finally to enter the global economy, the country as a whole may soon fall off the roster of the newly industrialized economies.

Unlike those at the political center, the leaders of region states—interested chief executive officers, heads of local unions, politicians at city and state levels—often welcome and encourage foreign capital investment. They do not go abroad to attract new plants and factories only to appear back home on television vowing to protect local companies at any cost. These leaders tend to possess an international outlook that can help defuse many of the usual kinds of social tensions arising over issues of "foreign" versus "domestic" inputs to production.

In the United States, for example, the Japanese have already established about 120 "transplant" auto factories throughout the Mississippi Valley. More are on the way. As their share of the U.S. auto industry's production grows, people in that region who look to these plants for their livelihoods and for the tax revenues needed to support local communities will stop caring whether the plants belong to U.S.or Japanese-based companies. All they will care about are the regional economic benefits of having them there. In effect, as members of the Mississippi Valley region state, they will have leveraged the contribution of these plants to help their region become an active participant in the global economy.

Region states need not be the enemies of central governments. Handled gently, region states can provide the opportunity for eventual prosperity for all areas within a nation's traditional political control. When political and industrial leaders accept and act on these realities, they help build prosperity. When they do not— falling back under the spell of the nationalist economic illusion—they may actually destroy it.

Consider the fate of Silicon Valley, that great early engine of much of America's microelectronics industry. In the beginning it was an extremely open and entrepreneurial environment. Of late, however, it has become notably protectionist—creating industry associations, establishing a polished lobbying presence in Washington and turning to "competitiveness" studies as a way to get more federal funding for research and development. It has also begun to discourage, and even to bar, foreign investment, let alone foreign takeovers. The result is that Boise and Denver now prosper in electronics; Japan is developing a Silicon Island on Kyushu; Taiwan is trying to create a Silicon Island of its own; and Korea is nurturing a Silicon Peninsula. This is the worst of all possible worlds: no new money in California and a host of newly energized and well-funded competitors.

Elsewhere in California, not far from Silicon Valley, the story is quite different. When Hollywood recognized that it faced a severe capital shortage, it did not throw up protectionist barriers against foreign money. Instead, it invited Rupert Murdoch into 20th Century Fox, C. Itoh and Toshiba into Time-Warner, Sony into Columbia, and Matsushita into MCA. The result: a $10 billion infusion of new capital and, equally important, $10 billion less for Japan or anyone else to set up a new Hollywood of their own.

Political leaders, however reluctantly, must adjust to the reality of economic regional entities if they are to nurture real economic flows. Resistant governments will be left to reign over traditional political territories as all meaningful participation in the global economy migrates beyond their well-preserved frontiers.

Canada, as an example, is wrongly focusing on Quebec and national language tensions as its core economic and even political issue. It does so to the point of still wrestling with the teaching of French and English in British Columbia, when that province's economic future is tied to Asia. Furthermore, as NAFTA takes shape the "vertical" relationships between Canadian and U.S. regions—Vancouver and Seattle (the Pacific Northwest region state); Toronto, Detroit and Cleveland (the Great Lakes region state)—will become increasingly important. How Canadian leaders deal with these new entities will be critical to the continuance of Canada as a political nation.

In developing economies, history suggests that when GNP per capita reaches about $5,000, discretionary income crosses an invisible threshold. Above that level people begin wondering whether they have reasonable access to the best and cheapest available products and whether they have an adequate quality of life. More troubling for those in political control, citizens also begin to consider whether their government is doing as well by them as it might.

Such a performance review is likely to be unpleasant. When governments control information—and in large measure because they do—it is all too easy for them to believe that they "own" their people. Governments begin restricting access to certain kinds of goods or services or pricing them far higher than pure economic logic would dictate. If market-driven levels of consumption conflict with a government's pet policy or general desire for control, the obvious response is to restrict consumption. So what if the people would choose otherwise if given the opportunity? Not only does the government withhold that opportunity but it also does not even let the people know that it is being withheld.

Regimes that exercise strong central control either fall on hard times or begin to decompose. In a borderless world the deck is stacked against them. The irony, of course, is that in the name of safeguarding the integrity and identity of the center, they often prove unwilling or unable to give up the illusion of power in order to seek a better quality of life for their people. There is at the center an understandable fear of letting go and losing control. As a result, the center often ends up protecting weak and unproductive industries and then passing along the high costs to its people—precisely the opposite of what a government should do.

The Goal Is to Raise Living Standards

The Clinton administration faces a stark choice as it organizes itself to address the country's economic issues. It can develop policy within the framework of the badly dated assumption that success in the global economy means pitting one nation's industries against another's. Or it can define policy with the awareness that the economic dynamics of a borderless world do not flow from such contrived head-to-head confrontations, but rather from the participation of specific regions in a global nexus of information, skill, trade and investment.

If the goal is to raise living standards by promoting regional participation in the borderless economy, then the less Washington constrains these regions, the better off they will be. By contrast, the more Washington intervenes, the more citizens will pay for automobiles, steel, semiconductors, white wine, textiles or consumer electronics—all in the name of "protecting" America. Aggregating economic policy at the national level—or worse, at the continent-wide level as in Europe—inevitably results in special interest groups and vote-conscious governments putting their own interests first.

The less Washington interacts with specific regions, however, the less it perceives itself as "representing" them. It does not feel right. When learning to ski, one of the toughest and most counterintuitive principles to accept is that one gains better control by leaning down toward the valley, not back against the hill. Letting go is difficult. For governments region-based participation in the borderless economy is fine, except where it threatens current jobs, industries or interests. In Japan, a nation with plenty of farmers, food is far more expensive than in Hong Kong or Singapore, where there are no farmers. That is because Hong Kong and Singapore are open to what Australia and China can produce far more cheaply than they could themselves. They have opened themselves to the global economy, thrown their weight forward, as it were, and their people have reaped the benefits.

For the Clinton administration, the irony is that Washington today finds itself in the same relation to those region states that lie entirely or partially within its borders as was London with its North American colonies centuries ago. Neither central power could genuinely understand the shape or magnitude of the new flows of information, people and economic activity in the regions nominally under its control. Nor could it understand how counterproductive it would be to try to arrest or distort these flows in the service of nation-defined interests. Now as then, only relaxed central control can allow the flexibility needed to maintain the links to regions gripped by an inexorable drive for prosperity.

Has Globalization Created a Borderless World?

Janet Ceglowski

The newest buzzword in the popular business press is *globalization*, a word that evokes images of a world in which goods, services, capital, and information flow across seamless national borders. In this world, the choices over where to produce, shop, invest, and save are no longer confined within national borders but have taken on a decidedly global orientation. Some analysts speculate that globalization has blurred the economic distinctions between countries, creating a "borderless world" in which economic decisions are made without reference to national boundaries. For instance, in describing the sphere in which the major industrial economies operate, Kenichi Ohmae asserts that "national borders have effectively disappeared and, along with them, the economic logic that made them useful lines of demarcation in the first place."

The view that national borders have become economically meaningless is controversial. But, if correct, it has potentially important implications for the world's economies and their policymakers. One current concern is that, by enhancing access to the labor resources and products of low-wage countries, globalization could already be stunting workers' living standards in relatively high-wage countries like the United States.[1] A truly borderless world would place great limits on the ability both to confine the effects of domestic economic policy within national borders and to insulate countries from foreign economic shocks. In such a world, financial capital, production activities, and even workers could move in response to better opportunities elsewhere in the world almost as easily as they could within a given country, thereby undermining efforts to maintain economic or financial conditions at home that diverge substantially from those abroad.

The overall level of international economic activity has escalated in recent years, spurred by a variety of factors ranging from innovations in information technology to efforts by national governments to liberalize and deregulate markets. The result has been an impressive expansion in world trade, investment in overseas operations, and international flows of financial capital. Casual observation suggests that international economic developments are attracting greater attention from policymakers, producers, and even individuals in their roles as workers and consumers. Both the growth in international economic activity and heightened public awareness are indications of strengthening economic ties between countries. The United States has participated in this trend and, by most measures, is considerably more open today than it was even 25 years ago.

Does all this mean that national borders no longer matter for economic decisions? This article assesses the relevance of the "borderless world" view for U.S. product markets. Although the U.S. economy has become more open, recent research finds that national borders continue to affect U.S. trade flows and product prices. In fact, the estimates of the border's effects are substantial. A number of factors could be responsible for this finding, including government-imposed barriers to trade, fluctuations in exchange rates, and a variety of noneconomic factors such as national historical and cultural ties. Even in the current environment of global and regional trade liberalization, there is little reason to expect that the influence of these factors on U.S. product markets is about to disappear.

Global and Regional Integration: Evidence for U.S. Product Markets

National economies are linked through trade in goods and services, cross-border flows of financial assets, and labor migration. International economic integration is the process by which reducing barriers between national economies strengthens these ties. In the economics literature, integration traditionally has been associated with explicit government actions to lower tariffs and other artificial barriers to the international movement of goods, services, and inputs. Recent advances in communication and information technologies have also promoted economic integration by enhancing knowledge of and access to foreign consumers and products. Both trade liberalization and advances in communication and information continue to be operative factors in the U.S. economy.

Have U.S. product markets become more integrated with the world economy as a result?[2] One common approach to quantifying the strength of an economy's ties with the rest of the world is to measure the share of its economic activity made up of exchanges with other countries. A larger share is indicative of a more "open" economy, one with stronger links to the world economy. According to this measure, markets for goods in the United States have become more open. Measured

Table I
U.S. Trade in Goods and Services Relative to U.S. GDP
(annual averages; in percent)

	1970–71	1980–81	1990–91	1995–96
Merchandise,				
excluding military	8.0	16.5	15.4	18.5
of which: exports	4.0	7.8	6.9	8.0
imports	4.0	8.7	8.5	10.5
Private services	1.8	2.5	4.2	4.8
of which: exports	0.9	1.4	2.5	2.9
imports	0.9	1.1	1.7	1.9
Merchandise & services	9.8	19.0	19.6	23.3
of which: exports	4.9	9.2	9.4	10.9
imports	4.9	9.8	10.2	12.4

Notes: The totals are the sums of the individual percentages for exports and imports. Private services trade is calculated as total services trade minus transfers under U.S. military sales contracts, direct defense expenditures, and U.S. government miscellaneous services.

Source: Author's calculations based on data from Bureau of Economic Analysis

relative to gross domestic product (GDP), merchandise trade more than doubled between 1970–71 and 1995–96 as a result of significant growth in both exports and imports (Table 1). Much of that gain occurred in the 1970s, so that by 1980–81 merchandise trade was 16.5 percent of GDP. The expansion in U.S. trade resumed in the 1990s, albeit at a somewhat slower pace. Though smaller in value than goods trade, services trade has grown even faster: measured relative to GDP, it has nearly tripled since 1970–71. Together, exports and imports of goods and services have expanded from under 10 percent of GDP in 1970–71 to over 23 percent in 1995–96.[3]

Do similar measures show evidence of growing *regional* integration? Recent trade agreements between the United States, Canada, and Mexico have created a tri-national free trade area; the Canada–United States Free Trade Agreement (CUSFTA) liberalized trade between the United States and Canada in 1989 and the North American Free Trade Agreement (NAFTA) extended the free trade area to Mexico in 1994. As a result, numerous formal barriers to trade and investment between the three countries have been or will be eliminated. The reduction in economic barriers should promote greater integration of the three economies. In fact, merchandise trade with Canada and Mexico grew from 2.3 percent of U.S. GDP in 1970–71 to 5.4 percent in 1995–96 (Table 2). Some of that growth predates the creation of the North American free trade area, suggesting an ongoing

Table 2
U.S. Trade with Canada and Mexico Relative to U.S. GDP
(annual averages; in percent)

	1970–71	*1980–81*	*1990–91*	*1995–96*
Merchandise	2.3	3.9	4.1	5.4
of which: Canada	2.0	2.9	3.0	3.8
Mexico	0.3	1.0	1.1	1.6
Private services	NA	NA	0.71	0.69
of which: Canada	0.30	0.28	0.45	0.44
Mexico	NA	NA	0.26	0.25

Notes: The individual percentages for Canada and Mexico represent the ratios of the sum of exports and imports to U.S. GDP. The totals for merchandise and services are the sums of the individual percentages for Canada and Mexico.

Source: Author's calculations based on data from Bureau of Economic Analysis

process of economic integration between the United States and the two other NAFTA countries. However, the recent trade agreements could have played a part in the significant gain since 1990–91. They might also be a factor in the sustained rise in the share of private services trade with Canada.

Is the U.S. Border Irrelevant?

The preceding analysis indicates that U.S. product markets have become more integrated with global markets. There is some indication of the same phenomenon at the regional level. But evidence of greater economic integration is not the same as evidence that national borders no longer matter for the worldwide distribution of goods and services. Although this distinction may appear to be simply a matter of degree, it is important. In a truly borderless world, the strength of the economic ties between markets would not depend on whether they are located in the same country. In particular, consumers and producers within a given country would not trade more among themselves simply because of shared nationality. In the language of economic integration, borderless product markets would be tantamount to complete integration.

Do borders still matter for U.S. product markets? The border between the United States and Canada is the most likely place to find evidence that they don't. Complete economic integration requires that there be no trade barriers between countries. Therefore, the strongest evidence of borderless product markets should be found among countries that have largely eliminated barriers to trade between them. The United States and Canada are clear candidates: not only have CUSFTA and NAFTA eliminated numerous barriers to bilateral trade but, for many goods, tariffs and other formal trade barriers between the United States and Canada were low or nonexistent well before the recent trade agreements.

Several other features of the two countries favor the development of strong bilateral economic links. Geographic proximity is one such feature. Greater distances between markets mean larger costs of transporting goods and services between them, encumbering trade and the development of close economic ties.[4] But the United States and Canada share a long border, much of which is easily negotiated by land or water. Moreover, some Canadian cities are closer to urban centers in the United States than they are to other major Canadian cities. Indeed, over three-fourths of Canada's population lives within 100 miles of the U.S. border. The nearness of the two countries extends beyond mere physical proximity: Canada and the United States share a number of social, political, and cultural traditions, and a majority of people in both countries speak the same language. Both the geographic proximity and cultural similarities of the two countries are propitious for bilateral trade and other cross-border economic activities.

In fact, Canada and the United States have long been major destinations for each other's products and foreign investment. They currently exchange close to $1 billion in goods and services each day, making theirs among the world's largest bilateral trade flows. But how are we to gauge whether this cross-border economic activity is evidence that the U.S.-Canada border no longer matters? One approach would be to evaluate the economic ties between a Canadian market (say, Toronto) and a U.S. market (say, Philadelphia). The strength of the ties between any such pair of markets could depend on a number of factors, including the geographic distance between them and the composition and sizes of their respective economies. But if economic activity were unaffected by the political border between Canada and the United States, the strength of the ties would not depend on the fact that the two markets are located in different countries. Evidence to the contrary would imply that the border does matter and that the two economies cannot be characterized as completely integrated.

Recent research finds that the relatively innocuous U.S.-Canada border has significant economic effects. The evidence is twofold. First, studies of Canadian merchandise trade reveal that the average Canadian province trades much more with other Canadian provinces than with U.S. states of similar economic size and geographic distance.[5] Ontario, for instance, is roughly equidistant from British Columbia and the state of Washington. Yet in 1990, it traded over seven times more with British Columbia than with Washington, despite the fact that Washington's economy was almost twice the size of British Columbia's. This suggests significant home bias in Canadian merchandise trade vis-a-vis the United States.

Second, evidence also comes from comparisons of consumer prices in the United States and Canada. If the U.S.-Canada border were economically irrelevant, there would be no large, persistent differences between the prices of identical products in Canadian and U.S. markets, once they were expressed in terms of the same currency. As every consumer has experienced firsthand, price differentials for the same good can and do exist at any single point in time. According to economic theory, however, the actions of buyers in search of low prices and sellers in pursuit of profits should minimize these price differences over time. Economists acknowledge that this process can take a considerable amount of time. They also recognize that prices of similar products in different locations may not be exactly equalized, owing to such factors as the cost of transporting the products between locations. When markets are integrated, however, the forces of competition should ensure that such prices move in parallel with one another over the long run. Yet recent research finds little evidence of such a correspondence between the U.S. dollar prices of consumer goods in U.S. and Canadian markets, even in the long run.[6]

The empirical evidence clearly indicates that the border has economic effects—that is, the border "matters"—for product markets in the United States and Canada. This conclusion may not be terribly surprising. After all, the free trade arrangement between Canada and the United States stops far short of establishing an economic union. A more interesting issue concerns the magnitude of the border's effects. That is, if the border matters, does it matter a lot? The answer appears to be yes. By one estimate, a Canadian province engages in 20 times more merchandise trade with another Canadian province than with an equidistant U.S. state of comparable economic size.[7] Preliminary evidence indicates the home bias is apt to be even larger for U.S.-Canada services trade.[8] Another study translates the impact of the U.S.-Canadian border on consumer prices into an equivalent physical distance, estimating that crossing the border is equivalent to adding a distance of 1780 miles between markets.[9] Whether measured in miles or trade volumes, the economic effect of the U.S.-Canada border is considerable.

Two conclusions can be inferred from this evidence. First, the U.S.-Canada border has a surprisingly large impact on both trade patterns and product prices in the two-country region. Second, if the relatively open U.S.-Canada border exhibits such substantial economic effects, it is likely that borders have even greater impacts on trade flows and relative prices between the United States and other countries. But why do borders appear to have such large effects?

The Economic Role of the Border

National borders can influence economic activity in a number of ways. As political and legal boundaries, they provide a means for governments to erect barriers to international flows of goods, services, and factors of production. These measures take a variety of forms and are instituted for a number of reasons. Tariffs drive a wedge between a domestic market and foreign supplies, frequently with the intention of offering protection to domestic industries.[10] The same is true of quotas, nontariff trade barriers that impose quantitative restrictions on imports.

Other so-called nontariff barriers often have the same effect but may or may not be erected for trade policy purposes. This broad category of barriers includes technical standards, licensing and certification requirements, health and safety regulations, border formalities, and government procurement practices. There are numerous instances in which regulators have been accused of imposing measures to protect domestic industries under the guise of other concerns such as the environment or public health. For example, in the early 1990s, Ontario levied a 10-cent tax on all beer sold in cans. The stated objective was to encourage container re-use. But U.S. beer manufacturers viewed the tax as protectionist because, unlike Canadian beer, most American beer is sold in cans and is thus subject to the levy. Practically speaking, of course, determining whether a specific nontariff barrier was intended to shelter domestic markets from foreign competition or had some other primary objective is often difficult.

Other examples of government-imposed barriers include controls on international flows of capital and labor, limitations on holdings of foreign exchange, and market-entry and ownership restrictions. All of these measures differentiate the products and inputs of the domestic economy from those originating outside the border, effectively contributing to the establishment of an economic frontier between a country and the rest of the world.

Tariffs and other formal barriers to trade between the United States and Canada have long been lower than in most other parts of the world. Thus, it is unlikely that they can account for the lion's share of the estimated border effects. A potentially larger effect could come from past trade policies. High tariffs were key components of Canada's National Policy, which was instituted in the latter part of the 19th century. The policy sought to promote economic development and east-west transportation and trade links within Canada. To the extent that it led to the integration of Canadian markets and the formation of strong internal distribution networks, this policy could bear some responsibility for the current home bias in Canadian merchandise trade.[11] Informal trade barriers or nontariff barriers in both countries could also contribute to the segmentation of U.S. and Canadian markets.

The economic impact attributed to the border might actually reflect the effects of geographic distance between markets. If transportation and information costs increase with distance, trade flows should be larger between markets that are geographically close to one another than between more distant markets. For the same reasons, price differentials across markets should be smaller when the markets are close to one another. Indeed, geographic distance is a significant factor in both merchandise trade flows and price dispersion within the U.S.-Canada region. But the border between Canada and the United States appears to have a separate effect on both measures of economic integration. As stated earlier, trade between two Canadian provinces is substantially greater than that between a province and an equidistant U.S. state. Moreover, even after controlling for distance, the variability of consumer prices between a city in Canada and a city in the United States is considerably higher than that between either two U.S. cities or two Canadian cities.[12]

Borders are usually demarcations between currency areas. Consequently, most international transactions require the exchange of one currency for another. Currency exchanges typically entail some small cost associated with translating one currency into another. A small cost for each of millions of transactions can amount to a considerable sum; one estimate places foreign-exchange costs in Germany at 1 percent of GDP.[13] However, there is a risk of substantially larger costs when a contract between parties in two countries calls for future payment. Between the time the price is set and settlement is made, unexpected changes in the value of the exchange rate will alter the ultimate price of the transaction for one of the parties involved. Unlike exchanges within a single country or currency area, international transactions often entail exchange-rate risk. This risk could act as a barrier to international trade. In empirical studies of international trade, currency risk is commonly measured by the volatility of the relevant exchange rate. However, perhaps because financial instruments such as forward exchange contracts are available to reduce or eliminate currency risk, such studies have yielded mixed results, and there is currently no consensus among economists that exchange-rate volatility has had a significant negative impact on trade volumes.

When price comparisons are used to measure border effects, the exchange rate matters in a different way. International price comparisons are made by using the nominal exchange rate to translate prices into a common currency. However, the nominal exchange rate is typically more variable than product prices. By implication, much of the variation in the relative dollar prices of Canadian and U.S. consumer products could simply reflect fluctuations in the nominal exchange rate between the two countries. Indeed, the empirical evidence indicates that changes in the exchange rate are significant factors in the volatility of relative U.S.-Canadian prices. But they are far from the whole story.[14]

Several economists have noted that consumers exhibit a distinct home bias, preferring to deal with firms in their own country and to purchase domestic products. Little is known about the precise reasons for this preference, but a number of factors may be involved. To the extent that they define social boundaries, national borders may also represent the economic effects of distinct tastes, history, traditions, and cultures. Alternatively, a preference for home products may simply reflect ignorance about or lack of access to alternatives. Regions within a common border typically share networks of associations, as well as legal, financial, and regulatory systems. Not only can this ease the acquisition of information but, once obtained, such knowledge is often universally applicable within the border. In addition, marketing and distribution networks for goods, services, and inputs may be more integrated within each country than they are across borders.[15] These networks may make it easier to learn about and gain access to domestic products, contributing to a home bias. Although it is difficult to measure the contribution of these factors to the economic role of the border, they should not be dismissed as necessarily trivial.

Conclusion

Despite evidence that the U.S. economy has become more open, recent empirical research finds that the border between the United States and Canada has a very large impact on bilateral trade flows and relative prices. Given the relative openness of the U.S.-Canada border, it is unlikely that the border's effects are any less significant between product markets in the United States and other countries. This contradicts the notion that globalization has already rendered national borders economically meaningless. But because most of the evidence is based on relatively recent data, it is not known whether the border's economic impacts are actually smaller now than in the past.

The reasons for the border's substantial effects are not yet completely understood. Consequently, it is difficult to speculate how recent advances in communication like the Internet will ultimately reduce the economic boundaries between nations. However, the effects of the border appear to extend beyond the economic impacts of geographic distance and formal trade barriers. By implication, merely liberalizing trade or reducing transportation costs between national markets may not be enough to cause the border to disappear.

NOTES

1. This is, itself, a hotly debated issue among economists. The debate centers on the impact of trade on jobs, wages, and income distribution. See, for instance, the article by Paul Krugman and Robert Z. Lawrence and the symposium papers in the *Journal of Economic Perspectives,* 9 (Summer, 1995), pp. 15–80.

2. While this paper is concerned with the economic integration of U.S. markets for goods and services, the term can also be applied to markets for inputs like labor and financial capital. By and large, labor market integration is limited by government-imposed barriers to international migration. In contrast, financial capital is perceived as highly mobile internationally. That view is supported by the fact that, at least for the major currencies, interest rate differentials between identical offshore and domestic assets are insignificant. But as Martin Feldstein observes, this merely reveals that financial capital can and does move across national borders. In fact, despite the substantial holdings of foreign stocks and bonds, recent research indicates that investors exhibit a strong home bias in their investment portfolios (see the articles by Kenneth French and James Poterba; and Linda Tesar and Ingrid Werner). The implication is that international capital markets are not fully integrated.

3. It could be argued that trade statistics underestimate the extent of product market integration because they do not fully account for the contributions of companies' overseas operations. For example, foreign companies have invested heavily in U.S. production facilities over the last 15 years or so. The result has been a significant rise in the level of economic activity of foreign companies operating in the United States. In fact, the Bureau of Economic Analysis estimates that the output of U.S. affiliates of foreign companies has grown faster than total U.S. output; as a share of gross output originating in private industries, it has increased from 2.3 percent in 1977 to 6 percent in 1995.

4. James Rauch argues that for all but a few relatively standardized products such as those traded in organized global markets, greater distances can also raise the costs of locating appropriate sellers or buyers in foreign markets.

5. See the papers by John McCallum and John Helliwell. It is possible that the effects attributed to the border actually derive from differences in the composition of state and provincial production. That is, interprovincial trade could exceed trade between Canadian provinces and U.S. states not because of the border, but simply because the provinces can obtain more of what they want from other provinces. However, when McCallum explicitly

controls for this possibility, he finds that it does not account for the large effect of the border on provincial trade patterns.

6. John Rogers and Michael Jenkins analyze ratios of U.S. prices to Canadian prices (both expressed in U.S. dollars) for various categories of consumer products. In constructing the ratios, they carefully pair U.S. consumer products with similar Canadian products to ensure that they are comparing the prices of like goods. Even so, they fail to find evidence of a stable, long-run relationship between most product pairs. In a related study, Charles Engel compares the variability of price ratios for pairs of consumer products in the United States and Canada. He reports that the variation in the dollar price ratio of similar Canadian and U.S. consumer products is typically much larger than the variation in the price ratio of two different consumer goods in either the United States or Canada.

7. This estimate comes from the studies by McCallum and Helliwell. Shang-Jin Wei comes up with much smaller estimates of home bias for the merchandise trade of a broader sample of industrialized countries. However, reconciling Wei's findings with those for U.S.-Canadian merchandise trade is complicated by conceptual and measurement differences in the two sets of studies.

8. See the paper by Helliwell and McCallum. This is likely for two reasons. First, the free trade agreements between the U.S. and Canada did not include some service sectors, such as health, transportation, basic telecommunications, and legal services. Second, national regulations in two important service sectors, broadcasting and finance, could limit the bilateral exchange of these services.

9. See Engel and Rogers (1996). Their study covers the period 1978–93 while McCallum's analysis of merchandise trade is based on data for 1988. Because the two studies include data from the period prior to the implementation of the Canada-United States Free Trade Agreement, it might be supposed that their estimates overstate the current impact of the U.S.-Canada border. However, Engel and Rogers find that the border's effect is no smaller when data prior to 1990 are excluded. Likewise, Helliwell's update of McCallum's work finds comparable estimates for merchandise trade through 1990. This could reflect the fact that the effective trade barriers between the United States and Canada were already low before the agreement. An alternative interpretation is that adjustment to the free trade agreement was not complete by the early 1990s.

10. Tariffs also raise revenue for the government.

11. It could be argued that Canada's current trade patterns are appropriate in view of its strong internal distribution networks. But a quick glance at a map suggests that, were it not for Canada's National Policy, Ontario might today have stronger links with, say, New York than with British Columbia.

12. See Engel and Rogers' 1996 paper.

13. See "When the Walls Come Down," *The Economist,* July 5, 1997, pp. 61–63.

14. Engel and Rogers (1996) explore the possibility that the effect attributed to the U.S.-Canada border is, in fact, the product of fluctuations in nominal exchange rates and rigidity in local prices. They find that while local price rigidity is responsible for part of the measured border effect, it accounts for less than half of it.

15. See the 1995 paper by Engel and Rogers for a model of international trade with marketing costs.

REFERENCES

Engel, Charles. "Real Exchange Rates and Relative Prices," *Journal of Monetary Economics,* 32 (1993), pp. 35–50.
Engel, Charles, and John Rogers. "Regional Patterns in the Law of One Price: The Roles

of Geography vs Currencies," Working Paper 5395, National Bureau of Economic Research (1995).

Engel, Charles, and John Rogers. "How Wide Is the Border?" *American Economic Review,* 86 (December, 1996), pp. 1112–25.

Feldstein, Martin. "Tax Policy and International Capital Flows," Working Paper 4851, National Bureau of Economic Research (1994).

French, Kenneth, and James Poterba. "Investor Diversification and International Equity Markets," *American Economic Review,* 81 (May, 1991), pp. 222–26.

Helliwell, John. "Do National Borders Matter for Quebec's Trade?" *Canadian Journal of Economics,* 29 (August, 1996), pp. 507–22.

Helliwell, John, and John McCallum. "National Borders Still Matter for Trade," *Policy Options,* 13 (July/August, 1995), pp. 44–48.

Krugman, Paul, and Robert Z. Lawrence. "Trade, Jobs, and Wages," *Scientific American* (April, 1994), pp. 44–49.

McCallum, John. "National Borders Matter: Canada-U.S. Regional Trade Patterns," *American Economic Review,* 85 (June, 1995), pp. 615–23.

Ohmae, Kenichi. *The Borderless World.* New York: Harper Business, 1990.

Rauch, James. "Networks Versus Markets in International Trade," Working Paper 5617, National Bureau of Economic Research (1996).

Rogers, John, and Michael Jenkins. "Haircuts or Hysteresis? Sources of Movements in Real Exchange Rates," *Journal of International Economics,* 38 (1995), pp. 339–60.

Tesar, Linda, and Ingrid Werner. "Home Bias and the Globalization of Securities Markets," Working Paper 4218, National Bureau of Economic Research (1992).

Wei, Shang-Jin. "Intra-national versus International Trade: How Stubborn Are Nations in Global Integration?" Working Paper 5531, National Bureau of Economic Research (1996).

The Real New World Order

Anne-Marie Slaughter

The State Strikes Back

Many thought that the new world order proclaimed by George Bush was the promise of 1945 fulfilled, a world in which international institutions, led by the United Nations, guaranteed international peace and security with the active support of the world's major powers. That world order is a chimera. Even as a liberal internationalist ideal, it is infeasible at best and dangerous at worst. It requires a centralized rule-making authority, a hierarchy of institutions, and universal membership. Equally to the point, efforts to create such an order have failed. The United Nations cannot function effectively independent of the major powers that compose it, nor will those nations cede their power and sovereignty to an international institution. Efforts to expand supranational authority, whether by the U.N. secretary-general's office, the European Commission, or the World Trade Organization (WTO), have consistently produced a backlash among member states.

The leading alternative to liberal internationalism is "the new medievalism," a back-to-the-future model of the 21st century. Where liberal internationalists see a need for international rules and institutions to solve states' problems, the new medievalists proclaim the end of the nation-state. Less hyperbolically, in her article, "Power Shift," in the January/February 1997 *Foreign Affairs,* Jessica T.

Reprinted with permission from *Foreign Affairs*, Vol. 76, No. 5, 1997. © 1997 by the Council on Foreign Relations, Inc.

Mathews describes a shift away from the state—up, down, and sideways—to supra-state, sub-state, and, above all, nonstate actors. These new players have multiple allegiances and global reach.

Mathews attributes this power shift to a change in the structure of organizations: from hierarchies to networks, from centralized compulsion to voluntary association. The engine of this transformation is the information technology revolution, a radically expanded communications capacity that empowers individuals and groups while diminishing traditional authority. The result is not world government, but global governance. If government denotes the formal exercise of power by established institutions, governance denotes cooperative problem-solving by a changing and often uncertain cast. The result is a world order in which global governance networks link Microsoft, the Roman Catholic Church, and Amnesty International to the European Union, the United Nations, and Catalonia.

The new medievalists miss two central points. First, private power is still no substitute for state power. Consumer boycotts of transnational corporations destroying rain forests or exploiting child labor may have an impact on the margin, but most environmentalists or labor activists would prefer national legislation mandating control of foreign subsidiaries. Second, the power shift is not a zero-sum game. A gain in power by nonstate actors does not necessarily translate into a loss of power for the state. On the contrary, many of these nongovernmental organizations (NGOs) network with their foreign counterparts to apply additional pressure on the traditional levers of domestic politics.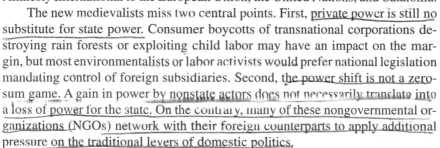

A new world order is emerging, with less fanfare but more substance than either the liberal internationalist or new medievalist visions. The state is not disappearing, it is disaggregating into its separate, functionally distinct parts. These parts—courts, regulatory agencies, executives, and even legislatures—are networking with their counterparts abroad, creating a dense web of relations that constitutes a new, transgovernmental order. Today's international problems terrorism, organized crime, environmental degradation, money laundering, bank failure, and securities fraud—created and sustain these relations. Government institutions have formed networks of their own, ranging from the Basle Committee of Central Bankers to informal ties between law enforcement agencies to legal networks that make foreign judicial decisions more and more familiar. While political scientists Robert Keohane and Joseph Nye first observed its emergence in the 1970s, today transgovernmentalism is rapidly becoming the most widespread and effective mode of international governance.

Compared to the lofty ideals of liberal internationalism and the exuberant possibilities of the new medievalism, transgovernmentalism seems mundane. Meetings between securities regulators, antitrust or environmental officials, judges, or legislators lack the drama of high politics. But for the internationalists of the 1990s—bankers, lawyers, businesspeople, public-interest activists, and criminals—transnational government networks are a reality. Wall Street looks to the Basle Committee rather than the World Bank. Human rights lawyers are more likely to develop transnational litigation strategies for domestic courts than to petition the U.N. Committee on Human Rights.

Moreover, transgovernmentalism has many virtues. It is a key element of a bipartisan foreign policy, simultaneously assuaging conservative fears of a loss of sovereignty to international institutions and liberal fears of a loss of regulatory power in a globalized economy. While presidential candidate Pat Buchanan and Senator Jesse Helms (R-N.C.) demonize the U.N. and the WTO as supranational bureaucracies that seek to dictate to national governments, Senators Ted Kennedy (D-Mass.) and Paul Wellstone (D-Mich.) inveigh against international capital mobility as the catalyst of a global "race to the bottom" in regulatory standards. Networks of bureaucrats responding to international crises and planning to prevent future problems are more flexible than international institutions and expand the regulatory reach of all participating nations. This combination of flexibility and effectiveness offers something for both sides of the aisle.

Transgovernmentalism also offers promising new mechanisms for the Clinton administration's "enlargement" policy, aiming to expand the community of liberal democracies. Contrary to Samuel Huntington's gloomy predictions in *The Clash of Civilizations and the New World Order* (1996), existing government networks span civilizations, drawing in courts from Argentina to Zimbabwe and financial regulators from Japan to Saudi Arabia. The dominant institutions in these networks remain concentrated in North America and Western Europe, but their impact can be felt in every corner of the globe. Moreover, disaggregating the state makes it possible to assess the quality of specific judicial, administrative, and legislative institutions, whether or not the governments are liberal democracies. Regular interaction with foreign colleagues offers new channels for spreading democratic accountability, governmental integrity, and the rule of law.

An offspring of an increasingly borderless world, transgovernmentalism is a world order ideal in its own right, one that is more effective and potentially more accountable than either of the current alternatives. Liberal internationalism poses the prospect of a supranational bureaucracy answerable to no one. The new medievalist vision appeals equally to states' rights enthusiasts and supranationalists, but could easily reflect the worst of both worlds. Transgovernmentalism, by contrast, leaves the control of government institutions in the hands of national citizens, who must hold their governments as accountable for their transnational activities as for their domestic duties.

Judicial Foreign Policy

Judges are building a global community of law. They share values and interests based on their belief in the law as distinct but not divorced from politics and their view of themselves as professionals who must be insulated from direct political influence. At its best, this global community reminds each participant that his or her professional performance is being monitored and supported by a larger audience.

National and international judges are networking, becoming increasingly aware of one another and of their stake in a common enterprise. The most informal level of transnational judicial contact is knowledge of foreign and international judicial decisions and a corresponding willingness to cite them. The Israeli Supreme Court and the German and Canadian constitutional courts have long researched U.S. Supreme Court precedents in reaching their own conclusions on questions like freedom of speech, privacy rights, and due process. Fledgling constitutional courts in Central and Eastern Europe and in Russia are eagerly following suit. In 1995, the South African Supreme Court, finding the death penalty unconstitutional under the national constitution, referred to decisions from national and supranational courts around the world, including ones in Hungary, India, Tanzania, Canada, and Germany and the European Court of Human Rights. The U.S. Supreme Court has typically been more of a giver than a receiver in this exchange, but Justice Sandra Day O'Connor recently chided American lawyers and judges for their insularity in ignoring foreign law and predicted that she and her fellow justices would find themselves "looking more frequently to the decisions of other constitutional courts."

Why should a court in Israel or South Africa cite a decision by the U.S. Supreme Court in reaching its own conclusion? Decisions rendered by outside courts can have no authoritative value. They carry weight only because of their intrinsic logical power or because the court invoking them seeks to gain legitimacy by linking itself to a larger community of courts considering similar issues. National courts have become increasingly aware that they and their foreign counterparts are often engaged in a common effort to delimit the boundaries of individual rights in the face of an apparently overriding public interest. Thus, the British House of Lords recently rebuked the U.S. Supreme Court for its decision to uphold the kidnapping of a Mexican doctor by U.S. officials determined to bring him to trial in the United States.

Judges also cooperate in resolving transnational or international disputes. In cases involving citizens of two different states, courts have long been willing to acknowledge each other's potential interest and to defer to one another when such deference is not too costly. U.S. courts now recognize that they may become involved in a sustained dialogue with a foreign court. For instance, Judge Guido Calabresi of the Second Circuit recently allowed a French litigant to invoke U.S. discovery provisions without exhausting discovery options in France, reasoning that it was up to the French courts to identify and protest any infringements of French sovereignty. U.S. courts would then respond to such protests.

Judicial communication is not always harmonious, as in a recent squabble between a U.S. judge and a Hong Kong judge over an insider trading case. The U.S. judge refused to decline jurisdiction in favor of the Hong Kong court on grounds that "in Hong Kong they practically give you a medal for doing this sort of thing [insider trading]." In response, the Hong Kong judge stiffly defended the adequacy of Hong Kong law and asserted his willingness to apply it. He also chided his American counterpart, pointing out that any conflict "should be approached in the spirit of judicial comity rather than judicial competitiveness." Such conflict is to be expected among diplomats, but what is striking here is the two courts' view of themselves as quasi-autonomous foreign policy actors doing battle against international securities fraud.

The most advanced form of judicial cooperation is a partnership between national courts and a supranational tribunal. In the European Union (EU), the European Court of Justice works with national courts when questions of European law overlap national law. National courts refer cases up to the European Court, which issues an opinion and sends the case back to national courts; the supranational recommendation guides the national court's decision. This cooperation marshals the power of domestic courts behind the judgment of a supranational tribunal. While the Treaty of Rome provides for this reference procedure, it is the courts that have transformed it into a judicial partnership.

Finally, judges are talking face to face. The judges of the supreme courts of Western Europe began meeting every three years in 1978. Since then they have become more aware of one another's decisions, particularly with regard to each other's willingness to accept the decisions handed down by the European Court of Justice. Meetings between U.S. Supreme Court justices and their counterparts on the European Court have been sponsored by private groups, as have meetings of U.S. judges with judges from the supreme courts of Central and Eastern Europe and Russia.

The most formal initiative aimed at bringing judges together is the recently inaugurated Organization of Supreme Courts of the Americas. Twenty-five supreme court justices or their designees met in Washington in October 1995 and drafted the OCSA charter, dedicating the organization to "promot[ing] and strengthen[ing] judicial independence and the rule of law among the members, as well as the proper constitutional treatment of the judiciary as a fundamental branch of the state." The charter calls for triennial meetings and envisages a permanent secretariat. It required ratification by 15 supreme courts, achieved in spring 1996. An initiative by judges, for judges, it is not a stretch to say that OCSA is the product of judicial foreign policy.

Champions of a global rule of law have most frequently envisioned one rule for all, a unified legal system topped by a world court. The global community of law emerging from judicial networks will more likely encompass many rules of law, each established in a specific state or region. No high court would hand down definitive global rules. National courts would interact with one another and with supranational tribunals in ways that would accommodate differences but acknowledge and reinforce common values.

The Regulatory Web

The densest area of transgovernmental activity is among national regulators. Bureaucrats charged with the administration of antitrust policy, securities regulation, environmental policy, criminal law enforcement, banking and insurance supervision—in short, all the agents of the modern regulatory state—regularly collaborate with their foreign counterparts.

National regulators track their quarry through cooperation. While frequently ad hoc, such cooperation is increasingly cemented by bilateral and multilateral agreements. The most formal of these are mutual legal assistance treaties, whereby two states lay out a protocol governing cooperation between their law enforcement agencies and courts. However, the preferred instrument of cooperation is the memorandum of understanding, in which two or more regulatory agencies set forth and initial terms for an ongoing relationship. Such memorandums are not treaties; they do not engage the executive or the legislature in negotiations, deliberation, or signature. Rather, they are good-faith agreements, affirming ties between regulatory agencies based on their like-minded commitment to getting results.

"Positive comity," a concept developed by the U.S. Department of Justice, epitomizes the changing nature of transgovernmental relations. Comity of nations, an archaic and notoriously vague term beloved by diplomats and international lawyers, has traditionally signified the deference one nation grants another in recognition of their mutual sovereignty. For instance, a state will recognize another state's laws or judicial judgments based on comity. Positive comity requires more active cooperation. As worked out by the Antitrust Division of the U.S. Department of Justice and the EU's European Commission, the regulatory authorities of both states alert one another to violations within their jurisdiction, with the understanding that the responsible authority will take action. Positive comity is a principle of enduring cooperation between government agencies.

In 1988 the central bankers of the world's major financial powers adopted capital adequacy requirements for all banks under their supervision—a significant reform of the international banking system. It was not the World Bank, the International Monetary Fund, or even the Group of Seven that took this step. Rather, the forum was the Basle Committee on Banking Supervision, an organization composed of 12 central bank governors. The Basle Committee was created by a simple agreement among the governors themselves. Its members meet four times a year and follow their own rules. Decisions are made by consensus and are not formally binding; however, members do implement these decisions within their own systems. The Basle Committee's authority is often cited as an argument for taking domestic action.

National securities commissioners and insurance regulators have followed the Basle Committee's example. Incorporated by a private bill of the Quebec National Assembly, the International Organization of Securities Commissioners has no formal charter or founding treaty. Its primary purpose is to solve problems affecting international securities markets by creating a consensus for enactment of national legislation. Its members have also entered into information-sharing agreements on their own initiative. The International Association of Insurance Supervisors follows a similar model, as does the newly created Tripartite Group, an international coalition of banking, insurance, and securities regulators the Basle Committee created to improve the supervision of financial conglomerates.

Pat Buchanan would have had a field day with the Tripartite Group, denouncing it as a prime example of bureaucrats taking power out of the hands of American voters. In fact, unlike the international bogeymen of demagogic fantasy, transnational regulatory organizations do not aspire to exercise power in the international system independent of their members. Indeed, their main purpose is to help regulators apprehend those who would harm the interests of American voters. Transgovernmental networks often promulgate their own rules, but the purpose of those rules is to enhance the enforcement of national law.

Traditional international law requires states to implement the international obligations they incur through their own law. Thus, if states agree to a 12-mile territorial sea, they must change their domestic legislation concerning the interdiction of vessels in territorial waters accordingly. But this legislation is unlikely to overlap with domestic law, as national legislatures do not usually seek to regulate global commons issues and interstate relations.

Transgovernmental regulation, by contrast, produces rules concerning issues that each nation already regulates within its borders: crime, securities fraud, pollution, tax evasion. The advances in technology and transportation that have fueled globalization have made it more difficult to enforce national law. Regulators benefit from coordinating their enforcement efforts with those of their foreign counterparts and from ensuring that other nations adopt similar approaches.

The result is the nationalization of international law. Regulatory agreements between states are pledges of good faith that are self-enforcing, in the sense that each nation will be better able to enforce its national law by implementing the agreement if other nations do likewise. Laws are binding or coercive only at the national level. Uniformity of result and diversity of means go hand in hand, and the makers and enforcers of rules are national leaders who are accountable to the people.

Bipartisan Globalization

Secretary of State Madeleine Albright seeks to revive the bipartisan foreign policy consensus of the late 1940s. Deputy Secretary of State Strobe Talbott argues that promoting democracy worldwide satisfies the American need for idealpolitik as well as realpolitik. President Clinton, in his second inaugural address, called for a "new government for a new century," abroad as well as at home. But bipartisanship is threatened by divergent responses to globalization, democratization is a tricky business, and Vice President Al Gore's efforts to "reinvent government" have focused on domestic rather than international institutions. Transgovernmentalism can address all these problems.

Globalization implies the erosion of national boundaries. Consequently, regulators' power to implement national regulations within those boundaries declines both because people can easily flee their jurisdiction and because the flows of capital, pollution, pathogens, and weapons are too great and sudden for any one regulator to control. The liberal internationalist response to these assaults on state regulatory power is to build a larger international apparatus. Globalization thus leads to internationalization, or the transfer of regulatory authority from the national level to an international institution. The best example is not the WTO itself, but rather the stream of proposals to expand the WTO's jurisdiction to global competition policy, intellectual property regulation, and other trade-related issues. Liberals are likely to support expanding the power of international institutions to guard against the global dismantling of the regulatory state.

Here's the rub. Conservatives are more likely to favor the expansion of globalized markets without the internationalization that goes with it, since internationalization, from their perspective, equals a loss of sovereignty. According to Buchanan, the U.S. foreign policy establishment "want[s] to move America into a New World Order where the World Court decides quarrels between nations; the WTO writes the rules for trade and settles all disputes; the IMF and World Bank order wealth transfers from continent to continent and country to country; the Law of the Sea Treaty tells us what we may and may not do on the high seas and ocean floor, and the United Nations decides where U.S. military forces may and may not intervene." The rhetoric is deliberately inflammatory, but echoes resound across the Republican spectrum.

Transgovernmental initiatives are a compromise that could command bipartisan support. Regulatory loopholes caused by global forces require a coordinated response beyond the reach of any one country. But this coordination need not come from building more international institutions. It can be achieved through transgovernmental cooperation, involving the same officials who make and implement policy at the national level. The transgovernmental alternative is fast, flexible, and effective.

A leading example of transgovernmentalism in action that demonstrates its bipartisan appeal is a State Department initiative christened the New Transatlantic Agenda. Launched in 1991 under the Bush administration and reinvigorated by Secretary of State Warren Christopher in 1995, the initiative structures the relationship between the United States and the EU, fostering cooperation in areas ranging from opening markets to fighting terrorism, drug trafficking, and infectious disease. It is an umbrella for ongoing projects between U.S. officials and their European counterparts. It reaches ordinary citizens, embracing efforts like the Transatlantic Business Dialogue and engaging individuals through people-to-people exchanges and expanded communication through the Internet.

Democratization, Step by Step

Transgovernmental networks are concentrated among liberal democracies but are not limited to them. Some nondemocratic states have institutions capable of cooperating with their foreign counterparts, such as committed and effective regulatory agencies or relatively independent judiciaries. Transgovernmental ties can strengthen institutions in ways that will help them resist political domination, corruption, and incompetence and build democratic institutions in their countries, step by step. The Organization of Supreme Courts of the Americas, for instance, actively seeks to strengthen norms of judicial independence among its members, many of whom must fend off powerful political forces.

Individuals and groups in nondemocratic countries may also "borrow" government institutions of democratic states to achieve a measure of justice they cannot obtain in their own countries. The court or regulatory agency of one state may be able to perform judicial or regulatory functions for the people of another. Victims of human rights violations, for example, in countries such as Argentina, Ethiopia, Haiti, and the Philippines have sued for redress in the courts of the United States. U.S. courts accepted these cases, often over the objections of the executive branch, using a broad interpretation of a moribund statute dating back to 1789. Under this interpretation, aliens may sue in U.S. courts to seek damages from foreign government officials accused of torture, even if the torture allegedly took place in the foreign country. More generally, a nongovernmental organization seeking to prevent human rights violations can often circumvent their own government's corrupt legislature and politicized court by publicizing the plight of victims abroad and mobilizing a foreign court, legislature, or executive to take action.

Responding to calls for a coherent U.S. foreign policy and seeking to strengthen the community of democratic nations, President Clinton substituted the concept of "enlargement" for the Cold War principle of "containment." Expanding transgovernmental outreach to include institutions from nondemocratic states would help expand the circle of democracies one institution at a time.

A New World Order Ideal

Transgovernmentalism offers its own world order ideal, less dramatic but more compelling than either liberal internationalism or the new medievalism. It harnesses the state's power to find and implement solutions to global problems. International institutions have a lackluster record on such problem-solving; indeed, NGOs exist largely to compensate for their inadequacies. Doing away with the state, however, is hardly the answer. The new medievalist mantra of global governance is "governance without government." But governance without government is governance without power, and government without power rarely works. Many pressing international and domestic problems result from states' insufficient power to establish order, build infrastructure, and provide minimum social services. Private actors may take up some slack, but there is no substitute for the state.

Transgovernmental networks allow governments to benefit from the flexibility and decentralization of nonstate actors. Jessica T. Mathews argues that "businesses, citizens' organizations, ethnic groups, and crime cartels have all readily adopted the network model," while governments "are quintessential hierarchies, wedded to an organizational form incompatible with all that the new technologies make possible." Not so. Disaggregating the state into its functional components makes it possible to create networks of institutions engaged in a common enterprise even as they represent distinct national interests. Moreover, they can work with their subnational and supranational counterparts, creating a genuinely new world order in which networked institutions perform the functions of a world government—legislation, administration, and adjudication—without the form.

These globe-spanning networks will strengthen the state as the primary player in the international system. The state's defining attribute has traditionally been sovereignty, conceived as absolute power in domestic affairs and autonomy in relations with other states. But as Abram and Antonia Chayes observe in *The New Sovereignty* (1995), sovereignty is actually "status—the vindication of the state's existence in the international system." More importantly, they demonstrate that in contemporary international relations, sovereignty has been redefined to mean "membership . . . in the regimes that make up the substance of international life." Disaggregating the state permits the disaggregation of sovereignty as well, ensuring that specific state institutions derive strength and status from participation in a transgovernmental order.

Transgovernmental networks will increasingly provide an important anchor for international organizations and nonstate actors alike. U.N. officials have already learned a lesson about the limits of supranational authority; mandated cuts in the international bureaucracy will further tip the balance of power toward national regulators. The next generation of international institutions is also likely to look more like the Basle Committee, or, more formally, the Organization of Economic Cooperation and Development, dedicated to providing a forum for transnational problem-solving and the harmonization of national law. The disaggregation of the state creates opportunities for domestic institutions, particularly courts, to make common cause with their supranational counterparts against their fellow branches of government. Nonstate actors will lobby and litigate wherever they think they will have the most effect. Many already realize that corporate self-regulation and states' promises to comply with vague international agreements are no substitute for national law.

The spread of transgovernmental networks will depend more on political and professional convergence than on civilizational boundaries. Trust and awareness of a common enterprise are more vulnerable to differing political ideologies and corruption than to cultural differences. Government networks transcend the traditional divide between high and low politics. National militaries, for instance, network as extensively as central bankers with their counterparts in friendly states. Judicial and regulatory networks can help achieve gradual political convergence, but are unlikely to be of much help in the face of a serious economic or military threat. If the coming conflict with China is indeed coming, transgovernmentalism will not stop it.

The strength of transgovernmental networks and of transgovernmentalism as a world order ideal will ultimately depend on their accountability to the world's peoples. To many, the prospect of transnational government by judges and bureaucrats looks more like technocracy than democracy. Critics contend that government institutions engaged in policy coordination with their foreign counterparts will be barely visible, much less accountable, to voters still largely tied to national territory.

Citizens of liberal democracies will not accept any form of international regulation they cannot control. But checking unelected officials is a familiar problem in domestic politics. As national legislators become increasingly aware of transgovernmental networks, they will expand their oversight capacities and develop networks of their own. Transnational NGO networks will develop a similar monitoring capacity. It will be harder to monitor themselves.

Transgovernmentalism offers answers to the most important challenges facing advanced industrial countries: loss of regulatory power with economic globalization, perceptions of a "democratic deficit" as international institutions step in to fill the regulatory gap, and the difficulties of engaging nondemocratic states. Moreover, it provides a powerful alternative to a liberal internationalism that has reached its limits and to a new medievalism that, like the old Marxism, sees the state slowly fading away. The new medievalists are right to emphasize the dawn of a new era, in which information technology will transform the globe. But government networks are government for the information age. They offer the world a blueprint for the international architecture of the 21st century.

4

Conflict and Security in a New World Order

Much of the writing on globalization presents it as a positive and enabling force. Kofi Annan, the Secretary General of the United Nations, recognizes the centrality of globalization but raises significant questions about its promise and perils. Politics and political development, he believes, have suffered from benign neglect with the rise of globalization, and developing nations are now increasingly aware of its downside. Indeed, for them globalization may be a concept foisted on them by capitalist centers of the West. Thus he concludes that if globalization is to succeed, it must do so equally for the rich and poor. Michael T. Klare's perspective is that global schisms are leading to new battle lines: "Many of the most severe and persistent threats to global peace are arising not from conflicts among major political entities but from increased discord within states, societies, and civilizations along ethnic, racial, religious, linguistic, caste, or class, lines." Klare echoes Annan in arguing that the widening gap between rich and poor is also causing increasing resentment. He expresses concern about the erosion or disappearance of central state authority in some developing countries. As a result of disintegrating state authority, David Keen sees the emergence of an "organised chaos"; individuals are increasingly taking into their own hands security functions that were once the responsibility of the state.

Finally, Walter Laqueur raises the disturbing specter of postmodern terrorism. He believes, however, that terrorists are less likely to use nuclear weapons than chemical weapons and least likely to use biological weapons. One of his bleak conclusions is that all of this leads to a new definition of terrorism, and therefore to a new global threat.

The Politics of Globalization

Kofi Annan

I speak to you at a time of global turmoil, of economic crisis, political challenge and conflict throughout much of the world. To cast a glance on the map of the world is to be not only concerned, but humbled. Concerned, of course, because long-simmering *intra*-state conflicts have in recent months intensified and been joined by *inter*-state tensions from Africa to Asia.

Humbled, because we all perhaps have been surprised by the swiftness with which these crises have accumulated in the space of twelve months. Any belief that either the end of major ideological competition or the revolutionary process of economic globalization would prevent conflict has been revealed as utterly wishful thinking. And yet, since these crises and conflicts are the product of human folly and human evil, I am convinced that they can be solved by human wisdom and human effort. But if we are to solve them, we must rededicate ourselves to addressing the *political* roots as well as the economic roots of the problems now gripping much of the world. That is why I have chosen to speak to you today about the politics of globalization.

To many, it is the phenomenon of globalization that distinguishes our era from any other. Globalization, we are told, is redefining not only the way we engage the world, but how we communicate with each other. We speak and hear often about the economics of globalization—of its promise and its perils.

Rarely, however, are the *political* roots of globalization addressed in a way

Address delivered to Harvard University, sponsored by the Harvard Academy for International and Area Studies, Cambridge, Massachusetts, 17 September 1998.

that would help us understand its *political* consequences—both in times of progress and in times of crisis. Rarely, indeed, are the *political* aspects of globalization recognized by either its friends or its foes.

Today, globalization is rapidly losing its luster in parts of the world. What began as a currency crisis in Thailand fourteen months ago has, so far, resulted in a contagion of economic insolvency and political paralysis. Globalization is seen by a growing number not as a friend of prosperity, but as its enemy; not as a vehicle for development, but as an ever-tightening vise increasing the demands on states to provide safety-nets while limiting their ability to do so.

At a time when the very value of globalization is being questioned, it may be prudent to revisit the role of politics and good governance in sustaining a successful process of globalization. Before doing so, however, let me say that great efforts are being made in every part of the world to contain and reverse the negative impact of globalization.

The fundamental recognition that lasting prosperity is based on legitimate politics has been joined by a growing appreciation of the need to maximize the benefits of the market while minimizing its costs in social justice and human poverty. To do so, regulatory systems must be improved in every part of the world; solid and sustainable safety-nets must be crafted to shield the poorest and most vulnerable; and transparency must be advanced on all sides.

Globalization is commonly understood to describe those advances in technology and communications that have made possible an unprecedented degree of financial and economic interdependence and growth. As markets are integrated, investments flow more easily, competition is enhanced, prices are lowered and living standards everywhere are improved.

For a very long time, this logic was borne out by reality. Indeed, it worked so well that in many cases underlying political schisms were ignored in the belief that the rising tide of material growth would eliminate the importance of political differences.

Today, we look back on the early 1990s as a period of savage wars of genocide in Bosnia and Rwanda that cruelly mocked the political hubris attending the end of Communism. Soon, we may well look back on the late 1990s as a period of economic crisis and political conflict that with equal cruelty mocked the political hubris attending the heyday of Globalism.

In time, these twin awakenings—rude as they have been—may be recalled as a form of blessing in disguise, for they will have reminded us that any peace and every prosperity depend on legitimate, responsive politics.

They will have shown beyond a doubt that the belief in the ability of markets to resolve all divisions neglected the reality of differences of interest and outlook; differences that *can* be resolved peacefully, but *must* be resolved politically.

In a sense, it may be said that politics and political development as a whole suffered a form of benign neglect during globalization's glory years. Extraordinary growth rates seemed to justify political actions which otherwise might have invited dissent. Autocratic rule which denied basic civil and political rights was legitimized by its success in helping people escape centuries of poverty. What was lost in the exuberance of material wealth was the value of politics. And not just any politics: the politics of good governance, liberty, equity and social justice.

The development of a society based on the rule of law; the establishment of legitimate, responsive, uncorrupt government; respect for human rights and the rights of minorities; freedom of expression; the right to a fair trial—these essential, universal pillars of democratic pluralism were in too many cases ignored. And the day the funds stopped flowing and the banks started crashing, the cost of political neglect came home.

Throughout much of the developing world, the awakening to globalization's down side has been one of resistance and resignation, a feeling that globalization is a false God foisted on weaker states by the capitalist centres of the West. Globalization is seen, not as a term describing objective reality, but as an ideology of predatory capitalism.

Whatever reality there is in this view, the perception of a siege is unmistakable. Millions of people are suffering; savings have been decimated; decades of hard-won progress in the fight against of poverty are imperiled. And unless the basic principles of equity and liberty are defended in the political arena and advanced as critical conditions for economic growth, they may suffer rejection. Economic despair will be followed by political turmoil and many of the advances for freedom of the last half-century could be lost.

In this growing backlash against globalization, one can discern three separate categories of reaction. All three threaten to undermine globalization's prospects. All three reflect globalization's neglect of political values. All three call for a response at the global level to what is, at root, a global challenge.

The first, perhaps most dangerous reaction, has been one of nationalism. From the devastated economies of Asia to the indebted societies of Africa, leaders in search of legitimacy are beginning to view globalization, and its down side, as a process that has weakened them vis-a-vis their rivals and diminished them in the eyes of their allies. Globalization is presented as a foreign invasion that will destroy local cultures, regional tastes and national traditions.

Even more troubling, political leaders are increasingly seeking to sustain popular support amidst economic difficulties by exploiting historic enmities and fomenting trans-border conflict. That these steps will do nothing to improve their nations' lot—indeed just the opposite—must be evident even to them. But the costs of globalization have given them a rhetorical vehicle with which to distract their peoples' attentions from the penury of tomorrow to the pride of today.

The irony, of course, is that globalization's promise was based on the notion that trading partners become political partners, and that economic interdependence would eliminate the potential for political and military conflict. This notion is not new. In the early years of this century, the rapid expansion in trade and commerce even led some to predict an end to conflict. However, no degree of economic interdependence between Germany and Britain prevented the First World War. But this lesson was soon forgotten.

It was assumed that the political nature of inter-state relations had been transformed by a quantum leap similar if not equal to that which has revolutionized technology in the information age.

The fallacy of this doctrine—that trade precludes conflict—is not simply that nations and peoples often act out of a complex web of interests that may or may not favour economic progress. Power politics, hegemonic interests, suspicion, rivalry, greed, and corruption are no less decisive in the affairs of state than rational economic interests. The doctrine also underestimates the degree to which governments often find that the relentless pace of globalization threatens their ability to protect their citizens. Without addressing this concern, globalization cannot succeed.

The second reaction has been the resort to illiberal solutions—the call for the man on the white horse, the strong leader who in a time of crisis can act resolutely in the nation's interests. The raw, immediate appeal of this idea seems most apparent in newly liberalized nations with weak political systems, incapable of reacting with effectiveness or legitimacy in the face of economic crisis.

As central power disintegrates and breadlines grow, there is a growing temptation to forget that democracy is a condition for development—and not its reward. Again—and again falsely—democracy is seen as a luxury and not a necessity, a blessing to be wished for, not a right to be fought for.

Here, too, there is an irony: the proponents of globalization always argued that greater trade would naturally lead to greater prosperity, which in turn would sustain a broad middle class. As a consequence, democratic rule would take firm and lasting root, securing respect for individual liberties and human rights. This, too, proved to be overly optimistic.

Some of globalization's proponents believed too much in the ability and inclination of trade and economic growth to foster democracy. Others, too little in the importance of democratic values such as freedom of speech and freedom of information in sustaining firm and lasting economic growth. Traders will trade, with or without political rights. Their prosperity alone, however, will not secure democratic rule.

In all the debates of the post-Cold War years about whether political liberalization should precede economic liberalization or vice versa, one question was left out. What if, regardless of which comes first, the other does not follow? What if economic liberalization, however profitable in the short term, will never beget a political liberalization that is not already integral to economic progress? What if political liberalization, however desirable on its own, is no guarantee of economic growth, at least in the short term?

These are the questions that globalization's friends must face—and answer —in *political* terms, if they are to win the argument against those who would seek solutions in tyranny. Freedom itself is too valuable, its spirit too important for progress, to be bargained away in the struggle for prosperity.

The third reaction against the forces of globalization has been a politics of populism. Embattled leaders may begin to propose forms of protectionism as a way to offset losses supposedly incurred by too open an embrace of competition, and too free a system of political change. Their solution is for a battered nation to turn away and turn inward, tend to its own at whatever cost, and rejoin the global community only when it can do so from a position of strength.

In this reaction, globalization is made the scapegoat of ills which more often have domestic roots of a political nature. Globalization, having been employed as political cover by reformers wishing to implement austerity programs, comes to be seen as a force of evil by those who would return to imagined communities of earlier times.

Notwithstanding its flaws and failed assumptions, this reaction is a real challenge with real power. Those who would defend the policies of openness, transparency and good governance must find ways to answer these critics at two levels: at the level of principle and at the level of practical solutions which can provide some kind of economic insurance against social despair and instability

The lesson of this reaction is that economic integration in an interdependent world is neither all-powerful nor politically neutral. It is seen in strictly political terms, particularly in times of trouble, and so must be defended in political terms. Otherwise, the populists and the protectionists will win the argument between isolation and openness, between the particular and the universal, between an imaginary past and a prosperous future. And they must not win.

If globalization is to succeed, it must succeed for poor and rich alike. It must deliver rights no less than riches. It must provide social justice and equity no less than economic prosperity and enhanced communication. It must be harnessed to the cause not of capital alone, but of development and prosperity for the poorest of the world. It must address the reactions of nationalism, illiberalism and populism with political answers expressed in political terms.

Political liberty must be seen, once and for all, as a necessary condition for lasting economic growth, even if not a sufficient one. Democracy must be accepted as the midwife of development, and political and human rights must be recognized as key pillars of any architecture of economic progress.

This is, undoubtedly, a tall order. But it is one that must be met, if globalization is not to be recalled in years hence as simply an illusion of the power of trade over politics, and human riches over human rights. As the sole international organization with universal legitimacy and scope, the United Nations has an interest—indeed an obligation—to help secure the equitable and lasting success of globalization.

We have no magic bullet with which to secure this aim, no easy answers in our common effort to confront this challenge. But we do know that the limitations on the ability of any state or any organization to affect the processes of globalization call for a global, concerted effort.

If this effort is to make a genuine difference, it is clear that the creation of lasting political institutions must form a first line of response. Such steps must, however, be combined with a clear and balanced acceptance of the roots of the precipitous collapse of so many economies. To some extent, this collapse was rooted in flaws and failures of already existing economies characterized by unsound policies, corruption and illiberal politics.

However, we must not be blind to the fact that irresponsible lending practices and aggressive investment policies pursued by outsiders played their part, too. Without improvements in these practices, we cannot expect political reform to succeed in creating the basis for lasting economic growth. All sides matter; all sides must play a role.

I have argued today that politics are at the root of globalization's difficulties, and that politics will be at the heart of any solutions. But where will solutions be found? In the heyday of globalization, it was assumed that all nations, once secure in prosperity, would turn to multilateral institutions out of maturity; today, I believe, they may turn to those same institutions out of necessity.

The challenge facing the United Nations is to ensure that the difficulties facing globalization do not become an impediment to global cooperation, but rather give such cooperation new life and new promise.

We will do so in two key ways: by emphasizing in all our development work the importance of civil society and institutional structures of democracy at the national level; and by seeking to strengthen the effectiveness of multilateralism in sustaining free economies while securing genuine protection for the poorest and most vulnerable of our world.

After World War II, there was a recognition that ultimately, economic problems were political and security problems. There was a recognition that prosperity and peace are *political* achievements, not simply natural consequences either of trade or of technological progress.

We owe the wisdom of this view and the consequences of its implementation to one man in particular, Franklin Delano Roosevelt. In his fourth inaugural address, President Roosevelt—a founder of the United Nations and surely the greatest Harvard Man of this century—made a passionate plea for global engagement:

"We have learned that we cannot live alone, at peace; that our own well-being is dependent on the well-being of other nations, far away. We have learned that we must live as men, and not as ostriches, nor as dogs in the manger. We have learned to be citizens of the world, members of the human community."

In this era, we have learned our lessons, too: that democracy is the condition for true, lasting and equitable development; that the rewards of globalization must be seen not only at the centre, but also, at the margins; and that without free, legitimate and democratic politics, no degree of prosperity can satisfy humanity's needs nor guarantee lasting peace—*even* in the age of Globalization.

Redefining Security

THE NEW GLOBAL SCHISMS

Michael T. Klare

Geopolitical boundaries—notably those separating rival powers and major military blocs—have constituted the principal "fault lines" of international politics during much of the twentieth century. Throughout the cold war, the world's greatest concentrations of military strength were to be found along such key dividing lines as the Iron Curtain between East and West in Europe and the demilitarized zone between North and South Korea.

When the cold war ended, many of these boundaries quickly lost their geopolitical significance. With the reunification of Germany and the breakup of the Soviet Union, the divide between East and West in Europe ceased to have any meaning. Other key boundaries—for example, the demilitarized zone in Korea—retained their strategic importance, but elsewhere thousands of miles of previously fortified frontier became open borders with a minimal military presence. The strategic alliances associated with these divisions also lost much of their prominence: the Warsaw Treaty Organization was eliminated altogether, while NATO was given new roles and missions in order to forestall a similar fate.

Battle Lines of the Future

The changes associated with the cold war's end have been so dramatic and profound that it is reasonable to question whether traditional assumptions regarding

Reprinted with permission from *Current History* (November 1996). © 1996 Current History, Inc.

the nature of global conflict will continue to prove reliable in the new, post–cold war era. In particular, one could question whether conflicts between states (or groups of states) will remain the principal form of international strife, and whether the boundaries between them will continue to constitute the world's major fault lines. Certainly the outbreak of ethnonationalist conflict in the former Yugoslavia and several other former communist states has focused fresh attention on internal warfare, as has the persistence of tribal and religious strife in such countries as Afghanistan, Burundi, Liberia, Rwanda, Somalia, Sri Lanka, and Sudan.

Nevertheless, traditional concepts retain great currency among security analysts. Although the Iron Curtain has disappeared, it is argued, similar schisms of a geographic or territorial nature will arise to take its place. Indeed, several theories have been advanced positing the likely location of these schisms.

Some analysts contend that the territorial schisms of earlier periods—notably those produced by military competition among the major powers—will be revived in the years ahead. Professor Kenneth Waltz of the University of California at Berkeley suggests that such competition will eventually reappear, with Germany, Japan, or some other rising power such as China building its military strength in order to contest America's global paramountcy. "Countries have always competed for wealth and security, and the competition has often led to conflict," he wrote in *International Security*'s summer 1993 issue. "Why should the future be different from the past?"

More novel, perhaps, is the suggestion that the principal schisms of the post–cold war era are to be found along the peripheries of the world's great civilizations: Western (including Europe and North America), Slavic-Orthodox (including Russia, Ukraine, and Serbia), Japanese, Islamic, Confucian (China), Latin American, and African. First propounded by Harvard's Samuel Huntington in the summer 1993 issue of *Foreign Affairs,* this argument holds that the economic and ideological antagonisms of the nineteenth and twentieth centuries will be superseded in the twenty-first by antagonisms over culture and cultural identity. "Nation-states will remain the most powerful actors in world affairs," Huntington wrote, "but the principal conflicts of global politics will occur between nations and groups of different civilizations." Although the boundaries between civilizations are not as precise as those between sovereign states, he noted, these loose frontiers will be the site of major conflict. "The clash of civilizations will dominate global politics. The fault lines between civilizations will be the battle lines of the future."

Others have argued that the world's future fault lines will fall not between the major states or civilizations, but between the growing nexus of democratic, market-oriented societies and those "holdout" states that have eschewed democracy or defied the world community in other ways. Such "pariah" states or "rogue" powers are said to harbor aggressive inclinations, to support terrorism, and to seek the production of nuclear or chemical weapons. "[We] must face the reality of recalcitrant and outlaw states that not only choose to remain outside the family [of nations] but also to assault its basic values," wrote President Clinton's national security adviser, Anthony Lake, in the March-April 1994 *Foreign Affairs.* Lake

placed several nations in this category—Cuba, North Korea, Iran, Iraq, and Libya
—and other writers have added Sudan and Syria. But while there is disagreement
about which of these states might actually fall into the "outlaw" category, Lake
and other proponents of this analysis hold that the United States and its allies must
work together to "contain" the rogue states and frustrate their aggressive designs.

While these assessments of the world security environment differ in many
of their particulars, they share a common belief that the "battle lines of the future"
(to use Huntington's expression) will fall along geographically defined boundaries, with the contending powers (and their friends and allies) arrayed on opposite
sides. This, in turn, leads to similar policy recommendations that generally entail
the maintenance of sufficient military strength by the United States to defeat any
potential adversary or combination of adversaries.

It is certainly understandable that many analysts have proceeded from traditional assumptions regarding the nature of conflict when constructing models of
future international relations, but it is not at all apparent that such assessments will
prove reliable. While a number of crises since the end of the cold war appear to
have followed one of the three models described, many have not. Indeed, the most
intense conflicts of the current period—including those in Algeria, Angola, Bosnia, Burma, Burundi, Haiti, Kashmir, Liberia, Rwanda, Somalia, Sri Lanka, and
Sudan—cannot be fully explained using these models. Moreover, other forms of
contemporary violence—terrorism, racial and religious strife, gang warfare, violence against women, and criminal violence—have shown no respect for geography or civilizational identity whatsoever, erupting in virtually every corner of the
world.

The Threat from Within

A fresh assessment of the world security environment suggests that the major
international schisms of the twenty-first century will not always be definable in
geographic terms. Many of the most severe and persistent threats to global peace
and stability are arising not from conflicts between major political entities but
from increased discord within states, societies, and civilizations along ethnic, racial, religious, linguistic, caste, or class lines.

The intensification and spread of internal discord is a product of powerful
stresses on human communities everywhere. These stresses—economic, demographic, sociological, and environmental—are exacerbating the existing divisions
within societies and creating entirely new ones. As a result, we are seeing the
emergence of new or deepened fissures across international society, producing
multiple outbreaks of intergroup hostility and violence. These cleavages cannot
be plotted on a normal map, but can be correlated with other forms of data: economic performance, class stratification, population growth, ethnic and religious
composition, environmental deterioration, and so on. Where certain conditions
prevail—a widening gulf between rich and poor, severe economic competition
between neighboring ethnic and religious communities, the declining habitability
of marginal lands—internal conflict is likely to erupt.

This is not to say that traditional geopolitical divisions no longer play a role in world security affairs. But it does suggest that such divisions may have been superseded in importance by the new global schisms.

For Richer and Poorer: The Widening Gap

The world has grown much richer over the past 25 years. According to the Worldwatch Institute, the world's total annual income rose from $10.1 trillion in 1970 to approximately $20 trillion in 1994 (in constant 1987 dollars). This increase has been accompanied by an improved standard of living for many of the world's peoples. But not all nations, and not all people in the richer nations, have benefited from the global increase in wealth: some countries, mostly concentrated in Africa and Latin America, have experienced a net decline in gross domestic product over the past few decades, while many of the countries that have achieved a higher GDP have experienced an increase in the number of people living in extreme poverty. Furthermore, the gap in national income between the richest and the poorest nations continues to increase, as does the gap between rich and poor people within most societies.

These differentials in economic growth rates, along with the widening gap between rich and poor, are producing dangerous fissures in many societies. As the masses of poor see their chances of escaping acute poverty diminish, they are likely to become increasingly resentful of those whose growing wealth is evident. This resentment is especially pronounced in the impoverished shantytowns that surround many of the seemingly prosperous cities of the third world. In these inhospitable surroundings, large numbers of people—especially among the growing legions of unemployed youth—are being attracted to extremist political movements like the Shining Path of Peru and the Islamic Salvation Front of Algeria, or to street gangs and drug-trafficking syndicates. The result is an increase in urban crime and violence.

Deep economic cleavages are also emerging in China and the postcommunist states of Eastern Europe and the former Soviet Union. Until the recent introduction of market reforms in these countries, the financial gap between rich and poor was kept relatively narrow by state policy, and such wealth as did exist among the bureaucratic elite was kept well hidden from public view. With the onset of capitalism the economic plight of the lowest strata of these societies has become considerably worse, while the newly formed entrepreneurial class has been able to accumulate considerable wealth—and to display it in highly conspicuous ways. This has generated new class tensions and provided ammunition for those who, like Gennadi Zyuganov of Russia's reorganized Communist Party, seek the restoration of the old, state-dominated system.

Equally worrisome is the impact of growing income differentials on intergroup relations in multiethnic societies. In most countries the divide between rich and poor is not the only schism that matters: of far greater significance are the divisions between various strata of the poor and lower middle class. When such divisions coincide with ethnic or religious differences—that is, when one group of poor people finds itself to be making less economic progress than a similar group of a different ethnic composition—the result is likely to be increased ethnic antagonisms and, at the extreme, increased intergroup violence. This is evident in Pakistan, where violent gang warfare in Karachi has been fueled by economic competition between the indigenous inhabitants of the surrounding region and several waves of Muslim immigrants from India and Bangladesh; it is also evident in Sri Lanka, where efforts by the Sinhalese to deny employment opportunities to the Tamils helped spark a deadly civil war.

Kindling Ethnic Strife

According to information assembled by the Stockholm International Peace Research Institute (SIPRI), ethnic and religious strife figured prominently in all but 3 of the 31 major armed conflicts under way in 1994. And while several long-running ethnic and sectarian conflicts have subsided in recent years, most analysts believe that such strife is likely to erupt repeatedly in the years ahead.

It is true that many recent ethnic and religious conflicts have their roots in clashes or invasions that occurred years ago. It is also true that the violent upheavals that broke out in the former Yugoslavia and the former Soviet Union drew upon deep-seated ethnic hostilities, even if these cleavages were not generally visible during much of the communist era (when overt displays of ethnic antagonism were prohibited by government decree). In this sense, the ethnic fissures that are now receiving close attention from international policymakers are not really new phenomena. Nevertheless, many of these schisms have become more pronounced since the end of the cold war, or have exhibited characteristics that are unique to the current era.

Greatly contributing to the intensity of recent ethnic and religious strife is the erosion or even disappearance of central state authority in poor third world countries experiencing extreme economic, political, and environmental stress. In such countries—especially Burundi, Liberia, Rwanda, Somalia, and Zaire—the flimsy state structures established after independence are simply unable to cope with the demands of housing and feeding their growing populations with the meager resources at hand. In such circumstances people lose all confidence in the state's ability to meet their basic needs and turn instead to more traditional, kinship-based forms of association for help in getting by—a process that often results in competition and conflict among groups over what remains of the nation's scarce resources. This shift in loyalty from the state to group identity is also evident in Bosnia and parts of the former Soviet Union, where various ethnic factions have attempted to seize or divide up the infrastructure (and in some cases the territory) left behind by the communist regime.

Also contributing to the intensity of intergroup conflict in the current era is the spread of mass communications and other instruments of popular mobilization. These advances have contributed to what Professor James Rosenau of George Washington University calls a "skill revolution" in which individual citizens "have become increasingly competent in assessing where they fit in international affairs and how their behavior can be aggregated into significant collective out-comes."[1] This competence can lead to calls for greater personal freedom and de-mocracy. But it can also lead to increased popular mobilization along ethnic, religious, caste, and linguistic lines, often producing great friction and disorder within heterogeneous societies. An important case in point is India, where Hindu nationalists have proved adept at employing modern means of communication and political organization—while retaining traditional symbols and motifs—to en-courage anti-Muslim sentiment and thereby erode the authority of India's largely secular government.

Demographic Schisms

According to the most recent UN estimates, total world population is expected to soar from approximately 5.6 billion people in 1994 to somewhere between 8 billion and 12 billion by the year 2050—an increase that will undoubtedly place great strain on the earth's food production and environmental capacity. But the threat to the world's environment and food supply is not all that we have to worry about. Because population growth is occurring unevenly in different areas, with some of the highest rates of growth to be found in countries with the slowest rates of economic growth, future population increases could combine with other fac-tors to exacerbate existing cleavages along ethnic, religious, and class lines.

Overall, the populations of the less-developed countries (LDCs) are growing at a much faster rate than those of the advanced industrial nations. As a result, the share of world population accounted for by the LDCs rose from 69 percent in 1960 to 74 percent in 1980, and is expected to jump to nearly 80 percent in the year 2000. Among third world countries, moreover, there have been marked variations in the rate of population growth: while the newly industrialized nations of East Asia have experienced a sharp decline in the rate of growth, Africa and parts of the Middle East have experienced an increase. If these trends persist, the global distribution of population will change dramatically over the next few decades, with some areas experiencing a substantial increase in total population and others moderate or even negligible growth.

This is where other factors enter the picture. If the largest increases in pop-ulation were occurring in areas of rapid economic growth, the many young adults entering the job market each year would be able to find productive employment and would thus be able to feed and house their families. In many cases, howev-er, large increases in population are coinciding with low or stagnant economic growth, meaning that future job-seekers are not likely to find adequate employ-ment. This will have a considerable impact on the world security environment. At the very least, it is likely to produce increased human migration from rural areas (where population growth tends to be greatest) to urban centers (where most new jobs are to be found), and from poor and low-growth countries to more affluent ones. The former process is resulting in the rapid expansion of many third world cities, with an attendant increase in urban crime and intergroup friction (especial-ly where the new urban dwellers are of a different ethnic or tribal group from the original settlers); the latter is producing huge numbers of new immigrants in the developed and high-growth countries, often sparking hostility and sometimes violence from the indigenous populations.

Rapid population growth in poor countries with slow or stagnant economic growth has other implications for world security. In many societies it is leading to the hyperutilization of natural resources, particularly arable soil, grazing lands, forests, and fisheries, a process that severely complicates future economic growth (as vital raw materials are depleted) and accelerates the pace of environmental decline. It can also overwhelm the capacity of weak or divided governments to satisfy their citizens' basic needs, leading eventually to the collapse of states and to the intergroup competition and conflict described earlier. Finally, it could generate fresh international conflicts when states with slow population growth employ stringent measures to exclude immigrants from nearby countries with high rates of growth. While some of this is speculative, early signs of many of these phenomena have been detected. The 1994 United States intervention in Haiti, for instance, was partly motivated by a desire on Washington's part to curb the flow of Haitian "boat people" to the United States.

Endangered by Environment

As with massive population growth, the world has been bombarded in recent years with dire predictions about the consequences of further deterioration in the global environment. The continuing buildup of industrial gases in the earth's outer atmosphere, for example, is thought to be impeding the natural radiation of heat from the planet and thereby producing a gradual increase in global temperatures —a process known as "greenhouse warming." If such warming continues, global sea levels will rise, deserts will grow, and severe drought could afflict many important agricultural zones. Other forms of environmental degradation—the thinning of the earth's outer ozone layer, the depletion of arable soil through overcultivation, the persistence of acid rain caused by industrial emissions—could endanger human health and survival in other ways. As with population growth, these environmental effects will not be felt uniformly around the world but will threaten some states and groups more than others, producing new cleavages in human society.

The uneven impact of global environmental decline is being seen in many areas. The first to suffer are invariably those living in marginally habitable areas —arid grazing lands, coastal lowlands, tropical rainforests. As annual rainfall declines, sea levels rise, and forests are harvested, these lands become uninhabitable. The choice, for those living in such areas, is often grim: to migrate to the cities, with all of their attendant problems, or to move onto the lands of neighboring peoples (who may be of a different ethnicity or religion), producing new outbreaks of intergroup violence. This grim choice has fallen with particular severity on indigenous peoples, who in many cases were originally driven into these marginal habitats by more powerful groups. A conspicuous case in point is the Amazon region of Brazil, where systematic deforestation is destroying the habitat and lifestyle of the indigenous peoples and producing death, illness, and unwelcome migration to the cities.

States also vary in their capacity to cope with environmental crisis and the depletion of natural resources. While the wealthier countries can rebuild areas damaged by flooding or other disasters, relocate displaced citizens to safer regions, and import food and other commodities no longer produced locally, the poorer countries are much less capable of doing these things. As noted by Professor Thomas Homer-Dixon of the University of Toronto, "Environmental scarcity sharply raises financial and political demands on government by requiring huge spending on new infrastructure."[2] Because many third world countries cannot sustain such expenditures, he notes, "we have . . . the potential for a widening gap between demands on the state and its financial ability to meet these demands"—a gap that could lead to internal conflict between competing ethnic groups, or significant out-migration to countries better able to cope with environmental stresses.[3]

Finally, there is a danger that acute environmental scarcities will lead to armed interstate conflict over such vital resources as water, forests, and energy supplies. Some believe that the era of "resource wars" has already occurred in the form of recurring conflict over the Middle East's oil supplies and that similar conflicts will arise over control of major sources of water, such as the Nile, Euphrates, and Ganges Rivers.

The New Cartography

These new and growing schisms are creating a map of international security that is based on economic, demographic, and environmental factors. If this map could be represented in graphic terms, it would show an elaborate network of fissures stretching across human society in all directions—producing large concentrations of rifts in some areas and smaller clusters in others, but leaving no area entirely untouched. Each line would represent a cleavage in the human community, dividing one group (however defined) from another; the deeper and wider clefts, and those composed of many fault lines, would indicate the site of current or potential conflict.

These schisms, and their continued growth, will force policymakers to rethink their approach to international security. It is no longer possible to rely on strategies of defense and diplomacy that assume a flat, two-dimensional world of contending geopolitical actors. While such units still play a significant role in world security affairs, they are not the only actors that matter; nor is their interaction the only significant threat to peace and stability. Other actors, and other modes of interaction, are equally important. Only by considering the full range of security threats will it be possible for policymakers to design effective strategies for peace.

When the principal fault lines of international security coincided with the boundaries between countries, it was always possible for individual states to attempt to solve their security problems by fortifying their borders or by joining with other nations in regional defense systems like NATO and the Warsaw Pact. When the fault lines fall *within* societies, however, there are no clear boundaries to be

Sources of Human Insecurity

Income   1.3 billion people in developing countries live in poverty; 200 million people live below the poverty line in industrial countries.

Clean Water 1.3 billion people in developing countries do not have access to safe water.

Literacy   900 million adults worldwide are illiterate.

Food   800 million people in developing countries have inadequate food supplies; 500 million of this number are chronically malnourished, and 175 million are under the age of five.

Housing   500 million urban dwellers worldwide are homeless or do not have adequate housing; 100 million young people are homeless.

Preventable Between 15 million and 20 million people die annually because of star-
Death   vation or disease aggravated by malnutrition; 10 million people die each year because of substandard housing, unsafe water, or poor sanitation in densely populated cities.

Source: Adapted from Michael Renner, *Fighting for Survival: Environmental Decline, Social Conflict, and the New Age of Insecurity* (New York: Norton, 1996), p. 81.

defended and no role for traditional alliance systems. Indeed, it is questionable whether there is a role for military power at all: any use of force by one side in these disputes, however successful, will inevitably cause damage to the body politic as a whole, eroding its capacity to overcome the problems involved and to provide for its long-term stability. Rather than fortifying and defending borders, a successful quest for peace must entail strategies for easing and erasing the rifts in society, by eliminating the causes of dissension or finding ways to peacefully bridge the gap between mutually antagonistic groups.

The new map of international security will not replace older, traditional types. The relations between states will still matter in world affairs, and their interactions may lead, as they have in the past, to major armed conflicts. But it will not be possible to promote international peace and stability without using the new map as well, and dealing with the effects of the new global schisms. Should we fail to do so, the world of the next century could prove as violent as the present one.

NOTES

1. James N. Rosenau, "Security in a Turbulent World," *Current History,* May 1995, p. 194.
2. Thomas Homer-Dixon, "Environmental Scarcity and Intergroup Conflict," in Michael T. Klare and Daniel C. Thomas, eds., *World Security: Challenges for a New Century* (New York: St. Martin's Press, 1994), pp. 298–299.
3. ibid.

Organised Chaos

NOT THE NEW WORLD WE ORDERED

David Keen

Having seen the Cold War recede, elements of the American right have now come out in a cold sweat. A combination of real and imagined threats has created something of a moral panic in the vacuum left by the collapse of communism, as analysts have highlighted the perils of disintegrating states, of "Islamic fundamentalism," the "clash of civilisations," of "mindless tribal violence" and ethnic nationalism. For those afflicted by a rather bizarre nostalgia for the days of nuclear brinkmanship, the Soviet Union may have been the Red Devil, but at least it was the Red Devil we knew. Now the threats are seemingly more diffuse, more invisible, more difficult to comprehend. It is as if, thirty years after the United States entered the Vietnam war, the enemy has once more taken to the jungle.

In his widely read article "The Coming Anarchy," which drew on West African examples in particular, Robert Kaplan outlined a nightmarish vision of young men as a seething mass of "loose molecules" waiting to ignite into violence.[1]

His vision of order and chaos was well summed up in a *Panorama* programme on BBC Television in March 1995, when he observed: "You have a lot of people in London and Washington who fly all over the world, who stay in luxury hotels, who think that English is dominating every place, but yet they have no idea what is out there. Out there is that thin membrane of luxury hotels, of things that work, of civil order, which is proportionately getting thinner and thinner and thinner."

Both Kaplan and the influential military historian Martin van Creveld have

From *The World Today,* January 1996, pp. 14–17. © 1996 by *The World Today,* a publication of the Royal Institute of International Affairs. Reprinted with permission.

often portrayed violence as essentially irrational. In *The Transformation of War*,[2] van Creveld noted that ". . . the reason why fighting can never be a question of interest is—to put it bluntly—that dead men have no interests . . . Warfare constitutes the great proof that man is not motivated by selfish interest." Meanwhile, Kaplan's "Balkan ghosts" emphasised the long-standing ethnic enmities underpinning conflict in the Balkans.

This kind of analysis can easily feed into rightist political agendas, notably the idea that "we in the West" need somehow to steel ourselves against the coming anarchy, whether through isolationism, or a strong military, or both. Kaplan and van Creveld have both been warmly received by the US military and foreign-policy establishment. Kaplan's analysis of the Balkans was taken by some as justifying Western inaction in the face of allegedly entrenched antagonisms. Van Creveld's talk of the need for the military to adapt to new and diverse forms of conflict has found a receptive ear in Washington.

Meanwhile, the "Fortress Europe" and "Fortress America" lobbies have been lent a degree of intellectual, or quasi-intellectual, support. Van Creveld suggested, on *Panorama*, that gathering chaos would lead to attempts at mass emigration and that Western governments might want to "blow a couple of those boats out of the water" as an example to the rest. In reference to the recent Italian conflict with Albanian immigrants, van Creveld added: "This may be in the long run a more humane solution both for the Italians . . . and for the immigrants."

An Alternative System of Profit and Power

Of course, it is undeniable that the thawing of the Cold War has indeed contributed to a variety of recent conflicts, and that ethnic nationalism, in particular, has proved to be a major source of violence with the collapse of the communist bloc. To put it mildly, this is not quite the new world that we ordered.

But at least two elements of the new moral panic need questioning. The first is the perception that contemporary patterns of violence somehow represent a kind of chaos, a kind of irrationalism, that is breaking through previous patterns of order and repression based on Cold War antagonisms. The second is the (related) suggestion that this new and somehow incomprehensible threat is best met by some combination of fight and flight—in other words, by arming ourselves against the gathering chaos, while at the same time attempting to isolate ourselves from it as much as possible.

What is most conspicuously missing from many accounts of the "new world disorder" is any sense of the vested interests, political and economic, which are driving the apparent "chaos"—and indeed the vested interests that may be driving its depiction as chaos. Also damagingly absent is any adequate attention to what might be done to counter or cajole those who have a vested interest in violence and disorder.

Part of the problem is that we tend to regard conflict as, simply, a breakdown in a particular system, rather than as the emergence of another, alternative system of profit and power. For example, the emergence of "warlords" in many countries does not equate to "chaos"; rather, it is likely to represent a reconstituted system in which some of the activities previously conducted by the state—protection, taxation—are taken over by regional warlords.

Michel Foucault's analysis of the Gulag in the former Soviet Union can also be applied to violence more generally: the problem of causes cannot be dissociated from that of function.[3] In other words, it is not enough to enumerate the many causes of violence (as Kaplan does in an exhaustive list in his "Coming Anarchy" article); we need also to understand the functions of violence, and to wonder what can be done in the light of these functions.

Mindless Violence . . .
Mindless Analysis

Nor is it enough to point despairingly to "the collapse of the state" without understanding how international financial institutions have often wilfully undermined the state in favour of the "market economy," or how the state—from Sudan to former Yugoslavia to Sierra Leone—has sometimes sponsored its own demise, with elites attempting to foment violence to prop up their own positions of privilege. In these circumstances, labels like "chaos" and "mindless violence" can be actively—and even sometimes intentionally—disabling.

Faced with international analysts' depictions of "mindless violence" in troublespots around the globe, we need to ask whether it is the violence that is mindless or the analysis. Violence leading to devastating famine in southern Sudan in the late 1980s was typically depicted by the Sudanese government—and to a large extent by the US State Department—as arising from "long-standing ethnic hostility" between the Arab-speaking Baggara peoples of the north and the Dinka and Nuer in the south. Superimposed on this misleading portrayal was a habitual emphasis in the international media on the religious origins of a civil war between the "Islamic north" and the "Christian south."

What was damagingly absent was any coherent account of the role of the Sudanese government in supplying arms and granting immunity from prosecution to northern Baggara militias, who were encouraged to attack southern Sudanese occupying areas that were rich in fertile land and, critically, oil. Facing pressure to repay escalating international debts and unable to afford a large, salaried army, the Sudanese government resorted to a strategy of turning the dissatisfaction of the economically marginalised Baggara against the Dinka and the Nuer. Partly through inducing man-made famine, this strategy offered the prospect of depopulating oil-rich lands and decimating the principal supporters of the rebel Sudan People's Liberation Army (SPLA). It also offered an opportunity to confuse the international community, and deflect recriminations from the Sudanese government.

In the course of this violence and famine, the state had not so much collapsed as attempted to compensate for its economic weakness by dividing and manipulating civil society. At the same time, the violence, so far from being completely irrational, served a range of mundane functions, not only for central government but also for elements of the Baggara, who stood to gain from access to grazing land, stolen cattle and the cheap—or even free—labour of southern Sudanese captives and famine migrants.

This is not to say that these processes were not, in some sense, "evil." However, this was an evil that was driven by a complex set of economic and political pressures, including the exclusion of the (western Sudanese) Baggara cattle herders from the bulk of the benefits of a highly uneven pattern of development centring on Sudan's central-eastern region. Moreover—and in this respect the evolution of evil was not totally different from the famine in the Jewish ghettos of Poland—this was an evil which began as a plan for resettlement and dovetailed into the starvation of the displaced when it was found that local authorities were not keen, for a variety of pragmatic reasons, to receive waves of refugees.

A failure to get to grips with the rational aspects of this violence in Sudan tended to obscure the opportunities for reducing human suffering, while allowing the government, as later in Rwanda, to get away with the portrayal of violence as irrational and "tribal." Major international donors pressured the government on its macroeconomic policy, but largely turned a blind eye to the abuses of militias the government was arming and manipulating. The pattern of famine relief concentrating on refugee camps in Ethiopia and on government garrison towns in the south—tended to speed up the process of depopulating rural areas of the south, while at the same time giving the SPLA a reason to attack relief shipments. Meanwhile, the provision of inadequate relief to Baggara drought victims in the north tended to encourage them to turn south in search of a remedy for their own destitution.

In Sierra Leone, after an initial period of vacillation when rebellion broke out in 1991, the government responded by rapidly expanding its military from some 3,000 to around 14,000. It recruited militiamen who had spilled over from the conflict in Liberia, as well as Sierra Leonean boys as young as eight. This ragtag Sierra Leonean army, underpaid and under-trained, was sent to do battle with the rebels, who were concentrated in the fertile and diamond-rich south and east of the country. One of the results has been that government soldiers have repeatedly resorted to raiding and to illegal mining to supplement their inadequate incomes. They have tended to avoid pitched battles with the rebels, and have even sold arms, ammunition and uniforms to them, apparently in a bid to keep the conflict going—whilst at the same time making short-term cash.

Presently, according to evidence of eye witnesses during my visit to the country in the summer of 1995, Sierra Leonean civilians are threatened not only by rebels but also by government soldiers, who sometimes seem to be acting in concert with the rebels to control and partially depopulate resource-rich areas and divide the spoils between them. Although the government claimed to have retaken the diamond-rich eastern district of Kono from the rebels, these raids continued throughout the autumn of 1995, suggesting continuing government soldier involvement in the violence against civilians.

Among the reasons why the rebellion in Sierra Leone originally gathered force were the poor social services and a notable decline in educational opportunities, which were themselves a reflection of international pressures for financial austerity. Thus, although the conflict in Sierra Leone has led to a partial collapse of the state, with "government" increasingly confined to the capital, Freetown, the conflict was also partly caused by a collapsing state administration—most notably, a tottering educational system and an inadequately trained and funded army.

Privatising War

In effect, in many African countries, in particular, it is not just the social services which have been partially privatised as a result of pressure from international creditors, but also war itself. That is, financially strapped governments have delegated the right to inflict violence to unpaid or underpaid fighters who have made up for the lack of salary with an abundance of loot. In these circumstances, warfare threatens to veer out of the control even of the government which seeks to manipulate it. In Sudan, the Baggara have to some extent followed their own economic agenda, raiding Muslim and semi-Muslim groups in the north, fostering opposition rather than quelling it, and reaching an accommodation with the SPLA that allows the Baggara access to contested grazing lands. For government troops in Sierra Leone, the business of defeating the rebels has often taken second place to the business of making money.

Thus, the functions of war, for those carrying out the violence, may diverge from the military to the economic. If this happens, warfare may come to resemble a virus which "mutates," making it much more difficult for outsiders to tackle the virus, particularly if they do not understand the nature of this mutation.

Given the importance of pillage in warfare, the boundaries between war and crime may be quite indistinct. Stephen Ellis has shown how, in Liberia, young militiamen—few of whom have been paid or trained—have tended to base themselves in areas that are rich in diamonds, or where villagers were still producing crops, or where humanitarian convoys could be looted.[4] Looting of civilians and commandeering of slave labour has been commonplace. "Only rarely did the militias attack each other head-on. For the most part, they preyed on civilians," Ellis recently wrote in *African Affairs*. Meanwhile, senior commanders—adults— have preyed on the boy militiamen, duplicating the generally unhappy experience of boy soldiers in Sierra Leone.

The West African experience shows clearly how violence may be used to create or preserve trade monopolies, a goal that Lenin saw as feeding into international wars but which may also feed into civil wars. Having created a trading monopoly and a geographical area that can be taxed, rebel "warlords" may then be in a position to fund the increased use of violence, allowing them to preserve or enlarge their "mini-states." In Somalia, the ability of a particular clan to gain control of critical ports and roads has sometimes allowed it to increase its revenue and strengthen its military muscle, permitting a further expansion in the geographical territory it controls.[5]

The phenomenon of government forces "going soft" on the rebels has echoes around the world. For example, elements of the military in both Cambodia and Thailand appear to have an economic interest in collaborating with the Khmer Rouge, which occupies an area of Cambodia rich in diamonds and timber. In Peru, as John Simpson's book *In the Forests of the Night* demonstrates,[6] government soldiers have habitually set free rebel fighters from the Shining Path guerrilla movement, apparently in order to perpetuate insecurity in areas where officers can benefit from illegal trading—in this case, principally the trade in cocaine.

Many contemporary conflicts are reminiscent of medieval warfare, which tended to see widespread pillage and an avoidance of pitched battles. In those days too, pillage was particularly likely when soldiers' provisions ran out or their pay was in arrears. In her account of the fourteenth century, *A Distant Mirror,* Barbara Tuchman notes: "Above all, war was made to pay for itself through pillage. Booty and ransom were not just a bonus, but a necessity to take the place of arrears in pay and to induce enlistment."[7]

Although we have come to regard strong states capable of commanding a disciplined army as somehow "normal," these states only emerged in Europe from a long and difficult struggle with local warlords, as central rulers were handicapped by their own underpaid soldiers. In many parts of the world, a modern bureaucratic state has never been properly established; in others, the modern state is extremely fragile. Insofar as the resources available to states in Africa are diminishing—not least through programmes of structural adjustment—the opportunities for prospective warlords to challenge state sovereignty would appear to be considerable.

If many of the characteristics of contemporary wars are not confined simply to the contemporary era, neither are they confined to countries at war. Indeed, the blurring of war and crime may increasingly call into question the traditional distinction between countries at war and countries at peace. Just as poorly paid and trained soldiers may prove unable or unwilling to confront rebel forces in resource-rich areas, so also may poorly paid and trained policemen be unable or unwilling to confront criminals, particularly where these criminals are operating within a lucrative illegal economy such as drugs or prostitution.

In the Polish capital Warsaw, police officers may be offered the equivalent of three years' pay to turn a blind eye to activities in the drug and prostitution sectors. As with the Khmer Rouge and the international timber and diamond trade, the Polish criminals' links with international trading networks provide them with resources that give them a degree of immunity to suppression.

People Protecting People

In Sierra Leone, faced with the twin threat of rebel and government soldier attacks, many civilians are providing funding and personnel for nascent "civil defence groups." Although badly equipped, such groups have sometimes managed to intimidate undisciplined gunmen, including government soldiers, into tempering their abuses. Again, this is not a trend confined to "countries at war." In South Africa, we have seen the emergence of citizens' vigilante groups in response to soaring crime and a perceived weak response by poorly paid, poorly trained policemen. Both crime and the vigilante groups appear to provide a role and activity for under-employed young men half-trained by the resistance movement.

Even in Western countries like Britain, France and—notably—the United States, we have seen the emergence of areas of the inner city where the law cannot properly be enforced, not least because of the control which certain criminals are able to exert over the community on which the police depend for tip-offs and witnesses.

Where the state gives up—or is forced to give up—its responsibilities for protecting people, they will seek their own protection, and the consequences may not be good. Self-protection may mean throwing in your lot with a particular ethnic group, as has happened in former Yugoslavia. It will certainly mean securing some kind of arms, either, as Hans Magnus Enzensberger notes,[8] through the obliging international market or through access to existing arsenals, like those that have fuelled conflict in the Balkans and the Caucasus. Such violence may feed on intense fear, and may lurch in unpredictable directions.

The point, perhaps, is not to mourn the collapse of the state but to counteract it. For example, the Rwandan state requires a major injection of resources if it is to stand any chance of convincing Hutus and Tutsis alike that it is capable of administering measured punishment and measured clemency in the wake of the genocide. Earlier, as argued by the London-based human rights organisation African Rights, the international drive towards democratisation in Rwanda appeared to have run aground, in part due to the resource shortages brought about by internationally generated austerity packages.[9] Extremist Hutu factions defended their privileged position with a ruthlessness that embraced carefully planned genocide.

Battles against the State

In some ways, both right and left seem to have been waging a battle against the state. For the right, the principal enemies have been public services and state control of the economy. A critical blind-spot at home and abroad has been the fuelling of violence through lack of economic and educational opportunities. For the left, the state's instruments of "repression"—the army and police—have come in for attack, while left-leaning non-governmental organisations have tended to place "civil society" on a pedestal. Moreover, while the needs and, belatedly, the strategies of disaster victims have come under examination from the aid community—notably *after* large-scale human rights abuses have taken place—the needs and strategies of those carrying out human rights abuses have been largely ignored. As a result, opportunities for influencing the perpetrators have been missed. Prevention has been neglected in favour of cure or, more accurately, in favour of the band-aid of humanitarian relief.

It is true, particularly in the poorer parts of the world, that states have tended to act in the interests of a narrow elite, and that the police and army have often been instruments of repression. But perhaps, in the days of ethnic militias and unpaid soldiers, we are now realising more and more that "civil society" is not necessarily particularly civil, especially when it is manipulated by an elite that finds itself threatened by democracy and austerity. Properly salaried state officials, for all their faults, may have their uses. At the same time, we need to be aware of the covert manipulation of private militias outside state structures. The challenge, perhaps, is to rebuild the institutions of the state in such a way that do not recreate the resentments that have encouraged states to promote their own decline by fuelling the tensions in civil society.

The fall of communism in the eastern bloc has been hailed as a triumph for capitalism, peace and democracy. Yet it is by no means clear that these three "brothers" will ride together into the sunset at the "End of History." Whilst Marx predicted that socialism would lead to the withering away of the state, it may ultimately be capitalism that proves more effective in leading us towards that dubious goal, with all the attendant dangers to both peace and democracy. The more arms are being sold for profit, the more decentralised the means of violence are likely to become. And with large groups effectively excluded from the promised benefits of the free market, the temptation to resort to these arms—as in Sierra Leone—will be great.

The "anti-welfarist" culture is built on the assumption that, deprived of state support, people will use their own initiative; unfortunately, this is already proving to be all too true, as disgruntled young men demonstrate their "initiative" with the use of guns.

Of course, initiative can also include participation in other "free" markets, the—often international—markets in illegal drugs, illegal mining and resource depletion, and prostitution. Meanwhile underpaid government officials, who in countries like Sierra Leone have always tended to have an ambiguous relationship with the illegal economy, may increasingly follow the culture of individual initiative to the extent of accepting kickbacks that allow criminal gangs, and even "rebels," to operate with impunity. If capitalism, as Max Weber famously argued, was built on a set of moral values—the so-called "Protestant ethic" of working and saving—is it not quite possible that capitalism is destroying the moral values on which its continued existence, at least in forms compatible with peace and democracy, depends?

NOTES

1. Robert Kaplan, *Atlantic Monthly,* February 1994, pp. 44–76 [p. 34, this volume].
2. Martin van Creveld, *The Transformation of War* (New York: The Free Press, 1991).
3. *Power/Knowledge: Selected Interviews and Other Writings 1972–1977,* edited by C. Gordon (Brighton: Harvester Press, 1988).

4. Stephen Ellis, "Liberia 1989–1994: a study of ethnic and spiritual violence," *African Affairs,* April 1995.

5. For essential information, see Mark Bradbury, *The Somali Conflict: Prospects for Peace,* Oxfam Research Paper No. 9.

6. John Simpson, *In the Forests of the Night: Encounters in Peru with Terrorism, Drug-running and Military Oppression* (London: Arrow, 1994).

7. Barbara Tuchman, *A Distant Mirror: The Calamitous 14th Century* (London and Basingstoke: Papermack, 1989).

8. Hans Magnus Enzensberger, *Civil War* (London: Granta Books, 1994).

9. *Rwanda: Death, Despair and Defiance,* London, 1994.

Postmodern Terrorism

Walter Laqueur

New Rules for an Old Game

As the nineteenth century ended, it seemed no one was safe from terrorist attack. In 1894 an Italian anarchist assassinated French President Sadi Carnot. In 1897 anarchists fatally stabbed Empress Elizabeth of Austria and killed Antonio Cánovas, the Spanish prime minister. In 1900 Umberto I, the Italian king, fell in yet another anarchist attack; in 1901 an American anarchist killed William McKinley, president of the United States. Terrorism became the leading preoccupation of politicians, police chiefs, journalists, and writers from Dostoevsky to Henry James. If in the year 1900 the leaders of the main industrial powers had assembled, most of them would have insisted on giving terrorism top priority on their agenda, as President Clinton did at the Group of Seven meeting after the June bombing of the U.S. military compound in Dhahran, Saudi Arabia.

From this perspective the recent upsurge of terrorist activity is not particularly threatening. According to the State Department's annual report on the subject, fewer people died last year in incidents of international terrorism (165) than the year before (314). Such figures, however, are almost meaningless, because of both the incidents they disregard and those they count. Current definitions of terrorism fail to capture the magnitude of the problem worldwide.

Terrorism has been defined as the substate application of violence or threat-

Reprinted with permission from *Foreign Affairs*, Vol. 75, No. 5, 1996. © 1996 by the Council on Foreign Relations, Inc.

ened violence intended to sow panic in a society, to weaken or even overthrow the incumbents, and to bring about political change. It shades on occasion into guerrilla warfare (although unlike guerrillas, terrorists are unable or unwilling to take or hold territory) and even a substitute for war between states. In its long history terrorism has appeared in many guises; today society faces not one terrorism but many terrorisms.

Since 1900, terrorists' motivation, strategy, and weapons have changed to some extent. The anarchists and the left-wing terrorist groups that succeeded them, down through the Red Armies that operated in Germany, Italy, and Japan in the 1970s, have vanished; if anything, the initiative has passed to the extreme right. Most international and domestic terrorism these days, however, is neither left nor right, but ethnic-separatist in inspiration. Ethnic terrorists have more staying power than ideologically motivated ones, since they draw on a larger reservoir of public support.

The greatest change in recent decades is that terrorism is by no means militants' only strategy. The many-branched Muslim Brotherhood, the Palestinian Hamas, the Irish Republican Army (IRA), the Kurdish extremists in Turkey and Iraq, the Tamil Tigers of Sri Lanka, the Basque Homeland and Liberty (ETA) movement in Spain, and many other groups that have sprung up in this century have had political as well as terrorist wings from the beginning. The political arm provides social services and education, runs businesses, and contests elections, while the "military wing" engages in ambushes and assassinations. Such division of labor has advantages: the political leadership can publicly disassociate itself when the terrorists commit a particularly outrageous act or something goes wrong. The claimed lack of control can be quite real because the armed wing tends to become independent; the men and women with the guns and bombs often lose sight of the movement's wider aims and may end up doing more harm than good.

Terrorist operations have also changed somewhat. Airline hijackings have become rare, since hijacked planes cannot stay in the air forever and few countries today are willing to let them land, thereby incurring the stigma of openly supporting terrorism. Terrorists, too, saw diminishing returns on hijackings. The trend now seems to be away from attacking specific targets like the other side's officials and toward more indiscriminate killing. Furthermore, the dividing line between urban terrorism and other tactics has become less distinct, while the line between politically motivated terrorism and the operation of national and international crime syndicates is often impossible for outsiders to discern in the former Soviet Union, Latin America, and other parts of the world. But there is one fundamental difference between international crime and terrorism: mafias have no interest in overthrowing the government and decisively weakening society; in fact, they have a vested interest in a prosperous economy.

Misapprehensions, not only semantic, surround the various forms of political violence. A terrorist is not a guerrilla, strictly speaking. There are no longer any guerrillas, engaging in Maoist-style liberation of territories that become the base of a counter-society and a regular army fighting the central government—except perhaps in remote places like Afghanistan, the Philippines, and Sri Lanka. The term "guerrilla" has had a long life partly because terrorists prefer the label, for its more positive connotations. It also persists because governments and media in other countries do not wish to offend terrorists by calling them terrorists. The French and British press would not dream of referring to their countries' native terrorists by any other name but call terrorists in other nations militants, activists, national liberation fighters, or even "gun persons."

The belief has gained ground that terrorist missions by volunteers bent on committing suicide constitute a radical new departure, dangerous because they are impossible to prevent. But that is a myth, like the many others in which terrorism has always been shrouded. The bomber willing and indeed eager to blow himself up has appeared in all eras and cultural traditions, espousing politics ranging from the leftism of the Baader-Meinhof Gang in 1970s Germany to rightist extremism. When the Japanese military wanted kamikaze pilots at the end of World War II, thousands of volunteers rushed to offer themselves. The young Arab bombers on Jerusalem buses looking to be rewarded by the virgins in Paradise are a link in an old chain.

State-sponsored terrorism has not disappeared. Terrorists can no longer count on the Soviet Union and its Eastern European allies, but some Middle Eastern and North African countries still provide support. Tehran and Tripoli, however, are less eager to argue that they have a divine right to engage in terrorist operations outside their borders; the 1986 U.S. air strike against Libya and the various boycotts against Libya and Iran had an effect. No government today boasts about surrogate warfare it instigates and backs.

On the other hand, Sudan, without fanfare, has become for terrorists what the Barbary Coast was for pirates of another age: a safe haven. Politically isolated and presiding over a disastrous economy, the military government in Khartoum, backed by Muslim leaders, believes that no one wants to become involved in Sudan and thus it can get away with lending support to terrorists from many nations. Such confidence is justified so long as terrorism is only a nuisance. But if it becomes more than that, the rules of the game change, and both terrorists and their protectors come under great pressure.

Opportunities in Terrorism

History shows that terrorism more often than not has little political impact, and that when it has an effect it is often the opposite of the one desired. Terrorism in the 1980s and 1990s is no exception. The 1991 assassination of Rajiv Gandhi as he campaigned to retake the prime ministership neither hastened nor inhibited the decline of India's Congress Party. Hamas' and Hezbollah's stepped-up terrorism in Israel undoubtedly influenced the outcome of Israeli elections in May, but while it achieved its immediate objective of setting back the peace process on which Palestine Authority President Yasir Arafat has gambled his future, is a hard-line Likud government really in these groups' interests? On the other side, Yigal Amir, the right-wing orthodox Jewish student who assassinated Prime Minister Yitzhak Rabin last fall because he disapproved of the peace agreement with the Palestinians, might well have helped elect Rabin's dovish second-in-command, Shimon Peres, to a full term had the Muslim terrorists not made Israeli security an issue again.

Terrorists caused disruption and destabilization in other parts of the world, such as Sri Lanka, where economic decline has accompanied the war between the government and the Tamil Tigers. But in Israel and in Spain, where Basque extremists have been staging attacks for decades, terrorism has had no effect on the economy. Even in Algeria, where terrorism has exacted the highest toll in human lives, Muslim extremists have made little headway since 1992–93, when many predicted the demise of the unpopular military regime.

Some argue that terrorism must be effective because certain terrorist leaders have become president or prime minister of their country. In those cases, however, the terrorists had first forsworn violence and adjusted to the political process. Finally, the common wisdom holds that terrorism can spark a war or, at least, prevent peace. That is true, but only where there is much inflammable material: as in Sarajevo in 1914, so in the Middle East and elsewhere today. Nor can one ever say with certainty that the conflagration would not have occurred sooner or later in any case.

Nevertheless, terrorism's prospects, often overrated by the media, the public, and some politicians, are improving as its destructive potential increases. This has to do both with the rise of groups and individuals that practice or might take up terrorism and with the weapons available to them. The past few decades have witnessed the birth of dozens of aggressive movements espousing varieties of nationalism, religious fundamentalism, fascism, and apocalyptic millenarianism, from Hindu nationalists in India to neofascists in Europe and the developing world to the Branch Davidian cult of Waco, Texas. The earlier fascists believed in military aggression and engaged in a huge military buildup, but such a strategy has become too expensive even for superpowers. Now, mail-order catalogs tempt militants with readily available, far cheaper, unconventional as well as conventional weapons—the poor man's nuclear bomb, Iranian President Ali Akbar Hashemi Rafsanjani called them.

In addition to nuclear arms, the weapons of mass destruction include biological agents and man-made chemical compounds that attack the nervous system, skin, or blood. Governments have engaged in the production of chemical weapons for almost a century and in the production of nuclear and biological weapons for many decades, during which time proliferation has been continuous and access ever easier.[1] The means of delivery—ballistic missiles, cruise missiles, and aerosols—have also become far more effective. While in the past missiles were deployed only in wars between states, recently they have played a role in civil wars in Afghanistan and Yemen. Use by terrorist groups would be but one step further.

Until the 1970s most observers believed that stolen nuclear material constituted the greatest threat in the escalation of terrorist weapons, but many now think the danger could lie elsewhere. An April 1996 Defense Department report says that "most terrorist groups do not have the financial and technical resources to acquire nuclear weapons but could gather materials to make radiological dispersion devices and some biological and chemical agents." Some groups have state sponsors that possess or can obtain weapons of the latter three types. Terrorist groups themselves have investigated the use of poisons since the nineteenth century. The Aum Shinrikyo cult staged a poison gas attack in March 1995 in the Tokyo subway; exposure to the nerve gas sarin killed ten people and injured 5,000. Other, more amateurish attempts in the United States and abroad to experiment with chemical substances and biological agents for use in terrorism have involved the toxin that causes botulism, the poisonous protein rycin (twice), sarin (twice), bubonic plague bacteria, typhoid bacteria, hydrogen cyanide, vx (another nerve gas), and possibly the Ebola virus.

Often speculation of Al Quaeda's involvement.

To Use or Not to Use?

If terrorists have used chemical weapons only once and nuclear material never, to some extent the reasons are technical. The scientific literature is replete with the technical problems inherent in the production, manufacture, storage, and delivery of each of the three classes of unconventional weapons.

The manufacture of nuclear weapons is not that simple, nor is delivery to their target. Nuclear material, of which a limited supply exists, is monitored by the U.N. affiliated International Atomic Energy Agency. Only governments can legally procure it, so that even in this age of proliferation investigators could trace those abetting nuclear terrorists without great difficulty. Monitoring can overlook a more primitive nuclear weapon: nonfissile but radioactive nuclear material. Iranian agents in Turkey, Kazakhstan, and elsewhere are known to have tried to buy such material originating in the former Soviet Union.

Chemical agents are much easier to produce or obtain but not so easy to keep safely in stable condition, and their dispersal depends largely on climatic factors. The terrorists behind last year's attack in Tokyo chose a convenient target where crowds of people gather, but their sarin was apparently dilute. The biological agents are far and away the most dangerous: they could kill hundreds of thousands where chemicals might kill only thousands. They are relatively easy to procure, but storage and dispersal are even trickier than for nerve gases. The risk of contamination for the people handling them is high, and many of the most lethal bacteria and spores do not survive well outside the laboratory. Aum Shinrikyo reportedly released anthrax bacteria—among the most toxic agents known—on two occasions from a building in Tokyo without harming anyone.

Given the technical difficulties, terrorists are probably less likely to use nuclear devices than chemical weapons, and least likely to attempt to use biological weapons. But difficulties could be overcome, and the choice of unconventional weapons will in the end come down to the specialties of the terrorists and their access to deadly substances.

The political arguments for shunning unconventional weapons are equally weighty. The risk of detection and subsequent severe retaliation or punishment is great, and while this may not deter terrorists it may put off their sponsors and suppliers. Terrorists eager to use weapons of mass destruction may alienate at least some supporters, not so much because the dissenters hate the enemy less or have greater moral qualms but because they think the use of such violence counter-productive. Unconventional weapon strikes could render whole regions uninhab-itable for long periods. Use of biological arms poses the additional risk of an un-controllable epidemic. And while terrorism seems to be tending toward more indiscriminate killing and mayhem, terrorists may draw the line at weapons of super-violence likely to harm both foes and large numbers of relatives and friends —say, Kurds in Turkey, Tamils in Sri Lanka, or Arabs in Israel.

Furthermore, traditional terrorism rests on the heroic gesture, on the willing-ness to sacrifice one's own life as proof of one's idealism. Obviously there is not much heroism in spreading botulism or anthrax. Since most terrorist groups are as interested in publicity as in violence, and as publicity for a mass poisoning or nuclear bombing would be far more unfavorable than for a focused conventional attack, only terrorists who do not care about publicity will even consider the ap-plications of unconventional weapons.

Broadly speaking, terrorists will not engage in overkill if their traditional weapons—the submachine gun and the conventional bomb—are sufficient to con-tinue the struggle and achieve their aims. But the decision to use terrorist violence is not always a rational one; if it were, there would be much less terrorism, since terrorist activity seldom achieves its aims. What if, after years of armed struggle and the loss of many of their militants, terrorist groups see no progress? Despair could lead to giving up the armed struggle, or to suicide. But it might also lead to a last desperate attempt to defeat the hated enemy by arms not tried before. As one of Racine's heroes said of himself, their "only hope lies in their despair."

Apocalypse Soon

Terrorist groups traditionally contain strong quasi-religious, fanatical elements, for only total certainty of belief (or total moral relativism) provides justification for taking lives. That element was strong among the prerevolutionary Russian terrorists and the Romanian fascists of the Iron Guard in the 1930s, as it is among today's Tamil Tigers. Fanatical Muslims consider the killing of the enemies of God a religious commandment, and believe that the secularists at home as well as the State of Israel will be annihilated because it is Allah's will. Aum Shinrikyo doctrine held that murder could help both victim and murderer to salvation. Sec-tarian fanaticism has surged during the past decade, and in general, the smaller the group, the more fanatical.

As humankind approaches the end of the second millennium of the Christian era, apocalyptic movements are on the rise. The belief in the impending end of the world is probably as old as history, but for reasons not entirely clear, sects and movements preaching the end of the world gain influence toward the end of a century, and all the more at the close of a millennium. Most of the preachers of doom do not advocate violence, and some even herald a renaissance, the birth of a new kind of man and woman. Others, however, believe that the sooner the reign of the Antichrist is established, the sooner this corrupt world will be destroyed and the new heaven and earth foreseen by St. John in the Book of Revelation, Nostradamus, and a host of other prophets will be realized.[2]

Extremist millenarians would like to give history a push, helping create world-ending havoc replete with universal war, famine, pestilence, and other scourges. It is possible that members of certain Christian and Jewish sects that believe in Armageddon or Gog and Magog or the Muslims and Buddhists who harbor related extreme beliefs could attempt to play out a doomsday scenario. A small group of Israeli extremists, for instance, firmly believes that blowing up Temple Mount in Jerusalem would bring about a final (religious) war and the beginning of redemption with the coming of the Kingdom of God. The visions of Shoko Asahara, the charismatic leader of Aum Shinrikyo, grew increasingly apocalyptic, and David Koresh proclaimed the Last Day's arrival in the Branch Davidians' 1994 confrontation with Bureau of Alcohol, Tobacco, and Firearms agents.

Those who subscribe to such beliefs number in the hundreds of thousands and perhaps millions. They have their own subcultures, produce books and CDs by the thousands, and build temples and communities of whose existence most of their contemporaries are unaware. They have substantial financial means at their disposal. Although the more extreme apocalyptic groups are potentially terrorist, intelligence services have generally overlooked their activities; hence the shock over the subway attack in Tokyo and Rabin's assassination, to name but two recent events.

Apocalyptic elements crop up in contemporary intellectual fashions and extremist politics as well. For instance, extreme environmentalists, particularly the so-called restoration ecologists, believe that environmental disasters will destroy civilization as we know it—no loss, in their view—and regard the vast majority of human beings as expendable. From such beliefs and values it is not a large step to engaging in acts of terrorism to expedite the process. If the eradication of smallpox upset ecosystems, why not restore the balance by bringing back the virus? The motto of *Chaos International*, one of many journals in this field, is a quotation from Hassan I Sabbah, the master of the Assassins, a medieval sect whose members killed Crusaders and others in a "religious" ecstasy; everything is permitted, the master says. The premodern world and postmodernism meet at this point.

Future Shock

Scanning the contemporary scene, one encounters a bewildering multiplicity of terrorist and potentially terrorist groups and sects. The practitioners of terrorism as we have known it to this point were nationalists and anarchists, extremists of the left and the right. But the new age has brought new inspiration for the users of violence along with the old.

In the past, terrorism was almost always the province of groups of militants that had the backing of political forces like the Irish and Russian social revolutionary movements of 1900. In the future, terrorists will be individuals or like-minded people working in very small groups, on the pattern of the technology-hating Unabomber, who apparently worked alone sending out parcel bombs over two decades, or the perpetrators of the 1995 bombing of the federal building in Oklahoma City. An individual may possess the technical competence to steal, buy, or manufacture the weapons he or she needs for a terrorist purpose; he or she may or may not require help from one or two others in delivering these weapons to the designated target. The ideologies such individuals and minigroups espouse are likely to be even more aberrant than those of larger groups. And terrorists working alone or in very small groups will be more difficult to detect unless they make a major mistake or are discovered by accident.

Thus at one end of the scale, the lone terrorist has appeared, and at the other, state-sponsored terrorism is quietly flourishing in these days when wars of aggression have become too expensive and too risky. As the century draws to a close, terrorism is becoming the substitute for the great wars of the 1800s and early 1900s.

Proliferation of the weapons of mass destruction does not mean that most terrorist groups are likely to use them in the foreseeable future, but some almost certainly will, in spite of all the reasons militating against it. Governments, however ruthless, ambitious, and ideologically extreme, will be reluctant to pass on unconventional weapons to terrorist groups over which they cannot have full control; the governments may be tempted to use such arms themselves in a first strike, but it is more probable that they would employ them in blackmail than in actual warfare. Individuals and small groups, however, will not be bound by the constraints that hold back even the most reckless government.

Society has also become vulnerable to a new kind of terrorism, in which the destructive power of both the individual terrorist and terrorism as a tactic are infinitely greater. Earlier terrorists could kill kings or high officials, but others only too eager to inherit their mantle quickly stepped in. The advanced societies of today are more dependent every day on the electronic storage, retrieval, analysis, and transmission of information. Defense, the police, banking, trade, transportation, scientific work, and a large percentage of the government's and the private sector's transactions are on-line. That exposes enormous vital areas of national life to mischief or sabotage by any computer hacker, and concerted sabotage could render a country unable to function. Hence the growing speculation about info-terrorism and cyberwarfare.

An unnamed U.S. intelligence official has boasted that with $1 billion and 20 capable hackers, he could shut down America. What he could achieve, a terrorist could too. There is little secrecy in the wired society, and protective measures have proved of limited value: teenage hackers have penetrated highly secret systems in every field. The possibilities for creating chaos are almost unlimited even now, and vulnerability will almost certainly increase. Terrorists' targets will change: Why assassinate a politician or indiscriminately kill people when an attack on electronic switching will produce far more dramatic and lasting results? The switch at the Culpeper, Virginia, headquarters of the Federal Reserve's electronic network, which handles all federal funds and transactions, would be an obvious place to hit. If the new terrorism directs its energies toward information warfare, its destructive power will be exponentially greater than any it wielded in the past—greater even than it would be with biological and chemical weapons.

Still, the vulnerability of states and societies will be of less interest to terrorists than to ordinary criminals and organized crime, disgruntled employees of big corporations, and, of course, spies and hostile governments. Electronic thieves, whether engaged in credit card fraud or industrial espionage, are part of the system, using it rather than destroying it; its destruction would cost them their livelihood. Politically motivated terrorist groups, above all separatists bent on establishing states of their own, have limited aims. The Kurdish Workers Party, the IRA, the Basque ETA, and the Tamil Tigers want to weaken their enemies and compel them to make far-reaching concessions, but they cannot realistically hope to destroy them. It is also possible, however, that terrorist groups on the verge of defeat or acting on apocalyptic visions may not hesitate to apply all destructive means at their disposal.

All that leads well beyond terrorism as we have known it. New definitions and new terms may have to be developed for new realities, and intelligence services and policymakers must learn to discern the significant differences among terrorists' motivations, approaches, and aims. The Bible says that when the Old Testament hero Samson brought down the temple, burying himself along with the Philistines in the ruins, "the dead which he slew at his death were more than he slew in his life." The Samsons of a society have been relatively few in all ages. But with the new technologies and the changed nature of the world in which they operate, a handful of angry Samsons and disciples of apocalypse would suffice to cause havoc. Chances are that of 100 attempts at terrorist superviolence, 99 would fail. But the single successful one could claim many more victims, do more material damage, and unleash far greater panic than anything the world has yet experienced.

NOTES

1. Science fiction writers produced chemical weapons even earlier. In Jules Verne's *The Begum's Fortune*, a (German) scientist aims to wipe out the 250,000 inhabitants of (French) Franceville with one grenade of what he calls carbon acid gas, shot from a supergun.

2. According to Nostradamus, a "great King of terror" will come from heaven in July 1999. Millenarians face a problem when it comes to fixing the date; the Gospel of St. Matthew says that "no one knows the day and the hour, not even the angels in heaven." As the year 1000 approached, educated people were fully aware that the Christian calendar was inexact and could not be corrected—hence the assumption that the world could end almost anytime between 960 and 1040. For a comparative review of apocalyptic influences at the end of the nineteenth and the twentieth centuries, see Walter Laqueur, "Fin de Siècle—Once More with Feeling," *Journal of Contemporary History*, January 1996, pp. 5–47.

Part

5

Globalization and the Evolution of Democracy

Globalization can result in profound political changes. Factors such as the expansion of international commerce and easy access to new ideas through the media and technology have led to demands for changes such as the introduction of democratic institutions and practices.

For Francis Fukuyama, fundamental changes in world history are taking place. A larger process is occurring which he refers to as the total exhaustion of viable alternatives to Western liberalism. In this, he sees the end of history as the dialectical process envisaged by Karl Marx. While this article was originally published in 1989 and refers to the historical context of that time, it remains a thought-provoking and challenging essay because it expresses the idea that Western liberal democracy is, and will continue to be, the dominant paradigm. Indeed, many policy makers and academics still subscribe to this view.

In contrast, Fareed Zakaria and Robert D. Kaplan argue that democracies do not always live up to the Western ideal. Zakaria is concerned about the proliferation of "illiberal democracies." The presence of democracy does not necessarily bring about constitutional liberalism. Changes in different parts of the world, such as elections in sub-Saharan Africa or the demise of communism in Eastern Europe, have not always resulted in liberal constitutional systems. Democracy is thus more than its structural and institutional components. It must be considered in terms of its intrinsic qualities of liberal values and rights. Kaplan puts forward the controversial idea that with increasing corporate power, the masses become more indifferent and elites less accountable. In addition, he argues that democracy is successful only when it is a capstone to other social and economic achievements. As such, democracy may not best serve the world in the future. Each of these three essays forces the reader to reassess the universal applicability of Western models of democracy, and to recognize that its future is embattled rather than assured.

The End of History?

Francis Fukuyama

In watching the flow of events over the past decade or so, it is hard to avoid the feeling that something very fundamental has happened in world history. The past year has seen a flood of articles commemorating the end of the Cold War, and the fact that "peace" seems to be breaking out in many regions of the world. Most of these analyses lack any larger conceptual framework for distinguishing between what is essential and what is contingent or accidental in world history, and are predictably superficial. If Mr. Gorbachev were ousted from the Kremlin or a new Ayatollah proclaimed the millennium from a desolate Middle Eastern capital, these same commentators would scramble to announce the rebirth of a new era of conflict.

And yet, all of these people sense dimly that there is some larger process at work, a process that gives coherence and order to the daily headlines. The twentieth century saw the developed world descend into a paroxysm of ideological violence, as liberalism contended first with the remnants of absolutism, then bolshevism and fascism, and finally an updated Marxism that threatened to lead to the ultimate apocalypse of nuclear war. But the century that began full of self-confidence in the ultimate triumph of Western liberal democracy seems at its close to be returning full circle to where it started: not to an "end of ideology" or a convergence between capitalism and socialism, as earlier predicted, but to an unabashed victory of economic and political liberalism.

The triumph of the West, of the Western *idea,* is evident first of all in the total exhaustion of viable systematic alternatives to Western liberalism. In the past decade, there have been unmistakable changes in the intellectual climate of the world's two largest communist countries, and the beginnings of significant reform movements in both. But this phenomenon extends beyond high politics and it can be seen also in the ineluctable spread of consumerist Western culture in such diverse contexts as the peasants' markets and color television sets now omnipresent throughout China, the cooperative restaurants and clothing stores opened in the past year in Moscow, the Beethoven piped into Japanese department stores, and the rock music enjoyed alike in Prague, Rangoon, and Tehran.

What we may be witnessing is not just the end of the Cold War, or the passing of a particular period of postwar history, but the end of history as such: that is, the end point of mankind's ideological evolution and the universalization of Western liberal democracy as the final form of human government. This is not to say that there will no longer be events to fill the pages of *Foreign Affairs*'s yearly summaries of international relations, for the victory of liberalism has occurred primarily in the realm of ideas or consciousness and is as yet incomplete in the real or material world. But there are powerful reasons for believing that it is the ideal that will govern the material world *in the long run.* To understand how this is so, we must first consider some theoretical issues concerning the nature of historical change.

I

The notion of the end of history is not an original one. Its best known propagator was Karl Marx, who believed that the direction of historical development was a purposeful one determined by the interplay of material forces, and would come to an end only with the achievement of a communist utopia that would finally resolve all prior contradictions. But the concept of history as a dialectical process with a beginning, a middle, and an end was borrowed by Marx from his great German predecessor, Georg Wilhelm Friedrich Hegel.

For better or worse, much of Hegel's historicism has become part of our contemporary intellectual baggage. The notion that mankind has progressed through a series of primitive stages of consciousness on his path to the present, and that these stages corresponded to concrete forms of social organization, such as tribal, slave-owning, theocratic, and finally democratic-egalitarian societies, has become inseparable from the modern understanding of man. Hegel was the first philosopher to speak the language of modern social science, insofar as man for him was the product of his concrete historical and social environment and not, as earlier natural right theorists would have it, a collection of more or less fixed "natural" attributes. The mastery and transformation of man's natural environment through the application of science and technology was originally not a Marxist concept, but a Hegelian one. Unlike later historicists whose historical relativism degenerated into relativism *tout court,* however, Hegel believed that history culminated in an absolute moment—a moment in which a final, rational form of society and state became victorious.

It is Hegel's misfortune to be known now primarily as Marx's precursor, and it is our misfortune that few of us are familiar with Hegel's work from direct study, but only as it has been filtered through the distorting lens of Marxism. In France, however, there has been an effort to save Hegel from his Marxist interpreters and to resurrect him as the philosopher who most correctly speaks to our time. Among those modern French interpreters of Hegel, the greatest was certainly Alexandre Kojève, a brilliant Russian emigre who taught a highly influential series of seminars in Paris in the 1930s at the *Ecole Pratique des Hautes Etudes.*[1] While largely unknown in the United States, Kojève had a major impact on the intellectual life of the continent. Among his students ranged such future luminaries as Jean-Paul Sartre on the Left and Raymond Aron on the Right; postwar existentialism borrowed many of its basic categories from Hegel via Kojève.

Kojève sought to resurrect the Hegel of the *Phenomenology of Mind,* the Hegel who proclaimed history to be at an end in 1806. For as early as this Hegel saw in Napoleon's defeat of the Prussian monarchy at the Battle of Jena the victory of the ideals of the French Revolution, and the imminent universalization of the state incorporating the principles of liberty and equality. Kojève, far from rejecting Hegel in light of the turbulent events of the next century and a half, insisted that the latter had been essentially correct.[2] The Battle of Jena marked the end of history because it was at that point that the *vanguard* of humanity (a term quite familiar to Marxists) actualized the principles of the French Revolution. While there was considerable work to be done after 1806—abolishing slavery and the slave trade, extending the franchise to workers, women, blacks, and other racial minorities, etc.—the basic *principles* of the liberal democratic state could not be improved upon. The two world wars in this century and their attendant revolutions and upheavals simply had the effect of extending those principles spatially, such that the various provinces of human civilization were brought up to the level of its most advanced outposts, and of forcing those societies in Europe and North America at the vanguard of civilization to implement their liberalism more fully.

The state that emerges at the end of history is liberal insofar as it recognizes and protects through a system of law man's universal right to freedom, and democratic insofar as it exists only with the consent of the governed. For Kojève, this so-called "universal homogenous state" found real-life embodiment in the countries of postwar Western Europe—precisely those flabby, prosperous, self-satisfied, inward-looking, weak-willed states whose grandest project was nothing more heroic than the creation of the Common Market.[3] But this was only to be expected. For human history and the conflict that characterized it was based on the existence of "contradictions": primitive man's quest for mutual recognition, the dialectic of the master and slave, the transformation and mastery of nature, the struggle for the universal recognition of rights, and the dichotomy between proletarian and capitalist. But in the universal homogenous state, all prior contradictions are resolved and all human needs are satisfied. There is no struggle or conflict over "large" issues, and consequently no need for generals or statesmen; what remains is primarily economic activity. And indeed, Kojève's life was consistent with his teaching. Believing that there was no more work for philosophers as well, since Hegel (correctly understood) had already achieved absolute knowledge, Kojève left teaching after the war and spent the remainder of his life working as a bureaucrat in the European Economic Community, until his death in 1968.

To his contemporaries at mid-century, Kojève's proclamation of the end of history must have seemed like the typical eccentric solipsism of a French intellectual, coming as it did on the heels of World War II and at the very height of the Cold War. To comprehend how Kojève could have been so audacious as to assert that history has ended, we must first of all understand the meaning of Hegelian idealism.

II

For Hegel, the contradictions that drive history exist first of all in the realm of human consciousness, i.e. on the level of ideas[4]—not the trivial election year proposals of American politicians, but ideas in the sense of large unifying world views that might best be understood under the rubric of ideology. Ideology in this sense is not restricted to the secular and explicit political doctrines we usually associate with the term, but can include religion, culture, and the complex of moral values underlying any society as well.

Hegel's view of the relationship between the ideal and the real or material worlds was an extremely complicated one, beginning with the fact that for him the distinction between the two was only apparent.[5] He did not believe that the real world conformed or could be made to conform to ideological preconceptions of philosophy professors in any simple-minded way, or that the "material" world could not impinge on the ideal. Indeed, Hegel the professor was temporarily thrown out of work as a result of a very material event, the Battle of Jena. But while Hegel's writing and thinking could be stopped by a bullet from the material world, the hand on the trigger of the gun was motivated in turn by the ideas of liberty and equality that had driven the French Revolution.

For Hegel, all human behavior in the material world, and hence all human history, is rooted in a prior state of consciousness—an idea similar to the one expressed by John Maynard Keynes when he said that the views of men of affairs were usually derived from defunct economists and academic scribblers of earlier generations. This consciousness may not be explicit and self-aware, as are modern political doctrines, but may rather take the form of religion or simple cultural or moral habits. And yet this realm of consciousness *in the long run* necessarily becomes manifest in the material world, indeed creates the material world in its own image. Consciousness is cause and not effect, and can develop autonomously from the material world; hence the real subtext underlying the apparent jumble of current events is the history of ideology.

Hegel's idealism has fared poorly at the hands of later thinkers. Marx reversed the priority of the real and the ideal completely, relegating the entire realm of consciousness—religion, art, culture, philosophy itself—to a "superstructure" that was determined entirely by the prevailing material mode of production. Yet another unfortunate legacy of Marxism is our tendency to retreat into materialist or utilitarian explanations of political or historical phenomena, and our disinclination to believe in the autonomous power of ideas. A recent example of this is Paul Kennedy's hugely successful *The Rise and Fall of the Great Powers,* which ascribes the decline of great powers to simple economic overextension. Obviously, this is true on some level: an empire whose economy is barely above the level of subsistence cannot bankrupt its treasury indefinitely. But whether a highly productive modern industrial society chooses to spend 3 or 7 percent of its GNP on defense rather than consumption is entirely a matter of that society's political priorities, which are in turn determined in the realm of consciousness.

The materialist bias of modern thought is characteristic not only of people on the Left who may be sympathetic to Marxism, but of many passionate anti-Marxists as well. Indeed, there is on the Right what one might label the *Wall Street Journal* school of deterministic materialism that discounts the importance of ideology and culture and sees man as essentially a rational, profit maximizing individual. It is precisely this kind of individual and his pursuit of material incentives that is posited as the basis for economic life as such in economic textbooks.[6] One small example will illustrate the problematic character of such materialist views.

Max Weber begins his famous book, *The Protestant Ethic and the Spirit of Capitalism,* by noting the different economic performance of Protestant and Catholic communities throughout Europe and America, summed up in the proverb that Protestants eat well while Catholics sleep well. Weber notes that according to any economic theory that posited man as a rational profit-maximizer, raising the piece work rate should increase labor productivity. But in fact, in many traditional peasant communities, raising the piece-work rate actually had the opposite effect of *lowering* labor productivity: at the higher rate, a peasant accustomed to earning two and one-half marks per day found he could earn the same amount by working less, and did so because he valued leisure more than income. The choices of leisure over income, or of the militaristic life of the Spartan hoplite over the wealth of the Athenian trader, or even the ascetic life of the early capitalist entrepreneur over that of a traditional leisured aristocrat, cannot possibly be explained by the impersonal working of material forces, but come preeminently out of the sphere of consciousness—what we have labeled here broadly as ideology. And indeed, a central theme of Weber's work was to prove that contrary to Marx, the material mode of production, far from being the "base," was itself a "superstructure" with roots in religion and culture, and that to understand the emergence of modern capitalism and the profit motive one had to study their antecedents in the realm of the spirit.

As we look around the contemporary world, the poverty of materialist theories of economic development is all too apparent. The *Wall Street Journal* school of deterministic materialism habitually points to the stunning economic success of Asia in the past few decades as evidence of the viability of free market economics, with the implication that all societies would see similar development were they simply to allow their populations to pursue their material self-interest freely. Surely free markets and stable political systems are a necessary precondition to capitalist economic growth. But just as surely the cultural heritage of those Far Eastern societies, the ethic of work and saving and family, a religious heritage that does not, like Islam, place restrictions on certain forms of economic behavior, and other deeply ingrained moral qualities, are equally important in explaining their economic performance.[7] And yet the intellectual weight of materialism is such that not a single respectable contemporary theory of economic development addresses consciousness and culture seriously as the matrix within which economic behavior is formed.

Failure to understand that the roots of economic behavior lie in the realm of consciousness and culture leads to the common mistake of attributing material causes to phenomena that are essentially ideal in nature. For example, it is commonplace in the West to interpret the reform movements first in China and most recently in the Soviet Union as the victory of the material over the ideal—that is, a recognition that ideological incentives could not replace material ones in stimulating a highly productive modern economy, and that if one wanted to prosper one had to appeal to baser forms of self-interest. But the deep defects of socialist economies were evident thirty or forty years ago to anyone who chose to look. Why was it that these countries moved away from central planning only in the 1980s? The answer must be found in the consciousness of the elites and leaders ruling them, who decided to opt for the "Protestant" life of wealth and risk over the "Catholic" path of poverty and security.[8] That change was in no way made inevitable by the material conditions in which either country found itself on the eve of the reform, but instead came about as the result of the victory of one idea over another.[9]

For Kojève, as for all good Hegelians, understanding the underlying processes of history requires understanding developments in the realm of consciousness or ideas, since consciousness will ultimately remake the material world in its own image. To say that history ended in 1806 meant that mankind's ideological evolution ended in the ideals of the French or American Revolutions: while particular regimes in the real world might not implement these ideals fully, their theoretical truth is absolute and could not be improved upon. Hence it did not matter to Kojève that the consciousness of the postwar generation of Europeans had not been universalized throughout the world; if ideological development had in fact ended, the homogenous state would eventually become victorious throughout the material world.

I have neither the space nor, frankly, the ability to defend in depth Hegel's radical idealist perspective. The issue is not whether Hegel's system was right, but whether his perspective might uncover the problematic nature of many materialist explanations we often take for granted. This is not to deny the role of material factors as such. To a literal-minded idealist, human society can be built around any arbitrary set of principles regardless of their relationship to the material world. And in fact men have proven themselves able to endure the most extreme material hardships in the name of ideas that exist in the realm of the spirit alone, be it the divinity of cows or the nature of the Holy Trinity.[10]

But while man's very perception of the material world is shaped by his historical consciousness of it, the material world can clearly affect in return the viability of a particular state of consciousness. In particular, the spectacular abundance of advanced liberal economies and the infinitely diverse consumer culture made possible by them seem to both foster and preserve liberalism in the political sphere. I want to avoid the materialist determinism that says that liberal economics inevitably produces liberal politics, because I believe that both economics and politics presuppose an autonomous prior state of consciousness that makes them possible. But that state of consciousness that permits the growth of liberalism seems to stabilize in the way one would expect at the end of history if it is underwritten by the abundance of a modern free market economy. We might summarize the content of the universal homogenous state as liberal democracy in the political sphere combined with easy access to VCRs and stereos in the economic.

III

Have we in fact reached the end of history? Are there, in other words, any fundamental "contradictions" in human life that cannot be resolved in the context of modern liberalism, that would be resolvable by an alternative political-economic structure? If we accept the idealist premises laid out above, we must seek an answer to this question in the realm of ideology and consciousness. Our task is not to answer exhaustively the challenges to liberalism promoted by every crackpot messiah around the world, but only those that are embodied in important social or political forces and movements, and which are therefore part of world history. For our purposes, it matters very little what strange thoughts occur to people in Albania or Burkina Faso, for we are interested in what one could in some sense call the common ideological heritage of mankind.

In the past century, there have been two major challenges to liberalism, those of fascism and of communism. The former[11] saw the political weakness, materialism, anomie, and lack of community of the West as fundamental contradictions in liberal societies that could only be resolved by a strong state that forged a new "people" on the basis of national exclusiveness. Fascism was destroyed as a living ideology by World War II. This was a defeat, of course, on a very material level, but it amounted to a defeat of the idea as well. What destroyed fascism as an idea was not universal moral revulsion against it, since plenty of people were willing to endorse the idea as long as it seemed the wave of the future, but its lack of success. After the war, it seemed to most people that German fascism as well as its other European and Asian variants were bound to self-destruct. There was no material reason why new fascist movements could not have sprung up again after the war in other locales, but for the fact that expansionist ultranationalism, with its promise of unending conflict leading to disastrous military defeat, had completely lost its appeal. The ruins of the Reich chancellory as well as the atomic bombs dropped on Hiroshima and Nagasaki killed this ideology on the level of consciousness as well as materially, and all of the proto-fascist movements spawned by the German and Japanese examples like the Peronist movement in Argentina or Subhas Chandra Bose's Indian National Army withered after the war.

The ideological challenge mounted by the other great alternative to liberalism, communism, was far more serious. Marx, speaking Hegel's language, asserted that liberal society contained a fundamental contradiction that could not be resolved within its context, that between capital and labor, and this contradiction has constituted the chief accusation against liberalism ever since. But surely, the class issue has actually been successfully resolved in the West. As Kojève (among others) noted, the egalitarianism of modern America represents the essential achievement of the classless society envisioned by Marx. This is not to say that there are not rich people and poor people in the United States, or that the gap between them has not grown in recent years. But the root causes of economic inequality do not have to do with the underlying legal and social structure of our society, which remains fundamentally egalitarian and moderately redistributionist, so much as with the cultural and social characteristics of the groups that make it up, which are in turn the historical legacy of premodern conditions. Thus black poverty in the United States is not the inherent product of liberalism, but is rather the "legacy of slavery and racism" which persisted long after the formal abolition of slavery.

As a result of the receding of the class issue, the appeal of communism in the developed Western world, it is safe to say, is lower today than any time since the end of the First World War. This can be measured in any number of ways: in the declining membership and electoral pull of the major European communist parties, and their overtly revisionist programs; in the corresponding electoral success of conservative parties from Britain and Germany to the United States and Japan, which are unabashedly pro-market and anti-statist; and in an intellectual climate whose most "advanced" members no longer believe that bourgeois society is something that ultimately needs to be overcome. This is not to say that the opinions of progressive intellectuals in Western countries are not deeply pathological in any number of ways. But those who believe that the future must inevitably be socialist tend to be very old, or very marginal to the real political discourse of their societies.

One may argue that the socialist alternative was never terribly plausible for the North Atlantic world, and was sustained for the last several decades primarily by its success outside of this region. But it is precisely in the non-European world that one is most struck by the occurrence of major ideological transformations. Surely the most remarkable changes have occurred in Asia. Due to the strength and adaptability of the indigenous cultures there, Asia became a battleground for a variety of imported Western ideologies early in this century. Liberalism in Asia was a very weak reed in the period after World War I; it is easy today to forget how gloomy Asia's political future looked as recently as ten or fifteen years ago. It is easy to forget as well how momentous the outcome of Asian ideological struggles seemed for world political development as a whole.

The first Asian alternative to liberalism to be decisively defeated was the fascist one represented by Imperial Japan. Japanese fascism (like its German version) was defeated by the force of American arms in the Pacific war, and liberal democracy was imposed on Japan by a victorious United States. Western capitalism and political liberalism when transplanted to Japan were adapted and transformed by the Japanese in such a way as to be scarcely recognizable.[12] Many Americans are now aware that Japanese industrial organization is very different from that prevailing in the United States or Europe, and it is questionable what relationship the factional maneuvering that takes place with the governing Liberal Democratic Party bears to democracy. Nonetheless, the very fact that the essential elements of economic and political liberalism have been so successfully grafted onto uniquely Japanese traditions and institutions guarantees their survival in the long run. More important is the contribution that Japan has made in turn to world history by following in the footsteps of the United States to create a truly universal consumer culture that has become both a symbol and an underpinning of the universal homogenous state. V.S. Naipaul travelling in Khomeini's Iran shortly after the revolution noted the omnipresent signs advertising the products of Sony, Hitachi, and JVC, whose appeal remained virtually irresistible and gave the lie to the regime's pretensions of restoring a state based on the rule of the *Shariah*. Desire for access to the consumer culture, created in large measure by Japan, has played a crucial role in fostering the spread of economic liberalism throughout Asia, and hence in promoting political liberalism as well.

The economic success of the other newly industrializing countries (NICs) in Asia following on the example of Japan is by now a familiar story. What is important from a Hegelian standpoint is that political liberalism has been following economic liberalism, more slowly than many had hoped but with seeming inevitability. Here again we see the victory of the idea of the universal homogenous state. South Korea had developed into a modern, urbanized society with an increasingly large and well-educated middle class that could not possibly be isolated from the larger democratic trends around them. Under these circumstances it seemed intolerable to a large part of this population that it should be ruled by an anachronistic military regime while Japan, only a decade or so ahead in economic terms, had parliamentary institutions for over forty years. Even the former socialist regime in Burma, which for so many decades existed in dismal isolation from the larger trends dominating Asia, was buffeted in the past year by pressures to liberalize both its economy and political system. It is said that unhappiness with strongman Ne Win began when a senior Burmese officer went to Singapore for medical treatment and broke down crying when he saw how far socialist Burma had been left behind by its ASEAN neighbors.

But the power of the liberal idea would seem much less impressive if it had not infected the largest and oldest culture in Asia, China. The simple existence of communist China created an alternative pole of ideological attraction, and as such constituted a threat to liberalism. But the past fifteen years have seen an almost total discrediting of Marxism-Leninism as an economic system. Beginning with the famous third plenum of the Tenth Central Committee in 1978, the Chinese Communist party set about decollectivizing agriculture for the 800 million Chinese who still lived in the countryside. The role of the state in agriculture was reduced to that of a tax collector, while production of consumer goods was sharply increased in order to give peasants a taste of the universal homogenous state and thereby an incentive to work. The reform doubled Chinese grain output in only five years, and in the process created for Deng Xiao-ping a solid political base from which he was able to extend the reform to other parts of the economy. Economic statistics do not begin to describe the dynamism, initiative, and openness evident in China since the reform began.

China could not now be described in any way as a liberal democracy. At present, no more than 20 percent of its economy has been marketized, and most importantly it continues to be ruled by a self-appointed Communist party which has given no hint of wanting to devolve power. Deng has made none of Gorbachev's promises regarding democratization of the political system and there is no Chinese equivalent of *glasnost*. The Chinese leadership has in fact been much more circumspect in criticizing Mao and Maoism than Gorbachev with respect to Brezhnev and Stalin, and the regime continues to pay lip service to Marxism-Leninism as its ideological underpinning. But anyone familiar with the outlook and behavior of the new technocratic elite now governing China knows that Marxism and ideological principle have become virtually irrelevant as guides to policy, and that bourgeois consumerism has a real meaning in that country for the first time since the revolution. The various slowdowns in the pace of reform, the campaigns against "spiritual pollution" and crackdowns on political dissent are more properly seen as tactical adjustments made in the process of managing what is an extraordinarily difficult political transition. By ducking the question of political reform while putting the economy on a new footing, Deng has managed to avoid the breakdown of authority that has accompanied Gorbachev's *perestroika*. Yet the pull of the liberal idea continues to be very strong as economic power devolves and the economy becomes more open to the outside world. There are currently over 20,000 Chinese students studying in the U.S. and other Western countries, almost all of them the children of the Chinese elite. It is hard to believe that when they return home to run the country they will be content for China to be the only country in Asia unaffected by the larger democratizing trend. The student demonstrations in Beijing that broke out first in December 1986 and recurred recently on the occasion of Hu Yao-bang's death were only the beginning of what will inevitably be mounting pressure for change in the political system as well.

What is important about China from the standpoint of world history is not the present state of the reform or even its future prospects. The central issue is the fact that the People's Republic of China can no longer act as a beacon for illiberal forces around the world, whether they be guerrillas in some Asian jungle or middle class students in Paris. Maoism, rather than being the pattern for Asia's future, became an anachronism, and it was the mainland Chinese who in fact were decisively influenced by the prosperity and dynamism of their overseas co-ethnics —the ironic ultimate victory of Taiwan.

Important as these changes in China have been, however, it is developments in the Soviet Union—the original "homeland of the world proletariat"—that have put the final nail in the coffin of the Marxist-Leninist alternative to liberal democracy. It should be clear that in terms of formal institutions, not much has changed in the four years since Gorbachev has come to power: free markets and the cooperative movement represent only a small part of the Soviet economy, which remains centrally planned; the political system is still dominated by the Communist party, which has only begun to democratize internally and to share power with other groups; the regime continues to assert that it is seeking only to modernize socialism and that its ideological basis remains Marxism-Leninism; and, finally, Gorbachev faces a potentially powerful conservative opposition that could undo many of the changes that have taken place to date. Moreover, it is hard to be too sanguine about the chances for success of Gorbachev's proposed reforms, either in the sphere of economics or politics. But my purpose here is not to analyze events in the short-term, or to make predictions for policy purposes, but to look at underlying trends in the sphere of ideology and consciousness. And in that respect, it is clear that an astounding transformation has occurred.

Emigres from the Soviet Union have been reporting for at least the last generation now that virtually nobody in that country truly believed in Marxism-Leninism any longer, and that this was nowhere more true than in the Soviet elite, which continued to mouth Marxist slogans out of sheer cynicism. The corruption and decadence of the late Brezhnev-era Soviet state seemed to matter little, however, for as long as the state itself refused to throw into question any of the fundamental principles underlying Soviet society, the system was capable of functioning adequately out of sheer inertia and could even muster some dynamism in the realm of foreign and defense policy. Marxism-Leninism was like a magical incantation which, however absurd and devoid of meaning, was the only common basis on which the elite could agree to rule Soviet society.

What has happened in the four years since Gorbachev's coming to power is a revolutionary assault on the most fundamental institutions and principles of Stalinism, and their replacement by other principles which do not amount to liberalism *per se* but whose only connecting thread is liberalism. This is most evident in the economic sphere, where the reform economists around Gorbachev have become steadily more radical in their support for free markets, to the point where some like Nikolai Shmelev do not mind being compared in public to Milton Friedman. There is a virtual consensus among the currently dominant school of Soviet economists now that central planning and the command system of allocation are the root cause of economic inefficiency, and that if the Soviet system is ever to heal itself, it must permit free and decentralized decision-making with respect to investment, labor, and prices. After a couple of initial years of ideological confusion, these principles have finally been incorporated into policy with the promulgation of new laws on enterprise autonomy, cooperatives, and finally in 1988 on lease arrangements and family farming. There are, of course, a number of fatal flaws in the current implementation of the reform, most notably the absence of a thoroughgoing price reform. But the problem is no longer a *conceptual* one: Gorbachev and his lieutenants seem to understand the economic logic of marketization well enough, but like the leaders of a Third World country facing the IMF, are afraid of the social consequences of ending consumer subsidies and other forms of dependence on the state sector.

In the political sphere, the proposed changes to the Soviet constitution, legal system, and party rules amount to much less than the establishment of a liberal state. Gorbachev has spoken of democratization primarily in the sphere of internal party affairs, and has shown little intention of ending the Communist party's monopoly of power; indeed, the political reform seeks to legitimize and therefore strengthen the CPSU's rule.[13] Nonetheless, the general principles underlying many of the reforms—that the "people" should be truly responsible for their own affairs, that higher political bodies should be answerable to lower ones, and not vice versa, that the rule of law should prevail over arbitrary police actions, with separation of powers and an independent judiciary, that there should be legal protection for property rights, the need for open discussion of public issues and the right of public dissent, the empowering of the Soviets as a forum in which the whole Soviet people can participate, and of a political culture that is more tolerant and pluralistic—come from a source fundamentally alien to the USSR's Marxist-Leninist tradition, even if they are incompletely articulated and poorly implemented in practice.

Gorbachev's repeated assertions that he is doing no more than trying to restore the original meaning of Leninism are themselves a kind of Orwellian doublespeak. Gorbachev and his allies have consistently maintained that intraparty democracy was somehow the essence of Leninism, and that the various liberal practices of open debate, secret ballot elections, and rule of law were all part of the Leninist heritage, corrupted only later by Stalin. While almost anyone would look good compared to Stalin, drawing so sharp a line between Lenin and his successor is questionable. The essence of Lenin's democratic centralism was centralism, not democracy; that is, the absolutely rigid, monolithic, and disciplined dictatorship of a hierarchically organized vanguard Communist party, speaking in the name of the *demos*. All of Lenin's vicious polemics against Karl Kautsky, Rosa Luxemburg, and various other Menshevik and Social Democratic rivals, not to mention his contempt for "bourgeois legality" and freedoms, centered around his profound conviction that a revolution could not be successfully made by a democratically run organization.

Gorbachev's claim that he is seeking to return to the true Lenin is perfectly easy to understand: having fostered a thorough denunciation of Stalinism and Brezhnevism as the root of the USSR's present predicament, he needs some point in Soviet history on which to anchor the legitimacy of the CPSU's continued rule.

But Gorbachev's tactical requirements should not blind us to the fact that the democratizing and decentralizing principles which he has enunciated in both the economic and political spheres are highly subversive of some of the most fundamental precepts of both Marxism and Leninism. Indeed, if the bulk of the present economic reform proposals were put into effect, it is hard to know how the Soviet economy would be more socialist than those of other Western countries with large public sectors.

The Soviet Union could in no way be described as a liberal or democratic country now, nor do I think that it is terribly likely that *perestroika* will succeed such that the label will be thinkable any time in the near future. But at the end of history it is not necessary that all societies become successful liberal societies, merely that they end their ideological pretensions of representing different and higher forms of human society. And in this respect I believe that something very important has happened in the Soviet Union in the past few years: the criticisms of the Soviet system sanctioned by Gorbachev have been so thorough and devastating that there is very little chance of going back to either Stalinism or Brezhnevism in any simple way. Gorbachev has finally permitted people to say what they had privately understood for many years, namely, that the magical incantations of Marxism-Leninism were nonsense, that Soviet socialism was not superior to the West in any respect but was in fact a monumental failure. The conservative opposition in the USSR, consisting both of simple workers afraid of unemployment and inflation and of party officials fearful of losing their jobs and privileges, is outspoken and may be strong enough to force Gorbachev's ouster in the next few years. But what both groups desire is tradition, order, and authority; they manifest no deep commitment to Marxism-Leninism, except insofar as they have invested much of their own lives in it.[14] For authority to be restored in the Soviet Union after Gorbachev's demolition work, it must be on the basis of some new and vigorous ideology which has not yet appeared on the horizon.

If we admit for the moment that the fascist and communist challenges to liberalism are dead, are there any other ideological competitors left? Or put another way, are there contradictions in liberal society beyond that of class that are not resolvable? Two possibilities suggest themselves, those of religion and nationalism.

The rise of religious fundamentalism in recent years within the Christian, Jewish, and Muslim traditions has been widely noted. One is inclined to say that the revival of religion in some way attests to a broad unhappiness with the impersonality and spiritual vacuity of liberal consumerist societies. Yet while the emptiness at the core of liberalism is most certainly a defect in the ideology—indeed, a flaw that one does not need the perspective of religion to recognize[15]—it is not at all clear that it is remediable through politics. Modern liberalism itself was historically a consequence of the weakness of religiously-based societies which, failing to agree on the nature of the good life, could not provide even the minimal preconditions of peace and stability. In the contemporary world only Islam has offered a theocratic state as a political alternative to both liberalism and communism. But the doctrine has little appeal for non-Muslims, and it is hard to believe that the movement will take on any universal significance. Other less organized religious impulses have been successfully satisfied within the sphere of personal life that is permitted in liberal societies.

The other major "contradiction" potentially unresolvable by liberalism is the one posed by nationalism and other forms of racial and ethnic consciousness. It is certainly true that a very large degree of conflict since the Battle of Jena has had its roots in nationalism. Two cataclysmic world wars in this century have been spawned by the nationalism of the developed world in various guises, and if those passions have been muted to a certain extent in postwar Europe, they are still extremely powerful in the Third World. Nationalism has been a threat to liberalism historically in Germany, and continues to be one in isolated parts of "post-historical" Europe like Northern Ireland.

But it is not clear that nationalism represents an irreconcilable contradiction in the heart of liberalism. In the first place, nationalism is not one single phenomenon but several, ranging from mild cultural nostalgia to the highly organized and elaborately articulated doctrine of National Socialism. Only systematic nationalisms of the latter sort can qualify as a formal ideology on the level of liberalism or communism. The vast majority of the world's nationalist movements do not have a political program beyond the negative desire of independence *from* some other group or people, and do not offer anything like a comprehensive agenda for socio-economic organization. As such, they are compatible with doctrines and ideologies that do offer such agendas. While they may constitute a source of conflict for liberal societies, this conflict does not arise from liberalism itself so much as from the fact that the liberalism in question is incomplete. Certainly a great deal of the world's ethnic and nationalist tension can be explained in terms of peoples who are forced to live in unrepresentative political systems that they have not chosen.

While it is impossible to rule out the sudden appearance of new ideologies or previously unrecognized contradictions in liberal societies, then, the present world seems to confirm that the fundamental principles of socio-political organization have not advanced terribly far since 1806. Many of the wars and revolutions fought since that time have been undertaken in the name of ideologies which claimed to be more advanced than liberalism, but whose pretensions were ultimately unmasked by history. In the meantime, they have helped to spread the universal homogenous state to the point where it could have a significant effect on the overall character of international relations.

IV

What are the implications of the end of history for international relations? Clearly, the vast bulk of the Third World remains very much mired in history, and will be a terrain of conflict for many years to come. But let us focus for the time being on the larger and more developed states of the world who after all account for the greater part of world politics. Russia and China are not likely to join the developed nations of the West as liberal societies any time in the foreseeable future, but suppose for a moment that Marxism-Leninism ceases to be a factor driving the foreign policies of these states—a prospect which, if not yet here, the last few years have made a real possibility. How will the overall characteristics of a de-ideologized world differ from those of the one with which we are familiar at such a hypothetical juncture?

The most common answer is—not very much. For there is a very widespread belief among many observers of international relations that underneath the skin of ideology is a hard core of great power national interest that guarantees a fairly high level of competition and conflict between nations. Indeed, according to one academically popular school of international relations theory, conflict inheres in the international system as such, and to understand the prospects for conflict one must look at the shape of the system—for example, whether it is bipolar or multipolar—rather than at the specific character of the nations and regimes that constitute it. This school in effect applies a Hobbesian view of politics to international relations, and assumes that aggression and insecurity are universal characteristics of human societies rather than the product of specific historical circumstances.

Believers in this line of thought take the relations that existed between the participants in the classical nineteenth-century European balance of power as a model for what a deideologized contemporary world would look like. Charles Krauthammer, for example, recently explained that if as a result of Gorbachev's reforms the USSR is shorn of Marxist-Leninist ideology, its behavior will revert to that of nineteenth-century imperial Russia.[16] While he finds this more reassuring than the threat posed by a communist Russia, he implies that there will still be a substantial degree of competition and conflict in the international system, just as there was, say, between Russia and Britain or Wilhelmine Germany in the last century. This is, of course, a convenient point of view for people who want to admit that something major is changing in the Soviet Union, but do not want to accept responsibility for recommending the radical policy redirection implicit in such a view. But is it true?

In fact, the notion that ideology is a superstructure imposed on a substratum of permanent great power interest is a highly questionable proposition. For the way in which any state defines its national interest is not universal but rests on some kind of prior ideological basis, just as we saw that economic behavior is determined by a prior state of consciousness. In this century, states have adopted highly articulated doctrines with explicit foreign policy agendas legitimizing expansionism, like Marxism-Leninism or National Socialism.

The expansionist and competitive behavior of nineteenth-century European states rested on no less ideal a basis; it just so happened that the ideology driving it was less explicit than the doctrines of the twentieth century. For one thing, most "liberal" European societies were illiberal insofar as they believed in the legitimacy of imperialism, that is, the right of one nation to rule over other nations without regard for the wishes of the ruled. The justifications for imperialism varied from nation to nation, from a crude belief in the legitimacy of force, particularly when applied to non-Europeans, to the White Man's Burden and Europe's Christianizing mission, to the desire to give people of color access to the culture of Rabelais and Molière. But whatever the particular ideological basis, every "developed" country believed in the acceptability of higher civilizations ruling lower ones—including, incidentally, the United States with regard to the Philippines. This led to a drive for pure territorial aggrandizement in the latter half of the century and played no small role in causing the Great War.

The radical and deformed outgrowth of nineteenth-century imperialism was German fascism, an ideology which justified Germany's right not only to rule over non-European peoples, but over *all* non-German ones. But in retrospect it seems that Hitler represented a diseased bypath in the general course of European development, and since his fiery defeat, the legitimacy of any kind of territorial aggrandizement has been thoroughly discredited.[17] Since the Second World War, European nationalism has been defanged and shorn of any real relevance to foreign policy, with the consequence that the nineteenth-century model of great power behavior has become a serious anachronism. The most extreme form of nationalism that any Western European state has mustered since 1945 has been Gaullism, whose self-assertion has been confined largely to the realm of nuisance politics and culture. International life for the part of the world that has reached the end of history is far more preoccupied with economics than with politics or strategy.

The developed states of the West do maintain defense establishments and in the postwar period have competed vigorously for influence to meet a worldwide communist threat. This behavior has been driven, however, by an external threat from states that possess overtly expansionist ideologies, and would not exist in their absence. To take the "neo-realist" theory seriously, one would have to believe that "natural" competitive behavior would reassert itself among the OECD states were Russia and China to disappear from the face of the earth. That is, West Germany and France would arm themselves against each other as they did in the 1930s, Australia and New Zealand would send military advisers to block each others' advances in Africa, and the U.S.-Canadian border would become fortified. Such a prospect is, of course, ludicrous: minus Marxist-Leninist ideology, we are far more likely to see the "Common Marketization" of world politics than the disintegration of the EEC into nineteenth-century competitiveness. Indeed, as our experience in dealing with Europe on matters such as terrorism or Libya prove, they are much further gone than we down the road that denies the legitimacy of the use of force in international politics, even in self-defense.

The automatic assumption that Russia shorn of its expansionist communist ideology should pick up where the czars left off just prior to the Bolshevik Revolution is therefore a curious one. It assumes that the evolution of human consciousness has stood still in the meantime, and that the Soviets, while picking up currently fashionable ideas in the realm of economics, will return to foreign policy views a century out of date in the rest of Europe. This is certainly not what happened to China after it began its reform process. Chinese competitiveness and expansionism on the world scene have virtually disappeared: Beijing no longer sponsors Maoist insurgencies or tries to cultivate influence in distant African countries as it did in the 1960s. This is not to say that there are not troublesome aspects to contemporary Chinese foreign policy, such as the reckless sale of ballistic missile technology in the Middle East; and the PRC continues to manifest traditional great power behavior in its sponsorship of the Khmer Rouge against Vietnam. But the former is explained by commercial motives and the latter is a vestige of earlier ideologically-based rivalries. The new China far more resembles Gaullist France than pre-World War I Germany.

The real question for the future, however, is the degree to which Soviet elites have assimilated the consciousness of the universal homogenous state that is post-Hitler Europe. From their writings and from my own personal contacts with them, there is no question in my mind that the liberal Soviet intelligentsia rallying around Gorbachev has arrived at the end-of-history view in a remarkably short time, due in no small measure to the contacts they have had since the Brezhnev era with the larger European civilization around them. "New political thinking," the general rubric for their views, describes a world dominated by economic concerns, in which there are no ideological grounds for major conflict between nations, and in which, consequently, the use of military force becomes less legitimate. As Foreign Minister Shevardnadze put it in mid-1988:

> The struggle between two opposing systems is no longer a determining tendency of the present-day era. At the modern stage, the ability to build up material wealth at an accelerated rate on the basis of front-ranking science and high-level techniques and technology, and to distribute it fairly, and through joint efforts to restore and protect the resources necessary for mankind's survival acquires decisive importance.[18]

The post-historical consciousness represented by "new thinking" is only one possible future for the Soviet Union, however. There has always been a very strong current of great Russian chauvinism in the Soviet Union, which has found freer expression since the advent of *glasnost*. It may be possible to return to traditional Marxism-Leninism for a while as a simple rallying point for those who want to restore the authority that Gorbachev has dissipated. But as in Poland, Marxism-Leninism is dead as a mobilizing ideology: under its banner people cannot be made to work harder, and its adherents have lost confidence in themselves. Unlike the propagators of traditional Marxism-Leninism, however, ultranationalists in the USSR believe in their Slavophile cause passionately, and one gets the sense that the fascist alternative is not one that has played itself out entirely there.

The Soviet Union, then, is at a fork in the road: it can start down the path that was staked out by Western Europe forty-five years ago, a path that most of Asia has followed, or it can realize its own uniqueness and remain stuck in history. The choice it makes will be highly important for us, given the Soviet Union's size and military strength, for that power will continue to preoccupy us and slow our realization that we have already emerged on the other side of history.

V

The passing of Marxism-Leninism first from China and then from the Soviet Union will mean its death as a living ideology of world historical significance.

For while there may be some isolated true believers left in places like Managua, Pyongyang, or Cambridge, Massachusetts, the fact that there is not a single large state in which it is a going concern undermines completely its pretensions to being in the vanguard of human history. And the death of this ideology means the growing "Common Marketization" of international relations, and the diminution of the likelihood of large-scale conflict between states.

This does not by any means imply the end of international conflict *per se*. For the world at that point would be divided between a part that was historical and a part that was post-historical. Conflict between states still in history, and between those states and those at the end of history, would still be possible. There would still be a high and perhaps rising level of ethnic and nationalist violence, since those are impulses incompletely played out, even in parts of the post-historical world. Palestinians and Kurds, Sikhs and Tamils, Irish Catholics and Walloons, Armenians and Azeris, will continue to have their unresolved grievances. This implies that terrorism and wars of national liberation will continue to be an important item on the international agenda. But large-scale conflict must involve large states still caught in the grip of history, and they are what appear to be passing from the scene.

The end of history will be a very sad time. The struggle for recognition, the willingness to risk one's life for a purely abstract goal, the worldwide ideological struggle that called forth daring, courage, imagination, and idealism, will be replaced by economic calculation, the endless solving of technical problems, environmental concerns, and the satisfaction of sophisticated consumer demands. In the post-historical period there will be neither art nor philosophy, just the perpetual caretaking of the museum of human history. I can feel in myself, and see in others around me, a powerful nostalgia for the time when history existed. Such nostalgia, in fact, will continue to fuel competition and conflict even in the post-historical world for some time to come. Even though I recognize its inevitability, I have the most ambivalent feelings for the civilization that has been created in Europe since 1945, with its North Atlantic and Asian offshoots. Perhaps this very prospect of centuries of boredom at the end of history will serve to get history started once again.

NOTES

1. Kojève's best-known work is his *Introduction à la lecture de Hegel* (Paris: Editions Gallimard, 1947), which is a transcript of the *Ecole Practique* lectures from the 1930s. This book is available in English entitled *Introduction to the Reading of Hegel* arranged by Raymond Queneau, edited by Allan Bloom, and translated by James Nichols (New York: Basic Books, 1969).

2. In this respect Kojève stands in sharp contrast to contemporary German interpreters of Hegel like Herbert Marcuse who, being more sympathetic to Marx, regarded Hegel ultimately as an historically bound and incomplete philosopher.

3. Kojève alternatively identified the end of history with the postwar "American way of life," toward which he thought the Soviet Union was moving as well.

4. This notion was expressed in the famous aphorism from the preface to the *Philosophy of History* to the effect that "everything that is rational is real, and everything that is real is rational."

5. Indeed, for Hegel the very dichotomy between the ideal and material worlds was itself only an apparent one that was ultimately overcome by the self-conscious subject; in his system, the material world is itself only an aspect of mind.

6. In fact, modern economists, recognizing that man does not always behave as a *profit*-maximizer, posit a "utility" function, utility being either income or some other good that can be maximized: leisure, sexual satisfaction, or the pleasure of philosophizing. That profit must be replaced with a value like utility indicates the cogency of the idealist perspective.

7. One need look no further than the recent performance of Vietnamese immigrants in the U.S. school system when compared to their black or Hispanic classmates to realize that culture and consciousness are absolutely crucial to explain not only economic behavior but virtually every other important aspect of life as well.

8. I understand that a full explanation of the origins of the reform movements in China and Russia is a good deal more complicated than this simple formula would suggest. The Soviet reform, for example, was motivated in good measure by Moscow's sense of *insecurity* in the technological-military realm. Nonetheless, neither country on the eve of its reforms was in such a state of *material* crisis that one could have predicted the surprising reform paths ultimately taken.

9. It is still not clear whether the Soviet peoples are as "Protestant" as Gorbachev and will follow him down that path.

10. The internal politics of the Byzantine Empire at the time of Justinian revolved around a conflict between the so-called monophysites and monothelites, who believed that the unity of the Holy Trinity was alternatively one of nature or of will. This conflict corresponded to some extent to one between proponents of different racing teams in the Hippodrome in Byzantium and led to a not insignificant level of political violence. Modern historians would tend to seek the roots of such conflicts in antagonisms between social classes or some other modern economic category, being unwilling to believe that men would kill each other over the nature of the Trinity.

11. I am not using the term "fascism" here in its most precise sense, fully aware of the frequent misuse of this term to denounce anyone to the right of the user. "Fascism" here denotes any organized ultra-nationalist movement with universalistic pretensions— not universalistic with regard to its nationalism, of course, since the latter is exclusive by definition, but with regard to the movement's belief in its right to rule other people. Hence Imperial Japan would qualify as fascist while former strongman Stoessner's Paraguay or Pinochet's Chile would not. Obviously fascist ideologies cannot be universalistic in the sense of Marxism or liberalism, but the structure of the doctrine can be transferred from country to country.

12. I use the example of Japan with some caution, since Kojève late in his life came to conclude that Japan, with its culture based on purely formal arts, proved that the universal homogenous state was not victorious and that history had perhaps not ended. See the long note at the end of the second edition of *Introduction à la Lecture de Hegel,* 462–3.

13. This is not true in Poland and Hungary, however, whose Communist parties have taken moves toward true power-sharing and pluralism.

14. This is particularly true of the leading Soviet conservative, former Second Secretary Yegor Ligachev, who has publicly recognized many of the deep defects of the Brezhnev period.

15. I am thinking particularly of Rousseau and the Western philosophical tradition that flows from him that was highly critical of Lockean or Hobbesian liberalism, though one could criticize liberalism from the standpoint of classical political philosophy as well.

16. See his article, "Beyond the Cold War," *New Republic,* December 19, 1988.

17. It took European colonial powers like France several years after the war to admit

the illegitimacy of their empires, but decolonialization was an inevitable consequence of the Allied victory which had been based on the promise of a restoration of democratic freedoms.

18. *Vestnik Ministerstva Inostrannikh Del SSSR* no. 15 (August 1988), 27–46. "New thinking" does of course serve a propagandistic purpose in persuading Western audiences of Soviet good intentions. But the fact that it is good propaganda does not mean that its formulators do not take many of its ideas seriously.

The Rise of Illiberal Democracy

Fareed Zakaria

The Next Wave

The American diplomat Richard Holbrooke pondered a problem on the eve of the September 1996 elections in Bosnia, which were meant to restore civic life to that ravaged country. "Suppose the election was declared free and fair," he said, and those elected are "racists, fascists, separatists, who are publicly opposed to [peace and reintegration]. That is the dilemma." Indeed it is, not just in the former Yugoslavia, but increasingly around the world. Democratically elected regimes, often ones that have been reelected or reaffirmed through referenda, are routinely ignoring constitutional limits on their power and depriving their citizens of basic rights and freedoms. From Peru to the Palestinian Authority, from Sierra Leone to Slovakia, from Pakistan to the Philippines, we see the rise of a disturbing phenomenon in international life—illiberal democracy.

It has been difficult to recognize this problem because for almost a century in the West, democracy has meant *liberal* democracy—a political system marked not only by free and fair elections, but also by the rule of law, a separation of powers, and the protection of basic liberties of speech, assembly, religion, and property. In fact, this latter bundle of freedoms—what might be termed constitutional liberalism—is theoretically different and historically distinct from democracy. As the political scientist Philippe Schmitter has pointed out, "Liberalism, either as a conception of political liberty, or as a doctrine about economic policy, may have coincided with the rise of democracy. But it has never been immutably or unambiguously linked to its practice." Today the two strands of liberal democracy, interwoven in the Western political fabric, are coming apart in the rest of the world. Democracy is flourishing; constitutional liberalism is not.

Today, 118 of the world's 193 countries are democratic, encompassing a majority of its people (54.8 percent, to be exact), a vast increase from even a decade ago. In this season of victory, one might have expected Western statesmen and intellectuals to go one further than E. M. Forster and give a rousing three cheers for democracy. Instead there is a growing unease at the rapid spread of multiparty elections across south-central Europe, Asia, Africa, and Latin America, perhaps because of what happens *after* the elections. Popular leaders like Russia's Boris Yeltsin and Argentina's Carlos Menem bypass their parliaments and rule by presidential decree, eroding basic constitutional practices. The Iranian parliament—elected more freely than most in the Middle East—imposes harsh restrictions on speech, assembly, and even dress, diminishing that country's already meager supply of liberty. Ethiopia's elected government turns its security forces on journalists and political opponents, doing permanent damage to human rights (as well as human beings).

Naturally there is a spectrum of illiberal democracy, ranging from modest offenders like Argentina to near-tyrannies like Kazakstan and Belarus, with countries like Romania and Bangladesh in between. Along much of the spectrum, elections are rarely as free and fair as in the West today, but they do reflect the reality of popular participation in politics and support for those elected. And the examples are not isolated or atypical. Freedom House's 1996–97 survey, *Freedom in the World*, has separate rankings for political liberties and civil liberties, which correspond roughly with democracy and constitutional liberalism, respectively. Of the countries that lie between confirmed dictatorship and consolidated democracy, 50 percent do better on political liberties than on civil ones. In other words, half of the "democratizing" countries in the world today are illiberal democracies.[1]

Illiberal democracy is a growth industry. Seven years ago only 22 percent of democratizing countries could have been so categorized; five years ago that figure had risen to 35 percent.[2] And to date few illiberal democracies have matured into liberal democracies; if anything, they are moving toward heightened illiberalism. Far from being a temporary or transitional stage, it appears that many countries are settling into a form of government that mixes a substantial degree of democracy with a substantial degree of illiberalism. Just as nations across the world have become comfortable with many variations of capitalism, they could well adopt and sustain varied forms of democracy. Western liberal democracy might prove to be not the final destination on the democratic road, but just one of many possible exits.

Democracy and Liberty

From the time of Herodotus democracy has meant, first and foremost, the rule of the people. This view of democracy as a process of selecting governments, articulated by scholars ranging from Alexis de Tocqueville to Joseph Schumpeter to Robert Dahl, is now widely used by social scientists. In *The Third Wave*, Samuel P. Huntington explains why:

> Elections, open, free and fair, are the essence of democracy, the inescapable sine qua non. Governments produced by elections may be inefficient, corrupt, shortsighted, irresponsible, dominated by special interests, and incapable of adopting policies demanded by the public good. These qualities make such governments undesirable but they do not make them undemocratic. Democracy is one public virtue, not the only one, and the relation of democracy to other public virtues and vices can only be understood if democracy is clearly distinguished from the other characteristics of political systems.

This definition also accords with the commonsense view of the term. If a country holds competitive, multiparty elections, we call it democratic. When public participation in politics is increased, for example through the enfranchisement of women, it is seen as more democratic. Of course elections must be open and fair, and this requires some protections for freedom of speech and assembly. But to go beyond this minimalist definition and label a country democratic only if it guarantees a comprehensive catalog of social, political, economic, and religious rights turns the word democracy into a badge of honor rather than a descriptive category. After all, Sweden has an economic system that many argue curtails individual property rights, France until recently had a state monopoly on television, and England has an established religion. But they are all clearly and identifiably democracies. To have democracy mean, subjectively, "a good government" renders it analytically useless.

Constitutional liberalism, on the other hand, is not about the procedures for selecting government, but rather government's goals. It refers to the tradition, deep in Western history, that seeks to protect an individual's autonomy and dignity against coercion, whatever the source—state, church, or society. The term marries two closely connected ideas. It is *liberal* because it draws on the philosophical strain, beginning with the Greeks, that emphasizes individual liberty.[3] It is *constitutional* because it rests on the tradition, beginning with the Romans, of the rule of law. Constitutional liberalism developed in Western Europe and the United States as a defense of the individual's right to life and property, and freedom of religion and speech. To secure these rights, it emphasized checks on the power of each branch of government, equality under the law, impartial courts and tribunals, and separation of church and state. Its canonical figures include the poet John Milton, the jurist William Blackstone, statesmen such as Thomas Jefferson and James Madison, and philosophers such as Thomas Hobbes, John Locke, Adam Smith, Baron de Montesquieu, John Stuart Mill, and Isaiah Berlin. In almost all of its variants, constitutional liberalism argues that human beings have certain natural (or "inalienable") rights and that governments must accept a basic law, limiting its own powers, that secures them. Thus in 1215 at Runnymede, England's barons forced the king to abide by the settled and customary law of the land. In the

American colonies these laws were made explicit, and in 1638 the town of Hartford adopted the first written constitution in modern history. In the 1970s, Western nations codified standards of behavior for regimes across the globe. The Magna Carta, the Fundamental Orders of Connecticut, the American Constitution, and the Helsinki Final Act are all expressions of constitutional liberalism.

The Road to Liberal Democracy

Since 1945 Western governments have, for the most part, embodied both democracy and constitutional liberalism. Thus it is difficult to imagine the two apart, in the form of either illiberal democracy or liberal autocracy. In fact both have existed in the past and persist in the present. Until the twentieth century, most countries in Western Europe were liberal autocracies or, at best, semi-democracies. The franchise was tightly restricted, and elected legislatures had little power. In 1830 Great Britain, in some ways the most democratic European nation, allowed barely 2 percent of its population to vote for one house of Parliament; that figure rose to 7 percent after 1867 and reached around 40 percent in the 1880s. Only in the late 1940s did most Western countries become full-fledged democracies, with universal adult suffrage. But one hundred years earlier, by the late 1840s, most of them had adopted important aspects of constitutional liberalism— the rule of law, private property rights, and increasingly, separated powers and free speech and assembly. For much of modern history, what characterized governments in Europe and North America, and differentiated them from those around the world, was not democracy but constitutional liberalism. The "Western model" is best symbolized not by the mass plebiscite but the impartial judge.

The recent history of East Asia follows the Western itinerary. After brief flirtations with democracy after World War II, most East Asian regimes turned authoritarian. Over time they moved from autocracy to liberalizing autocracy, and, in some cases, toward liberalizing semi-democracy.[4] Most of the regimes in East Asia remain only semi-democratic, with patriarchs or one-party systems that make their elections ratifications of power rather than genuine contests. But these regimes have accorded their citizens a widening sphere of economic, civil, religious, and limited political rights. As in the West, liberalization in East Asia has included economic liberalization, which is crucial in promoting both growth and liberal democracy. Historically, the factors most closely associated with full-fledged liberal democracies are capitalism, a bourgeoisie, and a high per capita GNP. Today's East Asian governments are a mix of democracy, liberalism, capitalism, oligarchy, and corruption—much like Western governments circa 1900.

Constitutional liberalism has led to democracy, but democracy does not seem to bring constitutional liberalism. In contrast to the Western and East Asian paths, during the last two decades in Latin America, Africa, and parts of Asia, dictatorships with little background in constitutional liberalism have given way to democracy. The results are not encouraging. In the western hemisphere, with elections having been held in every country except Cuba, a 1993 study by the scholar

Larry Diamond determined that 10 of the 22 principal Latin American countries "have levels of human rights abuse that are incompatible with the consolidation of [liberal] democracy."[5] In Africa, democratization has been extraordinarily rapid. Within six months in 1990 much of Francophone Africa lifted its ban on multiparty politics. Yet although elections have been held in most of the 45 sub-Saharan states since 1991 (18 in 1996 alone), there have been setbacks for freedom in many countries. One of Africa's most careful observers, Michael Chege, surveyed the wave of democratization and drew the lesson that the continent had "overemphasized multiparty elections . . . and correspondingly neglected the basic tenets of liberal governance." In Central Asia, elections, even when reasonably free, as in Kyrgyzstan and Kazakstan, have resulted in strong executives, weak legislatures and judiciaries, and few civil and economic liberties. In the Islamic world, from the Palestinian Authority to Iran to Pakistan, democratization has led to an increasing role for theocratic politics, eroding long-standing traditions of secularism and tolerance. In many parts of that world, such as Tunisia, Morocco, Egypt, and some of the Gulf States, were elections to be held tomorrow, the resulting regimes would almost certainly be more illiberal than the ones now in place.

Many of the countries of Central Europe, on the other hand, have moved successfully from communism to liberal democracy, having gone through the same phase of liberalization without democracy as other European countries did during the nineteenth century. Indeed, the Austro-Hungarian empire, to which most belonged, was a classic liberal autocracy. Even outside Europe, the political scientist Myron Weiner detected a striking connection between a constitutional past and a liberal democratic present. He pointed out that, as of 1983, "every single country in the Third World that emerged from colonial rule since the Second World War with a population of at least one million (and almost all the smaller colonies as well) with a continuous democratic experience is a former British colony."[6] British rule meant not democracy—colonialism is by definition undemocratic—but constitutional liberalism. Britain's legacy of law and administration has proved more beneficial than France's policy of enfranchising some of its colonial populations.

While liberal autocracies may have existed in the past, can one imagine them today? Until recently, a small but powerful example flourished off the Asian mainland—Hong Kong. For 156 years, until July 1, 1997, Hong Kong was ruled by the British Crown through an appointed governor general. Until 1991 it had never held a meaningful election, but its government epitomized constitutional liberalism, protecting its citizens' basic rights and administering a fair court system and bureaucracy. A September 8, 1997, editorial on the island's future in *The Washington Post* was titled ominously, "Undoing Hong Kong's Democracy." Actually, Hong Kong has precious little democracy to undo; what it has is a framework of rights and laws. Small islands may not hold much practical significance in today's world, but they do help one weigh the relative value of democracy and constitutional liberalism. Consider, for example, the question of where you would rather live, Haiti, an illiberal democracy, or Antigua, a liberal semi-democracy. Your choice would probably relate not to the weather, which is pleasant in both, but to the political climate, which is not.

Absolute Sovereignty

John Stuart Mill opened his classic *On Liberty* by noting that as countries became democratic, people tended to believe that "too much importance had been attached to the limitation of power itself. That . . . was a response against rulers whose interests were opposed to those of the people." Once the people were themselves in charge, caution was unnecessary. "The nation did not need to be protected against its own will." As if confirming Mill's fears, consider the words of Alexandr Lukashenko after being elected president of Belarus with an overwhelming majority in a free election in 1994, when asked about limiting his powers: "There will be no dictatorship. I am of the people, and I am going to be for the people."

The tension between constitutional liberalism and democracy centers on the scope of governmental authority. Constitutional liberalism is about the limitation of power, democracy about its accumulation and use. For this reason, many eighteenth- and nineteenth-century liberals saw in democracy a force that could undermine liberty. James Madison explained in *The Federalist* that "the danger of oppression" in a democracy came from "the majority of the community." Tocqueville warned of the "tyranny of the majority," writing, "The very essence of democratic government consists in the absolute sovereignty of the majority."

The tendency for a democratic government to believe it has absolute sovereignty (that is, power) can result in the centralization of authority, often by extra-constitutional means and with grim results. Over the last decade, elected governments claiming to represent the people have steadily encroached on the powers and rights of other elements in society, a usurpation that is both horizontal (from other branches of the national government) and vertical (from regional and local authorities as well as private businesses and other nongovernmental groups). Lukashenko and Peru's Alberto Fujimori are only the worst examples of this practice. (While Fujimori's actions—disbanding the legislature and suspending the constitution, among others—make it difficult to call his regime democratic, it is worth noting that he won two elections and was extremely popular until recently.) Even a bona fide reformer like Carlos Menem has passed close to 300 presidential decrees in his eight years in office, about three times as many as all previous Argentinean presidents put together, going back to 1853. Kyrgyzstan's Askar Akayev, elected with 60 percent of the vote, proposed enhancing his powers in a referendum that passed easily in 1996. His new powers include appointing all top officials except the prime minister, although he can dissolve parliament if it turns down three of his nominees for the latter post.

Horizontal usurpation, usually by presidents, is more obvious, but vertical usurpation is more common. Over the last three decades, the Indian government has routinely disbanded state legislatures on flimsy grounds, placing regions under New Delhi's direct rule. In a less dramatic but typical move, the elected government of the Central African Republic recently ended the long-standing independence of its university system, making it part of the central state apparatus.

Usurpation is particularly widespread in Latin America and the states of the former Soviet Union, perhaps because both regions mostly have presidencies. These systems tend to produce strong leaders who believe that they speak for the people—even when they have been elected by no more than a plurality. (As Juan Linz points out, Salvador Allende was elected to the Chilean presidency in 1970 with only 36 percent of the vote. In similar circumstances, a prime minister would have had to share power in a coalition government.) Presidents appoint cabinets of cronies, rather than senior party figures, maintaining few internal checks on their power. And when their views conflict with those of the legislature, or even the courts, presidents tend to "go to the nation," bypassing the dreary tasks of bargaining and coalition-building. While scholars debate the merits of presidential versus parliamentary forms of government, usurpation can occur under either, absent well-developed alternate centers of power such as strong legislatures, courts, political parties, regional governments, and independent universities and media. Latin America actually combines presidential systems with proportional representation, producing populist leaders and multiple parties—an unstable combination.

Many Western governments and scholars have encouraged the creation of strong and centralized states in the Third World. Leaders in these countries have argued that they need the authority to break down feudalism, split entrenched coalitions, override vested interests, and bring order to chaotic societies. But this confuses the need for a legitimate government with that for a powerful one. Governments that are seen as legitimate can usually maintain order and pursue tough policies, albeit slowly, by building coalitions. After all, few claim that governments in developing countries should not have adequate police powers; the trouble comes from all the other political, social, and economic powers that they accumulate. In crises like civil wars, constitutional governments might not be able to rule effectively, but the alternative—states with vast security apparatuses that suspend constitutional rights—has usually produced neither order nor good government. More often, such states have become predatory, maintaining some order but also arresting opponents, muzzling dissent, nationalizing industries, and confiscating property. While anarchy has its dangers, the greatest threats to human liberty and happiness in this century have been caused not by disorder but by brutally strong, centralized states, like Nazi Germany, Soviet Russia, and Maoist China. The Third World is littered with the bloody handiwork of strong states.

Historically, unchecked centralization has been the enemy of liberal democracy. As political participation increased in Europe over the nineteenth century, it was accommodated smoothly in countries such as England and Sweden, where medieval assemblies, local governments, and regional councils had remained strong. Countries like France and Prussia, on the other hand, where the monarchy had effectively centralized power (both horizontally and vertically), often ended up illiberal and undemocratic. It is not a coincidence that in twentieth-century

Spain, the beachhead of liberalism lay in Catalonia, for centuries a doggedly independent and autonomous region. In America, the presence of a rich variety of institutions—state, local, and private—made it much easier to accommodate the rapid and large extensions in suffrage that took place in the early nineteenth century. Arthur Schlesinger Sr. has documented how, during America's first 50 years, virtually every state, interest group and faction tried to weaken and even break up the federal government.[7] More recently, India's semi-liberal democracy has survived because of, not despite, its strong regions and varied languages, cultures, and even castes. The point is logical, even tautological: pluralism in the past helps ensure political pluralism in the present.

Fifty years ago, politicians in the developing world wanted extraordinary powers to implement then-fashionable economic doctrines, like nationalization of industries. Today their successors want similar powers to privatize those very industries. Menem's justification for his methods is that they are desperately needed to enact tough economic reforms. Similar arguments are made by Abdalá Bucarem of Ecuador and by Fujimori. Lending institutions, such as the International Monetary Fund and the World Bank, have been sympathetic to these pleas, and the bond market has been positively exuberant. But except in emergencies like war, illiberal means are in the long run incompatible with liberal ends. Constitutional government is in fact the key to a successful economic reform policy. The experience of East Asia and Central Europe suggests that when regimes—whether authoritarian, as in East Asia, or liberal democratic, as in Poland, Hungary, and the Czech Republic—protect individual rights, including those of property and contract, and create a framework of law and administration, capitalism and growth will follow. In a recent speech at the Woodrow Wilson International Center in Washington, explaining what it takes for capitalism to flourish, Federal Reserve chairman Alan Greenspan concluded that, "The guiding mechanism of a free market economy . . . is a bill of rights, enforced by an impartial judiciary."

Finally, and perhaps more important, power accumulated to do good can be used subsequently to do ill. When Fujimori disbanded parliament, his approval ratings shot up to their highest ever. But recent opinion polls suggest that most of those who once approved of his actions now wish he were more constrained. In 1993 Boris Yeltsin famously (and literally) attacked the Russian parliament, prompted by parliament's own unconstitutional acts. He then suspended the constitutional court, dismantled the system of local governments, and fired several provincial governors. From the war in Chechnya to his economic programs, Yeltsin has displayed a routine lack of concern for constitutional procedures and limits. He may well be a liberal democrat at heart, but Yeltsin's actions have created a Russian super-presidency. We can only hope his successor will not abuse it.

For centuries Western intellectuals have had a tendency to view constitutional liberalism as a quaint exercise in rule-making, mere formalism that should take a back seat to battling larger evils in society. The most eloquent counterpoint to this view remains an exchange in Robert Bolt's play *A Man For All Seasons*. The fiery young William Roper, who yearns to battle evil, is exasperated by Sir Thomas More's devotion to the law. More gently defends himself.

More: What would you do? Cut a great road through the law to get after
    the Devil?
Roper: I'd cut every law in England to do that!
More: And when the last law was down, and the Devil turned on you—
    where would you hide Roper, the laws all being flat?

Ethnic Conflict and War

On December 8, 1996, Jack Lang made a dramatic dash to Belgrade. The French
celebrity politician, formerly minister of culture, had been inspired by the student
demonstrations involving tens of thousands against Slobodan Milošević, a man
Lang and many Western intellectuals held responsible for the war in the Balkans.
Lang wanted to lend his moral support to the Yugoslav opposition. The leaders of
the movement received him in their offices—the philosophy department—only
to boot him out, declare him "an enemy of the Serbs," and order him to leave the
country. It turned out that the students opposed Milošević not for starting the war,
but for failing to win it.

Lang's embarrassment highlights two common, and often mistaken, assumptions—that the forces of democracy are the forces of ethnic harmony and of peace.
Neither is necessarily true. Mature liberal democracies can usually accommodate
ethnic divisions without violence or terror and live in peace with other liberal democracies. But without a background in constitutional liberalism, the introduction of democracy in divided societies has actually fomented nationalism, ethnic
conflict, and even war. The spate of elections held immediately after the collapse
of communism were won in the Soviet Union and Yugoslavia by nationalist separatists and resulted in the breakup of those countries. This was not in and of itself
bad, since those countries had been bound together by force. But the rapid se-
cessions, without guarantees, institutions, or political power for the many minorities living within the new countries, have caused spirals of rebellion, repression,
and, in places like Bosnia, Azerbaijan, and Georgia, war.

Elections require that politicians compete for peoples' votes. In societies
without strong traditions of multiethnic groups or assimilation, it is easiest to organize support along racial, ethnic, or religious lines. Once an ethnic group is in
power, it tends to exclude other ethnic groups. Compromise seems impossible;
one can bargain on material issues like housing, hospitals, and handouts, but how
does one split the difference on a national religion? Political competition that is
so divisive can rapidly degenerate into violence. Opposition movements, armed
rebellions, and coups in Africa have often been directed against ethnically based
regimes, many of which came to power through elections. Surveying the breakdown of African and Asian democracies in the 1960s, two scholars concluded that
democracy "is simply not viable in an environment of intense ethnic preferences."
Recent studies, particularly of Africa and Central Asia, have confirmed this pessimism. A distinguished expert on ethnic conflict, Donald Horowitz, concluded,
"In the face of this rather dismal account . . . of the concrete failures of democracy in divided societies . . . one is tempted to throw up one's hands. What is the

point of holding elections if all they do in the end is to substitute a Bemba-dominated regime for a Nyanja regime in Zambia, the two equally narrow, or a southern regime for a northern one in Benin, neither incorporating the other half of the state?"[8]

Over the past decade, one of the most spirited debates among scholars of international relations concerns the "democratic peace"—the assertion that no two modern democracies have gone to war with each other. The debate raises interesting substantive questions (does the American Civil War count? do nuclear weapons better explain the peace?) and even the statistical findings have raised interesting dissents. (As the scholar David Spiro points out, given the small number of both democracies and wars over the last two hundred years, sheer chance might explain the absence of war between democracies. No member of his family has ever won the lottery, yet few offer explanations for this impressive correlation.) But even if the statistics are correct, what explains them? Kant, the original proponent of the democratic peace, contended that in democracies, those who pay for war—that is, the public—make the decisions, so they are understandably cautious. But that claim suggests that democracies are more pacific than other states. Actually they are more warlike, going to war more often and with greater intensity than most states. It is only with other democracies that the peace holds.

When divining the cause behind this correlation, one thing becomes clear: the democratic peace is actually the liberal peace. Writing in the eighteenth century, Kant believed that democracies were tyrannical, and he specifically excluded them from his conception of "republican" governments, which lived in a zone of peace. Republicanism, for Kant, meant a separation of powers, checks and balances, the rule of law, protection of individual rights, and some level of representation in government (though nothing close to universal suffrage). Kant's other explanations for the "perpetual peace" between republics are all closely linked to their constitutional and liberal character: a mutual respect for the rights of each other's citizens, a system of checks and balances assuring that no single leader can drag his country into war, and classical liberal economic policies—most importantly, free trade—which create an interdependence that makes war costly and cooperation useful. Michael Doyle, the leading scholar on the subject, confirms in his 1997 book *Ways of War and Peace* that without constitutional liberalism, democracy itself has no peace-inducing qualities:

> Kant distrusted unfettered, democratic majoritarianism, and his argument offers no support for a claim that all participatory polities—democracies—should be peaceful, either in general or between fellow democracies. Many participatory polities have been non-liberal. For two thousand years before the modern age, popular rule was widely associated with aggressiveness (by Thucydides) or imperial success (by Machiavelli) . . . The decisive preference of [the] median voter might well include "ethnic cleansing" against other democratic polities.

The distinction between liberal and illiberal democracies sheds light on another striking statistical correlation. Political scientists Jack Snyder and Edward

Mansfield contend, using an impressive data set, that over the last 200 years democratizing states went to war significantly more often than either stable autocracies or liberal democracies. In countries not grounded in constitutional liberalism,
the rise of democracy often brings with it hyper-nationalism and war-mongering.
When the political system is opened up, diverse groups with incompatible interests gain access to power and press their demands. Political and military leaders,
who are often embattled remnants of the old authoritarian order, realize that to
succeed they must rally the masses behind a national cause. The result is invariably aggressive rhetoric and policies, which often drag countries into confrontation and war. Noteworthy examples range from Napoleon III's France, Wilhelmine Germany, and Taisho Japan to those in today's newspapers, like Armenia and
Azerbaijan and Milošević's Serbia. The democratic peace, it turns out, has little to
do with democracy.

The American Path

An American scholar recently traveled to Kazakstan on a U.S. government-
sponsored mission to help the new parliament draft its electoral laws. His counterpart, a senior member of the Kazak parliament, brushed aside the many options
the American expert was outlining, saying emphatically, "We want our parliament
to be just like your Congress." The American was horrified, recalling, "I tried
to say something other than the three words that had immediately come screaming into my mind: 'No you don't!'" This view is not unusual. Americans in the
democracy business tend to see their own system as an unwieldy contraption that
no other country should put up with. In fact, the adoption of some aspects of the
American constitutional framework could ameliorate many of the problems associated with illiberal democracy. The philosophy behind the U.S. Constitution,
a fear of accumulated power, is as relevant today as it was in 1789. Kazakstan, as
it happens, would be particularly well-served by a strong parliament—like the
American Congress—to check the insatiable appetite of its president.

It is odd that the United States is so often the advocate of elections and ple-
biscitary democracy abroad. What is distinctive about the American system is not
how democratic it is but rather how undemocratic it is, placing as it does multiple constraints on electoral majorities. Of its three branches of government, one
—arguably paramount—is headed by nine unelected men and women with life
tenure. Its Senate is the most unrepresentative upper house in the world, with the
lone exception of the House of Lords, which is powerless. (Every state sends two
senators to Washington regardless of its population—California's 30 million
people have as many votes in the Senate as Arizona's 3.7 million—which means
that senators representing about 16 percent of the country can block any proposed
law.) Similarly, in legislatures all over the United States, what is striking is not the
power of majorities but that of minorities. To further check national power, state
and local governments are strong and fiercely battle every federal intrusion onto
their turf. Private businesses and other nongovernmental groups, what Tocqueville called intermediate associations, make up another stratum within society.

The American system is based on an avowedly pessimistic conception of human nature, assuming that people cannot be trusted with power. "If men were angels," Madison famously wrote, "no government would be necessary." The other model for democratic governance in Western history is based on the French Revolution. The French model places its faith in the goodness of human beings. Once the people are the source of power, it should be unlimited so that they can create a just society. (The French revolution, as Lord Acton observed, is not about the limitation of sovereign power but the abrogation of all intermediate powers that get in its way.) Most non-Western countries have embraced the French model—not least because political elites like the prospect of empowering the state, since that means empowering themselves—and most have descended into bouts of chaos, tyranny, or both. This should have come as no surprise. After all, since its revolution France itself has run through two monarchies, two empires, one proto-fascist dictatorship, and five republics.[9]

Of course cultures vary, and different societies will require different frameworks of government. This is not a plea for the wholesale adoption of the American way but rather for a more variegated conception of liberal democracy, one that emphasizes both parts of that phrase. Before new policies can be adopted, there lies an intellectual task of recovering the constitutional liberal tradition, central to the Western experience and to the development of good government throughout the world. Political progress in Western history has been the result of a growing recognition over the centuries that, as the Declaration of Independence puts it, human beings have "certain inalienable rights" and that "it is to secure these rights that governments are instituted." If a democracy does not preserve liberty and law, that it is a democracy is a small consolation.

Liberalizing Foreign Policy

A proper appreciation of constitutional liberalism has a variety of implications for American foreign policy. First, it suggests a certain humility. While it is easy to impose elections on a country, it is more difficult to push constitutional liberalism on a society. The process of genuine liberalization and democratization is gradual and long-term, in which an election is only one step. Without appropriate preparation, it might even be a false step. Recognizing this, governments and nongovernmental organizations are increasingly promoting a wide array of measures designed to bolster constitutional liberalism in developing countries. The National Endowment for Democracy promotes free markets, independent labor movements, and political parties. The U.S. Agency for International Development funds independent judiciaries. In the end, however, elections trump everything. If a country holds elections, Washington and the world will tolerate a great deal from the resulting government, as they have with Yeltsin, Akayev, and Menem. In an age of images and symbols, elections are easy to capture on film. (How do you televise the rule of law?) But there is life after elections, especially for the people who live there.

Conversely, the absence of free and fair elections should be viewed as one flaw, not the definition of tyranny. Elections are an important virtue of governance, but they are not the only virtue. Governments should be judged by yardsticks related to constitutional liberalism as well. Economic, civil, and religious liberties are at the core of human autonomy and dignity. If a government with limited democracy steadily expands these freedoms, it should not be branded a dictatorship. Despite the limited political choice they offer, countries like Singapore, Malaysia, and Thailand provide a better environment for the life, liberty, and happiness of their citizens than do either dictatorships like Iraq and Libya or illiberal democracies like Slovakia or Ghana. And the pressures of global capitalism can push the process of liberalization forward. Markets and morals can work together. Even China, which remains a deeply repressive regime, has given its citizens more autonomy and economic liberty than they have had in generations. Much more needs to change before China can even be called a liberalizing autocracy, but that should not mask the fact that much has changed.

Finally, we need to revive constitutionalism. One effect of the overemphasis on pure democracy is that little effort is given to creating imaginative constitutions for transitional countries. Constitutionalism, as it was understood by its greatest eighteenth-century exponents, such as Montesquieu and Madison, is a complicated system of checks and balances designed to prevent the accumulation of power and the abuse of office. This is done not by simply writing up a list of rights but by constructing a system in which government will not violate those rights. Various groups must be included and empowered because, as Madison explained, "ambition must be made to counteract ambition." Constitutions were also meant to tame the passions of the public, creating not simply democratic but also deliberative government. Unfortunately, the rich variety of unelected bodies, indirect voting, federal arrangements, and checks and balances that characterized so many of the formal and informal constitutions of Europe are now regarded with suspicion. What could be called the Weimar syndrome—named after interwar Germany's beautifully constructed constitution, which failed to avert fascism—has made people regard constitutions as simply paperwork that cannot make much difference. (As if any political system in Germany would have easily weathered military defeat, social revolution, the Great Depression, and hyperinflation.) Procedures that inhibit direct democracy are seen as inauthentic, muzzling the voice of the people. Today around the world we see variations on the same majoritarian theme. But the trouble with these winner-take-all systems is that, in most democratizing countries, the winner really does take all.

Democracy's Discontents

We live in a democratic age. Through much of human history the danger to an individual's life, liberty and happiness came from the absolutism of monarchies, the dogma of churches, the terror of dictatorships, and the iron grip of totalitarianism. Dictators and a few straggling totalitarian regimes still persist, but increasingly they are anachronisms in a world of global markets, information, and media. There are no longer respectable alternatives to democracy; it is part of the fashionable attire of modernity. Thus the problems of governance in the 21st century will likely be problems *within* democracy. This makes them more difficult to handle, wrapped as they are in the mantle of legitimacy.

Illiberal democracies gain legitimacy, and thus strength, from the fact that they are reasonably democratic. Conversely, the greatest danger that illiberal democracy poses—other than to its own people—is that it will discredit liberal democracy itself, casting a shadow on democratic governance. This would not be unprecedented. Every wave of democracy has been followed by setbacks in which the system was seen as inadequate and new alternatives were sought by ambitious leaders and restless masses. The last such period of disenchantment, in Europe during the interwar years, was seized upon by demagogues, many of whom were initially popular and even elected. Today, in the face of a spreading virus of illiberalism, the most useful role that the international community, and most importantly the United States, can play is—instead of searching for new lands to democratize and new places to hold elections—to consolidate democracy where it has taken root and to encourage the gradual development of constitutional liberalism across the globe. Democracy without constitutional liberalism is not simply inadequate, but dangerous, bringing with it the erosion of liberty, the abuse of power, ethnic divisions, and even war. Eighty years ago, Woodrow Wilson took America into the twentieth century with a challenge, to make the world safe for democracy. As we approach the next century, our task is to make democracy safe for the world.

NOTES

1. Roger Kaplan, ed., *Freedom Around the World, 1997*, New York: Freedom House, 1997, pp. 21–22. The survey rates countries on two 7-point scales, for political rights and civil liberties (lower is better). I have considered all countries with a combined score of between 5 and 10 to be democratizing. The percentage figures are based on Freedom House's numbers, but in the case of individual countries I have not adhered strictly to its ratings. While the *Survey* is an extraordinary feat—comprehensive and intelligent—its methodology conflates certain constitutional rights with democratic procedures, which confuses matters. In addition, I use as examples (though not as part of the data set) countries like Iran, Kazakstan, and Belarus, which even in procedural terms are semi-democracies at best. But they are worth highlighting as interesting problem cases since most of their leaders were elected, reelected, and remain popular.

2. *Freedom in the World: The Annual Survey of Political Rights and Civil Liberties, 1992–1993*, pp. 620–26; *Freedom in the World, 1989–1990*, pp. 312–19.

3. The term "liberal" is used here in its older, European sense, now often called classical liberalism. In America today the word has come to mean something quite different, namely policies upholding the modern welfare state.

4. Indonesia, Singapore, and Malaysia are examples of liberalizing autocracies, while South Korea, Taiwan, and Thailand are liberal semi-democracies. Both groups, however,

are more liberal than they are democratic, which is also true of the region's only liberal democracy, Japan; Papua New Guinea, and to a lesser extent the Philippines, are the only examples of illiberal democracy in East Asia.

5. Larry Diamond, "Democracy in Latin America," in Tom Farer, ed., *Beyond Sovereignty: Collectively Defending Democracy in a World of Sovereign States*, Baltimore: Johns Hopkins University Press, 1996, p. 73.

6. Myron Weiner, "Empirical Democratic Theory," in Myron Weiner and Ergun Ozbudun, eds., *Competitive Elections in Developing Countries*, Durham: Duke University Press, 1987, p. 20. Today there are functioning democracies in the Third World that are not former British colonies, but the majority of the former are the latter.

7. Arthur Schlesinger, Sr., *New Viewpoints in American History*, New York: Macmillan, 1922, pp. 220–40.

8. Alvin Rabushka and Kenneth Shepsle, *Politics in Plural Societies: A Theory of Democratic Instability*, Columbus: Charles E. Merill, pp. 62–92; Donald Horowitz, "Democracy in Divided Societies," in Larry Diamond and Mark F. Plattner, eds., *Nationalism, Ethnic Conflict and Democracy*, Baltimore: The Johns Hopkins University Press, 1994, pp. 35–55.

9. Bernard Lewis, "Why Turkey Is the Only Muslim Democracy," *Middle East Quarterly*, March 1994, pp. 47–48.

Was Democracy Just a Moment?

Robert D. Kaplan

In the fourth century A.D. Christianity's conquest of Europe and the Mediterranean world gave rise to the belief that a peaceful era in world politics was at hand, now that a consensus had formed around an ideology that stressed the sanctity of the individual. But Christianity was, of course, not static. It kept evolving, into rites, sects, and "heresies" that were in turn influenced by the geography and cultures of the places where it took root. Meanwhile, the church founded by Saint Peter became a ritualistic and hierarchical organization guilty of long periods of violence and bigotry. This is to say nothing of the evils perpetrated by the Orthodox churches in the East. Christianity made the world not more peaceful or, in practice, more moral but only more complex. Democracy, which is now overtaking the world as Christianity once did, may do the same.

The collapse of communism from internal stresses says nothing about the long-term viability of Western democracy. Marxism's natural death in Eastern Europe is no guarantee that subtler tyrannies do not await us, here and abroad. History has demonstrated that there is no final triumph of reason, whether it goes by the name of Christianity, the Enlightenment, or, now, democracy. To think that democracy as we know it will triumph—or is even here to stay—is itself a form of determinism, driven by our own ethnocentricity. Indeed, those who quote Alexis de Tocqueville in support of democracy's inevitability should pay heed to his ob-

Article originally appeared in *The Atlantic Monthly* (December 1997). Reprinted by permission of the author.

servation that Americans, because of their (comparative) equality, exaggerate "the scope of human perfectibility." Despotism, Tocqueville went on, "is more particularly to be feared in democratic ages," because it thrives on the obsession with self and one's own security which equality fosters.

I submit that the democracy we are encouraging in many poor parts of the world is an integral part of a transformation toward new forms of authoritarianism; that democracy in the United States is at greater risk than ever before, and from obscure sources; and that many future regimes, ours especially, could resemble the oligarchies of ancient Athens and Sparta more than they do the current government in Washington. History teaches that it is exactly at such prosperous times as these that we need to maintain a sense of the tragic, however unnecessary it may seem. The Greek historian Polybius, of the second century B.C., interpreted what we consider the Golden Age of Athens as the beginning of its decline. To Thucydides, the very security and satisfactory life that the Athenians enjoyed under Pericles blinded them to the bleak forces of human nature that were gradually to be their undoing in the Peloponnesian War.

My pessimism is, I hope, a foundation for prudence. America's Founders were often dismal about the human condition. James Madison: "Had every Athenian citizen been a Socrates, every Athenian assembly would still have been a mob." Thomas Paine: "Society is produced by our wants and government by our wickedness." It was the "crude" and "reactionary" philosophy of Thomas Hobbes, which placed security ahead of liberty in a system of enlightened despotism, from which the Founders drew philosophical sustenance. Paul A. Rahe, a professor of history at the University of Tulsa, shows in his superb three-volume *Republics Ancient and Modern* (1992) how the Founders partly rejected the ancient republics, which were based on virtue, for a utilitarian regime that channeled man's selfish, materialistic instincts toward benign ends. Man, Benjamin Franklin said in an apparent defense of Hobbesian determinism, is "a tool-making animal."

Democracies Are Value-Neutral

Hitler and Mussolini each came to power through democracy. Democracies do not always make societies more civil—but they do always mercilessly expose the health of the societies in which they operate.

In April of 1985 I found myself in the middle of a Sudanese crowd that had just helped to overthrow a military regime and replace it with a new government, which the following year held free and fair elections. Sudan's newly elected democracy led immediately to anarchy, which in turn led to the most brutal tyranny in Sudan's postcolonial history: a military regime that broadened the scope of executions, persecuted women, starved non-Muslims to death, sold kidnapped non-Muslim children back to their parents for $200, and made Khartoum the terrorism capital of the Arab world, replacing Beirut. In Sudan only 27 percent of the population (and only 12 percent of the women) could read. If a society is not in reasonable health, democracy can be not only risky but disastrous: during the last phases of the post–First World War German and Italian democracies, for example, the unemployment and inflation figures for Germany and the amount of civil unrest in Italy were just as abysmal as Sudan's literacy rates.

As an unemployed Tunisian student once told me, "In Tunisia we have a twenty-five percent unemployment rate. If you hold elections in such circumstances, the result will be a fundamentalist government and violence like in Algeria. First create an economy, then worry about elections." There are many differences between Tunisia and its neighbor Algeria, including the fact that Tunisia has been peaceful without democracy and Algeria erupted in violence in 1992 after its first election went awry and the military canceled the second. In Kurdistan and Afghanistan, two fragile tribal societies in which the United States encouraged versions of democracy in the 1990s, the security vacuums that followed the failed attempts at institutionalizing pluralism were filled by Saddam Hussein for a time in Kurdistan and by Islamic tyranny in much of Afghanistan. In Bosnia democracy legitimized the worst war crimes in Europe since the Nazi era. In sub-Saharan Africa democracy has weakened institutions and services in some states, and elections have been manipulated to restore dictatorship in others. In Sierra Leone and Congo-Brazzaville elections have led to chaos. In Mali, which Africa-watchers have christened a democratic success story, recent elections were boycotted by the opposition and were marred by killings and riots. Voter turnout was less than 20 percent. Even in Latin America, the Third World's most successful venue for democracy, the record is murky. Venezuela has enjoyed elected civilian governments since 1959, whereas for most of the 1970s and 1980s Chile was effectively under military rule. But Venezuela is a society in turmoil, with periodic coup attempts, rampant crime, and an elite that invests most of its savings outside the country; as a credit risk Venezuela ranks behind only Russia and Mexico. Chile has become a stable middle-class society whose economic growth rate compares to those of the Pacific Rim. Democratic Colombia is a pageant of bloodletting, and many members of the middle class are attempting to leave the country. Then there is Peru, where, all the faults of the present regime notwithstanding, a measure of stability has been achieved by a retreat from democracy into quasi-authoritarianism.

Throughout Latin America there is anxiety that unless the middle classes are enlarged and institutions modernized, the wave of democratization will not be consolidated. Even in an authentically democratic nation like Argentina, institutions are weak and both corruption and unemployment are high. President Carlos Menem's second term has raised questions about democracy's sustainability— questions that the success of his first term seemed to have laid to rest. In Brazil and other countries democracy faces a backlash from millions of badly educated and newly urbanized dwellers in teeming slums, who see few palpable benefits to Western parliamentary systems. Their discontent is a reason for the multifold increases in crime in many Latin American cities over the past decade.

Because both a middle class and civil institutions are required for successful democracy, democratic Russia, which inherited neither from the Soviet regime, remains violent, unstable, and miserably poor despite its 99 percent literacy rate.

Under its authoritarian system China has dramatically improved the quality of life for hundreds of millions of its people. My point, hard as it may be for Americans to accept, is that Russia may be failing in part because it is a democracy and China may be succeeding in part because it is not. Having traveled through much of western China, where Muslim Turkic Uighurs (who despise the Chinese) often predominate, I find it hard to imagine a truly democratic China without at least a partial breakup of the country. Such a breakup would lead to chaos in western China, because the Uighurs are poorer and less educated than most Chinese and have a terrible historical record of governing themselves. Had the student demonstrations in 1989 in Tiananmen Square led to democracy, would the astoundingly high economic growth rates of the 1990s still obtain? I am not certain, because democracy in China would have ignited turmoil not just in the Muslim west of the country but elsewhere, too; order would have decreased but corruption would not have. The social and economic breakdowns under democratic rule in Albania and Bulgaria, where the tradition of pre-communist bourgeois life is weak or non-existent (as in China), contrasted with more-successful democratic venues like Hungary and the Czech Republic, which have had well-established bourgeoisie, constitute further proof that our belief in democracy regardless of local conditions amounts to cultural hubris.

Look at Haiti, a small country only ninety minutes by air from Miami, where 22,000 American soldiers were dispatched in 1994 to restore "democracy." Five percent of eligible Haitian voters participated in an election last April, chronic instability continues, and famine threatens. Those who think that America can establish democracy the world over should heed the words of the late American theologian and political philosopher Reinhold Niebuhr:

> The same strength which has extended our power beyond a continent has also . . . brought us into a vast web of history in which other wills, running in oblique or contrasting directions to our own, inevitably hinder or contradict what we most fervently desire. We cannot simply have our way, not even when we believe our way to have the "happiness of mankind" as its promise.

The lesson to draw is not that dictatorship is good and democracy bad but that democracy emerges successfully only as a capstone to other social and economic achievements. In his "Author's Introduction" to *Democracy in America,* Tocqueville showed how democracy evolved in the West not through the kind of moral fiat we are trying to impose throughout the world but as an organic outgrowth of development. European society had reached a level of complexity and sophistication at which the aristocracy, so as not to overburden itself, had to confer a measure of equality upon other citizens and allocate some responsibility to them: a structured division of the population into peacefully competing interest groups was necessary if both tyranny and anarchy were to be averted.

The very fact that we retreat to moral arguments—and often moral arguments only—to justify democracy indicates that for many parts of the world the historical and social arguments supporting democracy are just not there. Realism has come not from us but from, for example, Uganda's President Yoweri Museveni, an enlightened Hobbesian despot whose country has posted impressive annual economic growth rates—10 percent recently—despite tribal struggles in the country's north. In 1986 Museveni's army captured the Ugandan capital of Kampala without looting a single shop; Museveni postponed elections and saw that they took place in a manner that ensured his victory. "I happen to be one of those people who do not believe in multi-party democracy," Museveni has written. "In fact, I am totally opposed to it as far as Africa today is concerned. . . . If one forms a multi-party system in Uganda, a party cannot win elections unless it finds a way of dividing the ninety-four percent of the electorate [that consists of peasants], and this is where the main problem comes up: tribalism, religion, or regionalism becomes the basis for intense partisanship." In other words, in a society that has not reached the level of development Toqueville described, a multi-party system merely hardens and institutionalizes established ethnic and regional divisions. Look at Armenia and Azerbaijan, where democratic processes brought nationalists to power upon the demise of the Soviet Union: each leader furthered his country's slide into war. A coup in Azerbaijan was necessary to restore peace and, by developing Azerbaijan's enormous oil resources, foster economic growth. Without the coup Western oil companies would not have gained their current foothold, which has allowed the United States to increase pressure on neighboring Iran at the same time that we attempt to normalize relations with Iran "on our terms."

Certainly, moral arguments in support of democracy were aired at the 1787 Constitutional Convention in Philadelphia, but they were tempered by the kind of historical and social analysis we now abjure. "The Constitution of the United States was written by fifty-five men—and one ghost," writes retired Army Lieutenant General Dave R. Palmer in *1794: America, Its Army, and the Birth of the Nation* (1994). The ghost was that of Oliver Cromwell, the archetypal man on horseback who, in the course of defending Parliament against the monarchy in the mid-seventeenth century, devised a tyranny worse than any that had ever existed under the English Kings. The Founders were terrified of a badly educated populace that could be duped by a Cromwell, and of a system that could allow too much power to fall into one person's hands. That is why they constructed a system that filtered the whims of the masses through an elected body and dispersed power by dividing the government into three branches.

The ghosts of today we ignore—like the lesson offered by Rwanda, where the parliamentary system the West promoted was a factor in the murder of hundreds of thousands of Tutsis by Hutu militias. In 1992, responding partly to pressure from Western governments, the Rwandan regime established a multi-party system and transformed itself into a coalition government. The new political parties became masks for ethnic groups that organized murderous militias, and the coalition nature of the new government helped to prepare the context for the events that led to the genocide in 1994. Evil individuals were certainly responsible for the mass murder. But they operated within a fatally flawed system, which our own ethnocentric hubris helped to construct. Indeed, our often moralistic attempts to impose Western parliamentary systems on other countries are not dissimilar to the attempts of nineteenth-century Western colonialists—many of whom were equally idealistic—to replace well-functioning chieftaincy and tribal patronage systems with foreign administrative practices.

The demise of the Soviet Union was no reason for us to pressure Rwanda and other countries to form political parties—though that is what our post–Cold War foreign policy has been largely about, even in parts of the world that the Cold War barely touched. The Eastern European countries liberated in 1989 already had, in varying degrees, the historical and social preconditions for both democracy and advanced industrial life: bourgeois traditions, exposure to the Western Enlightenment, high literacy rates, low birth rates, and so on. The post–Cold War effort to bring democracy to those countries has been reasonable. What is less reasonable is to put a gun to the head of the peoples of the developing world and say, in effect, "Behave as if you had experienced the Western Enlightenment to the degree that Poland and the Czech Republic did. Behave as if 95 percent of your population were literate. Behave as if you had no bloody ethnic or regional disputes."

States have never been formed by elections. Geography, settlement patterns, the rise of literate bourgeoisie, and, tragically, ethnic cleansing have formed states. Greece, for instance, is a stable democracy partly because earlier in the century it carried out a relatively benign form of ethnic cleansing—in the form of refugee transfers—which created a monoethnic society. Nonetheless, it took several decades of economic development for Greece finally to put its coups behind it. Democracy often weakens states by necessitating ineffectual compromises and fragile coalition governments in societies where bureaucratic institutions never functioned well to begin with. Because democracy neither forms states nor strengthens them initially, multi-party systems are best suited to nations that already have efficient bureaucracies and a middle class that pays income tax, and where primary issues such as borders and power-sharing have already been resolved, leaving politicians free to bicker about the budget and other secondary matters.

Social stability results from the establishment of a middle class. Not democracies but authoritarian systems, including monarchies, create middle classes—which, having achieved a certain size and self-confidence, revolt against the very dictators who generated their prosperity. This is the pattern today in the Pacific Rim and the southern cone of South America, but not in other parts of Latin America, southern Asia, or sub-Saharan Africa. A place like the Democratic Republic of Congo (formerly Zaire), where the per capita gross national product is less than $200 a year and the average person is either a rural peasant or an urban peasant; where there is little infrastructure of roads, sewers, and so on; and where reliable bureaucratic institutions are lacking, needs a leader like Bismarck or Jerry Rawlings—the Ghanaian ruler who stabilized his country through dictatorship and then had himself elected democratically—in place for years before he is safe from an undisciplined soldiery.

Foreign correspondents in sub-Saharan Africa who equate democracy with progress miss this point, ignoring both history and centuries of political philosophy. They seem to think that the choice is between dictators and democrats. But for many places the only choice is between bad dictators and slightly better ones. To force elections on such places may give us some instant gratification. But after a few months or years a bunch of soldiers with grenades will get bored and greedy, and will easily topple their fledgling democracy. As likely as not, the democratic government will be composed of corrupt, bickering, ineffectual politicians whose weak rule never had an institutional base to start with: modern bureaucracies generally require high literacy rates over several generations. Even India, the great exception that proves the rule, has had a mixed record of success as a democracy, with Bihar and other poverty-wracked places remaining in semi-anarchy. Ross Munro, a noted Asia expert, has documented how Chinese autocracy has better prepared China's population for the economic rigors of the post-industrial age than Indian democracy has prepared India's.

Of course, our post–Cold War mission to spread democracy is partly a pose. In Egypt and Saudi Arabia, America's most important allies in the energy-rich Muslim world, our worst nightmare would be free and fair elections, as it would be elsewhere in the Middle East. The end of the Cold War has changed our attitude toward those authoritarian regimes that are not crucial to our interests—but not toward those that are. We praise democracy, and meanwhile we are grateful for an autocrat like King Hussein, and for the fact that the Turkish and Pakistani militaries have always been the real powers behind the "democracies" in their countries. Obviously, democracy in the abstract encompasses undeniably good things such as civil society and a respect for human rights. But as a matter of public policy it has unfortunately come to focus on elections. What is in fact happening in many places requires a circuitous explanation.

The New Authoritarianism

The battle between liberal and neoconservative moralists who are concerned with human rights and tragic realists who are concerned with security, balance-of-power politics, and economic matters (famously, Henry Kissinger) is a variation of a classic dispute between two great English philosophers—the twentieth-century liberal humanist Isaiah Berlin and the seventeenth-century monarchist and translator of Thucydides, Thomas Hobbes.

In May of 1953, while the ashes of the Nazi Holocaust were still smoldering and Stalin's grave was fresh, Isaiah Berlin delivered a spirited lecture against "historical inevitability"—the whole range of belief, advocated by Hobbes and others, according to which individuals and their societies are determined by their past, their civilization, and even their biology and environment. Berlin argued that adherence to historical inevitability, so disdainful of the very characteristics that make us human, led to Nazism and communism—both of them extreme attempts to force a direction onto history. Hobbes is just one of many famous philosophers Berlin castigated in his lecture, but it is Hobbes's bleak and elemental philosophy that most conveniently sums up what Berlin and other moralists so revile. Hobbes suggested that even if human beings are nobler than apes, they are nevertheless governed by biology and environment. According to Hobbes, our ability to reason is both a mask for and a slave to our passions, our religions arise purely from fear, and theories about our divinity must be subordinate to the reality of how we behave. Enlightened despotism is thus preferable to democracy: the masses require protection from themselves. Hobbes, who lived through the debacle of parliamentary rule under Cromwell, published his translation of Thucydides in order, he said, to demonstrate how democracy, among other factors, was responsible for Athens's decline. Reflecting on ancient Athens, the philosopher James Harrington, a contemporary and follower of Hobbes, remarked that he could think of "nothing more dangerous" than "debate in a crowd."

Though the swing toward democracy following the Cold War was a triumph for liberal philosophy, the pendulum will come to rest where it belongs—in the middle, between the ideals of Berlin and the realities of Hobbes. Where a political system leans too far in either direction, realignment or disaster awaits.

In 1993 Pakistan briefly enjoyed the most successful period of governance in its history. The government was neither democratic nor authoritarian but a cross between the two. The unelected Prime Minister, Moin Qureshi, was chosen by the President, who in turn was backed by the military. Because Qureshi had no voters to please, he made bold moves that restored political stability and economic growth. Before Qureshi there had been violence and instability under the elected governments of Benazir Bhutto and Nawaz Sharif. Bhutto's government was essentially an ethnic-Sindhi mafia based in the south; Sharif's was an ethnic-Punjabi mafia from the geographic center. When Qureshi handed the country back to "the people," elections returned Bhutto to power, and chaos resumed. Finally, in November of last year, Pakistan's military-backed President again deposed Bhutto. The sigh of relief throughout the country was audible. Recent elections brought Sharif, the Punjabi, back to power. He is governing better than the first time, but communal violence has returned to Pakistan's largest city, Karachi. I believe that Pakistan must find its way back to a hybrid regime like the one that worked so well in 1993; the other options are democratic anarchy and military tyranny. (Anarchy and tyranny, of course, are closely related: because power abhors a vacuum, the one necessarily leads to the other. One day in 1996 Kabul, the Afghan capital, was ruled essentially by no one; the next day it was ruled by Taliban, an austere religious movement.)

Turkey's situation is similar to Pakistan's. During the Cold War, Turkey's military intervened when democracy threatened mass violence, about once every decade. But Turkish coups are no longer tolerated by the West, so Turkey's military has had to work behind the scenes to keep civilian governments from acting too irrationally for our comfort and that of many secular Turks. As elected governments in Turkey become increasingly circumscribed by the army, a quieter military paternalism is likely to evolve in place of periodic coups. The crucial element is not the name the system goes by but how the system actually works.

Peru offers another version of subtle authoritarianism. In 1990 Peruvian voters elected Alberto Fujimori to dismantle parts of their democracy. He did, and as a consequence he restored a measure of civil society to Peru. Fujimori disbanded Congress and took power increasingly into his own hands, using it to weaken the Shining Path guerrilla movement, reduce inflation from 7,500 percent to 10 percent, and bring investment and jobs back to Peru. In 1995 Fujimori won re-election with three times as many votes as his nearest challenger. Fujimori's use of deception and corporate-style cost-benefit analyses allowed him to finesse brilliantly the crisis caused by the terrorist seizure of the Japanese embassy in Lima. The commando raid that killed the terrorists probably never could have taken place amid the chaotic conditions of the preceding Peruvian government. Despite the many problems Fujimori has had and still has, it is hard to argue that Peru has not benefited from his rule.

In many of these countries Hobbesian realities—in particular, too many young, violence-prone males without jobs—have necessitated radical action. In a York University study published last year the scholars Christian G. Mesquida and Neil I. Wiener demonstrate how countries with young populations (young poor males especially) are subject to political violence. With Third World populations growing dramatically (albeit at slowing rates) and becoming increasingly urbanized, democrats must be increasingly ingenious and dictators increasingly tyrannical in order to rule successfully. Surveillance, too, will become more important on an urbanized planet; it is worth noting that the etymology of the word "police" is *polis,* Greek for "city." Because tottering democracies and despotic militaries frighten away the investors required to create jobs for violence-prone youths, more hybrid regimes will perforce emerge. They will call themselves democracies, and we may go along with the lie—but, as in Peru, the regimes will be decisively autocratic. (Hobbes wrote that Thucydides "praiseth the government of Athens, when . . . it was democratical in name, but in effect monarchical under Pericles." Polybius, too, recommended mixed regimes as the only stable form of government.) Moreover, if a shortage of liquidity affects world capital markets by 2000, as Klaus Schwab, the president of the World Economic Forum, and other experts fear may happen, fiercer competition among developing nations for scarcer investment money will accelerate the need for efficient neo-authoritarian governments.

The current reality in Singapore and South Africa, for instance, shreds our democratic certainties. Lee Kuan Yew's offensive neo-authoritarianism, in which the state has evolved into a corporation that is paternalistic, meritocratic, and decidedly undemocratic, has forged prosperity from abject poverty. A survey of business executives and economists by the World Economic Forum ranked Singapore No. 1 among the fifty-three most advanced countries appearing on an index of global competitiveness. What is good for business executives is often good for the average citizen: per capita wealth in Singapore is nearly equal to that in Canada, the nation that ranks No. 1 in the world on the United Nations' Human Development Index. When Lee took over Singapore, more than thirty years ago, it was a mosquito-ridden bog filled with slum quarters that frequently lacked both plumbing and electricity. Doesn't liberation from filth and privation count as a human right? Jeffrey Sachs, a professor of international trade at Harvard, writes that "good government" means relative safety from corruption, from breach of contract, from property expropriation, and from bureaucratic inefficiency. Singapore's reputation in these regards is unsurpassed. If Singapore's 2.8 million citizens ever demand democracy, they will just prove the assertion that prosperous middle classes arise under authoritarian regimes before gaining the confidence to dislodge their benefactors. Singapore's success is frightening, yet it must be acknowledged.

Democratic South Africa, meanwhile, has become one of the most violent places on earth that are not war zones, according to the security firm Kroll Associates. The murder rate is six times that in the United States, five times that in Russia. There are ten private-security guards for every policeman. The currency has substantially declined, educated people continue to flee, and international drug cartels have made the country a new transshipment center. Real unemployment is about 33 percent, and is probably much higher among youths. Jobs cannot be created without the cooperation of foreign investors, but assuaging their fear could require the kind of union-busting and police actions that democracy will not permit. The South African military was the power behind the regime in the last decade of apartheid. And it is the military that may yet help to rule South Africa in the future. Like Pakistan but more so, South Africa is destined for a hybrid regime if it is to succeed. The abundant coverage of South Africa's impressive attempts at coming to terms with the crimes of apartheid serves to obscure the country's growing problems. There is a sense of fear in such celebratory, backward-looking coverage, as if writing too much about difficulties in that racially symbolic country would expose the limits of the liberal humanist enterprise worldwide.

Burma, too, may be destined for a hybrid regime, despite the deification of the opposition leader and Nobel Peace laureate Aung San Suu Kyi by Western journalists. While the United States calls for democracy in and economic sanctions against Burma, those with more immediate clout—that is, Burma's Asian neighbors, and especially corporate-oligarchic militaries like Thailand's—show no compunction about increasing trade links with Burma's junta. Aung San Suu Kyi may one day bear the title of leader of Burma, but only with the tacit approval of a co-governing military. Otherwise Burma will not be stable. A rule of thumb is that governments are determined not by what liberal humanists wish but rather by what business people and others require. Various democratic revolutions failed in Europe in 1848 because what the intellectuals wanted was not what the emerging middle classes wanted. For quite a few parts of today's world, which have at best only the beginnings of a middle class, the Europe of the mid-nineteenth century provides a closer comparison than the Europe of the late twentieth century. In fact, for the poorest countries where we now recommend democracy, Cromwell's England may provide the best comparison.

As with the Christian religion (whose values are generally different for Americans than for Bosnian Serbs or for Lebanese Phalangists, to take only three examples), the nominal system of a government is less significant than the nature of the society in which it operates. And as democracy sinks into the soils of various local cultures, it often leaves less-than-nourishing deposits. "Democracy" in Cambodia, for instance, began evolving into something else almost immediately after the UN-sponsored elections there, in 1993. Hun Sen, one of two Prime Ministers in a fragile coalition, lived in a fortified bunker from which he physically threatened journalists and awarded government contracts in return for big bribes. His coup last summer, which toppled his co–Prime Minister and ended the democratic experiment, should have come as no surprise.

"World Government"

Authoritarian or hybrid regimes, no matter how illiberal, will still be treated as legitimate if they can provide security for their subjects and spark economic growth. And they will easily find acceptance in a world driven increasingly by financial markets that know no borders.

For years idealists have dreamed of a "world government." Well, a world government has been emerging—quietly and organically, the way vast developments in history take place. I do not refer to the United Nations, the power of which, almost by definition, affects only the poorest countries. After its peacekeeping failures in Bosnia and Somalia—and its $2 billion failure to make Cambodia democratic—the UN is on its way to becoming a supranational relief agency. Rather, I refer to the increasingly dense ganglia of international corporations and markets that are becoming the unseen arbiters of power in many countries. It is much more important nowadays for the leader of a developing country to get a hearing before corporate investors at the World Economic Forum than to speak before the UN General Assembly. Amnesty International now briefs corporations, just as it has always briefed national governments. Interpol officials have spoken about sharing certain kinds of intelligence with corporations. The Prime Minister of Malaysia, Mahathir Mohamad, is recognizing the real new world order (at least in this case) by building a low-tax district he calls a "multimedia supercorridor," with two new cities and a new airport designed specifically for international corporations. The world's most efficient peacemaking force belongs not to the UN or even to the great powers but to a South African corporate mercenary force called Executive Outcomes, which restored relative stability to Sierra Leone in late 1995. (This is reminiscent of the British East India Company, which raised armies transparently for economic interests.) Not long after Executive Outcomes left Sierra Leone, where only 20.7 percent of adults can read, that country's so-called model democracy crumbled into military anarchy, as Sudan's model democracy had done in the late 1980s.

Of the world's hundred largest economies, fifty-one are not countries but corporations. While the 200 largest corporations employ less than three-fourths of one percent of the world's work force, they account for 28 percent of world economic activity. The 500 largest corporations account for 70 percent of world trade. Corporations are like the feudal domains that evolved into nation-states;

they are nothing less than the vanguard of a new Darwinian organization of politics. Because they are in the forefront of real globalization while the overwhelming majority of the world's inhabitants are still rooted in local terrain, corporations will be free for a few decades to leave behind the social and environmental wreckage they create—abruptly closing a factory here in order to open an unsafe facility with a cheaper work force there. Ultimately, as technological innovations continue to accelerate and the world's middle classes come closer together, corporations may well become more responsible to the cohering global community and less amoral in the course of their evolution toward new political and cultural forms.

For instance, ABB Asea Brown Boveri Ltd. is a $36 billion-a-year multinational corporation divided into 1,300 companies in 140 countries; no one national group accounts for more than 20 percent of its employees. ABB's chief executive officer, Percy Barnevik, recently told an interviewer that this diversity is so that ABB can develop its own "global ABB culture—you might say an umbrella culture." Barnevik explains that his best managers are moved around periodically so that they and their families can develop "global personalities" by living and growing up in different countries. ABB management teams, moreover, are never composed of employees from any one country. Barnevik says that this encourages a "cross-cultural glue." Unlike the multiculturalism of the left, which masks individual deficiencies through collective—that is, ethnic or racial—self-esteem, a multinational corporation like ABB has created a diverse multicultural environment in which individuals rise or fall completely on their own merits. Like the hybrid regimes of the present and future, such an evolving corporate community can bear an eerie resemblance to the oligarchies of the ancient world. "Decentralization goes hand in hand with central monitoring," Barnevik says.

The level of social development required by democracy as it is known in the West has existed in only a minority of places—and even there only during certain periods of history. We are entering a troubling transition, and the irony is that while we preach our version of democracy abroad, it slips away from us at home.

The Shrinking Domain of "Politics"

I put special emphasis on corporations because of the true nature of politics: who does and who doesn't have power. To categorize accurately the political system of a given society, one must define the significant elements of power within it. Supreme Court Justice Louis Brandeis knew this instinctively, which is why he railed against corporate monopolies. Of course, the influence that corporations wield over government and the economy is so vast and obvious that the point needs no elaboration. But there are other, more covert forms of emerging corporate power.

The number of residential communities with defended perimeters that have been built by corporations went from 1,000 in the early 1960s to more than 80,000 by the mid-1980s, with continued dramatic increases in the 1990s. ("Gated communities" are not an American invention. They are an import from Latin America, where deep social divisions in places like Rio de Janeiro and Mexico City make them necessary for the middle class.) Then there are malls, with their own rules and security forces, as opposed to public streets; private health clubs as opposed to public playgrounds; incorporated suburbs with strict zoning; and other mundane aspects of daily existence in which—perhaps without realizing it, because the changes have been so gradual—we opt out of the public sphere and the "social contract" for the sake of a protected setting. Dennis Judd, an urban-affairs expert at the University of Missouri at St. Louis, told me recently, "It's nonsense to think that Americans are individualists. Deep down we are a nation of herd animals: micelike conformists who will lay at our doorstep many of our rights if someone tells us that we won't have to worry about crime and our property values are secure. We have always put up with restrictions inside a corporation which we would never put up with in the public sphere. But what many do not realize is that life within some sort of corporation is what the future will increasingly be about."

Indeed, a number of American cities are re-emerging as Singapores, with corporate enclaves that are dedicated to global business and defended by private security firms adjacent to heavily zoned suburbs. For instance, in my travels I have looked for St. Louis and Atlanta and not found them. I found only hotels and corporate offices with generic architecture, "nostalgic" tourist bubbles, zoned suburbs, and bleak urban wastelands; there was nothing distinctive that I could label "St. Louis" or "Atlanta." Last year's Olympics in Atlanta will most likely be judged by future historians as the first of the postmodern era, because of the use of social façades to obscure fragmentation. Peace and racial harmony were continually proclaimed to be Olympic themes—even though whites and blacks in Atlanta live in separate enclaves and the downtown is a fortress of office blocks whose streets empty at dusk. During the games a virtual army was required to protect visitors from terrorism, as at previous Olympics, and also from random crime. All this seems normal. It is both wonderful and frightening how well we adapt.

Universities, too, are being redefined by corporations. I recently visited Omaha, where the corporate community made it possible for the Omaha branch of the University of Nebraska to build an engineering school—even after the Board of Regents vetoed the project. Local corporations, particularly First Data Resources, wanted the school, so they worked with the Omaha branch of the university to finance what became less a school than a large information-science and engineering complex. "This is the future," said the chancellor of the Omaha campus, Del Weber. "Universities will have to become entrepreneurs, working with corporations *on curriculum* [emphasis mine] and other matters, or they will die." The California state university system, in particular the San Diego campus, is perhaps the best example of corporate-academic synergy, in which a school rises in prestige because its curriculum has practical applications for nearby technology firms.

Corporations, which are anchored neither to nations nor to communities, have created strip malls, edge cities, and Disneyesque tourist bubbles. Developments are not necessarily bad: they provide low prices, convenience, efficient work forces, and, in the case of tourist bubbles, safety. We need big corporations. Our society has reached a level of social and technological complexity at which goods and services must be produced for a price and to a standard that smaller businesses cannot manage. We should also recognize, though, that the architectural reconfiguration of our cities and towns has been an undemocratic event—with decisions in effect handed down from above by an assembly of corporate experts.

"The government of man will be replaced by the administration of things," the Enlightenment French philosopher Henri de Saint-Simon prophesied. We should worry that experts will channel our very instincts and thereby control them to some extent. For example, while the government fights drug abuse, often with pathetic results, pharmaceutical corporations have worked *through* the government and political parties to receive sanction for drugs such as stimulants and antidepressants, whose consciousness-altering effects, it could be argued, are as great as those of outlawed drugs.

The more appliances that middle-class existence requires, the more influence their producers have over the texture of our lives. Of course, the computer in some ways enhances the power of the individual, but it also depletes our individuality. A degree of space and isolation is required for a healthy sense of self, which may be threatened by the constant stream of other people's opinions on computer networks.

Democratic governance, at the federal, state, and local levels, goes on. But its ability to affect our lives is limited. The growing piles of our material possessions make personal life more complex and leave less time for communal matters. And as communities become liberated from geography, as well as more specialized culturally and electronically, they will increasingly fall outside the realm of traditional governance. Democracy loses meaning if both rulers and ruled cease to be part of a community tied to a specific territory. In this historical transition phase, lasting perhaps a century or more, in which globalization has begun but is not complete and loyalties are highly confused, civil society will be harder to maintain. How and when we vote during the next hundred years may be a minor detail for historians.

True, there are strong similarities between now and a century ago. In the 1880s and 1890s America experienced great social and economic upheaval. The combination of industrialization and urbanization shook the roots of religious and family life: sects sprouted, racist Populists ranted, and single women, like Theodore Dreiser's Sister Carrie, went to work in filthy factories. Racial tensions hardened as the Jim Crow system took hold across the South. "Gadgets" like the light bulb and the automobile brought an array of new choices and stresses. "The city was so big, now, that people disappeared into it unnoticed," Booth Tarkington lamented in *The Magnificent Ambersons.*

A hundred years ago millionaires' mansions arose beside slums. The crass accumulation of wealth by a relatively small number of people gave the period its name—the Gilded Age, after a satire by Mark Twain and Charles Dudley Warner about financial and political malfeasance. Around the turn of the century 12 percent of all American households controlled about 86 percent of the country's wealth.

But there is a difference, and not just one of magnitude. The fortunes made from the 1870s through the 1890s by John D. Rockefeller, Andrew Carnegie, J. P. Morgan, and others were *American* fortunes, anchored to a specific geographic space. The Gilded Age millionaires financed an economy of scale to fit the vast landscape that Abraham Lincoln had secured by unifying the nation in the 1860s. These millionaires funded libraries and universities and founded symphony orchestras and historical societies to consolidate their own civilization in the making. Today's fortunes are being made in a global economic environment in which an affluent global civilization and power structure are being forced even as a large stratum of our society remains rooted in place. A few decades hence it may be hard to define an "American" city.

Even J. P. Morgan was limited by the borders of the nation-state. But in the future who, or what, will limit the likes of Disney chairman Michael Eisner? The UN? Eisner and those like him are not just representatives of the "free" market. Neither the Founders nor any of the early modern philosophers ever envisioned that the free market would lead to the concentration of power and resources that many corporate executives already embody. Whereas the liberal mistake is to think that there is a program or policy to alleviate every problem in the world, the conservative flaw is to be vigilant against concentrations of power in government only—not in the private sector, where power can be wielded more secretly and sometimes more dangerously.

Umpire Regimes

This rise of corporate power occurs more readily as the masses become more indifferent and the elite less accountable. Material possessions not only focus people toward private and away from communal life but also encourage docility. The more possessions one has, the more compromises one will make to protect them. The ancient Greeks said that the slave is someone who is intent on filling his belly, which can also mean someone who is intent on safeguarding his possessions. Aristophanes and Euripides, the late-eighteenth-century Scottish philosopher Adam Ferguson, and Tocqueville in the nineteenth century all warned that material prosperity would breed servility and withdrawal, turning people into, in Tocqueville's words, "industrious sheep."

In moderate doses, apathy is not necessarily harmful. I have lived and traveled in countries with both high voter turnouts and unstable politics; the low voter turnouts in the United States do not by themselves worry me. The philosopher James Harrington observed that the very indifference of most people allows for a calm and healthy political climate. Apathy, after all, often means that the political situation is healthy enough to be ignored. The last thing America needs is more voters —particularly badly educated and alienated ones—with a passion for politics. But when voter turnout decreases to around 50 percent at the same time that the middle class is spending astounding sums in gambling casinos and state lotteries, joining private health clubs, and using large amounts of stimulants and anti-depressants, one can legitimately be concerned about the state of American society.

I recently went to a basketball game at the University of Arizona. It was just a scrimmage, not even a varsity game. Yet the stadium was jammed, and three groups of cheerleaders performed. Season tickets were almost impossible to obtain, even before the team won the national championship. Donating $10,000 to $15,000 to the university puts one in a good position to accumulate enough points to be eligible for a season ticket, though someone could donate up to $100,000 and still not qualify. I have heard that which spouse gets to keep tickets can be a primary issue in Tucson divorce cases. I noticed that almost everyone in the stands was white; almost everyone playing was black. Gladiators in Rome were almost always of racial or ethnic groups different from the Romans. "There may be so little holding these southwestern communities together that a basketball team is all there is," a Tucson newspaper editor told me. "It's a sports team, a symphony orchestra, and a church rolled into one." Since neither Tucson nor any other southwestern city with a big state university can find enough talent locally, he pointed out, community self-esteem becomes a matter of which city can find the largest number of talented blacks from far away to represent it.

We have become voyeurs and escapists. Many of us don't play sports but love watching great athletes with great physical attributes. The fact that basketball and football and baseball have become big corporate business has only increased the popularity of spectator sports. Basketball in particular—so fluid, and with the players in revealing shorts and tank tops—provides the artificial excitement that mass existence "against instinct," as the philosopher Bertrand Russell labeled our lives, requires.

Take the new kind of professional fighting, called "extreme fighting," that has been drawing sellout crowds across the country. Combining boxing, karate, and wrestling, it has nothing fake about it—blood really flows. City and state courts have tried, often unsuccessfully, to stop it. The spectators interviewed in a CNN documentary on the new sport all appeared to be typical lower-middle and middle class people, many of whom brought young children to the fights. Asked why they came, they said that they wanted to "see blood." The mood of the Colosseum goes together with the age of the corporation, which offers entertainment in place of values. The Nobel laureate Czeslaw Milosz provides the definitive view on why Americans degrade themselves with mass culture: "Today man believes that there is *nothing* in him, so he accepts *anything,* even if he knows it to be bad, in order to find himself at one with others, in order not to be alone." Of course, it is because people find so little in themselves that they fill their world with celebrities. The masses avoid important national and international news because much of it is tragic, even as they show an unlimited appetite for the details of Princess Diana's death. This willingness to give up self and responsibility is the sine qua non for tyranny.

The classicist Sir Moses Finley ended his austere and penetrating work *Politics in the Ancient World* (1983) with these words:

> The ideology of a ruling class is of little use unless it is accepted by those who are being ruled, and so it was to an extraordinary degree in Rome.

Then, when the ideology began to disintegrate within the elite itself, the consequence was not to broaden the political liberty among the citizenry but, on the contrary, to destroy it for everyone.

So what about our ruling class?

I was an expatriate for many years. Most expatriates I knew had utopian liberal beliefs that meant little, since few of them had much of a real stake in any nation. Their patriotism was purely nostalgic: a French friend would become tearful when her national anthem was played, but whenever she returned to France, she complained nonstop about the French. Increasingly, though, one can be an expatriate without living abroad. One can have Oriental rugs, foreign cuisines, eclectic tastes, exposure to foreign languages, friends overseas with whom one's life increasingly intertwines, and special schools for the kids—all at home. Resident expatriatism, or something resembling it, could become the new secular religion of the upper-middle and upper classes, fostered by communications technology. Just as religion was replaced by nationalism at the end of the Middle Ages, at the end of modern times nationalism might gradually be replaced by a combination of traditional religion, spiritualism, patriotism directed toward the planet rather than a specific country, and assorted other organized emotions. Resident expatriates might constitute an elite with limited geographic loyalty beyond their local communities, which provide them with a convenient and aesthetically pleasing environment.

An elite with little loyalty to the state and a mass society fond of gladiator entertainments form a society in which corporate Leviathans rule and democracy is hollow. James Madison in *The Federalist* considered a comparable situation. Madison envisioned an enormously spread-out nation, but he never envisioned a modern network of transportation that would allow us psychologically to inhabit the same national community. Thus his vision of a future United States was that of a vast geographic space with governance but without patriotism, in which the state would be a mere "umpire," refereeing among competing interests. Regional, religious, and communal self-concern would bring about overall stability. This concept went untested, because a cohesive American identity and culture did take root. But as Americans enter a global community, and as class and racial divisions solidify, Madison's concept is relevant anew.

There is something postmodern about this scenario, with its blend of hollow governance and fragmentation, and something ancient, too. Because of suburbanization, American communities will be increasingly segregated by race and class. The tendency both toward compromise and toward trusting institutions within a given community will be high, as in small and moderately sized European countries today, or as in ancient Greek city-states. Furthermore, prosperous suburban sprawls such as western St. Louis and western Omaha, and high-technology regions such as the Tucson-Phoenix corridor, North Carolina's Research Triangle, and the Portland-Seattle-Vancouver area will compete with one another and with individual cities and states for overseas markets, as North America becomes a more peaceful and productive version of chaotic, warring city-state Greece.

A continental regime must continue to function, because America's edge in information warfare requires it, both to maintain and to lead a far-flung empire of sorts, as the Athenians did during the Peloponnesian War. But trouble awaits us, if only because the "triumph" of democracy in the developing world will cause great upheavals before many places settle into more practical—and, it is to be hoped, benign—hybrid regimes. In the Middle East, for instance, countries like Syria, Iraq, and the Gulf sheikhdoms—with artificial borders, rising populations, and rising numbers of working-age youths—will not instantly become stable democracies once their absolute dictators and medieval ruling families pass from the scene. As in the early centuries of Christianity, there will be a mess.

Given the surging power of corporations, the gladiator culture of the masses, and the ability of the well-off to be partly disengaged from their own countries, what will democracy under an umpire regime be like?

The Return of Oligarchy?

Surprisingly, the Founders admired the military regime of Sparta. Only in this century has Sparta been seen as the forerunner of a totalitarian state. Why shouldn't men like Madison and George Washington have admired Sparta? Its division of power among two Kings, the elders, and the *ephors* ("overseers") approximated the system of checks and balances that the Founders desired in order to prevent the emergence of another Cromwell. Of course, Sparta, like Athens, was a two-tiered system, with an oligarchic element that debated and decided issues and a mass—*helots* ("serfs") in Sparta, and slaves and immigrants in Athens—that had few or no rights. Whether Sparta was a monarchy, an oligarchy, or a limited democracy—and whether Athens was oligarchic or democratic—still depends on one's viewpoint. According to Aristotle, "Whether the few or the many rule is accidental to oligarchy and democracy—the rich are few everywhere, the poor many." The real difference, he wrote, is that "oligarchy is to the advantage of the rich, democracy to the advantage of the poor." By "poor" Aristotle meant laborers, landowning peasants, artisans, and so on—essentially, the middle class and below.

Is it not conceivable that corporations will, like the rulers of both Sparta and Athens, project power to the advantage of the well-off while satisfying the twenty-first-century servile populace with the equivalent of bread and circuses? In other words, the category of politics we live with may depend more on power relationships and the demeanor of our society than on whether we continue to hold elections. Just as Cambodia was never really democratic, despite what the State Department and the UN told us, in the future we may not be democratic, despite what the government and media increasingly dominated by corporations tell us.

Indeed, the differences between oligarchy and democracy and between ancient democracy and our own could be far subtler than we think. Modern democracy exists within a thin band of social and economic conditions, which include flexible hierarchies that allow people to move up and down the ladder. Instead of clear-cut separations between classes there are many gray shades, with most people bunched in the middle. Democracy is a fraud in many poor countries outside this narrow band: Africans want a better life and instead have been given the right to vote. As new and intimidating forms of economic and social stratification appear in a world based increasingly on the ability to handle and analyze large quantities of information, a new politics might emerge for us, too—less like the kind envisioned by progressive reformers and more like the pragmatic hybrid regimes that are bringing prosperity to developing countries.

The classicist Sir Moses Finley has noted that what really separated the rulers from the ruled in the ancient world was literacy: the illiterate masses were subject to the elite's interpretation of documents. Analogous gulfs between rulers and ruled may soon emerge, not only because of differing abilities to process information and to master technology but also because of globalization itself. Already, barely literate Mexicans on the U.S. border, working in dangerous, Dickensian conditions to produce our VCRs, jeans, and toasters, earn less than 50 cents an hour, with no rights or benefits. Is that Western democracy or ancient-Greek-style oligarchy?

As the size of the U.S. population and the complexity of American life spill beyond the traditional national community, creating a new world of city-states and suburbs, the distance will grow between the citizens of the new city-states and the bureaucratic class of overseers in Washington. Those overseers will manage an elite volunteer military armed with information-age weapons, in a world made chaotic by the spread of democracy and its attendant neo-authoritarian heresies. We prevented the worst excesses of a "military-industrial complex" by openly fearing it, as President Dwight Eisenhower told us to do. It may be equally wise to fear a high-tech military complex today.

Precisely because the technological future in North America will provide so much market and individual freedom, this productive anarchy will require the supervision of tyrannies—or else there will be no justice for anyone. Liberty, after all, is inseparable from authority, as Henry Kissinger observed in *A World Restored: Metternich, Castlereagh, and the Problems of Peace 1812–1822* (1957). A hybrid regime may await us all. The future of the Third World may finally be our own.

And that brings us to a sober realization. If democracy, the crowning political achievement of the West, is gradually being transfigured, in part because of technology, then the West will suffer the same fate as earlier civilizations. Just as Rome believed it was giving final expression to the republican ideal of the Greeks, and just as medieval Kings believed they were giving final expression to the Roman ideal, we believe, as the early Christians did, that we are bringing freedom and a better life to the rest of humankind. But as the nineteenth-century Russian liberal intellectual Alexander Herzen wrote, "Modern Western thought will pass into history and be incorporated in it . . . just as our body will pass into the composition of grass, of sheep, of cutlets, and of men." I do not mean to say that the United States is in decline. On the contrary, at the end of the twentieth century we are the very essence of creativity and dynamism. We are poised to transform ourselves into something perhaps quite different from what we imagine.

6 The New Global Economy

If there is one discipline that has accepted the concept of globalization wholeheartedly, it is the study of political economy. Indeed, historical political economists have argued that the forces that we now call globalization have existed for centuries. The current era, however, is the first in which the international economic system has become truly *interdependent*. A web of interconnections between, within, and above states has tied together formerly disparate forces.

Jeffrey Sachs and Lester C. Thurow present comprehensive overviews of the complex phenomenon that is politico-economic globalization. They describe the benefits of greater integration while acknowledging potential dangers. Similarly, Dani Rodrik attempts to clarify what globalization is and is not. Ultimately, the article is an attempt to reconcile simultaneous changes in markets and society. In the process, Sachs, Thurow, and Rodrik address the multifaceted economic, political, and social consequences of globalization.

Three additional articles dramatically illustrate the specific problems and dangers associated with ever-increasing economic globalization. First, former Assistant Secretary of the Treasury Roger C. Altman warns of the risk of global markets spiraling out of control. Second, the manifesto of the Tupac Amaru Revolutionary Movement of Peru describes the negative effects of economic globalization on peripheral elements in this system. This view, although radical, has grown in popularity in recent years. The rebellion in Chiapas, Mexico, in 1994 was but one expression of the growing disaffection with the effects of globalization on the periphery. Indeed, Aihwa Ong demonstrates that globalization affects not only economic but also cultural relations. In particular, she argues that opposition to globalization will take the form of solidarity networks based on gender or kinship rather than class. Together these articles vividly demonstrate that globalization is not without its consequences.

Economic globalization, to paraphrase Rodrik, is not occurring in a vacuum. While all of these readings focus on the economic side of globalization, they also point out that international economics in today's world cannot be understood without taking into account its multilayered effects.

International Economics

UNLOCKING THE MYSTERIES OF GLOBALIZATION

Jeffrey Sachs

International economics is concerned with the trade and financial relations of national economies, and the effects of international trade and finance on the distribution of production, income, and wealth around the world and within nations. In recent years, international economics has been increasingly taken up with one central question: How will national economies perform now that nearly all of the world is joined in a single global marketplace? As a result of changes in economic policy and technology, economies that were once separated by high transport costs and artificial barriers to trade and finance are now linked in an increasingly dense network of economic interactions. This veritable economic revolution over the last 15 years has come upon us so suddenly that its fundamental ramifications for economic growth, the distribution of income and wealth, and patterns of trade and finance in the world economy are only dimly understood.

The most notable features of the new world economy are the increasing links between the high- and low-income countries. After all, the advanced income economies of Europe, Japan, and the United States have been linked significantly through trade flows at least since the 1960s. The great novelty of the current era is the extent to which the poorer nations of the world have been incorporated in the global system of trade, finance, and production as partners and market participants rather than colonial dependencies. For globalization enthusiasts, this development promises increased gains from trade and faster growth for both sides of the worldwide income divide. For skeptics, the integration of rich and poor nations promises increasing inequality in the former and greater dislocation in the latter.

Reprinted with permission from *Foreign Policy,* 110 (Spring 1998). © 1998 by the Carnegie Endowment for International Peace.

National economies are becoming more integrated in four fundamental ways —through trade, finance, production, and a growing web of treaties and institutions. The increased trade linkages are clear: In almost every year since World War II, international trade has grown more rapidly than global production, resulting in a rising share of exports and imports in the GDP of virtually every country [see chart on page 219]. In the past 15 years, cross-border financial flows have grown even more rapidly than trade flows. Foreign direct investment (in which foreign capital gains a controlling interest in a cross-border enterprise), in particular, has grown even more rapidly than overall capital flows.

The sharp rise in foreign direct investment underscores the enormous and increasing role of multinational corporations in global trade, and especially in global production. As scholars such as Peter Dicken have shown, with falling transport and communications costs, it is possible to "divide up the value chain" of production. Different stages of the production process of a single output can be carried out in different parts of the world, depending on the comparative advantages of alternative production sites. Semiconductor chips might be designed in the United States, where the basic wafers are also produced; these are then cut and assembled in Malaysia; and the final products are tested in and shipped from Singapore. These cross-border flows often occur within the same multinational firm. One stunning fact about current trade flows is that an estimated one-third of merchandise trade is actually composed of shipments among the affiliates of a single company, as opposed to arms-length transactions among separate exporters and importers.

The fourth major aspect of globalization is the increased harmonization of economic institutions. Part of this is a matter of imitation. Most of the developing world chose nonmarket, economic strategies of development upon independence after World War II. These state-led models of development came crashing down in the 1980s, followed by a massive shift toward market-based, private sector–led growth. [For further discussion, please see the article by Joseph Stiglitz and Lyn Squire in *Foreign Policy,* 110 (Spring 1998).] Beyond mere imitation, however, has come a significant rise in international treaty obligations regarding trade, investment policy, tax policy, intellectual property rights, banking supervision, currency convertibility, foreign investment policy, and even the control of bribery. A growing web of treaties ties nations together through multilateral obligations (such as the G-77 group, with 132 member countries), regional obligations (the European Union and other trade blocs), and bilateral obligations (for example, binational tax treaties between the United States and dozens of other governments).

The Implications of Globalization

The implications of globalization for both the developed and developing countries are currently the subject of intensive research and heated policy debates. Four main sets of issues are now under investigation. First, will globalization promote faster economic growth, especially among the four-fifths of the world's population (4.5 billion people) still living in developing countries? Second, will globalization promote or undermine macroeconomic stability? Are the sudden and unexpected collapses of emerging market economies in recent years (such as Mexico in 1994 and East Asia in 1997) the result of deep flaws in the globalization process, or are they manageable, perhaps avoidable bumps in the road to greater prosperity? Third, will globalization promote growing income inequality, and, if so, is the problem limited to low-skilled workers in the advanced economies, or is this inequality a deeper result of intensifying market forces in all parts of the world? Fourth, how should governmental institutions at all levels—regional, national, and international—adjust their powers and responsibilities in view of the emergence of a global market?

ECONOMIC GROWTH

Adam Smith famously declared in the *Wealth of Nations* that "the discovery of America, and that of a passage to the East Indies by the Cape of Good Hope are the two greatest and most important events recorded in the history of mankind." He reasoned that by "uniting, in some measure, the most distant parts of the world, by enabling them to relieve one another's wants, to increase one another's enjoyments, and to encourage one another's industry, their general tendency would seem to be beneficial." The discoveries, of course, were not enough to guarantee these benefits. Smith himself recognized that the depredations of imperialism had deprived the native inhabitants of the New World and the East Indies of most of the benefits of globalization in his day. In our century, two world wars, the Great Depression, and 40 years of post–World War II protectionism in most of the de-

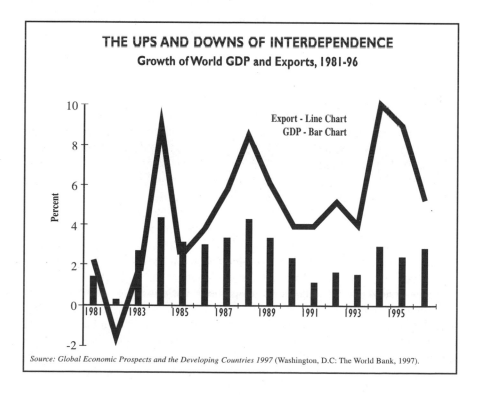

THE UPS AND DOWNS OF INTERDEPENDENCE
Growth of World GDP and Exports, 1981-96

Export - Line Chart
GDP - Bar Chart

Source: *Global Economic Prospects and the Developing Countries 1997* (Washington, D.C: The World Bank, 1997).

veloping world again frustrated Smith's vision of mutual gains from trade. Now, finally, can we envision the Smithian mechanism operating to worldwide advantage?

Much current theorizing on economic growth, such as the research by Gene Grossman and Elhanan Helpman, offers reasons for cheer. Smith's conjectures of dynamic gains to trade are at the core of many new mathematical models of "endogenous growth." These models stress that long-term growth depends on increased productivity and innovation, and that the incentives for both depend (as Smith conjectured) on the scope of the market. If innovators are selling into an expanded world market, they will generally have more incentive to innovate. If productivity is raised by refining the production process among a larger number of specialized subunits, and if each subunit faces fixed costs of production, then a larger market will allow these fixed costs to be spread over a larger production run.

One part of the argument has found strong empirical support in recent years. The fastest-growing developing countries in the past two decades have been those that succeeded in generating new export growth, especially in manufactured goods. Andrew Warner and I have demonstrated that economies that tried to go it alone by protecting their economies from imports through high trade barriers grew much less rapidly than more open export-oriented economies. Moreover, the manufactured exports of the developing countries have themselves exemplified the Smithian principle of division of labor. Steven Radelet and I found that in almost all cases of developing-country, export-led growth, the exports themselves have been part of a highly refined division of labor, in which final goods (e.g. automobiles, avionics, electronic machinery) are produced in multisite operations, with the labor-intensive parts of the production process reserved for the developing countries.

This kind of "new division of labor" in manufactures was inconceivable to early postwar development economists such as Raúl Prebisch, who counseled protectionism as the preferred path for industrialization in poor countries. These economists simply could not conceive of the production process being a complementary relationship between advanced and developing countries. In the standard theory, then, both sides of the great income divide stand to benefit from globalization: the developed countries by reaching a larger market for new innovations, and the developing economies by enjoying the fruits of those innovations while sharing in global production via multinational enterprises.

Modern theorizing still stresses, however, that the gains in growth might not in fact be shared by all. Two major theoretical exceptions that do find some supporting empirical evidence are most often discussed. The first exception is based on geography. The gains from trade depend on the transport costs between a national economy and the rest of the world being low enough to permit an extensive interaction between the economy and world markets. If the economy is geographically isolated—for example, landlocked in the high Andes or the Himalayas or Central Africa, as in the cases of Bolivia, Nepal, and Rwanda—the chances for extensive trade are extremely limited. Also, as MIT economist Paul Krugman has shown, the combination of increasing returns to scale and high transport costs may cause economic activity to concentrate somewhat accidentally in some areas at the expense of others. Climate may also have serious adverse effects. Generally speaking, the tropics impose additional burdens of infectious disease and often poor agricultural conditions (involving soil, water, and pests) not found in the temperate zones. For these reasons, a significant portion of the world's population may face severe geographical obstacles to development, despite the overall beneficial effects of globalization.

The second major theoretical exception, recognized in development thinking at least since Alexander Hamilton's call for protection of nascent U.S. industry, is the risk that producers of natural resources might get "trapped" into an unsatisfactory specialization of trade, thereby delaying or blocking the improvements in industry necessary for economic development. Kiminori Matsuyama was among the first to formulate a mathematical model to test this idea. Early evidence, derived from studies Warner and I conducted, gives some support to the "dynamic Dutch Disease" effect. Dutch Disease occurs when a boom in the natural resources that a country exports causes a national currency to strengthen, thereby undermining the profitability of nonresource-based industries. (The name comes from the de-industrialization that allegedly followed Holland's development of North Sea gas fields in the 1960s.) The "dynamic" effect is the supposed long-term loss of growth coming from the specialization in primary goods (e.g. gas exports) rather than manufactured products, which supposedly offer better opportunities for long term productivity growth.

The findings suggest that countries with large natural resource bases, such as the Persian Gulf oil exporters, find themselves uncompetitive in most manufacturing sectors. This condition, in turn, seems to be consistent with lower long-term growth, possibly because manufacturing rather than primary production (agriculture and mining) offers better possibilities for innovation, learning by doing, and productivity improvement in the long term. Economic theory suggests that some form of nonmarket intervention—ranging from the protection of nascent industries to the subsidization of manufacturing—could have beneficial effects in these circumstances. The practicalities of such real world interventions, however, are heatedly debated and open to question.

MACROECONOMIC STABILITY

In a famous cry of despair in the middle of the Great Depression, John Maynard Keynes, in his essay "National Self-Sufficiency," argued that economic entanglements through trade and finance added to global destabilization. He went so far as to declare "let goods be homespun whenever it is reasonably and conveniently possible; and, above all, let finance be primarily national."

After the depression, Keynes changed his mind and championed a postwar return to open trade based on convertible currencies. In his design of the new IMF, however, he kept to his view that financial flows ought to remain restricted so as to minimize the chance that international financial disturbances would create global macroeconomic instabilities. For this reason, the Articles of Agreement of the IMF call on member countries to maintain currencies that are convertible for current transactions (essentially trade and the repatriation of profits and interest) but not necessarily for capital flows.

As globalization has taken off in the past two decades, many forms of international capital flows have risen dramatically. Foreign direct investment, portfolio investment through country funds, bank loans, bond lending, derivatives (swaps, options, forward transactions), reinsurance, and other financial instruments have all grown enormously. Both developed and developing countries have increasingly opened their capital markets to foreign participation. In 1997, the IMF endorsed a move toward amending the Articles of Agreement to call for open capital flows. The Organization for Economic Cooperation and Development, World Trade Organization (WTO), and Bank for International Settlements have also increasingly sought international standards for the liberalization and supervision of international investment flows.

Economic theory generally asserts that trade in financial assets will benefit individual countries in ways analogous to trade in goods. Financial transactions, in theory, allow two kinds of gains from trade: increased diversification of risk and intertemporal gains (a better ability to borrow and lend over time, more consistent with desired patterns of investment and consumption). The theory, however, also hints at some limits to this optimistic view, and the experience of international financial liberalization gives real reason for pause. Perhaps Keynes' skepticism should still apply, despite our supposedly much enhanced capability to identify and manage financial risks.

The real meaning of the Mexican crash and the East Asian financial crisis is still far from clear, but both experiences have shown that unfettered financial flows from advanced to emerging markets can create profound destabilization. The problem, it seems, is that financial markets are subject to certain key "market failures" that are exacerbated, rather than limited, by globalization. One kind of failure is the tendency of underregulated and undercapitalized banks to gamble recklessly with depositor funds, since from the owner/management point of view, bank profits accrue to themselves, while bank losses get stuck with the government. Thus, international financial liberalization of a poorly capitalized banking system is an invitation to over-borrowing and eventual financial crisis.

The second kind of failure is financial panic, which comes when a group of creditors suddenly decides to withdraw loans from a borrower, out of fear that the other creditors are doing the same thing. Each lender flees for the exit because the last one out will lose his claims, assuming that the borrower does not have the liquid assets to cover a sudden withdrawal of loans. This kind of panic was once familiar in the form of bank runs, which used to afflict U.S. banks before the introduction of federal deposit insurance in 1934. It seems to be prevalent in international lending, especially in international bank loans to emerging markets. Both in Mexico in late 1994 and several East Asian economies in 1997 (Indonesia, Malaysia, the Philippines, and South Korea), once enthusiastic international bankers suddenly pulled the plug on new credits and the rollover of old credits. This withdrawal of funding sent the emerging markets into a tailspin, with falling production and the risk of outright international default. Emergency bailout loans led by the IMF aimed to block the defaults, but did not address the core causes of the crises [see box below].

These dramatic experiences are giving second thoughts in many quarters

A Brief History of Panic

One key risk of open capital flows is the pattern of booms and busts in international lending that contribute to instabilities in both creditor and debtor nations. In the 1820s, just after Latin American independence, British capital markets poured large sums into Latin American bonds and investment schemes. These crashed a few years later, giving the world its first developing-country debt crisis of modern times. The cycle of euphoric capital inflows, followed by "revulsion" and sudden outflows, has repeated itself every generation or so, including the defaults by U.S. states on British loans in the 1830s; the crisis of Egyptian and Ottoman debts in the 1870s; the defaulted loans to Caribbean countries in the early twentieth century; the worldwide defaults of the Great Depression; the developing-country debt crisis of the early 1980s; the Mexican crash of 1994; and now the East Asian financial crisis.

Crashes can occur when capital markets are exposed to "multiple equilibria," in which fears of bad outcomes can prove self-fulfilling. The scenario is similar to shouting "fire" in a theater. A small fire may pose no disaster if patrons quietly, calmly, and resolutely leave a crowded theater. But the same small fire may lead to disaster if patrons panic and trample one another to be the first ones out. Thus, if a debtor starts to weaken, a panicked withdrawal of short-term loans by nervous creditors can immediately lead to illiquidity of the debtor and then to bankruptcy, even if the debtor is fundamentally sound. Both the debtor and creditors lose by a creditor panic, as it produces a pure loss of market value.

A useful response to a panic is the provision of liquid funds to the afflicted debtor by a "lender of last resort." In a domestic banking panic, the lender of last resort is typically the central bank. In an international context, however, the debtor's central bank usually cannot be an adequate lender of last resort since the credits being withdrawn are in foreign currency. If the central bank's foreign exchange reserves are scarce (a fact that often helps to trigger the panic), then some kind of international lender of last resort might be needed—either a major creditor government—such as the United States in the case of the Mexican crisis—or an international lender of last resort—such as the IMF in the case of East Asia. The role of the IMF and other lending institutions continues to generate enormous debate. What should be the terms of "bailout loans?" What conditions should be attached to IMF programs? Should market forces be allowed to take their toll so that problems of moral hazard are avoided, as when bailouts lead to more irresponsible lending in the future? These issues sit at the center of the public policy debate on how to handle the Asian crisis.

—J.S.

to the pressures for rapid liberalization of international capital flows. While the official Washington community still presses for liberalization of the capital market, voices are being raised for putting a "spanner in the wheels" to slow capital movements with an aim toward preventing financial market panics. Ideas include the taxation of international transactions (such as the famous proposal of James Tobin to tax foreign exchange transactions to deter short-term currency speculation, or Chile's taxation of capital inflows); the direct limitation of short-term bank borrowing from abroad as a banking supervisory standard; and increased disclosure rules. Both the theory and practice of capital market liberalization are therefore in limbo.

INCOME DISTRIBUTION

Perhaps no aspect of globalization has been more controversial than the alleged effects of increased trade on income distribution. A series of claims are made that globalization is a major factor in increasing inequality, both in advanced and developing countries. Of course, within the United States, the main focus of debate is on advanced countries, especially the United States itself.

Over the past 25 years, international economics theory has mostly focused on two kinds of trade: intra-industry and inter-industry. The first kind, in which the United States sells cars to Europe while also importing European cars, is ostensibly based on gains from specialization under conditions of increasing returns to scale. The United States could itself produce "European-style" cars, so the argument goes, but chooses not to because it is less costly to have longer production runs of U.S. models, selling some of them to Europe to finance imports of the European models. Intra-industry trade, the theory holds, is a win-win situation for all. Consumers in both Europe and the United States enjoy an expanded range of products, and nobody suffers a loss of income, either absolute or relative.

Inter-industry trade involves the U.S. export of high technology goods to Asia, in return for inexpensive labor-intensive goods imported from Asia. In this case, trade is motivated by differing factor proportions. The United States produces goods that are intensive in physical capital and skills—advanced telecommunications equipment, for example—and imports goods that are intensive in labor—such as footwear and apparel. The theory suggests that both regions can gain overall from this kind of trade, though workers within each country may well lose. In the United States, for example, workers in the footwear and apparel sectors may lose their jobs in the face of increased low-wage competition, while skilled workers in Asia could conceivably lose out when skill-intensive goods are imported from the United States. More generally, according to basic Heckscher-Ohlin-Samuelson trade theory, unskilled U.S. workers may suffer relative and even absolute income declines, while skilled workers in the developing countries could similarly suffer a loss of relative and/or absolute income.

Since intra-industry trade is generally strongest among similar-income countries (e.g. U.S.–European trade), while inter-industry trade is strongest among dissimilar countries (e.g. U.S.–developing Asia), the income-distributional ramifications of trade between rich and poor countries are ostensibly more threatening to particular social groups, a point stressed early on by Krugman. It is therefore the increasing linkages of rich and poor countries that have become the corner-stone of political challenges to globalization.

Despite the hard work of researchers, there is still no consensus on the ef-fects of the globalized economy on income distribution within the advanced and emerging markets. Clearly, the period of dramatic globalization (especially dur-ing the 1980s and 1990s) has also been one of rising income inequality within the United States, and especially of a loss of relative income for low-skilled workers, consistent with basic trade theory. However, as with many important economic phenomena, the cause of this widening income inequality is almost surely multi-faceted. While trade might be one culprit, changes in technology such as the com-puter revolution might also favor skilled workers over unskilled ones, thereby contributing to the rising inequality. Most researchers agree that a combination of factors has played a role in the widening inequality, and the majority of them, including Krugman and Robert Lawrence, put the preponderant weight on tech-nology rather than trade. They do this for one main reason: The share of U.S. workers that are in direct competition with low-skilled workers in the emerging markets seems to be too small to explain the dramatic widening of inequalities since the end of the 1970s. Less than 5 percent of the U.S. labor market—in ap-parel, footwear, toys, assembly operations, and the like—appears to be in the "direct line of fire" of low-wage goods from Asia. If the United States is already out of the low-skill industries, then increased globalization in such goods cannot widen inequalities in the United States, and, in fact, would tend to benefit all households by offering less expensive consumer goods.

One problem with such estimates, however, is that they tend to be based on rather simple theoretical models of international trade. Conventional trade mea-sures may not pick up the additional channels through which globalization affects income distribution. Some researchers argue, for example, that increased global-ization limits the ability of union workers to achieve a "union wage premium" in collective bargaining because of the risk that firms will simply move overseas in response to higher union wages. Thus, the opening of international trade may have changed the bargaining power of workers vis-à-vis capital in ways not meas-ured by trade flows. More generally, the export of capital to low-wage countries can exacerbate inequalities caused by increased trade. Researchers have not yet uncovered large effects on wages and income distribution through these addition-al channels, but the scholarship devoted to these topics is still rather sparse.

Some sporadic evidence suggests that growing inequalities are not simply a problem of developed economies but also of developing economies. If the salary premium of skilled workers is rising in both developing and developed econo-mies, something more than inter-industry trade effects are at work. Part of the sto-ry could be technological change. Another possible factor (suggested recently by Robert Frank and Philip Cook) is that globalization is supporting a new "winner-take-all" approach in labor markets. The argument holds that skilled workers of all kinds, whether in sports, industry, science, or entertainment, find an expanding world market for their skills, while unskilled workers see no particular gains in an expanding market. Therefore, the scale of the world market would affect skilled workers differently from unskilled ones, leading to a worldwide rise in the market premium for skills. This hypothesis remains as yet almost completely unexamined empirically.

ECONOMIC GOVERNANCE

Without question, globalization is having a deep effect on politics at many levels. Most important, the national marketplace is losing its salience relative to international markets. This is causing a sea change in the role of the nation-state, relative to both local and regional governments on the one side, and multinational political institutions on the other.

In Smith's day, part of the market revolution was the removal of barriers to trade within nations and proto-nations. The freeing of trade among the German states in the Zollverein of 1834, and then the full unification of the German market with the establishment of the German Reich in 1871, exemplify the historical process. In most cases, nineteenth-century market capitalism and the importance of the national marketplace rose hand in hand, even as international trade was itself expanding. Generally speaking, the spread of capitalism within Europe, Japan, and North America gave impetus to the increasing importance of the national economy and thereby of the national government.

At the end of the twentieth century, the national market is being increasingly displaced by the international marketplace. After decades of experimentation, almost all countries have realized that the national market is simply too small to permit an efficient level of production in most areas of industry and even in many areas of services. Efficient production must be geared instead toward world markets. Moreover, globalization has proved a catalyst for internationally agreed-upon rules of behavior in trade, finance, taxation, and many other areas, thus prompting the rise of the WTO and other international institutions as the new bulwarks of the emerging international system. At the same time, communities, local governments, and regions within nations are increasingly asserting their claims to cultural and political autonomy. The nation is no longer their economic protector, and in peaceful regions of the world, the national government is no longer seen as a critical instrument of security. Consequently, regions as far-flung as Catalonia, Northern Italy, Quebec, and Scotland, as well as oblasts in Russia, provinces in China, and states in India, have taken globalization as their cue to pursue greater autonomy within the nation-state.

We are therefore in the midst of a startling, yet early, tug of war between polities at all levels. Where will the future of decision making, tax powers, and regulatory authorities reside: with localities, subnational regions, nation-states, or multilateral institutions (both within geographic regions such as the European Union and at the international level)? To the extent that increased regulatory, tax, and even judicial powers shift to the international setting, how should and will international institutions be governed in the future? Will there be a democracy deficit, as is now charged about decision making in the European Union? What will be the balance of political power between the developed and developing countries, especially as population and economic balances shift over time in favor of the now developing world? And crucially, what will be the balance of power between democratic and non-democratic polities at the world level? All of these issues are fresh, urgent, and likely to loom large on the research radar screens.

Sense and Nonsense in the Globalization Debate

Dani Rodrik

Globalization, Thomas Friedman of the *New York Times* has observed, is "the next great foreign policy debate." Yet as the debate expands, it gets more confusing. Is globalization a source of economic growth and prosperity, as most economists and many in the policy community believe? Or is it a threat to social stability and the natural environment, as a curious mix of interests ranging from labor advocates to environmentalists—and including the unlikely trio of Ross Perot, George Soros, and Sir James Goldsmith—argue? Has globalization advanced so far that national governments are virtually powerless to regulate their economies and use their policy tools to further social ends? Is the shift of manufacturing activities to low-wage countries undermining global purchasing power, thus creating a glut in goods ranging from autos to aircraft? Or is globalization no more than a buzzword and its impact greatly exaggerated?

There are good reasons to be concerned about the quality of the globalization debate. What we are witnessing is more a dialogue of the deaf than a rational discussion. Those who favor international integration dismiss globalization's opponents as knee-jerk protectionists who do not understand the principle of comparative advantage and the complexities of trade laws and institutions. Globalization's critics, on the other hand, fault economists and trade specialists for their narrow, technocratic perspective. They argue that economists are too enamored with their fancy models and do not have a good handle on how the real world works. The result is that there is too much opponent bashing—and too little learning—on each side.

Both sides have valid complaints. Much of the popular discussion about globalization's effect on American wages, to pick one important example, ignores the considerable research that economists have undertaken. A reasonably informed reader of the nation's leading op-ed pages could be excused for not realizing that a substantial volume of literature on the relationship between trade and inequality exists, much of which contradicts the simplistic view that Americans or Europeans owe their deteriorating fortunes to low-wage competition from abroad. The mainstream academic view actually is that increased trade with developing countries may account for at most 20 per cent of the reduction in the earnings of low-skilled American workers (relative to highly skilled workers) but not much more. One has to look elsewhere—to technological changes and deunionization, for example—to explain most of the increase in the wage gap between skilled and unskilled workers.

It is also true, however, that economists and proponents of trade have either neglected or pooh-poohed some of the broader complications associated with international economic integration. Consider the following questions: To what extent have capital mobility and the outsourcing of production increased the *substitutability* of domestic labor across national boundaries, thereby aggravating the economic insecurity confronting workers (in addition to exerting downward pressure on their wages)? Are the distributional implications of globalization—and certainly there are some—reconcilable with domestic concepts of distributive justice? Does trade with countries that have different norms and social institutions clash with and undermine long-standing domestic social bargains? To what extent does globalization undermine the ability of national governments to provide the public goods that their citizenries have come to expect, including social insurance against economic risks?

These are serious questions that underscore the potential of globally expanding markets to come into conflict with social stability, even as these markets provide benefits to exporters, investors, and consumers. Some of these questions have not yet been seriously scrutinized by economists. Others cannot be answered with economic and statistical analysis alone. But the full story of globalization cannot be told unless these broader issues are addressed as well.

The Limits of Globalization

Even with the revolution in transportation and communication and the substantial progress made in trade liberalization over the last three decades, national economies remain remarkably isolated from each other. This isolation has a critical implication, which has been repeatedly emphasized by economist Paul Krugman: Most governments in the advanced industrial world are not nearly as shackled by economic globalization as is commonly believed. They retain substantial autonomy in regulating their economies, in designing their social policies, and in maintaining institutions that differ from those of their trading partners.

The supposition that domestic economies are now submerged in a seamless, unified world market is belied by various pieces of evidence. Take the case of North America. Trade between Canada and the United States is among the freest in the world and is only minimally hampered by transport and communications costs. Yet a study by Canadian economist John McCallum has documented that trade between a Canadian province and a U.S. state (that is, *international* trade) is on average 20 times smaller than trade between two Canadian provinces (that is, *intranational* trade). Clearly, the U.S. and Canadian markets remain substantially delinked from each other. And if this is true of U.S.–Canadian trade, it must be all the more true of other bilateral trade relationships.

The evidence on the mobility of physical capital also contradicts current thought. Popular discussions take it for granted that capital is now entirely free to cross national borders in its search for the highest returns. As economists Martin Feldstein and Charles Horioka have pointed out, if this were true, the level of investment that is undertaken in France would depend only on the profitability of investment in France, and it would have no relationship to the available savings in France. Actually, however, this turns out to be false. Increased savings in one country translate into increased investments in that country almost one for one. Despite substantial crossborder money flows, different rates of return among countries persist and are not equalized by capital moving to higher-return economies.

One can easily multiply the examples. U.S. portfolios tend to be remarkably concentrated in U.S. stocks. The prices of apparently identical goods differ widely from one country to another despite the fact that the goods can be traded. In reality, national economies retain a considerable degree of isolation from each other, and national policymakers enjoy more autonomy than is assumed by most recent writings on the erosion of national sovereignty.

The limited nature of globalization can perhaps be better appreciated by placing it into historical context. By many measures, the world economy was more integrated at the height of the gold standard in the late 19th century than it is now. In the United States and Europe, trade volumes peaked before World War I and then collapsed during the interwar years. Trade surged again after 1950, but neither Europe nor the United States is significantly more open today (gauging by ratios of trade to national income) than it was under the gold standard. Japan actually exports less of its total production today than it did during the interwar period.

Globalization Matters

It would be a mistake to conclude from this evidence that globalization is irrelevant. Due to the increased importance of trade, the options available to national policymakers have narrowed appreciably over the last three decades. The oft-mentioned imperative of maintaining "international competitiveness" now looms much larger and imparts a definite bias to policymaking.

Consider labor market practices. As France, Germany, and other countries have shown, it is still possible to maintain labor market policies that increase the cost of labor. But globalization is raising the overall social cost of exercising this option. European nations can afford to have generous minimum wages and benefit levels if they choose to pay the costs. But the stakes—the resulting unemployment levels—have been raised by the increased international mobility of firms.

The consequences are apparent everywhere. In Japan, large corporations have started to dismantle the postwar practice of providing lifetime employment, one of Japan's most distinctive social institutions. In France and Germany, unions have been fighting government attempts to cut pension benefits. In South Korea, labor unions have taken to the streets to protest the government's relaxation of firing restrictions. Developing countries in Latin America are competing with each other in liberalizing trade, deregulating their economies, and privatizing public enterprises.

Ask business executives or government officials why these changes are necessary, and you will hear the same mantra repeated over and over again: "We need to remain (or become) competitive in a global economy." As some of these changes appear to violate long-standing social bargains in many countries, the widespread populist reaction to globalization is perhaps understandable.

The anxieties generated by globalization must be seen in the context of the demands placed on national governments, which have expanded radically since the late 19th century. At the height of the gold standard, governments were not yet expected to perform social-welfare functions on a large scale. Ensuring adequate levels of employment, establishing social safety nets, providing medical and social insurance, and caring for the poor were not parts of the government agenda. Such demands multiplied during the period following the Second World War. Indeed, a key component of the implicit postwar social bargain in the advanced industrial countries has been the provision of social insurance and safety nets at home (unemployment compensation, severance payments, and adjustment assistance, for example) in exchange for the adoption of freer trade policies.

This bargain is clearly eroding. Employers are less willing to provide the benefits of job security and stability, partly because of increased competition but also because their enhanced global mobility makes them less dependent on the goodwill of their local work force. Governments are less able to sustain social safety nets, because an important part of their tax base has become footloose because of the increased mobility of capital. Moreover, the ideological onslaught against the welfare state has paralyzed many governments and made them unable to respond to the domestic needs of a more integrated economy.

More Trade, More Government

The postwar period has witnessed two apparently contradictory trends: the growth of trade and the growth of government. Prior to the Second World War, government expenditures averaged around 20 per cent of the gross domestic products (GDPs) of today's advanced industrialized countries. By the mid-1990s, that figure had more than doubled to 47 per cent. The increased role of government is

Forms of Social Insurance

All societies maintain provisions for social insurance to counter large drops in workers' and families' living standard, but that insurance takes different forms. In Europe and North America, income transfers paid out by the government are the predominant form of social insurance. Old-age pensions, unemployment compensation, disability insurance, and family support constitute the bulk of such transfers. The effect of these programs is twofold: They establish an income minimum for the citizenry regardless of employment status, and they reduce uncertainty regarding lifetime earnings for workers. In the United States, the Trade Adjustment Assistance (TAA) program targets workers who lose their jobs due to import competition. The TAA provides additional unemployment benefits, training subsidies, and relocation assistance. Comparatively few workers have benefited from TAA.

In Japan and other East Asian countries, income transfers are small compared with those in European nations. Many of the social insurance functions provided by the state in Western nations are in fact supplied by large enterprises in East Asia. These come in the form of lifetime-employment guarantees and employer-provided social services, ranging from housing and medical care to family support.

Many developing countries lack the administrative capacity to run income-transfer programs, and only a small share of the labor force is employed in the formal sector. In such countries, social insurance often takes yet another form: public-works programs and employment in the public sector, where jobs are typically more secure than in the private sector.

Government programs are not the only mechanism for reducing income risk. Private insurance, community support, and household transfers are also important. As markets spread and mobility increases, however, some of the informal mechanisms for alleviating income insecurity—such as community-based social services—will become harder to sustain.

particularly striking in countries like the United States (from 9 to 34 per cent), Sweden (from 10 to 69 per cent), and the Netherlands (from 19 to 54 per cent). The driving force behind the expansion of government during this period was the increase in social spending—and income transfers in particular.

It is not a coincidence that social spending increased alongside international trade. For example, the small, highly open European economies like Austria, the Netherlands, and Sweden have large governments in part as a result of their attempts to minimize the social impact of openness to the international economy. It is in the most open countries like Denmark, the Netherlands, and Sweden that spending on income transfers has expanded the most.

Indeed, there is a surprisingly strong association across countries between the degree of exposure to international trade and the importance of the government in the economy. The chart below shows the relationship between trade and spending on social protection (including unemployment insurance, pensions, and family benefits) in 21 countries for which the Organization for Economic Cooperation and Development (OECD) publishes crossnationally comparable data. The chart reveals an unmistakably positive correlation between a nation's openness to trade and the amount of its spending on social programs. At one end of the distribution we have the United States and Japan, which have the lowest trade shares in GDP and some of the lowest shares of spending on social protection. At the other end, Luxembourg, Belgium, and the Netherlands have economies with high degrees of openness and large income transfers. This relationship is not confined to OECD economies: Developing nations also exhibit this pattern. Furthermore, the extent to which imports and exports were important in a country's economy in the early 1960s provided a good predictor of how big its government would become in the ensuing three decades, regardless of how developed it was. All the available evidence points to the same, unavoidable conclusion: The social welfare state has been the flip side of the open economy.

International economic integration thus poses a serious dilemma: Globalization increases the demand for social insurance while simultaneously constraining

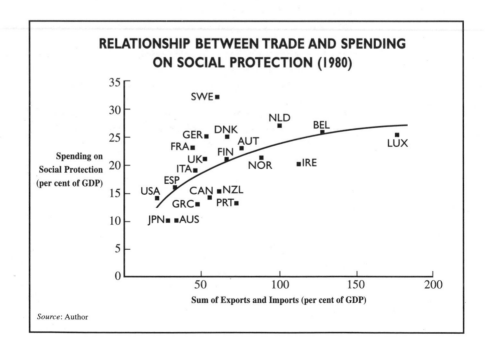

RELATIONSHIP BETWEEN TRADE AND SPENDING ON SOCIAL PROTECTION (1980)

Spending on Social Protection (per cent of GDP)

Sum of Exports and Imports (per cent of GDP)

Source: Author

the ability of governments to respond effectively to that demand. Consequently, as globalization deepens, the social consensus required to keep domestic markets open to international trade erodes.

Since the early 1980s, tax rates on capital have tended to decrease in the leading industrial nations, while tax rates on labor have continued generally to increase. At the same time, social spending has stabilized in relation to national incomes. These outcomes reflect the tradeoffs facing governments in increasingly open economies: The demands for social programs are being balanced against the need to reduce the tax burden on capital, which has become more globally mobile.

By any standard, the postwar social bargain has served the world economy extremely well. Spurred by widespread trade liberalization, world trade has soared since the 1950s. This expansion did not cause major social dislocations and did not engender much opposition in the advanced industrial countries. Today, however, the process of international economic integration is taking place against a backdrop of retreating governments and diminished social obligations. Yet the need for social insurance for the vast majority of the population that lacks international mobility has not diminished. If anything, this need has grown.

The question, therefore, is how the tension between globalization and the pressure to mitigate risks can be eased. If the vital role that social insurance played in enabling the postwar expansion of trade is neglected and social safety nets are allowed to dwindle, the domestic consensus in favor of open markets will be eroded seriously, and protectionist pressures will soar.

The Global Trade in Social Values

In the markets for goods, services, labor, and capital, international trade creates arbitrage—the possibility of buying (or producing) in one place at one price and selling at a higher price elsewhere. Prices thus tend to converge in the long run, this convergence being the source of the gains from trade. But trade exerts pressure toward another kind of arbitrage as well: arbitrage in national norms and social institutions. This form of arbitrage results, indirectly, as the costs of maintaining divergent social arrangements go up. As a consequence, open trade can conflict with long-standing social contracts that protect certain activities from the relentlessness of the free market. This is a key tension generated by globalization.

As the technology for manufactured goods becomes standardized and diffused internationally, nations with different sets of values, norms, institutions, and collective preferences begin to compete head on in markets for similar goods. In the traditional approach to trade policy, this trend is of no consequence: Differences in national practices and social institutions are, in effect, treated just like any other differences that determine a country's comparative advantage (such as endowments of physical capital or skilled labor).

In practice, however, trade becomes contentious when it unleashes forces that undermine the social norms implicit in domestic practices. For example, not all residents of advanced industrial countries are comfortable with the weakening of domestic institutions through the forces of trade, such as when child labor in

Honduras replaces workers in South Carolina or when cuts in pension benefits in France are called for in response to the requirements of the Treaty on European Union. This sense of unease is one way of interpreting the demands for "fair trade." Much of the discussion surrounding the new issues in trade policy—e.g., labor standards, the environment, competition policy, and corruption—can be cast in this light of procedural fairness.

Trade usually redistributes income among industries, regions, and individuals. Therefore, a principled defense of free trade cannot be constructed without addressing the question of the fairness and legitimacy of the practices that generate these distributional "costs." How comparative advantage is created matters. Low-wage foreign competition arising from an abundance of workers is different from competition that is created by foreign labor practices that violate norms at home. Low wages that result from demography or history are very different from low wages that result from government repression of unions.

From this perspective it is easier to understand why many people are often ill at ease with the consequences of international economic integration. Automatically branding all concerned groups as self-interested protectionists does not help much. This perspective also prepares us not to expect broad popular support for trade when trade involves exchanges that clash with (and erode) prevailing domestic social arrangements.

Consider labor rules, for example. Since the 1930s, U.S. laws have recognized that restrictions on "free contract" are legitimate to counteract the effects of unequal bargaining power. Consequently, the employment relationship in the United States (and elsewhere) is subject to a multitude of restrictions, such as those that regulate working hours, workplace safety, labor/management negotiations, and so forth. Many of these restrictions have been put in place to redress the asymmetry in bargaining power that would otherwise disadvantage workers vis-à-vis employers.

Globalization upsets this balance by creating a different sort of asymmetry: Employers can move abroad, but employees cannot. There is no substantive difference between American workers being driven from their jobs by their fellow *domestic* workers who agree to work 12-hour days, earn less than the minimum wage, or be fired if they join a union—all of which are illegal under U.S. law—and their being similarly disadvantaged by *foreign* workers doing the same. If society is unwilling to accept the former, why should it countenance the latter? Globalization generates an inequality in bargaining power that 60 years of labor legislation in the United States has tried to prevent. It is in effect eroding a social understanding that has long been settled.

Whether they derive from labor standards, environmental policy, or corruption, differences in domestic practices and institutions have become matters of international controversy. That is indeed the common theme that runs the gamut of the new issues on the agenda of the World Trade Organization (WTO). Conflicts arise both when these differences create trade—as in the cases of child labor or lax environmental policies—and when they reduce it—as industrial practices in Japan are alleged to do. As the *New York Times* editorialized on July 11, 1996, in connection with the Kodak-Fuji dispute on access to the photographic film market in Japan, "the Kodak case asks the WTO, in effect, to pass judgment on the way Japan does business."

The notions of "fair trade" and "leveling the playing field" that lie behind the pressures for putting these new issues on the trade agenda have been ridiculed by economists. But once it is recognized that trade has implications for domestic norms and social arrangements and that its legitimacy rests in part on its compatibility with these, such notions are not so outlandish. These sentiments are ways of addressing the concerns to which trade gives rise. Free trade among countries with different domestic practices requires an acceptance of either an erosion of domestic structures or the need for some degree of harmonization or convergence.

If this is the appropriate context in which demands for "fair trade" or "leveling the playing field" must be understood, it should also be clear that policymakers often take too many liberties in justifying their actions along such lines. Most of the pricing policies that pass as "unfair trade" in U.S. antidumping proceedings, for example, are standard business practice in the United States and other countries. While there may not be a sharp dividing line between what is fair and unfair in international trade, one clear sign that pure protectionism is at the root of a trade dispute is the prevalence of practices within the domestic economy that are identical or similar to those being protested in the international arena. Fairness cannot be eliminated from thinking about trade policy; but neither can it be invoked to justify trade restrictions when the practice in question does not conflict with domestic norms as revealed by actual practice.

Misunderstanding Trade

The tensions created by globalization are real. They are, however, considerably more subtle than the terminology that has come to dominate the debate. "Low-wage competition," "leveling the playing field," and "race to the bottom" are catchy phrases that often muddle the public's understanding of the real issues. A more nuanced debate and more imaginative solutions are badly needed.

A broader approach to this debate, one that takes into account some of the aspects discussed here, provides more credibility to the defenders of free trade in their attempts to clear up the misunderstandings that the opponents of trade often propagate. Journalist William Greider's recent book, *One World, Ready or Not— The Manic Logic of Global Capitalism,* illustrates the appeal that many of these misunderstandings retain in the minds of popular commentators on trade.

One of the main themes of this book—that the global expansion of markets is undermining social cohesion and is inexorably leading toward a major economic and political crisis—could be viewed as a more boldly expressed version of the potential danger that is highlighted above. Many of Greider's concerns—the consequences for low-skilled workers in the advanced industrial countries, the weakening of social safety nets, and the repression of political rights in some leading exporters like China and Indonesia—are indeed valid. However, the disregard for sound economic analysis and systematic empirical evidence that characterizes

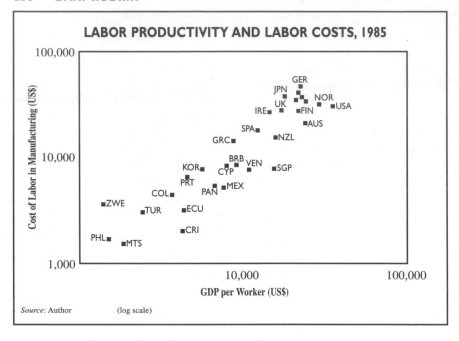

LABOR PRODUCTIVITY AND LABOR COSTS, 1985

Source: Author   (log scale)

Greider's book makes it both a very unreliable guide to understanding what is taking place and a faulty manual for setting things right.

A popular fallacy perpetuated in works like Greider's is that low wages are the driving force behind today's global trade. If that were so, the world's most formidable exporters would be Bangladesh and a smattering of African countries. Some Mexican or Malaysian exporting plants may approach U.S. levels in labor productivity, while local wages fall far short. Yet what is true for a small number of plants does not extend to economies as a whole and therefore does not have much bearing on the bulk of world trade.

The chart above shows the relationship between economy-wide labor productivity (GDP per worker) and labor costs in manufacturing in a wide range of countries. There is almost a one-to-one relationship between these two, indicating that wages are closely related to productivity. Low-wage economies are those in which levels of labor productivity are commensurately low. This tendency is of course no surprise to anyone with common sense. Yet much of the discourse on trade presumes a huge gap between wages and productivity in the developing country exporters.

Similarly, it is a mistake to attribute the U.S. trade deficit to the restrictive commercial policies of other countries—policies that Greider calls the "unbalanced behavior" of U.S. trading partners. How then can we explain the large U.S. deficit with Canada? If trade imbalances were determined by commercial policies, then India, as one of the world's most protectionist countries until recently, would have been running large trade surpluses.

Another misconception is that export-oriented industrialization has somehow failed to improve the livelihood of workers in East and Southeast Asia. Contrary to the impression one gets from listening to the opponents of globalization, life is significantly better for the vast majority of the former peasants who now toil in Malaysian or Chinese factories. Moreover, it is generally not the case that foreign-owned companies in developing countries provide working conditions that are inferior to those available elsewhere in the particular country; in fact, the reverse is more often true.

Perhaps the most baffling of the antiglobalization arguments is that trade and foreign investment are inexorably leading to excess capacity on a global scale. This is Greider's key argument and ultimately the main reason why he believes the system will self-destruct. Consider his discussion of Boeing's outsourcing of some of its components to the Xian Aircraft Company in China:

> When new production work was moved to Xian from places like the United States, the global system was, in effect, swapping highly paid industrial workers for very cheap ones. To put the point more crudely, Boeing was exchanging a $50,000 American machinist for a Chinese machinist who earned $600 or $700 a year. Which one could buy the world's goods? Thus, even though incomes and purchasing power were expanding robustly among the new consumers of China, the overall effect was an erosion of the world's potential purchasing power. If one multiplied the Xian example across many factories and industrial sectors, as well as other aspiring countries, one could begin to visualize why global consumption was unable to keep up with global production.

An economist would rightly point out that the argument makes little sense. The Chinese worker who earns only a tiny fraction of his American counterpart is likely to be commensurately less productive. Even if the Chinese worker's wages are repressed below actual productivity, the result is a transfer in purchasing power—to Boeing's shareholders and the Chinese employers—and not a diminution of global purchasing power. Perhaps Greider is thinking that Boeing's shareholders and the Chinese employers have a lower propensity to consume than the Chinese workers. If so, where is the evidence? Where is the global surplus in savings and the secular decline in real interest rates that we would surely have observed if income is going from low savers to high savers?

It may be unfair to pick on Greider, especially since some of his other conclusions are worth taking seriously. But the misunderstandings that his book displays are commonplace in the globalization debate and do not help to advance it.

Safety Nets, Not Trade Barriers

One need not be alarmed by globalization, but neither should one take a Panglossian view of it. Globalization greatly enhances the opportunities available to those who have the skills and mobility to flourish in world markets. It can help poor countries to escape poverty. It does not constrain national autonomy nearly as much as popular discussions assume. At the same time, globalization does exert downward pressure on the wages of underskilled workers in industrialized countries, exacerbate economic insecurity, call into question accepted social arrangements, and weaken social safety nets.

There are two dangers from complacency toward the social consequences of globalization. The first and more obvious one is the potential for a political backlash against trade. The candidacy of Patrick Buchanan in the 1996 Republican presidential primaries revealed that protectionism can be a rather easy sell at a time when broad segments of American society are experiencing anxieties related to globalization. The same can be said about the political influence of Vladimir Zhirinovsky in Russia or Jean-Marie Le Pen in France—influence that was achieved, at least in part, in response to the perceived effects of globalization. Economists may complain that protectionism is mere snake oil and argue that the ailments require altogether different medicine, but intellectual arguments will not win hearts and minds unless concrete solutions are offered. Trade protection, for all of its faults, has the benefit of concreteness.

Perhaps future Buchanans will ultimately be defeated, as Buchanan himself was, by the public's common sense. Even so, a second and perhaps more serious danger remains: The accumulation of globalization's side effects could lead to a new set of class divisions—between those who prosper in the globalized economy and those who do not; between those who share its values and those who would rather not; and between those who can diversify away its risks and those who cannot. This is not a pleasing prospect even for individuals on the winning side of the globalization divide: The deepening of social fissures harms us all.

National policymakers must not retreat behind protectionist walls. Protectionism would be of limited help, and it would create its own social tensions. Policymakers ought instead to complement the external strategy of liberalization with an internal strategy of compensation, training, and social insurance for those groups who are most at risk.

In the United States, President Bill Clinton's education initiatives represent a move in the right direction. However, the August 1996 welfare reform act could weaken social safety nets precisely at a time when globalization calls for the opposite. In Europe, as well, the pruning of the welfare state may exacerbate the strains of globalization.

Contrary to widespread belief, maintaining adequate safety nets for those at the bottom of the income distribution would not break the bank. Currently, old-age insurance is the most expensive income-transfer item for the advanced industrial countries. A reorientation of public resources away from pensions and toward labor-market and antipoverty programs would be a more appropriate way to address the challenges of globalization. This shift could be achieved while reducing overall public spending. Broad segments of the population in the industrial countries are understandably nervous about changing basic social-welfare arrangements. Therefore, political leadership will be required to render such changes palatable to these groups.

At the global level, the challenge is twofold. On the one hand, a set of rules that encourages greater harmonization of social and industrial policies on a voluntary basis is needed. Such harmonization could reduce tensions that arise from differing national practices. At the same time, flexibility sufficient to allow selective disengagement from multilateral disciplines needs to be built into the rules that govern international trade.

Currently, the WTO Agreement on Safeguards allows member states to impose temporary trade restrictions following an increase in imports—but only under a stringent set of conditions. One could imagine expanding the scope of the agreement to include a broader range of circumstances, reflecting concerns over labor standards, the environment, and even ethical norms in the importing country. The purpose of such an expanded "escape clause" mechanism would be to allow countries—under well-specified contingencies and subject to multilaterally approved procedures—greater breathing room to fulfill domestic requirements that conflict with free trade. If this flexibility could be achieved in exchange for a tightening of rules on antidumping, which have a highly corrosive effect on the world trading system, the benefits could be substantial.

Globalization is not occurring in a vacuum: It is part of a broader trend we may call marketization. Receding government, deregulation, and the shrinking of social obligations are the domestic counterparts of the intertwining of national economies. Globalization could not have advanced this far without these complementary forces at work. The broader challenge for the 21st century is to engineer a new balance between the market and society—one that will continue to unleash the creative energies of private entrepreneurship without eroding the social bases of cooperation.

The Nuke of the 90's

Roger C. Altman

In July 1945, a group of scientists huddled in the New Mexico dawn to witness the first nuclear explosion. They had created a terrible power, but one that nations have successfully controlled for more than 50 years. Now we have unleashed a very different but similarly awesome force, one capable of overthrowing governments and their policies almost overnight. And there are no systems in place for controlling it.

This force is the global financial marketplace. Strengthening for years, the markets have emerged as the ruling international authority, more potent than any military or political power. When arrayed against any nation, including the United States, they can impose previously unthinkable changes.

Such changes can sometimes be for the good. Indeed, the global markets have recently propelled many nations toward democracy. But there is a new and frightening downside, which we glimpsed in October but still haven't fully seen or understood. That is the risk of a chain reaction, a global market meltdown that could shatter confidence and plunge the world into recession or worse.

Imagine, for example, that Brazil's currency collapsed, losing more than half its value in a week. The country's banking system would totter while its stock and bond markets plummeted. Big international investors would race for the door, but not before sustaining heavy losses. Fearing that the Brazilian crisis would quickly spread to other Latin American markets, they would bail out of those too,

Article originally appeared in the *New York Times Magazine,* March 1, 1998. Reprinted by permission of the author.

causing them to plunge. The International Monetary Fund could not react quickly enough.

Now incurring wider losses, these same investors would try to protect themselves by pre-emptively selling in other foreign markets. This would trigger a stock market free fall in Asia and Europe, and then on Wall Street. Within a week, worldwide markets might lose an unprecedented quarter or more of their value. Stunned consumers and businesses would cut back their spending plans, fearing that the good times were over. This would be the financial shock that Alan Greenspan obliquely described as the one risk to the American economy today.

This risk of a global meltdown reflects the law of unintended consequences. The worldwide elimination of barriers to trade and capital, and the rise of communications technology, have created the global financial marketplace, which informed observers hailed for bringing private capital to the developing world, encouraging economic growth and democracy.

But in the past five years, as seamless 24-hour markets clicked in, the risks inherent in the new system became apparent. No one had envisioned such growth and the expansion of power that accompanied it. Average daily worldwide trading in financial instruments now may exceed $1 trillion. Yes, each day. This is largely carried out by huge financial institutions with short investment horizons.

The result is like an extraterrestrial force: gigantic flows of money, directed electronically, which dominate world finance and can change direction in an hour. They are beyond the control of any government or regulator. And there is no method of directly communicating with them.

Nations depend on stable currencies for facilitating imports and exports, for financing trade and budget deficits and for attracting investment capital. But their currencies are traded minute by minute around the world. As long as the markets look favorably on a nation's financial performance, there can be economic stability.

But if they render a negative verdict, the results can be disastrous. This is what happened to Mexico in late 1994, when it effectively went bankrupt. The markets suddenly judged Mexico's Government to be borrowing too much foreign capital on a short-term basis. Foreign investors fled, the peso plunged and the country couldn't pay off its debts. Over subsequent months, its economy contracted and bitter times set in. Only a controversial $20 billion in emergency financing organized by the United States kept Mexico from complete collapse.

Then last June, the global markets delivered a similarly harsh blow to Southeast Asia. It came out of the blue, and it followed years and years of celebrating the "miracle" economic rise of these "Asian tigers." Like the Titanic, they had acquired an aura of invincibility.

But that was shattered like a bullet exploding a glass. The markets judged that first Thailand, then Malaysia, Indonesia and South Korea were presiding over rickety banking systems loaded with bad loans. One by one their currencies were battered, some losing up to 70 percent of their value. The national treasuries all ran out of money trying to stop the plunge, and weakened economies followed. This time it was the International Monetary Fund that organized nearly $120 billion of emergency loans for these four countries to keep them breathing and prevent a domino effect elsewhere.

For the first time we saw what a worldwide collapse might look like. As the Asian financial crisis widened last October, the Hong Kong stock market, the region's biggest, began to fall. Then it plunged, down more than 10 percent in one day. This instantly triggered huge, same-day market declines across Europe and a shocking 554-point drop on Wall Street.

The next day, the world financial community held its breath, unsure whether the chain reaction would accelerate or abate. We were on the precipice. Luckily, markets stabilized, but those events may have been the tremor before the earthquake, and that was only four months ago.

High anxiety among the world's central bankers and finance ministers over the Asian crisis continues. Yes, they want to avoid calamitous impacts on South Korea and Indonesia, both strategically important countries. But their real fear is that the Asian market collapse will suddenly go global. Privately they consider that a real possibility.

What can be done to limit this risk of worldwide financial infection? There is only one bulwark, and it is the I.M.F., the world's emergency lender to nations in distress. But we need a vastly stronger and more alert I.M.F. to successfully contain those regional crises. Even now, global financial markets are unsure if the emergency I.M.F. financing for Indonesia is enough, or whether that nation will still default.

The huge Asian financing package has depleted the I.M.F.'s resources to an alarming degree. It needs a capital infusion from its shareholders, with the U.S. share even bigger than the $18 billion President Clinton has requested. The congressional outlook is uncertain. But a rejection of increased U.S. commitments could, by itself, destabilize world markets.

The managerial capabilities of the I.M.F. also require upgrading. Despite misgivings among finance ministers—who fear self-fulfilling prophecies—the fund must serve as an early-warning system for deteriorating national finances. Here at home, the major credit-rating agencies issue an alert if a corporation is faltering or if a city's debt load is getting too onerous. The I.M.F. should do the same.

Today, the I.M.F. expresses its concerns privately to governments with shaky finances. But these warnings are usually ignored by national political leaders, who have no interest in administering tough medicine.

Yet if the I.M.F. remained studiously apolitical, it could issue such warnings publicly, and financial markets would then apply the pressure for change. Yes, such admonitions could themselves trigger crises. But if the I.M.F. sounded the alarm early enough, it would more often move governments toward sounder finances and pull them back from the brink.

World leaders have discussed this warning capability for some time, but it was hard to take such an important step to ward off a danger that seemed, in previous years, to be hypothetical. We no longer have that excuse.

Anyone who thinks that the United States is immunized against all these risks is wrong. We may be in favor with these markets now, but that can change quickly. Indeed, the dollar set an all-time low against the yen only three years ago, causing much nervousness around the world. Should the markets move more strongly against our currency, even America's resources could not sustain its value. Like a long list of nations before us, we could be forced to raise interest rates drastically, which would probably throw the economy into a recession.

We saw some of this in 1978, when the dollar came under pressure. President Carter, trying to placate the markets, promised to adopt a tighter budget. The markets judged his promise weak and smashed the dollar down. One week later, the President had no choice but to announce yet a smaller deficit, even though it upset his political priorities.

We have entered an age of unprecedented financial power and risk. The strength of worldwide markets, already immeasurable, will only grow. Markets will be the dominant, worldwide force of the early 21st century, dwarfing that of the United States or any consortium of nations. And as with nuclear weapons, we are now permanently in their shadow.

New Rules

THE AMERICAN ECONOMY
IN THE NEXT CENTURY

Lester C. Thurow

The global economic environment in which the United States participates is undergoing tremendous and rapid change, but not for the first time. At the end of the nineteenth century, the invention of electricity sparked what some have called the second industrial revolution. Inventions such as underground transportation and streetcars made large cities possible for the first time. New industries developed, including electrical power and telecommunications, and old industries were transformed. The elevator reversed traditional rent differentials and made the top floors of buildings more valuable than the bottom floors for the first time in history. Light bulbs replaced oil and gas lamps, allowing economic and leisure activities to take place around the clock. As electric motors replaced steam engines, distributed power meant that the old linear factory could be abandoned and replaced with very different configurations of production.

Similarly, future historians studying the end of the twentieth century will refer to the major changes we are witnessing as the third industrial revolution. These changes are often called the "information revolution," but it is more accurate to say that we are entering an era of man-made, brain-power industries, for this revolution has replaced natural resources with human skills as mankind's most productive asset. The symbol of this new era is at hand: today, for the first time in history, the world's wealthiest man, Bill Gates, is a knowledge worker and not a petroleum magnate, as had been the case for the past hundred years. The political

Reprinted with permission from the *Harvard International Review* (Winter 1997/98).

and technical changes that define this third industrial revolution have important implications for the US economy and for US economic policy.

The Economic World to Come

The extent of this third industrial revolution far surpasses new information technologies. With the development of biotechnology, an era of partially man-made plants, animals, and even humans is dawning. New, custom-designed materials and intelligent, computer-controlled machines are rendering traditional production processes obsolete. Microelectronics and the computer are revolutionizing every sector of the economy—and not just the communication and information aspects of these industries. The oil industry, for example, harnessing acoustical sounding, deep-water production techniques, and horizontal drilling, has rapidly transformed itself into a knowledge-based industry. Some of the important new sectors that will develop from this revolution—computers, semiconductors, and electronic entertainment—are already visible. Others, such as electronic retailing, are in their infancy, and others have yet to be born.

A hundred years ago, local economies and local business gradually diminished in importance and were replaced by national economies and large national corporations. So today, national economies and national companies are gradually being replaced by a global economy characterized by multinational corporations. We are witnessing not only the expansion of world trade, but the emergence of an unprecedented global economy in which world trade will be a critical part of almost all business enterprise.

This transnational economy is already taking shape. Most national central banks are now irrelevant, as the world's money is essentially controlled by three key institutions: the US Federal Reserve Board, the Bank of Japan, and the German Bundesbank. Global capital markets, centered in London, Tokyo, and New York, are facilitating increased internationalization in every area of finance. Home mortgages from a local US bank, for example, are bundled with other home mortgages, securitized, and sold on global capital markets—perhaps to some foreign investment group. In this new, globalized financial world, even a local bank could thus find itself servicing international loans.

This globalization blurs national economic boundaries. Consider the accelerometer, a US$50 semiconductor chip that replaces about US$650 worth of mechanical sensors that control the air bags in cars. Today, accelerometers are assembled in the United States by skilled labor, shipped to the Philippines for testing, re-exported for packaging by mid-skill workers in Taiwan, and then sent to Germany where they are installed in BMW's, some of which are shipped to Singapore for final sale. By definition, an economy is the area over which capitalists arbitrage prices and wages, looking to buy at the lowest possible costs and sell at the highest possible prices. The case of the accelerometer illustrates how businesses now conduct arbitrage in one huge global marketplace. BMW manufactures each component of its vehicles wherever it can be most cheaply produced, regardless of national boundaries.

The Erosion of Nationality

Much of the sales and production of most of America's big corporations is now occurring overseas. Coca-Cola makes 80 percent of its sales outside of the United States. The meaning of "American corporation" changes when only one-fifth of the corporation's sales occur in the domestic market. Just as large national corporations once replaced small family businesses in the second industrial revolution, even larger multinational corporations are now replacing national corporations. These companies play a global game and, in many respects, regard countries in the same ways that large US corporations regard individual US states.

As corporations become increasingly mobile, countries will be forced to compete in order to encourage companies to establish headquarters and plants within their borders. Intel, for example, is receiving a huge subsidy from Israel in exchange for building a large semiconductor facility there. Such plants are essentially put up for bid; whichever country gives the company the best deal in terms of wages, skills, transportation costs, markets, taxes, and direct subsidies is rewarded by a corporate presence and the associated benefits. Though foreign companies do not yet negotiate directly with the US federal government to get anything beyond the normal level playing field, they have become very good at playing US states off against one another. Mercedes and BMW, for example, were able to negotiate large subsidies—hundreds of thousands of dollars in tax reductions and expenditures directed at their needs—with the states of Alabama and South Carolina.

Countries that once seemed uncompetitive have succeeded by offering special services to the global economy. The Cayman Islands, whose lax banking regulations have attracted customers weary of regulation in their home countries, have become the world's fifth largest banking center. Dummy corporations established in the Cayman Islands, for example, have allowed Taiwanese investors to pour money into mainland China despite official bans on such investment. And yet none of these businessmen ever goes to the Caymans—all the necessary transactions take place electronically.

Technology and globalization are rapidly changing the way businesses operate, limiting the ability of governments to restrict—or even control—economic activity.

Economic Interdependence

Put simply, globalization and multinationalization have reduced the powers of governments to regulate behavior and to set independent economic policies. Companies are no longer wedded to any one economy: they simply move their operations to locations where banking regulations, anti-trust policies, and the rules governing intellectual property rights are most favorable to their interests. Citibank, for example, does its investment banking in London to avoid US laws prohibiting banks from serving as both commercial and investment banks. European airlines buy large blocks of shares in US domestic airlines that would be illegal if the buyer were a US airline. Drug manufacturers move to India because it does not recognize patents on new drugs.

Americans have noticed this loss of governmental power less than others because it has been less real in the United States. As the United States has historically been the world's largest unified economy and most important power broker, the US government has retained more of its economic independence. The dollar is the world's unrivaled reserve currency. The United States holds the largest voting rights on the boards of global institutions such as the World Bank and the International Monetary Fund (IMF). US military protection was a valued commodity during the Cold War, and many countries were careful about crossing the United States economically to ensure the health of their alliance with Washington. But all of this is about to change: the United States will remain a large player in the world economic game, but it will soon be subject to the same limitations facing everyone else.

The Cold War is over, and other nations no longer have to defer to American economic views to ensure US support for the sake of their national security. Japan, no longer dependent on American protection against the Soviet Union, now finds it easier to withstand US pressure on economic issues. US influence is also declining at both the World Bank and the IMF. The United States is providing a smaller fraction of funding to both institutions, and eventually, its formal voting powers will be reduced to reflect this decreased involvement. The United States is no longer the world's biggest economy—it is the second, behind the European Common Market.

Euro-Blues

The most noticeable change in the US position will come with the introduction of the Euro in 1999. For the first time since the Second World War, investors and financiers will have a viable alternative to the US dollar, and the venerable greenback will become just another currency. A few years ago, the dollar was falling dramatically against the yen (down from 112 to 78 yen to the dollar) and other currencies, but there was no run on the dollar, even as holders of dollar reserves were losing a third of their real purchasing power. Why not? The answer, of course, is that there was no place to go. Individual European currencies were too small to allow inflows of hundreds of billions of dollars, and the Japanese market was still too regulated and too closed for the yen to be a good alternative. As a result, holders of thousands of billions of dollars in international reserves were forced to sustain enormous losses in the real value of their reserves. With no better alternative, few investors redenominated their selling prices or disposed of their dollar reserves despite the dollar's problems. Had the Euro been in place when the dollar was plunging, more investors would have abandoned the dollar, perhaps precipitating a frenzied sell-off.

With the advent of the Euro, the rest of the world is apt to become much less interested in holding US dollars, making it more difficult for the United States to borrow the funds necessary to sustain a permanently large trade deficit. The risks of a deficit are simply much greater with the Euro in place. The events that put an end to the current pattern of large US trade deficits will not flow from actions taken in the countries that directly run large trade surpluses with the United States. For them, decreased lending would harm the US sales of their corporations. The shift is also not likely to begin with official government reserves because no one would deliberately shake the world trading system. It will most likely start when private companies and banks decide that they hold too many dollars. The advent of the Euro will represent the elimination of 14 European currencies. This, in turn, will reduce the need for foreign exchanges reserves, mostly held in dollars, for most banks and companies. Middle Eastern oil sellers will likely want to start denominating some of their oil sales and holding some of their reserves in Euros. Others will follow suit. Financial economists will make a lot of money running sophisticated mathematical models to determine the exact amounts that should be moved from dollars to Euros and how much redenominating of sales from dollars to Euros should occur, and traders eager for commissions will urge their customers to make the suggested revisions in their portfolios. The momentum of global currency markets away from the dollar will be considerable.

The bottom line is simple: the United States is unlikely to be able to run a large trade deficit for very long after the Euro comes into existence—the funds necessary to sustain this deficit will not be forthcoming. To the extent that US imports are redenominated in Euros, the United States will also become a normal economy in that import prices will rise when the dollar goes down—something that does not happen when import prices are denominated in dollars. In the future, a falling dollar will translate into rising inflation in the United States. The French have been forthright in stating that one of their key reasons for supporting the Euro is that it will force the United States to face the same constraints that limit France and most other countries.

Economic Chess

In a global economy, competition resembles a three-dimensional chess game. First, the game is played at a national level. Americans pay taxes to the US government, and, in return, they receive a set of publicly provided benefits. A tax system out of line with the rest of the world may handicap US citizens, but government educational investments provide them with many of the skills they will later sell as individuals. The US government provides (or does not provide) the world-class infrastructure—telecommunications, transportation, and the like—that American companies need to be competitive, low-cost sellers. The government also finances the basic research that allows its citizens to build the new industries of the future, such as biotechnology, and to enjoy the economic benefits of being ahead of the rest of the world. Governments do not directly compete, but they build the platforms on which economic competition takes place. To the extent that the US government invests in education, infrastructure, and research, it is helping American companies and individual Americans compete.

Second, the game is played at the corporate level. If an Intel or a Microsoft can dominate the microchip or software markets and earn far above the average rates of return, those who work for such companies or own such companies share in the benefits. Corporations on the leading edge of technology are able to earn higher profits and pay higher wages. Any corporation's technical edge depends partly on its own skills, investments, and creativity, and partly on government investment. The success of the American biotechnology industry is a good example of the need for both. Government research investment created the knowledge base for the industry and paid for the training of the most highly skilled part of its work force, but the biotech companies used those skills and technology to create a multibillion dollar industry.

Even companies that successfully become multinational tend to keep far more than a proportional share of their very best jobs—top management, research, and product development—near their traditional home base. Phillips of the Netherlands is a good example: the company's foreign sales have resulted in a lot of good jobs for the Dutch. As headquarters for southern China, Hong Kong has become much richer than was when it had a stand-alone economy prior to China's opening up in 1978. Countries and the individuals in them benefit from having successful multinational companies. Successful American multinational companies make it possible for more Americans to be successful individually.

Thirdly, the global economic game is played on an individual level, where personal skills are sold on domestic or global markets. Those skills are partly generated by government investment in education, but they are also derived from what we as individuals invest in our own skills and the experiences we acquire. To make maximum use of them, it pays to work for a good multinational company with a technical edge. For those with the right skills working for the right companies, a global economy opens opportunities for higher wages and more successful careers.

One World, One Wage

Not long ago, unskilled US workers enjoyed what might have been called an "American premium." They were paid more than laborers with the same skills in other parts of the world simply because, as unskilled Americans, they would work with higher capital-to-labor ratios, better raw materials, and larger numbers of highly-skilled fellow workers than their foreign counterparts. As a result, America's unskilled workers were relatively more productive and thus earned higher wages than similar unskilled workers elsewhere in the world.

The American premium for the unskilled has disappeared. With better transportation and communications, the superior complementary inputs that once gave unskilled Americans a competitive edge can today be harnessed anywhere in the world. Foreign businesses take advantage of these opportunities to cut costs and earn greater profits. As a result, wages for the unskilled in the United States are falling, and wages for the unskilled in foreign countries are rising to meet them.

This phenomenon, referred to by economists as "factor price equalization," is steadily eroding the American premium.

In a global economy, the judgment that a country is competitively successful leaves a lot of important questions unanswered. Real per capita GDP in the United States rose 40 percent from 1970 to 1996. America was undoubtedly successful. Yet at the same time, 60 percent of the work force in 1995 was laboring for real wages below previous peaks. At the median, real wages for nonsupervisory workers were down 13 percent from peak 1973 levels. America was competitively successful, but a majority of Americans were not.

The problem is not, as some have suggested, that the US economy is witnessing the "end of work" and a lack of jobs. The US economy generated 12 million net new jobs in the last four years and has the lowest unemployment rates seen for a quarter of a century. The problem for most Americans is falling real wages. At the same time, with a booming stock market and the wage gains that the economy generated over the past three decades, the top 20 percent of the population has seen its earnings and wealth rise rapidly. For them, the global economy has been a golden opportunity.

America remains a competitive success, yet at the same time, it is running a record trade deficit of over US$200 billion. Some domestic producers—in the semiconductor and software industries, for example—are gaining global market share, but even more firms, such as auto-makers and oil companies, are losing. Yet this market share may well have been lost to foreign producers owned by the same corporate parent. American capitalists are successfully hedging their positions, but the average American laborer is not.

The factor price equalization that accompanies globalization calls for wage reductions for the unskilled, wage increases for the skilled, higher returns to capital, and lower returns to labor. Other factors such as a technological shift toward skill-intensive industries may be contributing to this trend, but the forces that derive from arbitrage and the resulting factor price equalization are certainly present as well. These forces do not lead to societal equality. The resulting inequalities can be reduced with greater public investments in the skills of the lowest wage-earners, but they probably cannot be eliminated.

Democracy and Capitalism

All of this creates a problem for democracies. Democracy and capitalism have very different core values. Democracy is founded on equality—one vote per citizen regardless of his intelligence or work ethic. Capitalism, however, is motivated by inequality: differences in economic returns create the incentive structure which encourages hard work and wise investment. Because investments in human or physical assets, and hence future income, depend on current income, wealth tends to generate wealth and poverty tends to be a trap. The economically fit are expected to drive the economically unfit out of existence: there are no equalizing feedback mechanisms in capitalism.

Slowing Down?

The United States' Gross Domestic Product (or GDP, the total value of all final goods produced in an economy) as a fraction of the world's GDP total grew from slightly under 2% in 1820 to about 15% in 1900 to a remarkable 30% in 1951. Since the Second World War, however, not only has the rate of US GDP growth slowed, it has slowed relative to rates in other countries. As a result, US influence in world economic organizations like the World Bank is gradually diminishing. Starting in the late 1960s, GDP growth rates fell for countries around the world, but US growth rates fell even faster, slipping below those of many other countries.

According to Michael French's *US Economic History Since 1945*, three schools of thought exist to explain this slowdown. The first points to the persistence of an absolute US productivity advantage in many sectors and suggests that the growth slowdown was due to short-term factors, such as the recessions of the 1980s and the rising value of the dollar. A second perspective holds that the decline in relative US GDP growth is a result of exceptionally appropriate economic policies in foreign nations and not due to US failings. A third argument is that the United States is indeed losing its ability to compete with other economies because of its low savings rates and insufficient investment in education. Recently, though, economic difficulty in Germany and in Asia has raised the possibility that US productivity growth may again rise relative to that of other countries.

Historically, the social-welfare state and social investment in education have been used to reconcile capitalism and democracy. The state took actions to equalize market outcomes—implementing progressive taxes, pensions, health care, special tax benefits for home mortgages, and unemployment insurance—and helped the individual develop marketable skills by way of public education to insure that differences in living standards did not grow too wide. Regardless of the results of such policies, this system put the state visibly on the side of equality. Low-income individuals knew that the state was taking actions to raise their absolute and relative earnings.

Today, economic globalization and the overburdened US social security system are putting this system at risk. Ever increasing consumption expenditures on ever more numerous elderly voters have to be financed by reducing social welfare benefits for other groups, by cutting social investments in the future (education, infrastructure, and research), or by raising payroll taxes. Globalization has rendered this last option impossible. Higher payroll taxes simply drive industries and employment abroad—as is now dramatically visible in Europe. Lower social investment in education, skills, infrastructure, and research makes US companies and workers less competitive in world markets. With lower earnings, they are less able and less willing to pay the taxes necessary to finance expensive social programs.

As a result, the system that has held democracy and capitalism together for the last century has started to unravel. As earnings distributions widen due to factor price equalization and a skill-intensive technological shift, and as the US government seems unable and unwilling to do anything about it, that majority which faces lower real earnings will sooner or later become disaffected with democracy. Resolving this difficulty—finding a new method of linking democracy and capitalism symbiotically—will perhaps be the most critical economic and political problem facing the United States in the twenty-first century.

The Gender and Labor Politics of Postmodernity

Aihwa Ong

The literature on export-industrialization and the feminization of industrial work challenges theory to catch up with lived realities. Reports from the new frontiers of industrial labor reveal a widening gap between our analytical constructs and workers' actual experiences. This puzzle arises from our limited theoretical grasp of the ingenuity of capitalist operations and the creativity of workers' responses in the late 20th century.

Modernization models of capitalist development (33, 85) predicted an increasing adoption of mass-assembly production (Fordism; see 35:279–318) and the gradual decline of cottage industries in the Third World. Yet, since the early 1970s, mixed systems based on free-trade zones, subcontracting firms, and sweatshops have come to typify industrialization in Asia, Central America, and elsewhere. Lapietz (55) argues that the current mix of mass production, subcontracting, and family-type firms represents a new regime of accumulation worldwide. Since the 1973 world recession, new patterns of "flexible accumulation" (55, 42) have come into play as corporations struggle in an increasingly competitive global arena. Flexible labor regimes, based primarily on female and minority workers, are now common in the Third World, as well as in poor regions of metropolitan countries.[1]

Another common assumption about industrialization is that "class consciousness" is the most fundamental category by means of which we are to understand workers' experiences. Furthermore, theorists construct workers' engagements with capitalism in terms both of a core-periphery framework and of other binary models such as metropolitan/ex-colonial formations and hegemonic/despotic labor regimes (13, 14, 30, 70, 107). Thus, the feminization of the transnational industrial force has also raised expectations that a female working class solidarity in the periphery will grow (22, 24, 26, 88). However, a closer look at ethnographic cases does not indicate the widespread emergence of class and/or feminist consciousness in developing countries. Instead, the range of engagements with capital that such an examination reveals, and the various forms of consciousness reported in the ethnographies, preclude the application of a single analytical rubric.

In this essay I analyze the links between flexible labor regimes and the distinctive labor worlds found in Asia and Mexico. I discuss easily available studies, of uneven ethnographic and methodological quality, conducted between 1970 and 1990. Rather than a homogeneous spread of Fordist production and "despotic" labor regimes, we find local milieux constituted by the unexpected conjunctures of labor relations and cultural systems, high-tech operations and indigenous values. First, I argue that industrial modes of domination go beyond production relations strictly construed; new techniques operating through the control of social spaces are a distinctive feature of postmodern regimes. Second, workers' struggles and resistances are often not based upon class interests or class solidarity, but comprise individual and even covert acts against various forms of control. The interest defended, or the solidarity built, through such acts are more often linked to kinship and gender than to class. To analyze the complex and shifting relations of domination and subordination (and insubordination), I substitute the concept of "cultural struggle" for class struggle.[2] In his historical study of the English working class, Thompson (103) argues that class is a cultural formation. Below, I suggest that the daily practices of workers in defending themselves against various modes of control are also struggles over cultural meanings, values, and goals. These cultural values are shaped, contested, and defended in different domains of power relations. While such conflicts may not necessarily result in structural transformation, the changes they effect in everyday attitudes and norms—or what Williams calls "structures of feeling" (112)—are part of the dynamics of civil society.

From World System to Flexible Accumulation

In the 1960s, developing economies greatly improved conditions for a new round of investments by foreign capital. Earlier attempts at import-substitution had failed, and the United Nations proposed a new plan building on the export functions already characteristic of ex-colonial countries. In addition to raw materials and crops, developing economies could export goods manufactured in "free-trade zones" (FTZs). To attract foreign capital, tax-free privileges in trade were combined with new incentives such as provision of buildings and utilities by the local government, and ease of profit repatriation (105). Export-industrialization seemed to complement the "green revolution" sponsored by the World Bank and International Monetary Fund (9, 67).

This two-pronged strategy for developing poor countries was elegantly simple. The commercializing rural economy would supply and feed the labor released for work in the "free-trade zones." Local governments were enticed by the promise that off-shore industrialization would boost foreign earnings, while solving the problems linked to rapid population growth, namely un- and under-employment. Host governments hoped that the large number of rural male migrants, the group thought to have the greatest potential for political unrest, would be absorbed by the new off-shore industries. Instead, foreign companies investing in the FTZs sought young single women, thus creating a new female industrial force where none had been envisioned (53, 67, 74, 88, 105).

By the 1970s, a network of industrial zones scattered throughout Southeast Asia opened up the region to industrial investments by Japanese transnational companies, to be quickly followed by Western corporations. At about the same time, the implementation of the *Maquiladora* (assembly plant) program along the US-Mexican Border opened up Mexico to North American firms (27:25–27).

To explain this corporate shift to overseas production scholars relied heavily on Wallerstein's (107) concept of the "modern world-system." He argues that European capitalism historically produced a transnational division of labor ("core, semi-periphery, and periphery") which reflected the degree of capitalist development achieved by each country drawn into global exchange relations. Employing Wallerstein's notion of different labor regimes in the core and periphery (107:99–106), Froebel et al (30) argued that the key principle of the "new international division of labor" was the search for cheap labor by transnational companies. Corporate activities divided the world economy into "core" metropolitan countries, from which most capital originates, and "peripheral" countries where capital can realize its greatest profits.

In recent years, the world-system model has come under criticism for its static and mechanical formulation. Observers note that a complex global economy has been created by the shifting operations of transnational corporations and their articulation with the ambitions of Third World governments (55:23).

Instead of exploiting a single global periphery, corporations tap into different labor pools, contributing to varying employment relations in unevenly developed countries and regions (55:23). Thus, Marxist geographers maintain that FTZs represent a transitional pattern of capital accumulation characterized by great instability and dynamism: "The geography of capitalism is uneven, to be sure; but it is, above all, inconstant" (55:4–5). Following the 1970s world recession, intensified competition in the global arena compelled a new pattern of accumulation marked by flexibile strategies. Mixed production systems were located anywhere in the world where optimal production, infrastructural, marketing, and political conditions existed. Such dispersal strategies became a means for the social reorganization of accumulation, pitting capital against capital, and one region of the world against another. Thus the Japanese move into the Pacific Rim area recalls the prewar "Great Co-Prosperity Sphere" strategy whereby Japan sought to make Asia the off-shore base of Japanese capitalist expansion (67, 68, 105). Today, Japan's "globalization" approach uses investment and aid to coordinate what commodities countries in Southeast Asia should produce (11, 115). American and European capital has also entered the arena, but at a lower level of investment and success. To achieve global dominance, Japanese and Western companies bypassed high production costs, labor militancy, and environmental concerns at home by moving to Southeast Asia or Mexico. Such rapid shifts with respect to labor markets and their attendant maneuvers in new financial markets enhance the flexibility and mobility that allow corporations to exert greater labor control worldwide (42:147).

In off-shore sites corporations seek a peculiar mix of benefits, including tax breaks, low labor costs, and access to markets—benefits that exist already or can be created. Flexible financial operations characterize each level of transaction. Depending on the host country, FTZ benefits include tax incentives, government services, and such features as "total or partial exemption from laws and decrees of the country concerned" (105:1); such advantages are negotiable as economic conditions change. An "inter-enclave, export-import type of transaction" allows transfer pricing (whereby profits are transferred from one site to another), thereby escaping local taxes (67:24–25). This mobility of capital from zone to zone reduces overall costs of production, while it strengthens the bargaining position of corporations vis-à-vis local governments competing for foreign investments. Firms choose countries like Singapore where maximization of profit is ensured not only by cheap labor but also by "nonwage" costs of production such as the general business environment, the advantageous infrastructure, efficiency, and the political environment (59:191). Access to large consumer markets also facilitates quick turnover of capital.

The most important recent experiment in corporate production is its flexible combination of mass assembly and subcontracting systems, of modern firms and home work as linked units dominated by transnational capital. In Southeast Asia and Mexico, export-manufacturing is not confined to FTZs but is increasingly dispersed in subcontracting arrangements that may include part-time work by peasants. In Malaysia, transnational production is carried out mainly in FTZ mass-assembly plants; these highly stratified systems employ hundreds to thousands of workers, about 80% of whom are female operators on the shop floor (74). By contrast, in Hong Kong, the prototypical export-industrial economy, most export production is undertaken by subcontracting family firms, many operating under sweatshop conditions (49; 89:20). Despite its high labor costs relative to other Asian enclaves, Hong Kong is favored by global companies precisely for its peculiar mix of family production units, legislation that ensures a disciplined and tractable labor force, "peaceful industrial relations," infrastructure, and flexibility in meeting market conditions (49, 89). Taiwanese export-industrialization is also based on a majority of small firms and a few FTZ plants (32, 53). In the Philippines, where wages are among the lowest in Asia (54), subcontracting reduces the visibility of transnational firms, enabling them to bypass further political and economic costs. For instance, only a quarter of Filipino garment workers are based in FTZs; the bulk of garment manufacturing depends on a four-tiered subcontracting system that relies mainly on village home-sewers (82). Similarly, Beneria & Roldan (10) report that outside the Mexican *maquiladora* zone, home work by housewives is a part of the low level of the segmented labor market; though hidden behind illegalities and mixed forms of production, it is indirectly controlled by industrial capital (10:68, 73–74).

Corporate reliance on mixed production systems in off-shore sites has produced an increasingly heterogeneous work force—including children, men, and imported labor. Along the US-Mexican border, recent labor shortage has led *maquiladoras* to use child and male labor in jobs initially reserved for young women (48, 61, 110). In China, Special Economic Zones (SEZs) have spawned home work in villages where women and children in their spare time make electronics gear, toys, and artificial flowers. Even SEZ-based factories illegally employed children as young as 10 to work up to 15 hours a day, at salaries less than half of the $40 paid to workers over 16 (56). Such flexible and varied labor arrangements organized by transnational firms have generated a range of heterogeneous workers, no longer strictly defined by space, age, or sex.

In other words, global firms increasingly come to share the labor pools used by service industries that depend on cheap labor. While FTZ jobs have generated out-migration of rural women throughout Asia (25), low wages and vulnerability to layoff have driven many to moonlight as prostitutes in China, Malaysia, Thailand, the Philippines, and Sri Lanka (3, 5, 7, 40, 54, 73, 79). This overall rise in demand for female labor from poor countries is linked to increasing demands in richer countries for consumer goods and services (81). For instance, Filipino women have been imported as maids into Hong Kong (some 52,000; see 8) and other Southeast Asian countries where local young women have flocked into factories (3). Female migrants from Thailand and Sri Lanka have also sought employment as maids and sex workers in places like the Gulf Emirates, Japan, and West Germany (7, 73, 93). As production capital roams the world seeking more flexible conditions of maximization, its labor needs become intertwined with those of transnational service industries, further blurring the traditional boundaries between different occupational, sectoral, and national groups.

Under postmodern capitalism, this proliferation of diverse work situations has produced a range of work experiences and histories. It challenges theories that assume that the form of worker consciousness in any one locale is significantly shaped by structural categories defined as core/periphery, metropolitan/ex-colonial, First World/Third World formations.

Modes of Regulation

DESPOTIC REGIMES?
The study of export-industrialization has contributed to the routine characterization of labor regimes in Asia and Mexico as "despotic" and "paternalistic." This perspective was developed by world-systems theorists concerned with the politi-

cal consequences of uneven capitalist development worldwide (13; 14:246). In Burawoy's formulation, "production politics" varies according to the degree of capitalist development in the core-periphery. He distinguishes between "relations of production" (through which surplus is appropriated and distributed by capital), and "relations in production" (the everyday relations between and among workers and managers) (14:13–15). The particular combination of these production relations is determined by core or periphery location. In advanced capitalist societies, "hegemonic" regimes prevail, with managers striking a balance between coercion and consent in regulating labor. In developing countries, where the state is bent on relative surplus extraction through production, labor control is "despotic," involving physical violence and often direct state intervention (13; 14:226–35). In Burawoy's view, core-periphery structural conditions account for differences in the behavior of workers, while the "'belief systems' people carry around in their heads" (i.e. cultural attitudes) are considered irrelevant factors in the formation of class consciousness (13:262; cf 103). The hegemonic/despotic model thus privileges class as a fundamental dynamic of social change, constructing a working class Other in conflict with capital, while treating as an afterthought the effects of pre-existing aspects of social organization like race, ethnicity, religion, and nationalism (e.g. see 17).

Besides their reductionist tendencies, the labels "despotic" and "paternalistic" have Orientalist overtones. While Burawoy explains "despotic" relations as the outcome of particular state-capital relations, other writers (52, 55:294; 58) suggest a singular set of cultural differences forming industrial systems in non-Western societies. This construction implies an Other who cannot benefit from the emancipatory promise of social change.[3] This usage also implies that despotic and paternalistic conduct is not found in advanced capitalist countries. Furthermore, Burawoy's argument that "brutal" forms of domination are found in despotic regimes, while coercion and consent prevail in hegemonic metropolitan systems discourages more fine-grained analysis of diverse forms of power relations in newly industrializing countries.

Below, I discuss the various forms of control that enforce and induce compliance, as well as call forth resistance, among women workers at Asian and Mexican industrial sites. The disciplinary schemes include power relations in the workplace and in society at large. In addition to the division of labor, new techniques of power operate through controlling a series of spaces—the body, the shop floor, the state, and the public sphere—defining permissible and impermissible cultural forms in society.

STATE INTERVENTION

Burawoy makes the important point that both competition among capitalists worldwide and the struggle between capital and labor in any country have historically been shaped by the state (13; 14:246). He argues that the "colonial/neo-colonial state" facilitates the transfer of surplus to advanced countries, while organizing conditions for production that are attractive to foreign capital. Asianists also stress the role of the state in securing conditions for profitable export-industrialization. They maintain that in the so-called newly industrializing countries (NICs), the outcomes of struggles between the colonial or "authoritarian" state and labor were crucial to the subsequent capitalist expansion (52). State suppression of workers in traditional industries greatly weakened labor movements before large-scale industrialization was undertaken. Anti-communism was a legitimating formula for authoritarian rule in Hong Kong (1920s), South Korea (1940s–1950s), Taiwan (1940s), and Singapore (1960s). Thus, export-oriented industrialization has often required state intervention to weaken labor movements and ensure industrial peace as conditions for the early success of industrialization in these countries (52:65). Modernization theorists (46, 59) argue that by disciplining labor, the state benefits the business climate and labor markets, producing conditions that will eventually permit an equitable income share for the working population.

A reliance on the "authoritarian state" model would imply that the state's primary role is to secure the material conditions for controlling, punishing, and rewarding the industrial labor force. While I do not wish to reify the state, its agencies and agents are crucial in preparing and regulating society for the disruptions of industrial development. Elsewhere, I have argued that capitalist discipline operates through overlapping networks of power relations in the workplace and the political domain, regulating daily practices, norms, and attitudes that give legitimacy to the unequal relations that sustain capitalism (74:4–5). Similarly Harvey and others (42:123; 55; 102) have maintained that the disciplining of the labor force is an intricate, long-drawn-out process involving a mixture of repression, habituation, co-option, and cooperation within the workplace and throughout society. Modern nation-states routinely regulate social life, promoting certain norms, practices, and identities, while marginalizing others (28, 29). In newly industrializing countries, one state function is to redefine the public spaces in which particular struggles between rural and town folk, between males and females, and among classes take place (see below). In many countries, state policies promoting a female industrial force produce challenges for young women as daughters, workers, and citizens.

KINSHIP AND GENDER: CLAIMS ON DAUGHTERS

Ethnographers of Asian workers in export industries have developed tropes emphasizing the junior status of the women—e.g. "working daughters" (89), "factory daughters" (113), and "village daughters" (63). Indeed, if we look at the figures for all off-shore industries, women tend to comprise the lower-paid half of the total industrial work force in developing countries. In 1980, over 50% of Hong Kong manufacturing workers were female, compared to 46% in Singapore (1978), 43% in Taiwan (1979), and nearly 40% in Korea. They are concentrated in a few industries: textiles, apparel, electronics, and footwear. Most are considered "secondary workers" by policymakers in the sense that they take lower wages than men in comparable work ranks, and perhaps consider wage work as an interlude before marriage. Thus branded as a secondary labor force, female workers are subjected to low wages, long hours, frequent overtime, little or no prospects for advancement, and generally uncertain employment. In these industries, foremen, technicians, supervisors, and labor contractors are almost all men, while shop floor operators and home workers are almost all young women. Thus, the "daughter" status at home is reproduced in the workplace, generating tensions between new feelings of personal freedom on the one hand, and the claims of family and society on the other.

For instance, Salaff notes that in the Hong Kong working class, parents viewed daughters as "poor long-term investments," and working daughters saw themselves paying back their natal families for giving them life and nurture before they left home (89:35). After marriage, these women helped to pay domestic expenses in return for increased influence in family matters (89:259). In a Chinese Taiwan case, Kung observes that women working in FTZs fulfilled and expanded "traditional roles/expectations of daughters" (53:xiv). It was a question of repaying parents the cost of bringing up a "useless" daughter—a child lost to the natal family after marriage (53:xv–xvii). Working daughters did not gain power, but because they helped to pay household expenses, mothers praised them for being more "filial" than sons, whose education was often paid for with their sisters' earnings (53:xv–xvii). Both writers view the Chinese family as an exchange system. The daughters' strength expended in wage work repaid the gift of life. In return for their "filial" conduct, Hong Kong daughters received economic support from their families (89:256). In Taiwan, working daughters were unwilling to challenge the distribution of domestic power because they viewed their families as their only source of affection and security (53:125). Thus, in both Hong Kong and Taiwan, the claims of the Chinese family on its members' labor, having as their ultimate goal ascent of the class ladder, serve to enforce workers' compliance with the demands of industrial employment, while at the same time they diminish class-based solidarity.

Socialist China adopted export-industrialization as part of its "four modernizations" in 1979. Andors (5) did preliminary research at the Shenzhen SEZ, where most of the industries—textiles, electronics, toys and tourism—were operated by Hong Kong subcontracting firms. Women, mainly single and under 35 years old, comprised 70% of the work force. They were recruited by a special labor contracting agency from rural home units that received compensation for releasing them. Although claimed to be among the best-paid workers in China, they were easily exploited by the contracting service and by factories that routinely demanded overtime. Separated from their families, working women did enjoy such new freedoms as living in singles' dormitories, having more buying power, and postponing marriage. These personal choices, including premarital sex, were already available to working women in Hong Kong and Taiwan, in recognition of their filial contribution to the family economy (89:266). Nevertheless, in socialist and capitalist Chinese communities, young working women did not attain social equality with men at home or in society at large.

Southeast Asian cases also indicate that industrial employment produced a break in customary practices that confined unmarried girls to the home. However, bilateral kinship organization and cultural norms exerted fewer claims on daughters than did the patrilineal Chinese system. The influx of factory jobs meant that young women had the opportunity to help households in a declining farm economy, or to escape from unbearable family situations (1–4, 7, 25, 62, 74, 76, 81, 82, 113, 114, 118; 63). For the first time, village girls had the chance to go away to work, to handle their own money, save for higher education, and choose their own husbands (e.g. 74:191–92), enjoying greater freedom from family claims than Chinese female workers. Wolf (114) mentions that young girls in Central Java eagerly sought wage work, often against their parents' wishes. Many kept their earnings for themselves and felt a sense of improved status (see also 62). In Malaysia, the earnings of village daughters helped furnish their parents' houses and improve daily consumption; the women themselves had discretionary income and could save for their weddings (2; 74:125–28).

These changes in the working daughter's status, with its mix of (and tension between) family obligations and growing personal autonomy, must modify sweeping assertions that pre-existing East and Southeast Asian "patriarchy" (20; 42:294; 58) alone is to blame for the construction of unequal industrial relations. Access to wages did gain young Asian women some personal forms of freedom, weakening customary family claims to varying degrees. In the Chinese cases, wage employment has allowed daughters to demonstrate how "filial" they can be, and thus to be considered "worthier" than before. In Southeast Asia, the unprecedented influx of young working women into public spaces produced a social backlash, generating demands for the regulation of female conduct (see below).

THE SEXUAL DIVISION OF LABOR AND TAYLORISM

Some scholars claim modern industrial organizations in Asian societies are rarely "paternalistic"; any "vestiges of kin relations" are dissolved in the workplace (89:3–4). In contrast, others assert that harsh and personal forms of control are features of peripheral Fordist systems (13; 42:192, 294; 58). However, the ethnographies suggest that the labor politics are neither exclusively despotic nor antipaternalistic but involve different disciplinary schemes institutionalized by local capitalist and cultural practices.

In Asia, the division of labor introduced by transnational firms separates managers and workers along lines of nationality, race, gender, and age. Central activities like research and finance are controlled by experts in the metropolitan headquarters, while the low-skilled and labor-intensive production processes employ young, poorly trained women in the off-shore sites (70, 72; see also 12:Ch. 4). For instance, Japanese industries based in Malaysia are headed by male Japanese managers and engineers. Malaysian Chinese and Indian men fill the mid-level professional ranks, while shop floor operators are mainly composed of young Malay women of rural origin (74:Ch. 7). This institutionalization of race, gender, and age inequalities in industrial enterprises is reflected by daily practices. Elson & Pearson (22) argue that the dialectic of gender and capital has the tendency to "intensify, decompose, and recompose" existing gender hierarchies, thereby incorporating gender inequalities in modern work relations. In Hong Kong, subcontracting agents simply rely on parental pressures at home to make the "girls" work for long hours and low wages (89:22–23). In contrast, Malaysia-based Japanese firms absorb Malay notions of male superiority into a "Pan Asian" philosophy that emphasizes the moral authority of the Japanese management, and of the managers, supervisors, and foremen over nubile female operators. Corporate discourse on the "Asian family" defines workers as "children" who should "obey their parents" (i.e. supervisors) in the factory (74:163, 170–78). Thus, despite claims that capitalism has destroyed traditional patriarchy (58, 89), these examples show that the industrial labor relations articulating with local norms often elaborate and reinvent principles of male and racial superiority (22, 73, 108).[4]

Such gender and race-based forms of domination help make "scientific management" (or Taylorism; see 101) an even more formidable apparatus for extracting surplus value. The essence of Fordist production, Taylorism is based on "time-motion" techniques that dictate precisely how each task is to be performed in order to obtain the highest level of productivity within a strict time economy (see 12:Ch. 4). The fragmentation of skills into simple procedures and the stripping away of individual judgment (separation of conception and execution) are intended by the system to treat workers as appendages of the machine.

FACTORY REGULATIONS: THE GAZE AND THE BODY

Foucault (28, 29) reminds us that some forms of modern power cannot be attributed directly to the reproduction of capitalist relations and labor power. He maintains that specific technologies of knowledge and power, associated with institutions like the prison, clinic, and school, produce discursive practices that enforce social regulation through establishing "the norm." In multinational enterprises, Taylorism is complemented by surveillance techniques that operate through the control of space.

Thus, it would be a mistake to think of scientific management as solely a process of technical detail-level control. It specifies exact bodily posture and requires tedious repetition of the same finger, eye, and limb movements, often for hours on end at the assembly line (74:164–67; see also 27:128; 89:101), a form of body discipline especially intolerable to neophyte factory women. In many enterprises, continual surveillance enforced the worker's compliance with the relentless Taylorist procedures (74:159). At a Malaysia-based microchip firm, male supervisors pressured female workers assembling thousands of components to achieve 100% efficiency; even trips to the locker-room were penalized. A Japanese director was pleased to note that the production rate of Malay workers exceeded that of Japanese ones at the corporate home base (74:162–63). In another plant, operators working under the strict eye of foremen were reported to almost double their daily output, especially when their efforts were sweetened by incremental cash allowances (74:166).

Other forms of spatial control include the deployment of workers on the shop floor in relative isolation from each other but under the constant surveillance of foremen, an arrangement that induces self-monitoring (74: Ch. 7; cf 60).[5] Factory women often felt they had few places left to hide; some complained of being spied upon in their locker-rooms (79). Furthermore, even unions were used to watch over workers. A Japanese factory based in Malaysia set up an in-house union to operate as a "grievance procedure system," or, in the words of a union leader, to act "as a watchdog, for both sides" (74:172–73).

Foucault notes that knowledge-power ultimately fastens on sex, making the body the ultimate site at which all strategies of control and resistance are registered (29:103). Ethnographic findings reveal that disciplinary practices frequently define the industrial presentation and workings of the body. Malay workers felt that the "tight work discipline" extended to regulation of clothing and footwear —policies that bodily constrained them (68:168). Japanese corporate policies in Malaysia defined Malay workers as "wards" under the moral custody of factory managers. By focusing on the young women's virginal status, the management capitalized on Malay fears about their daughters' vulnerability (79). Other techniques of control more closely monitored workers' bodies. In mass assembly factories from South Korea to Mexico, operators were subjected to humiliating innuendos about menstruation, and were required to request permission to use the toilet (6, 27, 38, 54, 79). In the Shenzhen SEZ, the normally quiescent workers went on strike in a toy factory after a pregnant woman, prevented from resting, fainted (56:47). Controlling the space of the worker's body is related to a wider corporate perception of women's "nature."

While Taylorism as a management policy aims to minimize the possibilities of resistance, by reducing workers to tools, disciplinary procedures seek to induce "docile bodies" (28) without resorting to "brutal" forms of control in the workaday life. However, electronics workers from Taiwan to Sri Lanka complain of the detail work that literally wears away at the "instruments of production"— for instance, eyes fitted to microscopes (7, 53, 72, 74). Indeed, neophyte workers, whose sensibilities were shaped by peasant and/or preindustrial cultures, often challenge the work process for its dehumanizing effects and accompanying forms of social control. Instead of opposing capital as an abstract entity, factory women's daily struggles against corporate policies—over body discipline, pressures for high productivity, and surveillance—aim to push back the varied norms and forms of domination (27, 61, 74, 79, 80; see below).

A mode of social regulation often ignored in our analysis of labor regimes and their effects on workers is the production of cultural discourses. Although Foucault does not see a necessary connection between discursive practices and the systematic domination of capitalism, Marxists maintain that as part of cultural production, images and discourses have a material basis in the symbolic reproduction of capitalism (42, 44, 112). There is much evidence that transnational capitalism has produced, along with microchips, discourses that naturalize the subordination of women in industrial enterprises.

Early in their operations, transnational companies explained their preferences for Third World female workers by producing a language defining them as "low grade" (meaning unskilled) and "docile." Bureaucrats in developing countries were quick to appeal to biology to woo foreign investments while gaining acceptance at home for the creation of a female industrial force. A Malaysian government brochure promoted "the oriental girl" as blessed with nimble fingers and thus "qualified by nature and inheritance" to contribute to assembly production

(74:152; 73; see also 22, 38, 57). Elsewhere (75), I have discussed how industrial discourses "disassemble" the female worker into eyes and fingers adapted for assembly work, at the same time reassembling other parts of their bodies according to commodified sexual images. Factories also pointed to other "natural" attributes of their female work force. A Japanese manager claimed that factories prefer "fresh female labor [that] after some training, is highly efficient" (74:153). Similarly, a manager in Cuidad Juarez on the Mexican border said he preferred women who were "unspoiled"—that is, young and inexperienced: "Women such as these are easier to shape to our requirements" (26:117). In Taiwan, factories sought young women from the remote areas said to "have a higher capacity for eating bitterness" (53:63). This language of essentialism and commodification creates an image of dull-witted work animals that can be trained for hard, tedious work. By implication, such a cultural (or is it a natural?) Other provides justification for the low wages offered.

Corporate practices also promoted a sexual image of Third World women workers. American firms in Malaysia and elsewhere in Southeast Asia encouraged extracurricular activities that stress consumerism, dating, and beauty competition (38). New sexual images, elaborated through make-up classes and newsletters, induce the consumption of commodities (e.g. Clairol toiletries) made available in company stores. Such emphasis on Western images of sex appeal engendered a desire for goods that working women could satisfy only by increasing their commitment to wage work (38, 53, 79, 89).

SOCIAL REGULATION: WOMEN IN PUBLIC SPACES

Throughout industrializing Asia and Mexico, the emergence of large female industrial forces has occasioned negative public commentary on the conduct of female workers. Douglas observes that persons in an interstitial position are often symbolized as dangerous and filthy, since they suggest a poorly articulated social system (21:120–24, 142–47; see also 95). As new workers, young women engage in activities that violate traditional boundaries (spatial, economic, social, and political) in public life, forcing a redefinition of the social order. Thus, states attempting to shape a new moral consensus on industrial development have found it necessary to regulate the activities of female workers along clearly marked gender lines, defining what is culturally appropriate and what is not.

In Malaysia, the influx of young rural women into industrial sites was widely considered as the cause of moral decadence in Malay-Muslim society. While the state promoted female industrial employment, the government-controlled media criticized factory women, citing their Westernized outfits, footloose behavior, and reputation as "micro-devils" and "bad women" (2, 4, 38, 57, 79). Islamic revivalists opposing industrial development viewed factory women, many of whom have deferred marriage, as would-be infidels indulging in the pleasures of consumer society. Malay working women were thus perceived as an Other invading (male) public spaces; while they were permitted to work, their social activities had to be curtailed. Religious leaders urged repentance, rejection of consumerism, and the embrace of a new sexual asceticism for young women (78, 79). Transnational companies that held religious classes in the workplace and monitored the behavior of workers were applauded by the religious authorities (79). Each vying to be more "Islamic" than the other, the state and revivalist movement competed in enforcing a moral discipline on working women in public life. By controlling female images and regulating their activities, this particular constitution of civil society makes it, like the FTZ, a place where women are free to work, but only under the male authority. Similarly, in West Java, Mather (62) reports that the "Islamic patriarchy" allied itself with factory managers to control the movement of workers between home and workplace. In Buddhist Thailand, rural women were pushed into wage work by cultural notions of a daughter's duty and the crime of ingratitude. While politicians warned that officials should not be "morally fastidious" and prohibit sexual entertainment, working women were accused of moral laxity (40:132–33; 63). These examples show that state encouragement of female industrial employment was paralleled by increased surveillance of their multiple "transgressions" (see 95), as viewed by dominant groups in society. While the conditions differ in each country, the widespread stigmatization of working women came to define public spheres where female productive activities were deemed necessary but their civil rights were not.

In contrast to the polarities noted above (e.g. virgin/whore, purity/immorality) that were used to regulate working women elsewhere, Chinese society in Taiwan evaluated such women according to a mind/body model (cf 87). As we have seen, mass-assembly work divided mental from physical labor to an extreme, making workers vulnerable to the Chinese cultural preference for mental over manual labor. Female industrial workers suffered from "damaged" identities (34), mainly because of the "low" nature of their work. Factory girls complained of being looked down upon by society because of their low-status job, which "does not give a person any face" (53:156–57). In complaints to Kung, they were especially bitter about being deprived of higher education (the "penality" of daughters) that would open the route to higher status (53:158–59). Doubly marginalized as daughters and as factory hands, these women were obstructed from attaining the education that would shield them from the social contempt attached to their jobs. Thus, in Taiwanese society, moral regulation marginalized factory women mainly because of their low occupational (class) rank, but also because of their sex.

Along the Mexican border, cross-racial constructions of workers' activities and identities appear to be a major part of social regulation (see 86). In Cuidad Juarez, Fernandez-Kelly reports the development of a "factory harem mentality." Although young women might have used their charms to attract suitors before, they were now encouraged to use sex as a bait and payment for access to jobs (26:129). A news article on Nogales notes a popular image of the Border Program as a place of sexual conquest where everyday talk included "innuendos about *maquiladora* managers who fornicate their way down assembly lines or companies that provide stud services as incentives" (110:39). An American manager in Nogales joked: "Imagine if we could harness sexual energy. When someone here has sex, the news travel . . . like electricity through a printed circuit" (110:31). Noting that "the only fun [female workers] ever have is love," he said that in the previous month, 10% of his workers had been pregnant.[6]

If the dominant discourse portrayed female operators as sexually wanton, implying that they were not such good workers, men were seen as emasculated by *maquila* work. In the early phases, most *maquilas* employed single women, but by 1983, more and more factories had turned to men and children under 14 years old (48, 61). In Nogales, American managers dealt with male workers by exploiting their sense of machismo. One said he tried to raise productivity by appealing to "the Mexican's pride" and "need to save face in front of others" (110:39). In Cuidad Juarez, Lugo (61) also observed the corporate manipulation of machismo to humiliate men who could not keep up with female workers. The factory men's sex talk and word games disclosed their sense of having been socially reduced (and thus becoming more woman-like). By accepting dominant images of male weakness, they unwittingly reproduced the very cultural categories now used to prod them to higher levels of productivity. The larger cultural significance of such corporate discourses is that *maquila* men are socially devalued for working in female-identified jobs.

The race/sex typing of workers (3) becomes most elaborated in situations where female workers participate in manufacturing and in service industries based overseas. In Sri Lanka, the post-1977 development pattern led to the simultaneous growth of FTZ industries, prostitution, and the export of servants and brides (7). In the process, the control of women shifted from male relatives to "alien male authorities—the factory supervisor, the employment agent, the government bureaucrat, the Western tourist, the Arab employer, or the Japanese farmer [who imports a bride]" (7:79). Sri Lankans alarmed at this mass entry of daughters into wage labor at home and abroad branded women workers with a sexual stigma (7:69). These workers thus join the mobile female labor force epitomized by Filipino women—as imported maids, nurses, mail-order brides, and entertainers in Asia and Europe (3, 24).[7] Such transnational formation of working relations may allow workers to escape social regulation in their home country temporarily, but it exposes them to other forms of domination abroad. They become migrant workers with few legal rights.

Ethnographies of working women in various locales encourage us to investigate the kinds of power such women are subjected to both at the workplace and in the wider society. In each locale, different modes of industrial and social domination promote certain cultural forms and identities, while undermining or suppressing others. In each case, the particular mix of production systems, state policies, and cultural forces both limit and enable workers' struggles (97:223; 84), a topic to which we now turn.

Cultural Struggles

The variety of industrial situations linked to flexible accumulation raises anew questions about workers' responses to capitalist transformation. Indigenous experiences of colonialism and capitalism are frequently assessed in terms of the concept of "class consciousness"—i.e. degree of recognition of class interests, organized action against capital, and even the goal of structural redistribution of power in society.[8] Although anthropologists have avoided a generic concept of class consciousness in discussing Third World experiences, scholars like Mintz (64:193; see also 45) would nevertheless consider unions and political parties as minimal evidence of the presence of "proletarians" in the Caribbean. In her important book, Nash (69:320–30) seeks in pre-Columbian rituals the class solidarity of Bolivian miners, but she then evaluates their consciousness according to strict Marxist criteria of class identity and union activity. By insisting on a single measure of class agency, we risk diluting the political significance of cultural resistances in encounters with capitalism.

A related tendency is to see the political importance of Third World workers in globalist terms. Vincent (106:232–62) notes that among the laboring poor in colonial Uganda, the sense of "no-classness" was a condition of their "subaltern" position in transnational capitalism. Comaroff analyzes the religious imagery of worker-peasants in South Africa as "simultaneously unique and yet one instance of a very general class of social movement" (15:194) that is "part of the second global culture" (15:254). Thus, anthropologists describe (and celebrate) the varied expressions of class/ethnic/religious consciousness in subaltern groups (i.e. the politically dominated), but often feel compelled to construct these struggles in the universalist terms of emergent collective consciousness. In a cautionary note, Spivak argues that the arena of the subaltern's consciousness is situational and uneven, and the subaltern's subjectivity is locally shaped and delimited (94:16–17).

Feminists influenced by the world-systems model also predict the emergence of solidarity among the transnational female labor force in developing economies (22, 24, 26, 88). In recent years, such feminist elaboration of a utopian discourse as an alternative to modernist, patriarchal narratives has itself come under criticism (41, 65, 66, 76, 94). These feminist critics argue that acknowledging the plurality of subject positions and self-representations puts us in a better position to understand different social realities. Without relying on totalizing "First" or "Third" World frameworks, a theory about the variable "subject-constitution" of subaltern women must link individual consciousness to the local workings of international capital (94:29).

Indeed, the ethnographic evidence on factory women in flexible labor systems indicates that they rarely construct their identities or organize themselves in terms of collective or global interests. Although demonstrations of female workers have been widely reported in Asia and Central America (3, 6, 7, 26, 36, 38, 50, 56, 74; M. B. Mills, unpublished), they tended to be wildcat strikes in individual firms. Union activities, especially in Asian FTZs, are controlled through company unions, or are otherwise severely limited (12, 57). What we do find are attempts to escape from or live with industrial systems without losing one's sense of human dignity.

Worker consciousness and subject-constitution, I would argue, must be investigated in contexts shaped by the intersection of state agencies, the local workings of capital, and already configured local power/culture realms (84). Instead of direct labor-capital confrontations, we discover workers' resistances in their oppositional tactics, embodied desires, and alternative interpretations and images. What seems key in their emerging consciousness is an awareness of how their status as daughter/young woman is linked to domination by family, industry, and society. In manipulating, contesting, or rejecting these claims, working women reassess and remake their identities and communities in ways important for social life.

ACCOMMODATION AND PERSONAL MOBILITY

At some industrial sites, factory women seemed overwhelmed by the needs of their families, a concern that restrains their capacity to participate in sustained social action. Industrialization in Mexico has generated a heterogeneous female working population variously employed in different labor systems. According to Fernandez-Kelly, workers in Cuidad Juarez included single women (17–25 years old) as well as older women who have been widowed, divorced, or separated from men. Female-headed households may have dependents (children, fathers, husbands, and boyfriends) who were unemployed or underemployed (26:48– 50). Since the border area is a transit point for US-bound, predominantly male migrants, many single women are compelled to seek wage work in the *maquila*. Companies prefer young, single, and childless women; older women with children can find work only in garment factories, where work conditions are worse (26:49– 51; see also 104:98). Working women often fall back on exchange networks that help them adjust to economic uncertainty as they enter and leave this unstable labor market (26:153–177). Others augment their wages by working as prostitutes or slipping across the border on weekends to work as maids (26:142–50; 110).

Beneria & Roldan (10) note that among home workers in Mexico City, young, single, and married "semi-prole" women routinely labored in and were discharged from various capitalist enterprises. They argue that this flexibility afforded by the informal economy produced sub-proletarianization among women, in contrast to more regular proletarianization of men (10:102–3). Since capital constantly creates and destroys job opportunities, the work conditions do not foster collective class or even gender consciousness. Although home workers are aware of oppression, "a configuration of ideological, economic and coercive mechanisms support[s] oppressive marital contracts." Women, because of limited resources, "could not renegotiate" their situations (10:160–161). Even in the absence of rebellion, each woman's awareness of her exploitation occasions reassessment of her status.[9]

In Taiwan, female workers unhappy with their jobs are in a better position to escape industrial employment. Kung reports that many feared reprimand, and were either resigned to the job conditions or planning to leave soon (53:106–7). They displayed not the classic type of class consciousness but acute consciousness of having to adjust to a low status (53:165). In their view, the company environment fostered manipulative behavior between superiors and inferiors as well as among workers themselves, thus sowing doubts and distrust about dealing effectively with conflicts (53:156–61). As in FTZs based elsewhere (26, 74, 89), women in Taiwan were reluctant to take leadership roles because of a sense of betraying the interests of the rank and file. The most common expression of discontent was a high rate of turnover, which further undermined community spirit. Besides, contrary to Western feminist expectations, most working daughters did not seek more equal relations at home and would gladly trade their "bitter" independence for the security of the college student who has a family to look after her needs (53:166–68). Thus, although initially family pressures denied daughters higher education and pushed them into factory employment, factory daughters developed a sense of self-direction through seeking better qualifications and jobs. In other words, they hoped eventually to evade production politics (and family claims) not by resisting control at work but by "graduating" from industrial employment altogether.

In mainland China, too, what was initially regarded as an opportunity has come to produce a sense of entrapment. Export-industrialization in Kwantung has increased class differentiation to the extent that few factory women wanted to marry local men because marriage would add to their work burden (5). Some hoped to achieve upward and geographical mobility by marrying Hong Kong tourists or entering Hong Kong prostitution rings (5:37–38). The potential stigma of being a prostitute seemed to them preferable to the status of a factory worker. Whether family or individually inspired, aspirations for upward mobility both conditioned the women's consciousness of their bitter fate and strengthened their resolve to escape it (cf 113:27). For many, the goal was not to stay and challenge the industrial system, but, like their Taiwanese sisters, to use factory jobs as a steppingstone to more lucrative employment elsewhere. Attaining such personal mobility also weakens family control over one's life. A sense of subjective rights began to replace traditional authority over one's fate.

BODILY TRUTHS AND CONTESTED CATEGORIES

In other cases, workers trapped in industrial enterprises frequently contest hegemonic representations of their situations. Factory women untutored in ideologies are capable of making alternative interpretations based on their own visceral experiences and cultural traditions. By thus challenging dominant discourse, they expand the space of political struggle in their everyday lives.

A few ethnographic accounts provide descriptions of women challenging dominant images of their purported "freedom" as factory workers. In Taiwan, female workers spoke of being shut up all day and wasting the "spring" of their youth, a bitter contrast to pre-factory days when the period before marriage seemed carefree (53:164–65). This sense of imprisonment is also felt by factory women in Malaysia who, released from the custody of their parents and widely accused of "unrestrained" conduct, felt "shackled" in the factory (79). An operator noted that her coworkers were ignorant of the wider industrial situation, "working as if they were imprisoned . . . like a frog beneath the coconut shell" (74:197). The theme of entrapment extends to their experience of work discipline. Malay women rejected corporate expressions of welfare concern, claiming that the management treated them as things, not human beings (74:167). Many found the relentless drive for higher productivity and disregard for worker fatigue intolerable. They also complained of bodily deprivations (aches and burns, insufficient sleep, skipped menstruation) that registered the grip of industrial discipline. More assertive workers tried to enforce traditional morality, demanding human empathy (*timbang rasa*) and justice from their foremen (74:167, 201–2). They sold their labor but not their right to human consideration.

Workers in Taiwan also contested categories and practices that treat them as extensions of machines. Seeing themselves as "mere assemblers," factory women did not expect their views to count for much. However, in their everyday conversations, they denounced workplace conditions in moral terms. Instead of using the language of class or sexual oppression, they posed questions of "how to be a person" (53:89). Foremen were described as "mean," "overly strict," "slippery," and "putting on airs" (53:94–98). Workers were therefore suspicious of perceived attempts to manipulate their emotions—i.e. foremen who chatted up workers, who took "pleasure" in ordering them around, and who made a habit of patting them on the shoulder (53:94–98). The refusal of such gestures echoes a Hong Kong worker who scornfully denounced implicit expectations that to get a slight pay raise one should "pat the horse's rump" (i.e. curry favor; 89:103). Like their Malaysian counterparts, these women wished to be treated with greater personal consideration, but they feared attempts to prime the pump. They complained that the companies did not allow for the development of human feelings (*kan-ching*) in the workplace, promoting instead opportunistic and impersonal behavior (53:98, 159–61). According to their cultural expectations, factory work was dehumanizing.

In mainland China, the introduction of capitalist methods of production in Hangzhou silk factories has produced similar policies for controlling female workers. In the discourse of economic reform, management emphasized higher productivity and the gendering of differences between manual labor (defined as women's work) and technical and mental labor (considered men's work). Using terms that echo corporate discourses in Southeast Asia, women were said to have nimble fingers but to lack the intellectual and leadership capabilities of men. Rofel (87) reports that although women workers subscribed to the sexual division of labor, they also used such gender images to subvert new pressures for higher productivity. They routinely cited family and female reasons for taking time off work. Using the same categories management uses has allowed workers to negotiate some work conditions, but they also thereby reproduce aspects of the larger culture, reinforcing the sense that women are inherently less productive than men (87:246–48).

The above examples indicate that dominant images of women workers—as footloose consumers, instruments of production, and the weaker sex—are contested or used by factory women to their own advantage. On the one hand, Malay and Taiwanese women felt factory work deprived them of their youth and of the kinds of pleasures and protection promised by local cultures. On the other, the shock of factory work led them to demand moral consideration and fairness. In different cultural idioms, these neophyte workers expressed a view of industrial work as an assault on the body as well as on the moral value of human beings (cf 23, 102, 109). By contesting hegemonic categories of human worth, factory women attempted "to seize language for their own purposes," engaging in "symbolic struggles over social position, identity and self-determination" (84:46–47). They thus found voices to validate their actual experiences, breaking the flow of meanings imposed on them, and thus directly defining their own lives.

CULTURAL RESISTANCE: TACTICS AND MOVEMENTS

In his notion of "everyday forms of resistance," Scott maintains that the oppositional practices of Malay peasants flourish precisely because they are outside hegemonic relations (92:335–36). This ethnographic observation is itself doubtful (e.g. see 74), and many would question a theoretical construction of subjects as external to power relations (29, 35, 39, 98, 112). As Foucault has argued, disciplinary technologies call forth counter-strategies within shifting fields of power (29:95). While Foucault emphasizes resistant tactics within discourse, De Certeau (19) identifies nonverbal ruses that proliferate in the interstices of a system of domination. This layer of moral resistance is derived from the basic, practical consciousness of subjects; and though often lacking an articulated awareness of its own, it can disrupt and subvert the established order, as we shall see below.

Reports on *maquila* production politics have been sparse, but despite their difficult employment situation and domestic responsibilities, Mexican workers do challenge industrial discipline. Fernandez-Kelly (26) and Lugo (61) provide accounts of female and male workers manipulating dominant sexual images to their own advantage, earning short-term reprieves or gains in the workplace.[10] Others briefly mention a form of covert resistance called *tortuosidad* whereby workers worked "at a turtle's pace" in response to speed-up pressures (80, 117). These scattered acts of resistance, sometimes not even recognized owing to management's view of "lazy" workers, did not collectively challenge the status quo, but they opposed the prevailing hegemonic interests.

My study of Malay factory women in Kuala Langat, Malaysia (74), indicates a range of resistance tactics that silently negotiated the contours of daily work relations. The Malay feminine ideal constrains young women from directly confronting their social superiors, yet female workers often resorted to isolated nonverbal acts to gain a symbolic and physical space despite contrary factory rules. Tactics to fool the system and lessen work demands included frequent absences from the shop floor, ostensibly to attend to "female" problems or to perform obligatory Islamic prayers (74, 79). At the workbench, operators sometimes feigned ignorance of the technical details of work, thus frustrating attempts to raise productivity rates. Even more hidden ruses were the destruction of microchips and jamming of machines; in both cases, the management was often unpleasantly surprised and unable to trace the culprits (74:210–13).

Subversion also takes the more startling form of spirit attacks on female workers, events that transfigure normal factory routines. Spirit possession is a complex phenomenon in Malay culture, but its repeated eruptions in modern factories can be partly accounted for in terms of work relations (1, 77). A worker attacked by a spirit wails, runs about creating havoc, struggles violently, and screams obscenities against restraining supervisors. In some cases (77; 74:205), the possessed exclaimed, "I am not to be blamed!" "Go away!" "I will kill you, let me go!" The effect on production was immediate. Other workers soon became infected, creating such a disturbance that a shutdown proved necessary, and the "hysterical women" were sent home.

Possession episodes were the inarticulate expression of individual anguish, transferred to the public sphere. The contortions of afflicted workers spoke of the ills experienced in the social body (77, 100). Some possession victims reported visions of fearsome old men at the workbench, spirits haunting bathrooms, or devils lurking in the microscopes. These "signs and symptoms" (100) of possession, though complexly motivated, constituted "a cryptic language of protest" (91) and social disease. Their vivid imagery defined the factory premises as a spiritually polluted place. To avoid attacks, young women had to be "spiritually vigilant" against fear and violation (74:207–9). Possession discourse thus contested the management's view of "mass hysteria" as caused by female physical weaknesses. Like other oppositional tactics, spirit attacks are not capable of identifying the common adversary but indirectly expressed the interests of others in a similar predicament.[11] The surreptitious foot-dragging, Luddite tactics, and possession rites count among the "polymorphous maneuvers and mobilities" (19:8) that, linking a basic sense of moral freedom, aesthetic creation, and practical action, have surprising effects on power relations, while managing to elude repression.

In contrast to Malay factory women, their South Korean counterparts are among the most militant in Asia, confronting a state more repressive of labor than other industrializing countries (6, 17, 50, 99). The growth of collective consciousness among South Korean female workers is also fostered by their relative social and geographical isolation. The Anglophone literature gives only tantalizing glimpses of the South Korean female workers' movements—"underground" struggles that while protracted and culturally elaborated tend not to be accessible to outsiders.

In South Korea, the dramatic performance of the economy has relied heavily on unskilled female labor, paid half the wages of comparable male workers (99:128). In 1969, a ban on strikes in foreign-invested firms was followed by the breakup of unions in the mid-1970s, through the New Community Factory Movement. In two large industrial estates, Oh (71) found most factories violated the Labor Standard Act by insisting on overtime and depriving workers of holidays and medical leaves. The work was arduous; textile workers, who routinely worked night shifts, put in an average of 10.5 hours per day but were paid "below sustenance wages" (71:192–93). Layoffs were not a bargaining option because of labor shortages. Companies therefore relied on "crude forms of control" by inventing rules requiring 20-hour work days (17:211).

Most female workers were single migrants from remote areas, who were thus cut off from family support (81). Socially isolated in the industrial estates, most of the female workers were under 25 years old, and many were adolescents. They were employed for an average of three years, and many had begun to stay on after marriage (71:191). Although most were "working daughters" supplementing family income, about 11% were primary income earners in their families. They lived in housing near the industrial zones where they could share stories and common circumstances on a daily basis. This led to the creation of a female class solidarity, further strengthened by women's wide experiences across different industries, and by their involvement in labor disputes (17). Furthermore, the large population and the expanding South Korean economy generated intense job competition between women and men. As a category, men were upgraded to more lucrative jobs, discarding "lower" ones to women (81). Most female workers desired wages at least equal to those of men, and wages were the main focus of their struggle (71). These factors refute the suggestion that because of "patriarchal family structures" Korean workers were relatively quiescent (19). In fact, labor disputes involving female workers have sharply increased since the mid-1970s but they have been underreported by the state (17:220).

In the late 1970s, when the national economy surpassed the "developing country" level, the Dong-Il Textile Company was engaged in a major labor dispute (71:186). Women workers rejected representatives of a puppet union led by men (6). The factory women determined that they could not depend on support from male union organizers, nor could they rely on sympathetic middle class women to lead them. Female workers began to organize and develop their own leadership. They told Kim (50) that they no longer needed students to awaken their consciousness: The time had come for "real laborers" to take care of themselves. In another context, Christian leaders were advised that they should leave after helping female workers to organize themselves (99).

Female workers, organized into different groups, have developed a whole repertoire of tactics and images expressing their struggles. In the Dong-Il Textile Company strike, women protested "miserable work conditions," poor food, imposed silence among coworkers, and prohibition from going to the toilets (6). They developed an anti-capitalist ideology that focused on "recover[ing] our human rights." At the climax of their struggle against the company union, women on a hunger strike faced off against police by stripping and singing union songs (6:235). The women were brutally beaten, and 72 were arrested. When the strikers presented their case to the regional union leader, he asked, "What sort of women are you, who prefer the labor movement to marriage?" (6:237). Because they chose to struggle as workers, women were apparently perceived as acting outside cultural traditions of femininity. Some of the women involved in this labor action were raped (99:133–34).

Thus, while male superiors tried to domesticate female protesters by using traditional forms of male control, the women workers drew on local and imported religious traditions for inspiration. Building resistance out of their daily suffering, workers found in shamanism a vital tradition for interpreting historical tragedies (51), while Christianity offered new concepts to articulate their oppression and the possibilities for change. Sun (99) argues that the goal of Korean feminist theology was to promote the full humanity of women by struggling to transform a society in which development depended on women's labor but disregarded improving women's status. Working women were said to be suspicious of bourgeois women's assertions that women would be liberated through work, when their work conditions were, "for the most part, exploitative and dehumanizing" (99:129). Instead of adopting bourgeois feminism, many female workers turned to Christianity. Some reported experiencing God's presence in their lives; their experiences led them to construct a new conception of power based on gender solidarity and human dignity. Sun observes that:

> [The women workers] cannot afford to see themselves as helpless victims: their survival depends on continued exercise of whatever personal powers they possess. They combine their strengths to survive and often assume responsibility for others in their struggle, sometimes even sacrificing their security—the safety of their bodies. By recognizing that the exercise of their power is an act of resistance, they reject both the dominant group's definition of them as powerless and dispensable, and the ideology of sexism which teaches that women are powerless and easily victimized (99:132).

South Korean female workers' struggles culminated in battles that extend beyond the workplace. They led to the emergence of a separate female labor movement in the 1987 mass labor struggle, the largest in Korean history (50). The conflict began with male workers at the Hyunda plant demanding "democratic labor unions." Women in the Masan FTZ were also inspired to strike; as a result, factory wages were raised from $4 to $7 a day in 1988 (see also 116). To a greater extent than the other cases, these South Korean worker movements have led to social changes, producing a new sense of effectiveness in the female workers, and posing questions about their gender identity and cultural community.

Conclusion

As I write this, the world speeds ahead. Corporations are retreating from off-shore manufacturing in developing countries where growing labor strife and rising wages since 1988, in addition to the declining US dollar, have increased production costs (116). More and more, Western companies are preferring sites in metropolitan countries where market access is optimal and ever increasing pools of immigrants and refugees supply the cheap labor (see 17, 43). Indeed, such changes in capital-labor engagements underline the need for theoretical flexibility on our part. I have suggested an alternative to the conventional framing of working-class experiences as a trajectory from the development of class consciousness to class struggle to structural change. Instead, I propose that we conceive of workers' experiences as cultural struggles—that is, workers struggle against new and varied forms of domination, and seek new ways of grappling with social realities. Such cultural resistance and production engender a new sense of self and community, potentially challenging the constitution of civil society.

Williams uses the phrase "structure of feeling" to describe such an emergent and fluid sensibility, a kind of "practical consciousness" derived from actively lived and felt relationships (112:132). A structure of feeling does not equate with an articulated formal system (ideology), shaped as it is by "a living and interrelating continuity," together with all its tensions (112:132). Above, I described the constitution of such "structures of feeling" in the context of class and other hegemonic forms of domination.

In different ethnographic contexts, institutions like the state, kinship, gender, and religion, as well as industrial enterprises, play important roles in constituting workers' activities and consciousness. Through their complex accommodations and resistances, the female workers under discussion here gained a sense of their particular oppressions and interests, but also achieved some degree of effectiveness and self-worth. Although such structures of feeling do not necessarily have significant political effects, they constitute a change in the everyday attitudes and practices of workers.

In negating hegemonic definitions daily, factory women came to explore new concepts of self, female status, and human worth. While many tactics of resistances were individual, and even covert, other forms of protest in the public sphere compelled a modification or renegotiation of power relations. In Kwantung and in Taiwan, factory daughters developed a sense of personal rights, while in South Korea, female workers learned to be sovereign subjects, acting as self-determining agents of social change. The latter have gone furthest in developing culturally new notions of human worth and individual rights, and in organizing resistance. They rejected traditional constructions of their status and selectively adopted foreign categories to articulate their own goals, as individuals and collectively. They have realized, to a greater extent than many female workers elsewhere, the liberating potential of the new structure of feeling. They achieved the voices to question the place of women in the economy, and to demand democratic practices in civil society. In viewing their silences, subterfuges, interpretations, and goals as "cultural struggle," we are merely acknowledging the role of subaltern women in making local histories, in their own ways.

NOTES

1. Flexible accumulation strategies in the Third World are also applied to particular sites in advanced capitalist countries. The mid-1970s world recession forced capitalists in metropolitan countries to restructure production in the face of rising labor costs and increased competition from developing countries (9). Informal or unregulated economic activities, long associated with Third World peasants, emerged in advanced economies; women, minorities, and immigrants furnished this low-waged labor (16, 37, 90). In the United States, this informalization—decentralized production, unaccounted labor, and earnings—included the assembly of electronics components, garment sweatshops, and home work (16, 26, 43, 83, 90, 97). This "downgraded" manufacturing sector (90) expanded alongside the service industries and depended on the same supply of native-born and immigrant women. Similarly, in Japan, female workers in Kyushu (called "Silicon Island") increasingly sought employment in electronics and service industries (31). Thus, flexibilization strategies disregard the traditional boundaries of the global "core-periphery," operating anywhere a peculiar mix of labor arrangements favors profit-maximization.

Such radical reorganization of production forms and spaces is sometimes referred to as "post-modern."

2. I borrow the phrase "cultural struggle" from Brackette Williams (111), who uses it in the more specific sense of battles over cultural ascendancy and cultural authenticity among different ethnic and class groupings in a nation-state.

3. See Ong (76) for a critique of the objectifying discourse of feminist studies on "women and development" in non-Western societies. For a discussion of Marz's notion of fetishism and the rendering of working classes, women, and minorities as "the other," see 42:104.

4. In Spivak's view, such particular collusions between local forms of "patriarchy" and transnational capitalism have made the subproletariat woman "the paradigmatic subject" of the international division of labor (94:29).

5. Metropolitan capitalism in places like California routinely uses electronics surveillance, an even more relentless form of control, in both industrial and office settings.

6. On a brief 1989 fieldtrip to Nogales, Mexico, I visited American factories, shantytowns, and service centers. Female workers and social workers reported that sexual harassment was a common occurrence in what they called "the *maquila* culture." A rape crisis center noted that the frequency of rapes of women and children was "alarmingly high." Aborted fetuses were sometimes found in *maquila* toilets. Rapists included factory supervisors, household members, and the police. Compared to the Malaysian situation, with which I am more familiar, sexual violence seemed a major force in the Border Program. The contrasting situations show the specific historical and cultural patterning of industrial regimes.

7. The importation of prostitutes and brides into regions being opened up for capitalist development, whether in colonial Southeast Asia or in California during the "gold rush," is the historical antecedent to these contemporary linkages between capital and women from poor countries.

8. See Mintz (64:187–95) for a succinct summary of basic assumptions about the classic type of class consciousness (cf 69:321, 325). Drawing a rigid distinction between "class-in-itself" (in the objective sense) and "class-for-itself" (when it develops collective interests) sometimes blinds analysts to the presence of class consciousness when the supposedly requisite behavior is absent.

9. After their factories were destroyed in the 1987 earthquake, garment workers in Mexico City formed the first female workers' union, mainly to help members and their families. See Kammer & Tolan (47) for a report on company unions, and Staudt (96) and Young (117) for problems in organizing *maquila* workers.

10. Hossfeld (43) identifies a similar tactic among immigrant workers in "the Silicon Valley," California. She reports that workers exploit the management's racist/sexist logic —such as the "lazy" Chicana or "China doll" stereotypes—so as to gain excuses for avoiding or easing work requirements.

11. Strathern (98) has argued that the question of agency goes beyond the independent actions of individuals, focusing on the interests "in terms of which they act." Their aims are neither "necessarily . . . independently conceived" (98:22) nor, in my view, fully conscious.

ACKNOWLEDGMENTS

Thanks to the following scholars: Allan Pred for guiding me through the geography of capital accumulation; Brackette Williams for her penetrating insights into racial and sexual exploitation; John Gumperz for explicating narrative forms; Scott Guggenheim for his trenchant remarks and refreshing perspective; and Carol Smith for her cautionary comments.

LITERATURE CITED

1. Ackerman, S., Lee, R. 1981. Communication and cognitive pluralism in a spirit possession event in Malaysia. *Am. Ethnol.* 8:789–99
2. Ackerman, S. 1984. The impact of industrialization on the social role of rural Malay women. In *Women in Malaysia,* ed. Hing Ai Yun, Nik S. Karim, Rokiah Talib, pp. 40–60. Petaling Jaya, Malaysia: Pelanduk Publ.
3. Aguilar, D. 1987. Women in the political economy of the Philippines. *Alternatives* 12(4):511–26
4. Amriah, B. 1989. Development and factory women—negative perceptions from a Malaysian source area. Commonw. Geogr. Bur., Gender and Dev., Univ. Newcastle, April: 16–21
5. Andors, P. 1988. Women and work in Shenzhen. *Bull. Concern. Asian Scholars* 20(3):22–41
6. Asian Women's Liberation Newsletter. Outcries of poor workers: appeal from South Korea. In *Third World—Second Sex,* ed. M. Davies, pp. 233–39. London: Zed Press
7. Bandarage, A. 1988. Women and capitalist development in Sri Lanka, 1977–87. *Bull. Concern. Asian Scholars* 20:57–81
8. Basler, B. 1990. For every (Hong Kong) household, those Filipino women. *The New York Times,* Aug. 28, A7
9. Bello, W., Kinley, D., Elinson, E. 1982. *Development Debacle: The World Bank in the Philippines.* San Francisco: Food First Publ.
10. Beneria, L., Roldan, M. 1987. *The Crossroads of Class and Gender: Industrial Homework, Subcontracting, and Household Dynamics in Mexico City.* Chicago: Univ. Chicago Press
11. Berger, M. 1990. Japan trying to export unique business style. *San Francisco Chronicle,* July 31, A6
12. Braverman, H. 1974. *Labor and Monopoly Capital: The Degradation Work in the Twentieth Century.* New York: Monthly Review Press
13. Burawoy, M. 1979. The anthropology of industrial work. *Annu. Rev. Anthropol.* 8:231–66
14. Burawoy, M. 1985. *The Politics of Production.* London: Verso
15. Camoroff, J. 1986. *Body of Power, Spirit of Resistance.* Chicago: Univ. Chicago Press
16. Castells, M., Portes, A. 1989. World underneath: the origins, dynamics, and effects of the informal economy. In *The Informal Economy,* ed. A. Portes, M. Castells, L. Benton, pp. 11–37. Baltimore: John Hopkins Univ. Press
17. Cho, S. K. 1985. The labor process and capital mobility: the limits of the new international division of labor. *Pol. & Soc.* 14(2):185–222
18. Cockburn, C. 1983. *Brothers: Male Domination and Technological Change.* London: Pluto Press
19. De Certeau, M. 1980. On the oppositional practices of everyday life. *Social Text* 3(Fall):3–43
20. Deyo, F. 1984. Export manufacturing and labor: the Asian case. In *Labor in the Capitalist World-Economy,* ed. C. Bergquist, pp. 267–88. Beverly Hills: Sage
21. Douglas, M. 1970. *Purity and Danger.* Harmondsworth: Penguin
22. Elson, D., Pearson, R. 1981. The subordination of women and the internationalisation of factory production. In *Of Marriage and the Market,* ed. K. Young, C. Wolkowitz, R. McCullagh, pp. 144–66. London: CSE Books
23. Engels, F. 1968. *The Condition of the Working Class in England.* Transl. W. O. Henderson, W. H. Chaloner. Stanford: Stanford Univ. Press
24. Enloe, C. 1989. *Bananas, Beaches and Bases.* Berkeley: Univ. Calif. Press
25. Fawcett, J. T., Khoo, S.-E., Smith, P. C., eds. 1984. *Women in the Cities of Asia.* Boulder: Westview

26. Fernandez-Kelly, M. P. 1983. *For We Are Sold, I and My People.* Albany: State Univ. NY Press
27. Fernandez-Kelly, M. P., Garcia, A. 1989. Informalization at the core: hispanic women, home work and the advanced capitalist state. See Ref. 16, pp. 247–64
28. Foucault, M. 1979. *Discipline and Punish: The Birth of the Prison.* Transl. A. Sheridan. New York: Vintage
29. Foucault, M. 1980. *The History of Sexuality. Vol. 1. Introduction.* Transl. R. Hurley. New York: Vintage
30. Froebel, F., Heinrichs, J., Kreye, O. 1980. *The New International Division of Labor.* Cambridge: Cambridge Univ. Press
31. Fujita, K. 1988. Women workers, state policy, and the international division of labor: the case of Silicon Island in Japan. *Bull. Concern. Asian Scholars* 20(3):42–53
32. Gates, H. 1979. Dependency and the part-time proletariat in Taiwan. *Modern China* 5:381–408
33. Geertz, C. 1962. *Peddlers and Princes.* Chicago: Univ. Chicago Press
34. Goffman, E. 1963. *Stigma: Notes on the Management of Spoiled Identity.* New York: Simon & Schuster
35. Gramsci, A. 1971. *Selections from the Prison Notebook.* New York: International Publ.
36. Gray, L., Bohlen, A., Fernandez-Kelly, M. P. 1987. *The Global Assembly Line* (16 mm film, 58 min., color). Wayne, NJ: New Day Films
37. Green, S. G. 1983. Silicon Valley's women workers: a theoretical analysis of sex-segregation in the electronics industry labor market. See Ref. 64, pp. 273–331
38. Grossman, R. 1979. Women's place in the integrated circuit. *Southeast Asia Chron.* 66:2–17
39. Guha, R., Spivak, G. C. 1988. *Selected Subaltern Studies.* New York: Oxford Univ. Press
40. Hanatrakul, S. 1988. Prostitution in Thailand. In *Development and Displacement: Women in Southeast Asia,* ed. G. Chandler, N. Sullivan, J. Branson, pp. 115–36. Monash Pap. Southeast Asia, No. 18. Clayton, Victoria, Aust.: Monash Univ.
41. Haraway, D. 1988. Situated knowledges: the science question in feminism and the privilege of partial perspective. *Fem. Stud.* 14(3):575–99
42. Harvey, D. 1989. *The Condition of Postmodernity.* Cambridge, MA: Basil Blackwell
43. Hossfeld, K.-J. 1990. "Their logic against them": contradictions in sex, race and class in the Silicon Valley. In *Women Workers and Global Restructuring,* ed. K. Ward, pp. 149–78. Ithaca: Cornell Univ. ILR Press
44. Jameson, F. 1985. Postmodernism, or the cultural logic of late capitalism. *New Left Rev.,* pp. 53–92
45. Jayawardena, C. 1968. Ideology and conflict in lower class communities. *Comp. Stud. Soc.* 10(14):416–46
46. Kamal, S., Young, M. L. 1987. Social forces, the state and the international division of labor: the case of Malaysia. In *Global Restructuring and Territorial Development,* ed. M. Castells, J. Henderson, pp. 169–201. London: Sage
47. Kammer, J., Tolan, S. 1989. "A farce": punchless Mexico unions have power to lure American firms. *The Ariz. Republic,* April 18, A1, A8
48. Kammer, J., Tolan, S. 1989. Many plants look other way when children apply for work. *The Ariz. Republic,* April 17, A11
49. Kelsey, M. 1986. Industrial Hong Kong: a case study of the relations of economic development. Unpubl. manuscript, Sociol. Dept., Univ. Calif. Berkeley
50. Kim, S. K. 1988. Women workers and the birth of labor unions in Masan, Korea. Presented at Annu. Meet. Am. Anthropol. Assoc., Phoenix
51. Kim, S. N. 1989. Lamentations of the dead: the historical imagery of violence on Cheju Island, South Korea. *J. Ritual Stud.* 3(2):251–71
52. Koo, H., Haggard, S., Deyo, F. 1986. Labor and development strategy in the East Asian NICS. *Items* 40(3/4):64–68

53. Kung, L. 1983. *Factory Women in Taiwan*. Ann Arbor: UMI Res. Press
54. Kyoko, S. 1980. Mariveles: servitude in the free trade zone. *Bull. Concern. Asian Scholars* 12(2):74–80
55. Lapietz, A. 1986. New tendencies in the international division of labor: regimes of accumulation and modes of regulation. In *Production, Work, Territory*, ed. A. Scott, M. Storper, pp. 16–39. Boston: Allen & Unwin
56. Lee, D., Brady, R. 1988. Long, hard days—at pennies an hour. *Bus. Week.* Oct. 31, pp. 46–47
57. Lim, L. Y. C. 1978. *Women Workers in Multinational Corporations: The Case of the Electronics Industry in Malaysia and Singapore*. Ann Arbor: Univ. Michigan, Women's Stud. Prog., Occ. Pap. No. 9
58. Lim, L. Y. C. 1983. Capitalism, imperialism and patriarchy: the dilemma of Third-World women workers in multinational factories. See Ref. 64, pp. 70–91
59. Lim, L. Y. C., Pang, E. F. 1985. Technology choice and employment creation: a case of three multinational enterprises in Singapore. In *The Pacific Challenge in International Business*, ed. W. C. Kim, P. K. Y. Young, pp. 157–194. Ann Arbor: UMI Res. Press
60. Lin, V. 1984. Productivity first: Japanese management methods in Singapore. *Bull. Concern. Asian Scholars* 16(4):12–25
61. Lugo, A. 1990. Cultural production and reproduction in Cuidad Juarez, Mexico: tropes at play among maquiladora workers. *Cult. Anthropol.* 5(2):173–96
62. Mather, C. 1983. Industrialization in the Tangerang Regency of West Java: women workers and the Islamic patriarchy. *Bull. Concern. Asian Scholars* 15(2):2–17
63. Mills, M. D. 1990. Between the bright city lights and the family hearth: the dilemma of village daughters in Bangkok. Anthropol. Dept., Univ. Calif., Berkeley
64. Mintz, S. W. 1974. The rural proletariat and the problem of the rural proletarian consciousness. In *Peasants and Proletarians*, ed. R. Cohen, P. Gutkind, P. Brazier, pp. 173–97. New York: Monthly Rev. Press
65. Mohanty, C. 1987. Feminist encounters: locating the politics of experience. *Copyright* 1:30–44
66. Moore, H. 1988. *Feminism and Anthropology*. Minneapolis: Univ. Minn. Press
67. Muto, I. 1977. The free trade zone and mystique of export-oriented industrialization. *AMPO.: Jpn.-Asia Q. Rev.*, Spec. Issue, pp. 9–32
68. Nakano, K. 1977. Japan's overseas investment patterns and FTZs. Spec. Iss. *AMPO. Jpn.-Asia Q. Rev.*, pp.33–50
69. Nash, J. 1985. *We Eat the Mines and the Mines Eat Us*. New York: Columbia Univ. Press
70. Nash, J., Fernandez-Kelly, M. P., eds. 1983. *Women and Men in the New International Division of Labor*. Albany: State Univ. NY Press
71. Oh, S. J. 1983. The living conditions of female workers in Korea. *Korea Observ.* 24(2):185–200
72. Ong, A. 1983. Global industries and Malay peasants in Peninsular Malaysia. See Ref. 64, pp. 426–41
73. Ong, A. 1985. Industrialization and prostitution in Southeast Asia. *Southeast Asia Chron.* 96:2–6
74. Ong, A. 1987. *Spirits of Resistance and Capitalist Discipline: Factory Women in Malaysia*. Albany: State Univ. NY Press
75. Ong, A. 1987. Disassembling gender in an electronics age. Review article. *Fem. Stud.* 13:609–27
76. Ong, A. 1988. Colonialism and modernity: feminist re-presentations of women in non-Western societies. *Inscriptions* 3/4:79–93
77. Ong, A. 1988. The production of possession: spirits and the multinational corporation in Malaysia. *Am. Ethnol.* 15:28–42
78. Ong, A. 1990. State versus Islam: families, women's bodies and the body politic in Malaysia. *Am. Ethnol.* 17(2):258–76

79. Ong, A. 1990. Japanese factories, Malay workers: class and sexual metaphors in Malaysia. In *Power and Difference: Gender in Island Southeast Asia,* ed. J. Atkinson, S. Errington. Palo Alto: Stanford Univ. Press
80. Pena, D. 1987. *Tortuosidad:* shopfloor struggles of female *maquiladora* workers. See Ref. 86, pp. 129–54
81. Phongpaichit, P. 1988. Two roads to the factory: industrialization strategies and women's employment in Southeast Asia. In *Structures of Patriarchy: Community and Household in Modernizing Asia,* ed. B. Agarwal, pp. 151–63. London: Zed Books Ltd.
82. Pineda-Ofreneo, R. 1988. Subcontracting in export-oriented industries: impact on Filipino working women. See Ref. 40, pp. 17–40
83. Portes, A., Sassen-Koob, S. 1987. Making in the underground: comparative material on the informal sector in Western market economies. *Am. J. Sociol.* 93:30–61
84. Pred, A. 1990. In other wor(l)ds: fragmented and integrated observations on gendered languages, gendered spaces and local transformation. *Antipode* 22(1): 33–52
85. Rostow, W. W. 1960. *Stages of Economic Growth: A Non-Communist Manifesto.* New York: Harper
86. Ruiz, V. L., Tiano, S., eds. 1987. *Women on the U.S.-Mexico Border.* Boston: Allen & Unwin
87. Rofel, L. 1989. Hegemony and productivity: workers in post-Mao China. In *Marxism and the Chinese Experience,* ed. A. Sirlik, M. Meisner, pp. 235–52. Armonk, NY: M. E. Sharpe
88. Safa, H. 1986. Runaway shops and female employment: the search for cheap labor. In *Women's Work,* ed. E. Leacock, H. Safa, pp. 58–71. South Hadley: Bergin & Garvey
89. Salaff, J. 1981. *Working Daughters of Hong Kong.* Cambridge: Cambridge Univ. Press
90. Sassen-Koob, S. 1984. Notes on the incorporation of Third World women into wage-labor through immigration and off-shore production. *Int. Migr. Rev.* 13:1144–67
91. Scheper-Hughes, N. 1991. The subversive body: illness and the micropolitics of resistance. In *Anthropology in the 1990s,* ed. R. Borowski. NY: McGraw Hill
92. Scott, J. 1986. *Weapons of the Weak.* New Haven: Yale Univ. Press
93. Siriporn, S. 1985. In pursuit of an illusion: Thai women in Europe. *Southeast Asia Chron.* 96:7–12
94. Spivak, G. H. 1988. Subaltern studies: deconstructing historiography. See Ref. 39, pp. 3–44
95. Stallybrass, P., White, A. 1986. *The Politics and Poetics of Transgression.* Ithaca: Cornell Univ. Press
96. Staudt, K. 1987. Programming women's empowerment: a case from Northern Mexico. See Ref. 86, pp. 155–73
97. Stroper, M., Walker, R. 1989. *The Capitalist Imperative: Territory, Technology and Industrial Growth.* NY: Basil Blackwell
98. Strathern, M. 1987. Introduction. In *Dealing with Inequality,* ed. M. Strathern, pp. 1–32. Cambridge: Cambridge Univ. Press
99. Sun, S. H. 1987. Women, work and theology in Korea. *J. Fem. Stud. Rel.* 3:125–34
100. Taussig, M. 1980. Reification and the consciousness of the patient. *So. Sci. Med.* 14B:3–13
101. Taylor, F. W. 1919. *Two Papers on Scientific Management.* London: Routledge & Sons
102. Thompson, E. P. 1967. Time, work discipline, and industrial capitalism. *Past & Present* 38:56–97
103. Thompson, E. P. 1962. *The Making of the English Working Class.* New York: Vintage
104. Tiano, S. 1987. *Maquiladoras* in Mexican: integration or exploitation? See Ref. 86, pp. 77–101
105. Tsuchiya, T. 1977. Introduction. *AMPO: Jpn.-Asia Q. Rev.,* Spec. Issue, pp. 1–32

106. Vincent, J. 1982. *Teso in Transformation.* Berkeley: Univ. Calif. Press
107. Wallerstein, I. 1974. *The Modern World-System I.* New York: Academic
108. Warren, K., Borque, S. 1987. Gender, technology, and development. *Daedalus* 116:173–97
109. Weber, M. 1958. *The Protestant Ethic and the Spirit of Capitalism.* Transl. T. Parsons. New York: Charles Scribners & Sons
110. Weisman, A. 1987. The other side of Nogales. *City Magazine, The Arizona Republic,* Tucson, Feb., pp. 34–41
111. Williams, B. F. 1989. Nationalism, traditionalism, and the problem of cultural inauthenticity. In *Nationalist Ideologies and the Production of National Cultures,* ed. R. C. Fox. Am. Ethnol. Soc. Monogr. Ser., No. 2. Washington, DC: Am. Anthropol. Assoc.
112. Williams, R. 1972. *Marxism and Literature.* London: Verso
113. Willis, P. 1977. *Learning to Labor: How Working Class Kids Get Working Class Jobs.* New York: Columbia Univ. Press
114. Wolf, D. 1990. Linking women's labor with the global economy: factory workers and their families in rural Java. See Ref. 43, pp. 25–47
115. Wysocki, B. Jr. 1990. Guiding hand: in Asia, Japan hopes to 'coordinate' what nations produce. *Wall Street J.,* August 20, A1, A4
116. Yang, D. J. et al. 1989. Is the era of cheap Asian labor over? *Bus. Week* May 15, 1989, pp. 45–46
117. Young, G. 1987. Gender identification and working-class solidarity among *maquila* workers in Cuidad Juarez: stereotypes and realities. See Ref. 86, pp. 105–27

Neo-Liberalism and Globalization

Tupac Amaru Revolutionary Movement (MRTA)

Extreme Poverty

In Latin America, the wave of privatizations demanded by the World Bank and the International Monetary Fund have ended up as a recipe for unemployment, throwing thousands of workers out onto the street to join what is already an army of the unemployed. The largely unresolved contradictions of our continent have become polarized. We believe that South America is the weak link in the transnational imperialist chain in the era of "globalization."

The political and economic ideas diffused by the imperialist bourgeoisie and their intelligentsia have no other purpose than to annihilate a section of our society. We will attempt to analyze these ideas in a scientific fashion. A task to which the "progressive and revolutionary" intelligentsia should contribute again, as it seems they entered into a period of self-censorship some time ago. As a political organization which has developed in the heart of the people, we will attempt to express these ideas in a language which is as simple as possible, without losing their scientific rigor. This method, and our practical actions, keep us in the hearts and minds of the people, despite the wishes of many who are still trying to make themselves believe the cries of victory for Fujimoriism, and others who announced our destruction at every possible opportunity, while apologizing for the dictatorship. It is not our intention to fall into using "fashionable terminology," but we consider it an obligation to clarify concepts, which some people formerly active in "revolu-

Originally appeared on the Web site *http://burn.ucsd.edu/~ats/MRTA/neo-lib.htm*

tionary" and "progressive" circles started using, thereby only creating confusion and false hopes in our people.

At a time when the so-called "neo-liberal model" is showing its true self, there have been a series of violent social protests, as in Mexico, Venezuela, Argentina, etc., which proves that it did not achieve the results they claimed it would, and that they can no longer sell false hopes to the millions of poor people pushed into conditions of extreme misery, in Peru, in our Andes, and in the whole of the continent.

"The Statements of Intentions"; Or a Program for the Neo-Colonies

In the shadows of the "Statements of Intentions" developed by the International Monetary Fund, they are proceeding to privatize the land, natural resources, and that which remains of our industry. These "Statements" are the real programs of the (neo-colonial) governments of Latin America and have been the cause of massive unemployment, poverty, and extreme misery, and they condemn millions of people to death through starvation, like in Somalia. It is in these conditions that the people of Peru and Latin America, and their revolutionary organizations, must plan a scientific and objective alternative to this murderous and genocidal system.

The Peruvian people have struggled against and survived the greatest economic genocide conceived by the ruling classes since the conquest. From 1975, the ruling class has been trying to put their neo-liberal plan into action, but the organized response of the masses has impeded this. However, in 1990, despite popular resistance, shock tactics were employed and we are now living with the brutal consequences.

Liberalism and Neo-Liberalism

This "model," theoretically originating from the theories of the liberal classics of Adam Smith and David Ricardo, is being applied in the age of globalization. However, if we emphasize our class differences with the classics of bourgeois economics, that does not mean to say that we overlook their contribution to general economic theory: the theory of work-value, which with other class elements serves as the basis by which the injustice of capitalist economic theory is revealed, where those who create the wealth which circulates in the world do not have access to it. Aside from the subjective question of justice and injustice, this system created the revolutionary class: the proletariat, which by its capacity to create wealth and by its form of social organization within the productive process is the only one capable of forging a radical alternative to capitalism. The crisis of capitalism is not created by the scarcity of goods, like in the economies before capitalism, but by their excess. From this point of view, the so-called "neo-liberals" are further from Smith and Ricardo than Marxism; their bourgeois apologists are neither willing nor able to enter into a debate about the "theory of value," and instead they attempt to reduce the creation of products and wealth to the omnipotent power of capital and the market. Maybe they do not want to know that capital exists as a product of the value accumulated and created by the workers, which is then concentrated and appropriated into private hands. On this point, which is the backbone of liberalism, there is no convergence with the neo-liberals. In the same way, the "free trade" proposed by the liberals has no connection with the commercial monopoly exercised by the globalizers, or multinational monopolists (imperialists). According to Jonathan Elliot in 1987: "It is calculated that on the world-market level, 40% of trade does not go through a free market but through internal trading (within the same companies)." In 1994, Jules Kagian said in "Middle East International" that: "In the United States, more than 80% of the income from goods sold abroad, quantified in dollars, does not come from exports but from sales by affiliated companies."

Globalization: The New Mask of Imperialism

The deification of the market is nothing other than the product of a development of national capital onto international levels, breaking down its physical barriers. This phenomena was studied at the start of this century and was named "imperialism" by Lenin. In this way the globalization of the economy is just the concentration of value created by world society in the multinationals. That is to say the upward fusion of productive, financial, and banking capital.

The number of multinational companies has risen from 7,000 in 1970 to 37,000 in 1992; i.e., former national companies have been merging with those from other countries and they maintain a dependence on the largest ones. The economic power of multinational companies is greater than that of many national states. Their sales for example have risen to 5.5 billion dollars, 90% of which are made in the imperialist (northern) countries and just 10% of which are made in the producer (southern) countries. The economic power of the multinationals gives them an unlimited political power over national states.

A Little Bit of History

The development of production created an antagonistic contradiction between the private ownership of the means of production and the socialization of production itself between capital and labor, and this resulted in many crises and two world wars. These wars allowed the victors to carve up the world markets again, and by so doing bury their crisis.

At the end of the Second World War, the fusion of capital via the multinationals permitted largely North American capital, through the Marshall Plan, to absorb that which remained of European and Japanese capital. The multinationals made the most of the high level of development achieved by labor in these countries. However, despite the fact that the workers were selling their labor in good conditions, due to the influence of competition from the socialist countries, it was possible to transcend neither the antagonistic contradictions between capital and labor, nor those between the socialized nature of production and the private appropriation of its products. Without this insight it would be impossible for us to explain the discontent and strikes in countries such as France.

It may be that the imperialists, or globalizers (to use the new terminology), have invested huge quantities of money to investigate how to avoid crises and violent uprisings, and that they have achieved a degree of mind control through the mass media, but they have not succeeded in curbing the discontent, which is growing day by day, and every time it becomes more difficult for them to make people believe that this system is not responsible for world problems; in the north they see the waves of immigrants and millions of dollars are sent as humanitarian "aid" to the "under-developed" countries. In the post-war era, they secured an internal market in the north, which increased in depth but not in extension. This has lead to the development of consumerism. This resulted in a bourgeoisfication of the working classes, dividing them from their historic task. The reasoning being that he who can satisfy his basic needs has no interest in social change. Even though they are conscious of the fact that their high standard of living comes from the extermination of whole peoples, after the natural resources of these nations have been plundered. The imperialist governments justify this by saying that the peoples of the south are lazy and ignorant. Despite this, they too have been affected by an incessant rise in unemployment, which although it may be concealed by the manipulation of statistics is still undeniably the case and removes an important sector of the population from the consumer market.

Another way by which they attempt to avoid or recover from their crises is by developing regional wars far from their centers, such as those based on religion, racism, territory, etc. These provide excellent markets for weapons.

But something terrible is happening in the world of globalization. Year by year profits are going down and the only way they have of recovering from this is by cutting wages and social benefits, and this has led to massive waves of redundancies, first in the countries of the south and more recently in their metropoles in the north. This tendency has no chance of being reversed. The difference is that in the north the social effects of these tendencies are dulled by the welfare state, something we do not have in the south.

The welfare state is deteriorating in the north, at the same time as the middle classes in Latin America are disappearing, increasing the flow of external and internal migration in an attempt to improve their living conditions.

The international proletariat and its organizations entered into a period of decline due to the influences of "welfare statism" and "reformism." This postponed the practical and theoretical development of world socialism for a long time. However, the enormous increase of the forces of production was not accompanied by an alternative program, which would not just have curbed the disproportionate increase in the exploitation of the forces of labor and the pillaging of the earth's resources. It is, for example, impossible to ignore the fact that today, despite the fact that the forces of production have been doubled many times since the last century and we have entered the phase of a revolution in information technology and cybernetics, people still work an eight hour day in the north and much longer in the south. It is therefore logical that there should be unemployment when one person is forced to do the work of two or three. It is within the capacity of any worker to realize that if the working day is not decreased by at least a third or even a half, then his destiny as redundant is assured. In Latin America, the famous privatizations, demanded by the IMF and World Bank, have been nothing more than a cause of unemployment. However, through the level of development of the forces of production achieved in Latin America and through the politicization of our working class, who have been forced into unemployment and are now in transit (including back to their old communities in the Andes), there has been a polarization of the unresolved contradictions in our continent.

We are the weak link in the imperialist chain. Our continent has passed through many ways, we have made many mistakes from which we believe we have learned and we now propose to construct a socialist alternative, because otherwise, if we stay in the realms of imperialist globalization, we are condemned to unemployment, misery, and extermination.

Part

7

Doing Business in the Information Age

In the past twenty years, the way in which business is done has fundamentally changed. Companies have become increasingly global. Concepts such as the workplace and trade have been profoundly altered by advances in technology, and the spread of both democracy and capitalism.

Thomas W. Malone and Robert J. Laubacher discuss how changes in computer technology have led to the possibility of a dramatic shift in the size and nature of companies. Powerful computers and new technologies and networks are changing the economic equation. Ideas of dominant and centralized business, they believe, will give way to a more elastic network. Individual workers will no longer be spatially bound, and the role of the manager may ultimately disappear in what they call an "e-lance economy."

Stephen J. Kobrin outlines a world in which currency as we know it is obsolete. But along with the change from cash commerce to a digital economy come a series of problems and risks. Kobrin lays out the costs and benefits of an e-commerce system, and suggests some preliminary solutions to key problems.

Finally, Gurcharan Das challenges the widely held notion that globalization requires businesses to apply standardized and preferably modern solutions, on a global level, in response to internationalization. Das details his experiences as a local businessman in a developing country, applying solutions to global challenges in a "local-friendly" manner. In particular, he suggests the utility of tapping into local diversity, and then applying insights learned on the local level to the global arena. In the course of outlining the utility of this approach, Das humanizes a business world that is increasingly homogenized and technologically dominated.

The Dawn of the E-Lance Economy

Thomas W. Malone and Robert J. Laubacher

In October of 1991, Linus Torvalds, a 21-year-old computer-science student at the University of Helsinki, made available on the Internet a kernel of a computer operating system he had written. Called Linux, it was a rudimentary version of the ubiquitous UNIX operating system, which for more than a decade had been a mainstay of corporate and academic computing. Torvalds encouraged other programmers to download his software—for free—and use it, test it, and modify it as they saw fit. A few took him up on the offer. They fixed bugs, tinkered with the original code, and added new features, and they too posted their work on the Internet.

As the Linux kernel grew, it attracted the attention of more and more programmers, who contributed their own ideas and improvements. The Linux community grew steadily, soon coming to encompass thousands of people around the world, all sharing their work freely with one another. Within three years, this loose, informal group, working without managers and connected mainly through the Internet, had turned Linux into one of the best versions of UNIX ever created.

Imagine, now, how such a software development project would have been organized at a company like IBM or Microsoft. Decisions and funds would have been filtered through layers of managers. Formal teams of programmers, quality assurance testers, and technical writers would have been established and assigned tasks. Customer surveys and focus groups would have been conducted, their findings documented in thick reports. There would have been budgets, milestones, deadlines, status meetings, performance reviews, approvals. There would have been turf wars, burnouts, overruns, delays. The project would have cost an enormous amount of money, taken longer to complete, and quite possibly produced a system less valuable to users than Linux.

For many executives, the development of Linux is most easily understood (and most easily dismissed) as an arcane story of hackers and cyberspace—a neat *Wired* magazine kind of story, but one that bears little relevance to the serious world of big business. This interpretation, while understandable, is shortsighted. What the Linux story really shows us is the power of a new technology—in this case, electronic networks—to fundamentally change the way work is done. The Linux community, a temporary, self-managed gathering of diverse individuals engaged in a common task, is a model for a new kind of business organization that could form the basis for a new kind of economy.

The fundamental unit of such an economy is not the corporation but the individual. Tasks aren't assigned and controlled through a stable chain of management but rather are carried out autonomously by independent contractors. These electronically connected freelancers—e-lancers—join together into fluid and temporary networks to produce and sell goods and services. When the job is done—after a day, a month, a year—the network dissolves, and its members become independent agents again, circulating through the economy, seeking the next assignment.

Far from being a wild hypothesis, the e-lance economy is, in many ways, already upon us. We see it not only in the development of Linux but also in the evolution of the Internet itself. We see it in the emergence of virtual companies, in the rise of outsourcing and telecommuting, and in the proliferation of freelance and temporary workers. Even within large organizations, we see it in the increasing importance of ad-hoc project teams, in the rise of "intrapreneurs," and in the formation of independent business units.[1]

All these trends point to the devolution of large, permanent corporations into flexible, temporary networks of individuals. No one can yet say exactly how important or widespread this new form of business organization will become, but judging from current signs, it is not inconceivable that it could define work in the twenty-first century as the industrial organization defined it in the twentieth. If it does, business and society will be changed forever.

Businesses of One

Business organizations are, in essence, mechanisms for coordination. They exist to guide the flow of work, materials, ideas, and money, and the form they take is strongly affected by the coordination technologies available. Until a hundred or so years ago, coordination technologies were primitive. Goods and messages were transported primarily by foot, horse, or boat, and the process was slow, unreliable, and often dangerous. Because there was no efficient way to coordinate disparate activities, most people worked near their homes, often by themselves, producing products or services for their neighbors. The business organizations that did exist —farms, shops, foundries—were usually small, comprising a few owners and employees. When their products had to reach distant consumers, they did so through a long series of transactions with various independent wholesalers, jobbers, shippers, storekeepers, and itinerant peddlers.

It was not until the second half of the nineteenth century, after railroad tracks had been laid and telegraph lines strung, that large, complex organizations became possible. With faster, more dependable communication and transportation, businesses could reach national and even international markets, and their owners had the means to coordinate the activities of large and dispersed groups of people. The hierarchical, industrial corporation was born, subsuming a broad array of functions and, often, a broad array of businesses, and it quickly matured to become the dominant organizational model of the twentieth century.

Despite all the recent talk of decentralized management, empowered employees, and horizontal processes, the large, industrial organization continues to dominate the economy today. We remain in the age of multinational megacompanies, and those companies appear to be rushing to meld into ever larger forms. The headlines of the business press tell the story: Compaq buys Digital. WorldCom buys MCI. Citibank merges with Travelers. Daimler-Benz acquires Chrysler. British Airways allies with American Airlines (which in turn allies with US Airways). Some observers, projecting this wave of consolidation into the future, foresee a world in which giant global corporations replace nations as the organizing units of humanity. We will be citizens of Sony or Shell or Wal-Mart, marching out every day to do battle with the citizens of Philips or Exxon or Sears.

Such a scenario certainly seems plausible. Yet when we look beneath the surface of all the M&A activity, we see signs of a counterphenomenon: the disintegration of the large corporation. People are leaving big companies and either joining much smaller companies or going into business for themselves as contract workers, freelancers, or temps. Twenty-five years ago, one in five U.S. workers was employed by a *Fortune* 500 company. Today the ratio has dropped to less than one in ten. The largest private employer in the United States is not General Motors or IBM or UPS. It's the temporary-employment agency Manpower Incorporated, which in 1997 employed 2 million people. While big companies control ever larger flows of cash, they are exerting less and less direct control over actual business activity. They are, you might say, growing hollow.

Even within large corporations, traditional command-and-control management is becoming less common. Decisions are increasingly being pushed lower down in organizations. Workers are being rewarded not for efficiently carrying out orders but for figuring out what needs to be done and then doing it. Some large industrial companies like Asea Brown Boveri and British Petroleum have broken themselves up into scores of independent units that transact business with one another almost as if they were separate companies. And in some industries, like investment banking and consulting, it is often easier to understand the existing organizations not as traditional hierarchies but as confederations of entrepreneurs, united only by a common brand name.

What underlies this trend? Why is the traditional industrial organization showing evidence of disintegration? Why are e-lancers proliferating? The answers lie in the basic economics of organizations. Economists, organizational theorists, and business historians have long wrestled with the question of why businesses grow large or stay small. Their research suggests that when it is cheaper to conduct transactions internally, within the bounds of a corporation, organizations grow larger, but when it is cheaper to conduct them externally, with independent entities in the open market, organizations stay small or shrink. If, for example, the owners of an iron smelter find it less expensive to establish a sales force than to contract with outside agencies to sell their products, they will hire salespeople, and their organization will grow. If they find that outside agencies cost less, they will not hire the salespeople, and their organization will not grow.

The coordination technologies of the industrial era—the train and the telegraph, the automobile and the telephone, the mainframe computer—made internal transactions not only possible but also advantageous. Companies were able to manage large organizations centrally, which provided them with economies of scale in manufacturing, marketing, distribution, and other activities. It made economic sense to directly control many different functions and businesses and to hire the legions of administrators and supervisors needed to manage them. Big was good.

But with the introduction of powerful personal computers and broad electronic networks—the coordination technologies of the twenty-first century—the economic equation changes. Because information can be shared instantly and inexpensively among many people in many locations, the value of centralized decision making and expensive bureaucracies decreases. Individuals can manage themselves, coordinating their efforts through electronic links with other independent parties. Small becomes good.

In one sense, the new coordination technologies enable us to return to the preindustrial organizational model of tiny, autonomous businesses—businesses of one or of a few—conducting transactions with one another in a market. But there's one crucial difference: electronic networks enable these microbusinesses to tap into the global reservoirs of information, expertise, and financing that used to be available only to large companies. The small companies enjoy many of the benefits of the big without sacrificing the leanness, flexibility, and creativity of the small.

In the future, as communications technologies advance and networks become more efficient, the shift to e-lancers promises to accelerate. Should that indeed take place, the dominant business organization of the future may not be a stable, permanent corporation but rather an elastic network that may sometimes exist for no more than a day or two. When a project needs to be undertaken, requests for proposals will be transmitted or electronic want ads posted, individuals or small teams will respond, a network will be formed, and new workers will be brought on as their particular skills are needed. Once the project is done, the network will disband. Following in the footsteps of young Linus Torvalds, we will enter the age of the temporary company.

The Temporary Company

From the 1920s through the 1940s, the movie business was controlled by big studios like MGM and Columbia. The studios employed actors, directors, screenwriters, photographers, publicists, even projectionists—all the people needed to produce a movie, get it into theaters, and fill the seats. Central managers determined which films to make and who would work on them. The film industry was a model of big-company, industrial organization.

By the 1950s, however, the studio system had disintegrated. The power had shifted from the studio to the individual. Actors, directors, and screenwriters became freelancers, and they made their own choices about which projects to work on. For a movie to be made, these freelancers would join together into a temporary company, which would employ different specialists as needed from day to day. As soon as the film was completed, the temporary company would go out of existence, but the various players would, in time, join together in new combinations to work on new projects.

The shift in the film business from permanent companies to temporary companies shows how entire industries can evolve, quite rapidly, from centralized structures to network structures. And such transformations are by no means limited to the idiosyncratic world of Hollywood. Consider the way many manufacturers are today pursuing radical outsourcing strategies, letting external agents perform more of their traditional activities. The U.S. computer-display division of the Finnish company Nokia, for example, chose to enter the U.S. display market with only five employees. Technical support, logistics, sales, and marketing were all subcontracted to specialists around the country. The fashion accessories company Topsy Tail, which has revenues of $80 million but only three employees, never even touches its products through the entire supply chain. It contracts with various injection-molding companies to manufacture its goods; uses design agencies to create its packaging; and distributes and sells its products through a network of independent fulfillment houses, distributors, and sales reps. Nokia's and Topsy Tail's highly decentralized operations bear more resemblance to the network model of organization than to the traditional industrial model.

For another, broader example, look at what's happened to the textile industry in the Prato region of Italy. In the early 1970s, Massimo Menichetti inherited his family's business, a failing textile mill. Menichetti quickly broke up the firm into eight separate companies. He sold a major portion of equity—between one-third and one-half—to key employees, and he required that at least 50% of the new companies' sales come from customers that had not been served by the old company. Within three years, the eight new businesses had achieved a complete turnaround, attaining significant increases in machine utilization and productivity.

Following the Menichetti model, many other big mills in Prato broke themselves up into much smaller pieces. By 1990, more than 15,000 small textile firms, averaging fewer than five employees, were active in the region. The tiny firms built state-of-the-art factories and warehouses, and they developed cooperative ventures in such areas as purchasing, logistics, and R&D, where scale economies could be exploited. Textile production in the area tripled during this time, despite the fact that the textile industry was in decline throughout the rest of Europe. And the quality of the products produced in the Prato region rose as innovation flourished. Textiles from Prato have now become the preferred material for fashion designers around the world.

Playing a key role in the Prato textile industry are brokers, known as *impannatori,* who act as conduits between the small manufacturing concerns and the textile buyers. The impannatori help coordinate the design and manufacturing process by bringing together appropriate groups of businesses to meet the particular needs of a customer. They have even created an electronic market, which serves as a clearinghouse for information about projected factory utilization and upcoming requirements, allowing textile production capacity to be traded like a commodity.

The Prato experience shows that an economy can be built on the network model, but Prato, it could be argued, is a small and homogeneous region. How would a complex, diverse industry operate under the network model? The answer is: far more easily than one might expect. As a thought experiment, let's take a journey forward in time, into the midst of the twenty-first century, and see how automobiles, the archetypal industrial product, are being designed.

General Motors, we find, has split apart into several dozen separate divisions, and these divisions have outsourced most of their traditional activities. They are now small companies concerned mainly with managing their brands and funding the development of new types and models of cars. A number of independent manufacturers perform fabrication and assembly on a contract basis for anyone who wants to pay for it. Vehicles are devised by freelance engineers and designers, who join together into small, ever shifting coalitions to work on particular projects. A coalition may, for example, focus on engineering an electrical system or on designing a chassis, or it may concentrate on managing the integration of all of the subsystems into complete automobiles.

These design coalitions take many forms. Some are organized as joint ventures; some share equity among their members; some are built around electronic markets that set prices and wages. All are autonomous and self-organizing, and all depend on a universal, high-speed computer network—the descendant of the Internet—to connect them to one another and exchange electronic cash. A highly developed venture-capital infrastructure monitors and assesses the various teams and provides financing to the most promising ones.

In addition to being highly efficient, with little managerial or administrative overhead, this market-based structure has spurred innovation throughout the automotive industry. While much of the venture capital goes to support traditional design concepts, some is allocated to more speculative, even wild-eyed, ideas, which if successful could create enormous financial rewards. A small coalition of engineers may, for example, receive funds to design a factory for making individualized lighting systems for car grilles. If their idea pans out, they could all become multimillionaires overnight. And the next day, they might dissolve their coalition and head off to seek new colleagues and new challenges.

Over the past few years, under the auspices of the Massachusetts Institute of Technology's initiative on Inventing the Organizations of the 21st Century, we have worked with a group of business professors and executives to consider the different ways business might be organized in the next century.[2] The automotive design scenario we've just laid out was discussed and refined by this group, and we subsequently shared it with managers and engineers from big car companies. They not only agreed that it was a plausible model for car design but also pointed out that the auto industry was in some ways already moving toward such a model. Many automakers have been outsourcing more and more of their basic design work, granting ever greater autonomy to external design agencies.

A shift to an e-lance economy would bring about fundamental changes in virtually every business function, not just in product design. Supply chains would become ad hoc structures, assembled to fit the needs of a particular project and disassembled when the project ended. Manufacturing capacity would be bought and sold in an open market, and independent, specialized manufacturing concerns would undertake small batch orders for a variety of brokers, design shops, and even consumers. Marketing would be performed in some cases by brokers, in other cases by small companies that would own brands and certify the quality of the merchandise sold under them. In still other cases, the ability of consumers to share product information on the Internet would render marketing obsolete; consumers would simply "swarm" around the best offerings. Financing would come less from retained earnings and big equity markets and more from venture capitalists and interested individuals. Small investors might trade shares in ad hoc, project-based enterprises over the Internet.

Business would be transformed fundamentally. But nowhere would the changes be as great as in the function of management itself.

The Transformation of Management

In the mid-1990s, when the Internet was just entering the consciousness of most business executives, the press was filled with disaster stories. The Internet, the pundits proclaimed, was about to fall into disarray. Traffic on the World Wide Web was growing too fast. There were too many Web sites, too many people on-line. Demand was outstripping capacity, and it was only a matter of months before the entire network crashed or froze.

It never happened. The Internet has continued to expand at an astonishing rate. Its capacity has doubled every year since 1988, and today more than 90 million people are connected to it. They use it to order books and flowers, to check on weather conditions in distant cities, to trade stocks and commodities, to send messages and spread propaganda, and to join discussion groups on everything from soap operas to particle physics.

So who's responsible for this great and unprecedented achievement? Who oversaw what is arguably the most important business development of the last 50 years? No one. No one controls the Internet. No one's in charge. No one's the leader. The Internet grew out of the combined efforts of all its users, with no central management. In fact, when we ask people whether they think the Internet could have grown this fast for this long if it had been managed by a single company—AT&T, for example—most say no. Managing such a massive and unpredictable explosion of capacity and creativity would have been beyond the skills of even the most astute and capable executives. The Internet *had* to be self-managed.

The Internet is the greatest model of a network organization that has yet emerged, and it reveals a startling truth: in an e-lance economy, the role of the traditional business manager changes dramatically and sometimes disappears completely. The work of the temporary company is coordinated by the individuals who compose it, with little or no centralized direction or control. Brokers, venture capitalists, and general contractors all play key roles—initiating projects, allocating resources, and coordinating work—but there need not be any single point of oversight. Instead, the overall results *emerge* from the individual actions and interactions of all the different players in the system.

Of course, this kind of coordination occurs all the time in a free market, where products ranging from cars to copying machines to soft drinks all get produced and consumed without any centralized authority deciding how many or what kinds of these products to make. More than two hundred years ago, Adam Smith called this kind of decentralized coordination the invisible hand of the market, and we usually take for granted that it is the most effective way for companies to interact with one another.

But what if this kind of decentralized coordination were used to organize all the different kinds of activities that today go on *inside* companies? One of the things that allow a free market to work is the establishment and acceptance of a set of standards—the "rules of the game"—that governs all the transactions. The rules of the game can take many forms, including contracts, systems of ownership, and procedures for dispute resolution. Similarly, for an e-lance economy to work, whole new classes of agreements, specifications, and common architectures will need to evolve.

We see this already in the Internet, which works because everyone involved with it conforms to certain technical specifications. You don't have to ask anyone for permission to become a network provider or a service provider or a user; you just have to obey the communication protocols that govern the Internet. Standards are the glue that holds the Internet together, and they will be the glue that binds temporary companies together and helps them operate efficiently.

To return to our auto industry scenario, car designers would be able to work independently because they would have on-line access to highly detailed engineering protocols. These standards would ensure that individual component designs are compatible with the overall design of the vehicle. Headlight designers, for example, would know the exact space allocated for the light assembly as well as the nature of any connections that need to be made with the electrical and control systems.

Standards don't have to take the form of technical specifications. They may take the form of routinized processes, such as we see today in the medical community. When doctors, nurses, and technicians gather to perform emergency surgery, they usually all know what process to follow, what role each will play, and how they'll interact with one another. Even if they've never worked together before, they can collaborate effectively without delay. In other cases, the standards may simply be patterns of behavior that come to be accepted as norms—what might today be referred to as the culture of a company or "the way things are done" in an industry.

One of the primary roles for the large companies that remain in the future may be to establish rules, standards, and cultures for network organizations operating partly within and partly outside their own boundaries. Some global consulting firms already operate in more or less this way. For example, McKinsey & Company has established a strong organizational culture with well-understood norms for how people are selected and promoted and how they are expected to work with others in the company. But the top managers do not tell individual partners what kind of work to do, which clients to work for, or which people to select for their consulting teams. Instead, the partners make largely autonomous decisions about what they will do and how they will do it. In other words, the value the firm provides to its members comes mainly from the standards—the rules of the game—it has established, not from the strategic or operational skills of its top managers.

As more large companies establish decentralized, market-based organizational structures, the boundaries between companies will become much less important. Transactions within organizations will become indistinguishable from transactions between organizations, and business processes, once proprietary, will freely cross organizational boundaries. The key role for many individuals—whether they call themselves managers or not—will be to play their parts in shaping a network that neither they nor anyone else controls.

Thinking about the Future

Most of what you've just read is, of course, speculative. Some of it may happen; some of it may not. Big companies may split apart, or they may stay together but adopt much more decentralized structures. The future of business may turn out to be far less revolutionary than we've sketched out, or it may turn out to be far more revolutionary. We're convinced, though, of one thing—an e-lance economy, though a radical concept, is by no means an impossible or even an implausible concept. Most of the necessary building blocks—high-bandwidth networks, data interchange standards, groupware, electronic currency, venture capital micromarkets—either are in place or are under development.

What is lagging behind technology is our imagination. Most people are not able to conceive of a completely new economy where much of what they know about doing business no longer applies. Mitch Resnick, a colleague of ours at MIT, says that most people are locked into a "centralized mind-set." When we look up into the sky and see a flock of birds flying in formation, we tend to assume that the bird in front is the leader and that the leader is somehow determining the organization of all the other birds. In fact, biologists tell us, each bird is following a simple set of rules—behavioral standards—that result in the emergence of the organization. The bird in the front is no more important than the bird in the back or the bird in the middle. They're all equally essential to the pattern that they're forming.

The reason it's so important for us to recognize and to challenge the biases of our existing mind-set is that the rise of an e-lance economy would have profound implications for business and society, and we should begin considering those implications sooner rather than later. An e-lance economy might well lead to a flowering of individual wealth, freedom, and creativity. Business might become much more flexible and efficient, and people might find themselves with much more time for leisure, for education, and for other pursuits. A Golden Age might dawn.

On the other hand, an e-lance economy might lead to disruption and dislocation. Loosed from its traditional moorings, the business world might become chaotic and cutthroat. The gap between society's haves and have-nots might widen, as those lacking special talents or access to electronic networks fall by the wayside. The safety net currently formed by corporate benefit programs, such as health and disability insurance, might unravel.[3] E-lance workers, separated from the communities that companies create today, may find themselves lonely and alienated. All of these potential problems could likely be avoided, but we won't be able to avoid them if we remain blind to them.

Twenty-four years from now, in the year 2022, the *Harvard Business Review* will be celebrating its one hundredth year of publication. As part of its centennial celebration, it may well publish a series of articles that look back on recent business history and contemplate the massive changes that have taken place. The authors may write about the industrial organization of the twentieth century as merely a transitional structure that flourished for a relatively brief time. They may comment on the speed with which giant companies fragmented into the myriad microbusinesses that now dominate the economy. And they may wonder why, at the turn of the century, so few saw it coming.

NOTES

1. For more about the influence of information technology on business organizations, see Thomas W. Malone, "Is 'Empowerment' Just a Fad? Control, Decision-Making, and Information Technology," *Sloan Management Review,* Winter 1997, p. 23; Thomas W. Malone, JoAnne Yates, and Robert I. Benjamin, "Electronic Markets and Electronic

Hierarchies," *Communications of the ACM,* June 1987, p. 484; and Thomas W. Malone and John F. Rockart, "Computers, Networks, and the Corporation," *Scientific American,* September 1991, p. 128.

2. See Robert J. Laubacher, Thomas W. Malone, and the MIT Scenario Working Group, "Two Scenarios for 21st Century Organizations: Shifting Networks of Small Firms or All-Encompassing 'Virtual Countries'?" MIT Initiative on Inventing the Organizations of the 21st Century Working Paper No. 001 (Cambridge, Mass.: January 1997) available on the World Wide Web at http://ccs.mit.edu/21c/21CWP001.html.

3. Workers' guilds, common in the Middle Ages, may again rise to prominence, taking over many of the welfare functions currently provided by big companies. See Robert J. Laubacher and Thomas W. Malone, "Flexible Work Arrangements and 21st Century Workers' Guilds," MIT Initiative on Inventing the Organizations of the 21st Century Working Paper No. 004 (Cambridge, Mass.: October 1997) available on the World Wide Web at http://ccs.mit.edu/21c/21CWP004.html.

Electronic Cash and the End of National Markets

Stephen J. Kobrin

Twenty-six years ago, Raymond Vernon's *Sovereignty at Bay* proclaimed that "concepts such as national sovereignty and national economic strength appear curiously drained of meaning." Other books followed, arguing that sovereignty, the nation-state, and the national economy were finished—victims of multinational enterprises and the internationalization of production. While sovereign states and national markets have outlasted the chorus of Cassandras, this time the sky really may be falling. The emergence of electronic cash and a digitally networked global economy pose direct threats to the very basis of the territorial state.

Let us begin with two vignettes. Fact: Smugglers fly Boeing 747s loaded with illicit drugs into Mexico and then cram the jumbo jets full of cash—American bills —for the return trip. Fiction: Uncle Enzo, Mafia CEO, pays for intelligence in the digital future of Neal Stephenson's novel *Snow Crash*: "He reaches into his pocket and pulls out a hypercard and hands it toward Hiro. It says 'Twenty-Five Million Hong Kong Dollars.' Hiro reaches out and takes the card. Somewhere on earth, two computers swap bursts of electronic noise and the money gets transferred from the Mafia's account to Hiro's."

The 747s leaving Mexico are anachronisms, among the last surviving examples of the physical transfer of large amounts of currency across national borders. Most money has been electronic for some time: Virtually all of the trillions of dollars, marks, and yen that make their way around the world each day take the form

Reprinted with permission from *Foreign Policy* 107 (Summer 1997). © 1997 by the Carnegie Endowment for International Peace.

of bytes—chains of zeros and ones. Only at the very end of its journey is money transformed into something tangible: credit cards, checks, cash, or coins.

Hypercards are here. Mondex, a smart card or electronic purse, can be "loaded" with electronic money from an automatic teller machine (ATM) or by telephone or personal computer using a card-reading device. Money is spent either by swiping the card through a retailer's terminal or over the Internet by using the card reader and a personal computer. An electronic wallet allows anonymous card-to-card transfers.

It is not just the current technology of electronic cash (e-cash) or even what might be technologically feasible in the future that presents policymakers with new challenges. Rather, policymakers must confront directly the implications of this technology—and, more generally, the emergence of an electronically networked global economy—for economic and political governance. As the U.S. comptroller of the currency, Eugene Ludwig, has noted, "There is clearly a freight train coming down the tracks. . . . Just because it hasn't arrived yet doesn't mean we shouldn't start getting ready."

Electronic Money

Many different forms of "electronic money" are under development, but it is useful to look at three general categories: electronic debit and credit systems; various forms of smart cards; and true digital money, which has many of the properties of cash.

Electronic debit and credit systems already exist. When a consumer uses an ATM card to pay for merchandise, funds are transferred from his or her account to the merchant's. Credit cards are used to make payments over the Internet. Computer software such as Intuit provides electronic bill payment, and it is but a short step to true electronic checks—authenticated by a digital signature—that can be transmitted to the payee, endorsed, and deposited over the Internet. Electronic debit and credit systems represent new, more convenient means of payment, but not new payment systems. A traditional bank or credit card transaction lies at the end of every transaction chain.

Smart cards and digital money represent new payment systems with potentially revolutionary implications. Smart cards are plastic "credit" cards with an embedded microchip. Many are now used as telephone or transit payment devices. They can be loaded with currency from an ATM or via a card reader from a telephone or personal computer, currency which can then be spent at businesses, vending machines, or turnstiles that have been equipped with appropriate devices. At this most basic level, a smart card is simply a debit card that does not require bank approval for each transaction; clearance takes place each day and the value resides in third-party accounts. There is no reason, however, that smart cards have to be limited in this way.

Banks or other institutions could provide value on smart cards through loans, payments for services, or products. The immediate transfer of funds between bank accounts is not necessary; units of value can circulate from card to card—and from user to user—without debiting or crediting third-party accounts. Assuming confidence in the creating institution, "money" could be created on smart cards and could circulate almost indefinitely before redemption.

Finally, electronic money can take true digital form, existing as units of value in the form of bytes stored in the memory of personal computers that may or may not be backed up by reserve accounts of real money. The money could be downloaded from an account, supplied as a loan or as payment, or bought with a credit card over the Internet. As long as digital cash can be authenticated *and* there is confidence in its continued acceptance, it could circulate indefinitely, allowing peer-to-peer payments at will. These are big "ifs," but they are well within the realm of the possible.

Imagine a world where true e-cash is an everyday reality. Whether all of the following assumptions are correct or even immediately feasible is unimportant; some form of e-cash is coming, and we need to begin the process of thinking about its as-yet-unexplored consequences for economic and political governance.

The year is 2005. You have a number of brands of e-cash on your computer's hard drive: some withdrawn from a bank in Antigua, some borrowed from Microsoft, and some earned as payment for your services. You use the digital value units (DVUs) to purchase information from a Web site, pay bills, or send money to your daughter in graduate school. Peer-to-peer payments are easy: You can transfer DVUs to any computer, anyplace in the world, with a few keystrokes.

Your e-cash is secure and can be authenticated easily. It is also anonymous; governments have not been able to mandate a technology that leaves a clear audit trail. Public-key encryption technology and digital signatures allow blind transactions; the receiving computer knows that the DVUs are authentic without knowing the identity of the payer. Your e-cash can be exchanged any number of times without leaving a trace of where it has been. It is virtually impossible to alter the value of your e-cash at either end of the transaction (by adding a few more zeros to it, for example).

DVUs are almost infinitely divisible. Given the virtually negligible transaction cost, it is efficient for you to pay a dollar or two to see a financial report over the Internet or for your teenager to rent a popular song for the few minutes during which it is in vogue. Microtransactions have become the norm.

E-cash is issued—actually created—by a large number of institutions, bank and nonbank. Electronic currencies (e-currencies) have begun to exist on their own; many are no longer backed by hard currency and have developed value separately from currencies issued by central banks. DVUs circulate for long periods of time without being redeemed or deposited. Consumer confidence in the issuer is crucial; as with electronic commerce (e-commerce) in general, brand names have become critical.

The early 21st century is described as a world of competing e-currencies, a throwback to the 19th-century world of private currencies. The better known brands of e-cash are highly liquid and universally accepted. It is a relatively simple matter for you to set up filters in your electronic purse to screen out e-currencies that you do not want to accept.

Governance in the Digital World

E-cash and the increasing importance of digital markets pose problems for central government control over the economy and the behavior of economic actors; they also render borders around national markets and nation-states increasingly permeable—or, perhaps, increasingly irrelevant. In a world where true e-cash is an everyday reality, the basic role of government in a liberal market economy and the relevance of borders and geography will be drastically redefined.

While at first glance this concern appears to reflect a traditional break between domestic and international economic issues, in fact the advent of e-cash raises serious questions about the very idea of "domestic" and "international" as meaningful and distinct concepts. The new digital world presents a number of governance issues, described below.

• *Can central banks control the rate of growth and the size of the money supply?* Private e-currencies will make it difficult for central bankers to control—or even measure or define—monetary aggregates. Several forms of money, issued by banks and nonbanks, will circulate. Many of these monies may be beyond the regulatory reach of the state. At the extreme, if, as some libertarians imagine, private currencies dominate, currencies issued by central banks may no longer matter.

• *Will there still be official foreign exchange transactions?* E-cash will markedly lower existing barriers to the transfer of funds across borders. Transactions that have been restricted to money-center banks will be available to anyone with a computer. Peer-to-peer transfers of DVUs across national borders do not amount to "official" foreign exchange transactions. If you have $200 worth of DVUs on your computer and buy a program from a German vendor, you will probably have to agree on a mark to dollar price. However, transferring the DVUs to Germany is not an "official" foreign exchange transaction; the DVUs are simply revalued as marks. In fact, national currencies may lose meaning with the development of DVUs that have a universally accepted denomination. Without severe restrictions on individual privacy—which are not out of the question—governments will be hard-pressed to track, account for, and control the flows of money across borders.

• *Who will regulate or control financial institutions?* The U.S. Treasury is not sure whether existing regulations, which apply to both banks and institutions that act like banks (i.e., take deposits), would apply to all who issue (and create) e-cash. If nonfinancial institutions do not accept the extensive regulatory controls that banks take as the norm, can reserve or reporting requirements be enforced? What about consumer protection in the event of the insolvency of an issuer of e-cash, a system breakdown, or the loss of a smart card?

• *Will national income data still be meaningful?* It will be almost impossible to track transactions when e-cash becomes a widely used means of payment, on-line deals across borders become much easier, and many of the intermediaries that now serve as checkpoints for recording transactions are eliminated by direct, peer-to-peer payments. The widespread use of e-cash will render national economic data much less meaningful. Indeed, the advent of both e-cash and e-commerce raises fundamental questions about the national market as the basic unit of account in the international economic system.

• *How will taxes be collected?* Tax evasion will be a serious problem in an economy where e-cash transactions are the norm. It will be easy to transfer large sums of money across borders, and tax havens will be much easier to reach. Encrypted anonymous transactions will make audits increasingly problematic. Additionally, tax reporting and compliance relies on institutions and intermediaries. With e-cash and direct payments, all sorts of sales taxes, value-added taxes, and income taxes will be increasingly difficult to collect. More fundamentally, the question of jurisdiction—who gets to tax what—will become increasingly problematic. Say you are in Philadelphia and you decide to download music from a computer located outside Dublin that is run by a firm in Frankfurt. You pay with e-cash deposited in a Cayman Islands account. In which jurisdiction does the transaction take place?

• *Will e-cash and e-commerce widen the gap between the haves and the have-nots?* Participation in the global electronic economy requires infrastructure and access to a computer. Will e-cash and e-commerce further marginalize poorer population groups and even entire poor countries? This widened gap between the haves and the have-nots—those with and without access to computers—could become increasingly difficult to bridge.

• *Will the loss of seigniorage be important as governments fight to balance budgets?* Seigniorage originally referred to the revenue or profit generated due to the difference between the cost of making a coin and its face value; it also refers to the reduction in government interest payments when money circulates. The U.S. Treasury estimates that traditional seigniorage amounted to $773 million in 1994 and that the reduction in interest payments due to holdings of currency rather than debt could be as much as $3.5 billion per year. The Bank for International Settlements reports that the loss of seigniorage for its 11 member states will be more than $17 billion if smart cards eliminate all bank notes under $25.

• *Will fraud and criminal activity increase in an e-cash economy?* At the extreme—and the issue of privacy versus the needs of law enforcement is unresolved—transfers of large sums of cash across borders would be untraceable: There would be no audit trail. Digital counterfeiters could work from anywhere in the world and spend currency in any and all places. New financial crimes and forms of fraud could arise that would be hard to detect, and it would be extremely difficult to locate the perpetrators. The task of financing illegal and criminal activity would be easier by orders of magnitude. E-cash will lower the barriers to entry and reduce the risks of criminal activity.

Most of the issues raised in the recent National Research Council report on cryptography's role in the information society apply directly to electronic cash. Secure, easily authenticated, and anonymous e-cash requires strong encryption technology. Anonymous transactions, however, cannot be restricted to law-abiding citizens. Encryption makes it as difficult for enforcement authorities to track criminal activity as it does for criminals to penetrate legitimate transmissions. Should privacy be complete? Or should law enforcement authorities and national security agencies be provided access to e-cash transactions through escrowed encryption, for example? What about U.S. restrictions on the export of strong encryption technology? E-cash is global cash; how can governments limit its geographic spread? Can they even suggest that strong encryption algorithms be restricted territorially?

Geographic Space vs. Cyberspace

A recent U.S. Treasury paper dealing with the tax implications of electronic commerce argues that new communications technologies have "effectively eliminated national borders on the information highway." It is clear from the paper's subsequent discussion, however, that the more fundamental problem is that electronic commerce may "dissolve the link between an income-producing activity and a specific location."

The source of taxable income, which plays a major role in determining liability, is defined geographically in terms of where the economic activity that produces the income is located. Therein lies the rub: "Electronic commerce doesn't seem to occur in any physical location but instead takes place in the nebulous world of 'cyberspace.'" In a digital economy it will be difficult, or even impossible, to link income streams with specific geographic locations.

Digitalization is cutting money and finance loose from its geographic moorings. The framework of regulation that governs financial institutions assumes that customers and institutions are linked by geography—that spatial proximity matters. E-cash and e-commerce snap that link. What remains are systems of economic and political governance that are rooted in geography and are trying nonetheless to deal with e-cash and markets that exist in cyberspace. The obvious disconnect here will only worsen over time.

The geographical rooting of political and economic authority is relatively recent. Territorial sovereignty, borders, and a clear distinction between domestic and international spheres are modern concepts associated with the rise of the nation-state. Territorial sovereignty implies a world divided into clearly demarcated and mutually exclusive geographic jurisdictions. It implies a world where economic and political control arise from control over territory.

The international financial system—which consists of hundreds of thousands of computer screens around the globe—is the first international electronic marketplace. It will not be the last. E-cash is one manifestation of a global economy that is constructed in cyberspace rather than geographic space. The fundamental problems that e-cash poses for governance result from this disconnect between electronic markets and political geography.

The very idea of controlling the money supply, for example, assumes that geography provides a relevant means of defining the scope of the market. It assumes that economic borders are effective, that the flow of money across them can be monitored and controlled, and that the volume of money within a fixed geographic area is important. All of those assumptions are increasingly questionable in a digital world economy.

Many of our basic tax principles assume that transactions and income streams can be located precisely within a given national market. That assumption is problematic when e-cash is spent on a computer network. It is problematic when many important economic transactions cannot be located, or may not even take place, in geographic space.

The increasing irrelevance of geographic jurisdiction in a digital world economy markedly increases the risks of fraud, money-laundering, and other financial crimes. Asking where the fraud or money-laundering took place means asking Whose jurisdiction applies? and Whose law applies? We need to learn to deal with crimes that cannot be located in geographic space, where existing concepts of national jurisdiction are increasingly irrelevant.

The term "disintermediation" was first used to describe the replacement of banks as financial intermediaries by direct lending in money markets when interest rates rose. It is often used in the world of e-commerce to describe the elimination of intermediaries by direct seller-to-buyer transactions over the Internet. Many observers argue that e-cash is likely to disintermediate banks. Of more fundamental importance is the possibility that e-cash and e-commerce will disintermediate the territorial state.

To be clear, I argue that we face not the end of the state, but rather the diminished efficacy of political and economic governance that is rooted in geographic sovereignty and in mutually exclusive territorial jurisdiction. Questions such as, Where did the transaction take place? Where did the income stream arise? Where is the financial institution located? and Whose law applies? will lose meaning.

E-cash and e-commerce are symptoms, albeit important ones, of an increasing asymmetry between economics and politics, between an electronically integrated world economy and territorial nation-states, and between cyberspace and geographic space. How this asymmetry will be resolved and how economic and political relations will be reconstructed are two of the critical questions of our time.

What Is to Be Done?

The question asked here is not What is feasible? but What are the limits of the possible? Whether the picture presented here is correct in all—or even some—of its details is unimportant. A digital world economy is emerging. Imagining possible scenarios is necessary if we are to come to grips with the consequences of this revolution.

The purpose here is to raise problems rather than to solve them and to imagine possible futures and think about their implications for economic and political governance. A digital world economy will demand increasing international cooperation, harmonizing national regulations and legislation, and strengthening the authority of international institutions.

The harmonization of national regulations will help to prevent institutions, such as those issuing e-cash, from slipping between national jurisdictions or shop-

Electronic Cash: A Glossary

Digital data: Information coded into a series of zeros and ones that can be transmitted and processed electronically.

Digital signature: A code that allows absolute authentication of the origin and integrity of a document, check, or electronic cash that has been sent over a computer network. A blind signature allows authentication without revealing the identity of the sender.

Disintermediation: The substitution of direct transactions for those that are mediated. The term originated when rising interest rates caused savings to be withdrawn from banks—whose interest rates were capped—and invested in money market instruments that were the direct debts of borrowers. Banks were disintermediated. In electronic commerce, the term refers to the rise of direct buyer-to-seller relationships over the Internet, disintermediating wholesalers and retail outlets.

Electronic money: Units or tokens of monetary value that take digital form and are transmitted over electronic networks. Digital Value Units are the basic units of denomination of electronic money; they may or may not correspond to units of national currency.

Encryption: The coding of information for security purposes, such as credit card numbers or electronic cash used over the Internet. Public-key encryption uses a mathematical algorithm comprising a pair of strings of numbers to encrypt and decrypt the data. For example, the sender would encrypt the data with the receiver's public key and the receiver would decrypt with his or her private key.

Internet: A global network of linked networks that allows communication and the sharing of information among many different types of computers. The World Wide Web is a graphical system on the Internet that allows rapid movement between documents and computers through the use of embedded (hypertext) links.

Smart card: A plastic card, similar to a credit card, containing a microchip that can be used to retrieve, store, process, and transmit digital data like electronic cash or medical information.

ping for the nation with the least onerous regulations. However, it will not address the basic problem of the disconnect between geographic jurisdiction and an electronically integrated global economy.

If it is impossible to locate transactions geographically—if the flows of e-cash are outside of the jurisdictional reach of every country—then the harmonization of national regulations will accomplish little. The basic problem is not one of overlapping or conflicting jurisdictions; it stems from the lack of meaning of the very concept of "jurisdiction" in a digitalized global economy.

The erosion of the viability of territorial jurisdiction calls for strengthened international institutions. It calls for giving international institutions real authority to measure, to control, and, perhaps, to tax. The Basle Committee on Banking Supervision—an international body of bank regulators who set global standards—could perhaps be given the authority to collect information from financial institutions wherever they are located and formulate and enforce regulations globally. Interpol, or its equivalent, may have to be given jurisdiction over financial crimes, regardless of where they are committed. That does not mean a world government; it does mean a markedly increased level of international cooperation.

The questions we must face are whether territorial sovereignty will continue to be viable as the *primary* basis for economic and political governance as we enter the 21st century and what the implications will be for the American economy—and Americans in general—if we refuse to cooperate internationally in the face of an increasingly integrated global economy.

Local Memoirs of a Global Manager

Gurcharan Das

There was a time when I used to believe with Diogenes the Cynic that "I am a citizen of the world," and I used to strut about feeling that a "blade of grass is always a blade of grass, whether in one country or another." Now I feel that each blade of grass has its spot on earth from where it draws its life, its strength; and so is man rooted to the land from where he draws his faith, together with his life.

In India, I was privileged to help build one of the largest businesses in the world for Vicks Vaporub, a hundred-year-old brand sold in 147 countries and now owned by Procter & Gamble. In the process, I learned a number of difficult and valuable lessons about business and about myself. The most important lesson was this: to learn to tap into the roots of diversity in a world where global standardization plays an increasingly useful role.

"Think global and act local," goes the saying, but that's only half a truth. International managers must also think local and then apply their local insights on a global scale.

The fact is that truths in this world are unique, individual, and highly parochial. They say all politics is local. So is all business. But this doesn't keep either from being global. In committing to our work we commit to a here and now, to a particular place and time; but what we learn from acting locally is often universal in nature.

This is how globalization takes place. Globalization does not mean imposing homogeneous solutions in a pluralistic world. It means having a global vision and strategy, but it also means cultivating roots and individual identities. It means nourishing local insights, but it also means reemploying communicable ideas in new geographies around the world.

The more human beings belong to their own time and place, the more they belong to *all* times and places. Today's best global managers know this truth. They nourish each "blade of grass."

Managerial basics are the same everywhere, in the West and in the Third World. There is a popular misconception among managers that you need merely to push a powerful brand name with a standard product, package, and advertising in order to conquer global markets, but actually the key to success is a tremendous amount of local passion for the brand and a feeling of local pride and ownership.

I learned these lessons as a manager of international brands in the Third World and as a native of India struggling against the temptation to stay behind in the West.

On Going Home

I was four years old when India became free. Before they left, the British divided us into two countries, India and Pakistan, and on a monsoon day in August 1947 I suddenly became a refugee. I had to flee east for my life because I was a Hindu in predominantly Muslim West Punjab. I survived, but a million others did not, and another 12 million were rendered homeless in one of the great tragedies of our times.

I grew up in a middle-class home in East Punjab as the eldest son of a civil engineer who built canals and dams for the government. Our family budget was always tight: after paying for milk and school fees, there was little left to run the house. My mother told us heroic stories from the *Mahabharata* and encouraged in us the virtues of honesty, thrift, and responsibility to country.

I grew up in the innocence of the Nehru age when we still had strong ideals. We believed in secularism, democracy, socialism, and the U.N.; and we were filled with the excitement of building a nation.

I came to the United States at the age of 12, when the Indian government sent my father to Washington, D.C. on temporary assignment. When my family returned to India a few years later, I won a scholarship to Harvard College and spent four happy years on the banks of the Charles River. My tutor taught me that the sons of Harvard had an obligation to serve, and I knew that I must one day use my education to serve India.

In 1964, in the towering confidence of my 21 years, I returned home. Some of my friends thought I had made a mistake. They said I should have gone on to graduate school and worked for a few years in the West. In fact, I missed the West in the beginning and told myself that I would go back before long; but I soon became absorbed in my new job with Richardson-Vicks in Bombay, and like the man who came to dinner, I stayed on.

From a trainee, I rose to become CEO of the company's Indian subsidiary, with interim assignments at Vicks headquarters in New York and in the Mexican subsidiary. When I became CEO, the Indian company was almost bankrupt, but with the help of a marvelous all-Indian organization, I turned it around in the early 1980s and made it one of the most profitable companies on the Bombay Stock Exchange. In 1985 we were acquired by Procter & Gamble, and so began another exciting chapter in my life. We successfully incorporated the company into P&G without losing a single employee, and we put ourselves on an aggressive growth path, with an entry first into sanitary napkins and then into one of the largest detergent markets in the world.

At three stages in my life, I was tempted to settle in the West. Each time I could have chosen to lead the cosmopolitan life of an expatriate. Each time I chose to return home. The first after college; the second when I was based in the New York office of Vicks, where I met my Nepali wife with her coveted Green Card (which we allowed to lapse); the third when I was in Mexico running our nutritional foods business, when once again I came home to earn a fraction of what I would have earned abroad.

Apart from a lurking wish to appear considerable in the eyes of those I grew up with, I ask myself why I keep returning to India. I have thrice opted for what appeared to be the less rational course in terms of career and money. The only remotely satisfying answer I have found comes from an enigmatic uncle of mine who once said, "You've come back, dear boy, because as a child you listened to the music of your mother's voice. They all say, 'I'll be back in a few years,' but the few years become many, until it is too late and you are lost in a lonely and homeless crowd."

Yet I think of myself as a global manager within the P&G world. I believe my curious life script has helped to create a mind-set that combines the particular with the universal, a mind-set rooted in the local and yet open and nonparochial, a mind-set I find useful in the global management of P&G brands.

On One-Pointed Success

I first arrived on the island of Bombay on a monsoon day after eight years of high school and college in America. That night, 15-foot waves shattered thunderously against the rocks below my window as the rain advanced from the Arabian sea like the disciplined forward phalanx of an army.

The next morning I reported for duty at Richardson-Vicks' Indian headquarters, which turned out to be a rented hole-in-the-wall with a dozen employees. This was a change after the company's swank New York offices in midtown Manhattan, where I had been interviewed. That evening my cousin invited me for dinner. He worked in a big British company with many factories, thousands of employees, and plush multistoried marble offices. I felt ashamed to talk about my job.

"How many factories do you have?" he wanted to know.

"None," I said.

"How many salesmen do you have?" he asked.

"None," I said.

"How many employees?"

"Twelve."

"How big are your offices?"

"A little smaller than your house."

Years later I realized that what embarrassed me that night turned out to be our strength. All twelve of our employees were focused on building our brands without the distraction of factories, sales forces, industrial relations, finance and other staff departments. Our products were made under contract by Boots, an English drug company; they were distributed under contract by an outside distribution house with 100 salesmen spread around the country; our external auditors had arranged for someone to do our accounting; and our lawyers took care of our government work. We were lean, nimble, focused, and very profitable.

All my cousin's talk that night revolved around office politics, and all his advice was about how to get around the office bureaucracy. It was not clear to me how his company made decisions. But he was a smart man, and I sensed that with all his pride in working for a giant organization, he had little respect for its bureaucratic style.

If marketing a consumer product is what gives a company its competitive advantage, then it seems to me it should spend all its time building marketing and product muscle and employ outside suppliers to do everything else. It should spin off as many services as someone else is willing to take on and leave everyone inside the company focused on one thing—creating, retaining, and satisfying consumers.

There is a concept in Yoga called one-pointedness (from the Sanskrit *Ekagrata*). All twelve of us were one-pointedly focused on making Vicks a household name in India, as if we were 12 brand managers. I now teach our younger managers the value of a one-pointed focus on consumer satisfaction, which P&G measures every six months for all of its major brands.

Concentrating on one's core competence thus was one of the first lessons I learned. I learned it because I was face-to-face with the consumer, focused on the particular. Somehow I feel it would have taken me longer to learn this lesson in a glass tower in Manhattan.

As so often in life, however, by the time I could apply the lesson I had learned, we had a thousand people, with factories, sales forces, and many departments that were having a lot of fun fighting over turf. I believe that tomorrow's big companies may well consist of hundreds of small decentralized units, each with a sharp focus on its particular customers and markets.

On the Kettle That Wrote My Paycheck

For months I believed that my salary came from the payroll clerk, so I was especially nice to her. (She was also the boss's secretary.) Then one day I discovered the most important truth of my career—I realized who really paid my salary.

Soon after I joined the company, my boss handed me a bag and a train ticket and sent me "up-country." A man of the old school, he believed that you learned marketing only in the bazaar, so I spent 10 of my first 15 months on the road and saw lots of up-country bazaars.

On the road, I typically would meet our trade customers in the mornings and consumers in the evenings. In the afternoons everyone slept. One evening I knocked on the door of a middle-class home in Surat, a busy trading town 200 miles north of Bombay. The lady of the house reluctantly let me in. I asked her, "What do you use for your family's coughs and colds?" Her eyes lit up, her face became animated. She told me that she had discovered the most wonderful solution. She went into the kitchen and brought back a jar of Vicks Vaporub and a kettle. She then showed me how she poured a spoon of Vaporub into the boiling kettle and inhaled the medicated vapors from the spout.

"If you don't believe me, try it for yourself," she said. "Here, let me boil some water for you."

Before I could reply she had disappeared into the kitchen. Instead of drinking tea that evening we inhaled Vicks Vaporub. As I walked back to my hotel, I felt intoxicated: I had discovered it was she who paid my salary. My job also became clear to me: I must reciprocate her compliment by striving relentlessly to satisfy her needs.

The irony is that all the money a company makes is made *outside* the company (at the point of sale), yet the employees spend their time *inside* the company, usually arguing over turf. Unfortunately, we don't see customers around us when we show up for work in the mornings.

When I became the CEO of the company I made a rule that every employee in every department had to go out every year and meet 20 consumers and 20 retailers or wholesalers in order to qualify for their annual raise. This not only helps to remind us who pays our salaries, we also get a payoff in good ideas to improve our products and services.

The idea of being close to the customer may be obvious in the commercial societies of the West, but it was not so obvious 20 years ago in the protected, bureaucratic Indian environment. As to the lady in Surat, we quickly put her ideas into our advertising. She was the first consumer to show me a global insight in my own backyard.

Of Chairs, Armchairs, and Monsoons

Two years after I joined, I was promoted. I was given Vicks Vaporub to manage, which made me the first brand manager in the company. I noticed we were building volume strongly in the South but having trouble in the North. I asked myself whether I should try to fix the North or capitalize on the momentum in the South. I chose the latter, and it was the right choice. We later discovered that North Indians don't like to rub things on their bodies, yet the more important lesson was that it is usually better to build on your strength than to try and correct a weakness. Listen to and respect the market. Resist the temptation to impose your will on it.

We were doing well in the South partially because South Indians were accustomed to rubbing on balms for headaches, colds, bodyaches, insect bites, and a host of other minor maladies. We had a big and successful balm competitor, Amrutanjan, who offered relief for all these symptoms. My first impulse was to try to expand the use of Vaporub to other symptoms in order to compete in this larger balm market.

My boss quickly and wisely put a stop to that. In an uncharacteristically loud voice, he explained that Vaporub's unique function was to relieve colds.

"Each object has a function," he said. "A chair's function is to seat a person. A desk is to write on. You don't want to use a chair for writing and a desk for sitting. You never want to mix up functions."

A great part of Vaporub's success in India has been its clear and sharp position in the consumer's mind. It is cold relief in a jar, which a mother rubs tenderly on her child's cold at bedtime. As I thought more about balms, I realized that they were quite the opposite. Adults rub balms on themselves for headaches during the day. Vaporub was succeeding precisely because it was not a balm; it was a rub for colds.

Every brand manager since has had to learn that same lesson. It is of the utmost importance to know who you are and not be led astray by others. Tap into your roots when you are unsure. You cannot be all things to all people.

This did not prevent us from building a successful business with adults, but as my boss used to say, "Adult colds, that is an armchair. But it is still a chair and not a desk."

When I took over the brand we were spending most of our advertising rupees in the winter, a strategy that worked in North America and other countries. However, my monthly volume data stubbornly suggested that we were shipping a lot of Vaporub between July and September, the hot monsoon season. "People must be catching lots of colds in the monsoon," I told my boss, and I got his agreement to bring forward a good chunk of our media to the warm monsoon months. Sure enough, we were rewarded with an immediate gain in sales.

I followed this up by getting our agency to make a cinema commercial (we had no television at that time) showing a child playing in the rain and catching cold. We coined a new ailment, "wet monsoon colds," and soon the summer monsoon season became as important as the winter in terms of sales.

Another factor in our success was the introduction of a small 5-gram tin, which still costs 10 cents and accounts for 40% of our volume. At first it was not successful, so we had to price it so that it was cheaper to buy four 5-gram tins than a 19-gram jar. The trade thought we were crazy. They said henceforth no one would buy the profitable jar; they would trade down to the tin. But that didn't happen. Why? Because we had positioned the tin for the working class. We were right in believing that middle class consumers would stay loyal to the middle-class size.

Moves like these made us hugely successful and placed us first in the Indian market share by far. But instead of celebrating, my boss seemed depressed. He called me into his office, and he asked me how much the market was growing.

"Seven percent," I said.

"Is that good?"

"No," I replied. "But *we* are growing twenty percent, and that's why we're now number one in India."

"I don't give a damn that we are number one in a small pond. That pond has to become a lake, and then an ocean. We have to grow the market. Only then will we become number one in the world."

Thus I acquired another important mind-set: when you are number one, you must not grow complacent. Your job is to grow the market. You always must benchmark yourself against the best in the world, not just against the local competition. In the Third World this is an especially valuable idea, because markets there are so much less competitive.

Being receptive to regional variations, tapping the opportunity that the monsoon offered, introducing a size for the rural and urban poor, and learning to resist complacency and grow the market—all are variations on the theme of local thinking, of tapping into the roots of pluralism and diversity.

On Not Reinventing the Wheel

We could not have succeeded in building the Vicks business in India without the support of the native traders who took our products deep into the hinterland, to every nook and corner of a very large country. Many times we faced the temptation to set up an alternative Western-style distribution network. Fortunately, we never gave in to it. Instead, we chose each time to continue relying on the native system.

Following the practice of British companies in India, we appointed the largest wholesaler in each major town to become our exclusive stock point and direct customer. We called this wholesaler our stockist. Once a month our salesman visited the stockist, and together they went from shop to shop redistributing our products to the retailers and wholesalers of the town. The largest stockist in each state also became our Carrying-and-Forwarding Agent (in other words, our depot) for re-shipping our goods to stockists in smaller towns. Over time, our stockists expanded their functions. They now work exclusively on P&G business under the supervision of our salesmen; they hire local salesmen who provide interim coverage of the market between the visits of our salesmen; they run vans to cover satellite villages and help us penetrate the interior; they conduct local promotions and advertising campaigns; and they are P&G's ambassadors and lifeline in the local community. The stockists perform all these services for a five percent commission, and our receivables are down to six days outstanding.

In our own backyard, we found and adopted an efficient low-cost distribution system perfected by Indian traders over hundreds of years. Thank God we chose to build on it rather than reinvent the wheel.

On Taking Ancient Medicine

We learned our most important lesson about diversity and tapping into roots shortly after I became head of the company in the early 1980s. We found ourselves against a wall. The chemists and pharmacists had united nationwide and decided to target our company and boycott our products in their fight for higher margins from the entire industry. At the same time, productivity at our plant was falling, while wages kept rising. As a result, our profitability had plummeted to two percent of sales.

Beset by a hostile environment, we turned inward. The answer to our problems came as a flash of insight about our roots, for we suddenly realized that Vicks Vaporub and other Vicks products were all-natural, herbal formulas. All their ingredients were found in thousand-year-old Sanskrit texts. What was more, this ancient *Ayurvedic* system of medicine enjoyed the special patronage of the government. If we could change our government registration from Western medicine to Indian medicine, we could expand our distribution to food shops, general stores, and street kiosks and thus reduce dependence on the pharmacists. By making our products more accessible, we would enhance consumer satisfaction and build competitive advantage. What was more, a new registration would also allow us to set up a new plant for Vicks in a tax-advantaged "backward area," where we could raise productivity dramatically by means of improved technology, better work practices, and lower labor costs.

I first tested the waters with our lawyers, who thought our solution to the problem quite wonderful. We then went to the government in Delhi, which was deeply impressed to discover all the elements of Vaporub's formula in the ancient texts. They advised us to check with the local FDA in Bombay. The regulators at the FDA couldn't find a single fault with our case and, to our surprise and delight, promptly gave us a new registration.

Lo and behold, all the obstacles were gone! Our sales force heroically and rapidly expanded the distribution of our products to the nondrug trade, tripling the outlets which carried Vicks to roughly 750,000 stores. Consumers were happy that they could buy our products at every street corner. At the same time we quickly built a new plant near Hyderabad, where productivity was four times what it was in our Bombay plant. Our after-tax profits rose from 2% to 12% of sales, and we became a blue chip on the Bombay Stock Exchange.

Finally, we decided to return the compliment to the Indian system of medicine. We persuaded our headquarters to let us establish an R&D Center to investigate additional all-natural, Ayurvedic therapies for coughs and colds. When I first mooted this idea, my bosses at the head office in the United States practically fell off their chairs. Slowly, however, the idea of all-natural, safe, and effective remedies for a self-limiting ailment sold around the world under the Vicks name grew on them.

We set up labs in Bombay under the leadership of a fine Indian scientist who had studied in the United States. They began by creating a computerized data bank of herbs and formulas from the ancient texts; they invented a "finger-printing" process to standardize herbal raw materials with the help of computers; and they organized clinical trials in Bombay hospitals to confirm the safety and efficacy of the new products. We now have two products being successfully sold in the Indian market—Vicks Vaposyrup, an all-natural cough liquid, and Vicks Hotsip, a hot drink for coughs and colds. The lab today is part of P&G's global health-care research effort and has 40 scientists and technicians working with state-of-the-art equipment.

Of Local Passions and Golden Ghettos

The story of Vicks in India brings up a mistaken notion about how multinationals build global brands. The popular conception is that you start with a powerful brand name, add standardized product, packaging and advertising, push a button, and bingo—you are on the way to capturing global markets. Marlboro, Coke, Sony Walkman, and Levis are cited as examples of this strategy.

But if it's all so easy, why have so many powerful brands floundered? Without going into the standardization vs. adaptation debate, the Vicks story demonstrates at least one key ingredient for global market success: *the importance of local passion.* If local managers believe a product is theirs, then local consumers will believe it too. Indeed, a survey of Indian consumers a few years ago showed that 70% believed Vicks was an Indian brand.

What is the universal idea behind Vicks Vaporub's success in India? What is it that made it sell? Was it "rubbing it on the child with tender, loving care?" Could that idea be revived in the United States? Some people argue that the United States has become such a rushed society that mothers no longer have time to use a bedtime rub on their children when they've got a cold. Others feel that Vaporub could make its marketing more meaningful by striking a more contemporary note.

The Vicks story shows that a focus on the particular brings business rewards. But there are also psychic rewards for the manager who invests in the local. Going back to my roots reinvigorated me as a person and brought a certain fullness to my life. Not only was it pleasant to see familiar brown faces on the street, it also was enormously satisfying to be a part of the intense social life of the neighborhood, to experience the joys and sorrows of politics, and to share in the common fate of the nation. But at another level I also began to think of my work as a part of nation building, especially training and developing the next generation of young managers who would run the company and the country. It discharged a debt to my tutor at Harvard and a responsibility that we all have to the future.

Equally, it seems to me, there are powerful though less obvious psychic rewards for an international manager on transfer overseas who chooses to get involved in the local community. When such people approach the new country with an open mind, learn the local language, and make friends with colleagues and neighbors, they gain access to the wealth of a new culture. Not only will they be more effective as managers, they also will live fuller, richer lives.

Unfortunately, my experience in Mexico indicates that many expatriate managers live in "golden ghettos" of ease with little genuine contact with locals other than servants. Is it any surprise that they become isolated and complain of rootlessness and alienation in their new environment? The lesson for global companies is to give each international manager a local "mentor" who will open doors to the community. Ultimately, however, it is the responsibility of individual managers to open their minds, plunge into their local communities, and try to make them their own.

On Global Thinking

It would be wrong to conclude from the Vicks story that managing a global brand is purely a local affair. On the contrary, the winners in the new borderless economy will be the brands and companies that make best use of the richness of experience they get from their geographical diversity. Multinational companies have a natural advantage over local companies because they have talented people solving similar problems for identical brands in different parts of the world, and these brand managers can learn from each other's successes and failures. If a good idea emerges in Egypt, a smart brand manager in Malaysia or Venezuela will at least give it a test.

The Surat lady's teakettle became the basis of a national campaign in India. "One-pointedness" emerged from a hole-in-the-wall in Bombay, but it became the fulcrum on which we built a world-class business over a generation. Advertising for colds during the hot monsoon months seems highly parochial, but it taught us the importance of advertising year round in other places. The stockist system found applicability in Indonesia and China. Even the strange Ayurvedic system of medicine might plausibly be reapplied in the form of efficacious herbal remedies for common ailments in Western countries.

Business truths are invariably local in origin, but they are often expressions of fundamental human needs that are the same worldwide. Local insights with a universal character thus can become quickly global—though only in the hands of flexible, open-minded managers who can translate such ideas into new circumstances with sensitivity and understanding. My admonition to think local is only half the answer. Managers also must remember to think global. The insights we glean from each microcosm are ultimately universal.

Organizational specialists often express a fear that companies will demotivate their local managers by asking them to execute standardized global marketing packages. If they impose these standardized marketing solutions too rigidly, then this fear may be justified. However, this does not happen in successful companies. In fact, the more common disease in a global company is the "not invented here" syndrome, which especially afflicts subsidiaries and managers whose local triumphs have left them arrogant and unwilling to learn from successes in other parts of the world.

We in India were no different. But slowly and painfully we learned that useful lessons can emerge anywhere. For all our efforts to tap into the roots of Indian pluralism, we were dealing with a global brand. The product itself, the positioning, and the packaging were basically the same everywhere. Global brands are not free-for-alls, with each subsidiary doing its own thing. It took us six months, for example, to persuade our marketing people to try a new advertising idea for Vaporub that came from Mexico. It asked the consumer to use Vaporub on three parts of the body to obtain three types of relief. When we finally tried "Three-by-Three" in our advertising, it worked brilliantly.

It is deeply wrong to believe that going global is a one-stop, packaged decision. Local managers can add enormous value as they tap into local roots for insights. But it is equally wrong to neglect the integrity of the brand's core elements. Smart global managers nourish each blade of grass without neglecting the garden as a whole.

On Karma

Although the principles of managing a business in the Third World are the same as in the West, there are still big differences between the two. For me, the greatest of these is the pervasive reality of poverty.

I have lost the towering confidence of my youth, when I believed that socialism could wipe away poverty. The problem of socialism is one of performance, not vision. If it worked, we would all be socialists. Ironically, the legacy of the collectivist bias in Indian thinking has been the perpetuation of poverty. We created an over-regulated private sector and an inefficient public sector. We did not allow the economy to grow and produce the surplus that might have paid for direct poverty programs. We created an exploitative bureaucracy that fed on itself. Today, happily, we are righting the balance by liberalizing the economy, reducing state control, and restoring legitimacy to the market. I am confident that these changes will foster the entrepreneurialism and economic vitality India needs to create prosperity and eliminate the destitution of so many of its people.

Despite the problems, I find managers in India and other poor countries more optimistic than their counterparts in rich nations. The reason is that we believe our children will be better off than our parents were, and this idea is a great source of strength. We see our managerial work as nation building. We are the benign harbingers of technology and modernity. As we learn to manage complex enterprises, we empower people with the confidence they need to become responsible, innovative, and self-reliant.

It seems to come down to commitment. In committing to our work we commit to a here and now, to a particular place and time. The meaning in our lives comes from nourishing a particular blade of grass. It comes from absorbing ourselves so deeply in the microcosm of our work that we forget ourselves, especially our egos. The difference between subject and object disappears. The Sanskrit phrase *nishkama karma* describes this state of utter absorption, in which people act for the sake of the action, not for the sake of the reward from the action. This is also the meaning of happiness.

Part

8

Forecasting the Future: Innovations, Technology, Winners, and Losers

Throughout history, changes in global relations have been driven by technological innovations that have altered the way in which economic interactions occur. The evolution of democracy and the changing nature of borders and security are altering political interactions. Technological innovation also affects the ecological and cultural environment in which we live. In sum, globalization as a process is driven by a series of interlocking innovations. Part 8 examines technological innovations that may dominate the next wave of globalization, and how countries are expected to cope with the consequences.

Paul Kennedy examines global trends in economics, the environment, politics, demographics, and technological innovations in order to forecast which states will succeed and which will lose out in the next century. Ultimately Kennedy concludes that the developed world is in the best position to succeed in the twenty-first century, and that this advantage has actually grown as a direct result of the consequences of technological innovations. Kennedy's analysis demonstrates that globalization benefits the already well-off, those actively involved in the new global system.

William E. Halal, Michael D. Kull, and Ann Leffmann attempt to forecast the dominant technologies for the first thirty years of the next century. While information technology is currently the leading sector, it will be followed by innovations in genetics, alternative energy sources, transportation, space exploration, and perhaps the very nature or function of the modern nation-state. Joseph F. Coates, John B. Mahaffie, and Andy Hines emphasize the promise of genetics. They suggest that biotechnology can offer large-scale benefits in areas such as economic growth, industry, global development, health care, species management, and even human destiny.

Preparing for the 21st Century

WINNERS AND LOSERS

Paul Kennedy

I.

Evcryone with an interest in international affairs must be aware that broad, global forces for change are bearing down upon humankind in both rich and poor societies alike. New technologies are challenging traditional assumptions about the way we make, trade, and even grow things. Automated workplaces in Japan intimate the end of the "factory system" that first arose in Britain's Industrial Revolution and spread around the world. Genetically engineered crops, cultivated in biotech laboratories, threaten to replace naturally grown sugar, vanilla, coconut oil, and other staple farm produce, and perhaps undermine field-based agriculture as we know it. An electronically driven, twenty-four-hour-a-day financial trading system has created a global market in, say, yen futures over which nobody really has control. The globalization of industry and services permits multinationals to switch production from one country to another (where it is usually cheaper), benefitting the latter and hurting the former.

In addition to facing these technology-driven forces for change, human society is grappling with the effects of fast-growing demographic imbalances throughout the world. Whereas birthrates in richer societies plunge well below the rates that would replace their populations, poorer countries are experiencing a popula-

This article appeared in *The New York Review of Books,* February 11, 1993, pp. 32–44. From *Preparing for the Twenty-First Century* by Paul Kennedy. © 1993 by Paul Kennedy. Reprinted by permission of Random House, Inc.

tion explosion that may double or even treble their numbers over the next few decades. As these fast-swelling populations press upon the surrounding forests, grazing lands, and water supplies, they inflict dreadful damage upon local environments and may also be contributing to that process of global warming first created by the industrialization of the North a century and a half ago. With overpopulation and resource depletion undermining the social order, and with a global telecommunications revolution bringing television programs like *Dallas* and *Brideshead Revisited* to viewers everywhere from Central America to the Balkans, a vast illegal migration is under way as millions of families from the developing world strive to enter Europe and North America.

Although very different in form, these various trends from global warming to twenty-four-hour-a-day trading are *transnational* in character, crossing borders all over our planet, affecting local communities and distant societies at the same time, and reminding us that the earth, for all its divisions, is a single unit. Every country is challenged by these global forces for change, to a greater or lesser extent, and most are beginning to sense the need to prepare themselves for the coming twenty-first century. Whether *any* society is at present "well prepared" for the future is an open question;[1] but what is clear is that the regions of the globe most affected by the twin impacts of technology and demography lie in the developing world. Whether they succeed in harnessing the new technologies in an environmentally prudent fashion, and at the same time go through a demographic transition, will probably affect the prospects of global peace in the next century more than any other factor. What, then, are their chances?

Before that question can be answered, the sharp contrasts among the developing countries in the world's different regions need to be noted here.[2] Perhaps nothing better illustrates those differences than the fact that, in the 1960s, South Korea had a per capita GNP exactly the same as Ghana's (US $230), whereas today it is ten to twelve times more prosperous.[3] Both possessed a predominantly agrarian economy and had endured a half-century or more of colonial rule. Upon independence, each faced innumerable handicaps in their effort to "catch up" with the West, and although Korea possessed a greater historical and cultural coherence, its chances may have seemed less promising, since it had few natural resources (apart from tungsten) and suffered heavily during the 1950–1953 fighting.

Decades later, however, West African states remain among the most poverty-stricken countries in the world—the per capita gross national products of Niger, Sierra Leone, and Chad today, for example, are less than $500[4]—while Korea is entering the ranks of the high-income economies. Already the world's thirteenth largest trading nation, Korea is planning to become one of the richest countries of all in the twenty-first century,[5] whereas the nations of West Africa face a future, at least in the near term, of chronic poverty, malnutrition, poor health, and underdevelopment. Finally, while Korea's rising prosperity is attended by a decrease in population growth, most African countries still face a demographic explosion that erodes any gains in national output.

This divergence is not new, for there have always been richer and poorer societies; the prosperity gap in the seventeenth century—between, say, Amsterdam and the west coast of Ireland, or between such bustling Indian ports as Surat and Calcutta[6] and the inhabitants of New Guinean hill villages—must have been marked, although it probably did not equal the gulf between rich and poor nations today. The difference is that the twentieth-century global communications revolution has made such disparities widely known. This can breed resentments by poorer peoples against prosperous societies, but it can also provide a desire to emulate (as Korea emulated Japan). The key issue here is: What does it take to turn a "have not" into a "have" nation? Does it simply require imitating economic techniques, or does it involve such intangibles as culture, social structure, and attitudes toward foreign practices?

This discrepancy in performance between East Asia and sub-Saharan Africa clearly makes the term "third world" misleading. However useful the expression might have been in the 1950s, when poor, nonaligned, and recently decolonized states were attempting to remain independent of the two superpower blocs,[7] the rise of super-rich oil-producing countries a decade later already made the term questionable. Now that prosperous East Asian societies—Korea, Taiwan, and Singapore—possess higher per capita GNPs than Russia, Eastern Europe, and even West European states like Portugal, the word seems less suitable than ever. With Taiwanese or Korean corporations establishing assembly plants in the Philippines, or creating distribution networks within the European Community, we need to recognize the differences that exist among non-Western economies. Some scholars now categorize *five* separate types of "developing" countries in assessing the varied potential of societies in Asia, Africa, and Latin America.[8]

Relative national growth in the 1980s confirms these differences. Whereas East Asian economies grew on average at an impressive annual rate of 7.4 percent, those in Africa and Latin America gained only 1.8 and 1.7 percent respectively[9] —and since their populations grew faster, the net result was that they slipped backward, absolutely and relatively. Differences of economic structure also grew in this decade, with African and other primary commodity-producing countries eager for higher raw-material prices, whereas the export-oriented manufacturing nations of East Asia sought to keep commodity prices low. The most dramatic difference occurred in the shares of world trade in manufactures, a key indicator of economic competitiveness. Thus, while some scholars still refer to a dual world economy[11] of rich and poor countries, what is emerging is increasing differentiation. Why is this so?

The developing countries most successfully catching up with the West are the trading states of the Pacific and East Asia. Except for Communist regimes there, the Pacific rim countries (including the western provinces of Canada and the United States, and in part Australia) have enjoyed a lengthy boom in manufacturing, trade, and investment; but the center of that boom is on the *Asian* side of the

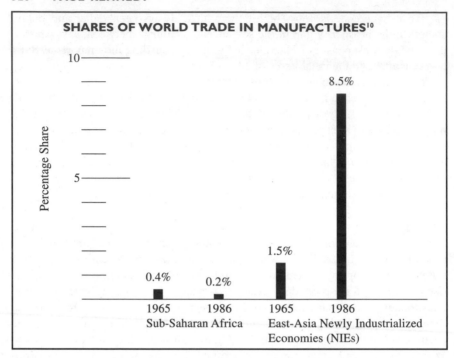

SHARES OF WORLD TRADE IN MANUFACTURES[10]

Pacific, chiefly fuelled by Japan's own spectacular growth and the stimulus given to neighboring economies and trans-Pacific trade. According to one source:

> In 1962 the Western Pacific (notably East Asia) accounted for around 9 percent of world GNP, North America for 30 percent, and Western Europe for 31 percent. Twenty years later, the Western Pacific share had climbed to more than 15 percent, while North America's had fallen to 28 percent and Europe's to 27 percent. By the year 2000 it is likely that the Western Pacific will account for around one-quarter of world GNP, with the whole Pacific region increasing its share from just over 43 percent to around half of world GNP.[12]

East Asia's present boom is not, of course, uniform, and scholars distinguish between the different stages of economic and technological development in this vast region. Roughly speaking, the divisions would be as follows:

(a) Japan, now the world's largest or second largest financial center and, increasingly, the most innovative high-tech nation in the nonmilitary field;

(b) the four East Asian "tigers" or "dragons," the Newly Industrialized Economies (NIEs) of Singapore, Hong Kong, Taiwan, and South Korea, of which the latter two possess bigger populations and territories than the two port-city states, but all of which have enjoyed export-led growth in recent decades;

(c) the larger Southeast Asian states of Thailand, Malaysia, and Indonesia which, stimulated by foreign (chiefly Japanese) investment, are becoming involved in manufacturing, assembly, and export—it is doubtful whether the Philippines should be included in this group;

(d) finally, the stunted and impoverished Communist societies of Vietnam, Cambodia, and North Korea, as well as isolationist Myanmar pursuing its "Burmese Way to Socialism."

Because of this staggered level of development, economists in East Asia invoke the image of the "flying geese," with Japan the lead bird, followed by the East Asian NIEs, the larger Southeast Asian states, and so on. What Japan produced in one decade—relatively low-priced toys, kitchenware, electrical goods—will be imitated by the next wave of "geese" in the decade following, and by the third wave in the decade after that. However accurate the metaphor individually, the overall picture is clear; these birds are flying, purposefully and onward, to an attractive destination.

Of those states, it is the East Asian NIEs that have provided the clearest example of successful transformation. Although distant observers may regard them as similar, there are notable differences in size, population,[13] history, and political system. Even the economic structures are distinct; for example, Korea, which began its expansion at least a decade later than Taiwan (and democratized itself even more slowly), is heavily dependent upon a few enormous industrial conglomerates, or *chaebol*, of whom the top four alone (Samsung, Hyundai, Lucky-Goldstar, and Daewoo) have sales equal to half Korea's GNP. By contrast, Taiwan possesses many small companies, specializing in one or two kinds of products. While Taiwanese are concerned that their firms may lose out to foreign giants, Koreans worry that the *chaebol* will find it increasingly difficult to compete in large-scale industries like petrochemicals and semiconductors and shipbuilding at the same time.[14]

Despite such structural differences, these societies each contain certain basic characteristics, which, *taken together,* help to explain their decade-upon-decade growth. The first, and perhaps the most important, is the emphasis upon education. This derives from Confucian traditions of competitive examinations and respect for learning, reinforced daily by the mother of the family who complements what is taught at school.

To Western eyes, this process—like Japan's—appears to concentrate on rote learning and the acquisition of technical skills, and emphasizes consensus instead of encouraging individual talent and the habit of questioning authority. Even if some East Asian educators would nowadays admit that criticism, most believe that their own educational mores create social harmony and a well-trained work force. Moreover, the uniformity of the system does not exclude intense individual competitiveness; in Taiwan (where, incidentally, twelve members of the fourteen-member cabinet of 1989 had acquired Ph.D.s abroad), only the top one-third of each year's 110,000 students taking the national university entrance examinations are selected, to emphasize the importance of college education.[15]

Perhaps nothing better illustrates this stress upon learning than the fact that Korea (43 million population) has around 1.4 million students in higher education, compared with 145,000 in Iran (54 million), 15,000 in Ethiopia (46 million), and 159,000 in Vietnam (64 million); or the further fact that already by 1980 "as many engineering students were graduating from Korean institutions as in the United Kingdom, West Germany and Sweden combined."[16]

The second common characteristic of these countries is their high level of national savings. By employing fiscal measures, taxes, and import controls to encourage personal savings, large amounts of low-interest capital were made available for investment in manufacture and commerce. During the first few decades of growth, personal consumption was constrained and living standards controlled—by restrictions upon moving capital abroad, or importing foreign luxury goods—in order to funnel resources into industrial growth. While average prosperity rose, most of the fruits of economic success were plowed back into further expansion. Only when economic "take-off" was well under way has the system begun to alter; increased consumption, foreign purchases, capital investment in new homes, all allow internal demand to play a larger role in the country's growth. In such circumstances, one would expect to see overall savings ratios decline. Even in the late 1980s, however, the East Asian NIEs still had high national savings rates:

Comparative Savings Ratios, 1987[17]

Taiwan	38.8%
Malaysia	37.8%
Korea	37.0%
Japan	32.3%
Indonesia	29.1%
US	12.7%

The third feature has been a strong political system within which economic growth is fostered. While entrepreneurship and private property are encouraged, the "tigers" never followed a laissez-faire model. Industries targeted for growth were given a variety of supports—export subsidies, training grants, tariff protection from foreign competitors. As noted above, the fiscal system was arranged to produce high savings ratios. Taxes assisted the business sector, as did energy policy. Trade unions operated under restrictions. Democracy was constrained by the governor of Hong Kong, *dirigiste* administrations in Singapore, and the military regimes in Taiwan and Korea. Only lately have free elections and party politics been permitted. Defenders of this system argued that it was necessary to restrain libertarian impulses while concentrating on economic growth, and that democratic reforms are a "reward" for the people's patience. The point is that domestic politics were unlike those in the West yet did not hurt commercial expansion.

The fourth feature was the commitment to exports, in contrast to the policies of India, which emphasize locally produced substitutes for imports, and the consumer-driven policies of the United States. This was traditional for a small, bustling trading state like Hong Kong, but it involved substantial restructuring in Taiwan and Korea, where managers and workers had to be trained to produce what foreign customers wanted. In all cases, the value of the currency was kept low, to increase exports and decrease imports. Moreover, the newly industrialized economies of East Asia took advantage of favorable global circumstances: labor costs were much lower than in North America and Europe, and they benefitted from an open international trading order, created and protected by the United States, while shielding their own industries from foreign competition.

Eventually, this led to large trade surpluses and threats of retaliation from European and American governments, reminding us of the NIEs' heavy dependence upon the current international economic system. The important thing, however, is that they targeted export-led growth in manufactures, whereas other developing nations continued to rely upon commodity exports and made little effort to cater to foreign consumers' tastes.[18] Given this emphasis on trade, it is not surprising to learn that Asia now contains seven of the world's twelve largest ports.

Finally, the East Asian NIEs possess a local model, namely Japan, which Yemen, Guatemala, and Burkina Faso simply do not have. For four decades East Asian peoples have observed the dramatic success of a non-Western neighbor, based upon its educational and technical skills, high savings ratios, long-term, state-guided targeting of industries and markets, and determination to compete on world markets, though this admiration of Japan is nowadays mixed with a certain alarm at becoming members of a yen block dominated by Tokyo. While the Japanese domestic market is extremely important for the East Asian NIEs, and they benefit from Japanese investments, assembly plants, engineers, and expertise, they have little enthusiasm for a new Greater East Asia co-prosperity sphere.[19]

The benefits of economic success are seen not merely in East Asia's steadily rising standards of living. Its children are on average four or five inches taller than they were in the 1940s, and grow up in some of the world's healthiest countries:

> A Taiwanese child born in 1988 could expect to live 74 years, only a year less than an American or a West German, and 15 years longer than a Taiwanese born in 1952; a South Korean born in 1988 could expect 70 years on earth, up from 58 in 1965. In 1988 the Taiwanese took in 50 percent more calories each day than they had done 35 years earlier. They had 200 times as many televisions, telephones and cars per household; in Korea the rise in the possession of these goods was even higher.[20]

In addition, the East Asian NIEs enjoy some of today's highest literacy rates, once again confirming that they are altogether closer to "first" world nations than poor, developing countries:

Comparative Living Standards[21]

	Life Expectancy at Birth (years), 1987	Adult Literacy Rate (%), 1985	GNP per capita, 1988 US$
Niger	45	14	300
Togo	54	41	310
India	59	43	340
SINGAPORE	73	86	9,070
SOUTH KOREA	70	95	5,000
Spain	77	95	7,740
New Zealand	75	99	10,000

Will this progress last into the twenty-first century? Politically, Hong Kong's future is completely uncertain, and many companies are relocating their headquarters elsewhere; Taiwan remains a diplomatic pariah-state because of Beijing's traditional claims; and South Korea still worries about the unpredictable, militarized regime in the north. The future of China—and of Siberia—is uncertain, and causes concern. The 1980s rise in Asian stock-market prices (driven by vast increases in the money supply) was excessive and speculative, and destined to tumble. Protectionist tendencies in the developed world threaten the trading states even more than external pressures to abandon price supports for local farmers. A rise in the value of the Korean and Taiwanese currencies has cut export earnings and reduced their overall rate of growth. Some Japanese competitors have moved production to neighboring low-cost countries such as Thailand or southern China. Sharp rises in oil prices increase the import bills. High wage awards (in Korea they increased by an average 14 percent in 1988, and by 17 percent in 1989) affect labor costs and competitiveness. The social peace, precarious in these recent democracies, is damaged by bouts of student and industrial unrest.[22]

On the other hand, these may simply be growing pains. Savings ratios are still extremely high. Large numbers of new engineers and technicians pour out of college each year. The workers' enhanced purchasing power has created a booming domestic market, and governments are investing more in housing, infrastructure, and public facilities. The labor force will not grow as swiftly as before because of the demographic slowdown, but it will be better educated and spend more.[23] A surge in overseas investments is assisting the long-term balance of payments. As the populous markets of Indonesia, Thailand, and Malaysia grow at double-digit rates, there is plenty of work for the trading states. A hardening of the currency can be met by greater commitment to quality exports, high rates of industrial investment, and a move into newer, high-technology manufacture—in imitation of the 1980s re-tooling of Japanese industry when its currency hardened swiftly. Nowhere else in the world would growth rates of "only" 5 or 6 percent be considered worrying, or a harbinger of decline. Barring a war in East Asia, or a widespread global slump, the signs are that the four "tigers" are better structured than most to grow in wealth and health.

2.

For confirmation of that remark, one need only consider the present difficult condition of Latin America, which lost ground in the 1980s just as East Asia was gaining it. Here again, distinctions have to be made between various countries within the continent, with its more than 400 million people in an area almost 7 million square miles stretching from the Rio Grande to Antarctica, and with a range of political cultures and socioeconomic structures. Argentina, which around 1900 had a standard of living suggesting that it was a "developed" economy, is very different from Honduras and Guyana. Similarly, population change in Latin America occurs in three distinct forms: such nations as Bolivia, the Dominican Republic, and Haiti have high fertility rates and lower life expectancies; a middle group— Brazil, Colombia, Mexico, Venezuela, Costa Rica, and Panama—is beginning to experience declines in fertility and longer life expectancy; and the temperate-zone countries of Argentina, Chile, and Uruguay have the demographic characteristics of developed countries.[24]

Despite this diversity, there are reasons for considering Latin America's prospects as a whole: the economic challenges confronting the region are similar, as are its domestic politics—in particular, the fragility of its recently emerged democracies; and each is affected by its relationship with the developed world, especially the United States.

Several decades ago, Latin America's future appeared encouraging. Sharing in the post-1950 global boom, benefitting from demand for its coffee, timber, beef, oil, and minerals, and enjoying foreign investments in its agriculture, industry, and infrastructure, the region was moving upward. In the thirty years after 1945, its production of steel multiplied twenty times, and its output of electric energy, metals, and machinery grew more than tenfold.[25] Real gross domestic product (GDP) per person rose at an annual average of 2.8 percent during the 1960s and spurted to an annual average increase of 3.4 percent in the 1970s. Unfortunately, the growth then reversed itself, and between 1980 and 1988 Latin America's real GDP per person steadily fell by an annual average of 0.9 percent.[26] In some states, such as Peru and Argentina, real income dropped by as much as one quarter during the 1980s. With very few exceptions (Chile, Colombia, the Dominican Republic, Barbados, the Bahamas), most Latin American countries now have per capita GDPs lower than they were a decade earlier, or even two decades earlier (see chart below).

The reasons for this reversal offer a striking contrast to the East Asian NIEs. Instead of encouraging industrialists to target foreign markets and stimulate the economy through export-led growth, many Latin American governments pursued a policy of import substitution, creating their own steel, cement, paper, automo-

Per Capita GDP of Latin American Countries[27]
(1988 US Dollars)

Country	1960	1970	1980	1988
Chile	1,845	2,236	2,448	2,518
Argentina	2,384	3,075	3,359	2,862
Uruguay	2,352	2,478	3,221	2,989
Brazil	1,013	1,372	2,481	2,449
Paraguay	779	931	1,612	1,557
Bolivia	634	818	983	724
Peru	1,233	1,554	1,716	1,503
Ecuador	771	904	1,581	1,477
Colombia	927	1,157	1,595	1,739
Venezuela	3,879	4,941	5,225	4,544
Guyana	1,008	1,111	1,215	995
Suriname	887	2,337	3,722	3,420
Mexico	1,425	2,022	2,872	2,588
Guatemala	1,100	1,420	1,866	1,502
Honduras	619	782	954	851
El Salvador	832	1,032	1,125	995
Nicaragua	1,055	1,495	1,147	819
Costa Rica	1,435	1,825	2,394	2,235
Panama	1,264	2,017	2,622	2,229
Dominican Republic	823	987	1,497	1,509
Haiti	331	292	386	319
Jamaica	1,610	2,364	1,880	1,843
Trinidad & Tobago	3,848	4,927	8,116	5,510
Barbados	2,000	3,530	3,994	4,233
Bahamas	8,448	10,737	10,631	11,317

biles, and electronic-goods industries, which were given protective tariffs, government subsidies, and tax-breaks to insulate them from international competition. As a result, their products became less attractive abroad.[28] Moreover, while it was relatively easy to create a basic iron and steel industry, it proved harder to establish high-tech industries like computers, aerospace, machine-tools, and pharmaceuticals—most of these states therefore still depend on imported manufactured goods, whereas exports chiefly consist of raw materials like oil, coffee, and soybeans.[29]

Secondly, economic growth was accompanied by lax financial policies and an increasing reliance upon foreign borrowings. Governments poured money not only into infrastructure and schools but also into state-owned enterprises, large bureaucracies, and oversized armed forces, paying for them by printing money and raising loans from Western (chiefly US) banks and international agencies. The result was that public spending's share of GDP soared, price inflation accelerated, and was further increased by index-linked rises in salaries and wages. Inflation became so large that it was difficult to comprehend, let alone to combat. According to the 1990 *World Resources* report, "in 1989, for example, annual inflation in Nicaragua was more than 3,400 percent; in Argentina inflation reached 3,700 percent, in Brazil almost 1,500 percent, and in Peru nearly 3,000 percent. Ecuador, with only 60 percent inflation, did comparatively well."[30] In such circumstances the currency becomes worthless, as does the idea of seeking to raise national savings rates for long-term capital investment.

Another result is that some Latin American countries find themselves among the most indebted in the world, as the chart below shows. Total Latin American indebtedness now equals about $1,000 for every man, woman, and child. But instead of being directed into productive investment, that money has been wasted domestically or disappeared as "capital flight" to private accounts in United States and European banks. This has left most countries incapable of repaying even the interest on their loans. Defaults on loans (or suspension of interest payments) then produced a drying up of capital from indignant Western banks and a net capital *outflow* from Latin America just when it needed capital to aid economic growth.[32] Starved of foreign funds and with currencies made worthless by hyperinflation, many countries are in a far worse position than would have been imagined twenty-five years ago.[33] For a while, it was even feared that the region's financial problems might undermine parts of the international banking system. It now appears that the chief damage will be in the continent itself, where 180 million people (40 percent) are living in poverty—a rise of 50 million alone in the 1980s.

Given such profligacy, and the conservative, "anti–big government" incumbents in the White House during the 1980s, it was predictable that Latin America would come under pressure—from the World Bank, the IMF, private bankers, Washington itself—to slash public spending, control inflation, and repay debts. Such demands were easier said than done in the existing circumstances. Islands of democracy (e.g., Costa Rica) did exist, but many states were ruled by right-wing military

Growth of Latin American Indebtedness (Selected Countries)[31]

Country	Total External Debt (billion US$)			Long-Term Public Debt as a Percentage of GNP		
	1977	1982	1987	1977	1982	1987
Argentina	8.1	32.4	53.9	10	31	62
Brazil	28.3	68.7	109.4	13	20	29
Chile	4.9	8.5	18.7	28	23	89
Guyana	0.4	0.9	1.2	100	158	353
Honduras	0.6	1.6	3.1	29	53	71
Jamaica	1.1	2.7	4.3	31	69	139
Mexico	26.6	78.0	93.7	25	32	59
Venezuela	9.8	27.0	29.0	10	16	52

dictatorships or social revolutionaries; internal guerrilla wars, military *coups d'état,* labor unrest were common. Even as democracy began to reassert itself in the 1980s, the new leaders found themselves in a near-impossible situation: inheritors of the high external debts contracted by the outgoing regimes, legatees in many cases of inflationary index-linked wage systems, targets of landowner resentment and/or of guerrilla attacks, frustrated by elaborate and often corrupt bureaucracies, and deficient in trained personnel. While grappling with these weaknesses, they discovered that the Western world, which applauded the return to democracy, was unsympathetic to fresh lending, increasingly inclined to protectionism, and demanding unilateral measures (e.g., in the Amazon rain forests) to stop global warming.

Two other weaknesses have also slowed any hoped-for recovery. One is the unimpressive accomplishments of the educational systems. This is not due to an absence of schools and universities, as in parts of Africa. Many Latin American countries have extensive public education, dozens of universities, and high adult literacy rates; Brazil, for example, has sixty-eight universities, Argentina forty-one.[34] The real problem is neglect and under-investment. One citizen bemoaned the collapse in Argentina as follows:

> Education, which kept illiteracy at bay for more than a century, lies in ruins. The universities are unheated and many public schools lack panes for their window frames. Last summer [1990] an elementary school teacher with ten years' experience earned less than $110 a month. An associate professor at the Universidad de Buenos Aires, teaching ten hours a week, was paid $37 a month. A doctor's salary at a municipal hospital was $120 a month. . . . At times, teachers took turns teaching, or cut their class hours, because they and their students could not afford transportation.[35]

Presumably, if resources were available, those decaying educational and health-care structures could be resuscitated, helping national recovery; but where the capital can be raised in present circumstances is difficult to see. Moreover, in the strife-torn countries of Central America there is little education to begin with; in Guatemala, the latest census estimated that 63 percent of those ten years of age and older were illiterate, while in Honduras the illiteracy rate was 40 percent.[36] Unfortunately, it is in the educationally most deprived Latin American countries that resources are being eroded by swift population increases.

Despite these disadvantages, recent reports on Latin America have suggested that the "lost decade" of the 1980s will be followed by a period of recovery. The coming of democratic regimes, the compromises emerging from protracted debt-recycling talks, the stiff economic reforms (cutting public spending, abandoning indexation) to reduce inflation rates, the replacement of "state protectionism with import liberalization and privatization,"[37] the conversion of budget deficits into surpluses—all this has caused the Inter-American Development Bank to argue that "a decisive and genuine takeoff" is at hand, provided the new policies are sustained.[38] Growth has resumed in Argentina, Mexico, and Venezuela. Even investment bankers are reported to be returning to the continent.

Whether these changes are going to be enough remains uncertain, especially since the newly elected governments face widespread resentment at the proposed reforms. As one commentator put it, "Much of Latin America is entering the 1990s in a race between economic deterioration and political progress."[39] Whereas Spain, Portugal, and Greece moved to democracy while enjoying reasonable prosperity, Latin America (like Eastern Europe) has to make that change as its economies flounder—which places immense responsibilities upon the political leadership.

Although it can be argued that the region's future is in its own hands, it will also be heavily influenced by the United States. In many ways, the US–Latin America leadership is similar to that between Japan and the East Asian NIEs, which are heavily dependent upon Japan as their major market and source of capital.[40] Yet there is more to this relationship than Latin America's economic dependence upon the United States, whose banking system has also suffered because of Latin American indebtedness. United States exports, which are fifty times larger to this region than to Eastern Europe, were badly hurt by Latin America's economic difficulties, and they would benefit greatly from a resumption of growth. The United States' own environment may now be threatened by the diminution of the Amazon and Central American rain forests. Its awful drug problem, driven by domestic demand, is fuelled by Latin American supplies—more than 80 percent of the cocaine and 90 percent of the marijuana entering the United States are produced or move through this region.

Finally, the population of the United States is being altered by migration from Mexico, the Caribbean, and Central America; if there should be a widespread socioeconomic collapse south of the Rio Grande, the "spillover" effects will be felt across the United States. Instead of being marginalized by the end of the cold war, Latin America may present Washington with formidable and growing challenges —social, environmental, financial, and ultimately political.[41] Thus, while the region's own politicians and citizens have to bear the major responsibility for recovery, richer nations—especially the United States—may find it in their own best interest to lend a hand.

3.

If these remarks disappoint readers in Brazil or Peru, they may care to glance, in grim consolation, at the world of Islam. It is one thing to face population pressures, shortage of resources, educational/technological deficiencies, and regional conflicts, which would challenge the wisest governments. But it is another when regimes themselves stand in angry resentment of global forces for change instead of (as in East Asia) selectively responding to such trends. Far from preparing for the twenty-first century, much of the Arab and Muslim world appears to have difficulty in coming to terms with the nineteenth century, with its composite legacy of secularization, democracy, laissez-faire economics, industrial and commercial linkages among different nations, social change, and intellectual questioning. If one needed an example of the importance of cultural attitudes in explaining a society's response to change, contemporary Islam provides it.

Before analyzing the distinctive role of Islamic culture, one should first note the danger of generalizing about a region that contains such variety. After all, it is not even clear what *name* should be used to describe this part of the earth. To term it the "Middle East"[42] is, apart from its Atlantic-centered bias, to leave out such North African states as Libya, Tunisia, Algeria, and Morocco. To term it the "Arab World"[43] is to exclude Iran (and, of course, Israel), the Kurds, and the non-Muslim tribes of southern Sudan and Mauritania. Even the nomenclature Islam, or the Muslim world, disguises the fact that millions of Catholics, Copts, and Jews live in these lands, and that Islamic societies extend from West Africa to Indonesia.[44]

In addition, the uneven location of oil in the Middle East has created a division between super-rich and dreadfully poor societies that has no equivalent in Central America or sub-Saharan Africa.[45] Countries like Kuwait (2 million), the United Arab Emirates (1.3 million), and Saudi Arabia (11.5 million) enjoy some of the world's highest incomes, but exist alongside populous neighbors one-third as rich (Jordan, Iran, Iraq) or even one-tenth as rich (Egypt, Yemen). The gap is accentuated by different political systems: conservative, anti-democratic, traditionalist in the Gulf sheikdoms; demagogic, populist, militarized in countries such as Libya, Syria, Iraq, and Iran.

The 1990 Iraqi attack upon Kuwait, and the different responses of the Saudi elites on the one hand and the street masses in Amman or Rabat on the other, illustrated this divide between "haves" and "have-nots" in the Muslim world. The presence of millions of Egyptian, Yemeni, Jordanian, and Palestinian *Gastarbeiter* in the oil-rich states simply increased the mutual resentments, while the Saudi and Emirate habit of giving extensive aid to Iraq during its war against Iran, or to Egypt to assist its economic needs, reinforces the impression of wealthy but precarious regimes seeking to achieve security by bribing their larger, jealous neighbors.[46] Is it any wonder that the unemployed, badly housed urban masses, despairing of their own secular advancement, are attracted to religious leaders or "strongmen" appealing to Islamic pride, a sense of identity, and resistance to foreign powers and their local lackeys?

More than in any other developing region, then, the future of the Middle East and North Africa is affected by issues of war and conflict. The region probably contains more soldiers, aircraft, missiles, and other weapons than anywhere else in the world, with billions of dollars of armaments having been supplied by Western, Soviet, and Chinese producers during the past few decades. In view of the range and destructiveness of these weapons, another Arab-Israeli war would be a nightmare, yet many Muslim states still regard Israel with acute hostility. Even if the Arab-Israeli antagonism did not exist, the region is full of other rivalries, between Syria and Iraq, Libya and Egypt, Iran and Iraq, and so on. Vicious one-man dictatorships glare threateningly at arch-conservative, antidemocratic, feudal sheik-doms. Fundamentalist regimes exist from Iran to the Sudan. Terrorist groups in exile threaten to eliminate their foes. Unrest among the masses puts a question mark over the future of Egypt, Algeria, Morocco, Jordan.[47] The recent fate of Lebanon, instead of serving as a warning against sectarian fanaticism, is more often viewed as a lesson in power politics, that the strong will devour the weak.

To the Western observer brought up in Enlightenment traditions—or, for that matter, to economic rationalists preaching the virtues of the borderless world—the answer to the Muslim nations' problems would appear to be a vast program of *education,* not simply in the technical, skills-acquiring sense but also to advance parliamentary discourse, pluralism, and a secular civic culture. Is that not the reason, after all, for the political stability and economic success of Scandinavia or Japan today?

If that argument is correct, then such an observer would find few of those features in contemporary Islam. In countries where fundamentalism is strong, there is (obviously) little prospect of education or advancement for the female half of the population.[48] Where engineers and technicians exist, their expertise has all too often been mobilized for war purposes, as in Iraq. Tragically, Egypt possesses a large and bustling university system but a totally inadequate number of jobs for graduates and skilled workers, so that millions of both are underemployed. In Yemen, to take an extreme example, the state of education is dismal. By contrast, the oil-rich states have poured huge resources into schools, technical institutes, and universities, but these alone are insufficient to create an "enterprise culture" that would produce export-led manufacturing along East Asian lines. Ironically, possession of vast oil reserves could be a disadvantage, since it reduces the incentive to rely upon the skills and quality of the people, as occurs in countries (Japan, Switzerland) with few natural resources. Such discouraging circumstances may also explain why many educated and entrepreneurial Arabs, who passionately wanted their societies to borrow from the West, have emigrated.

It is difficult to know whether the reason for the Muslim world's troubled condition is cultural or historical. Western critics pointing to the region's religious intolerance, technological backwardness, and feudal cast of mind often forget that, centuries before the Reformation, Islam led the world in mathematics, cartography, medicine, and many other aspects of science and industry; and contained libraries, universities, and observatories, when Japan and America possessed none and Europe only a few. These assets were later sacrificed to a revival of traditionalist thought and the sectarian split between Shi'ite and Sunni Muslims, but Islam's retreat into itself—its being "out of step with History," as one author termed it[49]—was probably also a response to the rise of a successful, expansionist Europe.

Sailing along the Arab littoral, assisting in the demise of the Mughal Empire, penetrating strategic points with railways, canals, and ports, steadily moving into North Africa, the Nile Valley, the Persian Gulf, the Levant, and then Arabia itself, dividing the Middle East along unnatural boundaries as part of a post–First World War diplomatic bargain, developing American power to buttress and then replace European influences, inserting an Israeli state in the midst of Arab peoples, instigating coups against local popular leaders, and usually indicating that this part of the globe was important only for its oil—the Western nations may have contributed more to turning the Muslim world into what it is today than outside commentators are willing to recognize.[50] Clearly, the nations of Islam suffer many self-inflicted problems. But if much of their angry, confrontational attitudes toward the international order today are due to a long-held fear of being swallowed up by the West, little in the way of change can be expected until that fear is dissipated.

4.

The condition of sub-Saharan Africa—"the third world's third world," as it has been described—is even more desperate.[51] When one considers recent developments such as perestroika in the former Soviet Union, the coming integration of Europe, and the economic miracle of Japan and the East Asian NIEs, remarked a former president of Nigeria, General Olusegun Obasanjo, and "contrasting all this with what is taking place in Africa, it is difficult to believe that we inhabit the same historical time."[52] Recent reports upon the continent's plight are extraordinarily gloomy, describing Africa as "a human and environmental disaster area," as "moribund," "marginalized," and "peripheral to the rest of the world," and having so many intractable problems that some foreign development experts are abandoning it to work elsewhere. In the view of the World Bank, virtually everywhere else in the world is likely to experience a decline in poverty by the year 2000 *except* Africa, where things will only get worse.[53] "Sub-Saharan Africa," concludes one economist, "suffers from a combination of economic, social, political, institutional and environmental handicaps which have so far largely defied development efforts by the African countries and their donors."[54] How, an empathetic study asks, can Africa survive?[55]

The unanimity of views is remarkable, given the enormous variety among the forty-five states that comprise sub-Saharan Africa.[56] Nine of them have fewer than one million people each, whereas Nigeria contains about 110 million. Some lie in the desert, some in tropical rain forests. Many are rich in mineral deposits, others have only scrubland. While a number (Botswana, Cameroun, Congo, Gabon, Kenya) have seen significant increases in living standards since independence, they are the exception—suggesting that the obstacles to growth on East Asian lines are so deep-rooted and resistant to the "development strategies" of foreign experts and/or their own leaders that it may require profound changes in attitude to achieve recovery.

This was not the mood thirty years ago, when the peoples of Africa were gaining their independence. True, there was economic backwardness, but this was assumed to have been caused by decades of foreign rule, leading to dependency upon a single metropolitan market, monoculture, lack of access to capital, and so on. Now that Africans had control of their destinies, they could build industries, develop cities, airports, and infrastructure, and attract foreign investment and aid from either Western powers or the USSR and its partners. The boom in world trade during the 1950s and 1960s, and demand for commodities, strengthened this optimism. Although some regions were in need, Africa as a whole was self-sufficient in food and, in fact, a net food exporter. Externally, African states were of increasing importance at the United Nations and other world bodies.

What went wrong? The unhappy answer is "lots of things." The first, and perhaps most serious, was that over the following three decades the population mushroomed as imported medical techniques and a reduction in malaria-borne mosquitoes drastically curtailed infant mortality. Africa's population was already increasing at an average annual rate of 2.6 percent in the 1960s, jumped to 2.9 percent during the 1970s, and increased to over 3 percent by the late 1980s, implying a doubling in size every twenty-two years; this was, therefore, the highest rate for any region in the world.[57]

In certain countries, the increases were staggering. Between 1960 and 1990, Kenya's population quadrupled, from 6.3 million to 25.1 million, and Côte d'Ivoire's jumped from 3.8 million to 12.6 million. Altogether Africa's population—including the North African states—leapt from 281 to 647 million in three decades.[58] Moreover, while the majority of Africans inhabit rural settlements, the continent has been becoming urban at a dizzying speed. Vast shanty-cities have already emerged on the edges of national capitals (such as Accra in Ghana, Monrovia in Liberia, and Lilongwe in Malawi). By 2025, urban dwellers are predicted to make up 55 percent of Africa's total population.

The worst news is that the increase is unlikely to diminish in the near future. Although most African countries spend less than 1 percent of GNP on health care and consequently have the highest infant mortality rates in the world—in Mali, for example, there are 169 infant deaths for every 1,000 live births—those rates are substantially less than they were a quarter century ago and will tumble further in the future, which is why demographers forecast that Africa's population in 2025 will be nearly three times that of today.[59]

There remains one random and tragic factor which may significantly affect all these (late 1980s) population projections—the AIDS epidemic, which is especially prevalent in Africa. Each new general study has raised the global total of people who are already HIV positive. For example, in June 1991, the World Health Organization abandoned its earlier estimate that 25–30 million people throughout the world would be infected by the year 2000, and suggested instead that the total could be closer to 40 million, and even that may be a gross underestimate.[60] Without question, Africa is the continent most deeply affected by AIDS, with entire families suffering from the disease. Tests of pregnant women in certain African families reveal that 25–30 percent are now HIV positive.[61] Obviously, this epidemic would alter the earlier projections of a doubling or trebling of Africa's total population over the next few decades—and in the worst possible way: family sizes would still be much larger than in most other regions of the globe, but tens of millions of Africans would be dying of AIDS, further crushing the world's most disadvantaged continent.

The basic reason why the present demographic boom will not otherwise be halted swiftly is traditional African belief-systems concerning fecundity, children, ancestors, and the role of women. Acutely aware of the invisible but pervasive presence of their ancestors, determined to expand their lineage, regarding childlessness or small families as the work of evil spirits, most Africans seek to have as many children as possible; a woman's virtue and usefulness are measured by the number of offspring she can bear. "Desired family size," according to polls of African women, ranges from five to nine children. The social attitudes that lead women in North America, Europe, and Japan to delay childbearing—education, career ambitions, desire for independence—scarcely exist in African societies; where such emerge, they are swiftly suppressed by familial pressures.[62]

This population growth has not been accompanied by equal or larger increases in Africa's productivity, which would of course transform the picture. During the 1960s, farm output was rising by around 3 percent each year, keeping pace with the population, but since 1970 agricultural production has grown at only half that rate. Part of this decline was caused by the drought, hitting countries south of the Sahara. Furthermore, existing agricultural resources have been badly eroded by overgrazing—caused by the sharp rise in the number of cattle and goats —as well as by deforestation in order to provide fuel and shelter for the growing population. When rain falls, the water runs off the denuded fields, taking the topsoil with it.

None of this was helped by changes in agricultural production, with farmers encouraged to grow tea, coffee, cocoa, palm oil, and rubber for export rather than food for domestic consumption. After benefitting from high commodity prices in the early stages, producers suffered a number of blows. Heavy taxation on cash crops, plus mandatory governmental marketing, reduced the incentives to increase output; competition grew from Asian and Latin American producers; many African currencies were overvalued, which hurt exports; and in the mid-1970s, world commodity prices tumbled. Yet the cost of imported manufactures and foodstuffs remained high, and sub-Saharan Africa was badly hurt by the quadrupling of oil prices.[63]

These blows increased Africa's indebtedness in ways that were qualitatively new. Early, postcolonial borrowings were driven by the desire for modernization, as money was poured into cement works, steel plants, airports, harbors, national airlines, electrification schemes, and telephone networks. Much of it, encouraged from afar by international bodies like the World Bank, suffered from bureaucratic interference, a lack of skilled personnel, unrealistic planning, and inadequate basic facilities, and now lies half-finished or (where completed) suffers from lack of upkeep. But borrowing to pay for imported oil, or to feed half the nation's population, means that indebtedness rises without any possible return on the borrowed funds. In consequence, Africa's total debt expanded from $14 billion in 1973 to $125 billion in 1987, when its capacity to repay was dropping fast; by the mid-1980s, payments on loans consumed about half of Africa's export earnings, a proportion even greater than for Latin American debtor nations. Following repeated debt reschedulings, Western bankers—never enthusiastic to begin with—virtually abandoned private loans to Africa.[64]

As a result, Africa's economy is in a far worse condition now than at independence, apart from a few countries like Botswana and Mauritius. Perhaps the most startling illustration of its plight is the fact that "excluding South Africa, the nations of sub-Saharan Africa with their 450 million people have a total GDP less than that of Belgium's 11 million people"; in fact, the entire continent generates roughly 1 percent of the world GDP.[65] Africa's share of world markets has shriveled just as East Asia's share has risen fast. Plans for modernization lie unrealized. Manufacturing still represents only 11 percent of Africa's economic activity—scarcely up from the 9 percent share in 1965; and only 12 percent of the continent's exports is composed of manufactures (compared with Korea's 90 percent). There is a marked increase in the signs of decay: crumbling infrastructure, power failures, broken-down communications, abandoned projects, and everywhere the pressure of providing for increasing populations. Already Africa needs to import 15 million tons of maize a year to achieve minimal levels of food consumption, but with population increasing faster than agricultural output, that total could multiply over the next decade—implying an even greater diversion of funds from investment and infrastructure.[66]

Two further characteristics worsen Africa's condition. The first is the prevalence of wars, *coups d'état,* and political instability. This is partly the legacy of the European "carve-up" of Africa, when colonial boundaries were drawn without regard for the differing tribes and ethnic groups,[67] or even of earlier conquests by successful tribes of neighboring lands and peoples; Ethiopia, for example, is said to contain 76 ethnic groups and 286 languages.[68] While it is generally accepted that those boundaries cannot be unscrambled, most of them are clearly artificial. In extreme cases like Somalia, the "state" has ceased to exist. And in most other African countries, governments do not attract the loyalty of citizens (except perhaps kinsmen of the group in power), and ethnic tensions have produced innumerable civil wars—from Biafra's attempt to secede from Nigeria, to the conflict between Arab north and African south in the Sudan, to Eritrean struggles to escape from Ethiopia, to the Tutsi-Hutu struggle in Burundi, to clashes and suppressions and guerrilla campaigns from Uganda to the Western Sahara, from Angola to Mozambique.[69]

These antagonisms have often been worsened by struggles over ideology and government authority. The rulers of many new African states rapidly switched either to a personal dictatorship, or single-party rule. They also embraced a Soviet or Maoist political economy, instituting price controls, production targets, forced industrialization, the takeover of private enterprises, and other features of "scientific socialism" that—unknown to them—were destroying the Soviet econ-omy. Agriculture was neglected, while bureaucracy flourished. The result was the disappearance of agricultural surpluses, inattention to manufacturing for the world market, and the expansion of party and government bureaucracies, exacer-bating the region's problems.

The second weakness was the wholly inadequate investment in human re-sources and in developing a culture of entrepreneurship, scientific inquiry, and technical prowess. According to one survey, Africa has been spending less than $1 each year on research and development per head of population, whereas the United States was spending $200 per head. Consequently, Africa's scientific pop-ulation has always trailed the rest of the world:

Numbers of Scientists and Engineers per Million of Population[70]

Japan	3,548
US	2,685
Europe	1,632
Latin America	209
Arab States	202
Asia (minus Japan)	99
Africa	53

In many African countries—Malawi, Zambia, Lesotho—government spend-ing on education has fallen, so that, after some decades of advance, a smaller share of children are now in school. While there is a hunger for learning, it cannot be satisfied beyond the secondary level except for a small minority. Angola, for ex-ample, had 2.4 million pupils in primary schools in 1982–1983, but only 153,000 in secondary schools and a mere 4,700 in higher education.[71] By contrast, Swe-den, with a slightly smaller total population, had 570,000 in secondary education and 179,000 in higher education.[72]

Despite these relative weaknesses, some observers claim to have detected signs of a turnaround. With the exception of intransigent African socialists,[73] many leaders are now attempting to institute reforms. In return for "structural adjustments," that is, measures to encourage free enterprise, certain African societies have secured additional loans from Western nations and the World Bank. The latter organization has identified past errors (many of them urged on African governments and funded by itself), and encouraged economic reforms. Mozambique, Ghana, and Zambia have all claimed recent successes in reversing negative growth, albeit at consider-able social cost.

Democratic principles are also returning to the continent: the dismantling of apartheid in South Africa, the cease-fire in Angola, the independence of Namibia, the success of Botswana's record of democracy and prosperity, the cries for re-forms in Gabon, Kenya, and Zaire, the rising awareness among African intellec-tuals of the transformations in East Asia, may all help—so the argument goes—to change attitudes, which is the prerequisite for recovery.[74] Moreover, there are local examples of economic self-improvement, cooperative ventures to halt erosion and improve yields, and village-based schemes of improvement.[75] This is, after all, a continent of enormous agricultural and mineral resources, provided they can be sensibly exploited.

Despite such signs of promise, conditions are likely to stay poor. Population increases countered only by the growing toll of AIDS victims, the diminution of grazing lands and food supplies, the burdens of indebtedness, the decay of infrastructures and reduced spending on health care and education, the residual strength of animist religions and traditional belief-systems, the powerful hold of corrupt bureaucracies and ethnic loyalties . . . all those tilt against the relatively few African political leaders, educators, scientists, and economists who perceive the need for changes.

What does this mean for Africa's future? As the Somalian disaster unfolds, some observers suggest that parts of the continent may be taken over and administered from the outside, rather like the post-1919 League of Nations mandates. By contrast, other experts argue that disengagement by developed countries might have the positive effect of compelling Africans to begin a *self-driven* recovery, as well as ending the misuse of aid monies.[76] Still others feel that Africa cannot live without the West, although its leaders and people will have to abandon existing habits, and development aid must be more intelligently applied.[77] Whichever view is correct, the coming decade will be critical for Africa. Even a partial recovery would give grounds for hope; on the other hand, a second decade of decline, together with a further surge in population, would result in catastrophe.

5.

From the above, it is clear that the developing countries' response to the broad forces for global change is going to be uneven. The signs are that the gap between success and failure will widen; one group enjoys interacting beneficial trends, while others suffer from linked weaknesses and deficiencies.[78]

This is most clearly the case with respect to demography. As noted earlier, the commitment of the East Asian trading states to education, manufacturing, and export-led growth produced a steady rise in living standards, and allowed those societies to make the demographic transition to smaller family sizes. This was in marked contrast to sub-Saharan Africa where, because of different cultural attitudes and social structures, improved health care and rising incomes led, *not* to a drop in population growth, but to the opposite. Just before independence in 1960, for example, the average Kenyan woman had 6.2 children, whereas by 1980 she had 8.2[79]—and that in a period when Africa's economic prospects were fading.

In Africa's case the "global trend" which drives all others is, clearly, the demographic explosion. It spills into every domain—overgrazing, local conflicts over water and wood supplies, extensive unplanned urbanization, strains upon the educational and social structures, reliance upon imported food supplies (at the cost of increasing indebtedness), ethnic tensions, domestic unrest, border wars. Only belatedly are some African governments working to persuade families to limit their size as people become aware that access to family planning, plus improved educational opportunities for women, produce significant declines in birth rates. Against such promising indications stand the many cultural, gender-related, and economic forces described above that encourage large families. This resistance to change is aided by Africa's general lack of resources. Raising Somalia's female literacy rate (6 percent) to South Korea's (88 percent) to produce a demographic transition sounds fine until one considers how so ambitious a reform could be implemented and paid for. Unfortunately, as noted above, the projections suggest that, as Africa's population almost trebles over the next few decades, the only development curtailing it could be the rapid growth of AIDS.[80]

In many parts of Latin America, the demographic explosion will also affect the capacity to handle globally driven forces for change. While wide differences in total fertility rates exist between the moderate-climate countries and those in the tropics, the overall picture is that Latin America's population, which was roughly equal to that of United States and Canada in 1960, is increasing so swiftly that it will be more than double the latter in 2025.[81] Even if birth-rates are now declining in the larger countries, there will still be enormous increases: Mexico's population will leap to 150 million by 2025 and Brazil's to 245 million.[82] This implies a very high incidence of child poverty and malnutrition, further strain upon already inadequate health-care and educational services, the crowding of millions of human beings into a dozen or more "mega-cities," pollution, the degradation of grazing land, forests, and other natural resources. In Mexico, for example, 44 million people are without sewers and 21 million without potable water, which means that when disease (e.g., cholera) strikes, it spreads swiftly.[83] These are not strong foundations upon which to improve the region's relative standing in an increasingly competitive international economic order.

In this regard, many Muslim states are in a similar or worse position; in no Arab country is the population increasing by less than 2 percent a year,[84] and in most the rate is considerably higher. The region's total population of more than 200 million will double in less than twenty-five years and city populations are growing twice as fast as national averages. This puts enormous pressures upon scarce food, water, and land resources, and produces unbalanced populations. Already, in most Arab countries at least four out of every ten people are under the age of fifteen—the classic recipe for subsequent social unrest and political revolution. One in five Egyptian workers is jobless, as is one in four Algerian workers.[85] In what is widely regarded as the most turbulent part of the world, therefore, demography is contributing to the prospects of future unrest year by year. Even the Israeli-Palestine quarrel has become an issue of demography, with the influx of Soviet Jews seen as countering the greater fertility of the Palestinians.

There is, moreover, little likelihood that population growth will fall in the near future. Since infant mortality rates in many Muslim countries are still high, further improvements in prenatal care will produce rises in the numbers surviving, as is happening in the Gulf States and Saudi Arabia:

Comparative Infant Mortality Rates[86]
(Infant deaths per 1,000 live births)

	1965–1970	1985–1990
Algeria	150	74
Egypt	170	85
Sudan	156	108
Yemen Arab Republic	186	116
Saudi Arabia	140	71
Kuwait	55	19
Iraq	111	69
Japan	16	5
US	22	10
Sweden	13	6

As elsewhere, politics intrudes; many regimes are deliberately encouraging women to have large families, arguing that this adds to the country's military strength. "Bear a child," posters in Iraq proclaim, "and you pierce an arrow in the enemy's eye."[87] Countries such as Iraq and Libya offer many incentives for larger families, as do the Gulf States and Saudi Arabia, anxious to fill their oil-rich lands with native-born rather than foreign workers. Only in Egypt are propaganda campaigns launched to curb family size, but even if that is successful—despite resistance from the Muslim Brotherhood—present numbers are disturbing. With a current population of over 55 million Egyptians, six out of ten of whom are under twenty, and with an additional one million being born every eight months, the country is in danger of bursting at the seams during the next few decades.

6.

For much the same reasons, we ought to expect a differentiated success rate among developing countries in handling environmental challenges, with the newly industrializing East Asian economies way ahead of the others. This is not to ignore significant local schemes to improve the ecology that are springing up in Africa and the interesting proposals for "sustainable development" elsewhere in the developing world,[88] or to forget that industrialization has caused environmental damage in East Asia, from choked roads to diminished forests. Yet the fact is that nations with lots of resources (capital, scientists, engineers, technology, a per capita GNP of over US $4,000) are better able to deal with environmental threats than those without money, tools, or personnel. By contrast, it is the poorer societies (Egypt, Bangladesh, Ethiopia) that, lacking financial and personnel resources, find it difficult to respond to cyclones, floods, drought, and other natural disasters—with their devastated populations augmenting the millions of refugees and migrants. Should global warming produce sea-level rises and heightened storm surges, teeming island populations from the Caribbean to the Pacific are in danger of being washed away.[89]

Finally, it is the population explosion in Latin America and South Asia and Africa that is the major cause for the overgrazing, soil erosion, salinization, and clearing of the tropical rain forests, which, while contributing to global warming, also hurts the local populations and exacerbates regional struggles for power. Elsewhere, in the Middle East for example, supplies of water are the greatest concern, especially in view of growing demographic pressures. The average Jordanian now uses only one-third the amount of domestic water consumed in Israel and has little hope of increasing the supply, yet Jordan's population, which is now roughly equal to Israel's, is expected to double during the next twenty years.[90]

With all governments in the region striving to boost agricultural output and highly sensitive to famine and unrest among their peasant farmers, the search for secure water influences domestic politics, international relations, and spending priorities. Egypt worries that either the Sudan or Ethiopia might dam the Nile in order to increase irrigation. Syria and Iraq have taken alarm at Turkey's new Ataturk dam, which can interrupt the flow of the Euphrates. Jordan, Syria, and Israel quarrel over water rights in the Litani, Yarmuk, and Jordan river valleys, as do Arabs and Jews over well supplies in the occupied West Bank. Saudi Arabia's ambition to grow wheat is draining its aquifers, and the same will occur with Libya's gigantic scheme to tap water from under the Sahara.[91] As more and more people struggle for the same—or diminishing—amounts of water, grand ideas about preparing for the twenty-first century look increasingly irrelevant; surviving *this* century becomes the order of the day.

What are the implications for these societies of the new technologies being developed by Western scientists? The revolution in biotech farming, for example, is of great relevance to developing countries, even if the consequences will be mixed. Improved strains of plants and more sophisticated pesticides and fertilizers could, potentially, enhance yields in the developing world, reduce pressures upon marginal lands, restore agricultural self-sufficiency, improve the balance of payments, and raise standards of living. Since much biotech does not involve expensive enterprise, we could witness farmers' groups experimenting with new seeds, improved breeding techniques, cultivation of gene tissue, regional gene-banks, and other developments.

Yet it is also possible that giant pharmaceutical and agro-chemical firms in the "first" world may monopolize much of the knowledge—and the profits—that this transformation implies. Surpluses in global foodstuffs caused by the biotech revolution could be used to counter malnutrition. They could also undermine commodity prices and hurt societies in which most inhabitants were employed in agriculture. Removing food production from the farm to the laboratory—which is what is implied by recent breakthroughs in biotech agriculture—would undercut agrarian societies, which is why some biotech experts in the development field call for serious planning in "agricultural conversion," that is, conversion into other economic activities.[92]

While the uses of biotechnology are relatively diverse, that is not the case with robotics and automated manufacture. The requirements for an indigenous robotics industry—capital, an advanced electronics sector, design engineers, a dearth of skilled labor—suggest that countries like Taiwan and Korea may follow Japan's example out of concern that Japan's automation will make their own products uncompetitive. On the other hand, automated factories assembling goods more swiftly, regularly, and economically than human beings pose a challenge to *middle-income* economies (Malaysia, Mexico), whose comparative advantage would be undercut. As for countries without a manufacturing base, it is difficult to see how the robotics revolution would have any meaning—except to further devalue the resource which they possess in abundance, masses of impoverished and under-educated human beings.

Finally, the global financial and communications revolution, and the emergence of multinational corporations, threatens to increase the gap between richer and poorer countries, even in the developing world. The industrial conglomerates of Korea are now positioning themselves to become multinational, and the East Asian NIEs in general are able to exploit the world economy (as can be seen in their trade balances, stock-markets, electronics industries, strategic marketing alliances, and so on). Furthermore, if the increasingly borderless world rewards entrepreneurs, designers, brokers, patent-owners, lawyers, and dealers in high value-added services, then East Asia's commitment to education, science, and technology can only increase its lead over other developing economies.

By contrast, the relative lack of capital, high-technology, scientists, skilled workers, and export industries in the poorer countries makes it difficult for them to take part in the communications and financial revolution, although several countries (Brazil, India) clearly hope to do so. Some grimmer forecasts suggest the poorer parts of the developing world may become more marginalized, partly because of the reduced economic importance of labor, raw materials, and food-stuffs, partly because the advanced economies may concentrate upon greater knowledge-based commerce among themselves.

7.

Is there any way of turning these trends around? Obviously, a society strongly influenced by fundamentalist mullahs with a dislike of "modernization" is unlikely to join the international economy; and it does not *have* to enter the borderless world if its people believe that it would be healthier, spiritually if not economically, to remain outside. Nor ought we to expect that countries dominated by selfish, authoritarian elites bent upon enhancing their military power—developing world countries spent almost $150 billion on weapons and armies in 1988 alone—will rush to imitate Japan and Singapore.

But what about those societies that wish to improve themselves yet find that they are hampered by circumstances? There are, after all, many developing countries, the vast majority of which depend upon exporting food and raw materials. With dozens of poor countries seeking desperately to sell their cane sugar or bananas or timber or coffee in the global market, prices fall and they are made more desperate.[93] Moreover, although much international aid goes to the developing world, in fact far more money flows out of impoverished countries of Africa, Asia, and Latin America and *into* the richer economies of Europe, North America, and Japan—to the tune of at least $43 billion each year.[94] This outward flow of interest repayments, repatriated profits, capital flight, royalties, fees for patents and information services, makes it difficult for poorer countries to get to their feet; and even if they were able to increase their industrial output, the result might be a large rise in "the costs of technological dependence."[95] Like their increasing reliance upon Northern suppliers for food and medical aid, this has created another dependency relationship for poorer nations.

In sum, as we move into the next century the developed economies appear to have all the trump cards in their hands—capital, technology, control of communications, surplus foodstuffs, powerful multinational companies[96]—and, if anything, their advantages are growing because technology is eroding the value of labor and materials, the chief assets of developing countries. Although nominally independent since decolonization, these countries are probably more dependent upon Europe and the United States than they were a century ago.

Ironically, three or four decades of efforts by developing countries to gain control of their own destinies—nationalizing Western companies, setting up commodity-exporting cartels, subsidizing indigenous manufacturing to achieve import substitution, campaigning for a new world order based upon redistribution of the existing imbalances of wealth—have all failed. The "market," backed by governments of the developed economies, has proved too strong, and the struggle against it has weakened developing economies still further—except those (like Korea and Taiwan) which decided to join.

While the gap between rich and poor in today's world is disturbing, those who have argued that this gap is unjust have all too often supported heavy-handed state interventionism and a retreat from open competition, which preserved indigenous production in the short term but rendered it less efficient against those stimulated by market forces. "Scientific socialism for Africa" may still appeal to some intellectuals,[97] but by encouraging societies to look inward it made them less well equipped to move to newer technologies in order to make goods of greater sophistication and value. And a new "world communications order," as proposed a few years ago by UNESCO to balance the West's dominance, sounds superficially attractive but would in all likelihood become the pawn of bureaucratic and ideological interests rather than function as an objective source of news reporting.

On the other hand, the advocates of free market forces often ignore the vast political difficulties which governments in developing countries would encounter in abolishing price controls, selling off national industries, and reducing food subsidies. They also forget that the spectacular commercial expansion of Japan and the East Asian NIEs was carried out by strong states which eschewed laissez faire. Instead of copying either socialist or free market systems, therefore, the developing countries might imitate East Asia's "mixed strategies" which combine official controls and private enterprise.[98]

Although the idea of a mixed strategy is intriguing, how can West or Central African countries imitate East Asia without a "strong state" apparatus, and while having a weak tradition of cooperation between government and firms, far lower educational achievements, and a different set of cultural attitudes toward family size or international economics? With the global scene less welcoming to industrializing newcomers, how likely are they to achieve the same degree of success as the East Asian NIEs did, when they "took off" a quarter-century ago?[99] Even if, by an economic miracle, the world's poorest fifty nations *did* adopt the Korean style of export-led growth in manufactures, would they not create the same crisis of overproduction as exists in the commodity markets today?

How many developing nations will be able to follow East Asia's growth is impossible to tell. The latest *World Development Report* optimistically forecast significant progress across the globe, provided that poorer nations adopted "market friendly" policies and richer nations eschewed protectionism.[100] Were Taiwan and Korea to be followed by the larger states of Southeast Asia such as Malaysia and Thailand, then by South Asia and a number of Latin American countries, that would blur the North-South divide and make international economic alignments altogether more variegated. Moreover, sustained manufacturing success among developing countries *outside* East Asia might stimulate imitation elsewhere.

At the moment, however, the usual cluster of factors influencing relative economic performance—cultural attitudes, education, political stability, capacity to carry out long-term plans—suggests that while a small but growing number of countries is moving from a "have-not" to a "have" status, many more remain behind. The story of winners and losers in history will continue, therefore, only this time modern communications will remind us all of the growing disparity among the world's nations and regions.

NOTES

1. Discussed further in my new book, *Preparing for the Twenty-First Century* (Random House, 1993).

2. For reasons of size and organization, China and India (containing around 37 percent of the world's population) are not treated here: for coverage, see Chapter 9, "India and China," of *Preparing for the Twenty-First Century*.

3. *World Tables 1991* (Washington, DC: World Bank, 1991), pp. 268–269, 352–353.

4. *World Tables 1991,* pp. 268–269, 352–353.

5. See the World Bank publication *Trends in Developing Economies,* 1990, pp. 299–303, for Korea.

6. For descriptions, see F. Braudel, *Civilization and Capitalism: Vol. 3, The Perspective of the World* (Harper and Row, 1986), pp. 506–511.

7. See P. Lyon, "Emergence of the Third World," in H. Bull and A. Watson, editors, *The Expansion of International Society* (Oxford University Press, 1983), p. 229 ff.; G. Barraclough, *An Introduction to Contemporary History* (Penguin, 1967), chapter 6, "The Revolt Against the West."

8. J. Ravenhill, "The North-South Balance of Power," *International Affairs,* Vol. 66, No. 4 (1990), pp. 745–746. See also, J. Cruickshank, "The Rise and Fall of the Third World: A Concept Whose Time Has Passed," *World Review,* February 1991, pp. 28–29. Ravenhill's divisions are high-income oil-exporting countries; industrializing economies with strong states and relatively low levels of indebtedness (Taiwan, etc.); industrializing economies with the state apparatus under challenge and/or with debt problems (Argentina, Poland); potential newly industrializing countries (Malaysia, Thailand); primary commodity producers (in sub-Saharan Africa, Central America).

9. Ravenhill, "The North-South Balance of Power," p. 732.

10. S. Fardoust and A. Dhareshwan, *Long-Term Outlook for the World Economy: Issues and Projections for the 1990s,* a World Bank report (February 1990), p. 9, Table 3.

11. W. L. M. Adriaansen and J. G. Waardensburg, editors, *A Dual World Economy* (Groningen: Wolters-Noordhoff, 1989).

12. P. Drysdale, "The Pacific Basin and Its Economic Vitality," in J. W. Morley, editor, *The Pacific Basin: New Challenges for the United States* (Academy of Political Science with the East Asian Institute and the Center on Japanese Economy and Business, 1986), p. 11.

13. While Korea has a population of around 43 million and Taiwan about 20 million, Hong Kong possesses 5.7 million and Singapore only 2.7 million.

14. See especially, "Taiwan and Korea: Two Paths to Prosperity," *The Economist,* July 14, 1990, pp. 19–21; also "South Korea" (survey), *The Economist,* August 18, 1990. There is a useful comparative survey in L. A. Veit, "Time of the New Asian Tigers," *Challenge,* July–August 1987, pp. 49–55.

15. N. D. Kristof, "In Taiwan, Only the Strong Get US Degrees," *The New York Times,* March 26, 1989, p. 11.

16. Figures taken, respectively, from J. Paxton, editor, *The Statesman's Yearbook 1990–1991* (St. Martin's Press, 1990); and from R. N. Gwynne, *New Horizons? Third World Industrialization in an International Framework* (New York/London: Wiley, 1990), p. 199.

17. Lest this 1987 figure appear too distant, note that Korea's sixth Five-Year Plan calls for a national savings rate of 33.5 percent in the early 1990s: see *Trends in Developing Economies,* p. 300. This table is taken from p. 31 (Table 10) of T. Fukuchi and M. Kagami, editors, *Perspectives on the Pacific Basin Economy: A Comparison of Asia and Latin America* (Tokyo: Asian Club Foundation, Institute of Developing Economics, 1990).

18. The table on p. 4 (Table 1) of Fukuchi and Kagami shows the different rates of growth, and of export's share of total GDP, of the Asian Pacific nations compared with those of Latin America. See also H. Hughes, "Catching Up: The Asian Newly Industrializing Economies in the 1990s," *Asian Development Review,* Vol. 7, No. 2 (1989), p. 132 (and Table 3).

19. "The Yen Block" (Survey), *The Economist,* July 15, 1989; "Japan Builds A New Power Base," *Business Week,* March 20, 1989, pp. 18–25.

20. "Taiwan and Korea: Two Paths to Prosperity," *The Economist,* p. 19; "South Korea: A New Society," *The Economist,* April 15, 1989, pp. 23–25.

21. "Development Brief," *The Economist,* May 26, 1990, p. 81, for the first two columns; the GNP per capita comes from *World Development Report,* 1990, pp. 178–179.

22. "When a Miracle Stalls," *The Economist,* October 6, 1990, pp. 33–34 (on Taiwan); *Trends in Developing Economies,* 1990, pp. 299–300 (Korea); R. A. Scalapino, "Asia and the United States: The Challenges Ahead," *Foreign Affairs,* Vol. 69, No. 1 (1989–1990), especially pp. 107–112; "Hong Kong, In China's Sweaty Palm," *The Economist,* November 5, 1988, pp. 19–22.

23. See the detailed forecasts in "Asia 2010: The Power of People," *Far Eastern Economist Review,* May 17, 1990, pp. 27–58. On industrial retooling, see pp. 8–9 of "South Korea" (Survey), *The Economist,* August 18, 1990.

24. N. Sadik, editor, *Population: The UNFPA Experience,* (New York University Press, 1984), chapter 4, "Latin America and the Caribbean," pp. 51–52.

25. A. F. Lowenthal, "Rediscovering Latin America," *Foreign Affairs,* Vol. 69, No. 4 (Fall 1990), p. 34.

26. Figure from "Latin America's Hope," *The Economist,* December 9, 1989, p. 14.

27. Taken from page 5 of G. W. Landau et al., *Latin America at a Crossroads* (The Trilateral Commission, 1990), which reports the source as being *Economic and Social Progress in Latin America: 1989 Report* (Washington, DC: Inter-American Development Bank, 1989), Table B1, p. 463.

28. As mentioned earlier, Japan and its East Asian emulators also sought to protect fledgling domestic industries, but that was in order to create a strong base from which to mount an export offensive—*not* to establish an economic bastion within which their industries would be content to remain.

29. For details, see the various national entries in *The Statesman's Year-Book 1990–91*; and *The Economist World Atlas and Almanac* (Prentice Hall, 1989), pp. 131–157. R. N. Gwynne's *New Horizons?* has useful comments on Latin America's "inward-oriented industrialization" (chapter 11), which he then contrasts with East Asia's "outward orientation" (chapter 12).

30. World Resources Institute, *World Resources 1990–91* (Oxford University Press, 1990), p. 39.

31. *World Resources 1990–91*, p. 240.

32. In 1989, the net transfer of capital leaving Latin America was around $25 billion.

33. For the above, see pp. 33–48 of *World Resources 1990–91*: "Latin America At a Crossroads," B. J. McCormick, *The World Economy: Patterns of Growth and Change* (Oxford University Press, 1988), chapter 13; "Latin American debt: The banks' great escape," *The Economist,* February 11, 1989, pp. 73–74.

34. For educational details, see *The Statesman's Year-Book 1990–91*, pp. 95, 236; for literacy rates, see especially those of Uruguay, Costa Rica, Argentina, and Venezuela in the table "Development Brief," *The Economist,* May 26, 1990, p. 81.

35. T. E. Martinez, "Argentina: Living with Hyperinflation," *The Atlantic Monthly,* December 1990, p. 36.

36. *The Statesman's Year-Book 1990–91*, pp. 584, 605.

37. T. Kamm, "Latin America Edges Toward Free Trade," *The Wall Street Journal,* November 30, 1990, p. A10.

38. C. Farnsworth, "Latin American Economies Given Brighter Assessments," *The New York Times,* October 30, 1990; "Latin America's New Start," *The Economist,* June 9, 1990, p. 11; N. C. Nash, "A Breath of Fresh Economic Air Brings Change to Latin America," *The New York Times,* November 13, 1991, pp. A1, D5.

39. "Latin America's Hope," *The Economist,* December 9, 1989, p. 15; Nash, "A Breath of Fresh Economic Air Brings Change to Latin America."

40. J. Brooke, "Debt and Democracy," *The New York Times,* December 5, 1990, p. A16; P. Truell, "As the U.S. Slumps, Latin America Suffers," *The Wall Street Journal,* November 19, 1990, p. 1.

41. For these arguments, see especially Lowenthal's fine summary, "Rediscovering Latin America," in *Foreign Affairs*; also G. A. Fauriol, "The Shadow of Latin American Affairs," *Foreign Affairs,* Vol. 69, No. 1 (1989–1990), pp. 116–134; and M. D. Hayes, "The U.S. and Latin America: A Lost Decade?" *Foreign Affairs,* Vol. 68, No. 1 (1988–1989), pp. 180–198.

42. This is the subdivision preferred by *The Economist World Atlas and Almanac,* pp. 256–271, which discusses the North African states (except Egypt) in a later section, under "Africa."

352   **PAUL KENNEDY**

43. "The Arab World" (survey), *The Economist,* May 12, 1990.
44. See "Religions," p. 21 of the *Hammond Comparative World Atlas* (Hammond, Inc., 1993 edition).
45. The few oil-producing countries in Africa, such as Gabon and Nigeria, still have relatively low per capita GNPs compared with the Arab Gulf states.
46. G. Brooks and T. Horwitz, "Shaken Sheiks," *The Wall Street Journal,* December 28, 1990, pp. A1, A4.
47. "The Arab World," *The Economist,* p. 12.
48. In 1985, adult female literacy in the Yemen Arab Republic was a mere 3 percent, in Saudi Arabia 12 percent, in Iran 39 percent. On the other hand, many women from the middle and upper-middle classes in Muslim countries are educated, which suggests that poverty, as much as culture, plays a role.
49. M. A. Heller, "The Middle East: Out of Step with History," *Foreign Affairs,* Vol. 69, No. 1 (1989–1990), pp. 153–171.
50. See also the remarks by S. F. Wells and M. A. Bruzonsky, editors, *Security in the Middle East: Regional Change and Great Power Strategies* (Westview Press, 1986), pp. 1–3.
51. D. E. Duncan, "Africa: The Long Good-bye," *The Atlantic Monthly,* July 1990, p. 20.
52. J. A. Marcum, "Africa: A Continent Adrift," *Foreign Affairs,* Vol. 68, No. 1 (1988–1989), p. 177. See also the penetrating article by K. R. Richburg, "Why Is Black Africa Overwhelmed While East Asia Overcomes?" *The International Herald Tribune,* July 14, 1992, pp. 1, 6.
53. C. H. Farnsworth, "Report by World Bank Sees Poverty Lessening by 2000 Except in Africa," *The New York Times,* July 16, 1990, p. A3; Marcum, "Africa: A Continent Adrift"; Duncan, "Africa: The Long Good-bye"; and "The bleak continent," *The Economist,* December 9, 1989, pp. 80–81.
54. B. Fischer, "Developing Countries in the Process of Economic Globalisation," *Intereconomics* (March/April 1990), p. 55.
55. J. S. Whitaker, *How Can Africa Survive?* (Council on Foreign Relations Press, 1988).
56. As will be clear from the text, this discussion excludes the Republic of South Africa.
57. T. J. Goliber, "Africa's Expanding Population: Old Problems, New Policies," *Population Bulletin,* Vol. 44, No. 3 (November 1989), pp. 4–49, an outstandingly good article.
58. *World Resources 1990–91,* p. 254.
59. *World Resources 1990–91,* p. 254 (overall population growth to 2025), and p. 258 (infant mortality). L. K. Altman, "W.H.O Says 40 Million Will Be Infected With AIDS by 2000," *The New York Times,* June 18, 1991, p. C3 (for percentage of GNP devoted to health care).
60. L. K. Altman, "W.H.O. Says 40 Million Will Be Infected With AIDS Virus by 2000"; and for further figures, see Kennedy, *Preparing for the Twenty-First Century,* chapter 3.
61. K. H. Hunt, "Scenes From a Nightmare," *The New York Times Magazine,* August 12, 1990, pp. 26, 50–51.
62. See Whitaker, *How Can Africa Survive?,* especially chapter 4, "The Blessings of Children," for a fuller analysis; and J. C. Caldwell and P. Caldwell, "High Fertility in Sub-Saharan Africa," *Scientific American,* May 1990, pp. 118–125.
63. "The bleak continent," *The Economist;* Whitaker, *How Can Africa Survive?,* chapters 1 and 2; Goliber, "Africa's Expanding Population," pp. 12–13.
64. Whitaker, *How Can Africa Survive?;* Duncan, "Africa: The Long Good-bye."
65. "Fruits of Containment" (op-ed), *The Wall Street Journal,* December 18, 1990, p.

A14, for the Africa-Belgium comparison; H. McRae, "Visions of tomorrow's world," *The Independent* (London), November 26, 1991, for Africa's share of world GDP.

66. "Aid to Africa," *The Economist,* December 8, 1990, p. 48.

67. In this regard, East Asian nations like Taiwan and Korea, possessing coherent indigenous populations, are once again more favorably situated.

68. *The Economist World Atlas and Almanac* (Prentice Hall, 1989), p. 293.

69. Apart from the country by country comments in *The Economist World Atlas and Almanac,* see also K. Ingham, *Politics in Modern Africa: The Uneven Tribal Dimension* (Routledge, 1990); "Africa's Internal Wars of the 1980s—Contours and Prospects," United States Institute of Peace, *In Brief,* No. 18 (May 1990).

70. T. R. Odhiambo, "Human resources development: problems and prospects in developing countries," *Impact of Science on Society,* No. 155 (1989), p. 214.

71. *The Statesman's Yearbook 1989,* p. 84; Goliber, "Africa's Expanding Population," p. 15.

72. *The Statesman's Yearbook 1989,* pp. 1,159–1,160 (certain smaller groups of students are excluded from these totals).

73. P. Lewis, "Nyerere and Tanzania: No Regrets at Socialism," *The New York Times,* October 24, 1990.

74. "Wind of change, but a different one," *The Economist,* July 14, 1990, p. 44. See also the encouraging noises made—on a country by country basis—in the World Bank's own *Trends in Developing Economies,* 1990, as well as in its 1989 publication *Sub-Saharan Africa: From Crisis to Sustainable Growth* (summarized in "The bleak continent," *The Economist,* pp. 80–81).

75. See especially P. Pradervand, *Listening to Africa: Developing Africa from the Grassroots* (Greenwood, 1989); B. Schneider, *The Barefoot Revolution* (London: I. T. Publications, 1988); K. McAfee, "Why the Third World Goes Hungry," *Commonweal,* June 15, 1990, pp. 384–385.

76. See Edward Sheehan's article "In the Heart of Somalia," *The New York Review,* January 14, 1993. See also Duncan, "Africa: The Long Goodbye," p. 24; G. Hancock, *Lords of Poverty: The Power, Prestige, and Corruption of the International Aid* (Atlantic Monthly Press, 1989); G. B. N. Ayittey, "No More Aid for Africa," *The Wall Street Journal,* October 18, 1991 (op-ed), p A 14.

77. Whitaker, *How Can Africa Survive?,* p. 231.

78. See, for example, the conclusions in B. Fischer, "Developing Countries in the Process of Economic Globalisation," pp. 55–63.

79. Caldwell and Caldwell, "High Fertility in Sub-Saharan Africa," *Scientific American,* p. 88.

80. "AIDS in Africa," *The Economist,* November 24, 1989, p. 1B; E. Eckholm and J. Tierney, "AIDS in Africa: A Killer Rages On," *The New York Times,* September 16, 1990, pp. 1, 4; C. M. Becker, "The Demo-Economic Impact of the AIDS Pandemic in Sub-Saharan Africa," *World Development,* Vol. 18, No. 12 (1990), pp. 1,599–1,619.

81. *World Resources 1990–91,* p. 254. The US-Canada total in 1960 was 217 million to Latin America's 210 million; by 2025 it is estimated to be 332 million to 762 million.

82. *World Resources 1990–91,* p. 254.

83. Apart from chapters 2 and 4 of *Preparing for the Twenty-First Century,* see again *World Resources 1990–91,* pp. 33–48; T. Wicker, "Bush Ventures South," *The New York Times,* December 9, 1990, p. E17; T. Golden, "Mexico Fights Cholera But Hates to Say Its Name," *The New York Times,* September 14, 1991, p. 2.

84. "The Arab World," *The Economist,* p. 4.

85. "The Arab World," p. 6; Y. F. Ibrahim, "In Algeria, Hope for Democracy But Not Economy," *The New York Times,* July 26, 1991, pp. A1, A6.

86. *World Resources 1990–91,* pp. 258–259.

87. As quoted in "The Arab World," p. 5.

88. See again Pradervand, *Listening to Africa.* Also important is D. Pearce et al., *Sustainable Development: Economics and Environment in the Third World* (Gower, 1990).

89. F. Gable, "Changing Climate and Caribbean Coastlines," *Oceanus,* Vol. 30, No. 4 (Winter 1987–1988), pp. 53–56; G. Gable and D. G. Aubrey, "Changing Climate and the Pacific," *Oceanus,* Vol. 32, No. 4 (Winter 1989–1990), pp. 71–73.

90. "The Arab World," p. 12.

91. *World Resources 1990–91,* pp. 176–177; *State of the World 1990,* pp. 48–49.

92. C. Juma, *The Gene Hunters: Biotechnology and the Scramble for Seeds* (Princeton University Press, 1989).

93. D. Pirages, *Global Technopolitics: The International Politics of Technology and Resources* (Brooks-Cole, 1989), p. 152.

94. McAfee, "Why the Third World Goes Hungry," p. 380.

95. See P. K Ghosh, editor, *Technology Policy and Development: A Third World Perspective* (Greenwood, 1984), p. 109.

96. C. J. Dixon et al., editors, *Multinational Corporations and the Third World* (Croom Helm, 1986).

97. For a good example, B. Onimode, *A Political Economy of the African Crisis* (Humanities Press International, 1988), especially p. 310 ff.

98. M. Clash, "Development Policy, Technology Assessment and the New Technologies," *Futures,* November 1990, p. 916.

99. L. Cuyvers and D. Van den Bulcke, "Some Reflections on the 'Outward-oriented' Development Strategy of the Far Eastern Newly Industrialising Countries," especially pp. 196–197, in Adriaansen and Waardenburg, *A Dual World Economy.*

100. *World Development Report 1991: The Challenge of Development,* a World Bank report (Oxford University Press, 1991). See also the World Bank's *Global Economic Prospects and the Developing Countries* (1991).

Emerging Technologies

WHAT'S AHEAD FOR 2001–2030

William E. Halal, Michael D. Kull, and Ann Leffmann

Revolutionary innovation is now occurring in all scientific and technological fields. This wave of unprecedented change is driven primarily by advances in information technology, but it is much larger in scope. We are not dealing simply with an Information Revolution but with a *Technology* Revolution.

To anticipate developments in this Technology Revolution, the George Washington University Forecast of Emerging Technologies was launched at the start of the 1990s. We have now completed four iterations of our Delphi survey—in 1990, 1992, 1994, and 1996—giving us a wealth of data and experience. We now can offer a reasonably clear picture of what can be expected to happen in technology over the next three decades.

Time horizons play a crucial role in forecasting technology. Forecasts of the next five to 10 years are often so predictable that they fall into the realm of market research, while those more than 30 or 40 years away are mostly speculation. This leaves a 10- to 20-year window in which to make useful forecasts. It is this time frame that our Forecast addresses.

The Forecast uses diverse methods, including environmental scanning, trend analysis, Delphi surveys, and scenario building. Environmental scanning is used to identify emerging technologies. Trend analysis guides the selection of the most important technologies for further study, and a modified Delphi survey is used to obtain forecasts. Instead of using the traditional Delphi method of providing

Article originally published in *The Futurist*, November-December 1997. Reprinted by permission of the World Future Society.

respondents with immediate feedback and requesting additional estimates in order to arrive at a consensus, we conduct another survey after an additional time period of about two years.

Finally, the results are portrayed in time periods to build scenarios of unfolding technological change. By using multiple methods instead of relying on a single approach, the Forecast can produce more robust, useful estimates.

For our latest survey, conducted in 1996, we selected 85 emerging technologies representing the most crucial advances that can be foreseen. We then submitted the list of technologies to our panel of futurists for their judgments as to when (or if) each technological development would enter the mainstream, the probability it would happen, and the estimated size of the economic market for it. In short, we sought a forecast as to when each emerging technology will have actually "emerged."

The respondents include prominent futurists, forecasters, and technical experts, such as authors Marvin Cetron and Joseph F. Coates and mathematician Olaf Helmer, the co-inventor of the Delphi technique. Panelists only respond to questions when they feel confident that they know enough to render an informed judgment. Their responses have shown remarkable consistency: Overall, the average variance appears to be on the order of plus or minus three years.

Infotech to Lead Parade

The results indicate that a wave of major technological advances seems likely to arrive during the next three decades. Highly important technological innovations

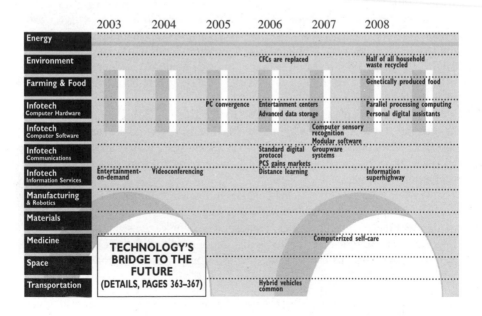

are occurring in all fields, and most of the new technologies under study will arrive between the years 2003 and 2025. It seems clear that almost all fields of endeavor are undergoing a serious transformation that will, in turn, transform society.

The four information-technology fields—computer hardware, computer software, communications, and information services—appear to lead this wave of innovation by about five years.

This finding fits our theory that information technology serves as the principal factor now driving the Technology Revolution.

Space appears to be the lagging field. Some relatively simple space technologies are likely to arrive fairly soon, particularly the privatization of space efforts, but almost all serious technologies seem destined to wait about 30–60 years for their development and implementation. Space programs can be most readily postponed because the payoffs are uncertain and distant; furthermore, serious space exploration beyond the solar system will require technological breakthroughs that transcend our present knowledge of physics.

Highlights of Latest Survey

Information technologies may lead all others, but advances may be slower to come than conventional wisdom currently suggests. Entertainment-on-demand is not expected until 2003, and the time when half of all goods in the United States are sold through information services will not come until 2018.

Personal digital assistants will not be adopted by the majority of people until 2008. Personal computers may soon be able to incorporate television, telephone,

	2009	2010	2011	2012	2013	2014	2015	2016
		Alternative energy sources	Organic energy sources					Energy efficiency
		Green environmental methods					Industrial ecology	Fossil fuels cut greenhouse gas; Recycled goods
				Farm chemicals drop by one-half		Aquaculture	Precision farming; Alternative/organic farming; Hydroponic produce	
					Optical computers			
	Intelligent agents; Ubiquitous computing environment	Expert systems		Machine learning; Computer language translation			Neural networks	
	Broadband networks							
	Electronic banking/cash				Online publishing			Nanotechnology; Sophisticated robots
			Mass customization	Computer-integrated manufacturing			Factory jobs drop to 10%	Material composites
			Buckyballs and buckytubes		Half of autos recyclable	Ceramic engines	Superconducting materials	
	Holistic health care				Gene therapy; Major diseases cured	Computerized vision implants		
			Electric cars are common					Fuel-cell electric cars; Intelligent transportation systems

and interactive video, but our panel did not see this or a Web-TV with telephone capabilities in wide use until 2005 or 2006.

Software also has a way to go. Although search engines are used on the Web, we will not see intelligent software agents in routine use until 2009. Expert systems, once heralded as the decision-making software for the 1990s, have a 72% chance of finding routine use by 2010. Computer programs that can learn and adjust their own programming will not be commonly available until 2012. Language translation has a similar fate, not achieving widespread use until 2012.

Computerized medical systems should be in common use by 2007. Two years later, holistic health practices will be well integrated into medicine. Gene therapy will be eradicating inherited diseases by 2013. Growing genetically similar or cloned organs is likely by 2018.

Automation and computer-integrated manufacturing should result in the proportion of factory jobs declining from 20% of the current work force to less than 10% by 2015. The helpful robot servants may arrive in 2016.

Promising advances in nanotechnology and microscopic machines could lead to the development of self-assembling and intelligent materials around 2026 or 2027. A form of carbon known as buckminster-fullerene, or "Buckyballs," will become significant in developing new materials by 2011.

Genetic engineering should allow the routine production of new strains of plants and animals by 2008. In 2015, the majority of farmers will have adopted organic or alternative farming methods, and the use of chemical fertilizers and pesticides will have declined by 2012 to less than half of current usage. However, automated farming and urban greenhouses will not appear until 2020.

By 2010 or so we should expect manufacturers to have adopted "green" meth-

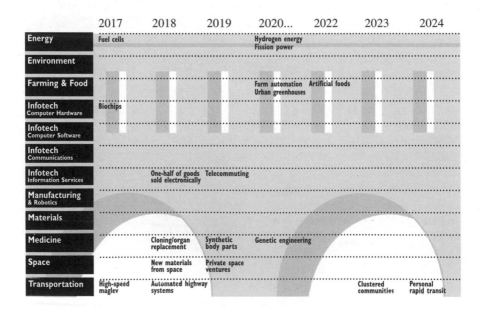

ods, and a significant portion of energy will be derived from renewable sources and biomass. Improvements in fossil-fuel efficiency will reduce greenhouse-gas emissions by one-half by 2016.

The technologies that may have the most direct impact on daily lives are in transportation. By 2017, high-speed rail systems will connect major cities of the developed world. Around this time, we will see automated highway systems and intelligent transportation systems commonly used to reduce traffic congestion.

Space remains the most intriguing frontier, but advances here are the most difficult to forecast since they require massive project planning, coordination with the government, and, increasingly, international collaboration. The exploration of Mars will begin with the completion of a manned mission in 2037. Five years after that, in 2042, a spaceship or probe will be launched to explore a neighboring star system.

The 2001–2010 Decade

The data allow us to create a longitudinal scenario covering the first three decades of the new millennium.

In the first decade of the twenty first century, the Information Revolution should mature, producing major advances in all fields. Multimedia interconnectivity will allow people to interact seamlessly across diverse information media and geographic borders. Virtual reality and large flat panel displays will take the place of the computer monitor, permitting simultaneous viewing of several applications at once, virtual meetings, and group collaboration.

Education, entertainment, commerce, and tourism will enter a new era of

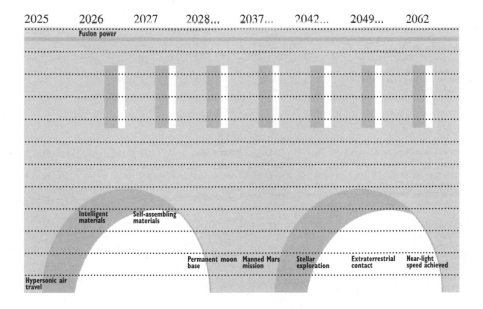

The Technological Road Ahead

Here is a chronology based on the George Washington University Forecast of Emerging Technologies.

The panel estimated the probability (in percent) of each forecast being realized by a given date as well as the likely market demand for it (in dollars). The number in parentheses indicates the technological category of each forecast in the list of 85 forecasts on pages 363–367.

Technology and Category (see pages 363–367 for details)	Probability (in percent)	Demand (in millions of dollars)	Technology and Category (see pages 363–367 for details)	Probability (in percent)	Demand (in millions of dollars)
2003			**2015**		
Entertainment-on-demand (7)	84%	$90 million	Neural networks (5)	61%	$28 million
2004			Alternative/organic farming (3)	57	76
Videoconferencing (7)	83	44	Superconducting materials (9)	56	43
2005			Industrial ecology (2)	55	48
PC convergence (4)	84	111	Hydroponic produce (3)	53	40
2006			**2016**		
Entertainment centers (4)	83	109	Nanotechnology (8)	66	31
Distance learning (7)	78	41	Recycled goods (2)	66	126
CFCs are replaced (2)	77	52	Sophisticated robots (8)	64	130
Advanced data storage (4)	75	44	Energy efficiency (1)	61	49
Standard digital protocol (6)	70	70	Fossil fuels cut greenhouse gas (2)	59	46
Hybrid vehicles common (12)	69	87	Fuel-cell electric cars (12)	58	116
PCS gains markets (6)	56	42	Intelligent transportation systems (12)	58	90
2007			Material composites (9)	53	100
Computerized self-care (10)	82	87	**2017**		
Groupware systems (6)	75	33	High-speed maglev (12)	58	120
Computer sensory recognition (5)	73	34	Biochips (4)	54	58
Modular software (5)	72	47	Fuel cells (1)	53	61
2008			**2018**		
Parallel processing computing (4)	80	64	New materials from space (11)	57	21
Information Superhighway (6)	78	74	One-half of goods sold electronically (7)	55	208
Genetically produced food (3)	75	67	Automated highway systems (12)	55	70
Personal digital assistants (4)	75	54	Cloning/organ replacement (10)	53	63
Half of all household waste recycled (2)	74	53	**2019**		
2009			Private space ventures (11)	62	60
Intelligent agents (5)	79	28	Synthetic body parts (10)	58	68
Ubiquitous computing environment (5)	75	32	Telecommuting (7)	56	468
Broadband networks (6)	70	103	**2020**		
Electronic banking/cash (7)	70	69	Farm automation (3)	60	82
Holistic health care (10)	61	55	Urban greenhouses (3)	53	55
2010			Genetic engineering (10)	53	21
Alternative energy sources (1)	77	46	Hydrogen energy (1)	50	102
"Green" environmental methods (2)	73	90	Fission power (1)	46	26
Expert systems (5)	72	59	**2022**		
2011			Artificial foods (3)	39	75
Mass customization (8)	73	330	**2023**		
Electric cars are common (12)	70	102	Clustered communities (12)	53	85
Organic energy sources (1)	60	43	**2024**		
Buckyballs and buckytubes (9)	59	20	Personal rapid transit (12)	43	62
2012			**2025**		
Computer-integrated manufacturing (8)	73	124	Hypersonic air travel (12)	48	91
Machine learning (5)	67	31	**2026**		
Computer language translation (5)	65	41	Intelligent materials (9)	57	66
Farm chemicals drop by one-half (3)	60	27	Fusion power (1)	50	113
2013			**2027**		
Gene therapy (10)	63	63	Self-assembling materials (9)	56	82
Online publishing (7)	60	66	**2028**		
Major diseases cured (10)	58	116	Permanent moon base (11)	55	32
Half of autos recyclable (9)	58	51	**2037**		
2014			Manned Mars mission (11)	59	30
Optical computers (4)	64	67	**2042**		
Ceramic engines (9)	58	49	Stellar exploration (11)	51	47
Aquaculture (3)	56	52	**2049**		
Computerized vision implants (10)	56	32	Extraterrestrial contact (11)	33	45
2015			**2062**		
Precision farming (3)	69	71	Near-light speed achieved (11)	43	75
Factory jobs drop to 10% (8)	67	150			

electronic access. Sophisticated software will aid consumers and professionals by providing intelligent agents to filter news and mail. Expert systems may see routine use as surrogate doctors, lawyers, and other professionals.

The medical community will have accepted the validity of holistic methods and computerized self-care. New genetic strains of plants and animals will provide designer foods and customized farming.

Alternative forms of energy, environmental management, and transportation will also seriously begin to alter lifestyles. Pollution control and highly effective recycling efforts will become normal in developed countries, which may allow developing countries such as China to leapfrog "dirty" industrialization in favor of "clean" and sustainable development.

The 2011–2020 Decade

The early 2010s will witness the most striking technological advances in terms of number, scope, and sophistication that civilization has ever seen.

Electronic working, learning, shopping, and publishing will become a way of life, much as automobiles became a way of life a few decades ago. More powerful computers incorporating optical technologies and biochips will begin to simulate the human brain in sensory recognition and thought processing.

This will be the decade of information technology diffusion, transforming other fields. Academic research will be performed anywhere, at any library, with any colleagues. Travelers can know where they are or where their baggage is at any given moment through satellite global positioning networks, and much of travel itself will become virtual.

Information technology will allow parents to check on their kids, farmers to check on their crops, and states to check on criminals. Automated factories will translate personal details of a consumer's taste into mass-customized products that suit individual needs. Blue-collar jobs will dwindle to less than 10% of the work force.

Gene therapy will cure or prevent diseases, and genetic pioneers may try to improve the genome of normal humans who want to be smarter, stronger, or longer-lived. Farmers will genetically manipulate plants to improve yields and make crops resistant to pests and spoilage. The cloning and/or manufacture of body organs should help increase lifespans. Composite materials, nanotechnology, and a variety of other methods will permit the production of almost any physical object, while maglev trains, fuel-cell powered cars, and intelligent transportation systems should allow vastly improved mobility.

The 2021–2030 Decade

The third decade of the twenty-first century will see expansion into bold new frontiers, notably advanced materials, exotic forms of transportation, and space. The capabilities of intelligent and self-assembling materials, fusion power, artificial foods, and other advanced technologies will improve dramatically.

Nations will find their influence declining relative to multinational corporations and virtual or "clustered" communities. This trend is likely to create tension between local versus global concerns. A worldwide consensus will be needed for progress on complex, controversial problems of population, environmental sustainability, space development, and human bioengineering. No single nation can readily provide the resources necessary to mount huge projects such as an advanced space program or a planetary energy grid. If society wishes to pursue these goals, a profound restructuring of international relations lies ahead.

Plans for Forecast Project's Future

The George Washington University Forecast has reached its current state of development by dint of continual improvements during and between four iterations covering almost an entire decade. More improvements are anticipated: We are in the process of refining the clarity and focus of the question series and of strengthening the panel through more rigorous selection methods. These plans should make the next forecast, to be conducted in 1998, significantly better.

An experimental Web site has been developed that allows individuals to access the latest results electronically and to enter their own estimates. We are now considering the possibility of using this idea to replace the biennial round-by-round approach to provide a continuous stream of data. Individuals on the Web could enter their estimates, and these would be compared with the expert panelists. The role of the research team would be to identify emerging technologies and serve as the system's gatekeepers.

With some support, we can easily envision this concept being expanded to the point where it would become a national, or even international system that draws on the estimates of thousands of people to provide continually updated forecasts online. In addition to gaining far more sophisticated data, such a system would also serve the crucial purpose of engaging students, scholars, policy makers, and the public in a stimulating educational dialogue that raises the general level of understanding of technological change. We anticipate this advance by the end of 1998.

The authors have conducted the Forecast without funding. Sponsors are currently being sought to support more ambitious plans. We hope that the encouraging potential of our approach will prove attractive to interested foundations who wish to lend their resources toward improving the Forecast.

The study makes one overwhelming conclusion abundantly clear: The Technology Revolution seems destined to transform modern civilization. And because the wave of historic innovation is so unprecedented that it is likely to change continuously even as we move through it, there is little alternative but to constantly monitor and forecast progress in science and technology in order to guide progress more wisely.

THE EMERGING TECHNOLOGIES FROM
THE FORECAST PROJECT

Here is a summary of the 85 emerging technologies, grouped in 12 categories, together with the Forecast panel's consensus estimate of the year each will occur.

I. Energy

Alternative energy sources: A significant portion (10%) of energy usage is derived from alternative energy sources, such as geothermal, hydroelectric, solar/photoelectric. 2010

Energy efficiency: Energy efficiency improves by 50% through innovations in transportation, industrial processing, environmental control, etc. 2016

Fuel cells: Fuel cells, converting fuels to electricity, are commonly used (30%). 2017

Organic energy sources: Biological materials, such as crops, trees, and other forms of organic matter, are used as significant (10%) energy sources. 2011

Fission power: Fission nuclear power is used for 50% of electricity generation. 2020

Hydrogen energy: Hydrogen becomes routinely used in energy systems. 2020

Fusion power: Fusion nuclear power is used commercially for electricity produc tion. 2026

2. Environment

CFCs are replaced: The majority of CFCs (chlorofluorocarbons) are replaced by materials that do not damage the ozone layer. 2006

Household waste: One-half of the waste from households in developed countries is recycled. 2008

"Green" manufacturing: Most manufacturers adopt "green" methods that minimize environmental pollution. 2010

Recycled goods: The majority of manufactured goods use recycled materials. 2016

Fossil fuels produce less greenhouse gas: Improvements in fossil fuel energy efficiency and greater use of alternative energy sources reduce "greenhouse" gas emissions by one-half from current volumes. 2016

Industrial ecology: The majority of manufacturing facilities use industrial ecology (eco-industrial parks operating as a closed system) to reduce waste pollution. 2006

3. Farming & Food

Genetically produced food: Genetic engineering techniques are routinely used to produce new strains of plants and animals. 2008

Farm chemicals drop: The use of chemical fertilizers and pesticides declines by half. 2012

Alternative/organic farming: The majority of farming in industrialized countries incorporates alternative/organic farming techniques into traditional methods. 2015

Aquaculture: Seafood grown using aquaculture provides the majority of seafood consumed. 2014

Farm automation: Automation of farming methods, using technology such as robotics, is common (over 30%). 2020

Precision farming: Computerized control of irrigation, seeding, fertilizer, pesticides, etc., is common (over 30%). 2015

Urban greenhouses: Urban production of fruits and vegetables using greenhouses and/or other intensive production systems is common (over 30%). 2020

Hydroponic produce: Produce grown using hydroponic methods is common (over 30%). 2015

Artificial foods: Artificial meats, vegetables, bread, etc., are commonly (over 30%) consumed. 2022

4. Infotech Computer Hardware

Personal digital assistants: Hand-held microcomputers are used by the majority of people to manage their work and personal affairs. 2008

Parallel processing: Supercomputers using massive parallel processing are commonly used (30%). 2008

PCs include interactive television: Personal computers incorporate television, telephone, and interactive video transmission. 2005

Entertainment center: An entertainment center combining interactive television, telephone, and computer capability is commercially available for home use. 2006

Optical computers: Computers using photons rather than electrons to code information enter the commercial marketplace. 2014

Advanced data storage: More advanced forms of data storage (optical, non-volatile semiconductor, magnetic memory, etc.) are standard on multimedia personal computers. 2006

Biochips: "Biochips" that store data in molecular bonds are commercially available. 2017

5. Infotech Computer Software

Modular software: The majority of software is generated automatically using software modules (object-oriented programming, CASE tools, etc.). 2007

Expert systems: Routine use of expert systems helps decision making in management, medicine, engineering, and other fields. 2010

Computer sensory recognition: Voice, handwriting, and optical recognition features allow ordinary personal computers to interact with humans. 2007

Computer translation: Computers are able to routinely translate languages in real-time with the accuracy and speed necessary for effective communications. 2012

Intelligent agents: Knowbots, navigators, and other intelligent software agents routinely filter and retrieve information for users. 2009

Ubiquitous computing environment: Embedded processors in common objects are integrated into the workplace and home. 2009

Neural networks: Computations are commonly (more than 30%) performed by neural networks using parallel processors. 2015

Machine learning: Computer programs are commonly available that learn by trial and error in order to adjust their behavior. 2012

6. Infotech Communications

Personal communication systems: PCS has a significant (10%) share of the market for voice communications. 2006

Standard digital protocol: Most communications systems (80%) in industrialized countries adopt a standard digital protocol. 2006

Information superhighway: Most people (80%) in developed countries access an information superhighway. 2008

Groupware systems: Groupware systems are routinely used for simultaneously working and learning together at multiple sites. 2007

Broadband networks: ISDN, ATM, fiber optics, etc., connect the majority of homes and offices. 2009

7. Infotech Information Services

Entertainment-on-demand: A variety of movies, TV shows, sports, and other forms of entertainment can be selected electronically at home on demand. 2003

Videoconferencing: Teleconferencing is routinely used in industrialized countries for business meetings. 2004

Online publishing: The majority of books and publications are published online. 2007

Electronic banking and cash: Electronic banking, including electronic cash, replaces paper, checks, and cash as the principal means of commerce. 2009

Electronic sales: Half of all goods in the United States are sold through information services. 2018

Telecommuting: Most employees (80%) perform their jobs at least partially from remote locations by telecommuting. 2019

Distance learning: Schools and colleges commonly use computerized teaching programs and interactive television lectures and seminars, as well as traditional methods. 2006

8. Manufacturing & Robotics

Computer-integrated manufacturing: CIM is used in most (80%) factory operations. 2012

Factory jobs decline below 10%: Due to automation, factory jobs decline to less than 10% of the work force. 2015

Mass customization: Mass customization of cars, appliances, and other products is commonly (30%) available. 2011

Sophisticated robots: Robots that have sensory input, make decisions, learn, and are mobile become commercially available. 2016

Nanotechnology: Microscopic machines and/or nanotechnology are developed into commercial applications. 2016

9. Materials

Ceramic engines: Ceramic engines are mass-produced for commercial vehicles. 2014

Half of all autos are recyclable: Recyclable plastic composites are used in making half of all automobiles. 2013

Superconducting materials: Superconducting materials are commonly used (30%) for transmitting electricity in electronic devices, such as energy, medical, and communications applications. 2015

Material composites: Material composites replace the majority of traditional metals in product designs. 2016

"Buckyballs": The form of carbon known as "Buckyballs" (or "Buckytubes") is instrumental in developing new materials. 2011

Self-assembling materials: Self-assembling materials are routinely used commercially. 2027

Intelligent materials: Smart materials are routinely used in homes, offices, and vehicles. 2026

10. Medicine

Self-care: Computerized information systems are commonly used for medical care, including diagnosis, dispensing prescriptions, monitoring medical conditions, and self-care. 2007

Holistic health care: Holistic approaches to health care, both physical and mental, become accepted by the majority of the medical community. 2009

Genetic engineering of children: Parents can routinely choose characteristics of their children through genetic engineering. 2020

Gene therapy: Genetic therapy is routinely used to prevent and/or cure an inherited disease. 2013

Organ replacement: Living organs and tissue produced genetically are routinely used for replacement. 2019

Synthetic body parts: Artificial organs and tissue produced synthetically are routinely used for replacement. 2019

Computerized vision: Computerized vision implants are commercially available to correct eye defects. 2014

Major disease cured: A cure or preventive treatment for a major disease such as cancer or AIDS is found. 2013

11. Space

Private space ventures: Private corporations perform the majority of space launches as private ventures. 2019

Manned mission to Mars: A manned mission to Mars is completed. 2037

Permanent moon base: A permanently manned moon base is established. 2028

Stellar exploration: A spaceship is launched to explore a neighboring star system. 2042

New materials from space: Chemicals, metals, etc., that cannot be created on Earth are developed in space, where conditions allow it due to such factors as the absence of gravity and air pollution. 2018

Spaceships travel at near-light speed: Spaceships or probes reach 80% or more of the speed of light. 2062

Extraterrestrial contact: Intelligent life is contacted elsewhere in the universe. 2049

12. Transportation

High-speed trains: High-speed rail or maglev trains are available between most major cities in developed countries. 2017

Hybrid vehicles: Vehicles that combine electric and internal combustion engines are commercially available. 2006

Electric cars: Battery-powered electric cars are commonly (30%) available. 2006

Fuel-cell cars: Electric cars powered by fuel cells are commonly (30%) available. 2016

Hypersonic planes: Aircraft traveling at more than five times the speed of sound are used for the majority of transoceanic flights. 2025

Automated highways: Automated highway systems are commonly (30%) used to control speed, steering, braking, etc. 2018

Intelligent transportation: Intelligent transportation systems are commonly (30%) used to reduce highway congestion. 2016

Personal rapid transit: Car-like capsules on guide rails or other personal rapid transit systems are installed in most metropolitan areas. 2024

Clustered communities: Clustered, self-contained communities in urban areas reduce the need for local transportation. 2023

William E. Halal, Michael D. Kull, and Ann Leffmann

Panel for Latest George Washington University Forecast

About 45 well-known futurists and technical experts have participated in George Washington University's Forecast of Emerging Technologies.

Among participants in the 1996 Forecast were **Marvin J. Cetron,** president of Forecasting International, Ltd.; **Joseph F. Coates,** principal of Coates and Jarratt, Inc.; **Jerome C. Glenn,** coordinator of the United Nations University's Millennium Project Feasibility Study; **Theodore J. Gordon,** retired chairman of The Futures Group; **Olaf Helmer,** co-inventor of the Delphi Technique; **Harold A. Linstone,** editor of the journal *Technological Forecasting and Social Change;* **Joseph P. Martino,** Technological Forecasting Editor of THE FUTURIST; and **John L. Petersen,** author of *Out of the Blue* and *The Road to 2015.*

[EDITOR'S NOTE: The latest version of the George Washington University Forecast is on the World Wide Web at http://www.gwforecast.gwu.edu]

The Promise of Genetics

*Joseph F. Coates, John B. Mahaffie,
and Andy Hines*

Genetics will be a key enabling technology of the twenty-first century, rivaling information technology, materials technology, and energy technology in importance.

The effects of all of these enabling technologies will be far-reaching across business and society, but advances in genetics in particular will be fundamental to many science and technology areas and societal functions, including health and medicine, food and agriculture, nanotechnology, and manufacturing.

One benefit of genetics that is already highly visible is in forensics. DNA identification will significantly enhance criminology. It may contribute to declines in violent crime, the identification of deadbeat parents, and the prevention of fraud. It may even deter rape and murder, as potential perpetrators fear leaving their DNA "fingerprints" on the scene.

Rising public interest in genetics is tied to the growing realization that humanity is capable of directly shaping its own and other species' evolution. We will no longer have to wait for nature's relatively slow natural selection. Genetics will bring the capability of speeding and redirecting evolution along paths of our choice. Eliminating genetic diseases, for instance, might take centuries through natural selection but could be accomplished in decades through genetic manipulation.

Article originally appeared in *The Futurist,* September-October 1997. This article draws upon the authors' book *2025: Scenarios of U.S. and Global Society Reshaped by Science and Technology* (Oakhill Press, 1997). Reprinted by permission.

This power will doubtless inspire a profound global debate about how genetics should and should not be used.

The Genetic Economy

On the economic front, genetics could reward those who invest in it for the long haul. It is an industry for patient capital. Its spread over many industries will make it an increasingly important factor in the global economy.

Genetics is not a typical industry, in that it is not measured as a separate entity. It will be a part of, or embedded in, so many industries that government statisticians will not attempt such a measure. A good guess is that genetics will account for about 20% of gross domestic product, or roughly $2 trillion in 2025.

The early emphasis on using genetics to improve human health and battle disease will be supplemented with more exotic applications, such as manufacturing and materials, human enhancement, energy, environmental engineering, and species restoration and management. The food and agriculture industries, for example, are steadily expanding their use of genetics. Advances will come from applying what seem like isolated breakthroughs into a systems framework. For example, researchers working on eradicating a species of locust may develop a microorganism useful in converting crop wastes into biomass energy.

Genetics and Species Management

The genomes of many animals, fish, insects, and microorganisms will be worked out, leading to more refined management, control, and manipulation of their health and propagation—or their elimination.

• **Designer animals.** Routine genetic programs will be used to enhance animals used for food production, recreation, and even pets. Goats, for example, are especially well suited to genetic manipulation. In affluent nations, goats will be used for producing pharmaceutical compounds; in less-developed nations, goats will produce high-protein milk.

Livestock will be customized to increase growth, shorten gestation, and enhance nutritional value. Farmers will be able to order the genes they want from gene banks for transmission to local biofactories, where the animals with the desired characteristics will then be produced and shipped.

Transgenic animals, sharing the genes of two or more species, may be created to withstand rough environments. Genes from the hardy llama in South America, for example, could be introduced into camels in the Middle East—and vice versa—to greatly expand the range of each. Some species will be introduced into entirely new areas. Parrots may be modified to withstand cold North American temperatures, becoming a boon to bird watchers in the United States.

Transgenic pets may become popular: Genes from mild-mannered Labrador retrievers could be put into pit bull terrier genomes.

• **Pest control.** Genetics will play a central role in pest management. The arms race between insects and pesticides has been marked by humans winning battles, but insects winning the war. Genetics will turn the tide.

One method is to breed pheromones into surrounding plants to lure pests away from their intended prey. Pests will also be sterilized through genetic engineering to disrupt their populations. Genetically engineered resistance to pests will be common through such techniques as inducing the plants to produce their own protective or repellant compounds.

Insects that carry disease will also be targeted through genetic engineering to control their populations. It is hoped that malaria will soon be eliminated this way.

• **Boosting plants.** Future farmers may have near total control over plant genetics. Plants will give higher yields and be more resistant to disease, frost, drought, and stress. They will have higher protein, lower oil, and more efficient photosynthesis rates than ever before. Natural processes such as ripening will be enhanced and controlled.

Genetics will allow farmers to customize and fine-tune crops, building in flavor, sweeteners, and preservatives, while increasing nutritional value. [See box, "Future Foods: The New Genetic Menu," page 373.]

The first step in agrogenetics is to identify disease-resistant genes; the second step is to put them into plants. Eventually, plants will be genetically engineered to produce specific prevention factors against likely disease invaders.

Forestry will also benefit from genetics. Genetic manipulation will result in superior tree strains with disease resistance and improved productivity. Trees will be routinely engineered to allow nonchemical pulping for use in paper making. Genetic forests will also help in the global restoration of many denuded areas.

• **Engineering microorganisms.** Manufacturers will use engineered microorganisms to produce commodity and specialty chemicals, as well as medicines, vaccines, and drugs. Groups of microorganisms, often working in sequence as living factories, will produce useful compounds. They will also be widely used in agriculture, mining, resource upgrading, waste management, and environmental cleanup. Oil- and chemical-spill cleanups are a high-profile application.

The development of so-called suicidal microorganisms will be an important factor. Engineered microorganisms would self-destruct by expressing a suicide gene after their task is accomplished. These would be developed in response to fears of runaways—that is, harmful genetically engineered microorganisms that rapidly spread destructive power. They would be particularly useful in the bioremediation of solid and hazardous waste sites and in agricultural applications such as fertilizers.

Genetics in Industry

Genetics will first become a force in improving human health, food, and agriculture. But over the next few decades it will have a greater impact across many industries, such as chemical engineering, environmental engineering, manufacturing, energy, and information technology. It will even contribute to the burgeoning field of artificial life.

GENETICS IN 2025

Application	*Genetics' Potential Impacts*
Health	Eliminate almost 2,000 single gene diseases, such as Huntington's Chorea. Cut in half the diseases with genetic predispositions, including dozens of cancers.
Behavior	Substantial reduction of schizophrenia. Education overhauled to tailor learning to individual genetic/cognitive profiles.
Forensics	Reduction in auto thefts, kidnapping, fraud, and other crimes due to DNA identification and security systems.
Livestock	Revival of pork industry with custom-designed varieties, such as ultra-lean pork.
Fisheries	Overwhelmed natural fisheries supplemented by aquafarms specializing in transgenic specialty fish.
Pest management	Crop loss due to pests reduced by two-thirds in the United States; Lyme disease eliminated.
Crops	Intermittent blights eliminated, allowing record yields of Irish potatoes, Kansas wheat, and Japanese rice.
Food	The number of foods making up 90% of the typical human diet rises from six to 37; foods are customized according to consumers' taste, preparation, and storage needs.
Forestry	Superior strains of trees allow worldwide tree coverage to double.
Microorganisms	Specialty chemicals, medicines, and foods are produced in bioreactors, enhancing agriculture, mining, waste management, and other industries.
Chemical engineering	Databases of molecules allow more rapid and accurate design of chemicals.
Environmental engineering	Bioremediation becomes primary cleanup mechanism in many hazardous waste sites.
Materials	One-third of people in affluent nations use biosensors to monitor their health.
Manufacturing	Bioreactors exploiting biological processes approaching the nanoscale are in widespread use for manufacturing nondurable goods.
Energy	Conversion efficiency of biomass triples. Oil recovery is enhanced.
Infotech	Genetic algorithms are applied to software programming, enabling neural network computers that mimic the intelligence level of chimps.

Source: *2025: Scenarios of U.S. and Global Society Reshaped by Science and Technology.*

Chemical engineering, for example, has begun "biologizing"—i.e., incorporating an understanding of complex biological interactions. Genetics will help the chemical industry shift away from bulk chemicals to higher value-added products, such as food additives or industrial enzymes used as biocatalysts.

Genetic engineering will also help to clean the environment and may be used to create totally artificial environments, such as in space and seabed stations or even for terraforming Mars.

Manufacturing, too, will become "biologized" and more like breeding. Manufacturing applications of genetics will include molecular engineering for pharmaceuticals and other compounds, rudimentary DNA chips, biosensors, and nanotechnology based on biological principles such as self-assembly.

A key consideration in biologizing will be society's commitment to sustainability, which could drive a search for environmentally benign manufacturing strategies. Biological approaches, while slower than mechanistic ones, could prove more sustainable. In the future, all industrial enzymes may be produced by genetic engineering. Already, recombinant DNA is used in cheese making, wine making, textiles, and paper production. Bioreactors, in which engineered living cells are used as biocatalysts, will be used for new kinds of manufacturing, such as making new tree species.

Linkages may be found between genetics and information technology: Researchers are striving for ways to take advantage of the fact that genes are pure information. A whole new discipline is evolving: "bioinformatics" to manage and interpret the flood of new biological and genomic data. A science of biological computing is also likely to evolve and compete successfully with silicon-based computing.

Genetics and information technology would work together in advanced computers. Biophotonic computers using biomolecules and photonic processors could be the fastest switching systems ever built.

Genetics and Global Development

Genetics could be a tool for igniting a second Green Revolution in agriculture. Synthetic soil supplements, crop strains that accommodate a land's existing conditions, and integrated pest management techniques could be a boon to developing countries, such as India, facing burgeoning population growth on increasingly tired and overworked cropland.

Another potential economic benefit of genetics may be in tourism. Kenya, for instance, could promote tourism associated with wildlife by strengthening its indigenous species. Genetics could be used to rescue lions and elephants from extinction by boosting their food supply or developing vaccines to prevent viral attacks.

Like Kenya, Brazil has an economic opportunity in protecting and enhancing its biodiversity. Brazil's niche would be in pharmaceuticals and other chemicals, and it could tap its lush tropical forests—storehouses of over half the world's plant and animal species. Genes that promote rapid growth could be engineered into the native rain-forest tree species, thus helping to save forests once thought to be lost forever.

Genetics to Improve Human Health

Genetics will increasingly enable health professionals to identify, treat, and prevent the 4,000 or more genetic diseases and disorders that our species is heir to. Genetics will become central to diagnosis and treatment, especially in testing for predispositions and in therapies. By 2025, there will likely be thousands of diagnostic procedures and treatments for genetic conditions.

Genetic diagnostics can detect specific diseases, such as Down syndrome, and behavioral predispositions, such as depression. Treatments include gene-based pharmaceuticals, such as those using antisense DNA to block the body's process of transmitting genetic instructions for a disease process. In future preventive therapies, harmful genes will be removed, turned off, or blocked. In some cases, healthy replacement genes will be directly inserted into fetuses or will be administered to people via injection, inhalation, retroviruses, or pills. These therapies will alter traits and prevent diseases.

Future Foods: The New Genetic Menu

Restaurants and grocery stores will offer future diners far more exotic choices than ever before, thanks to genetics that permit flavors, textures, and other properties from one species to be introduced into another.

Some items on tomorrow's menu might include:
- "Protrout," super-protein trout.
- Ultra-lean "Pig-No-More."
- "Octo-squid."
- "Beetatoes."
- "Beefison," meat with venison's flavor and beef's bulk.
- "Shrimpsters," less-squishy oysters produced with shrimp genes.
- Swordfish-flavored tuna.
- Duck-flavored pork.
- Seaweed dip seasoned with spring onion genes.
- A quail–chicken transgenic fowl dubbed "quicken."

Ultimately, genetic chefs may produce crossover transgenics: plants with animal genes and animals with plant genes, giving new meaning to "chocolate milk" and "duck à l'orange."

Source: *2025: Scenarios of U.S. and Global Society Reshaped by Science and Technology.*

Although genetics will be the greatest driver of advances in human health in the twenty-first century, it will not be a panacea for all human health problems. Health is a complex of interacting systems. The benefits of genetics will also be weighted more heavily to future generations, because prevention will be such an important component. Genetic therapies will ameliorate conditions in middle-aged and older people, but those conditions will not even exist in future generations. For example, psoriasis may be brought under control for many via gene therapy; if an effective prenatal diagnosis can be developed, then no future child would ever need be born with the condition.

Genetics and Human Destiny

The greatest genetic challenge of the twenty-first century will be human enhancement. The human species is the first to influence its own evolution. Already, we have seen the use of human growth hormone for more than its original intent as a treatment for dwarfism. In many instances, use of HGH has been cosmetic rather than medically indicated.

In the future, genetics may also be used for mental enhancement. Parents lacking math skills, for example, may shop for genes that predispose their bearer to mathematical excellence and have these genes inserted prenatally or postnatally into their children. Other parents may select traits such as artistic ability, musical talent, charm, honesty, or athletic prowess for their children.

Of course, some challenging social questions are bound to arise as genetics leads to increasingly talented and intelligent children growing up in a society in which they are in many ways superior to their parents, teachers, and government authorities. Optimists may anticipate a more informed and enlightened society. Pessimists would worry about older people being warehoused in communities or homes for the genetically impaired.

Part

9

"Think Global, Act Local": The Environment

International politics is generally the result of actions taken by nation-states, representing their own interests. Increasingly, leaders concerned with the national interest also have to consider what is best for the planet as a whole. Policies that appear to have short-term economic advantage for any single nation may have long-term deleterious global consequences, as well as negative effects on the nation that adopted the policies in the first place. The ability of nation-states to resolve environmental problems that affect all nations may prove to be the ultimate test of globalization.

Vinod Thomas and Tamara Belt point out that in the past, rapidly growing countries have chosen economic development over protection of the environment, leading to irreversible environmental losses and high clean-up costs. They show ways this unhealthy combination can be minimized in the future. Bill McKibben believes that we may be living during "a special moment in history" when there may be the capacity, understanding, and will to take the actions necessary to save the planet. Unless we are prepared to do now what is necessary—and assume the burden that will follow—the opportunity may be lost forever. Eugene Linden treats the lure and expansion of mega-cities throughout the world and the problems they pose to nations and to international peace and security.

Growth and the Environment

ALLIES OR FOES?

Vinod Thomas and Tamara Belt

Over the past quarter of a century, economic growth per capita in the southeast part of East Asia—Indonesia, Malaysia, Singapore, and Thailand—averaged 5 percent a year. Socioeconomic well-being improved enormously. In Indonesia, Malaysia, and Thailand, the percentage of the population living below the poverty line is estimated to have declined by some 50–70 percent. Starting from even earlier periods, Hong Kong, Japan, Korea, Singapore, and Taiwan Province of China made dramatic economic gains. Over the past decade and a half, China experienced very high growth rates and a sharp reduction in poverty.

At the same time, environmental losses in East Asia have surpassed in many respects those of other regions. For example, 9 of the world's 15 cities with the highest levels of particulate air pollution are in this region. About 20 percent of land covered by vegetation suffers from soil degradation owing to waterlogging, erosion, and overgrazing at levels above world averages. Fifty to 75 percent of coastlines and marine protected areas are classified as areas with highly threatened biodiversity, and the region has witnessed some of the highest deforestation rates in the world.

One lesson is that rapid growth can be a great ally of poverty reduction when supported by certain policy fundamentals. In East Asia these have included substantial and efficient investments in education, a relatively good income and asset distribution, a labor-intensive export orientation, and an emphasis on agricultural

This article originally appeared in *Finance & Development,* June 1997. © 1997 by the International Monetary Fund and the International Bank for Reconstruction and Development/The World Bank. Reprinted by permission.

development. A second lesson, however, is that rapid growth has come at the expense of the environment. Rapid growth does not automatically improve the environment—environmental policies must also be put in place.

To be sure, many growth-inducing policies, such as clarifying property rights, investing in sanitation, improving education (especially for girls), and sound economic policies, help to improve resource use and contribute to a better environment. But in crucial areas, such as the control of pollution or sustainable forest use, environmental actions such as imposing taxes and standards, investing in technology, improving production methods, and recycling are necessary. Rapidly growing economies are learning this lesson the hard way and some are now taking corrective actions.

It is also interesting to focus on Central America. For a variety of economic and sociopolitical reasons, the Central American economies have grown slowly in recent decades, although their potential for sustainable development remains high. An exception is Costa Rica, a country with a strong record in promoting human development. But, more generally, the economies of Central America have been dominated by traditional exports, which have faced declining terms of trade; by a highly unequal income distribution; and by inadequate educational investments—all exacerbated by political instability. Costa Rica remains a notable exception. Because growth rates have been low, poverty levels have remained stubbornly high—as in other regions with slow growth. Environmental quality has deteriorated—there are large deforested areas, soil degradation, overfishing, and polluted water in coastal zones.

The experiences of East Asia and Central America show that both slow- and fast-growing economies can suffer from severe environmental degradation. The question then is whether, with the right priorities and policies, the environment can be protected irrespective of the pace of growth.

Growth per se is not to be blamed for environmental degradation, but, in some respects, rapid growth appears to make the problem worse. When the sources of environmental problems—underpriced resources (forests, water, or air), weak institutions, and nuclear property rights—are not addressed adequately, rapid growth seems to aggravate them. However, growth and high incomes can mitigate environmental degradation and improve resource use if accompanied by timely environmental actions.

Grow First and Clean Up Later?

The human and ecological costs of environmental deterioration have been widely studied. In many instances, convincing evidence is available of the large social gains from environmental actions. And yet, environmental actions have been inadequate. The literature has emphasized a basic reason: the divergence between what is beneficial to society and what is beneficial for the private individual. When coupled with the lack of resources at low income levels, the pattern worldwide has been to grow first and clean up later.

Experience that calls this approach into question is accumulating. For one thing, it is a costly strategy socially and ecologically, and might threaten the sustainability of growth itself. Furthermore, new institutional arrangements, technologies, production methods, and targeted investments are beginning to offer opportunities to address growth and environmental protection in ways that are good for government finances as well as for private business.

The high costs of cleaning up later. Ecological damage is often irreversible. Cleaning up later is not an option when terrestrial and aquatic biodiversity has been lost because of habitat destruction. For example, pollution and destructive fishing techniques have damaged a large proportion of coral reefs in some areas. As up to one-fourth of all marine species and one-fifth of known marine fish species live in coral reef ecosystems, the loss of reef habitats disproportionately threatens a high percentage of the ocean's plant and animal life. Complete reversal of this damage is unlikely; therefore, efforts need to focus on preserving global biological resources before they are damaged.

Environmental pollution causes considerable health costs, which are compounded when pollution control is postponed. Some of the evidence comes from widely publicized episodes—for example, mercury poisoning from a manufacturing firm in Minamata, Japan resulting in severe neurological afflictions ("Minamata Disease") for people in the area since the mid-1950s, or exposure to toxic materials causing acute illness or death as in the Bhopal, India tragedy of 1984. Other evidence, even if less visible, is widely prevalent, such as the steady health losses to children and adults from air pollution.

The cost is usually far less than the benefits to society of investing in pollution control. In this regard, an ounce of prevention is worth a pound of cure. It is usually cheaper to control pollution at its source through policy reforms, especially by removing subsidies, than by investing in pollution control later.

Better use of resources. With proper concern for the environment, scarce resources can be put to high-return and sustainable uses. For example, in parts of Southeast Asia, uplands can be used for sustainable planting of fruit trees or other perennials rather than for planting maize or cassava for a few years and then abandoning cultivation as yields decline. Similarly, in areas of Latin America, forests can be protected for their higher social value rather than converted to ranches that generate negative returns. And in many cases, putting a resource to multiple uses generates a large net benefit. For example, management of tropical forests for multiple uses that include nontimber goods, water and soil conservation, biological diversity, and other environmental services, as well as timber, could generate higher social returns as well as revenue.

Bringing in revenue. Applying pollution taxes, in addition to inducing lower emissions and better conservation of resources, can raise revenues that allow governments to scale back more distortionary forms of taxation. In Thailand, for example, a 10 percent tax on the coal and lignite used in manufacturing could yield a return of 1 to 2 percent of government revenue. The cost of such a tax is usually a fraction of the estimated health benefits it helps to produce.

It's good business. Finally, there is the economy-wide link between a country's competitiveness and the environment. In one direction, trade liberalization without environmental policies makes the environment more vulnerable. The higher prices for forest resources resulting from trade liberalization can lead to excessive deforestation if property rights are unclear and logging rights fail to incorporate the resource costs. In the other direction, trade liberalization can increase the profitability of industries that have environmental safeguards in place.

How Can It Be Done?

Although the record is limited, innovative approaches in East Asia and Latin America offer the promise of growth with sustainable resource use. To take one example, a coalition of conservation and research organizations in El Salvador developed an ecolabeling initiative, ECO-OK, to give coffee farmers the incentives and information to produce coffee in an eco-friendly way. The program simultaneously raises awareness and motivates consumers to seek products from socially and environmentally responsible farms. ECO-OK products meet environmental standards that protect rain-forests, workers, and wildlife.

User charges and tradable resource rights. Experience with market-based instruments and regulations, notwithstanding the obstacles to their enforcement, illustrates the range of policies that are possible and widens the debate on options. In East Asia, considerable progress has been made in removing subsidies on gasoline, diesel, and kerosene. In Latin America, there are several examples of the application of market-based instruments (see table). Some have been ineffective in achieving their full objectives as a result of institutional weaknesses such as under-funding, unclear jurisdiction, monitoring requirements, and legal design requirements. Nevertheless, there are some promising examples:

• *Resource user charges.* Brazil, Colombia, and Venezuela charge a forestry tax when tree harvesting is not compensated by equivalent reforestation. So far the taxes have been set at too low a level, and enforcement has been weak; nonetheless, the principle is sound.

• *Joint Implementation Agreements.* Central America is relatively advanced in the creation of agreements for carbon sequestration through forest protection under Joint Implementation programs. Costa Rica has just initiated such an agreement with Norway. The development of such agreements will depend in part on an emerging international consensus, but initial activities are promising.

Participation and community involvement. Where institutions are weak or enforcement is expensive, public participation and community involvement can be effective in enforcing sustainable resource use and adapting local conditions to development needs. Traditional communities have known and used this approach for ages. It could be strengthened for today's market economy, as evidenced in Japan. The local government and resident groups in Japan negotiate with firms to arrive at a detailed written agreement on emissions levels. Between 1971 and 1991, the number of agreements increased from approximately 2,000 to 37,000. Once standards were agreed upon, they were effectively implemented. This consensual approach benefits local governments, residents, and companies alike.

Mainstreaming environmental concerns. A crucial approach involves mainstreaming environmental concerns in national plans and policies. This means that

Protecting the environment
Application of market-based instruments in Latin America

	Credit subsidies	Tax/tariff relief	Deposit-refund schemes	Waste fees and levies	Forestry taxation	Pollution charges	Earmarked renewable resource taxes	Earmarked conventional tax levy	Tradable permits	Eco-labeling	Liability insurance
Barbados	✔	✔	✔	✔							
Bolivia			✔	✔	✔				☆	✔	✔
Brazil	✔	✔	✔	✔	✔	✔	✔	✔		✔	✔
Chile			✔	✔					✔	✔	
Colombia	✔	✔	✔	✔	✔	✔	✔	✔			✔
Ecuador	✔	✔	✔	✔			✔			✔	
Jamaica		✔	✔	✔		☆					
Mexico	✔		✔	✔		✔		✔	☆	✔	
Peru			✔								
Trinidad and Tobago	✔	✔									✔
Venezuela	✔	✔	✔		✔						

Source: Richard M. Huber, Jack Ruitenbeek, and Ronaldo Seroa da Motta, 1996, "Market Based Instruments for Environmental Policymaking in Latin America and the Caribbean," World Bank, Washington.
✔ In place.
☆ Under introduction.

the environmental consequences of actions pursued by finance and planning, as well as environmental, ministries are made explicit within core economic policies. In some countries innovative approaches to confront environmental problems are beginning to be applied. Mainstreaming them would mean that these options are put on the table at the time key fiscal, trade, and industrial policies are discussed. Their benefits and costs would be revealed, providing the basis to pursue the best approaches.

Inserting the environment into policy-making can produce much stronger results for economic growth and environmental sustainability than responding to individual environmental concerns along the way. Practical ways to do this are beginning to emerge, and there would be great benefit from disseminating them. More generally, integrating environmental awareness in education programs, especially at the early stages, and influencing values and behavior would be a fundamental step in mainstreaming environmental concerns.

Uncertainties

Tough questions remain with respect to both policy choices and the implementation of environmental actions. Win-win policy choices (for example, reducing energy subsidies to benefit both economic performance and the environment) should be relatively easy for the policymaker to make. Pushing ahead with them should therefore be a high priority. But even in this case, there will be winners and losers from the changes, requiring the policymaker to manage the political economy of reforms.

Policy choices involving trade-offs to the policymaker are more difficult to make, even if society would benefit on balance (for example, financial investments for pollution control that produce net gains in health and welfare). This difficulty is compounded if the benefits accrue later and especially if future benefits involve uncertainty, or if some of the benefits accrue to the rest of the world (for example, part of the gains from biodiversity from the protection of forests). Financial constraints make the decision hard to take even if it is socially beneficial.

Higher incomes eventually contribute to the demand for a more sustainable environment, especially in the so-called "brown" areas such as urban pollution. Higher incomes also provide the resources to help address the problem. However, this chain of events is particularly delayed in the case of the "green" dimensions of the environment, which faces severe deterioration in the early phases of rapid growth. And they also involve unacceptable thresholds of degradation, and irreversible losses, such as biodiversity. Protecting the "green" aspects during rapid growth remains a tough challenge.

Countries' institutional capacity to make, implement, and enforce difficult decisions is a key consideration. Even the best solutions require the support of well-functioning markets and property rights. Where trade-offs are involved, additional measures to align the social and private benefits (through taxes, quotas, investments, etc.) are needed. When the benefits go beyond individual countries, financial and institutional arrangements across borders might be called for.

These dilemmas need to be recognized. Clearly, priorities have to be set, resource limits acknowledged, and systemic processes put in place to help make tough choices. There is a growing body of experience on how innovative approaches can help address trade-offs and institutional rigidities. Meanwhile, the evidence on the high costs of not taking these measures is mounting.

Conclusion

In the main, the experience of rapidly growing countries has been to grow first and clean up later. However, this neglect of the environment has resulted in irreversible losses and high cleanup costs. Current experiences and policies, even if limited, demonstrate that it is possible to protect the environment, promote growth, and enhance competitiveness at the same time. Most developing countries can benefit from both the positive and the negative lessons of rapid growth elsewhere. If they can take economic and environmental actions now, they could become the "green tigers" of the future.

REFERENCES

Daniel Esty, 1997, "Environmental Protection During the Transition to a Market Economy," in Wing Woo, Steven Parker, and Jeffrey Sachs, eds., *Economies in Transition, Asia and Europe,* (Cambridge, Massachusetts: MIT Press).
Jeffrey S. Hammer and Sudhir Shetty, 1995, "East Asia's Environment," World Bank Discussion Paper No. 287 (Washington).
Andrew Steer, 1996, "Ten Principles of the New Environmentalism," *Finance & Development* (December).
World Resources Institute, UNEP, UNDP, and World Bank, 1996, *World Resources, 1996–97* (New York: Oxford University Press).

A Special Moment in History

Bill McKibben

Beware of people preaching that we live in special times. People have preached that message before, and those who listened sold their furniture and climbed up on rooftops to await ascension, or built boats to float out the coming flood, or laced up their Nikes and poisoned themselves in some California subdivision. These prophets are the ones with visions of the seven-headed beast, with a taste for the hair shirt and the scourge, with twirling eyes. No, better by far to listen to Ecclesiastes, the original wise preacher, jaded after a thousand messiahs and a thousand revivals.

> One generation passes away, and another generation comes; but the earth abides forever. . . . That which has been is what will be, that which is done is what will be done, and there is nothing new under the sun. Is there anything of which it may be said, "See, this is new"? It has already been in ancient times before us.

And yet, for all that, we may live in a special time. We may live in the strangest, most thoroughly different moment since human beings took up farming, 10,000 years ago, and time more or less commenced. Since then time has flowed in one direction—toward *more,* which we have taken to be progress. At first the momentum was gradual, almost imperceptible, checked by wars and the Dark Ages and plagues and taboos; but in recent centuries it has accelerated, the curve

Article originally appeared in *The Atlantic Monthly* (May 1998). Reprinted by permission of the author.

of every graph steepening like the Himalayas rising from the Asian steppe. We have climbed quite high. Of course, fifty years ago one could have said the same thing, and fifty years before that, and fifty years before *that*. But in each case it would have been premature. We've increased the population fourfold in that 150 years; the amount of food we grow has gone up faster still; the size of our economy has quite simply exploded.

But now—now may be the special time. So special that in the Western world we might each of us consider, among many other things, having only one child— that is, reproducing at a rate as low as that at which human beings have ever voluntarily reproduced. Is this really necessary? Are we finally running up against some limits?

To try to answer this question, we need to ask another: *How many of us will there be in the near future?* Here is a piece of news that may alter the way we see the planet—an indication that we live at a special moment. At least at first blush the news is hopeful. *New demographic evidence shows that it is at least possible that a child born today will live long enough to see the peak of human population.*

Around the world people are choosing to have fewer and fewer children—not just in China, where the government forces it on them, but in almost every nation outside the poorest parts of Africa. Population growth rates are lower than they have been at any time since the Second World War. In the past three decades the average woman in the developing world, excluding China, has gone from bearing six children to bearing four. Even in Bangladesh the average has fallen from six to fewer than four; even in the mullahs' Iran it has dropped by four children. If this keeps up, the population of the world will not quite double again; United Nations analysts offer as their mid-range projection that it will top out at 10 to 11 billion, up from just under six billion at the moment. The world is still growing, at nearly a record pace—we add a New York City every month, almost a Mexico every year, almost an India every decade. But the rate of growth is slowing; it is no longer "exponential," "unstoppable," "inexorable," "unchecked," "cancerous." If current trends hold, the world's population will all but stop growing before the twenty-first century is out.

And that will be none too soon. There is no way we could keep going as we have been. The *increase* in human population in the 1990s has exceeded the *total* population in 1600. The population has grown more since 1950 than it did during the previous four million years. The reasons for our recent rapid growth are pretty clear. Although the Industrial Revolution speeded historical growth rates considerably, it was really the public-health revolution, and its spread to the Third World at the end of the Second World War, that set us galloping. Vaccines and antibiotics came all at once, and right behind came population. In Sri Lanka in the late 1940s life expectancy was rising at least a year every twelve months. How much difference did this make? Consider the United States: if people died throughout this century at the same rate as they did at its beginning, America's population would be 140 million, not 270 million.

If it is relatively easy to explain why populations grew so fast after the Second World War, it is much harder to explain why the growth is now slowing.

Experts confidently supply answers, some of them contradictory: "Development is the best contraceptive"—or education, or the empowerment of women, or hard times that force families to postpone having children. For each example there is a counterexample. Ninety-seven percent of women in the Arab sheikhdom of Oman know about contraception, and yet they average more than six children apiece. Turks have used contraception at about the same rate as the Japanese, but their birth rate is twice as high. And so on. It is not AIDS that will slow population growth, except in a few African countries. It is not horrors like the civil war in Rwanda, which claimed half a million lives—a loss the planet can make up for in two days. All that matters is how often individual men and women decide that they want to reproduce.

Will the drop continue? It had better. UN mid-range projections assume that women in the developing world will soon average two children apiece—the rate at which population growth stabilizes. If fertility remained at current levels, the population would reach the absurd figure of 296 billion in just 150 years. Even if it dropped to 2.5 children per woman and then stopped falling, the population would still reach 28 billion.

But let's trust that this time the demographers have got it right. Let's trust that we have rounded the turn and we're in the home stretch. Let's trust that the planet's population really will double only one more time. Even so, this is a case of good news, bad news. The good news is that we won't grow forever. The bad news is that there are six billion of us already, a number the world strains to support. One more near-doubling—four or five billion more people—will nearly double that strain. Will these be the five billion straws that break the camel's back?

Big Questions

We've answered the question *How many of us will there be?* But to figure out how near we are to any limits, we need to ask something else: *How big are we?* This is not so simple. Not only do we vary greatly in how much food and energy and water and minerals we consume, but each of us varies over time. William Catton, who was a sociologist at Washington State University before his retirement, once tried to calculate the amount of energy human beings use each day. In hunter-gatherer times it was about 2,500 calories, all of it food. That is the daily energy intake of a common dolphin. A modern human being uses 31,000 calories a day, most of it in the form of fossil fuel. That is the intake of a pilot whale. And the average American uses six times that—as much as a sperm whale. We have become, in other words, different from the people we used to be. Not kinder or unkinder, not deeper or stupider—our natures seem to have changed little since Homer. We've just gotten bigger. We appear to be the same species, with stomachs of the same size, but we aren't. It's as if each of us were trailing a big Macy's-parade balloon around, feeding it constantly.

So it doesn't do much good to stare idly out the window of your 737 as you fly from New York to Los Angeles and see that there's *plenty* of empty space down there. Sure enough, you could crowd lots more people into the nation or onto the planet. The entire world population could fit into Texas, and each person could have an area equal to the floor space of a typical U.S. home. If people were willing to stand, everyone on earth could fit comfortably into half of Rhode Island. Holland is crowded and is doing just fine.

But this ignores the balloons above our heads, our hungry shadow selves, our sperm-whale appetites. As soon as we started farming, we started setting aside extra land to support ourselves. Now each of us needs not only a little plot of cropland and a little pasture for the meat we eat but also a little forest for timber and paper, a little mine, a little oil well. Giants have big feet. Some scientists in Vancouver tried to calculate one such "footprint" and found that although 1.7 million people lived on a million acres surrounding their city, those people required 21.5 million acres of land to support them—wheat fields in Alberta, oil fields in Saudi Arabia, tomato fields in California. People in Manhattan are as dependent on faraway resources as people on the Mir space station.

Those balloons above our heads can shrink or grow, depending on how we choose to live. All over the earth people who were once tiny are suddenly growing like Alice when she ate the cake. In China per capita income has doubled since the early 1980s. People there, though still Lilliputian in comparison with us, are twice their former size. They eat much higher on the food chain, understandably, than they used to: China slaughters more pigs than any other nation, and it takes four pounds of grain to produce one pound of pork. When, a decade ago, the United Nations examined sustainable development, it issued a report saying that the economies of the developing countries needed to be five to ten times as large to move poor people to an acceptable standard of living—with all that this would mean in terms of demands on oil wells and forests.

That sounds almost impossible. For the moment, though, let's not pass judgment. We're still just doing math. There are going to be lots of us. We're going to be big. But lots of us in relation to what? Big in relation to what? It could be that compared with the world we inhabit, we're still scarce and small. Or not. So now we need to consider a third question: *How big is the earth?*

Any state wildlife biologist can tell you how many deer a given area can support—how much browse there is for the deer to eat before they begin to suppress the reproduction of trees, before they begin to starve in the winter. He can calculate how many wolves a given area can support too, in part by counting the number of deer. And so on, up and down the food chain. It's not an exact science, but it comes pretty close—at least compared with figuring out the carrying capacity of the earth for human beings, which is an art so dark that anyone with any sense stays away from it.

Consider the difficulties. Human beings, unlike deer, can eat almost anything and live at almost any level they choose. Hunter-gatherers used 2,500 calories of energy a day, whereas modern Americans use seventy-five times that. Human beings, unlike deer, can import what they need from thousands of miles away. And human beings, unlike deer, can figure out new ways to do old things. If, like deer, we needed to browse on conifers to survive, we could cross-breed lush new strains, chop down competing trees, irrigate forests, spray a thousand chemicals, freeze or dry the tender buds at the peak of harvest, genetically engineer new strains—and advertise the merits of maple buds until everyone was ready to switch. The variables are so great that professional demographers rarely even bother trying to figure out carrying capacity. The demographer Joel Cohen, in his potent book *How Many People Can the Earth Support?* (1995), reports that at two recent meetings of the Population Association of America exactly none of the more than 200 symposia dealt with carrying capacity.

But the difficulty hasn't stopped other thinkers. This is, after all, as big a question as the world offers. Plato, Euripides, and Polybius all worried that we would run out of food if the population kept growing; for centuries a steady stream of economists, environmentalists, and zealots and cranks of all sorts have made it their business to issue estimates either dire or benign. The most famous, of course, came from the Reverend Thomas Malthus. Writing in 1798, he proposed that the growth of population, being "geometric," would soon outstrip the supply of food. Though he changed his mind and rewrote his famous essay, it's the original version that people have remembered—and lambasted—ever since. Few other writers have found critics in as many corners. Not only have conservatives made Malthus's name a byword for ludicrous alarmism, but Karl Marx called his essay "a libel on the human race," Friedrich Engels believed that "we are forever secure from the fear of overpopulation," and even Mao Zedong attacked Malthus by name, adding, "Of all things in the world people are the most precious."

Each new generation of Malthusians has made new predictions that the end was near, and has been proved wrong. The late 1960s saw an upsurge of Malthusian panic. In 1967 William and Paul Paddock published a book called *Famine—1975!,* which contained a triage list: "Egypt: Can't-be-saved. . . . Tunisia: Should Receive Food. . . . India: Can't-be-saved." Almost simultaneously Paul Ehrlich wrote, in his best-selling *The Population Bomb* (1968), "The battle to feed all of humanity is over. In the 1970s, the world will undergo famines— hundreds of millions of people will starve to death." It all seemed so certain, so firmly in keeping with a world soon to be darkened by the first oil crisis.

But that's not how it worked out. India fed herself. The United States still ships surplus grain around the world. As the astute Harvard social scientist Amartya Sen points out, "Not only is food generally much cheaper to buy today, in constant dollars, than it was in Malthus's time, but it also has become cheaper during recent decades." So far, in other words, the world has more or less supported us. Too many people starve (60 percent of children in South Asia are stunted by malnutrition), but both the total number and the percentage have dropped in recent decades, thanks mainly to the successes of the Green Revolution. Food production has tripled since the Second World War, outpacing even population growth. We may be giants, but we are clever giants.

So Malthus was wrong. Over and over again he was wrong. No other prophet has ever been proved wrong so many times. At the moment, his stock is especially low. One group of technological optimists now believes that people will continue to improve their standard of living precisely *because* they increase their numbers. This group's intellectual fountainhead is a brilliant Danish economist named Ester Boserup—a sort of anti-Malthus, who in 1965 argued that the gloomy cleric had it backward. The more people, Boserup said, the more progress. Take agriculture as an example: the first farmers, she pointed out, were slash-and-burn cultivators, who might farm a plot for a year or two and then move on, not returning for maybe two decades. As the population grew, however, they had to return more frequently to the same plot. That meant problems: compacted, depleted, weedy soils. But those new problems meant new solutions: hoes, manure, compost, crop rotation, irrigation. Even in this century, Boserup said, necessity-induced invention has meant that "intensive systems of agriculture replaced extensive systems," accelerating the rate of food production.

Boserup's closely argued examples have inspired a less cautious group of popularizers, who point out that standards of living have risen all over the world even as population has grown. The most important benefit, in fact, that population growth bestows on an economy is to increase the stock of useful knowledge, insisted Julian Simon, the best known of the so-called cornucopians, who died earlier this year. We might run out of copper, but who cares? The mere fact of shortage will lead someone to invent a substitute. "The main fuel to speed our progress is our stock of knowledge, and the brake is our lack of imagination," Simon wrote. "The ultimate resource is people—skilled, spirited, and hopeful people who will exert their wills and imaginations for their own benefit, and so, inevitably, for the benefit of us all."

Simon and his ilk owe their success to this: they have been right so far. The world has behaved as they predicted. India hasn't starved. Food is cheap. But Malthus never goes away. The idea that we might grow too big can be disproved only for the moment—never for good. We might always be on the threshold of a special time, when the mechanisms described by Boserup and Simon stop working. It is true that Malthus was wrong when the population doubled from 750 million to 1.5 billion. It is true that Malthus was wrong when the population doubled from 1.5 billion to three billion. It is true that Malthus was wrong when the population doubled from three billion to six billion. Will Malthus still be wrong fifty years from now?

Looking at Limits

The case that the next doubling, the one we're now experiencing, might be the difficult one can begin as readily with the Stanford biologist Peter Vitousek as with anyone else. In 1986 Vitousek decided to calculate how much of the earth's "primary productivity" went to support human beings. He added together the grain we ate, the corn we fed our cows, and the forests we cut for timber and paper; he added the losses in food as we overgrazed grassland and turned it into desert. And when he was finished adding, the number he came up with was 38.8 percent. We use 38.8

percent of everything the world's plants don't need to keep themselves alive; directly or indirectly, we consume 38.8 percent of what it is possible to eat. "That's a relatively large number," Vitousek says. "It should give pause to people who think we are far from any limits." Though he never drops the measured tone of an academic, Vitousek speaks with considerable emphasis: "There's a sense among some economists that we're *so* far from any biophysical limits. I think that's not supported by the evidence."

For another antidote to the good cheer of someone like Julian Simon, sit down with the Cornell biologist David Pimentel. He believes that we're in big trouble. Odd facts stud his conversation—for example, a nice head of iceberg lettuce is 95 percent water and contains just fifty calories of energy, but it takes 400 calories of energy to grow that head of lettuce in California's Central Valley, and another 1,800 to ship it east. ("There's practically no nutrition in the damn stuff anyway," Pimentel says. "Cabbage is a lot better, and we can grow it in upstate New York.") Pimentel has devoted the past three decades to tracking the planet's capacity, and he believes that we're already too crowded—that the earth can support only two billion people over the long run at a middle-class standard of living, and that trying to support more is doing great damage. He has spent considerable time studying soil erosion, for instance. Every raindrop that hits exposed ground is like a small explosion, launching soil particles into the air. On a slope, more than half of the soil contained in those splashes is carried downhill. If crop residue—cornstalks, say—is left in the field after harvest, it helps to shield the soil: the raindrop doesn't hit as hard. But in the developing world, where firewood is scarce, peasants burn those cornstalks for cooking fuel. About 60 percent of crop residues in China and 90 percent in Bangladesh are removed and burned, Pimentel says. When planting season comes, dry soils simply blow away. "Our measuring stations pick up Chinese soil in the Hawaiian air when ploughing time comes," he says. "Every year in Florida we pick up African soils in the wind when they start to plough."

The very things that made the Green Revolution so stunning—that made the last doubling possible—now cause trouble. Irrigation ditches, for instance, water 17 percent of all arable land and help to produce a third of all crops. But when flooded soils are baked by the sun, the water evaporates and the minerals in the irrigation water are deposited on the land. A hectare (2.47 acres) can accumulate two to five tons of salt annually, and eventually plants won't grow there. Maybe 10 percent of all irrigated land is affected.

Or think about fresh water for human use. Plenty of rain falls on the earth's surface, but most of it evaporates or roars down to the ocean in spring floods. According to Sandra Postel, the director of the Global Water Policy Project, we're left with about 12,500 cubic kilometers of accessible runoff, which would be enough for current demand except that it's not very well distributed around the globe. And we're not exactly conservationists—we use nearly seven times as much water as we used in 1900. Already 20 percent of the world's population lacks access to potable water, and fights over water divide many regions. Already the

Colorado River usually dries out in the desert before it reaches the Sea of Cortez, making what the mid-century conservationist Aldo Leopold called a "milk and honey wilderness" into some of the nastiest country in North America. Already the Yellow River can run dry for as much as a third of the year. Already only two percent of the Nile's freshwater flow makes it to the ocean. And we need more water all the time. Producing a ton of grain consumes a thousand tons of water—that's how much the wheat plant breathes out as it grows. "We estimated that biotechnology might cut the amount of water a plant uses by ten percent," Pimentel says. "But plant physiologists tell us that's optimistic—they remind us that water's a pretty important part of photosynthesis. Maybe we can get five percent."

What these scientists are saying is simple: human ingenuity can turn sand into silicon chips, allowing the creation of millions of home pages on the utterly fascinating World Wide Web, but human ingenuity cannot forever turn dry sand into soil that will grow food. And there are signs that these skeptics are right—that we are approaching certain physical limits.

I said earlier that food production grew even faster than population after the Second World War. Year after year the yield of wheat and corn and rice rocketed up about three percent annually. It's a favorite statistic of the eternal optimists. In Julian Simon's book *The Ultimate Resource* (1981) charts show just how fast the growth was, and how it continually cut the cost of food. Simon wrote, "The obvious implication of this historical trend toward cheaper food—a trend that probably extends back to the beginning of agriculture—is that real prices for food will continue to drop. . . . It is a fact that portends more drops in price and even less scarcity in the future."

A few years after Simon's book was published, however, the data curve began to change. That rocketing growth in grain production ceased; now the gains were coming in tiny increments, too small to keep pace with population growth. The world reaped its largest harvest of grain per capita in 1984; since then the amount of corn and wheat and rice per person has fallen by six percent. Grain stockpiles have shrunk to less than two months' supply.

No one knows quite why. The collapse of the Soviet Union contributed to the trend—cooperative farms suddenly found the fertilizer supply shut off and spare parts for the tractor hard to come by. But there were other causes, too, all around the world—the salinization of irrigated fields, the erosion of topsoil, the conversion of prime farmland into residential areas, and all the other things that environmentalists had been warning about for years. It's possible that we'll still turn production around and start it rocketing again. Charles C. Mann, writing in *Science,* quotes experts who believe that in the future a "gigantic, multi-year, multi-billion-dollar scientific effort, a kind of agricultural 'person-on-the-moon project,'" might do the trick. The next great hope of the optimists is genetic engineering, and scientists have indeed managed to induce resistance to pests and disease in some plants. To get more yield, though, a cornstalk must be made to put out another ear, and conventional breeding may have exhausted the possibilities. There's a sense that we're running into walls.

We won't start producing *less* food. Wheat is not like oil, whose flow from the spigot will simply slow to a trickle one day. But we may be getting to the point where gains will be small and hard to come by. The spectacular increases may be behind us. One researcher told Mann, "Producing higher yields will no longer be like unveiling a new model of a car. We won't be pulling off the sheet and there it is, a two-fold yield increase." Instead the process will be "incremental, torturous, and slow." And there are five billion more of us to come.

So far we're still fed; gas is cheap at the pump; the supermarket grows ever larger. We've been warned again and again about approaching limits, and we've never quite reached them. So maybe—how tempting to believe it!—they don't really exist. For every Paul Ehrlich there's a man like Lawrence Summers, the former World Bank chief economist and current deputy secretary of the Treasury, who writes, "There are no . . . limits to carrying capacity of the Earth that are likely to bind at any time in the foreseeable future." And we are talking about the future—nothing can be *proved*.

But we can calculate risks, figure the odds that each side may be right. Joel Cohen made the most thorough attempt to do so in *How Many People Can the Earth Support?* Cohen collected and examined every estimate of carrying capacity made in recent decades, from that of a Harvard oceanographer who thought in 1976 that we might have food enough for 40 billion people to that of a Brown University researcher who calculated in 1991 that we might be able to sustain 5.9 billion (our present population), but only if we were principally vegetarians. One study proposed that if photosynthesis was the limiting factor, the earth might support a trillion people; an Australian economist proved, in calculations a decade apart, that we could manage populations of 28 billion and 157 billion. None of the studies is wise enough to examine every variable, to reach by itself the "right" number. When Cohen compared the dozens of studies, however, he uncovered something pretty interesting: the median low value for the planet's carrying capacity was 7.7 billion people, and the median high value was 12 billion. That, of course, is just the range that the UN predicts we will inhabit by the middle of the next century. Cohen wrote,

> The human population of the Earth now travels in the zone where a substantial fraction of scholars have estimated upper limits on human population size. . . . The possibility must be considered seriously that the number of people on the Earth has reached, or will reach within half a century, the maximum number the Earth can support in modes of life that we and our children and their children will choose to want.

Earth2

Throughout the 10,000 years of recorded human history the planet—the physical planet—has been a stable place. In every single year of those 10,000 there have been earthquakes, volcanoes, hurricanes, cyclones, typhoons, floods, forest fires, sandstorms, hailstorms, plagues, crop failures, heat waves, cold spells, blizzards, and droughts. But these have never shaken the basic predictability of the planet as a whole. Some of the earth's land areas—the Mediterranean rim, for instance—have been deforested beyond recovery, but so far these shifts have always been local.

Among other things, this stability has made possible the insurance industry—has underwritten the underwriters. Insurers can analyze the risk in any venture because they know the ground rules. If you want to build a house on the coast of Florida, they can calculate with reasonable accuracy the chance that it will be hit by a hurricane and the speed of the winds circling that hurricane's eye. If they couldn't, they would have no way to set your premium—they'd just be gambling. They're always gambling a little, of course: they don't know if that hurricane is coming next year or next century. But the earth's physical stability is the house edge in this casino. As Julian Simon pointed out, "A prediction based on past data can be sound if it is sensible to assume that the past and the future belong to the same statistical universe."

So what does it mean that alone among the earth's great pools of money and power, insurance companies are beginning to take the idea of global climate change quite seriously? What does it mean that the payout for weather-related damage climbed from $16 billion during the entire 1980s to $48 billion in the years 1990–1994? What does it mean that top European insurance executives have begun consulting with Greenpeace about global warming? What does it mean that the insurance giant Swiss Re, which paid out $291.5 million in the wake of Hurricane Andrew, ran an ad in the *Financial Times* showing its corporate logo bent sideways by a storm?

These things mean, I think, that the possibility that we live on a new earth cannot be discounted entirely as a fever dream. Above, I showed attempts to calculate carrying capacity for the world as we have always known it, the world we were born into. But what if, all of a sudden, we live on some other planet? On Earth2?

In 1955 Princeton University held an international symposium on "Man's Role in Changing the Face of the Earth." By this time anthropogenic carbon, sulfur, and nitrogen were pouring into the atmosphere, deforestation was already widespread, and the population was nearing three billion. Still, by comparison with the present, we remained a puny race. Cars were as yet novelties in many places. Tropical forests were still intact, as were much of the ancient woods of the West Coast, Canada, and Siberia. The world's economy was a quarter its present size. By most calculations we have used more natural resources since 1955 than in all of human history to that time.

Another symposium was organized in 1987 by Clark University, in Massachusetts. This time even the title made clear what was happening—not "Man and Nature," not "Man's Role in Changing the Face of the Earth," but "The Earth as Transformed by Human Actions." Attendees were no longer talking about local changes or what would take place in the future. "In our judgment," they said, "the biosphere has accumulated, or is on its way to accumulating, such a magnitude and variety of changes that it may be said to have been transformed."

Many of these changes come from a direction that Malthus didn't consider. He and most of his successors were transfixed by *sources*—by figuring out whether and how we could find enough trees or corn or oil. We're good at finding more stuff; as the price rises, we look harder. The lights never did go out, despite many predictions to the contrary on the first Earth Day. We found more oil, and we still have lots and lots of coal. Meanwhile, we're driving big cars again, and why not? As of this writing, the price of gas has dropped below a dollar a gallon across much of the nation. Who can believe in limits while driving a Suburban? But perhaps, like an audience watching a magician wave his wand, we've been distracted from the real story.

That real story was told in the most recent attempt to calculate our size—a special section in *Science* published last summer. The authors spoke bluntly in the lead article. Forget man "transforming" nature—we live, they concluded, on "a human-dominated planet," where "no ecosystem on Earth's surface is free of pervasive human influence." It's not that we're running out of stuff. What we're running out of is what the scientists call "sinks"—places to put the by-products of our large appetites. Not garbage dumps (we could go on using Pampers till the end of time and still have empty space left to toss them away) but the atmospheric equivalent of garbage dumps.

It wasn't hard to figure out that there were limits on how much coal smoke we could pour into the air of a single city. It took a while longer to figure out that building ever higher smokestacks merely lofted the haze farther afield, raining down acid on whatever mountain range lay to the east. Even that, however, we are slowly fixing, with scrubbers and different mixtures of fuel. We can't so easily repair the new kinds of pollution. These do not come from something going wrong—some engine without a catalytic converter, some waste-water pipe without a filter, some smokestack without a scrubber. New kinds of pollution come instead from things going as they're supposed to go—but at such a high volume that they overwhelm the planet. They come from normal human life—but there are so many of us living those normal lives that something abnormal is happening. And that something is so different from the old forms of pollution that it confuses the issue even to use the word.

Consider nitrogen, for instance. Almost 80 percent of the atmosphere is nitrogen gas. But before plants can absorb it, it must become "fixed"—bonded with carbon, hydrogen, or oxygen. Nature does this trick with certain kinds of algae and soil bacteria, and with lightning. Before human beings began to alter the nitrogen cycle, these mechanisms provided 90–150 million metric tons of nitrogen a year. Now human activity adds 130–150 million more tons. Nitrogen isn't pollution—it's essential. And we are using more of it all the time. Half the industrial nitrogen fertilizer used in human history has been applied since 1984. As a result, coastal waters and estuaries bloom with toxic algae while oxygen concentrations dwindle, killing fish; as a result, nitrous oxide traps solar heat. And once the gas is in the air, it stays there for a century or more.

Or consider methane, which comes out of the back of a cow or the top of a termite mound or the bottom of a rice paddy. As a result of our determination to raise more cattle, cut down more tropical forest (thereby causing termite populations to explode), and grow more rice, methane concentrations in the atmosphere are more than twice as high as they have been for most of the past 160,000 years. And methane traps heat—very efficiently.

Or consider carbon dioxide. In fact, concentrate on carbon dioxide. If we had to pick one problem to obsess about over the next fifty years, we'd do well to make it CO_2—which is not pollution either. Carbon *mon*oxide is pollution: it kills you if you breathe enough of it. But carbon *di*oxide, carbon with two oxygen atoms, can't do a blessed thing to you. If you're reading this indoors, you're breathing more CO_2 than you'll ever get outside. For generations, in fact, engineers said that an engine burned clean if it produced only water vapor and carbon dioxide.

Here's the catch: that engine produces a *lot* of CO_2. A gallon of gas weighs about eight pounds. When it's burned in a car, about five and a half pounds of carbon, in the form of carbon dioxide, come spewing out the back. It doesn't matter if the car is a 1958 Chevy or a 1998 Saab. And no filter can reduce that flow —it's an inevitable by-product of fossil-fuel combustion, which is why CO_2 has been piling up in the atmosphere ever since the Industrial Revolution. Before we started burning oil and coal and gas, the atmosphere contained about 280 parts CO_2 per million. Now the figure is about 360. Unless we do everything we can think of to eliminate fossil fuels from our diet, the air will test out at more than 500 parts per million fifty or sixty years from now, whether it's sampled in the South Bronx or at the South Pole.

This matters because, as we all know by now, the molecular structure of this clean, natural, common element that we are adding to every cubic foot of the atmosphere surrounding us traps heat that would otherwise radiate back out to space. Far more than even methane and nitrous oxide, CO_2 causes global warming—the greenhouse effect—and climate change. Far more than any other single factor, it is turning the earth we were born on into a new planet.

Remember, this is not pollution as we have known it. In the spring of last year the Environmental Protection Agency issued its "Ten-Year Air Quality and Emissions Trends" report. Carbon monoxide was down by 37 percent since 1986, lead was down by 78 percent, and particulate matter had dropped by nearly a quarter. If you lived in the San Fernando Valley, you saw the mountains more often than you had a decade before. The air was *cleaner,* but it was also *different*—richer with CO_2. And its new composition may change almost everything.

Ten years ago I wrote a book called *The End of Nature,* which was the first volume for a general audience about carbon dioxide and climate change, an early attempt to show that human beings now dominate the earth. Even then global warming was only a hypothesis—strong and gaining credibility all the time, but a hypothesis nonetheless. By the late 1990s it has become a fact. For ten years, with heavy funding from governments around the world, scientists launched satellites, monitored weather balloons, studied clouds. Their work culminated in a long-awaited report from the UN's Intergovernmental Panel on Climate Change, released in the fall of 1995. The panel's 2,000 scientists, from every corner of the globe, summed up their findings in this dry but historic bit of understatement: "The balance of evidence suggests that there is a discernible human influence on global climate." That is to say, we are heating up the planet—substantially. If we don't reduce emissions of carbon dioxide and other gases, the panel warned, temperatures will probably rise 3.6° Fahrenheit by 2100, and perhaps as much as 6.3°.

You may think you've already heard a lot about global warming. But most of our sense of the problem is behind the curve. Here's the current news: the changes are already well under way. When politicians and businessmen talk about "future risks," their rhetoric is outdated. This is not a problem for the distant future, or even for the near future. The planet has already heated up by a degree or more. We are perhaps a quarter of the way into the greenhouse era, and the effects are already being felt. From a new heaven, filled with nitrogen, methane, and carbon, a new earth is being born. If some alien astronomer is watching us, she's doubtless puzzled. This is the most obvious effect of our numbers and our appetites, and the key to understanding why the size of our population suddenly poses such a risk.

Stormy and Warm

What does this new world feel like? For one thing, it's stormier than the old one. Data analyzed last year by Thomas Karl, of the National Oceanic and Atmospheric Administration, showed that total winter precipitation in the United States had increased by 10 percent since 1900 and that "extreme precipitation events"— rainstorms that dumped more than two inches of water in twenty-four hours and blizzards—had increased by 20 percent. That's because warmer air holds more water vapor than the colder atmosphere of the old earth; more water evaporates from the ocean, meaning more clouds, more rain, more snow. Engineers designing storm sewers, bridges, and culverts used to plan for what they called the "hundred-year storm." That is, they built to withstand the worst flooding or wind that history led them to expect in the course of a century. Since that history no longer applies, Karl says, "there isn't really a hundred-year event anymore . . . we seem to be getting these storms of the century every couple of years." When Grand Forks, North Dakota, disappeared beneath the Red River in the spring of last year, some meteorologists referred to it as "a 500-year flood"—meaning, essentially, that all bets are off. Meaning that these aren't acts of God. "If you look out your window, part of what you see in terms of the weather is produced by ourselves," Karl says. "If you look out the window fifty years from now, we're going to be responsible for more of it."

Twenty percent more bad storms, 10 percent more winter precipitation— these are enormous numbers. It's like opening the newspaper to read that the average American is smarter by 30 IQ points. And the same data showed increases in drought, too. With more water in the atmosphere, there's less in the soil, according to Kevin Trenberth, of the National Center for Atmospheric Research. Those parts of the continent that are normally dry—the eastern sides of mountains, the plains and deserts—are even drier, as the higher average temperatures evaporate more of what rain does fall. "You get wilting plants and eventually drought faster than you would otherwise," Trenberth says. And when the rain does come, it's often so intense that much of it runs off before it can soak into the soil.

So—wetter and drier. *Different.*

In 1958 Charles Keeling, of the Scripps Institution of Oceanography, set up the world's single most significant scientific instrument in a small hut on the slope of Hawaii's Mauna Loa volcano. Forty years later it continues without fail to track the amount of carbon dioxide in the atmosphere. The graphs that it produces show that this most important greenhouse gas has steadily increased for forty years. That's the main news.

It has also shown something else of interest in recent years—a sign that this new atmosphere is changing the planet. Every year CO_2 levels dip in the spring, when plants across the Northern Hemisphere begin to grow, soaking up carbon dioxide. And every year in the fall decaying plants and soils release CO_2 back into the atmosphere. So along with the steady upward trend, there's an annual seesaw, an oscillation that is suddenly growing more pronounced. The size of that yearly tooth on the graph is 20 percent greater than it was in the early 1960s, as Keeling reported in the journal *Nature,* in July of 1996. Or, in the words of Rhys Roth, writing in a newsletter of the Atmosphere Alliance, the earth is "breathing deeper." More vegetation must be growing, stimulated by higher temperatures. And the earth is breathing earlier, too. Spring is starting about a week earlier in the 1990s than it was in the 1970s, Keeling said.

Other scientists had a hard time crediting Keeling's study—the effect seemed so sweeping. But the following April a research team led by R. B. Myneni, of Boston University, and including Keeling, reached much the same conclusion by means of a completely different technique. These researchers used satellites to measure the color of sunlight reflected by the earth: light bouncing off green leaves is a different color from light bouncing off bare ground. Their data were even more alarming, because they showed that the increase was happening with almost lightning speed. By 1991 spring above the 45th parallel—a line that runs roughly from Portland, Oregon, to Boston to Milan to Vladivostok—was coming eight days earlier than it had just a decade before. And that was despite increased snowfall from the wetter atmosphere; the snow was simply melting earlier. The earlier spring led to increased plant growth, which sounds like a benefit. The area above the 45th parallel is, after all, the North American and Russian wheat belt. But as Cynthia Rosenzweig, of NASA's Goddard Institute for Space Studies, told *The New York Times,* any such gains may be illusory. For one thing, the satellites were measuring biomass, not yields; tall and leafy plants often produce less grain. Other scientists, the *Times* reported, said that "more rapid plant growth can make for less nutritious crops if there are not enough nutrients available in the soil." And it's not clear that the grain belt will have the water it needs as the climate warms. In 1988, a summer of record heat across the grain belt, harvests plummeted, because the very heat that produces more storms also causes extra evaporation. What *is* clear is that fundamental shifts are under way in the operation of the planet. And we are very early yet in the greenhouse era.

The changes are basic. The freezing level in the atmosphere—the height at which the air temperature reaches 32°F—has been gaining altitude since 1970 at the rate of nearly fifteen feet a year. Not surprisingly, tropical and subtropical glaciers are melting at what a team of Ohio State researchers termed "striking" rates. Speaking at a press conference last spring, Ellen Mosley-Thompson, a member of the Ohio State team, was asked if she was sure of her results. She replied, "I don't know quite what to say. I've presented the evidence. I gave you the example of the Quelccaya ice cap. It just comes back to the compilation of what's happening at high elevations: the Lewis glacier on Mount Kenya has lost forty percent of its mass; in the Ruwenzori range all the glaciers are in massive retreat. Everything, virtually, in Patagonia, except for just a few glaciers, is retreating. . . . We've seen . . . that plants are moving up the mountains. . . . I frankly don't know what additional evidence you need."

As the glaciers retreat, a crucial source of fresh water in many tropical countries disappears. These areas are "already water-stressed," Mosley-Thompson told the Association of American Geographers last year. Now they may be really desperate.

As with the tropics, so with the poles. According to every computer model, in fact, the polar effects are even more pronounced, because the Arctic and the Antarctic will warm much faster than the Equator as carbon dioxide builds up. Scientists manning a research station at Toolik Lake, Alaska, 170 miles north of the Arctic Circle, have watched average summer temperatures rise by about seven degrees in the past two decades. "Those who remember wearing down-lined summer parkas in the 1970s—before the term 'global warming' existed—have peeled down to T-shirts in recent summers," according to the reporter Wendy Hower, writing in the *Fairbanks Daily News-Miner.* It rained briefly at the American base in McMurdo Sound, in Antarctica, during the southern summer of 1997—as strange as if it had snowed in Saudi Arabia. None of this necessarily means that the ice caps will soon slide into the sea, turning Tennessee into beachfront. It simply demonstrates a radical instability in places that have been stable for many thousands of years. One researcher watched as emperor penguins tried to cope with the early breakup of ice: their chicks had to jump into the water two weeks ahead of schedule, probably guaranteeing an early death. They (like us) evolved on the old earth.

You don't have to go to exotic places to watch the process. Migrating red-winged blackbirds now arrive three weeks earlier in Michigan than they did in 1960. A symposium of scientists reported in 1996 that the Pacific Northwest was warming at four times the world rate. "That the Northwest is warming up fast is not a theory," Richard Gammon, a University of Washington oceanographer, says. "It's a known fact, based on simple temperature readings."

The effects of that warming can be found in the largest phenomena. The oceans that cover most of the planet's surface are clearly rising, both because of melting glaciers and because water expands as it warms. As a result, low-lying Pacific islands already report surges of water washing across the atolls. "It's nice weather and all of a sudden water is pouring into your living room," one Marshall Islands resident told a newspaper reporter. "It's very clear that something is happening in the Pacific, and these islands are feeling it." Global warming will be like a much more powerful version of El Niño that covers the entire globe and lasts forever, or at least until the next big asteroid strikes.

If you want to scare yourself with guesses about what might happen in the near future, there's no shortage of possibilities. Scientists have already observed large-scale shifts in the duration of the El Niño ocean warming, for instance. The Arctic tundra has warmed so much that in some places it now gives off more carbon dioxide than it absorbs—a switch that could trigger a potent feedback loop, making warming ever worse. And researchers studying glacial cores from the Greenland Ice Sheet recently concluded that local climate shifts have occurred with incredible rapidity in the past—18° in one three-year stretch. Other scientists worry that such a shift might be enough to flood the oceans with fresh water and reroute or shut off currents like the Gulf Stream and the North Atlantic, which keep Europe far warmer than it would otherwise be. (See "The Great Climate Flip-flop," by William H. Calvin, January *Atlantic*.) In the words of Wallace Broecker, of Columbia University, a pioneer in the field, "Climate is an angry beast, and we are poking it with sticks."

But we don't need worst-case scenarios: best-case scenarios make the point. The population of the earth is going to nearly double one more time. That will bring it to a level that even the reliable old earth we were born on would be hard-pressed to support. Just at the moment when we need everything to be working as smoothly as possible, we find ourselves inhabiting a new planet, whose carrying capacity we cannot conceivably estimate. We have no idea how much wheat this planet can grow. We don't know what its politics will be like: not if there are going to be heat waves like the one that killed more than 700 Chicagoans in 1995; not if rising sea levels and other effects of climate change create tens of millions of environmental refugees; not if a 1.5° jump in India's temperature could reduce the country's wheat crop by 10 percent or divert its monsoons.

The arguments put forth by cornucopians like Julian Simon—that human intelligence will get us out of any scrape, that human beings are "the ultimate resource," that Malthusian models "simply do not comprehend key elements of people"—all rest on the same premise: that human beings change the world mainly for the better.

If we live at a special time, the single most special thing about it may be that we are now apparently degrading the most basic functions of the planet. It's not that we've never altered our surroundings before. Like the beavers at work in my back yard, we have rearranged things wherever we've lived. We've leveled the spots where we built our homes, cleared forests for our fields, often fouled nearby waters with our waste. That's just life. But this is different. In the past ten or twenty or thirty years our impact has grown so much that we're changing even those places we don't inhabit—changing the way the weather works, changing the plants and animals that live at the poles or deep in the jungle. This is total. Of all the remarkable and unexpected things we've ever done as a species, this may be the biggest. Our new storms and new oceans and new glaciers and new spring-times—these are the eighth and ninth and tenth and eleventh wonders of the modern world, and we have lots more where those came from.

We have gotten very large and very powerful, and for the foreseeable future we're stuck with the results. The glaciers won't grow back again anytime soon; the oceans won't drop. We've already done deep and systemic damage. To use a human analogy, we've already said the angry and unforgivable words that will haunt our marriage till its end. And yet we can't simply walk out the door. There's no place to go. We have to salvage what we can of our relationship with the earth, to keep things from getting any worse than they have to be.

If we can bring our various emissions quickly and sharply under control, we *can* limit the damage, reduce dramatically the chance of horrible surprises, preserve more of the biology we were born into. But do not underestimate the task. The UN's Intergovernmental Panel on Climate Change projects that an immediate 60 percent reduction in fossil-fuel use is necessary just to stabilize climate at the current level of disruption. Nature may still meet us halfway, but halfway is a long way from where we are now. What's more, we can't delay. If we wait a few decades to get started, we may as well not even begin. It's not like poverty, a concern that's always there for civilizations to address. This is a timed test, like the SAT: two or three decades, and we lay our pencils down. It's *the* test for our generations, and population is a part of the answer.

Changing "Unchangeable" Needs

When we think about overpopulation, we usually think first of the developing world, because that's where 90 percent of new human beings will be added during this final doubling. In *The Population Bomb,* Paul Ehrlich wrote that he hadn't understood the issue emotionally until he traveled to New Delhi, where he climbed into an ancient taxi, which was hopping with fleas, for the trip to his hotel. "As we crawled through the city, we entered a crowded slum area. . . . the streets seemed alive with people. People eating, people washing, people sleeping. People visiting, arguing, and screaming. . . . People, people, people, people."

We fool ourselves when we think of Third World population growth as producing an imbalance, as Amartya Sen points out. The white world simply went through its population boom a century earlier (when Dickens was writing similar descriptions of London). If UN calculations are correct and Asians and Africans will make up just under 80 percent of humanity by 2050, they will simply have returned, in Sen's words, "to being proportionately almost exactly as numerous as they were before the European industrial revolution."

And of course Asians and Africans, and Latin Americans, are much "smaller" human beings: the balloons that float above their heads are tiny in comparison with ours. Everyone has heard the statistics time and again, usually as part of an attempt to induce guilt. But hear them one more time, with an open mind, and try to think strategically about how we will stave off the dangers to this planet. Pretend it's not a moral problem, just a mathematical one.

• An American uses seventy times as much energy as a Bangladeshi, fifty times as much as a Malagasi, twenty times as much as a Costa Rican.

• Since we live longer, the effect of each of us is further multiplied. In a year an American uses 300 times as much energy as a Malian; over a lifetime he will use 500 times as much.

• Even if all such effects as the clearing of forests and the burning of grass-lands are factored in and attributed to poor people, those who live in the poor world are typically responsible for the annual release of a tenth of a ton of carbon each, whereas the average is 3.5 tons for residents of the "consumer" nations of Western Europe, North America, and Japan. The richest tenth of Americans—the people most likely to be reading this magazine—annually emit eleven tons of carbon apiece.

• During the next decade India and China will each add to the planet about ten times as many people as the United States will—but the stress on the natural world caused by new Americans may exceed that from new Indians and Chinese com-bined. The 57.5 million Northerners added to our population during this decade will add more greenhouse gases to the atmosphere than the roughly 900 million added Southerners.

These statistics are not eternal. Though inequality between North and South has steadily increased, the economies of the poor nations are now growing faster than those of the West. Sometime early in the next century China will pass the United States as the nation releasing the most carbon dioxide into the atmosphere, though of course it will be nowhere near the West on a per capita basis.

For the moment, then (and it is the moment that counts), we can call the United States the most populous nation on earth, and the one with the highest rate of growth. Though the U.S. population increases by only about three million people a year, through births and immigration together, each of those three million new Americans will consume on average forty or fifty times as much as a person born in the Third World. My daughter, four at this writing, has already used more stuff and added more waste to the environment than most of the world's residents do in a lifetime. In my thirty-seven years I have probably outdone small Indian villages.

Population growth in Rwanda, in Sudan, in El Salvador, in the slums of Lagos, in the highland hamlets of Chile, can devastate *those places.* Growing too fast may mean that they run short of cropland to feed themselves, of firewood to cook their food, of school desks and hospital beds. But population growth in those places doesn't devastate *the planet.* In contrast, we easily absorb the modest an-nual increases in our population. America seems only a little more crowded with each passing decade in terms of our daily lives. You can still find a parking spot. But the earth simply can't absorb what we are adding to its air and water.

So if it is we in the rich world, at least as much as they in the poor world, who need to bring this alteration of the earth under control, the question becomes how.

Many people who are sure that controlling population is the answer overseas are equally sure that the answer is different here. If those people are politicians and engineers, they're probably in favor of our living more efficiently—of designing new cars that go much farther on a gallon of gas, or that don't use gas at all. If they're vegetarians, they probably support living more simply—riding bikes or buses instead of driving cars.

Both groups are utterly correct. I've spent much of my career writing about the need for cleverer technologies and humbler aspirations. Environmental damage can be expressed as the product of Population × Affluence × Technology. Surely the easiest solution would be to live more simply and more efficiently, and not worry too much about the number of people.

But I've come to believe that those changes in technology and in lifestyle are not going to occur easily and speedily. They'll be begun but not finished in the few decades that really matter. Remember that the pollution we're talking about is not precisely pollution but rather the inevitable result when things go the way we think they should: new filters on exhaust pipes won't do anything about that CO_2. We're stuck with making real changes in how we live. We're stuck with dramatically reducing the amount of fossil fuel we use. And since modern Westerners are practically machines for burning fossil fuel, since virtually everything we do involves burning coal and gas and oil, since we're wedded to petroleum, it's going to be a messy breakup.

So we need to show, before returning again to population, why simplicity and efficiency will not by themselves save the day. Maybe the best place to start is with President Bill Clinton—in particular his reaction to global warming. Clinton is an exquisite scientific instrument, a man whose career is built on his unparalleled ability to sense minute changes in public opinion. He understands our predicament. Speaking to the United Nations early last summer, he said plainly, "We humans are changing the global climate. . . . No nation can escape this danger. None can evade its responsibility to confront it, and we must all do our part."

But when it comes time to do our part, we don't. After all, Clinton warned of the dangers of climate change in 1993, on his first Earth Day in office. In fact, he solemnly promised to make sure that America produced no more greenhouse gases in 2000 than it had in 1990. But he didn't keep his word. The United States will spew an amazing 15 percent more carbon dioxide in 2000 than it did in 1990. It's as if we had promised the Russians that we would freeze our nuclear program and instead built a few thousand more warheads. We broke our word on what history may see as the most important international commitment of the 1990s.

What's important to understand is why we broke our word. We did so because Clinton understood that if we were to keep it, we would need to raise the price of fossil fuel. If gasoline cost $2.50 a gallon, we'd drive smaller cars, we'd drive electric cars, we'd take buses—and we'd elect a new President. We can hardly blame Clinton, or any other politician. His real goal has been to speed the pace of economic growth, which has been the key to his popularity. If all the world's leaders could be gathered in a single room, the one thing that every last socialist, Republican, Tory, monarchist, and trade unionist could agree on would be the truth of Clinton's original campaign admonition: "It's the economy, stupid."

The U.S. State Department had to send a report to the United Nations explaining why we would not be able to keep our Earth Day promise to reduce greenhouse-gas emissions; the first two reasons cited were "lower-than-expected fuel prices" and "strong economic growth." The former senator Tim Wirth, who until recently was the undersecretary of state for global affairs, put it nakedly: the United States was missing its emissions targets because of "more prolonged economic activity than expected."

America's unease with real reductions in fossil-fuel use was clear at last year's mammoth global-warming summit in Kyoto. With utility executives and Republican congressmen stalking the halls, the U.S. delegation headed off every attempt by other nations to strengthen the accord. And even the tepid treaty produced in Kyoto will meet vigorous resistance if it ever gets sent to the Senate.

Changing the ways in which we live has to be a fundamental part of dealing with the new environmental crises, if only because it is impossible to imagine a world of 10 billion people consuming at our level. But as we calculate what must happen over the next few decades to stanch the flow of CO_2, we shouldn't expect that a conversion to simpler ways of life will by itself do the trick. One would think offhand that compared with changing the number of children we bear, changing consumption patterns would be a breeze. Fertility, after all, seems biological—hard-wired into us in deep Darwinian ways. But I would guess that it is easier to change fertility than lifestyle.

Perhaps our salvation lies in the other part of the equation—in the new technologies and efficiencies that could make even our wasteful lives benign, and table the issue of our population. We are, for instance, converting our economy from its old industrial base to a new model based on service and information. Surely that should save some energy, should reduce the clouds of carbon dioxide. Writing software seems no more likely to damage the atmosphere than writing poetry.

Forget for a moment the hardware requirements of that new economy—for instance, the production of a six-inch silicon wafer may require nearly 3,000 gallons of water. But do keep in mind that a hospital or an insurance company or a basketball team requires a substantial physical base. Even the highest-tech office is built with steel and cement, pipes and wires. People working in services will buy all sorts of things—more software, sure, but also more sport utility vehicles. As the Department of Energy economist Arthur Rypinski says, "The information age has arrived, but even so people still get hot in the summer and cold in the winter. And even in the information age it tends to get dark at night."

Yes, when it gets dark, you could turn on a compact fluorescent bulb, saving three-fourths of the energy of a regular incandescent. Indeed, the average American household, pushed and prodded by utilities and environmentalists, has installed one compact fluorescent bulb in recent years; unfortunately, over the same period it has also added seven regular bulbs. Millions of halogen torchère lamps have been sold in recent years, mainly because they cost $15.99 at Kmart. They also suck up electricity: those halogen lamps alone have wiped out all the gains achieved by compact fluorescent bulbs. Since 1983 our energy use per capita has been increasing by almost one percent annually, despite all the technological advances of those years.

As with our homes, so with our industries. Mobil Oil regularly buys ads in leading newspapers to tell "its side" of the environmental story. As the company pointed out recently, from 1979 to 1993 "energy consumption per unit of gross domestic product" dropped 19 percent across the Western nations. This sounds good—it's better than one percent a year. But of course the GDP grew more than two percent annually. So total energy use, and total clouds of CO_2, continued to increase.

It's not just that we use more energy. There are also more of us all the time, even in the United States. If the population is growing by about one percent a year, then we have to keep increasing our technological efficiency by that much each year—and hold steady our standard of living—just to run in place. The President's Council on Sustainable Development, in a little-read report issued in the winter of 1996, concluded that "efficiency in the use of all resources would have to increase by more than fifty percent over the next four or five decades just to keep pace with population growth." Three million new Americans annually means many more cars, houses, refrigerators. Even if everyone consumes only what he consumed the year before, each year's tally of births and immigrants will swell American consumption by one percent.

We demand that engineers and scientists swim against that tide. And the tide will turn into a wave if the rest of the world tries to live as we do. It's true that the average resident of Shanghai or Bombay will not consume as lavishly as the typical San Diegan or Bostonian anytime soon, but he will make big gains, pumping that much more carbon dioxide into the atmosphere and requiring that we cut our own production even more sharply if we are to stabilize the world's climate.

The United Nations issued its omnibus report on sustainable development in 1987. An international panel chaired by Gro Harlem Brundtland, the Prime Minister of Norway, concluded that the economies of the developing countries needed to grow five to ten times as large as they were, in order to meet the needs of the poor world. And that growth won't be mainly in software. As Arthur Rypinski points out, "Where the economy is growing really rapidly, energy use is too." In Thailand, in Tijuana, in Taiwan, every 10 percent increase in economic output requires 10 percent more fuel. "In the Far East," Rypinski says, "the transition is from walking and bullocks to cars. People start out with electric lights and move on to lots of other stuff. Refrigerators are one of those things that are really popular everywhere. Practically no one, with the possible exception of people in the high Arctic, doesn't want a refrigerator. As people get wealthier, they tend to like space heating and cooling, depending on the climate."

In other words, in doing the math about how we're going to get out of this fix, we'd better factor in some unstoppable momentum from people on the rest of the planet who want the very basics of what we call a decent life. Even if we airlift solar collectors into China and India, as we should, those nations will still burn more and more coal and oil. "What you can do with energy conservation in those situations is sort of at the margin," Rypinski says. "They're not interested in fifteen-thousand-dollar clean cars versus five-thousand-dollar dirty cars. It was hard enough to get Americans to invest in efficiency; there's no feasible amount of largesse we can provide to the rest of the world to bring it about."

The numbers are so daunting that they're almost unimaginable. Say, just for argument's sake, that we decided to cut world fossil-fuel use by 60 percent— the amount that the UN panel says would stabilize world climate. And then say that we shared the remaining fossil fuel equally. Each human being would get to produce 1.69 metric tons of carbon dioxide annually—which would allow you to drive an average American car nine miles a day. By the time the population increased to 8.5 billion, in about 2025, you'd be down to six miles a day. If you carpooled, you'd have about three pounds of CO_2 left in your daily ration— enough to run a highly efficient refrigerator. Forget your computer, your TV, your stereo, your stove, your dishwasher, your water heater, your microwave, your water pump, your clock. Forget your light bulbs, compact fluorescent or not.

I'm not trying to say that conservation, efficiency, and new technology won't help. They will—but the help will be slow and expensive. The tremendous momentum of growth will work against it. Say that someone invented a new furnace tomorrow that used half as much oil as old furnaces. How many years would it be before a substantial number of American homes had the new device? And what if it cost more? And if oil stays cheaper per gallon than bottled water? Changing basic fuels—to hydrogen, say—would be even more expensive. It's not like running out of white wine and switching to red. Yes, we'll get new technologies. One day last fall *The New York Times* ran a special section on energy, featuring many up-and-coming improvements: solar shingles, basement fuel cells. But the same day, on the front page, William K. Stevens reported that international negotiators had all but given up on preventing a doubling of the atmospheric concentration of CO_2. The momentum of growth was so great, the negotiators said, that making the changes required to slow global warming significantly would be like "trying to turn a supertanker in a sea of syrup."

There are no silver bullets to take care of a problem like this. Electric cars won't by themselves save us, though they would help. We simply won't live efficiently enough soon enough to solve the problem. Vegetarianism won't cure our ills, though it would help. We simply won't live simply enough soon enough to solve the problem.

Reducing the birth rate won't end all our troubles either. That, too, is no silver bullet. But it would help. There's no more practical decision than how many children to have. (And no more mystical decision, either.)

The bottom-line argument goes like this: The next fifty years are a special time. They will decide how strong and healthy the planet will be for centuries to come. Between now and 2050 we'll see the zenith, or very nearly, of human population. With luck we'll never see any greater production of carbon dioxide or toxic chemicals. We'll never see more species extinction or soil erosion. Greenpeace recently announced a campaign to phase out fossil fuels entirely by midcentury, which sounds utterly quixotic but could—if everything went just right— happen.

So it's the task of those of us alive right now to deal with this special phase, to squeeze us through these next fifty years. That's not fair—any more than it was fair that earlier generations had to deal with the Second World War or the Civil War or the Revolution or the Depression or slavery. It's just reality. We need in these fifty years to be working simultaneously on all parts of the equation—on our ways of life, on our technologies, and on our population.

As Gregg Easterbrook pointed out in his book *A Moment on the Earth* (1995), if the planet does manage to reduce its fertility, "the period in which human numbers threaten the biosphere on a general scale will turn out to have been much, much more brief" than periods of natural threats like the Ice Ages. True enough. But the period in question happens to be our time. That's what makes this moment special, and what makes this moment hard.

The Exploding Cities
of the Developing World

Eugene Linden

Vulnerable Giants

The rhythm of history has been the rise, collapse, and occasional rebirth of cities. Until recently urban populations waxed and waned as disease, changes in trade and technology, and shifting political fortunes rewarded some cities and penalized others. In this century the rhythm has been interrupted in the developing world, where urban populations almost always rise. Lured by the bright lights, or driven from the countryside by political and economic turmoil, population pressures, and ecological breakdown, billions of people have been migrating to the cities.

This influx strains the resources, leadership, and infrastructure of already overburdened countries. Migrants from the desperately poor interior of sub-Saharan Africa continue to come to Kinshasa, Zaire, despite the collapse of its economy and services, which has led to rampant disease and malnutrition and brought the city to the edge of anarchy. Pakistanis pour into Karachi despite factional violence characterized by car bombings and gun battles in the streets. Question marks hang in the polluted air over megacities like Rio de Janeiro, São Paulo, Jakarta, Mexico City, Cairo, Delhi, and Beijing and tens of thousands of smaller cities in Asia, Africa, and Latin America. Many First World cities are also coping with waves of poor newcomers at a time when their tax base is eroding as companies

Reprinted with permission from *Foreign Affairs,* Vol. 75, No. 1, 1996. © 1996 by the Council on Foreign Relations, Inc.

and well-to-do citizens move out, driven away by high costs, crime, and a deteriorating quality of life.

More and more, the fate of cities determines the fate of nations and regions. Karachi, for instance, accounts for half of government revenues in Pakistan and 20 percent of GDP. It is the country's financial center and only port and has the highest concentration of literate people. Given the ties between Karachi's ethnic groups and powerful tribes elsewhere in the country, if the current factional violence in the city intensifies, unrest could engulf the rest of Pakistan's well-armed populace, perhaps leading to international conflicts and large cross-border movements of people.

With ever-increasing global integration, problems that arise in one city can quickly spread throughout its region and even worldwide. The health of cities in the developed world depends in some measure on developing nations' efforts to control new diseases and drug-resistant strains of old ones incubating in their slums. Moreover, as Earth becomes more and more crowded, how successfully developing world cities absorb continuing migration will have much to do with whether tides of humanity overwhelm nations and regions in years to come. The developed world ignores at its peril the problems of Third World cities.

Mismeasure of a Metropolis

At the turn of the century roughly five percent of the world's people lived in cities with populations over 100,000. Today an estimated 45 percent—slightly more than 2.5 billion people—live in urban centers. In recent years the most explosive growth has been in the developing world. Between 1950 and 1995 the number of cities in the developed world with populations greater than 1 million more than doubled, from 49 to 112; in the same period, million-plus cities in the developing world increased sixfold, from 34 to 213. The United Nations estimates that rural numbers will remain virtually steady while urban populations continue to soar: by 2025, it predicts, more than 5 billion people, or 61 percent of humanity, will be living in cities.

Determining what steps governments might take to lessen the shocks of this coming era of giant cities calls for information not available today. It is difficult, for example, to get a fix on something as elementary as the size of the larger cities. In 1992 some estimates put the population of Mexico City at 20 million. Now the United Nations sets the number at 15.6 million—a difference bigger than Baghdad. Karachi may have 9.5 million residents, or it may have 12 million; São Paulo, at 16 million, has several million fewer than in earlier estimates. Part of the problem is the uncertainty of census data—where there has been a census at all—in nations that do not have the resources to conduct an efficient count and where squatters and legal residents may have sound reasons for evading the tally.

Migration to the cities is also difficult to analyze or predict. Often it is a product of both the pull of perceived opportunities and services in the metropolis and the push of rural unemployment caused by the mechanization of agriculture, oversubdivision of farmland, and environmental degradation. In China's rural Sichuan province, for example, where the land cannot come close to supporting the people on it, workers are squeezed out to join the country's "floating population" of some 100 million souls.

The conventional wisdom has been that megacities will continue to grow to horrific size. Experience, however, has sometimes proved otherwise, as in Mexico. As economic and political power was consolidated in Mexico City from the 1940s onward, peasants flocked to the capital, drawn by the prospect of jobs and lavishly subsidized transportation, health care, and education. Since the mid-1980s, however, when Mexico began opening its markets, many companies producing for domestic consumption have closed down; the job losses and cutbacks in government spending hit the capital disproportionately, and immigration has moderated in response. What might be called the rising cost of admission, as scarcity of land, water, and other resources drives up prices in the capital, is also having an effect. In recent years Mexicans have followed jobs to secondary cities like Monterrey. Thus U.N. projections for Mexico City's population at century's end have been halved since 1973, from 32 million to 16.4 million, and have been wildly off the mark for other cities, from Rio de Janeiro to Seoul.

The emphasis on megacities, argues David Satterthwaite of the International Institute for Environment and Development in London, is based on misapprehensions about what made them big and diverts attention from the real problems. There are probably 30,000 urban centers in the developing world, he says. "We concentrate on perhaps 100 of them." The fastest-growing cities on the planet, after all, are not the giant metropolises but anonymous secondary cities—agglomerations like El Alto, a sprawling collection of 500,000 people in Bolivia that has been expanding nine percent a year with virtually no planning and a haphazard infrastructure. The infant mortality rate in the million-plus Indian city of Kanpur is nearly four times that in Delhi. The second-rank cities must deal with all the problems facing a Karachi or Jakarta without the national attention and international assistance that go to the more visible megacities.

The Diseased City

The general picture of the developing world in the latter half of the twentieth century painted by international institutions is one of tremendous progress in improving health and raising incomes: child mortality has been cut in half and incomes have more than doubled, according to the World Bank. These statistics, however, have been skewed by the tremendous health gains and economic growth of China and the newly industrializing Asian Tigers. Roughly one billion people —more than at any other time in history—live in households too poor to obtain enough food to provide nourishment for normal work, points out James Gustave Speth, the current head of the U.N. Development Programme. Another two billion live in conditions Speth describes as deplorable. About 1.5 billion poor people now live in cities, and many of them see their prospects dimming and family and community ties dissolving at the same time that assaults on their personal well-being have risen sharply.

Even the greatest and most enduring cities seem vulnerable when one considers the natural, political, and economic upheavals they must contend with. Poverty, unemployment, disease, crime, and pollution have plagued urban centers for 10,000 years, since the earliest cities developed around granaries and armories in Mesopotamia and Anatolia. There is reason to believe, however, that while the individual problems facing cities are not new, an unholy synergy created in the developing world when explosive population growth, industrialization, and capital scarcity meet means dangers on an unprecedented scale.

After the decline of ancient Rome, nearly 1,800 years passed before a city again reached a population of one million, as London did in the nineteenth century. Until then, crowded slums without running water or sewers and inadequate public health procedures allowed microbes to flourish, and epidemics regularly decimated populations. Advances in sanitation and the discovery of antibiotics have given humanity a century's respite from the ravages of infectious disease. But many epidemiologists fear this period is drawing to a close as urban growth outruns the installation of sanitation in the developing world and resilient microbes discover opportunities in the stressed immune systems of the urban poor.

Diseases transmitted by insects are staging a comeback from the ditches and trash heaps of squatter settlements. Mosquito hosts for the larvae of the parasite that causes filariasis can breed in polluted water. *Anopheles stephensi* mosquitoes need cleaner water but find it in open water tanks and the irrigated urban gardens of India and Africa. The malaria they carry is now the leading cause of hospital visits and deaths from infectious disease in Latin America and Africa, according to Carolyn Stephens, an epidemiologist at the London School of Hygiene and Tropical Medicine. The mosquito that transmits dengue has also benefited from urbanization, multiplying in old tires, flowerpots, and water drums.

While diseases vary from city to city, one motif the megacities of the developing world share is pollution. To live in Mexico City or Delhi is to live in a place where the basic elements of life—air, water, and soil—have become inimical to health. Many of the cities in China have five to ten times the levels of particulates and sulfur dioxide found in the air of First World cities; a recent sampling in Guangzhou revealed concentrations of these pollutants among the highest ever measured anywhere. In Beijing and other Chinese metropolises ordinary people have been driven to riot by pollution ranging from incessant noise to choking clouds of coal dust. In some parts of Poland the land and water have been so poisoned by toxic waste that ten percent of babies are born with birth defects. Inadequate zoning regulations and enforcement, antiquated technologies, corruption, rising consumption, and burgeoning populations all play a part.

Pollution also has a role in the renewed spread of infectious disease. Untreated sewage flowing into the Bay of Bengal off Bangladesh made its way into the bilge tanks of a freighter headed for South America; a relatively new strain of cholera came along for the ride. According to Paul Epstein, an epidemiologist at the Harvard School of Public Health, when the tanker emptied its bilge off Peru, the microbe found a home in algal blooms in the coastal waters that had been nurtured by sewage from Lima. From there the cholera made its way into cities as people ate contaminated shellfish. Since arriving in Latin America in 1991, the disease has struck 320,000 people and killed 2,600.

Stephens' work has shown that poor people in cities die disproportionately from both infectious diseases and chronic illnesses, such as cancer and heart disease, associated with more developed societies. She and others argue that disease, along with pollution, is a symptom of a larger threat to urban dwellers: poverty. Many people endure these risks in the hope that work in the city will pay enough for them to move their families out of harm's way. But as cities continue to swell because of migration and births, workers face crowds of competitors like themselves. Beijing is now home to an estimated one million floating workers in search of jobs. Unemployment rates in scores of African cities top 20 percent and are unlikely to drop soon.

Disease, squalor, hopelessness, stress, and the decline of traditional cultural constraints in the atomized contemporary city conspire to aggravate yet another health hazard: violence. Homicides and other violence accounted for 86 percent of all deaths among teenage boys in São Paulo in a study Stephens conducted. Karachi, with roughly four million unemployed, many of them teens, has an endless supply of recruits for its ethnic militias and drive-by assassination teams. "You have a lot of people sitting around idly, and a lot of guns," says a World Bank official. "All you need is a little ideology and you can get your own army." The mixture helps fuel the Islamic uprising in Algerian cities and a crime wave in Rio that has driven the middle class into garrisons and encouraged vigilante justice.

Finally, there is war, which, as the stories that have emerged from Monrovia, Mogadishu, and Kigali show, inflicts unique horrors on those trapped in cities that at the best of times have trouble taking care of the injured, the hungry, and the displaced. Even without the stresses of war, the quality of life for the poor has declined to the point where observers who long believed city dwellers had the advantage now recognize that large numbers of impoverished urbanites are worse off than the rural poor.

Violence, disorder, pollution, and disease can ultimately become so severe that authorities abdicate, foreign investors retreat, and a city begins to slide into chaos. Karachi has flirted with this threshold in the past and after a few years of growth may be approaching it again. Kinshasa has long since crossed the line, and its slow contraction shows how a city dies from government corruption and incompetence.

Kinshasa Descending

Kinshasa should be one of the more prosperous cities in sub-Saharan Africa. It is the capital of a country blessed with vast forests, rich agricultural lands, one of the world's great rivers, and huge reserves of copper, cobalt, manganese, and diamonds (now essentially privatized as a source of cash for the elite). During the Cold War, Zaire received billions in development aid, much of which disappeared, along with the nation's wealth, into the pockets of President Mobutu Sese Seko and his kleptocratic officials. Even so, the capital city of roughly four million people began the decade with an excellent water system, cheap and reliable electricity, and functioning public transportation.

In September 1991, however, ordinary citizens joined unpaid government troops in rioting and looting, reducing the city to a shambles; roughly $1 billion in goods changed hands. Foreign workers, many of whom provided critical services for the utilities, fled the city. Over the last three years Kinshasa has seen its formal economy shrink 40 percent. Thousands of government jobs have disappeared, the infrastructure has slowly crumbled, and businesspeople have replaced store windows with concrete facades and steel gates in anticipation of new rounds of civil disorder. Carjackers and gangs of bandits rove the streets. Those lucky enough to have work are paid in a shaky currency. Following rises of 8,500 percent in 1993 and 6,000 percent in 1994, inflation has been cut to three digits, but the economy is still extremely vulnerable. Many people eat only every other day, long-vanquished diseases such as plague are returning, and AIDS, tuberculosis, malaria, sleeping sickness, cholera, and river blindness spread.

What amazes visitors is that the city continues to function at all. Most Kinshasans live by what is facetiously called Article 25 of the constitution—*débrouil-toi,* or getting by on your own. A lively informal economy has sprung up and proved much more efficient than the bloated, corrupt state-owned organizations. People grow crops and raise livestock on every available patch of ground. Families share good fortune and bad. Enterprising traders work the markets. Still, only food from outside donors has prevented outright starvation.

The situation is particularly frustrating because, as one U.S. State Department official put it, "Given the wealth of the nation, it would not take a lot to restore a semblance of order to the economy." The interim government of Prime Minister Kengo wa Dondo has wrested control of the central bank from Indiang Kabul, a Mobutu loyalist, and installed Patrice Djamboleka, a seasoned civil servant, who has imposed some discipline. But hopes for a savior are dim, as Mobutu has entangled most of the nation's best and brightest in his web of corruption. "There are no virgins in Zaire," it is said.

Swollen Cities, Weakened States

The world's major cities already cast a long shadow, and as they absorb the great majority of those born in the coming decades, their economic and electoral significance will only grow—along with the danger of conflict as cities protect their interests.

How long, for instance, will China's central government be able to maintain control of booming coastal provinces dominated by industrial cities as the economy opens up and these local units gain clout? With the capitalist genie escaping from the bottle, the central government has less and less to offer in return for its claims on productivity. An attempt to reassert central control could cause provinces like Guangdong to break away and declare themselves free economic zones.

Internal migration may also drive coastal cities to break with China. The 100 or 120 million surplus workers in the country gravitate toward cities in search of employment; Vaclav Smil of the University of Manitoba estimates that at any given time China's major urban centers each house between 500,000 and two million recent arrivals. Cities such as Guangzhou, which in 1990 averaged 5.7 people per room (the average in the United States is 0.5), are already too crowded to absorb migrants. Yet the great urban migration has only just begun in China, which is still more than 70 percent rural.

China may be fast approaching other limits. After a tenfold increase in agricultural productivity between 1978 and 1988, there may not be much room for improved yields. Recently the country went from being a net exporter to a net importer of grain. Factors including political turmoil following the death of paramount leader Deng Xiaoping, consolidation of land holdings, or protracted drought could trigger an enormous increase in the already heavy migration to the cities among China's rural population of 800 million. The government has allowed grain prices to jump more than 60 percent over the past year, possibly to boost rural incomes and encourage people to remain on the land. This, however, is a delicate game because higher food prices might inflame the urban poor. Should migration increase, the prosperous cities and provinces might try to close their gates, leaving rural China to cope with millions of desperate unemployed peasants. According to Jack Goldstone, a specialist on revolt and rebellion in China who teaches at the University of California at Davis, the tensions created by the contrast between coastal prosperity and rural poverty might even tear the country apart. This pattern of population pressures leading to collapse into warlord-led states, Goldstone argues, has bedeviled the region since antiquity.

Cities of Hope?

Despite these dangers, many economists view China's migrants in a positive light. Urbanization has long been seen as a necessary step in economic development (although studies of Brazil and Mexico have shown that urbanization does not necessarily lead to development). Urban living carries built-in incentives to have smaller families, take mass transportation, recycle garbage, use energy, water, and space carefully, and do other things deemed desirable in a crowded world with limited resources. In fact, the shift to the cities may be a major reason behind the present rapid drop in birthrates throughout the developing world. Concentration in urban areas may well be the only efficient way to house people and still preserve agricultural acreage and wilderness, given inexorable population growth.

But more than anything else, cities are a prism for the genius of civilizations. As Lewis Mumford put it, they are a "symbol of the possible," and this is true in the developing world no less than the developed. Cities are where entrepreneurs hatch their schemes and find the markets and financing to bring them to fruition, where the elites of technology, industry, and the arts meet to brainstorm, and where deep shifts in culture and politics might begin with an unexpected encounter.

Faced with budgetary restraints and capital scarcity, some developing world cities have adopted creative approaches to fundamental problems. Calcutta, Ho Chi Minh City, and Jakarta, for instance, have been experimenting with sewage treatment that uses wetland plants like water hyacinth and duckweed to purify waste naturally. Alternative energy sources such as wind and solar power are getting a much better reception in the developing world than they did in the developed, fossil fuel–based systems having been adjudged expensive, dirty, and a drain on foreign exchange.

Some urban cheerleaders foresee South-to-North technology transfers as cities in the developed world encounter dilemmas familiar to poorer countries, while confronting a similar scarcity of capital. One possibility is suggested by the Speedy Line, designed to meet mass transit needs in Curitiba, Brazil. Essentially a bus line with loading platforms and dedicated lanes, the Speedy Line achieves speeds and passenger capacity approaching that of a subway system at one-300th the cost. Moreover, it can be installed in six months, which means, notes Curitiba's former mayor, Jaime Lerner, "you don't have to waste a generation building a subway." Vancouver and Lyons are among the cities examining the idea's potential.

During the past few years Curitiba, a state capital in a predominantly agricultural region of southern Brazil, has become the poster child for the hopes of the developing world city. Its economy is now based on a healthy mix of manufacturing, services, and commerce. Although its 2.2 million citizens have an average annual income of only about $2,000, Curitiba offers amenities and services many First World cities fail to deliver. The city has managed to increase open space per capita by a factor of 100 since 1970 even as its population grew by 164 percent; today citizens enjoy nearly four times the open space available to New Yorkers. Curitiba has feeding centers for street children, immaculate public housing, and innovative programs like one in which the poor in neighborhoods beyond the reach of sanitation trucks trade garbage for fresh vegetables. Lerner argues that parks and good public transportation bolster ordinary people's dignity, and says, "If people feel respected, they will assume responsibility to help solve other problems."

What does Curitiba have that other cities don't? Most notably, quality leadership. Lerner and an idealistic team of technocrats with experience in urban planning have guided the city since 1970. When Lerner left office recently, he was the most popular mayor in Brazilian history. Now that he has been elected governor of Parana and a member of his mayoral administration, Rafael Greca, has succeeded him in Curitiba, the city and state may be able to mount a coordinated response to rural-urban migration, the one seemingly intractable problem for this successful city in a poor country.

Curitiba, the Indian city of Bangalore, and a few other examples may indicate that the real problem facing poorer cities is not so much population growth or their resource base but a lack of competent leadership and sound regulations and policies that last beyond one administration. But the extreme rarity of success stories in the array of struggling municipalities suggests that this does not explain why so many cities are having trouble creating an environment in which citizens and businesses can prosper. Self-reliance among the indigent is also insufficient to pull a city up. There are those who say, get government out of the way of business, allow the poor to own their plots and homes, and watch human resourcefulness do the rest. This logic resonates with the libertarian mood of the times, but action tends to stop where the neighborhood stops, and a city is much more than a series of adjoining neighborhoods.

In fact, the fortunes of cities are increasingly hostage to factors beyond their control. Population pressures and the integration of the world economy have unleashed forces that can overwhelm a city, however well managed. To a degree, all poor cities today are at the mercy of a restless $4 trillion in institutional capital that roams the world like a giant ocean bird looking for profitable places to alight. When investment fund managers lose confidence in a nation's fiscal policies, as happened in Mexico in the fall of 1994, a country's or region's share of that capital can vanish, leaving cities to deal with the consequences of a ruined currency.

Even seemingly permanent foreign investments have become flighty. Competition among cities for what Adrian Atkinson of the Development Planning Unit of University College, London, calls "footloose foreign industry attracted to cheap labor" places constraints on the current panacea for improving the lot of the poor: jobs. Jabotatek, the name given to greater Jakarta, the Indonesian capital, has enjoyed formidable growth in manufacturing jobs since the 1970s as foreign investment took advantage of labor as cheap as $1.50 a day. Since the industries that have created those jobs import the bulk of their raw materials, they could move elsewhere if costs rise or a more attractive labor market beckons. This leaves workers little hope of better wages or working conditions, since their government is loath to impose costs that might scare away foreign money. Meanwhile unrelenting migration from overpopulated agricultural areas creates a situation in which ever more people could be chasing ever fewer jobs in an economic downturn. Atkinson writes, "The city could, in this situation, become a mass graveyard."

As the global population climbs by nearly 100 million a year, starker limits appear on the horizon. Successful export-based economies can generate the money to buy food elsewhere, but somebody has to produce it. Even today China is simply too populous to count on exports to release its economy from inherent agricultural and resource limitations. Though the largest grain producer in the world, China has quickly become the second-largest importer of grain as well. Worldwide grain reserves, an estimated 48-day supply, are at their lowest level since the agricultural community began tabulating global statistics in 1963. Any disruption of the world market by either weather or grain exporters imposing export controls to protect their consumers could cause a staggering free-for-all over grain. Lester Brown of the Worldwatch Institute in Washington asks: what happens to countries that cannot compete with China and other hungry giants?

The usually optimistic International Food Policy Research Institute recently warned that the world cannot expect new breakthroughs to replicate the gains won during the now-sputtering Green Revolution. According to the World Bank, food production failed to keep pace with population growth in 75 countries during the 1980s, and 15 developing countries saw per capita food production decrease more than 20 percent during the decade. In per capita terms, fish production, fresh water, and arable land have all declined since 1980. As surpluses vanish, higher prices may temporarily spur production, but scores of developing countries may find themselves priced out of the market.

As limits begin to appear—or, equally important, are perceived to appear—the potential for strife and disorder rises, particularly if there are huge disparities in wealth within a city or society. The interplay between scarce land in the countryside, urban migration, and conflict in the cities is complicated, but the scramble for resources in a developing world city can create an environment ripe for exploitation by thugs and gangs. Thomas Homer-Dixon, director of the Peace and Conflict Studies Program at the University of Toronto, argues that crime and social instability resulting from environmental degradation and scarcity of land can prevent a society from establishing independent courts, open and honest markets, and other institutions necessary if it is to decouple its economy from resource limitations.

Other threats loom further off. Sometime in the next century, cities may have to deal with the serious consequences of climate change. Thirty of the world's 50 largest cities lie near coasts; a one-meter rise in the oceans caused by global warming would place an estimated 300 million people directly at risk. Many foreign investors already steer clear of Bangladesh because of its vulnerability to typhoons; a sea-level rise of one meter would put 16 percent of that densely populated country under water.

City dwellers have proved their resilience many times over. Kinshasa refuses to die, and Monrovia and Mogadishu still function despite hellish upheavals. But throughout history cities have explred, and there is no reason to believe the cycle has been permanently interrupted. One can envision a future in which the world's urban population swells from the 300 million of 1950 to perhaps 6 billion in 2050 without widespread collapse, but such a scenario is unlikely, if for no other reason than that it would run counter to the rhythm of history. In its own interest, the more developed world should help the developing cities with investments that promote family planning, foster education for girls as well as boys, improve sanitation and health care, and better the lot of those in rural areas. Broadcasting the rare success stories like Curitiba would also be useful. The world will have an opportunity to spotlight the problems of developing world cities at the U.N. conference on cities in Istanbul in June.

If the world's cities cannot absorb the unprecedented influx, masses of the desperate may overwhelm entire nations and regions. As populations grow and cities become more crowded, the margin for error narrows and the cost of mistakes rises. If peaceful, functioning cities are to exist in 2050, a law-abiding, harmonious, hard-working, ecology-conscious citizenry must be supported by enlightened leaders. Little in the cities of today suggests that this will come to pass.

Part

10 An Emerging Global Culture?

The spread of technology, easy access to the international media, the availability of standardized foods and products, and the pervasive influence of American popular culture are changing how people in different parts of the world think and act. This process of change is hard to control, and its inroads are often difficult to gauge or regulate.

For Peter L. Berger, the emergence of a global culture would help to create a more peaceful world. However, there is also the fear that the end result might be a worldwide "airport culture" in which the diversity of different civilizations will be homogenized and vulgarized.

In many parts of the world, English has become the language of choice for business transactions and for communication through the Internet. For Madelaine Drohan and Alan Freeman, the globalization of a particular language, in this case English, is directly connected to the political power of its people. English as a global language now seems to divide the world into haves and have-nots. Popular music and the easy availability of Western television and movies are transforming all political, social, and cultural expectations. The presence of McDonald's hamburgers in Beijing, Moscow, and other parts of the world is changing the types of food that a particular people may have eaten for centuries. The Internet brings messages to women and young people that might never have penetrated the walls of tradition even five years ago. Joshua A. Fishman, on the other hand, sees the potential for a more pluralistic linguistic environment, dominated by regional languages. In particular, he highlights the advantages of multilingualism. However, Fishman sees the pressures of globalization as contributing to communal conflict based on language.

David Rothkopf takes a much more positive view of these changes; the decline of cultural distinctions may be a measure of progress because it enhances civilization and understanding. In his argument he maintains that it would be in the interest of the United States to encourage the disappearance of fault lines separating nations, and it should do all that is possible to export its values. Despite what appears to be the emergence of a global, homogenized, Americanized culture, a recent article in *The Economist* casts doubt on this conclusion.

Four Faces of Global Culture

Peter L. Berger

The term "globalization" has become somewhat of a cliché. It serves to explain everything from the woes of the German coal industry to the sexual habits of Japanese teenagers. Most clichés have a degree of factual validity; so does this one. There can be no doubt about the fact of an ever more interconnected global economy, with vast social and political implications, and there is no shortage of thoughtful, if inconclusive, reflection about this great transformation. It has also been noted that there is a cultural dimension, the obvious result of an immense increase in worldwide communication. If there is economic globalization, there is also cultural globalization. To say this, however, is only to raise the question of what such a phenomenon amounts to.

Again, there can be no doubt about some of the facts. One can watch CNN in an African safari lodge. German investors converse in English with Chinese apparatchiks. Peruvian social workers spout the rhetoric of American feminism. Protestant preachers are active in India, while missionaries of the Hare Krishna movement return the compliment in Middle America. Both hope and fear attach to these facts.

The hope is that a putative global culture will help to create a more peaceful world. If a global culture is in the making, then perhaps a global civil society might come into being. Ever since John Locke re-emerged from Eastern Europe speaking with a Polish accent, a great amount of hope has been invested in the notion of civil society, that agglomerate of intermediate institutions that Tocqueville saw as the foundation of a vital democracy. Civil society depends on a consensus on civic virtues, and that, after all, is what a culture is supposed to supply. The French sociologist Danièle Hervieu-Léger (in her contribution to the forthcoming volume *The Limits of Social Cohesion,* edited by me) speaks of an "ecumenism of human rights." The same idea is conveyed in a much cruder form by the advertisements of the Benetton company. Whether the idea is couched in sophisticated or crude terms, it too has an evident factual basis. It is also reasonable to hope that a world in which there would be a greater consensus on human rights would also be a more peaceful world.

But there is also fear attached to the prospect of cultural globalization, fear of a worldwide "airport culture" in which the rich diversity of human civilizations will be homogenized and vulgarized. This fear has been vocalized in the rhetoric of "Asian values" that has attained a certain political significance in recent years, as well as in the rhetoric of the various movements of Islamic resurgence. Similar fear, in less virulent form, can be observed elsewhere, for example in the worries about cultural homogenization among Euroskeptics. One of the arguments made by those who opposed Austria's joining the European Union was that Austrians would no longer be able to refer to potatoes as *Erdäpfel,* a homey word that was suddenly imbued with the genius of Austrian identity, but would have to use the High German word *Kartoffeln.* Of course this was silly. But the desire to preserve distinct cultural traditions and a distinct cultural identity in the intense economic and political pressure cooker of the new Europe is not silly at all. The fear, like the hope, is not without foundation.

A more nuanced understanding of cultural globalization will have to take account of both the homogenizing forces and the resistances to them. Benjamin Barber made a move toward such an understanding in his book *Jihad vs. McWorld* (1995). Most recently, and in a more subtle way, Samuel Huntington has discussed the same issues in his *Clash of Civilizations and the Remaking of World Order* (1996), a book to which the present observations are greatly indebted. Huntington, whose view of the contemporary world cannot be accused of being overly optimistic, ends his book with a call to search for commonalities between the contending civilizations, a dialogue of cultures. One need not agree with every aspect of his analysis to agree with his conclusion. A dialogue between cultures, however, presupposes a clearer understanding of all the processes at work, both those of cultural globalization and of resistance to it. It is proposed here that there are at least four distinct processes of cultural globalization going on simultaneously, relating in complex ways both to each other and to the many indigenous cultures on which they impinge.

Davos: From Boardroom to Bedroom

First is what Huntington nicely calls the "Davos culture" (after the annual World Economic Summit that meets in that Swiss luxury resort). This culture is globalized as a direct accompaniment of global economic processes. Its carrier is international business. It has obvious behavioral aspects that are directly functional in economic terms, behavior dictated by the accoutrements of contemporary business. Participants in this culture know how to deal with computers, cellular phones, airline schedules, currency exchange, and the like. But they also dress alike, exhibit the same amicable informality, relieve tensions by similar attempts at humor, and of course most of them interact in English. Since most of these cultural traits are of Western (and mostly American) provenance, individuals coming from different backgrounds must go through a process of socialization that will allow them to engage in this behavior with seemingly effortless spontaneity. This is not always easy. A growing number of consultants in "diversity management" are making a good living advising corporations on how to affect this sort of socialization as smoothly as possible.

But it would be a mistake to think that the "Davos culture" operates only in the offices, boardrooms, and hotel suites in which international business is transacted. It carries over into the lifestyles and presumably also the values of those who participate in it. Thus, for example, the frenetic pace of contemporary business is carried over into the leisure activities and the family life of business people. There is a yuppie style in the corporation, but also in the body-building studio and in the bedroom. And notions of costs, benefits, and maximization spill over from work into private life.

The "Davos culture" is a culture of the elite and (by way of what sociologists call "anticipatory socialization") of those aspiring to join the elite. Its principal social location is in the business world, but since elites intermingle, it also affects at least the political elites. There is, as it were, a yuppie *internationale*. Some years ago, while the apartheid regime was still in power in South Africa, a friend of mine had lunch with a representative of the African National Congress at the United Nations. To my friend's surprise, this individual spent most of the lunch talking about apartment costs in Manhattan. While this yuppification of a representative of what then still understood itself as an anti-capitalist revolutionary movement might have had an ironic aspect, it was a cultural trait that turned out to be very useful a few years later. A number of people from both sides have reported how, when they first met, young ANC exiles and young Afrikaners were surprised by their similar lifestyle preferences and personal values. These were certainly not derived from their respective historical traditions; rather, they were, precisely, commonalities rooted in the "Davos culture." There have been similar reports about the first meetings between young Israelis and Palestinians leading up to the Oslo agreements. Whether one is edified by this spectacle or not, it may be that commonalities in taste make it easier to find common ground politically.

While cultural globalization facilitates interaction between elites, it creates difficulties between these elites and the non-elite populations with whom they must deal. Many moral and ideological conflicts in contemporary societies pit an elite culture against a resentful mass of culturally accredited and economically underprivileged people. As Huntington points out, these resentments may lead to the emergence of a nationalist or religious counter-elite. Also, individuals who participate in the "Davos culture" with reasonable success vary in their ability to balance this participation with other parts of their lives. While some, as previously pointed out, may allow yuppie behavior and values to inundate their private lives, others seek more complicated compromises. On my last visit to Hong Kong I happened to stray into a Buddhist temple and came upon a truly graphic vignette: In front of an altar, facing a large statue of the Buddha, stood a middle-aged man wearing a dark business suit over stocking feet. He was burning incense and at the same time talking on his cellular phone.

Faculty Club International

Both critics and advocates of contemporary global capitalism mainly think in terms of the "Davos culture" and its ramifications in popular culture ("Davos" in interaction with "McWorld"). Yet there are at least two other quite different types of cultural globalization going on. One of these is what one might call the "faculty club culture." Essentially, this is the internationalization of the Western intelligentsia, its values and ideologies. To put it graphically, if the "Davos culture" tries to sell computer systems in India, the "faculty club culture" tries to promote feminism or environmentalism there—a rather different agenda.

While this culture has also penetrated the business world (and in turn has been penetrated by it), its principal carrier is not business. Rather, it is carried by foundations, academic networks, non-governmental organizations, and some governmental and multinational agencies (such as development agencies with social and cultural missions). It too is primarily an elite culture, though here again there are those who aspire to it from the lower echelons of cultural enterprises (say, schoolteachers or social workers who read the books and periodicals that reflect the views emanating from the great cultural centers).

More importantly, the "faculty club culture" spreads its beliefs and values through the educational system, the legal system, various therapeutic institutions, think tanks, and at least some of the media of mass communication. If this culture internationalizes the Western intelligentsia, it also internationalizes the conflicts in which this intelligentsia has been engaged on its home territories. James Hunter has written very insightfully about the American "culture wars" (first in his 1991 book with that title). These conflicts can now be observed worldwide, though always of course subject to local modifications.

A good example of this second process of cultural globalization is the anti-smoking movement, arguably one of the most successful movements in developed societies over the last twenty years or so. Before then it was a small, marginal sect, hardly noticed in public discourse; today, especially in North America and Western Europe, it has largely achieved the goal proclaimed early on by one of its spokesmen—to make smoking an activity engaged in privately by consenting adults. The reasons for this stunning success need not concern us here. The point is that this movement, clearly a product of Western intellectuals, was disseminated worldwide by an alliance of governmental and non-governmental organizations.

In a series of conferences, the World Health Organization propagated the anti-smoking cause internationally. At one of the early conferences the travel expenses of all participants from developing societies were paid by the Scandinavian development agencies (the conference was held in Stockholm). These participants, mostly from health and education ministries, came from countries with horrendous health problems and the campaign against smoking was not high on their list of priorities. As was to be expected, they re-ordered their priorities given the incentives to do so. Ironically, the concepts of neo-Marxist dependency theory, which have not been very good at interpreting the transformations of advanced capitalism, fit rather well in the globalization of the "faculty club culture." Here there is overwhelming "dependency," with an indigenous "comprador class" carrying out the agendas devised in the cultural centers of the "metropolis."

There are obvious tensions between the first and second processes of cultural globalization. Clearly, the anti-smoking movement collides with the interests of the tobacco industry. More generally, both feminism and environmentalism collide with notions of economic efficiency held by the international economic elite. At this time, the most visible conflict is between the "ecumenism of human rights," carried out by a multitude of non-governmental organizations, and the belief of the "Davos culture" that all good things, including human rights, will eventually result from the global establishment of successful market economies. And of course there are also tensions between the "faculty club culture" and various indigenous movements of cultural revitalization. The recent women's conference in Beijing pitted mostly Western feminists against an odd alliance of Islamists and the Vatican. Most significant politically, the Western-centered human rights community is meeting with strong opposition in a sizable number of non-Western countries.

The McWorld Culture

Third, of course, is popular culture. Here Barber's term "McWorld" fits best. And it is this culture that is most credibly subsumed under the category of Westernization, since virtually all of it is of Western, and more specifically American, provenance. Young people throughout the world dance to American music, wiggling their behinds in American jeans and wearing T-shirts with messages (often misspelled) about American universities and other consumer items. Older people watch American sitcoms on television and go to American movies. Everyone, young and old, grows taller and fatter on American fast foods. Here indeed is a case of cultural hegemony, and it is not surprising that others, such as French ministers of culture and Iranian mullahs (not to mention the now defunct Soviet Komsomol functionaries), greatly resent the fact.

These critics of "cultural imperialism" also understand that the diffusion of popular culture is not just a matter of outward behavior. It carries a significant freight of beliefs and values. Take the case of rock music. Its attraction is not just due to a particular preference for loud, rhythmic sound and dangerously athletic dancing. Rock music also symbolizes a whole cluster of cultural values—concerning self-expression, spontaneity, released sexuality, and, perhaps most importantly, defiance of the alleged stodginess of tradition. The consumption of American popular culture has, as it were, sacramental character. Paraphrasing the Book of Common Prayer, these items of consumption are visible signs of an invisible grace—or curse. The hegemony becomes clear by the asymmetry of consumption. Mexicans eat *hamburguesas,* Americans eat tacos. But the Mexicans are consuming whole chunks of American values "in, with, and under" the American hamburgers; the Americans are certainly *not* absorbing non-culinary aspects of Mexican culture by eating tacos.

A couple of years ago, I met a representative of Hallmark greeting cards for the Chinese province of Guandong (a market of some sixty million people). He was happy to report that his product was selling very well. When asked which greeting cards were most popular, he said Valentine cards. "You see, young Chinese men are quite shy with members of the opposite sex. It is difficult for them to express their feelings. It is much easier to send a Valentine card." I did not know what to say to this and mumbled something about how there must be a lot of work translating the texts into Chinese. "Oh no," he said, "they want the cards to be in English."

The people in charge of the globalization of popular culture are, of course, members or aspiring members of the "Davos" elite. The aforementioned Hallmark representative evinced all the characteristics of a successful, with-it yuppie. But the consumers of these cultural exports are a vastly broader population. The indigenous reactions once again vary from complete acceptance to complete rejection, with many degrees of compromise in between. Complete acceptance generally leads to a conflict between the generations, and presumably an important motive for such acceptance among young people is to outrage one's parents. Complete rejection is difficult, even under repressive regimes (the Komsomol functionaries, after trying repression, finally had to compromise by inventing something they would call "Soviet rock"). There are many and complex degrees of compromise, some of them puzzling to the outsider.

A few years ago I visited the Meiji Grand Shrine in Tokyo. I was in the company of my hosts, who were pious adherents of Shinto. When inviting me to go to the Shrine with them, they asked me solicitously whether my religious feelings would be offended by their venerating the Meiji Emperor; I replied courteously (and perhaps rashly) that this would be quite all right. I then stood with them, holding incense sticks in my hands and bowing to the deafening accompaniment of drums being beaten by a row of Shinto priests lined up behind us. I re-emerged from the Shrine somewhat dazed, reflecting that I had just been praying to a dead Japanese potentate. Outside the Shrine was a large park filled with hundreds of young people, fervently dancing to rock music blaring from numerous portable radios. I had noticed some young people inside the Shrine and wondered whether they were now joining the crowd in the park. I asked my hosts whether they saw any contradiction between what was going on inside and outside the Shrine. They were actually puzzled by my question. Certainly not, they replied after a moment of reflection, "Japanese culture has always been successful in integrating elements coming from abroad." One of the most interesting questions about contemporary Japan is whether my hosts were correct in their sanguine view about the absorptive capacity of Japanese culture.

Evangelical Protestantism

Fourthly (though perhaps not finally), a distinctive process of globalization is provided by Evangelical Protestantism, especially in its Pentecostal version (which accounts for something like 80 percent of its worldwide growth). Its globalizing force is best seen by comparing it with the other dynamic religious phenomenon of our time, that of the Islamic resurgence. While the latter has been limited to countries that have always been Muslim and to Muslim diaspora communities, Evangelical Protestantism has been exploding in parts of the world to which this religious tradition has always been alien, indeed, mostly unknown. The most dramatic explosion has occurred in Latin America (it was magisterially described in David Martin's 1990 book, *Tongues of Fire*). But the same variety of Protestantism has been rapidly growing in East Asia (with the notable exception of Japan), in all the Chinese societies (including, despite oppression, the People's Republic), in the Philippines, the South Pacific, and throughout sub-Saharan Africa. There are recent, as yet vague, accounts of an incipient growth in Eastern Europe. And while the origins of this religion are in the United States (the "metropolis"), its new incarnations are thoroughly indigenized and independent of foreign missionaries or financial support.

Evangelical Protestantism brings about a cultural revolution in its new territories (in that respect it is very different from its social function on its American homeground). It brings about radical changes in the relations between men and women, in the upbringing and education of children, in the attitudes toward traditional hierarchies. Most importantly, it inculcates precisely that "Protestant ethic" that Max Weber analyzed as an important ingredient in the genesis of modern capitalism—a disciplined, frugal, and rationally oriented approach to work. Thus, despite its indigenization (converts in Mexico and Guatemala sing American gospel songs in Mayan translation), Evangelical Protestantism is the carrier of a pluralistic and modernizing culture whose original location is in the North Atlantic societies.

It is not clear at this point how this startlingly new phenomenon relates to the previously enumerated processes of cultural globalization. It certainly enters into conflicts with indigenous cultures. Most of the persecution of Christians recently publicized by human rights organizations—notably in China, in the Islamic world, and (sporadically) in Latin America—has been directed against Evangelical Protestants. What is clear is that this type of Protestantism is creating a new international culture, increasingly self-conscious as such (here the relation to American Evangelicals *is* relevant), with vast social, economic, and political ramifications. While the new Protestantism should not be misunderstood as a movement of social protest or reform (its motives are overwhelmingly personal and religious), it has large and unintended consequences. These are decidedly favorable to pluralism, to the market economy, and to democracy. It should be observed here that there may be other globalizing popular movements, but Evangelicalism is clearly the most dynamic.

Four faces of globalization: each is distinctive, each relates to the other three in complex ways. Yet they have important common features. The two perhaps most important features have already been mentioned—their Western, principally American, provenance, and related to this, their relation to the English language.

The Western provenance of these processes has given credibility to the frequent charge that they are part and parcel of Western imperialism, with the United States being the core of this malevolent phenomenon. The charge will not hold up. The "Davos culture" is today fully internationalized. It is centered as much in Tokyo and Singapore as it is in New York and London. One could more plausibly speak of an imperialism of the global capitalist system, but that is simply to attach a pejorative term to the fact of an immensely powerful global reality. The concepts of neo-Marxist theory simply do not fit it. As already mentioned, those concepts are somewhat more apt in describing the globalization of the "faculty club culture." Feminist or environmentalist agitators in Bangladesh can indeed be described as agents of a Western-based "cultural imperialism," but it is difficult to see how their activity benefits global capitalism. Multinational corporations do indeed make large profits from the distribution of popular culture, but there is no coercion involved in their success. No one is forcing Japanese teenagers to enjoy rock music or young men in China to express their emotions in terms derived from American romanticism.

Claudio Véliz (in his 1994 book *The New World of the Gothic Fox*) has made this point very tellingly in his description of the collapse of Latin American tradition before the onslaught of "Anglo-Saxon" values and lifestyles, notably those connected with a pluralistic society. He has used a good metaphor to denote this process, proposing that "Anglo-Saxon" culture is now in its "Hellenistic" phase. That is, it is no longer diffused by means of imperial power, British or American; rather, it has become a cultural force in itself, with large numbers of people clamoring to share it. As to Evangelical Protestantism, both leftist intellectuals and Roman Catholic bishops have portrayed it as a gigantic CIA plot, especially in Latin America, but a look at the empirical evidence presents a very different picture, one of a vital, autonomous movement no longer dependent on support from the outside.

If cultural globalization today represents the "Hellenistic" phase of a civilization originating in the northern parts of Europe and America, the English language is its *koiné* (the "basic Greek" that served as the lingua franca of late classical antiquity and that, among other things, became the language of the New Testament). We live, as Véliz puts it, in "a world made in English," and he points out that no other language appears to be a viable successor to English in the foreseeable future. By now there are very straightforward practical reasons for this hegemony of the English language. However much this may enrage intellectuals in certain places (France, for example, or Quebec), English has become *the* medium of international economic, technological, and scientific communication. The millions of people learning English all over the world do so in order to participate in this global communication, not (with few exceptions) because they want to read Shakespeare or Melville in the original. However, one does not use a language innocently. Every language carries a freight of values, of sensibilities, of approaches to reality, all of which insinuate themselves into the consciousness of those who speak it. It makes sense to assume that the attractiveness of English, especially in its American form, is due at least in part to its capacity to express the sensibilities of a dynamic, pluralistic, and rationally innovative world. This is even true of Evangelical Protestantism, which mostly expresses itself in languages other than English, but whose leaders and young people learn English in order to be in touch with the Evangelical centers in the United States. In doing so, they may get more than they bargained for. The road from the Christian Broadcasting Network to Oprah Winfrey is disturbingly straight.

The picture I have sketched is huge and exceedingly complex. There are many aspects of it that are not yet fully understood. There is a very large research agenda here. But one conclusion can be ventured: If one is to heed Huntington's call for a dialogue between cultures, one must pay as much attention to the manner in which the different processes of cultural globalization relate to each other as to their relation with many indigenous cultures. This then will not just be a dialogue between "the West and the rest," but a considerably more complicated enterprise.

English Rules

Madelaine Drohan and Alan Freeman

When the leaders of the European Union's 15 countries gathered in Amsterdam last month it fell to their Dutch hosts to keep journalists covering the meeting posted on what was going on. Among them, the leaders spoke Europe's 11 official languages. Add reporters from Japan, Poland, Hungary and the Czech Republic and there were at least 15 languages represented in the room. But when Dutch Foreign Minister Hans Van Mierlo began to talk, he chose English.

A lone Dutch reporter protested. He was drowned out by cries of "English! English!" by the majority, who wanted to hear the facts delivered in the language they may not speak perfectly but could at least understand. And increasingly these days—not just in Europe but around the world—that language is English.

The British Empire might be in full retreat with the handover of Britain's last significant possession, Hong Kong. But from Bengal to Belize and Las Vegas to Lahore, the language that spread from Britain through military might, political power, technology and sheer coincidence is rapidly becoming the first global *lingua franca*. The reason is obvious: The American cultural and economic colossus.

Native Mandarin Chinese speakers still far outnumber those whose mother tongue is English. But English is No. 1 when those who speak it as a second, third or fourth language are counted.

A quick look at the nightly television news provides ample evidence of English's ascendancy:

• In Africa, residents of Kinshasa, Zaire, jeer as the motorcade of ousted

Reprinted with permission from *The Globe and Mail* (Toronto), 27 July 1998.

strongman Mobutu Sese Seko passes on the way to the airport. "We don't have to speak French anymore!" they shout. Rebel leader Laurent Kabila, who speaks fluent English, decides he will not only change the name of the country to the Democratic Republic of Congo, he will also adopt English as an official language.

• In Asia, students at a technical institute in the Cambodian capital of Phnom Penh mount a street protest against mandatory French classes. Cambodia, like Zaire, was colonized by French speakers whose legacy was their language. The students want to learn English.

• In Eastern Europe, military officers in the Polish, Hungarian and Czech armies (which were invited to join NATO this week) are hitting the school books again in preparation for the expansion of the military alliance. It has 16 members but only one dominant working language: English.

There's much to be said for having a global language. It can cut down on misunderstandings, provide wider access to sources of knowledge and improve and speed up communications.

But it can also lead to arrogance and complacency on the part of native English speakers, and a sense of grievance and inferiority in other language groups. Canadians need look no further than Quebec to see a prime example.

The English juggernaut is often blamed for the death of minority languages. Half of the world's 6,500 languages are expected to disappear in the next century. English is not always the culprit. Many minority languages have been overwhelmed by dominant languages such as Chinese or Russian.

But because English is in wider use around the globe, it comes in for more blame. And because language and culture are closely intertwined, there is a danger of backlash. "We are very concerned that English could be perceived as damaging to other languages," says Caroline Moore of the British Council, a state-funded group that promotes Britain and British culture. Ms. Moore is part of a team that is looking into the future of English. It predicts that English will remain the biggest global language for the foreseeable future. "But we're mindful of what happened to French and Latin," says Ms. Moore.

There is nothing inherent in English to explain why it has spread so far, says British linguist David Crystal in his book, *English as a Global Language*. He dismisses the suggestion that it is popular because it is simpler to learn, has just a few nouns with gender (such as "ship," often referred to as "her") or that it is more democratic because it does not have a class-based structure. "A language becomes an international language for one chief reason: the political power of its people—especially their military power."

Prof. Crystal points to the spread of Greek, Latin, Arabic, Spanish, Portuguese and French by their respective armies and navies to illustrate his point. There have been exceptions, he admits. One of the most notable is the failure of the French-speaking Normans to force the English to speak their language after they invaded Britain in 1066. "Perhaps if the Normans had taken up residence in larger numbers, or if good political relations between England and France had lasted longer, or if English had not already been well-established since Anglo-Saxon times, the outcome might have been different. This book would then, in all probability, have been written about (and in) French."

Like the Roman legions who spread Latin through Europe, it was British colonial soldiers, explorers and traders who initially spread English. In the modern world, the British have been replaced by the Americans, who now run the world's remaining superpower—in English.

The collapse of the Soviet Union has suddenly meant that Russian has lost influence as a language of power. Throughout Eastern Europe, millions of Poles, Hungarians and Czechs who used to be forced to learn Russian have gratefully dropped that language in favour of English, which is not only the language of commerce and mass culture but of their future military allies.

"In this department, everybody speaks English," says Colonel Grzegorz Wisniewski, deputy director at the Department for NATO Cooperation at Poland's Defence Ministry in Warsaw. "It's a prerequisite." For military officers such as Col. Wisniewski, the collapse of the Warsaw Pact presented a linguistic as well as a geopolitical challenge. After years of studying Russian, they realized that without English their careers would go nowhere. "I didn't study English before 1989 because I didn't think I would use this language or travel widely," says Col. Wisniewski, who now speaks English fluently.

School children were told during Soviet times that Russian was a global language. Now, throughout Eastern Europe, Russian is definitely out. And while German has economic influence and French continues to have a certain status in Romania, English is clearly the second language of choice throughout the region. At the recent Warsaw Book Fair, the official poster was in English, and even German books were presented in stalls that carried English signs announcing, "Books from Germany."

Geopolitical changes elsewhere have served to strengthen English as well. In South Africa, the collapse of apartheid has undermined the official position of Afrikaans in favour of English. Elsewhere in Africa, the French language is in retreat as French influence wanes. It started when the Hutu-led government in Rwanda, allied with France, was replaced three years ago by a Tutsi-led force that invaded from English-speaking Uganda. In neighbouring Zaire, where France supported Mr. Mobutu until the bitter end, the Congolese have happily renounced French in favour of English.

"The fact is that the French language is identified by the majority of Africans with support for the worst dictatorships," says François-Xavier Verschave, president of Survie, a Paris-based non-governmental organization with an interest in Africa. He remembers hearing a speech by the newly installed president of Rwanda in late 1995. "He took out two versions of his speech, one in English and the other in French. He decided purposely to read the one in English. The French ambassador, who was sitting next to me, turned green."

In Asia, English has become the *lingua franca* of business, displacing French in such places as Vietnam, Laos and Cambodia. The desire to do business with the Americans and other English-speaking countries has been a powerful incentive. "Anyone will learn a language if it's going to pay them," says Prof. Crystal.

The move to English has been further encouraged by countries in ASEAN, the Association of South East Asian Nations, which is led by Indonesia, Malaysia and Thailand. The foundations for English in the region were laid by the British through trade, which in some places, such as Hong Kong and Penang, Malaysia, led to the establishment of British schools.

One of Canada's most important foreign-aid projects in the Pacific Rim region provides training in English as a second language to a couple of hundred Indochinese officials a year at a base in Singapore. (The Canadian government is also contemplating a program to encourage executives from France to study English in Canada on the grounds that they will feel more comfortable in a country where French is also an official language.)

In Korea and Japan, English has become the second language of choice as well. "The fact of life is that when you sit down with a Japanese or Korean official, 95 per cent of them are reasonably proficient in English," says a Canadian diplomat. That proficiency in English has benefited the British because Japanese and Korean firms looking for a foothold in Europe have established their factories in Britain, where they feel comfortable with the language.

The British also gain to the tune of at least £800-million a year from foreigners travelling to Britain to study English or attend English universities. Teaching English to Asians has become a big source of foreign exchange in Australia as well. In many parts of the world, English prospers because it's perceived as a neutral language in the battle between national groups. That's the case in Belgium, where French and Flemish speakers increasingly refuse to speak each other's language, leaving English to prosper as an alternative. And it's the case in India, which is producing some of the world's best English-language literature. A recent issue of *The New Yorker* was devoted entirely to English writing coming out of India.

English is also thriving in Spain, Portugal and Italy, which have traditionally had more linguistic affinity with French. Diogo Vaz Guedes, a Portuguese businessman who studied French at the Lycée in Lisbon, says he never gets to use it any more. He sends his children to the local British school.

Anyone who doubts that English has become the dominant language of business need only go to the World Economic Forum, which attracts the world's business and political elite to Davos, Switzerland, each year. If you want to network in the corridors or try to conduct international negotiations over dinner, no other language goes as far. In the first few years after the Berlin Wall came down, the countries of Eastern Europe required interpreters for their representatives to Davos. The representatives were soon replaced by more polished delegates who spoke fluent English.

Multinational companies, like multinational institutions, must establish a common language or languages, and English is usually chosen or figures in the mix. At the headquarters of Airbus—a consortium of French, English, German and Spanish companies—in Toulouse, France, the working language is English.

While America's victory in the Cold War can be credited to its economic and military might, it isn't just nuclear weapons and Stealth bombers that are winning the linguistic war for English. It is also the power of Hollywood and American popular culture.

English is the language of T-shirts, rap music, advertising and MTV. American culture is an export industry that outranks aerospace exports when it comes to global penetration. And every can of Coke, rock-music CD or McDonald's hamburger spreads that culture a little bit further. Berlin's recently opened branch of Planet Hollywood features a video of the superstar owners, including movie star Arnold Schwarzenegger, welcoming patrons to the restaurant. But the Austrian-born hulk doesn't speak a word of his native German. He speaks English.

In the world of advertising, the use of English is growing not just in the ads themselves but also in the contracts and correspondence between advertisers and agencies. "When I write letters in French or Dutch I still use the terms camera-ready or layout because they are the ones everyone understands," says Barbara Captijn, director of North American Media Experts, an agency based in The Hague with a transatlantic clientele.

In the world of technology, English is particularly pervasive perhaps because many of the advances have been made in English-speaking countries. Ms. Moore of the British Council points out that Britain controlled the telegraph in the early days, giving it a potent tool with which to spread its language far and wide. The first radio broadcast was made in English. The first telephone call took place in English. And now the Internet is dominated by English because so much of it was constructed by and for Americans.

The steady march of the English language hasn't come without opposition. In France, there are efforts to counter its use on product labels and on the Internet. A recent survey suggested that 84 per cent of all web sites are in English. French President Jacques Chirac has warned that if the trend continues, future French generations will be economically and culturally marginalized: "The danger exists of a loss of influence for other major languages and a total eradication of smaller languages," he said.

Losing linguistic ground globally is harder for the French than most, says Prof. Crystal, because French was a world language in the 18th century, unlike most other languages. "The French really are very, very upset about the world dominance of English." This adds an emotional element to the debate—as is the case in Quebec.

Like residents of a river valley desperately trying to plug the breach in a dam above them with a thimble of putty, Quebec's language bureaucrats are doing their best to stop the flood of English on the Internet. They recently ordered a Montreal-area computer store to translate an English-only web site into French, arguing that French-speaking Quebeckers have a right to advertising in their own language. The Quebec government has also encouraged computer buffs to develop an alternative vocabulary to compete with the English terms used on the Internet.

In Russia, President Boris Yeltsin and Moscow Mayor Yuri Luzhkov have complained vociferously about the widespread use of English on store signs and advertising billboards. In a move that will be familiar to Canadians, the Moscow mayor has introduced a law requiring that store signs be predominantly in Russian and that all imported food products carry a Russian-language translation of the ingredients.

In the Netherlands over the past decade language activist groups have complained they have had trouble finding Dutch product descriptions. The Dutch are open-minded about language and are considered the linguists of Europe, with 96 per cent of children in secondary school studying English. Even so, there are signs that the spread of English has gone too far for some. A billboard in The Hague advertising Calvin Klein jeans was recently defaced. "Keep English in England," read the message scrawled in Dutch on the sign, "English has no place in Holland." Ms. Captijn, the advertising director, says she was shocked when she saw the graffiti. "I went home and told my husband: 'There's starting to be a backlash.'"

Even when people have a positive attitude toward speaking English, it can lead to misunderstandings. Sometimes the message gets garbled by people with an inadequate grasp of the language. And sometimes a perfect command of English masks the fact that the parties having the conversation come from different cultures. Didier Savignat, director of the Alliance Française in London, uses the example of the business lunch as a potential pitfall. "In France, lunches are longer and they are more leisure than business," he says. "In England, it's the reverse." The lesson: Executives need to learn each other's culture as well as their language to have smooth relations.

Widespread use of English by people whose proficiency doesn't match their enthusiasm can lead to distorted messages, such as when television reporters interview people in foreign countries for news items shown in English-speaking countries. "You rarely see a TV report where foreigners are speaking their own language and it's dubbed or has subtitles," complains Mr Savignat of Alliance Française. Coverage of the coup in Zaire/Congo provided many such interviews. "People were speaking very broken English. And you wonder, did they say what they meant?"

It's easier and cheaper for reporters to talk to English speakers because they are immediately accessible and there is no cost for a translator. But it also leads to faulty perceptions. During the pro-democracy demonstrations last winter in Serbia, viewers of CNN and other English-language TV networks would be forgiven if they thought that Vuk Draskovic was the most important leader of the opposition movement, rather than Zoran Djindjic. Mr. Djindjic led a larger and better-organized political party. But Mr. Draskovic speaks fluent English and so won the contest for air time.

Hardest to take for many non-English speakers is the way that adoption of English as a global language has divided the world into a new set of haves and have-nots: Opportunities for knowledge, jobs and advancement may be open to the English speakers and closed to the others. Career ads in French newspapers published in Belgium are often in English, because multinationals increasingly regard mastery of the language as a job prerequisite.

Since English is generally the language of the wealthy and better-educated in

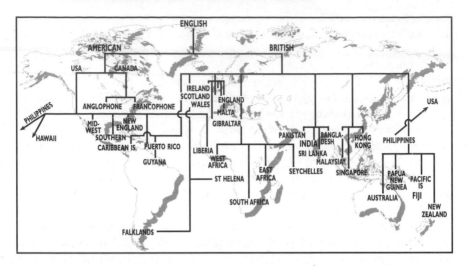

many countries, there is a danger that the language is seen as a hurdle to advancement rather than a key to a wider world.

The strength of English also threatens to leave English speakers complacent about learning other languages. Who hasn't heard English speakers on holiday in a foreign country seemingly under the impression that if they just speak loud enough the non-English-speaking hotel clerk, waiter or operator will understand them?

The minister in charge of education in Scotland recently deplored the fact that only 12 per cent of Scottish students over the age of 16 studied a foreign language last year, compared with 36 per cent as recently as 1975. By contrast, the latest statistics show 96 per cent of German high-school students study English and another 25 per cent study French.

Prof. Crystal says he is heartened by evidence in the United States that businessmen are starting to realize that if they want to maintain their position in global markets they have to make a greater effort to speak to people in their native language. This, and the fact that the United Nations and the European Union have recently come out with statements on linguistic rights, has made him hopeful that English will not eventually bulldoze all other languages in its path.

But the danger is there. "The situation is undoubtedly pretty dire as far as linguistic diversity is concerned," he says. But if countries act now to strengthen minority languages so they can exist alongside a dominant language such as English, the future needn't be grim.

Those Canadians who have acquired a second language either through their parents or by dint of hard work know how much this broadens and enriches their lives. Languages are like windows on the world, each providing a slightly different view. Globally we will all be poorer if we opt for a unilingual future—viewing the world from a single perspective—when a multilingual future is still possible and, ultimately, desirable.

The New Linguistic Order

Joshua A. Fishman

As you read this sentence, you are one of approximately 1.6 billion people—nearly one-third of the world's population—who will use English in some form today. Although English is the mother tongue of only 380 million people, it is the language of the lion's share of the world's books, academic papers, newspapers, and magazines. American radio, television, and blockbuster films export English-language pop culture worldwide. More than 80 percent of the content posted on the Internet is in English, even though an estimated 44 percent of online users speak another language in the home. Not surprisingly, both the global supply of and the demand for English instruction are exploding. Whether we consider English a "killer language" or not, whether we regard its spread as benign globalization or linguistic imperialism, its expansive reach is undeniable and, for the time being, unstoppable. Never before in human history has one language been spoken (let alone semi-spoken) so widely and by so many.

With unprecedented reach comes a form of unprecedented power. Although language is synonymous with neither ideology nor national interest, English's role as the medium for everything from high-stakes diplomacy to air traffic control confers certain advantages on those who speak it. Predominantly English-speaking countries account for approximately 40 percent of the world's total gross domestic product. More and more companies worldwide are making English competency a prerequisite for promotions or appointments. The success of politi-

Reprinted with permission from *Foreign Policy,* 113 (Winter 1998/99). © 1998 by the Carnegie Endowment for International Peace.

cians around the world also increasingly depends on their facility in English. When newly elected German chancellor Gerhard Schroeder and French president Jacques Chirac met in September to discuss future cooperation, they spoke neither French nor German, but English. And English is the official language of the European Central Bank, despite the fact that the United Kingdom has not joined the European Monetary Union, the bank is located in Frankfurt, and only 10 percent of the bank's staff are British. The predominance of English has become such a sore point within the European Union that its leadership now provides incentives for staff members to learn any other official languages.

Yet professional linguists hesitate to predict far into the future the further globalization of English. Historically, languages have risen and fallen with the military, economic, cultural, or religious powers that supported them. Beyond the ebb and flow of history, there are other reasons to believe that the English language will eventually wane in influence. For one, English actually reaches and is then utilized by only a small and atypically fortunate minority. Furthermore, the kinds of interactions identified with globalization, from trade to communications, have also encouraged regionalization and with it the spread of regional languages. Arabic, Chinese, Hindi, Spanish, and a handful of other regional tongues already command a significant reach—and their major growth is still ahead. Finally, the spread of English and these regional languages collectively—not to mention the sweeping forces driving them—have created a squeeze effect on small communities, producing pockets of anxious localization and local-language revival resistant to global change.

Love Thy Neighbor's Language

English came to Massachusetts the same way it did to Mumbai: on a British ship. For all the talk of Microsoft and Disney, the vast reach of English owes its origins to centuries of successful colonization by England. Of the 100 colonies that achieved independence between 1940 and 1990, 56 were former British colonies and 1 was an American possession. Almost every colony that won its independence from England either kept English as an official language or at least recognized its utility.

The continued spread of English today is both a consequence of and a contributor to globalization. Some factors are obvious: the growth in international trade and multinational corporations; the ever widening reach of American mass media; the expanding electronic network created by the Internet; and the linguistic impact of American songs, dress, food, sports, and recreation. Other factors are perhaps less visible but no less powerful, such as the growth in the study of English overseas and the swelling number of students who go abroad to study in English-speaking countries. In 1992, almost half of the world's million-plus population of foreign students were enrolled at institutions in six English mother-tongue countries: Australia, Canada, Ireland, New Zealand, the United Kingdom, and the United States.

Yet globalization has done little to change the reality that, regardless of location, the spread of English is closely linked to social class, age, gender, and profession. Just because a wide array of young people around the world may be able to sing along to a new Madonna song does not mean that they can hold a rudimentary conversation in English, or even understand what Madonna is saying. The brief formal educational contact that most learners have with English is too scant to produce lasting literacy, fluency, or even comprehension. Indeed, for all the enthusiasm and vitriol generated by grand-scale globalization, it is the growth in regional interactions—trade, travel, the spread of religions, interethnic marriages—that touches the widest array of local populations. These interactions promote the spread of regional languages.

Consider the case of Africa, where some 2,000 of the modern world's approximately 6,000 languages are spoken and 13 percent of the world's population lives. English is neither the only nor even the best means to navigate this linguistic obstacle course. Throughout East Africa, Swahili is typically the first language that two strangers attempt upon meeting. The average East African encounters Swahili in a variety of contexts, from the market, elementary education, and government "how to" publications, to popular radio programming and films. New movies from India are often dubbed in Swahili and shown in towns and villages throughout Kenya, Tanzania, and Uganda. In West Africa, some 25 million people speak Hausa natively and perhaps double that number speak it as a second or third language, due in large part to burgeoning regional commerce at local markets throughout the region. Since most Hausa speakers are Muslim, many of them also attend Koranic schools where they learn Arabic, itself a major regional language in North Africa. Thus, many Africans are trilingual on a functional basis: local mother tongues when among "their own," Hausa for trade and secular literacy, and Arabic for prayer and Koranic study. Hausa speakers firmly believe that Hausa has great prospects as a unifying language for even more of West Africa than it already reaches. Its main competition will not likely come from English but rather from other regional languages such as Woloff—which is also spreading in markets in and around Senegal—and Pidgin English.

Increased regional communication, informal market interaction, and migration are driving regional language spread around the world just as they are in Africa. Mandarin Chinese is spreading throughout China and in some of its southern neighbors. Spanish is spreading in the Americas. Hundreds of varieties of Pidgin English have emerged informally among diverse groups in Australia, the Caribbean, Papua New Guinea, and West Africa. The use of French is still increasing in many former French colonies, albeit much more slowly than at its peak of colonial influence. Hindi is reaching new learners in multilingual, multiethnic India. And Arabic is spreading in North Africa and Southeast Asia both as the language of Islam and as an important language of regional trade.

Some regional languages are spreading in part due to the efforts of organizations and government committees. France spends billions of francs annually to support French-language conferences, schools, and media that promote French

LINGUISTIC TOP 10
The World's Foremost Languages by Number of Native Speakers

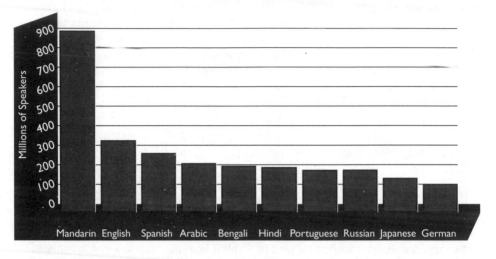

Source: *Ethnologue* (Dallas: Summer Institute of Linguistics, 1996).
Note: Arabic includes all regional variations.

as a vehicle for a common French culture. Muslim organizations in the Middle East spread knowledge about Islam worldwide with an extensive array of English pamphlets and other literature, but they cultivate their ties with each other in Arabic. Moreover, in promoting Islam within their borders, many governments seek to Arabize local ethnic minorities (for example Berbers in Morocco and Christians in Sudan). The German government funds 78 Goethe Institutes, scattered from Beirut to Jakarta, that offer regular German language courses as well as German plays, art exhibits, lectures, and film festivals. Singapore, a tiny country with four official languages, is in the nineteenth year of its national "Speak Mandarin" campaign. Singapore designed the campaign to encourage dialect-speaking Chinese to adopt a common language and facilitate the use of Mandarin as a regional tongue.

The importance of regional languages should increase in the near future. Popular writers, itinerant merchants, bazaar marketers, literacy advocates, relief workers, filmmakers, and missionaries all tend to bank on regional lingua francas whenever there is an opportunity to reach larger, even if less affluent, populations. In many developing areas, regional languages facilitate agricultural, industrial, and commercial expansion across local cultural and governmental boundaries. They also foster literacy and formal adult or even elementary education in highly multilingual areas. Wherever the local vernaculars are just too many to handle, regional languages come to the fore.

Home Is Where the Tongue Is

For all the pressures and rewards of regionalization and globalization, local identities remain the most ingrained. Even if the end result of globalization is to make the world smaller, its scope seems to foster the need for more intimate local connections among many individuals. As Bernard Poignant, mayor of the town of Quimper in Brittany, told the *Washington Post,* "Man is a fragile animal and he needs his close attachments. The more open the world becomes the more ties there will be to one's roots and one's land."

In most communities, local languages such as Poignant's Breton serve a strong symbolic function as a clear mark of "authenticity." The sum total of a community's shared historical experience, authenticity reflects a perceived line from a culturally idealized past to the present, carried by the language and traditions associated (sometimes dubiously) with the community's origins. A concern for authenticity leads most secular Israelis to champion Hebrew among themselves while also acquiring English and even Arabic. The same obsession with authenticity drives Hasidic Jews in Israel or the Diaspora to champion Yiddish while also learning Hebrew and English. In each case, authenticity amounts to a central core of cultural beliefs and interpretations that are not only resistant to globalization but are actually reinforced by the "threat" that globalization seems to present to these historical values. Scholars may argue that cultural identities change over time in response to specific reward systems. But locals often resist such explanations and defend authenticity and local mother tongues against the perceived threat of globalization with near religious ardor.

As a result, never before in history have there been as many standardized languages as there are today: roughly 1,200. Many smaller languages, even those with far fewer than one million speakers, have benefited from state-sponsored or voluntary preservation movements. On the most informal level, communities in Alaska and the American northwest have formed Internet discussion groups in an attempt to pass on Native American languages to younger generations. In the Basque, Catalan, and Galician regions of Spain, such movements are fiercely political and frequently involve staunch resistance to the Spanish government over political and linguistic rights. Projects have ranged from a campaign to print Spanish money in the four official languages of the state to the creation of language immersion nursery and primary schools. Zapatistas in Mexico are championing the revival of Mayan languages in an equally political campaign for local autonomy.

In addition to invoking the subjective importance of local roots, proponents of local languages defend their continued use on pragmatic grounds. Local tongues foster higher levels of school success, higher degrees of participation in local government, more informed citizenship, and better knowledge of one's own culture, history, and faith. Navajo children in Rough Rock, Arizona, who were schooled initially in Navajo were found to have higher reading competency in English than those who were first schooled in English. Governments and relief agencies can also use local languages to spread information about industrial and agricultural techniques as well as modern health care to diverse audiences. Development workers in West Africa, for example, have found that the best way to teach the vast number of farmers with little or no formal education how to sow and rotate crops for higher yields is in these local tongues. From Asturian to Zulu, the world's practical reliance on local languages today is every bit as great as the identity roles these languages fulfill. Nevertheless, both regionalization and globalization require that more and more speakers and readers of local languages be multiliterate.

Looking Ahead

Since all larger language communities have opted to maintain their own languages in the face of globalization, it should come as no surprise that many smaller ones have pursued the same goal. If Germans can pursue globalization and yet remain German-speaking among themselves, why should Telegus in India not aspire to do the same?

Multilingualism allows a people this choice. Each language in a multilingual society has its own distinctive functions. The language characteristically used with intimate family and friends, the language generally used with coworkers or neighbors, and the language used with one's bosses or government need not be one and the same. Reading advanced technical or economic material may require literacy in a different language than reading a local gossip column. As long as no two or more languages are rivals for the same societal function, a linguistic division of labor can be both amicable and long-standing. Few English speakers in India, for example, have given up their local mother tongues or their regional languages. Similarly, in Puerto Rico and Mexico, English is typically "a sometime tongue," even among those who have learned it for occupational or educational rewards.

There will of course be conflict, not to mention winners and losers. Language conflict occurs when there is competition between two languages for exclusive use in the same power-related function—for example, government or schooling. Most frequently, this friction occurs when one regional or local language seeks to usurp roles traditionally associated with another local tongue. In the Soviet era, Moscow took an aggressive line on local languages, instituting Russian as the sole language of education and government in the Baltics and Central Asia. In the 1990s, however, many of these states have slowly deemphasized Russian in schools, government, and even theaters and publishing houses, in favor of their national tongues. Estonia, Latvia, and Lithuania have passed the strictest laws, placing education, science, and culture within the exclusive purview of their national languages and (until just recently) leaving ethnic Russians out in the cold.

Even though local and regional regimes are most likely to use language for political ends, global languages (including English, *the* language of globalization) can also foster conflict. France's anxiety over the spread of English is well documented. The government in Paris forbids English in advertising and regulates the number of English-language films that may be shown in the country. A cabinet-level official, the minister of culture and communication, is responsible for monitoring the well-being of the national tongue. The Académie Française, France's national arbiter of language and style, approves official neologisms for Anglo-American slang to guard the French language against "corruption." Yet French schools are introducing students to English earlier and earlier.

Those who speak and master the languages of globalization often suggest that "upstart" local tongues pose a risk to world peace and prosperity. Throughout most of recorded history, strong languages have refused to share power with smaller ones and have accused them of making trouble—disturbing the peace and promoting ethnic violence and separatism. Purging Ireland of Gaelic in the nineteenth century, however, did not convince many Irish of their bonds with England. Those who fear their own powerlessness and the demise of their beloved languages of authenticity have reasons to believe that most of the trouble comes from the opposite end of the language-and-power continuum. Small communities accuse these linguistic Big Brothers of imperialism, linguicide, genocide, and mind control.

Globalization, regionalization, and localization are all happening concurrently. They are, however, at different strengths in different parts of the world at any given time. Each can become enmeshed in social, cultural, economic, and even political change. English is frequently the language of choice for Tamils in India who want to communicate with Hindi-speaking northerners. Ironically, for many Tamils—who maintain frosty relations with the central authorities in Delhi—English seems less like a colonial language than does Hindi. In Indonesia, however, English may be associated with the military, the denial of civil rights, and the exploitation of workers, since the United States has long supported Jakarta's oligarchic regime. Although English is spreading among Indonesia's upper classes, the government stresses the use of Indonesia's official language, Bahasa Indonesia, in all contact with the general public. Local languages are denied any symbolic recognition at all. The traditional leadership and the common population in Java, heirs to a classical literary tradition in Javanese, resent the favoritism shown to English and Indonesian. Spreading languages often come to be hated because they can disadvantage many as they provide advantages for some.

English itself is becoming regionalized informally and orally, particularly among young people, because most speakers today use it as a second or third language. As students of English are increasingly taught by instructors who have had little or no contact with native speakers, spoken English acquires strong regional idiosyncrasies. At the same time, however, English is being globalized in the realms of business, government, entertainment, and education. However, Hindi and Urdu, Mandarin Chinese, Spanish, and vernacular varieties of Arabic can all expect a boom in these areas in the years to come—the result of both a population explosion in the communities that speak these tongues natively and the inevitable migrations that follow such growth.

The smallest languages on the world scene will be squeezed between their immediate regional neighbors on one side and English on the other. Most purely local languages (those with fewer than a million speakers) will be threatened with extinction during the next century. As a result, many smaller communities will not only seek to foster their own tongues but also to limit the encroachments of more powerful surrounding languages. Even in a democratic setting, "ethnolinguistic democracy" is rarely on the agenda. The U.S. government was designed to protect the rights of individuals; it is no accident that its founding fathers chose not to declare an official language. Yet given the vocal opposition to Spanish-language and bilingual education in many quarters of the United States, it seems not everyone holds the right to choose a language as fundamental.

What is to come of English? It may well gravitate increasingly toward the higher social classes, as those of more modest status turn to regional languages for more modest gains. It might even help the future of English in the long run if its proponents sought less local and regional supremacy and fewer exclusive functions in the United Nations and in the world at large. A bully is more likely to be feared than popular. Most non-native English speakers may come to love the language far less in the twenty-first century than most native English speakers seem to anticipate. Germans are alarmed that their scientists are publishing overwhelmingly in English. And France remains highly resistant to English in mass media, diplomacy, and technology. Even as English is widely learned, it may become even more widely disliked. Resentment of both the predominance of English and its tendency to spread along class lines could in the long term prove a check against its further globalization.

There is no reason to assume that English will always be necessary, as it is today, for technology, higher education, and social mobility, particularly after its regional rivals experience their own growth spurts. Civilization will not sink into the sea if and when that happens. The decline of French from its peak of influence has not irreparably harmed art, music, or diplomacy. The similar decline of German has not harmed the exact sciences. Ancient Greek, Aramaic, Latin, and Sanskrit—once world languages representing military might, sophistication, commerce, and spirituality—are mere relics in the modern world. The might of English will not long outlive the technical, commercial, and military ascendancy of its Anglo-American power base, particularly if a stronger power arises to challenge it. But just because the use of English around the world might decline does not mean the values associated today with its spread must also decline. Ultimately, democracy, international trade, and economic development can flourish in any tongue.

In Praise of Cultural Imperialism?

David Rothkopf

The gates of the world are groaning shut. From marble balconies and over the airwaves, demagogues decry new risks to ancient cultures and traditional values. Satellites, the Internet, and jumbo jets carry the contagion. To many people, "foreign" has become a synonym for "danger."

Of course, now is not the first time in history that chants and anthems of nationalism have been heard. But the tide of nationalism sweeping the world today is unique. For it comes in reaction to a countervailing global alternative that—for the first time in history—is clearly something more than the crackpot dream of visionaries. It is also the first time in history that virtually every individual at every level of society can sense the impact of international changes. They can see and hear it in their media, taste it in their food, and sense it in the products that they buy. Even more visceral and threatening to those who fear these changes is the growth of a global labor pool that during the next decade will absorb nearly 2 billion workers from emerging markets, a pool that currently includes close to 1 billion unemployed and underemployed workers in those markets alone. These people will be working for a fraction of what their counterparts in developed nations earn and will be only marginally less productive. You are either someone who is threatened by this change or someone who will profit from it, but it is almost impossible to conceive of a significant group that will remain untouched by it.

Globalization has economic roots and political consequences, but it also has

Reprinted with permission from *Foreign Policy,* 107 (Summer 1997). © 1997 by the Carnegie Endowment for International Peace.

brought into focus the power of culture in this global environment—the power to bind and to divide in a time when the tensions between integration and separation tug at every issue that is relevant to international relations.

The impact of globalization on culture and the impact of culture on globalization merit discussion. The homogenizing influences of globalization that are most often condemned by the new nationalists and by cultural romanticists are actually positive; globalization promotes integration and the removal not only of cultural barriers but of many of the negative dimensions of culture. Globalization is a vital step toward both a more stable world and better lives for the people in it.

Furthermore, these issues have serious implications for American foreign policy. For the United States, a central objective of an Information Age foreign policy must be to win the battle of the world's information flows, dominating the airwaves as Great Britain once ruled the seas.

Culture and Conflict

Culture is not static; it grows out of a systematically encouraged reverence for selected customs and habits. Indeed, *Webster's Third New International Dictionary* defines culture as the "total pattern of human behavior and its products embodied in speech, action, and artifacts and dependent upon man's capacity for learning and transmitting knowledge to succeeding generations." Language, religion, political and legal systems, and social customs are the legacies of victors and marketers and reflect the judgment of the marketplace of ideas throughout popular history. They might also rightly be seen as living artifacts, bits and pieces carried forward through the years on currents of indoctrination, popular acceptance, and unthinking adherence to old ways. Culture is used by the organizers of society—politicians, theologians, academics, and families—to impose and ensure order, the rudiments of which change over time as need dictates. It is less often acknowledged as the means of justifying inhumanity and warfare. Nonetheless, even a casual examination of the history of conflict explains well why Samuel Huntington, in his *The Clash of Civilizations?* [p. 3, this volume], expects conflict along cultural fault lines, which is precisely where conflict so often erupts. Even worse is that cultural differences are often sanctified by their links to the mystical roots of culture, be they spiritual or historical. Consequently, a threat to one's culture becomes a threat to one's God or one's ancestors and, therefore, to one's core identity. This inflammatory formula has been used to justify many of humanity's worst acts.

Cultural conflicts can be placed into three broad categories: religious warfare, ethnic conflict, and conflict between "cultural cousins," which amounts to historical animosity between cultures that may be similar in some respects but still have significant differences that have been used to justify conflict over issues of proximity, such as resource demands or simple greed.

Religion-based conflicts occur between Christians and Muslims, Christians and Jews, Muslims and Jews, Hindus and Muslims, Sufis and Sunis, Protestants and Catholics, and so forth. Cultural conflicts that spring from ethnic (and in some cases religious) differences include those between Chinese and Vietnamese,

Chinese and Japanese, Chinese and Malays, Normans and Saxons, Slavs and Turks, Armenians and Azerbaijanis, Armenians and Turks, Turks and Greeks, Russians and Chechens, Serbs and Bosnians, Hutus and Tutsis, blacks and Afrikaners, blacks and whites, and Persians and Arabs. Conflicts between "cultural cousins" over resources or territory have occurred between Britain and France, France and Germany, Libya and Egypt, and many others.

Another category that might be included in our taxonomy is quasi-cultural conflict. This conflict is primarily ideological and is not deeply enough rooted in tradition to fit within standard definitions of culture, yet it still exhibits most if not all of the characteristics of other cultural clashes. The best example here is the Cold War itself, a conflict between political cultures that was portrayed by its combatants in broader cultural terms: "godless communists" versus "corrupt capitalists." During this conflict, differences regarding the role of the individual within the state and over the distribution of income produced a "clash of civilizations" that had a relatively recent origin.

Finally, as a reminder of the toll that such conflicts take, one need only look at the 20th century's genocides. In each one, leaders used culture to fuel the passions of their armies and other minions and to justify their actions among their people. One million Armenians; tens of millions of Russians; 10 million Jews, Gypsies, and homosexuals; 3 million Cambodians; and hundreds of thousands of Bosnians, Rwandans, and Timorese all were the victims of "culture"—whether it was ethnic, religious, ideological, tribal, or nationalistic in its origins. To be sure, they fell victim to other agendas as well. But the provocative elements of culture were to these accompanying agendas as Joseph Goebbels was to Adolf Hitler—an enabler and perhaps the most insidious accomplice. Historians can, of course, find examples from across the ages of "superior" cultures eradicating "inferior" opponents—in the American West, among the native tribes of the Americas and Africa, during the Inquisition, and during the expansion of virtually every empire.

Satellites as Cultural Death Stars

Critics of globalization argue that the process will lead to a stripping away of identity and a blandly uniform, Orwellian world. On a planet of 6 billion people, this is, of course, an impossibility. More importantly, the decline of cultural distinctions may be a measure of the progress of civilization, a tangible sign of enhanced communications and understanding. Successful multicultural societies, be they nations, federations, or other conglomerations of closely interrelated states, discern those aspects of culture that do not threaten union, stability, or prosperity (such as food, holidays, rituals, and music) and allow them to flourish. But they counteract or eradicate the more subversive elements of culture (exclusionary aspects of religion, language, and political/ideological beliefs). History shows that bridging cultural gaps successfully and serving as a home to diverse peoples requires certain social structures, laws, and institutions that transcend culture. Furthermore, the history of a number of ongoing experiments in multiculturalism, such as in the European Union, India, South Africa, and the United States, suggests that workable, if not perfected, integrative models exist. Each is built on the idea that tolerance is crucial to social well-being, and each at times has been threatened by both intolerance and a heightened emphasis on cultural distinctions. The greater public good warrants eliminating those cultural characteristics that promote conflict or prevent harmony, even as less-divisive, more personally observed cultural distinctions are celebrated and preserved.

The realization of such integrative models on a global scale is impossible in the near term. It will take centuries. Nor can it be achieved purely through rational decisions geared toward implementing carefully considered policies and programs. Rather, current trends that fall under the broad definitional umbrella of "globalization" are accelerating a process that has taken place throughout history as discrete groups have become familiar with one another, allied, and commingled —ultimately becoming more alike. Inevitably, the United States has taken the lead in this transformation; it is the "indispensable nation" in the management of global affairs and the leading producer of information products and services in these, the early years of the Information Age.

The drivers of today's rapid globalization are improving methods and systems of international transportation, devising revolutionary and innovative information technologies and services, and dominating the international commerce in services and ideas. Their impact affects lifestyles, religion, language, and every other component of culture.

Much has been written about the role of information technologies and services in this process. Today, 15 major U.S. telecommunications companies, including giants like Motorola, Loral Space & Communications, and Teledesic (a joint project of Microsoft's Bill Gates and cellular pioneer Craig McCaw), offer competing plans that will encircle the globe with a constellation of satellites and will enable anyone anywhere to communicate instantly with anyone elsewhere without an established telecommunications infrastructure on the ground near either the sender or the recipient. (Loral puts the cost of such a call at around $3 per minute.)

Technology is not only transforming the world; it is creating its own metaphors as well. Satellites carrying television signals now enable people on opposite sides of the globe to be exposed regularly to a wide range of cultural stimuli. Russian viewers are hooked on Latin soap operas, and Middle Eastern leaders have cited CNN as a prime source for even local news. The Internet is an increasingly global phenomenon with active development under way on every continent.

The United States dominates this global traffic in information and ideas. American music, American movies, American television, and American software are so dominant, so sought after, and so visible that they are now available literally everywhere on the Earth. They influence the tastes, lives, and aspirations of virtually every nation. In some, they are viewed as corrupting.

France and Canada have both passed laws to prohibit the satellite dissemination of foreign—meaning American—content across their borders and into the homes of their citizens. Not surprisingly, in many other countries—fundamentalist Iran, communist China, and the closely managed society of Singapore—central governments have aggressively sought to restrict the software and programming

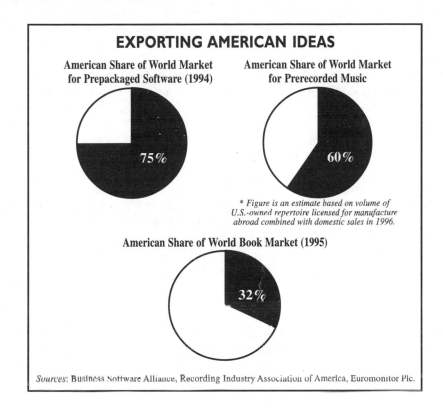

EXPORTING AMERICAN IDEAS

American Share of World Market for Prepackaged Software (1994)

75%

American Share of World Market for Prerecorded Music

60%

* Figure is an estimate based on volume of U.S.-owned repertoire licensed for manufacture abroad combined with domestic sales in 1996.

American Share of World Book Market (1995)

32%

Sources: Business Software Alliance, Recording Industry Association of America, Euromonitor Plc.

that reach their citizens. Their explicit objective is to keep out American and other alien political views, mores, and, as it is called in some parts of the Middle East, "news pollution." In these countries, the control of new media that give previously closed or controlled societies virtually unlimited access to the outside world is a high priority. Singapore has sought to filter out certain things that are available over the Internet—essentially processing all information to eliminate pornography. China has set up a "Central Leading Group" under the State Planning Commission and the direct supervision of a vice premier to establish a similar system that will exclude more than just what might be considered obscene.

These governments are the heirs of King Canute, the infamous monarch who set his throne at the sea's edge and commanded the waves to go backward. The Soviet Union fell in part because a closed society cannot compete in the Information Age. These countries will fare no better. They need look no further than their own élites to know this. In China, while satellite dishes are technically against the law, approximately one in five citizens of Beijing has access to television programming via a dish, and almost half of the people of Guangzhou have access to satellite-delivered programming. Singapore, the leading entrepôt of Southeast Asia, is a hub in a global network of business centers in which the lives of the élites are virtually identical. Business leaders in Buenos Aires, Frankfurt, Hong Kong, Johannesburg, Istanbul, Los Angeles, Mexico City, Moscow, New Delhi, New York, Paris, Rome, Santiago, Seoul, Singapore, Tel Aviv, and Tokyo all read the same newspapers, wear the same suits, drive the same cars, eat the same food, fly the same airlines, stay in the same hotels, and listen to the same music. While the people of their countries remain divided by culture, they have realized that to compete in the global marketplace they must conform to the culture of that marketplace.

The global marketplace is being institutionalized through the creation of a series of multilateral entities that establish common rules for international commerce. If capital is to flow freely, disclosure rules must be the same, settlement procedures consistent, and redress transparent. If goods are also to move unimpeded, tariff laws must be consistent, customs standards harmonized, and product safety and labeling standards brought into line. And if people are to move easily from deal to deal, air transport agreements need to be established, immigration controls standardized, and commercial laws harmonized. In many ways, business is the primary engine driving globalization, but it would be a mistake to conclude that the implications of globalization will be limited primarily to the commercial arena.

In politics, for example, as international organizations arise to coordinate policy among many nations on global issues such as trade, the environment, health, development, and crisis management, a community of international bureaucrats is emerging. These players are as comfortable operating in the international environment as they would be at home, and the organizations that they represent in effect establish global standards and expectations—facilitating the progress of globalization.

The community of nations increasingly accepts that such supranational entities are demanded by the exigencies of the times; with that acceptance also comes a recognition that the principal symbol of national identity—namely sovereignty—must be partially ceded to those entities. The United States in particular seems to have problems with this trend. For example, the United States was involved in creating the World Trade Organization and now undermines its effectiveness by arbitrarily withdrawing from its efforts to blunt the effects of the Helms-Burton act. Still, the recognition that sometimes there are interests greater than national interests is a crucial step on the path to a more peaceful, prosperous world.

Toward a Global Culture

It is in the general interest of the United States to encourage the development of a world in which the fault lines separating nations are bridged by shared interests. And it is in the economic and political interests of the United States to ensure that if the world is moving toward a common language, it be English; that if the world is moving toward common telecommunications, safety, and quality standards, they be American; that if the world is becoming linked by television, radio, and music, the programming be American; and that if common values are being developed, they be values with which Americans are comfortable.

These are not simply idle aspirations. English is linking the world. American information technologies and services are at the cutting edge of those that are enabling globalization. Access to the largest economy in the world—America's—is the primary carrot leading other nations to open their markets.

Indeed, just as the United States is the world's sole remaining military superpower, so is it the world's only information superpower. While Japan has become quite competitive in the manufacture of components integral to information systems, it has had a negligible impact as a manufacturer of software or as a force behind the technological revolution. Europe has failed on both fronts. Consequently, the United States holds a position of advantage at the moment and for the foreseeable future.

Some find the idea that Americans would systematically seek to promote their culture to be unattractive. They are concerned that it implies a sense of superiority on Americans' part or that it makes an uncomfortable value judgment. But the realpolitik of the Information Age is that setting technological standards, defining software standards, producing the most popular information products, and leading in the related development of the global trade in services are as essential to the well-being of any would-be leader as once were the resources needed to support empire or industry.

The economic stakes are immense considering the enormous investments that will be made over the next 10 years in the world's information infrastructure. The U.S. government estimates that telecommunications investment in Latin America alone during this period will top $150 billion. China will spend a similar amount, as will the member states of the Association of South East Asian Nations. In fact, the market for telecommunications services is expected to top $1 trillion by the turn of the century.

During the decade ahead, not only will enormous sums be directed toward the establishment of the global network of networks that the Clinton administration has dubbed the "Global Information Infrastructure," but those sums will pay for the foundations of a system that will dictate decades of future choices about upgrades, systems standards, software purchases, and services. At the same time, new national and international laws will be written, and they will determine how smoothly information products and services may flow from one market to another. Will steps be taken to ensure that Internet commerce remains truly free? What decisions will be made about the encryption of data that will impact not only the security of information markets but the free flow of ideas and the rights of individuals in the Information Age? Will governments allow the democratizing promise of the Internet to enable virtually anyone with a computer to contact anyone else?

The establishment of the Global Information Infrastructure is not just an enormous commercial opportunity for the world's information leader. The development of the rules governing that infrastructure will shape the nature of global politics decisively, either enhancing or undermining freedoms, thereby either speeding or slowing the pace of integration, understanding, and tolerance world-wide. The nature of individual and national relations will be transformed. Those wires and constellations of satellites and invisible beams of electronic signals crisscrossing the globe will literally form the fabric of future civilization.

Consequently, it could not be more strategically crucial that the United States do whatever is in its power to shape the development of that infrastructure, the rules governing it, and the information traversing it. Moreover, even if much of this process of developing what we might call the "infosphere" is left to the mar-ketplace (as it should be), governments will control crucial elements of it. Gov-ernments will award many of the biggest infrastructure development contracts offered in the next decade: Some will assist their national companies in trying to win those contracts, and state officials will meet to decide the trade rules that will govern international traffic in the world's telecommunications markets, the glo-bal regulatory environment, encryption standards, privacy standards, intellectual property protections, and basic equipment standards. Governments will determine whether these are open or closed markets and what portion of development dollars will be targeted at bringing the benefits of these technologies to the poor to help counteract information inequities. Already some government intercessions into this marketplace have failed. Notably, Japan's efforts to shape the development of high-definition television standards sent that nation down an analog path in what turned out to be a digital race. Yet there are many places where there is an important role for governments and where the United States should have a care-fully considered overarching policy and an aggressive stance to match.

Exporting the American Model

Many observers contend that it is distasteful to use the opportunities created by the global information revolution to promote American culture over others, but that kind of relativism is as dangerous as it is wrong. American culture is fundamen-tally different from indigenous cultures in so many other locales. American culture is an amalgam of influences and approaches from around the world. It is melded—consciously in many cases—into a social medium that allows individual freedoms and cultures to thrive. Recognizing this, Americans should not shy away from do-ing that which is so clearly in their economic, political, and security interests—and so clearly in the interests of the world at large. The United States should not hes-itate to promote its values. In an effort to be polite or politic, Americans should not deny the fact that of all the nations in the history of the world, theirs is the most just, the most tolerant, the most willing to constantly reassess and improve itself, and the best model for the future. At the same time, Americans should not fall under the spell of those like Singapore's Lee Kuan Yew and Malaysia's Mahathir bin-Mohamad, who argue that there is "an Asian way," one that non-Asians should not judge and that should be allowed to dictate the course of events for all those operating in that corner of the world. This argument amounts to self-interested po-litical rhetoric. Good and evil, better and worse coexist in this world. There are absolutes, and there are political, economic, and moral costs associated with failing to recognize this fact.

Repression is not defensible whether the tradition from which it springs is Confucian, Judeo-Christian, or Zoroastrian. The repressed individual still suffers, as does society, and there are consequences for the global community. Real costs accrue in terms of constrained human creativity, delayed market development, the diversion of assets to enforce repression, the failure of repressive societies to adapt well to the rapidly changing global environment, and the dislocations, struggles, and instability that result from these and other factors. Americans should promote their vision for the world, because failing to do so or taking a "live and let live" stance is ceding the process to the not-always-beneficial actions of others. Using the tools of the Information Age to do so is perhaps the most peaceful and powerful means of advancing American interests.

If Americans now live in a world in which ideas can be effectively exported and media delivery systems are powerful, they must recognize that the nature of those ideas and the control of those systems are matters with which they should be deeply concerned. Is it a threat to U.S. interests, to regional peace, to American markets, and to the United States's ability to lead if foreign leaders adopt models that promote separatism and the cultural fault lines that threaten stability? It certainly is. Relativism is a veil behind which those who shun scrutiny can hide. Whether Americans accept all the arguments of Huntington or not, they must recognize that the greater the cultural value gaps in the world, the more likely it is that conflict will ensue. The critical prerequisite for gaining the optimum benefits of global integration is to understand which cultural attributes can and should be tolerated—and, indeed, promoted—and which are the fissures that will become fault lines.

It is also crucial that the United States recognize its limitations. Americans can have more influence than others, but they cannot assure every outcome. Rather, the concerted effort to shape the development of the Global Information Infrastructure and the ideas that flow within it should be seen merely as a single component of a well-rounded foreign and security policy. (And since it is not likely to be an initiative that is widely liked or admired or enhanced through explicit promotion, it is not an approach that should be part of American public diplomacy efforts.)

Of course, implementing such an approach is not going to be easy in an America that is wracked by the reaction to and the backlash against globalization. Today, the extreme left and right wings of both major political parties are united in a new isolationist alliance. This alliance has put the brakes on 60 years of expanding free trade, has focused on the threats rather than the promise posed by such critical new relationships as those with China and other key emerging markets, and has seized on every available opportunity to disengage from the world or to undermine U.S. abilities to engage or lead effectively. It will take a committed effort by the president and cooperation from leaders on Capitol Hill to overcome the political opposition of the economic nationalists and neoisolationists. It will not happen if those in leadership positions aim simply to take the path of least political resistance or to rest on the accomplishments of the recent past. In a time of partisan bickering, when the emphasis of top officials has shifted from governing to politicking, there is a risk that America will fail to rise to these challenges. While the Clinton administration has broken important ground in developing a Global Information Infrastructure initiative and in dealing with the future of the Internet, encryption issues, and intellectual property concerns, these efforts are underfunded, sometimes managed to suit political rather than strategic objectives, shortsighted (particularly the steps concerning encryption, in which rapid changes and the demands of the marketplace are being overlooked), and poorly coordinated. At the same time, some of America's most powerful tools of engagement—which come in the form of new trade initiatives—seemingly have been shelved. This problem is most clearly manifested in the fact that fast-track negotiating-authority approval has not yet been granted and in the real possibility that Congress will refuse to grant such approval before the turn of the century.

The Clinton administration and its successors must carefully consider the long-term implications of globalization, such as the impact of the rise of new markets on America's economic influence and how America can maintain its leadership role. Aspects of American culture will play a critical role in helping to ensure the continuation of that leadership. American cultural diversity gives the United States resources and potential links with virtually every market and every major power in the world. America's emphasis on the individual ensures that American innovation will continue to outstrip that of other nations. Working in its favor is the fact that the "Pax Americana" is a phenomenon of the early years of globalization and that the U.S. ascendancy to undisputed leadership came at the same time as the establishment of international institutions such as the United Nations, the World Bank, and the International Monetary Fund; thus, for all the challenges of adjustment, the United States has more leadership experience than any other nation in this new global environment. Also, though some may decry Americans' emphasis on "newness" and suggest that it is a result of their lack of an extensive history, it also represents a healthy lack of cultural "baggage": It is this emphasis on newness that puts the United States in the best position to deal with a world in which the rapidity of change is perhaps the greatest strategic challenge of all.

Identity without Culture

The opportunity lies before us as Americans. The United States is in a position not only to lead in the 21st century as the dominant power of the Information Age but to do so by breaking down the barriers that divide nations—and groups within nations—and by building ties that create an ever greater reservoir of shared interests among an ever larger community of peoples. Those who look at the post–Cold War era and see the "clash of civilizations" see only one possibility. They overlook the great strides in integration that have united the world's billions. They discount the factors that have led to global consolidation and the reality that those factors grow in power with each new day of the global era—integration is a trend that builds upon itself. They argue that America should prepare for the conflicts that may come in this interim period without arguing that it should accelerate the arrival of a new era with every means at its disposal.

Certainly, it is naive to expect broad success in avoiding future conflicts among cultures. But we now have tools at our disposal to diminish the disparities that will fuel some of those conflicts. While we should prepare for conflict, we should also remember that it is not mere idealism that demands that we work for integration and in support of a unifying global culture ensuring individual rights and enhancing international stability: It is also the ultimate realpolitik, the ultimate act of healthy self-interest.

Allowing ourselves to be swept up in the backlash against globalization would undermine America's ability to advance its self-interests. Americans must recognize that those interests and the issues pertaining to them reach across the disciplines of economics, politics, science, and culture. An interdisciplinary approach to international policymaking is thus required. We must also fully understand the new tools at our disposal. We must understand the profound importance and nature of the emerging infosphere—and its potential as a giant organic culture processor, democratic empowerer, universal connector, and ultimate communicator. Moreover, it is not enough to create and implement the right policies using the new tools at our disposal. Policymakers must better communicate the promise of this new world and make clear America's stake in that promise and the role Americans must play to achieve success. The United States does not face a simple choice between integration or separation, engagement or withdrawal. Rather, the choice is between leading a more peaceful world or being held hostage to events in a more volatile and violent one.

Culture Wars

France's Ministry of Culture does not look like the sort of place where pessimism ought to flourish. The ministry occupies a wing of Richelieu's magnificent Palais Royal, round the corner from the Comédie Française and just a short walk from the Louvre and the Opéra. On their way to lunch its inhabitants have to pick their way through throngs of tourists who have come from all over the world to admire France's cultural riches.

Yet pessimism flourishes here nonetheless. The ministry's officials are convinced that a rising tide of American popular culture is swamping France. And they spend much of their working lives administering a complex system of quotas and subsidies that are designed to protect French culture from total submersion.

The ministry has almost uniform support for its position among a French cultural elite worried about the threat that America poses, particularly to French film. Their concern is not, as sometimes claimed, that an upstart America hijacked the French national invention of Méliès and the Lumières. Rather it is that Hollywood is a Trojan horse bringing with it Disneyland Paris, fast-food chains and free advertising for American products from clothes to rock music. "America is not just interested in exporting its films," says Giles Jacob, the head of the Cannes Film Festival. "It is interested in exporting its way of life."

Editorial from *The Economist,* September 12, 1998, pp. 97–99. © 1998 by The Economist Newspaper Group, Inc. Reprinted by permission. Further reproduction prohibited. www.economist.com

These French people lead a world guerrilla army hoping to curb American cultural hegemony. In 1989 the French government persuaded the European Community to decree that 40% of TV programmes should be domestic. It also strengthened their complex system of support (which taxes cinema tickets to help French film production) by extending it to television programmes. In 1993 France threatened to sabotage the GATT trade round in order to exempt audio-visual materials from free trade agreements.

The French have found a powerful ally in Canada, which has long been terrified of being swamped by its closest neighbour. Of the films shown on Canadian screens, 96% are foreign, primarily American. Three-quarters of the music on Canadian radio is not Canadian. Four in five magazines sold on news-stands in Canada, and six in every ten books, are foreign, mainly American.

In June Canada organised a meeting in Ottawa about American cultural dominance. Nineteen countries attended, including Britain, Brazil and Mexico; the United States was pointedly excluded. At issue were ways of exempting cultural goods from treaties lowering trade barriers, on the view that free trade threatened national cultures. The Ottawa meeting followed a similar gathering in Stockholm, sponsored by the United Nations, which resolved to press for special exemptions for cultural goods in another global trade pact, the Multilateral Agreement on Investment.

What Exactly Is the Problem?

Quite apart from its recommended solutions, is the "resistance" to American cultural imperialism correct in its diagnosis of the problem? Lurking here are three distinct questions. Is Hollywood as powerful as its enemies imagine? Is there an identifiable thing you can sensibly label "American culture"? And does America's domination extend to every corner of the popular arts and entertainment?

A strong case can be made out that America dominates world cinema. It may not make most feature films. But American films are the only ones that reach every market in the world. (The highly successful films of India and Hong Kong hardly travel outside their regions.) In major markets around the world, lists of the biggest-grossing films are essentially lists of Hollywood blockbusters in slightly differing orders with one or two local films for variety. In the European Union the United States claimed 70% overall of the film market in 1996, up from 56% in 1987; even in Japan, America now accounts for more than half the film market. "Titanic" has grossed almost $1.8 billion worldwide. "Armageddon" and "Lethal Weapon 4" play well from Belgium to Brazil.

Hollywood's empire also appears to be expanding by the year. Hollywood now gets roughly half its revenues from overseas, up from just 30% in 1980. At the same time few foreign films make it big in the United States, where they have less than 3% of the market. Between 1995 and 1996 Europe's trade deficit with the United States in films and television grew from $4.8 billion to $5.65 billion.

Striking figures, to be sure. Yet the more one looks at many of these films the less distinctively American they become. One reason for Hollywood's success is that from the earliest days it was open to foreign talent and foreign money. Some of the great figures of Hollywood—Chaplin, Murnau, Stroheim, Hitchcock —were imports. And now, two of the most powerful studios, Columbia Tristar and Fox, are owned by foreign media conglomerates, Japan's Sony and Australia's News Corporation.

Several of Hollywood's most successful films have drawn heavily on international resources. "Three Men and a Baby," which helped to revive Disney after a fallow period in the mid-1980s, was a remake of a French comedy. "Total Recall" was made partly with French money, directed by a Dutchman and starred an Austrian, Arnold Schwarzenegger. "The English Patient" was directed by a Briton, shot in Italy, and starred French and British actresses.

It may even be argued that it is less a matter of Hollywood corrupting the world than of the world corrupting Hollywood. The more Hollywood becomes preoccupied by the global market, the more it produces generic blockbusters made to play as well in Pisa as Peoria. Such films are driven by special effects that can be appreciated by people with minimal grasp of English rather than by dialogue and plot. They eschew fine-grained cultural observation for generic subjects that anybody can identify with, regardless of national origins. There is nothing particularly American about boats crashing into icebergs or asteroids that threaten to obliterate human life.

Hollywood Is Not America

The very identification of Hollywood with American culture, particularly American high culture, is itself a mistake. So is confusing screen conduct with real conduct, although plenty of serious-minded people do seem to treat Hollywood as a ruinous influence on American manners and morals: Michael Medved, an American screenwriter turned cultural commentator, argues that, far from nurturing deep-rooted values, Hollywood helps destroy them. "Tens of millions of Americans now see the entertainment industry as an all-powerful enemy," he argues, "an alien force that assaults our most cherished values and corrupts our children." Making a point more about art than behaviour, Terry Teachout, a music critic, says that educated Americans would cheer if an earthquake reduced Hollywood's sound stages to rubble. "The 'enemy' at the gates is not the United States, free trade or even Walt Disney," he says with deliberate effect, "it is democracy."

Instead of treating the sovereignty of popular taste as something that underpins America's cultural domination of the world, many of America's neoconservatives (and some liberals) see it rather as a perilous solvent acting on the United States itself. The country, they fear, is dissolving into a babble of discordant ethnic voices without a common cultural identity or a shared national purpose. And they put much of the blame on the proliferation of foreign-language media outlets. One of the most popular television channels in Los Angeles is KMFX 34, which broadcasts in Spanish; there are also channels which broadcast exclusively in Korean, Cantonese and Japanese, and others that rent air-time for Yiddish and

Russian broadcasts. Even in the shadow of the Hollywood sign it is possible to live without bowing the knee to a majority culture.

The world's culture ministers might well reply that the inroads that Spanish and Korean television have made into the United States are as nothing compared with the inroads that American television has made into their home countries. The deregulation of television in the 1980s created a legion of upstart stations that were desperate for content—and much of the cheapest and most reliable content came from America.

Yet as new stations establish themselves they tend to drop generic American products in favour of local productions: audiences still prefer homegrown fare if given the choice. In every European country in 1997, the most popular television programme was a local production. "Navarro," an unmistakeably French action drama, has never had less than a 33% market share. Across the channel, "Inspector Morse," a much re-run British detective series, owes its lasting appeal to an Oxford setting and a curmudgeonly hero.

In Rock Music, Europe Rules

The strength of local ties is even more apparent in pop music, long supposed to provide the soundtrack to America's cultural hegemony. The United States has never enjoyed the same dominance of pop music as it has of cinema, having to share the global market with Britain. According to a just published book reporting the results of a rock-music poll of 200,000 people aged from nine to 62 in America and Europe, "The All-Time Top 1,000 Albums" (Virgin; £16.99. London Bridge; $24.95), seven of the ten most popular albums were British. As the rock market fragments into niches—from urban rap to techno—it is harder and harder to create global brands.

A few years ago few self-respecting teenagers would be caught dead listening to French or Swedish pop groups. (The Swedish group Abba was almost the definition of naff.) Now French groups such as Air and Daft Punk and Swedish groups such as Ace of Base and the Cardigans are decidedly cool. In Germany, the world's third-largest music market after the United States and Japan, local performers account for 48% of the DM6 billion ($3.5 billion) in yearly sales, double the percentage five years ago. Two leading music channels, Viva and Viva-2, now devote about 40% of their time to German titles. In Spain, 58% of the total $1 billion music sales are generated by Spanish and Latin American artists. In the French market, French rock groups account for nearly half the country's total sales. MTV makes different programmes for different regions.

As America's pop-music industry struggles with a stagnating international market, European groups are finding it easier to cross borders. Americans buy some $2 billion worth of Spanish music a year. Ace of Base's first record was one of the biggest selling debut records ever, dominating the American charts. German techno bands such as Mr. President have had a string of international successes. Ibiza is the capital of global dance music. Daft Punk sold 900,000 albums outside

France last year, earning some 77m francs ($13m). Even Iceland has a global star in Bjork.

So Long Broadway

The American empire is equally shaky in other areas of popular culture. The British have dominated popular musicals since the appearance of "Joseph and the Amazing Technicolour Dreamcoat" and "Jesus Christ Superstar" in the mid-1970s. Andrew Lloyd Webber and Cameron Macintosh revived what had become a geriatric art form with catchy tunes, clever lyrics, sumptuous sets and relentless marketing. They turned British musicals into both a major tourist attraction and an important export. "The Phantom of the Opera" has been seen by an estimated 52m people, pulling in more than £1.5 billion ($2.5 billion). Basle has a purpose-built theatre for "Phantom," Bochum, in Germany, has one for "Starlight Express" and Frankfurt has one for "Sunset Boulevard," complete with its own hotel.

As for fashion, the great houses of Paris and Milan dominate the high end of the market, London its street-wise, popular base. Walk down Rodeo Drive in Los Angeles, with its outlets for Gucci, Valentino and Armani, and America looks like the cultural colony, not Europe. Here too it is the British who are shaking up the industry. Jean-Paul Gaultier claims that he gets some of his best ideas by walking around London. Ex-punker Vivienne Westwood is a *grande dame* in Paris and Milan, and two big French houses recently put young British designers, John Galliano and Alexander McQueen, in charge.

Even in publishing and magazines—an area that particularly worries the Canadians—American domination is by no means clear-cut. The best-known magazine editor in the United States is an Englishwoman, Tina Brown, who is credited with reviving (before leaving) both "Vanity Fair" and "The New Yorker." Foreign companies control half of America's top 20 publishing houses. Earlier this year Bertelsmann, a German conglomerate, purchased America's biggest publisher, Random House, provoking headlines about American culture being sold to foreigners.

In fact, Bertelsmann may well be a stronger global force than its American-owned rivals. After the fall of the Berlin Wall it built a network of book clubs, publishers and record companies across the old Soviet block. It holds a stake in Prague's City Radio, owns the biggest newspaper in Hungary and in Slovakia, and has launched a glossy science magazine in Russia in a venture with the Orthodox Church.

Don't Protect

Even if America really were as powerful as its cultural adversaries imagine, the commonly suggested solution of protection would not be the answer. Take film, where there is no question about Hollywood's might. Quotas are about as suitable to the modern age as the horse and carriage. Anybody who wants to watch an American TV programme in prime time can flick through an ever-increasing number of channels—or rent a video. Quotas also have the perverse effect of encouraging the production of "quota quickies"—banal local productions designed only to satisfy official mandates and capture the subsidies that often come with them.

The case for subsidies is hardly more robust. Government handouts tend to go to the people who have least need of them. France's Centre National de la Cinématographie gives the biggest subsidies to the country's most successful film producers. One of the three British film companies that get grants from Britain's National Lottery is run by the producers of two of the most successful British films of recent years, "Four Weddings and a Funeral" and "Trainspotting." At best, this means that public money is used to subsidise films that would have been made anyway; at worst, it means that talented producers spend their time lobbying the government rather than making good films.

In some cases subsidies even end up supporting the sort of Hollywood fodder that they are meant to thwart. The past decade has seen a steady trek of Hollywood producers to Canada, particularly Toronto, in search of subsidies and a nice exchange rate. (Films and television shows made in Canada—even by foreigners—are eligible for government handouts; Canadian television channels also pay a premium for programmes that help them meet government requirements for Canadian content.) Toronto has doubled for New York City in more than 100 films (including "Moonstruck" and "I'll Take Manhattan") and TV series (including "Due South" and "Gangsters"). Alliance Communications, which produces "Due South," about a Canadian mountie who busts Chicago street gangs, calculates that the show would cost about 40% more to produce in Chicago.

Jeanne Moreau, the doyenne of French film actresses, suggests a more hopeful way of preserving French (and by implication other national) film industries. French film producers, she argues, should stop relying on protectionism ("an attitude born from fear") and should start believing in themselves again. They should realise that the building of new cinemas and the explosion of television channels provides them with an opportunity; "The beast needs to be fed," she laughs. They should learn from Hollywood's story-telling skills and from its *savoir-faire*. And they should form alliances with Hollywood studios to exploit its technical skills and its marketing might.

This answer has the merit of working with the grain of new technology and new Hollywood thinking. Some time ago studios began to set up or buy independent studios to reduce their dependence on extravagant blockbusters and reach beyond their most reliable audience of teenage morons. That restless quest for new ideas and fresh talent has now led them to create subsidiaries in Europe: Sony's Bridge in London; a Miramax office in Berlin and offshoots of Warner Brothers both there and in Paris.

Cultural protectionists might well complain that this is yet more evidence of America's remorseless penetration into European markets. Yet what is it that they object to—the Americanness of the company or the Americanness of its products? On balance, global companies, be they American-, Australian- or German-owned, do best when serving local markets, local ways and local tastes.

The United States will always have a big influence on popular culture. America has the advantage of a huge domestic market, a language that is becoming ubiquitous and a genius for marketing. Its worldwide image is of the nation that reached modernity first, inventing trends from blue jeans to rock 'n' roll, since widely adopted—and adapted—elsewhere. Whether they want to resist American modernity from fear or from envy, cultural protectionists are wrong to think they can direct taste through subsidies and quotas. And they err yet more if they think that, given a free choice, their citizens will prefer American to local artefacts. Those officials at France's Ministry of Culture have less to fear than they think.

RESOURCE BIBLIOGRAPHY

Robert Goehlert and Anthony Stamatoplos

This resource bibliography identifies selected basic resources related to global and area studies research. It is not comprehensive; rather, it is representative of the most useful sources currently available in print and on the World Wide Web. The bibliography contains three sections: (1) a bibliography of books and articles, (2) a survey of research guides, and (3) a selected list of Web sites.

The first section is a list of suggested supplementary readings relating to the concept of globalization. This bibliography includes books and articles focusing on global and international studies, from a variety of academic perspectives. The section includes articles and books that discuss different approaches to the concept of globalization from several disciplines, including anthropology, history, political science, and sociology. The bibliography draws upon the literature related to global, comparative, and area studies. The focus is on materials that are concerned with increasing awareness and knowledge of world and foreign affairs. We include materials on the concept of globalization, and new perspectives, methodologies, and interdisciplinary approaches to international studies. We also include materials discussing the history and future directions of area and international studies. The bibliography includes materials that are international, inter-area, and interdisciplinary in scope. There are articles and books on culture, politics, business, history, conflict, geography, and the social sciences.

The following are a few additional suggestions for updating the bibliography. To find additional monographic literature, one should use bibliographic databases, such as *Books in Print, WorldCat,* or *RLIN,* as well as the library's catalog. One should consult indexes and abstracts to identify articles of interest. The best indexes, in either print or electronic form, for finding articles in this area are *ABC POL SCI, ABI Inform, America: History and Life, Anthropological Literature, Arts and Humanities Citation Index, EconLit, GeoRef, Historical Abstracts, Humanities Index, International Political Science Abstracts, PAIS International, Readers' Guide to Periodical Literature, Social Sciences Citation Index, Social Sciences Index,* and *Sociological Abstracts.* One also should consult a librarian for assistance in finding materials.

The second section is a survey of research guides that provide reference materials about global and area studies. It does not include guides to archives, libraries, or other collections. We have annotated a number of the most important guides, and included an additional listing of un-annotated entries. Both lists are in alphabetical order by author. Because of their comprehensiveness, research guides to global and area studies continue to be useful; however, it is difficult to keep them current. Not all of these guides will be available in every library.

An important series of research guides not included here is the World Bibliographic Series published by ABC-Clio. There are over two hundred volumes available, and more are forthcoming. Each multidisciplinary volume covers all aspects of a single country, including its history, geography, economy, politics, culture, religion, and living conditions. The volumes are uniform in nature, and the annotated entries include books, articles, maps, documents, newspapers, and dissertations. In addition to volumes for individual countries, there are some that cover the principal regions of the world and major cities. Many will be found in most large public and academic libraries.

The third section is a selected list of major World Wide Web sites related to the study of globalization. The Web sites are listed in alphabetical order by name of the site. We have included the URL and a brief annotation. The World Wide Web is undoubtedly one of the most important resources in the field of education, as it is now a major source of information for researchers. While interesting and useful Web sites often are found serendipitously by following live links or using search engines and Web browsers, good print directories often can save time and make this task easier. As a result of the growing popularity and widespread use of the World Wide Web, numerous Web user guides and directories are being published and are available in print. Most large bookstores and libraries have a selection of such guides, many of which are published by recognized commercial and scholarly presses. Some cover a broad variety of resources, including Web pages, discussion groups, Gopher sites, and so on. Others are more narrowly focused, dealing with particular types of information, or selected subjects from specific points of view.

A major problem of print directories of the World Wide Web is that information changes constantly and becomes outdated, so that it is difficult for libraries to keep their collections of directories up-to-date. When searching in library catalogs for printed guides to the Web, one should use keywords that might appear as title or subject terms, such as "Internet" or "Web," and combine these with terms such as "guide" or "directory." One also should pay close attention to publication dates and frequency of publication.

On-line Web directories tend to be more focused. Web sites themselves may work well as on-line directories or catalogs, because most have live links to other sites. Sites that prove useful should be bookmarked and consulted regularly. A variety of methods can be used to find Web-based guides to international Web sources. Web pages of organizations and institutions tend to have links to similar or related sites, so one can follow links from known sites. One should use Web browsers and search engines to search for the pages of known organizations and institutions, or search by relevant keywords. In using any resource concerning the Web, one must keep in mind that no single print directory or Web site will be absolutely current or reliable. Sites come and go. Some are not well maintained or updated frequently, and addresses (URLs) change. It is best to use familiar sources, those that are known to provide good coverage on topics of interest, and those that are updated frequently. The sites selected here cover a range of topics related to the study of globalization.

It is impossible to use any single search engine to identify global and area studies sites that contain good listings of links or original source material. Perhaps the best way to find other Web sites is to start with the mega-sites listed in this section. The World Wide Web Virtual Libraries are also a good place to start. One of them is annotated in this resource bibliography. They are excellent sites and provide links to other related Virtual Libraries. Another good place to search is the IANWeb Resources (International Affairs Network), which is part of the World Wide Web Virtual Library. The International Affairs Network maintains a comprehensive collection of annotated links to international affairs resources on the Internet. Topics included are Area Studies, Country Information, and others related to globalization.

Bibliography

Abeles, Marc. "Political Anthropology: New Challenges, New Aims." *International Social Science Journal* 49 (September 1997): 319–332.

Abraham, Itty, and Ronald Kassimir. "Internationalization of the Social Sciences and Humanities." *Items* [Social Science Research Council] 51 (June–September 1997): 23–30.

Alexandre, Laurien. "Genderizing International Studies: Revisioning Concepts and Curriculum." *International Studies Notes* 14 (Winter 1989): 5–8.

Alger, Chadwick. "Peace Studies at the Crossroads: Where Else?" *Annals of the American Academy of Political and Social Science* 504 (July 1989): 117–127.

Andreopoulos, George, and Richard Claude, eds. *Human Rights Education for the Twenty-first Century*. Philadelphia: University of Pennsylvania Press, 1997. 636 pp.

Association of American Geographers. *Geography and International Knowledge*. Washington, D.C.: The Association, 1982. 24 pp.

Auletta, Ken. "The Next Corporate Order: American Keiretsu." *New Yorker* (October 20–27, 1997): 225–227.

Axtmann, Roland. "Society, Globalization and the Comparative Method." *History of the Human Sciences* [Great Britain] 6, 2 (1993): 53–74.

Axtmann, Roland, ed. *Globalization and Europe: Theoretical and Empirical Investigations*. London: Pinter, 1998. 214 pp.

Backman, Earl, ed. *Approaches to International Education*. New York: Macmillan, 1984. 356 pp.

Bates, Robert H. "Area Studies and the Discipline." *APSA-CP: Newsletter of the APSA Organized Section in Comparative Politics* 7 (Winter 1996): 1–2.

Bates, Robert H. "Area Studies and the Discipline: A Useful Controversy." *PS: Political Science and Politics* 30 (June 1997): 166–169.

Bates, Robert H. "Area Studies and Political Science: Rupture and Possible Synthesis." *Africa Today* 44 (April–June 1997): 123–131.

Bates, Robert H. "The Death of Comparative Politics?" *APSA-CP: Newletter of the APSA Organized Section in Comparative Politics* 7 (Summer 1996): 1–2.

Benavot, Aaron, et al. "Knowledge for the Masses: World Models and National Curricula 1920–1986." *American Sociological Review* 56 (February 1991): 85–100.

Bennett, Christine. *Comprehensive Multicultural Education: Theory and Practice.* 3rd ed. Boston: Allyn and Bacon, 1995. 452 pp.

Bennett, Wendell C. *Area Studies in American Universities.* New York: Social Science Research Council, 1951. 82 pp.

Beyer, Peter. "Globalizing Systems, Global Cultural Models and Religion(s)." *International Sociology* 13 (March 1998): 79–94.

Bird, A., et al. "A Conceptual Model of the Effects of Area Studies Training Programs and a Preliminary Investigation of the Model's Hypothesized Relationships." *International Journal of Intercultural Relations* 17, 4 (1993): 415–435.

Blodgett, Steven A. "A Research Agenda for the Internationalization of Higher Education in the United States: Some Thoughts on Next Steps." *International Education Forum* 16 (Spring 1996): 37–41.

Bonham, George. "Education and the World View." *Change Magazine* 12 (May–June 1980): 2–7.

Boulding, Kenneth, and Elise Boulding. *Introduction to the Global Society: Interdisciplinary Perspectives.* New York: Consortium for International Studies Education of the International Studies Association, 1974. 47 pp.

Boyce, James K. "Area Studies and the National Security State." *Bulletin of Concerned Asian Scholars* 29 (January–March 1997): 27–29.

Bradshaw, Michael J. "New Regional Geography, Foreign Area Studies and Perestroika." *Area* 22, 4 (1990): 315–322.

Braungart, Richard G. "At Century's End: Globalization, Paradoxes, and a New Political Agenda." *Journal of Political and Military Sociology* 25 (Winter 1997): 343–351.

Brzezinski, Zbigniew. "New Challenges to Human Rights." *Journal of Democracy* 8, 2 (1997): 3–8.

Bugliarello, George. "Telecommunities: The Next Civilization." *Futurist* 31 (September–October 1997): 23–26.

Bulman, Raymond F. "Discerning Major Shifts in the World-System: Some Help from Theology?" *Review* [Fernand Braudel Center] 19, 4 (1996): 383–400.

Burn, Barbara. *Expanding the International Dimensions of Higher Education.* San Francisco: Jossey-Bass Publishers, 1980. 176 pp.

Burn, Barbara. "International Education in a Troubled World." *Annals of the American Academy of Political and Social Science* 449 (May 1980): 17–30.

Buzan, Barry. "The Present as a Historic Turning Point." *Journal of Peace Research* 32, 4 (1995): 385–398.

Caporaso, James, and James Mittelman. "The Assault on Global Education." *PS: Political Science and Politics* 21 (Winter 1988): 36–44.

Carver, Terrell. "Time, Space and Speed: New Dimensions in Political Analysis." *New Political Science* 40 (Summer 1997): 33–44.

Cavusgil, S. Tamer, and Nancy Horn, eds. *Internationalizing Doctoral Education in Business.* East Lansing: Michigan State University Press, 1997. 317 pp.

Cerny, Philip G. "Globalization and Other Stories: The Search for a New Paradigm for International Relations." *International Journal* 51 (Autumn 1996): 617–637.

Cerny, Philip G. "Paradoxes of the Competition State: The Dynamics of Political Globalization." *Government and Opposition* 32 (Spring 1997): 251–274.

Chege, Michael. "The Social Science Area Studies Controversy from the Continental African Standpoint." *Africa Today* 44 (April–June 1997): 133–142.

Chomsky, Noam, et al. *The Cold War & the University: Toward an Intellectual History of the Postwar Years.* New York: W. W. Norton, 1997. 258 pp.

Clark, Ian. *Globalization and Fragmentation: International Relations in the Twentieth Century.* New York: Oxford University Press, 1997. 220 pp.

Clarke, Susan E., and Gary L. Gaile. "Local Politics in a Global Era: Thinking Locally, Acting Globally." *Annals of the American Academy of Political and Social Science* 551 (1997): 28–43.

Cleveland, Harlan. "Ten Keys to World Peace." *Futurist* 28 (July–August 1994): 15–21.

Clinton, William J. "The 21st Century Will Challenge Our Security." *Vital Speeches* 64, 1 (1997): 1–4.

Collins, H. Thomas. *Guidelines for Global and International Studies Education: Challenges, Culture, Connection.* New York: American Forum for Global Education, 1996. 19 pp.

Coombs, Philip. *The Fourth Dimension of Foreign Policy: Education and Cultural Affairs.* New York: Harper and Row, 1964. 158 pp.

Coyne, J. "Geography in Area Studies: Have British Geographers Missed the Boat?" *Journal of Geography in Higher Education* 8, 1 (1984): 3–9.

Cox, Michael. "Rebels without a Cause? Radical Theorists and the World System after the Cold War." *New Political Economy* 3 (November 1998): 445–461.

Cumings, Bruce. "Boundary Displacement: Area Studies and International Studies during and after the Cold War." *Bulletin of Concerned Asian Scholars* 29 (January–March 1997): 6–26.

Currie, Jan, and Janice Newson, eds. *Universities and Globalization: Critical Perspectives.* Thousand Oaks, Calif.: Sage Publications, 1998. 339 pp.

Daniels, John, and N. Caroline Daniels *Global Vision. Building New Models for the Corporation of the Future.* New York: McGraw-Hill, 1993. 197 pp.

Dell, David. "Readings for a Global Curriculum." *Change Magazine* 12 (May–June 1980): 70–76.

Desmond, Jane C., and Virginia R. Dominguez. "Resituating American Studies in a Critical Internationalism." *American Quarterly* 48 (September 1996): 475–490.

Diamond, Larry. "Is the Third Wave Over?" *Journal of Democracy* 7 (July 1996): 20–37.

Didsbury, Howard F., ed. *Futurevision: Ideas, Insights, and Strategies.* Bethesda, Md.: World Future Society, 1996. 366 pp.

Dugan, Maire. "Peace Studies at the Graduate Level." *Annals of the American Academy of Political and Social Science* 504 (July 1989): 72–79.

Dunn, David. "The Peace Studies Debate." *Political Quarterly* 56 (January–March 1985): 68–71.

During, Simon. "Popular Culture on a Global Scale: A Challenge for Cultural Studies?" *Critical Inquiry* 23 (Summer 1997): 808–833.

Ehrlich, Robert, ed. *Perspectives on Nuclear War and Peace Education.* New York: Greenwood Press, 1987. 242 pp.

Elliott, Anthony. "Symptoms of Globalization: Or, Mapping Reflexivity in the Postmodern Age." *Political Psychology* 16 (December 1995): 719–736.

Farmer, Rod. "International Education as a Worldcentric Perspective: Defining International Education." *New England Journal of History* 49 (Winter 1992–93): 52–55.

Fiero, Gloria. "Global Humanities: Pedagogy or Politics." *Interdisciplinary Humanities* 13 (Winter 1996): 5–11.

Foran, John. "The Future of Revolutions at the Fin-de-Siècle." *Third World Quarterly* 18 (December 1997): 791–820.

Forte, Maximilian C. "Globalization and World-Systems Analysis: Toward New Paradigms of a Geo-Historical Social Anthropology (A Research Review)." *Reviews* 21 (Winter 1998): 29–99.

Fung, C. Victor. "Rationales for Teaching World Musics." *Music Educators* 82 (July 1995): 36–40.

Ganderton, P. S. "Concepts of Globalization and Their Impact upon Curriculum Policy-

Making: Rhetoric and Reality—A Study of Australian Reform." *International Journal of Educational Development* 16, 4 (1996): 393–405.

George, Alexander. "The Two Cultures of Academia and Policymaking: Bridging the Gap." *Political Psychology* 15 (March 1994): 143–172.

Gill, Stephen. "Globalization, Market Civilization, and Disciplinary Neoliberalism." *Millennium: Journal of International Studies* 24 (Winter 1995): 399–424.

Giugni, Marco G. "The Other Side of the Coin: Explaining Crossnational Similarities between Social Movements" *Mobilization* 3 (March 1998): 89–105.

Goldsmith, Peter. "Globalization: The European Experience." *Journal of Legal Education* 46 (September 1996): 317–321.

Goodwin, Geoffrey. *The University Teaching of International Relations*. Oxford: Blackwell, 1951. 126 pp.

Greenfield, Liah. "Transcending the Nation's Worth." *Daedalus* 122, 31 (1993): 47–61.

Groennings, Sven, and David Wiley, eds. *Group Portrait: Internationalizing the Disciplines*. New York: American Forum, 1990. 468 pp.

Guyer, Jane I. "Distant Beacons and Immediate Steps: Area Studies, International Studies, and the Disciplines in 1996." *Africa Today* 44 (April–June 1997): 149–156.

Haass, Richard N., and Robert E. Litan. "Globalization and Its Discontents: Navigating the Dangers of a Tangled World." *Foreign Affairs* 77 (May–June 1998): 2–6.

Hall, Peter A., and Sidney Tarrow. "Globalization and Area Studies: When Is Too Broad Too Narrow?" *The Chronicle of Higher Education* (January 23, 1998): B4–5.

Hall, Robert. *Area Studies: With Special Reference to their Implications for Research in the Social Sciences*. New York: Social Science Research Council, 1947. 90 pp.

Halliday, Fred. "International Relations and Its Discontents." *International Affairs* 71 (October 1995): 733–746.

Hawkins, John N., Carlos Manuel Haro, Miriam A. Kazanjian, Gilbert W. Merkx, and David Wiley, eds. *International Education in the New Global Era: Proceedings of a National Policy Conference on the Higher Education Act, Title VI, and Fulbright-Hays Programs*. Los Angeles: International Studies and Overseas Programs, UCLA. 1998. 250 pp.

Heater, Derek. "Peace Studies: A Venerable Tradition." *Teaching Politics* 16 (September 1987): 275–284.

Heginbotham, Stanley J. "Rethinking International Scholarship: The Challenge of Transition from the Cold War Era." *Items* [Social Science Research Council] 48 (June–September 1994): 33–40.

Heilbrunn, J. "The News from Everywhere, Does Global Thinking Threaten Local Knowledge (The Social Science Research Council Debates the Future of Area Studies)." *Lingua Franca* 6 (May–June 1996): 48–56.

Hesselbein, Frances, et al., eds. *The Community of the Future*. San Francisco: Jossey-Bass, 1998. 285 pp.

Hettne, Bjorn. "Development, Security and World Order: A Regionalist Approach." *European Journal of Development Research* 9 (June 1997): 83–106.

Hewitt de Alcantera, Cynthia. "Uses and Abuses of the Concept of Governance." *International Social Science Journal* 50 (March 1998): 105–113.

Heyl, John. "A Research Agenda for the Internationalization of Higher Education in the United States: Comments on Research Categories." *International Education Forum* 16 (Spring 1996): 44–46.

Hicks, David, and Cathie Holden. "Exploring the Future: A Missing Dimension in Environmental Education." *Environmental Education Research* 1 (1995): 185–193.

Hill, Christopher, and Pamela Beshoff, eds. *Two Worlds of International Relations: Academics, Practitioners and the Trade in Ideas*. New York: Routledge, 1994. 233 pp.

Hoemeke, Thomas. "A Research Agenda for the Internationalization of Higher Education in the United States: Reaction and Comments." *International Education Forum* 16 (Spring 1996): 57–58.

Hood, Christopher. "Emerging Issues in Public Administration." *Public Administration* 73 (Spring 1995): 165–183.

Hoffman, Dorothy. *International Development in a Global Context.* Minneapolis: United Nations Association of Minnesota, 1988. 105 pp.

Holsti, Ole. "Case Teaching: Transforming Foreign Policy Courses with Cases." *International Studies Notes* 19 (Spring 1994): 7–13.

Hounshell, David A. "Pondering the Globalization of R & D: Some New Questions for Business Historians." *Business and Economic History* 25, 2 (1996): 131–143.

Hubert, Robert T., Blair A. Ruble, and Peter J. Stavrakis. "Post-Cold War 'International' Scholarship: A Brave New World or the Triumph of Form over Substance?" *Items* [Social Science Research Council] 49 (March 1995): 30–38.

Hurrell, Andrew, and Ngaire Woods. "Globalization and Inequality." *Millennium: Journal of International Studies* 24 (Winter 1995): 447–470.

Hursh, Heidi, and Jonathan Fore. *Global Issues for the 90s.* Denver, Colo.: Center for Teaching International Relations, 1993. 149 pp.

Institute of Advanced Projects. East-West Center, Honolulu, Hawaii, and International Programs, Michigan State University. *The International Programs of American Universities: An Inventory and Analysis.* 2nd ed. East Lansing: Michigan State University, 1966. 466 pp.

Jacobson, Harold K. "International Cooperation in the Twenty-first Century: Familiar Problems and New Challenges." *International Studies Review* 1, 1 (1997): 51–68.

Jameson, Fredric, and Masao Miyoshi, eds. *The Cultures of Globalization.* Durham, N.C.: Duke University Press, 1998. 393 pp.

Jancar-Webster, Barbara. "Environmental Studies: State of the Discipline." *International Studies Notes* 18 (Fall 1993): 1–4.

Jancar-Webster, Barbara. "An Overview of Area." *International Studies Notes* 19 (Fall 1994): 52–57.

Johnson, C. "Preconception vs. Observation, or the Contributions of Rational Choice Theory and Area Studies to Contemporary Political Science." *PS: Political Science and Politics* 30 (June 1997): 170–174.

Johnson, Donald. "Academic and Intellectual Foundations of Teacher Education in Global Perspectives." *Theory into Practice* 32 (Winter 1993). 3–13.

Kacowicz, Arie. "Teaching International Relations in a Changing World: Four Approaches." *PS: Political Science and Politics* 26 (March 1993): 76–81.

Karp, Basil. "Toward a Global Perspective in Education." *International Studies Notes* 14 (Winter 1989): 2–4.

Karp, Ivan. "Does Theory Travel? Area Studies and Cultural Studies." *Africa Today* 44 (July–September 1997): 281–295.

Keller, William W., and Louis W. Pauly. "Globalization at Bay." *Current History* 96 (November 1997): 370–376.

Kennedy, Paul. "Preparing for the 21st Century: Winners and Losers." *New York Review of Books* (February 11, 1993): 32–44.

Keohane, Robert O., and Lisa L. Martin. "The Promise of Institutionalist Theory." *International Security* 20 (Summer 1995): 39–51.

Kerr, Clark. "Education for Global Perspectives." *Annals of the American Academy of Political and Social Science* 442 (March 1979): 109–116.

Kerr, Clark. "International Learning and National Purposes in Higher Education." *American Behavioral Scientist* 35 (September–October 1991): 17–42.

Khosrowpour, Mehdi, and Aren Loch. *Global Information Technology Education: Issues and Trends.* Harrisburg, Pa.: Idea Group, 1993. 517 pp.

Kilgore, De Witt Douglas. "Undisciplined Multiplicity: The Relevance of an American Cultural Studies." *American Studies* 38 (Summer 1997): 31–41.

King, Anthony D., ed. *Culture, Globalization and the World System.* Minneapolis: University of Minnesota Press, 1997. 186 pp.

King, Charles. "Post-Sovietology: Area Studies of Social Science?" *International Affairs* 70 (April 1994): 291–298.

Kirk, Grayson. *The Study of International Relations in American Colleges and Universities.* New York: Council on Foreign Relations, 1947. 113 pp.

Klitgaard, Robert. "On Reviewing International Studies." *Journal of Higher Education* 52 (March–April 1981): 124–142.

Kothari, Rajni. "Globalization: A World Adrift." *Alternatives: Social Transformation and Humane Governance* 22 (April–June 1997): 227–267.

Kreidler, William. *Teaching Concepts of Peace and Conflict.* Cambridge, Mass.: Educators for Social Responsibility, 1991. 249 pp.

Kress, Gunther. "Internationalization and Globalization: Rethinking a Curriculum of Communication." *Comparative Education* 32 (June 1996): 185–196.

Krombach, Hayo. "International Relations as an Academic Discipline." *Millennium: Journal of International Studies* 21 (Summer 1992): 243–258.

Kushigian, Julia A., and Penny Parsekian, eds. *International Studies in the Next Millennium: Meeting the Challenge of Globalization.* Westport, Conn.: Praeger, 1998. 181 pp.

Lambert, Richard D. "Blurring the Disciplinary Boundaries: Area Studies in the United States." *American Behavioral Scientist* 33 (July–August 1990): 712–733.

Lambert, Richard D. "Domains and Issues in International Studies." *International Education Forum* 16 (Spring 1996): 1–19.

Lambert, Richard D. "International Studies: An Overview and Agenda." *Annals of the American Academy of Political and Social Science* 449 (May 1980): 151–164.

Laszlo, Ervin. "Essential Knowledge for Living in a World in Transformation." *Futures* 17 (February 1985): 2–23.

Leeds, Roger. "Graduate Education in International Affairs: A Discipline in Transition." *SAIS Review* 6 (Summer–Fall 1986): 205.

Little, Angela W. "Globalization and Educational Research: Whose Context Counts." *International Journal of Educational Development* 16 (October 1996): 427–438.

Lopez, George A., Jackie G. Smith, and Ron Pagnucco. "The Global Tide." *Bulletin of Atomic Scientists* 51 (July–August 1995): 33–39.

Low, Setha M. "Theorizing the City: Ethnicity, Gender and Globalization." *Critique of Anthropology* 17 (December 1997): 403–409.

Luhmann, Niklas. "Globalization or World Society: How to Conceive of Modern Society?" *International Review of Sociology* 7 (March 1997): 67–79.

McCaughey, Robert. *International Studies and Academic Enterprise: A Chapter in the Enclosure of American Learning.* New York: Columbia University Press, 1985. 301 pp.

McLaren, Peter. "Education and Globalization: An Environmental Perspective—An Interview with Edgar Gonzalez-Gaudiano." *International Journal of Educational Reform* 4 (January 1995): 72–78.

Marchand, Marianne H. "Reconceptualizing Gender and Development in an Era of Globalization." *Millennium: Journal of International Studies* 25 (Winter 1995): 577–604.

Marden, Peter. "Geographies of Dissent: Globalization, Identity, and the Nation." *Political Geography* 16 (January 1997): 37–64.

Marshall, Don D. "National Development and the Globalization Discourse: Confronting 'Imperative' and 'Convergence' Notions." *Third World Quarterly* 17 (December 1996): 875–901.

Marshall, Don D. "Understanding Late-Twentieth-Century Capitalism: Reassessing the Globalization Theme." *Government and Opposition* 31 (Spring 1996): 193–215.

Martin, Hans-Peter, and Harold Schumann. *The Global Trap: Globalization and the Assault on Prosperity and Democracy.* New York: Zed Books, 1997. 269 pp.

Martin, William G., and Mark Beittel. "Toward a Global Sociology? Evaluating Current Conceptions, Methods, and Practices." *Sociological Quarterly* 39 (Winter 1998): 139–161.

Mato, D. "On the Theory, Epistemology, and Politics of the Social Construction of Cultural Identities in the Age of Globalization: Introductory Remarks to Ongoing Debates." *Identities: Global Studies in Culture and Power* 3, 1–2 (1996): 61–72.

Mayall, James. "Globalization and International Relations." *Review of International Studies* 24 (April 1998): 239–250.

Mazlish, Bruce. "Psychohistory and the Question of Global Identity." *Psychohistory Review* 25 (Winter 1997): 165–176.

Miller, Morris. "Where Is Globalization Taking Us—Why We Need a New Woods, Bretton." *Futures* 27 (March 1995): 125–144.

Mitchell, Michael. "Explaining Third World Democracies." *PS: Political Science and Politics* 28 (March 1995): 83–85.

Mittelman, James H. "Rethinking the New Regionalism in the Context of Globalization." *Global Governance* 2 (May–August 1996): 189–213.

Moisy, Claude. "Myths of the Global Information Village." *Foreign Policy* 107 (Summer 1997): 78–87.

Morgenthau, Hans. "Area Studies and the Study of International Relations." *International Social Science Bulletin* 4 (1952): 647–655.

Nathan, James. "International Education and International Relations: Values and Implications of Contending Approaches." *Teaching Political Science* 3 (January 1976): 115 - 139.

Natoli, Salvatore. "How a Geographer Looks at Globalism." *International Journal of Social Education* 5 (Fall 1990): 22–37.

Nye, Joseph S., Jr. "What New World Order?" *Foreign Affairs* 71 (Spring 1992): 83–96.

Palmer, Norman. "From Retrospectives to New Perspectives in International Studies." *International Studies Notes* 12 (Fall 1986): 56–57.

Palmer, Norman. "The Study of International Relations in the United States: Perspectives of Half a Century." *International Studies Quarterly* 24 (September 1980): 343–363.

Parker, Franklin. "Essay on International and Multicultural Education." *Phi Delta Kappan* 51 (January 1970): 216–281.

Pennycook, Alastair. "The Diremptive/Redemptive Project: Postmodern Reflections on Culture and Knowledge in International Academic Relations." *Alternatives* 15 (Winter 1990): 53–81.

Peres, Shimon. "The End of Hunting Season in History." *New Perspectives Quarterly* 12 (Fall 1995): 49–52.

Perez-Baltodano, Andres. "The Study of Public Administration in Times of Global Interpenetration: A Historical Rationale for a Theoretical Model." *Journal of Public Administration Research and Theory* 7 (October 1997): 615–638.

Pieterse, Jan N. "Multiculturalism and Museums: Discourse about Others in the Age of Globalization." *Theory, Culture & Society* 14 (November 1997): 123–146.

Porter, David, ed. *Internet Culture.* New York: Routledge, 1997. 279 pp.

Prewitt, Kenneth. "Presidential Items." *Items* [Social Science Research Council] 50 (March 1996): 15–18.

Prewitt, Kenneth. "Presidential Items." *Items* [Social Science Research Council] 50 (June–September 1996): 31–40.

Prewitt, Kenneth. "Presidential Items." *Items* [Social Science Research Council] 50 (December 1996): 91–92.

Ratinoff, Luis. "Global Insecurity and Education: The Culture of Globalization." *Prospects* 25 (June 1995): 147–174.

Ray, James L. "Democratic Path to Peace." *Journal of Democracy* 8 (April 1997): 49–64.

Reinicke, Wolfgang H. "Global Public Policy." *Foreign Affairs* 76 (November–December 1997): 127–138.

Rex, John. "Ethnic Identity and the Nation State: The Political Sociology of Multi-Cultural Societies." *Social Identities* 1, 1 (1995): 21–34.

Richards, Huw. "Ageing Crisis Threat to Area Studies." *Times Higher Education Supplement* 1335 (June 5, 1998): 7–13.

Richards, Huw. "Area Studies Lose Their Appeal." *Times Higher Education Supplement* 1103 (December 24, 1993): 2–8.

Robertson, Roland, and Habib-Haque Khondker. "Discourses of Globalization: Preliminary Considerations." *International Sociology* 13 (March 1998): 25–40.

Robinson, William I. "Globalization: 9 Theses on Our Epoch." *Race & Class* 38 (October–December 1996): 13–31.

Robles, Alfredo, Jr. "How 'International' Are International Relations Syllabi?" *PS: Political Science and Politics* 26 (September 1993): 526–528.

Rosecrance, Richard. "A New Concert of Powers." *Foreign Affairs* 71 (Spring 1992): 64–80.

Roseneau, James N. "The Complexities and Contradictions of Globalization." *Current History* 96 (November 1997): 360–364.

Roseneau, James N. "The Dynamics of Globalization: Toward an Operational Formulation." *Security Dialogue* 27 (September 1996): 247–262.

Roseneau, James N. "Governance in the Twenty-First Century." *Global Governance* 1 (Winter 1995): 13–43.

Rossman, Parker. *The Emerging Worldwide Electronic University: Information Age Global Higher Education.* Westport, Conn.: Greenwood Press, 1992. 169 pp.

Roudometof, Victor. "Preparing for the 21st Century." *Sociological Forum* 12 (December 1997): 661–670.

Sanders, Bernie. "Globalization's the Issue." *Nation* 267 (September 28, 1998): 4–6.

Sassen, Saskia. *Globalization and Its Discontents: Essays on the New Mobility of People and Money.* New York: New Press, 1998. 253 pp.

Schaeffer, Robert K. *Understanding Globalization: The Social Consequences of Political, Economic, and Environmental Change.* Lanham, Md.: Rowman and Littlefield, 1997. 360 pp.

Schneider, Ann, and Llewellyn Howell. "The Discipline of International Studies." *International Studies Notes* 16–17 (Fall 1991–Winter 1992): 1–3.

Schott, Thomas. "World Science: Globalization of Institutions and Participation." *Science Technology & Human Values* 18 (Spring 1993): 196–208.

Schwab, Klaus, and Claude Smadja. "Power and Policy: The New Economic World Order." *Harvard Business Review* 72 (November–December): 40–46.

Schwartz, Benjamin. "Area Studies as a Critical Discipline." *Journal of Asian Studies* 40 (November 1980): 15–25.

Scott, Peter, ed. *The Globalization of Higher Education.* Philadelphia: Open University Press, 1998.

Shaw, Martin. "Global Society and Global Responsibility: The Theoretical, Historical and Political Limits of 'International Society.'" *Millennium: Journal of International Studies* 21 (Winter 1992): 421–434.

Shaw, Martin. "The State of Globalization: Towards a Theory of State Transformation." *Review of International Political Economy* 4 (Autumn 1997): 497–513.

Shea, Christopher. "Political Scientists Clash over Value of Area Studies." *The Chronicle of Higher Education* 43 (January 10, 1997): B4–5.

Sideri, Sandro. "Globalization and Regional Integration." *European Journal of Development Research* 9 (June 1997): 38–82.

Sivanandan, A. "Capitalism, Globalization, and Epochal Shifts: An Exchange." *Monthly Review: An Independent Socialist Magazine* 48, 9 (1997): 19–21.

Sjolander, Claire T. "The Rhetoric of Globalization: What's in a Wor(L)D." *International Journal* 51 (Autumn 1996): 603–616.

Smart, Barry. "Sociology, Globalization and Postmodernity: Comments on the Sociology for One World Thesis." *International Sociology* 9 (June 1994): 149–159.

Smart, Reginald. "Goals and Definitions of International Education: Agenda for Discussion." *International Studies Quarterly* 15 (December 1971): 442–464.

Smelser, Neil. "Internationization of Social Science Knowledge." *American Behavioral Scientist* 35 (September–October 1991): 65–91.

Smist, Frank, Jr. "International Education in an Age of Transition." *International Studies Notes* 16–17 (Fall 1991–Winter 1992): 43–46.

Smith, Hazel. "The Silence of the Academics: International Social Theory, Historical Materialism, and Political Values." *Review of International Studies* 22 (April 1996): 191–212.

Smith, Steve. "The Development of International Relations." *Teaching Politics* 14 (January 1985): 103–123.

Smith, Steve. "The Study of International Relations: Geographical and Methodological Divisions." *International Studies Notes* 10 (Fall 1983): 8–10.

Smouts, Marie Claude. "The Proper Use of Governance in International Relations." *International Social Science Journal* 50 (March 1998): 81–89.

Snarr, Michael T., and D. Neil Snarr, eds. *Introducing Global Issues.* Boulder, Colo.: Lynne Rienner Publishers, 1998.

Spark, Alasdair. "Wrestling with America: Media National Images and the Global Village." *Journal of Popular Culture* 29 (Spring 1996): 83–98.

Spybey, Tony. *Globalization and World Society.* Cambridge, Mass.: Polity Press, 1996. 187 pp.

Stewart, F. "Globalization and Education." *International Journal of Educational Development* 16, 4 (1996): 327–333.

Stone, Priscilla M. "The Remaking of African Studies." *Africa Today* 44 (April–June 1997): 179–186.

Sweeting, Anthony. "The Globalization of Learning: Paradigm or Paradox." *International Journal of Educational Development* 16 (October 1996): 379–391.

Sylvester, Christine. "Feminist Theory and Gender Studies in International Relations." *International Studies Notes* 16–17 (Fall 1991–Winter 1992): 32–38.

Tabb, W. K. "Globalization Is an Issue, the Power of Capital Is the Issue." *Monthly Review: An Independent Socialist Magazine* 49, 2 (1997): 20–30.

Talbott, S. "Globalization and Diplomacy: A Practitioner's Perspective." *Foreign Policy* 108 (1997): 69–83.

Tarrow, Sidney, and Kent Worcester. "European Studies after the Cold War." *The Chronicle of Higher Education* (April 6, 1994): B1–2.

Thullen, Manfred. "A Research Agenda for the Internationalization of Higher Education in the United States: Comments, Observations, Suggestions." *International Education Forum* 16, 1 (Spring 1996): 47–50.

Tomikura, Masaya. "Problems of Designing Global Simulation/Games." *Simulation & Gaming* 29 (December 1998): 456–472.

Tonelson, Alan. "Globalization: The Great American Non-debate." *Current History* 96 (November 1997): 353–359.

Turner, Bryan S. "Citizenship Studies: A General Theory." *Citizenship Studies* 1 (February 1997): 5–18.

Vanbergeijk, Peter A. G., and Nico W. Mensink. "Measuring Globalization." *Journal of World Trade* 31 (June 1997): 159–168.

van Elteren, Mel. "Conceptualizing the Impact of US Popular Culture Globally." *Journal of Popular Culture* 30 (Summer 1996): 47–89.

Vestal, Theodore. *International Education: Its History and Promise for Today.* Westport, Conn.: Praeger, 1994. 229 pp.

Waddington, David, ed. *Global Environmental Change Science: Education and Training.* New York: Springer, 1995. 270 pp.

Wallerstein, Immanuel. "The Rise and Future Demise of World-Systems Analysis." *Review* 21 (Winter 1998): 103–112.

Waltz, Kenneth N. "The Emerging Structure of International Politics." *International Security* 18 (Fall 1993): 44–79.

Ward, Robert, and Bryce Wood. "Foreign Area Studies and the Social Science Research Council." *Items* [Social Science Research Council] 28 (December 1974): 53–58.

Waters, Malcom. *Globalization.* London: Routledge, 1995.

Watts, Michael. "African Studies at the Fin De Siècle: Is It Really the Fin?" *Africa Today* 44 (April–June 1997): 185–192.

Williamson, J. G. "Globalization, Convergence, and History." *Journal of Economic History* 56 (June 1996): 277–306.

Winkler, Fred. "The Comparative Approach to the Survey of Western Civilization." *The History Teacher* 6 (November 1971): 71–76.

Wood, E. M. "Capitalism, Globalization, and Epochal Shifts—Reply." *Monthly Review: An Independent Socialist Magazine* 48, 9 (1997): 21–32.

Woods, Ngaire. "Globalization: Definitions, Debates and Implications." *Oxford Development Studies* 26 (February 1998): 5–13.

Young, Nigel J. "The Peace Movement, Peace Research, Peace Education and Peace Building: The Globalization of the Species Problem." *Bulletin of Peace Proposals* [Norway] 18, 3 (1987): 331–349.

Zamora, Mario, et al. *The Social Sciences and International Education: A Reader.* Dubuque, Iowa: Kendall/Hunt Publishing Company, 1989. 119 pp.

Research Guides

Cook, Chris. *The Facts on File World Political Almanac.* 3rd ed. New York: Facts on File, 1995. 536 pp.

This single volume reference book attempts to assemble the key facts and figures on the major political developments since World War II. It includes information on international political organizations, heads of state and governments, constitutions and legislatures, treaties and agreements, political parties, elections, and population. The volume includes a biographical dictionary and dictionary of political terms, events, and actions.

Droubay, Melvin. *Foreign Area Studies: A Beginning Guide to Sources and Methods.* Dubuque, Iowa: Kendall/Hunt, 1990. 124 pp.

This basic volume is a combination of resource guides and a set of research strategies and worksheets for teaching students how to develop basic research skills. The author discusses how to organize one's research and develop a method for one's research. The volume combines these strategies with a basic list of standard reference tools. The author also discusses identifying documents from individual countries and international agencies.

Janes, Robert. *Scholars' Guide to Washington, D.C., for Peace and International Security Studies.* Washington, D.C.: Woodrow Wilson Center Press, 1995. 407 pp.

This volume is a survey of Washington, D.C.–area collections, organizations, agencies, and scholarly resources for peace studies and international security. The volume covers topics such as international law, military history, environmental issues, disarmament, and peace theory. The book identifies over four hundred institutions, including archives, libraries, museums, photo and film collections, and data banks. For each institution there is a description of resources, activities, programs, and products. The work includes a personal papers index, subject index, library subject strength index, and organizations and institutions index.

Kurian, George. *Global Data Locator.* Lanham, Md.: Bernan Press, 1997. 375 pp.
This volume identifies the most important general global statistical source books available in print. It also identifies by subject statistical source books that are available in print. The volume identifies electronic databases, including CD-ROMs, online, and on tape. There are a list of publication by publishers and an index of publications by title.

Levinson, David, and Karen Christensen. *The Global Village Companion: An A-to-Z Guide to Understanding Current World Affairs.* Santa Barbara, Calif.: ABC-Clio, 1996. 438 pp.
This volume is a good starting place to find information about concepts and terms related to global studies. The volume includes over four hundred entries that describe over one thousand terms. In addition to individual definitions, the entries give historical and global significance of concepts. The work includes a detailed subject index, maps, and appendixes of countries, major international documents, and a chronology.

Additional Research Guides

Appiah, Kwame A., and Henry Louis Gates, eds. *The Dictionary of Global Culture.* New York: Knopf, 1997. 717 pp.

Atkins, Stephen. *Arms Control and Disarmament, Defense and Military, International Security, and Peace: An Annotated Guide to Sources, 1980–1987.* Santa Barbara, Calif.: ABC-Clio, 1989. 411 pp.

Baer, George, ed. *International Organizations, 1918–1945: A Guide to Research and Research Materials.* Rev. ed. Wilmington, Del.: Scholarly Resources, 1991. 213 pp.

Baratta, Joseph. *United Nations System.* New Brunswick, N.J.: Transaction Publishers, 1995. 511 pp.

Beckel, Lothar, ed. *Global Change: The Atlas of Global Change.* New York: Macmillan Library Reference USA, 1998. 164 pp.

Brine, Jenny. *COMECON: The Rise and Fall of an International Socialist Organization.* New Brunswick, N.J.: Transaction Publishers, 1992. 225 pp.

Carroll, Freda, and Barbara Zolynski. *Basic Sources of European Union Information.* Manchester, UK: European Information Association, 1996. 95 pp.

Clements, Frank. *Arab Regional Organizations.* New Brunswick, N.J.: Transaction Publishers, 1992. 198 pp.

Colas, Bernard, ed. *Global Economic Co-operation: A Guide to Agreements and Organizations.* 2nd ed. Tokyo: United Nations University Press, 1994. 557 pp.

Deans, Candace, and Shaun Dakin. *The Thunderbird Guide to International Business Resources on the World Wide Web.* New York: John Wiley, 1997. 142 pp.

Economist. *Economist Guide to Global Economic Indicators.* New York: Wiley, 1994. 216 pp.

Fenton, Thomas P., and Mary J. Heffron, eds. *Third World Resource Directory, 1994–1995: An Annotated Guide to Print and Audiovisual Resources from and about Africa, Asia, and Pacific, Latin America and Caribbean, and the Middle East.* Maryknoll, N.Y.: Orbis Books, 1994. 785 pp.

Flemming, Michael C., and Joseph G. Nellis, eds. *Instat: International Statistics Sources—Subject Guide to Sources of International Comparative Statistics.* New York: Routledge, 1995. 876 pp.

George Washington Journal of International Law and Economics. *Guide to International Legal Research.* 2nd ed. Salem, N.H.: Butterworth Legal Publishers, 1993. 536 pp.

Godan, Jurgen. *International Legal Bibliographies: A Worldwide Guide and Critique.* Ardsley-on-Hudson, N.Y.: Transnational Publishers, 1992. 388 pp.

Hajnal, Peter I., ed. *International Information: Documents, Publications, and Electronic Information of International Governmental Organizations.* 2nd ed. Englewood, Colo.: Libraries Unlimited, 1997. 528 pp.

Hall, Katherine. *International Human Rights Law: A Resource Guide.* Queenstown, Md.: Aspen Institute, Justice and Society Program, 1993. 82 pp.

Harris, Gordon. *Organization of African Unity.* New Brunswick, N.J.: Transaction Publishers, 1994. 139 pp.

Hoopes, David S. *The Global Guide to International Business.* New York: Facts on File, 1983. 847 pp.

Huq, A. M. Abdul. *The Global Economy: An Information Sourcebook.* Phoenix: Oryx Press, 1988. 171 pp.

Katz, Linda S. *Environmental Profiles: A Global Guide to Projects and People.* New York: Garland, 1993. 1,083 pp.

Kelleher, Ann, and Laura Klein. *Global Perspectives: A Handbook for Understanding Global Issues.* Upper Saddle River, N.J.: Prentice Hall, 1999.

Kohls, L. Robert, and Lynn Tyler. *A Select Guide to Area Studies Resources.* Rev. ed. Provo, Utah: Brigham Young University, David M. Kennedy Center International Studies, 1988. 47 pp.

Lane, Jan-Erik, David McKay, and Kenneth Newton, eds. *Political Data Handbook: OECD Countries.* 2nd ed. Oxford: Oxford University Press, 1997. 357 pp.

Larby, Patricia, and Harry Hannam. *The Commonwealth.* New Brunswick, N.J.: Transaction Publishers, 1993. 254 pp.

Levy-Livermore, Amnon, ed. *Handbook on the Globalization of the World Economy.* Northampton, Mass.: Edward Elgar, 1998. 748 pp.

Linacre, Edward. *Climate Change and Resources: A Reference and Guide.* London: Routledge, 1992. 366 pp.

Mitchell, Bruce M., and Robert E. Salsbury. *Multicultural Education: An International Guide to Research, Policies, and Programs.* Westport, Conn.: Greenwood Press, 1996. 383 pp.

Owen, Richard. *The Times Guide to World Organizations: Their Role and Reach in the New World Order.* London: Times Books, 1996. 254 pp.

Oyen, Else, S. M. Miller, and Syed Abdus, eds. *Poverty: A Global Review: Handbook on International Poverty Research.* Cambridge, Mass.: Scandinavian University Press, 1996. 620 pp.

Pagell, Ruth. *International Business Information: How to Find It, How to Use It.* 2nd ed. Phoenix, Ariz.: Oryx Press, 1997. 371 pp.

Paxton, John. *European Communities.* New Brunswick, N.J.: Transaction Publishers, 1992. 182 pp.

Salda, Anne C. M. *The International Monetary Fund.* New Brunswick, N.J.: Transaction Publishers, 1992. 295 pp.

Salda, Anne C. M. *World Bank.* New Brunswick, N.J.: Transaction Publishers, 1995. 306 pp.

Savitt, William, and Paula Bottorf. *Global Development: A Reference Handbook.* Santa Barbara, Calif.: ABC-Clio, 1995. 369 pp.

Schreiber, Mae. *International Trade Sources: A Research Guide.* New York: Garland, 1997. 327 pp.

Schwartz, Richard A. *The Cold War Reference Guide: A General History and Annotated Chronology with Selected Biographies.* Jefferson, N.C.: McFarland, 1997. 321 pp.

Shaaban, Marian, ed. *Guide to Country Information in International Governmental Organization Publications.* Bethesda, Md.: Congressional Information Service, 1996. 343 pp.

Sheinin, David. *Organization of American States.* Santa Barbara, Calif.: ABC-Clio, 1995. 209 pp.

Williams, Phil, comp. *North Atlantic Treaty Organization.* New Brunswick, N.J.: Transaction Publishers, 1994. 283 pp.

Wilson, Carol R. *The World Bank Group: A Guide to Information Sources.* New York: Garland, 1991. 322 pp.

Web Sites

Academic Council on the United Nations System
http://www.yale.edu/acuns
> This is the Web site of the ACUNS, headquartered at the Yale Center for International and Area Studies. It is an excellent site for anyone interested in the United Nations. It includes calendar information, newsletters, publications, documents, and links to other important sites.

Academic Research Institutions on the World Wide Web
http://www.aber.ac.uk/~inpwww/res/instit.htm
> This is a selective directory of research institutions, maintained by the Department of Politics at the University of Wales, Aberystwyth. The site provides links to the institutions listed, as well as to other international politics sites and resources.

Action Without Borders
http://www.idealist.org
> This is the Web site of Action Without Borders, formerly the Contact Center Network. It includes links to organizations, news and information sources, and other nonprofit directories. One can search the Idealist information system by organization name, keyword or a variety of fields.

Aspen Global Change Institute
http://gcrio.ciesin.org/agci-home.html
> This site contains information and news about the Institute and global change. It includes a link to a searchable database of article summaries on global change topics, and a list of publications and videos on global change.

British International Studies Association: BISA
http://snipe.ukc.ac.uk/international/bisa.dir/index.html
> This is the Web site of the British International Studies Association, which focuses on international affairs and international institutions. It includes information about the group, links to its newsletter, membership, grants, and its journal.

Canadian Institute of International Affairs Links to Other Sites in International Relations
http://www.ciia.org/links.htm
> This extensive set of links to Internet sites on international relations is maintained by the Canadian Institute of International Affairs. It includes links to sites related to conferences and meetings, electronic publications, educational programs, and organizations.

Carnegie Council on Ethics and International Affairs
http://www.cceia.org
> The Carnegie Council on Ethics and International Affairs is a non-profit organization

dedicated to research and teaching in ethics and international affairs. The Web site describes its projects, such as the Human Rights Initiative and the Environment and Development Values Project, its faculty development seminars and lecture series. The site also includes a partial listing of the Council's publications.

Carter Center
http://www.cartercenter.org
> This is the Web site of the public policy institute founded by Jimmy and Rosalynn Carter, former U.S. president and first lady. The site is searchable by term or phrase. It includes information and news about the Center, and links to other Internet resources.

CERES Global Knowledge Network
http://www.info.uniroma2.it/ceres
> This is the Web site of CERES Global Knowledge Network, a network that promotes environmentally sound product and process development. It provides information on the network and its activities, resources, and members, and links to related environmental sites.

CIBERWeb: Centers for International Business Education and Research
http://ciber.centers.purdue.edu
> This Web site includes links that are extremely useful for business outreach, curriculum development, research, conferences, faculty development in international business, and faculty development in language. The site provides information about CIBER publications and access to CIBERs. The site has a searchable document index.

Consortium for International Earth Science Information Network: CIESIN
http://www.ciesin.org
> This Web site promotes interdisciplinary study of global environmental change. It provides links to various interactive applications, data and meta-data resources, information systems and resources, education and other programs and services, and links to related Web and Gopher sites.

Council on Foreign Relations
http://www.foreignrelations.org
> Users can search the archives of *Foreign Affairs* magazine at this site and access publications, papers, and transcripts held by the Council on Foreign Relations. The Web page also provides lists of research projects, research staff, foreign affairs links, and career opportunities.

Department for International Development
http://www.dfid.gov.uk
> This is the home page of Britain's Department for International Development, formerly the Overseas Development Administration. The site provides information about the organization, press releases, speeches, and other publications.

Devline Home Page
http://www.ids.ac.uk
> This is the online information service of the British Library for Development Studies and is associated with the Institute of Development Studies. It includes a link to the Electronic Development and Environment Information System, which provides information on development and environmental issues, a directory, and links to electronic information resources on the Internet. Also included are links to the British Library for Development Studies catalogue and other databases, and a guide to courses on development studies in Britain.

DiploNet
http://www.clark.net/pub/diplonet/DiploNet.html

DiploNet is a network that focuses on the needs of diplomats in the post–cold war period. Topics include conflict management and resolution, peacemaking, and multilateral diplomacy.

Directory of Economic, Commodity and Development Organizations
http://www.imf.org/external/np/sec/decdo/about.htm
This is a guide to regional economic organizations and intergovernmental commodity development organizations, produced by the International Monetary Fund. It includes agencies, offices, and intergovernmental groups. The links are arranged alphabetically by organization. It also contains other IMF links.

Environmental Research Resources
http://darkwing.uoregon.edu/~rmitchel/envres.shtml
This site was created by Ronald Mitchell, political science professor at the University of Oregon. It is an extensive list of links arranged by topic on environmental organizations and issues.

Gateway to World History
http://www.hartford-hwp.com/gateway
This is a collection of Internet resources on world history. This site provides links to history-related sites, including sites covering various topics, geographic areas, images, electronic documents, history departments, and other resources.

Global Applied Research Network: GARNET
http://info.lut.ac.uk/departments/cv/wedc/garnet/grntweb.html
This site points to sites related to international applied research. It includes an archive, news, and information about the network. It also provides information about the GARNET electronic discussion group, newsletters, and other publications.

Global Business Network
http://www.gbn.org/home.html
This site includes links to organizations and individuals affiliated with the Global Business Network. This site provides information about the network's programs, consulting and educational services, and book club.

Global Change Master Directory
http://gomd.gsfc.nasa.gov
Maintained by NASA, this is a directory of information and data sources about earth sciences. The site includes links to earth science sites, as well as other related sites and resources. There also is a global change conference calendar.

GlobalLink
http://www.meshdesign.com/globallink
This site serves as a guide for locating international relations resources. It contains links to organizations, and to news and information sources.

Greenpeace USA
http://www.greenpeaceusa.org
This is the official Web site of Greenpeace USA. The site provides information and news about the organization, with links to other sites on related topics.

IAN Web Resources—Area Studies Resources
http://info.pitt.edu/~ian/resource/area.htm
This Web site, organized by the International Affairs Network, sponsored by the University of Pittsburgh, is a concise listing of area studies, institutes, networks, and other sources. It is arranged alphabetically by area and also has sections for related links. Other important sections of the overall site include individual countries, international organizations, primary documents, and university centers.

Information Technology and International Affairs
http://library.lib.binghamton.edu/subjects/polsci/infotech.html
    Maintained by the Binghamton University Libraries, this site provides an introduc-
    tion that describes the effects of information technology on international relations. It
    also links to sites related to current issues, treaties, and other contemporary issues in
    international technology.

Institute for Global Communications
http://www.igc.org/igc/index.html
    This is the Web site of the Institute for Global Communications. The site provides
    links to sites of the IGC, news, and projects. It includes an online directory of member
    organizations. The site is searchable, using the Excite! search engine.

Institute of Development Studies
http://www.ids.ac.uk/ids/ids.html
    This is the home page of the Institute of Development Studies, a research, teaching,
    and information center at the University of Sussex. It provides information and news
    about the institute and its activities. There also is information about IDS publications,
    and a Virtual Bookshop.

InterAction: American Council for Voluntary International Action
http://www.interaction.org
    This is the searchable Web page of the American Council for Voluntary International
    Action, a coalition of more than 150 non-profit organizations. This site includes links
    to sites of InterAction members, and various international topics.

International Business Resources on the World Wide Web
http://ciber.bus.msu.edu/busres.htm
    This site, maintained by the Center for International Business Education and Re-
    search at Michigan State University, provides links to news sources and periodicals,
    journals, research papers and articles, regional or country-specific information, in-
    ternational trade information, statistical data and information, government sources,
    and other indexes of business information. The site has a search capability to search
    by keyword.

International Commerce
http://www.icg.org/intelweb/commerce.html
    This site links to major international commerce sites such as CNN Financial network,
    EBN, *The Economist,* Nijenrode, National Trade Databank, FedWorld, World Bank/
    International Monetary Fund, and many other sites. It also is possible to search the site
    by keyword.

International Development Studies Network: IDSNet
http://www.idsnet.org
    Based in Canada, the IDSNet project supports international development educational
    programs around the world. This site includes lecture series essays, submitted papers,
    a public bulletin board, news links, and links to participating and related institutions
    and organizations.

International Institute for Sustainable Development: IISDnet
http://iisd.ca
    This is the Web page of the International Institute for Sustainable Development. It
    includes many internal links related to business, policy, and education, as well as
    institute publications. It also includes links to other sustainable development organi-
    zations and information services.

International Interactive Video Site Directory
http://www.indiana.edu/~global/giantproject.htm

This is a project of Indiana University's Center for the Study of Global Change's Global Interactive Academic Network (GIANT), which is a virtual academic community of scholars and students from around the world. This directory is a listing of more than 700 overseas interactive compressed video (IAV) sites in 64 countries. Included in the directory are foreign colleges and universities, governmental institutions, multinational corporations, and other businesses that allow public access to interactive video technology. Searches can be done by city or country. The directory includes technical data on IAV equipment, contact information, and other relevant materials, and is updated on a weekly basis. The site also lists links to other Web directories and sites that provide information on videoconferencing.

International Political Economy Network: IPNet
http://csf.Colorado.EDU/ipe
This site is sponsored by the International Political Economy Section of the International Studies Association. Its focus is on global political economy, with links to the IPNet electronic discussion group, archives, and bookstore, as well as subscriber home pages and education related sites.

International Relations
http://www.carleton.ca/polisci/graduate/intrel.html
Maintained by the Carleton University Department of Political Science, this site links to general international relations, international political economy, and international integration and organization. Other links relate to conflict and security, development, and journals and other publications.

International Relations Internet Sites: University of British Columbia Library
http://www.library.ubc.ca/poli/international.html
This site provides links to Internet sites related to international relations, conflict and peace studies, international economic development, and international and supranational organizations. The site is maintained by the University of British Columbia Library.

International Studies Associations Network
http://csf.Colorado.EDU/isa
This site provides links to selected networks and discussion groups related to international studies, and is affiliated with the International Studies Association. It includes an International Studies Association membership directory, and links to other associations and subject sites. There also is information about ISA conferences, workshops, and publications.

International Studies Resources on the Internet: A Cyberlibrary
http://www.etown.edu/home/selchewa/international_studies/firstpag.htm
This site is a library of Internet links on international studies. It includes a wide range of resources, such as maps, media sources, government and non-government sites, global and regional studies sites. It also includes various subjects such as business, economics, education, law, and religion.

ISN: International Relations and Security Network
http://www.isn.ethz.ch
ISN's Web site focuses on the fields of international relations and security. ISN is a cooperative project to promote free flow of unclassified information in the fields concerned and to facilitate dialogue and networking within the international security community. It features an annotated collection of links, a search engine, sources on current world affairs, and specialized fact databases. ISN also develops educational modules in these fields, and acts as a platform for networking, dialogue, and cooperation within the international security community.

Marshall McLuhan Center on Global Communications
http://www.mcluhanmedia.com
> The Center promotes the use of communications technologies in the teaching-learning environment. Awards are given to teachers who help students understand how the information age will affect global communications. The site provides information about the Center and its activities.

Member Institutions of the Association of Professional Schools of International Affairs
http://www.apsia.org/member_schools.html
> This Web site lists the members of the Association of Professional Schools of International Affairs. It is an excellent site for colleges and universities specializing in international affairs.

National Institute for Research Advancement's World Directory of Think Tanks
http://www.nira.go.jp/ice/tt-info/nwdtt96
> This is an international directory of public policy institutes, or think tanks, maintained by the National Institute for Research Advancement. It covers over 250 influential think tanks in 68 countries. Independent non-profit institutes are included; government organizations are excluded. It is arranged by country.

Online Intelligence Project—International Affairs Resources
http://www.interaccess.com/intelweb
> The site provides access to online foreign affairs information. It includes links to sites of the Department of State, intelligence community, foreign affairs, news sources, and other resources.

Peace Studies Association
http://sobek.colorado.edu/SOC/ORGS/peace.html
> This site presents information about the Peace Studies Association. It includes directories of board members, staff members, and charter members, and links to sociology resources and organizations.

Political Geography on the Internet
http://www.library.ubc.ca/poli/geography.html
> This site provides a list of links and resources on Political Geography from the Walter C. Koerner Library at the University of British Columbia.

Popnet: The Source for Global Population Information
http://www.popnet.org
> This Web site focuses on international population information. It includes a comprehensive directory of population-related sites, searchable by topic, keyword, organization, or by a clickable world map. It covers demographics statistics, economics, education, the environment, gender policy, and reproductive health. It also provides links to sites of government and international organizations, non-governmental organizations, university centers, associations, and discussion groups.

Resources for the Future
http://www.rff.org
> Resources for the Future is a nonprofit and nonpartisan organization, based in Washington, D.C., that conducts independent research on environmental and natural resource issues related to economics and other social sciences. This site provides information on research projects, upcoming events, resources, and funding.

Ronald Mitchell's Home Pages—International Research Resources
http://darkwing.uoregon.edu/~rmitchel/othres.shtml
> This Web site was created by Professor Ronald Mitchell at the University of Oregon Department of Political Science. It is an extensive list of links to resources related to

various aspects of international research, as well as links to Mitchell's other home pages.

Stockholm International Peace Research Institute: SIPRI
http://www.sipri.se
This is the home page of the Stockholm International Peace Research Institute, which focuses on international peace and security. It provides information about the institute, its research, publications, and activities. It also includes links to the library, an article database, various organizations, and selected Swedish sites.

Thunderbird International Resources
http://www.t-bird.edu/ibic
This site is part of the Web site of the American Graduate School of International Management. Maintained by Thunderbird's International Business Information Centre, it provides various information resources appropriate for international research and education, particularly related to business. Includes links to related Internet sites.

Trade Compass
http://www.tradecompass.com
This is the home page of Trade Compass, an Internet-based resource that offers products and services that facilitate international commerce via the Internet. This site provides global trade information, import/export, trade leads, logistics, research, and E-commerce information. In addition, the site is searchable by keyword.

Weatherhead Center for International Affairs—International Affairs Resources
http://data.fas.harvard.edu/cfia/links
This is part of the Web site of Harvard University's Weatherhead Center for International Affairs. It is quite an extensive list of online international affairs resources. These include government and non-government, educational organizations, and news sites.

Woodrow Wilson International Center for Scholars
http://wwlcs.si.edu
This is the Web site of the Woodrow Wilson International Center for Scholars. The site provides information and news about the center, and links to sites of related interests. It includes a directory of programs, projects, staff and board members.

World Policy Institute
http://worldpolicy.org/
The World Policy Institute, now part of the New School for Social Research, provides tables of contents for current issues of *World Policy Journal,* descriptions of its programs, and a list of fellows. A statement of its aims and its 1998 calendar also are included, as are descriptions of and links to its Arms Trade Research Center, the North American Project, and other projects. The North America Project page provides links to reports on Democracy and Human Rights in Mexico, the U.S., Haiti, and Guatemala, the International Bill of Rights, a page on human rights and the environment, and another on the death penalty.

World Resources Institute
http://www.wri.org
This site provides information and news about the World Resources Institute and its activities. It has links to many sites that focus on the environment. It also includes a list of publications on the global environment, links to World Resources Institute Web sites and external sites on various topics, and topic and geographical indexes.

Worldwatch Institute
http://www.worldwatch.org

The Worldwatch Institute promotes environmentally sustainable development by providing information and raising public awareness of global environmental threats. This site provides information about the Institute. Highlights from each issue of their *World-Watch* magazine, subscription information, annual indexes, press releases, and a catalog of publications can be accessed at this site.

World-Wide Web Virtual Library: International Affairs Resources
http://www.pitt.edu/~ian/ianres.html
This is part of the World-Wide Web Virtual Library, maintained by the International Affairs Network. It provides quite an extensive collection of international affairs sites, arranged by type, source, and topic. The lists of sites include brief annotations.

World-Wide Web Virtual Library: Museums
http://www.icom.org/vlmp
This is a directory of Web sites of museums, galleries, archives, and related resources. It is arranged by country and type. It includes links to selected virtual exhibitions and other World-Wide Web Virtual Library Pages.

Yale Library Selected Internet Resources: International Affairs
http://www.library.yale.edu/ia-resources/resource.htm
This is a Web site of international affairs links, selected by librarians at the Yale University Library. It includes a variety of resources: subject guides; discussion groups, mailing lists, and e-mail discussion groups; electronic publications and news sources; organizations and research institutions; libraries; data; reference tools; teaching resources and Web sites, arranged by subject and region.

CONTRIBUTORS *

Fouad Ajami is Majid Khadduri Professor of Middle Eastern Studies at The Johns Hopkins University. His most recent book is *The Dream Palace of the Arabs: A Generation's Odyssey* (1998).

Roger C. Altman, an investment banker, served in the U.S. Treasury Department under Presidents Carter and Clinton.

The Honorable Kofi Annan is Secretary-General of the United Nations.

Benjamin R. Barber is Whitman Professor of Political Science and Director of the Whitman Center at Rutgers University and the author of many books, including *Strong Democracy* (1984), *Jihad vs. McWorld* (1995), and *A Place for Us* (1998)

Tamara Bell is a consultant in the Environment and Natural Resources Division of the World Bank's Economic Development Institute.

Peter L. Berger is Professor of Sociology and Director of the Institute for the Study of Economic Culture at Boston University, which conducts research in several countries on the relationship of culture and social change.

John R. Bowen is Professor of Anthropology and Chair of the Program in Social Thought and Analysis at Washington University in St. Louis.

Janet Ceglowski is Associate Professor of Economics at Bryn Mawr College, Bryn Mawr, Pennsylvania.

Joseph F. Coates is President of the futures consulting firm Coates

---

* Wherever possible, biographical notes have been updated from those in the journals in which the articles originally appeared.

and Jarratt, Inc. He is adjunct faculty at the George Washington University and teaches courses on the future and technology.

Gurcharan Das is Vice President and Managing Director of world-wide strategic planning for health and beauty care at Procter & Gamble, and former chairman and managing director of Procter & Gamble, India.

Madelaine Drohan works for the European Bureau of the Toronto *Globe and Mail* and is based in London.

Joshua A. Fishman is Distinguished Professor Emeritus of the Ferkauf Graduate School of Psychology, Yeshiva University, and author of numerous books and articles on language and society. He most recently co-edited the *Handbook of Language and Ethnic Identity* (1999).

Alan Freeman works for the European Bureau of the Toronto *Globe and Mail* and is based in Berlin.

Francis Fukuyama is Omer L. and Nancy Hirst Professor of Public Policy at the Institute of Public Policy, George Mason University. He is also a consultant to the RAND Corporation in Washington, D.C., and Co-director of the New Sciences Project at the Johns Hopkins School for Advanced International Studies.

Robert Goehlert is librarian for economics, political science and criminal justice at Indiana University–Bloomington and library liaison to The Center for the Study of Global Change.

William E. Halal is Professor of Management in the Department of Management Science at the School of Business and Public Management, George Washington University. He has most recently co-edited the book *Twenty-First Century Economics: Perspectives of Socioeconomics for a Changing World* (1999).

Andy Hines, a former associate at the consulting firm Coates & Jarratt, Inc., is a contributing editor on emerging technologies to *The Futurist*.

Samuel P. Huntington is Eaton Professor of the Science of Government, director of the John M. Olin Institute for Strategic Studies at Harvard University, and Chairman of the Harvard Academy for International and Area Studies.

Robert D. Kaplan is a journalist and contributing editor to *The Atlantic Monthly,* reporting on assignment for the magazine from Europe, Africa, the Middle East, Asia, Latin America, and the United States.

David Keen is a research officer at Queen Elizabeth House, Oxford

University. His most recent book is *The Economic Functions of Violence in Civil Wars* (1998).

Paul M. Kennedy is J. Richardson Dilworth Professor of History and director of International Security Studies at Yale University. He most recently co-edited *Pivotal States: A New Framework for U.S. Policy in the Developing World.*

Michael T. Klare is Five College Professor of Peace and World Security Studies, and Director of the Five College Program in Peace and World Security Studies at Hampshire College. He is a member of the Committee on International Security Studies of the American Academy of Arts and Sciences.

Stephen J. Kobrin is William H. Wurster Professor of Multinational Management and Director of the Joseph H. Lauder Institute of Management and International Studies at the Wharton School, University of Pennsylvania.

Michael D. Kull is a doctoral fellow in the Department of Management Science at the School of Business and Public Management, George Washington University.

Walter Laqueur is Chairman of the International Research Council at the Center for Strategic and International Studies, Georgetown University. His most recent book is *The New Terrorism: Fanaticism and the Arms of Mass Destruction* (1999).

Robert J. Laubacher is a research associate for Inventing the Organizations of the 21st Century, an initiative of the Center for Coordination Science at the Sloan School of Management, Massachusetts Institute of Technology.

Ann Leffmann is a doctoral candidate in George Washington University's Department of Management Science.

Eugene Linden is a contributor at *Time.*

John B. Mahaffie is Vice President at the futures consulting firm Coates & Jarratt, Inc. He has authored numerous futures studies for corporations, government agencies, and nonprofit groups, and is a speaker on the future of science and technology, health and medicine, work and worklife, and other futures topics.

Thomas W. Malone is the Patrick J. McGovern Professor of Information Systems in the Sloan School of Management, Massachusetts Institute of Technology. He directs MIT's Center for Coordination Science and co-directs the institute's initiative, Inventing the Organizations of the 21st Century.

Bill McKibben is an essayist and the author of several books about the environment. His most recent book is *Maybe One: A Personal and Environmental Argument for Smaller Families* (1999).

Kenichi Ohmae is Chairman of the offices of McKinsey & Company in Japan.

Aihwa Ong is Professor of Anthropology at the University of California, Berkeley. Her most recent book is *Flexible Citizenship: The Cultural Logics of Transnationality* (1999).

Dani Rodrik is Rafiq Hariri Professor of International Political Economy and director of the CID Political Economy Program at the John F. Kennedy School of Government at Harvard University. His most recent book is *The New Global Economy and Developing Countries: Making Openness Work* (1999).

David Rothkopf is Adjunct Professor of International Affairs at Columbia University and managing director of Kissinger Associates.

Jeffrey Sachs is Galen L. Stone Professor of International Trade at Harvard University, the Director of the Harvard Institute for International Development and the Center for International Development, and a research associate of the National Bureau of Economic Research.

Eisuke Sakakibara is Director-General of the International Finance Bureau, the Japanese Ministry of Finance. The views expressed here are strictly personal and do not reflect those of the Ministry of Finance or the Japanese government.

Anne-Marie Slaughter is the J. Sinclair Armstrong Professor of International, Foreign, and Comparative Law and the director of Graduate and International Legal Studies at Harvard Law School. She teaches courses in international litigation, international law and international relations, and the law and politics of the European Court of Justice.

Anthony Stamatoplos is a reference and instructional librarian at Indiana University–Purdue University Indianapolis (IUPUI).

Vinod Thomas is the director of the World Bank's Economic Development Institute.

Lester C. Thurow is the Lemelson Professor of Management at the Sloan School of Management, Massachusetts Institute of Technology.

The Tupac Amaru Revolutionary Movement (MRTA) is a left-wing guerilla movement that was founded in Peru in 1984.

Fareed Zakaria is Managing Editor of *Foreign Affairs* and contributing editor to *Newsweek*.

INDEX

Abidjan (Ivory Coast), 37–38
Absolute sovereignty, 186–189
Advertising, 95
Africa, 176; anarchy and, 34–60; civil defense
  and, 146; colonialism and, 81–83;
  conditions of, 338–343; conflicts and,
  132, 144; crime and, 21–30, democracy
  and, 182, 185; disease and, 40–41;
  economic factors and, 134, 324–326, 349;
  English and, 428–430, 437; Kinshasa
  and, 410–411; Last Map and, 59–60;
  National Congress and, 421; Nigeria, 39–
  40; population and, 339–340, 384–385,
  399; religion and, 425; Sierra Leone, 34–
  36, 39
African Affairs (Ellis), 144
African Rights (organization), 140
Agency for International Development, 192
AIDS, 40, 339, 343
Ajami, Fouad, 46, 61, 63 70, 483
Akayev, Askar, 186
Akbar, M. J., 10
Alaska, 397
Albright, Madeleine, 118
Algeria: economic factors and, 134; military
  build-up of, 19–20; trends of, 344
Al-Hawali, Safar, 12
Allende, Salvador, 187
Altindag, Turkey, 47
Altman, Roger C., 240–243
Amazon region, 137–138
American Airlines, 291
American Consitution, 184
Amir, Yigal, 151
Amnesty International, 113
Anarchy, 34–35, 141, 149; African model and,
  34–42; cultural differences and, 45–47;
  dead past and, 47–51; the environment
  and, 42–45; future premonitions of, 36–

42; maps and, 51–53, 57–60; a new kind
  of war and, 54–57
Anderson, Benedict, 51–52
Angola, 342
Animism, 35
Annan, Kofi, 123, 123–130, 483
Anopheles stephensi (mosquito), 409
Antarctica, 397
Anthropocentrism, 77
Antichrist, 154–155
Apocalypse, 154–155
Arab world, 51, 68; Bosnia and, 14; kin-
  country syndrome and, 12–14; nuclear
  weapons and, 19; religious conflict and,
  10–11; terrorism and, 151; Western world
  and, 15–16
Arafat, Yasir, 151
Arbatov, Georgy, 15
Arctic Circle, 397
Argentina, 114; democracy and, 182; violence
  and, 283
Armageddon, 155
Asea Brown Boveri, 291
ASEAN. *See* Association of South East Asian
  Nations
Asia, 16, 18; American culture and, 450;
  conflicts and, 132; democracy and, 182,
  185–186; economic factors and, 94, 166,
  325–327, 349, 377–378; English and,
  429–431; environment and, 379–380;
  future of, 77; Islam and, 335–338;
  liberalism and, 168–169, 184; military
  reduction and, 19; population and, 346,
  399; privatization and, 188; religion and,
  425; trade and, 329; trends of, 343;
  values and, 420
Association of South East Asian Nations
  (ASEAN), 430–431
Atkinson, Adrian, 414

"Atlanticist" course, 17
Atmosphere Alliance, 396
ATMs, 301
Aum Shinrikyo cult, 154–155
Australia, 176; region states and, 100
Autarky, 25
Automobile industry, 98
Ayatollah Ali Khamenei, 12, 68
Ayatollah Khomeini, 65, 68

Baader-Meinhof Gang, 151
Baggara people (Sudan), 142–144
Balkans, crisis in, 67–68, 80–81, 84–85, 141, 152. *See also* Yugoslavia
Bangkok: investment and, 97; multinational corporations and, 96
Banks: electronic cash and, 300–303; English and, 436; governance and, 303–305. *See also* World Bank
Barber, Benjamin R., 1, 420, 423
Basle Committee of Central Bankers, 113, 121
Basle Committee on Banking Supervision, 117, 308
Basque Homeland and Liberty (ETA), 150, 157
Battle of Jena, 163–164, 174
Bayindir, Erduhan, 50
Bazargan, Mehdi, 65
BBC, 24
Belarus, 182
Belt, Tamara, 375
Berger, Peter L., 417
Berlin, Isaiah, 183
Bertelsmann, 458
Bharatiya Janata Party, 23
Bilateral trade flow, 105, 108
Biological weapons, 152–154, 157
Bjork, 458
Boise, Idaho, 98
Bolshevism, 161, 176
Bolt, Robert, 188
Bombay Stock Exchange, 311, 316
Book of Common Prayer, 424
Boots Company, 312
Borders, 109; economic factors and, 106–108; globalization and, 118–119; integration and, 102–104; region states and, 93–100; security and, 131–139; technology and, 324; transgovernmentalism and, 114; U.S./Canada, 104–107
Boserup, Ester, 388
Bosnia, 13–14, 126; democracy and, 181; ethnic strife and, 135
Bowen, John R., 61
Bradkovic, Vuk, 433
Branch Davidian cult, 152, 155
Braudel, Fernand, 64
Brazil, 97, 413; cities and, 410; environment and, 380; ethnic factors and, 95; genetics and, 372; population and, 407; urbanization and, 412

Britain: culture and, 459; centralization and, 187; democracy and, 185; education and, 328; English and, 420, 428–436; Industrial Revolution and, 322; internationalism and, 175; liberal democracy and, 184; music and, 457–458
British Airways, 291
British Columbia, 98, 105
British House of Lords, 115
British Petroleum, 291
Broadway, 458
Broecker, Wallace, 398
Brown, Tina, 458
Brundtland, Gro Harlem, 403
Bucarem, Abdala, 188
Buchanan, Pat, 114, 117, 119
Buddhism: apocalyptic beliefs and, 155. *See also* Religion
Burton, Sir Richard, 40–41
Bush, George, 112, 119
Business, 300, 306–308; American model and, 450–452; culture and, 446, 448; cyberspace and, 305–306; Das on, 309–319; developing countries and, 323–349; digital governance and, 303–305; e-lance economy and, 289–299; electronic cash and, 301–302; genetics and, 370–372; insurance, 392. *See also* Corporations; Economic factors
Buttimer, Anne, 57

Calabresi, Guido, 115
California: economic factors and, 94–95; Silicon Valley and, 98
Cambodia, 145; economic factors and, 327
Canada: courts and, 115; culture and, 446, 455, 459; dissolution of, 59–60; domestic protection and, 107; economic factors and, 98–99, 325; English and, 420, 429, 431, 434; NAFTA and, 94, 98–99; National Policy and, 107; regional integration and, 103; trade bias of, 105–106; United States and, 104–107
Canada–United States Free Trade Agreement (CUSFTA), 103–105
Cannes Film Festival, 454
Canovas, Antonio, 149
Capitalism, 161; crises of, 72–73; injustice of, 283; labor and, 284–286; liberal democracy and, 184; neoclassical paradigm and, 73–74; progressivism and, 71
Captijn, Barbara, 432–433
Cardigans, 457
Caricom, 8
Carnot, Sadi, 149
Cartography. *See* Maps
Catalonia, 113, 188
Catholicism, 165–166, 426; conflicts and, 444. *See also* Religion
Catton, William, 385

Ceglowski, Janet, 91
Central America: economic factors and, 378; environment and, 380
Central American Common Market, 8
Central Leading Group, 447
Centralization, 187–188
Centre National de la Cinématographie, 459
Cetron, Marvin J., 356, 367
Ceylon, 82. *See also* Sri Lanka
Chaebol (conglomerates), 327
Chaos, 140; alternative systems and, 141–142; conflict and, 142–144; protection and, 145–146; state and, 146–147; war privatization and, 144–145
Chayes, Abram, and Antonia Chayes, 121
Chemical weapons, 152–154, 157
Chicago, Abidjan, 37–38
China, 11, 15, 18; centralized states and, 187; conflicts and, 132; culture and, 446–447; economic factors and, 73, 94–95, 134, 330; English and, 428, 437; environment and, 45, 386, 400; expansionism and, 176–177; income and, 386; internationalism and, 174; liberalism and, 169–171; liberty and, 193; military build-up of, 19–20; multinational corporations and, 96; population and, 384, 407–408, 414, region states and, 100; religion and, 425; urban growth and, 411–412
Chirac, Jacques, 432, 436
Christianity, 67, 425, 427; apocalyptic beliefs and, 154–155; conflicts and, 142, 444; fundamentalism and, 173; internationalism and, 175–176; superficial, 35; vs Islam, 10–11, 46–47. *See also* Religion
Christopher, Warren, 119
Chrysler Corporation, 291
CIA, 426
Cities: disease and, 406–410; hope and, 412–415; Kinshasa, 410–411; mismeasurement and, 407–408; swollen, 411–412
Civilization: cultural differences and, 45–47; Jihad vs. McWorld and, 23–33; religious differences and, 8–12; universal, 15–16
Civilizations: Confucian-Islamic Connection and, 18–20; cultural fault lines and, 8–12, 45–47; Jihad vs. McWorld and, 23–33; kin-country syndrome and, 12–14; nature of, 4–5; next conflict pattern of, 3–4; progressivism and, 71–78; reasons for clashes of, 5–8; religion and, 8–12; torn countries and, 16–18; Western implications and, 15–16, 20–21
Clash of Civilizations and the New World Order, The (Huntington), 114
Clash of Civilizations?, The (Huntington), 444
Clash of Civilizations and the Remaking of World Order (Huntington), 420
Clausewitz, Carl von, 55
Clinton, Bill, 99–100, 401, 449, 452;

globalization and, 118; terrorism and, 149; transgovernmentalism and, 114
Coates, Joseph F., 321
Cohen, Joel, 387, 391
Cold War, 4, 8, 19, 78; aftermath of, 140–141; commemoration of, 161; fault lines and, 131; ideology and, 42–43; progressivism and, 71–72
Colombia, 380
Colonialism, legacy of, 81–83
Columbia Corporation, 98, 456
Comity of nations, 117
Committee on Human Rights, 113
Common Market, 163, 176, 178
Communism, 140–141, 147, 172, 176
Compaq, 291
Computers, 358, 364–366
Confederal option, 31–33
Conflicts, 3, 415; Africa and, 341–342; anarchy and, 34–60; Bosnia and, 126; cartography and, 57–60, 138–139; colonialism and, 81–83; culture and, 444–445, 454–460; demographic schisms and, 136–137; economic factors and, 134–135; elitism and, 146–147; environmental issues and, 42–45, 137–138; ethnic, 12, 79–89, 95, 135–136, 189–191, 444–445; fear and, 83–85; future wars and, 3–4, 54–57, 131–133; history and, 178; Kinshasa and, 410–411; Middle East and, 336–337; modernization and, 64–66; organized chaos and, 140–148; political choice and, 87–88; religion and, 444–445; Rwanda and, 126; state and, 125; threat from within and, 131–134; trade and, 127–128; Van Creveld on, 54–57, 140–141, West vs. Islam, 9–10
Confucian-Islamic Connection, 18–21, 66
Conrad, Joseph, 63
Constitutionalism, 183, 193
Consumer prices, 105–106
Coon, Carleton Stevens, 49–50
Corporations, 456; culture and, 446; e-lance economy and, 289–299; imperialism and, 284; medievalism and, 113; multinational, 96, 98–99. *See also* Business
Cosby Show, The, 26
Costa Rica, 380
Courts, 114–116
Crime, 113; cities and, 409; electronic, 157; genetics and, 368; war and, 144–145
Croats, 80–81, 84–85
Crystal, David, 429–430, 432, 434
Cuba, 133
Culture: Broadway and, 458; Davos, 420–424, 426; Evangelical Protestantism and, 425–427; future conflicts and, 3–4; globalization and, 419–427, 448–450; Hollywood and, 456–457; identity and, 452–453; imperialism and, 443–453; McWorld and,

423–425; protectionism and, 458; U.S. influence and, 454–460. *See also* Civilizations
Curitiba, Brazil, 413
Currency exchange, 107–108
CUSFTA. *See* Canada–United States Free Trade Agreement
Cyberspace, 305–306. *See also* Electronic cash; Internet
Cyberwarfare, 156–157

Daft Punk, 457
Daimler-Benz, 291
Das, Gurcharan, 287
Davos Economic Forum, 420–424, 426, 431
Débrouil-toi (self-sufficiency), 411
Deforestation, 137–138
Delphi technique, 355–356
Democracy, 10, 18, 128, 147; absolute sovereignty and, 186–189; American path of, 191–192; capitalism and, 27, 72; confederal option and, 31–33; conflict and, 189–191; constrainment of, 328; darkening future of, 29–31; discontents of, 193–194; foreign policy and, 192–193; globalization and, 118; ideology and, 161; liberal, 184–186; liberty and, 182–184; next wave and, 181–182; peace and, 190–191; rise of illiberal, 181–195; Russia and, 73; transgovernmentalism and, 119–120
Demographic schisms. *See* Schisms
Deng Xiaoping, 11, 412
Denver, Colorado, 98
Deudney, Daniel, 44
Development Planning Unit, 414
Dhahran bombing, 149
Diamond, Larry, 185
Digital Corporation, 291
Diogenes, 309
Disaggregation, 120–121
Discretionary income, 99
Disease, 40–41; cities and, 409–410; ebola, 154; malaria, 40–41, 409
Disintermediation, 307
Disney Corporation, 454–456
Distant Mirror, A (Tuchman), 145
Diversity, ethnic, 85
Djamboleka, Patrice, 411
Djindjic, Zoran, 433
DNA, 368, 372
Doyle, Michael, 190
Drohan, Madelaine, 417
DVUs (digital value units), 302–303

"Earth as Transformed by Human Actions, The" (symposium), 392
Earth Day, 393, 401
East Timor, 85–86
Easterbrook, Gregg, 405

Ebola virus, 154
Ecole Pratique des Hautes Etudes, 163
Ecological imperative, 24, 27
Economic Cooperation Organization, 7
Economic factors: American model and, 450–452; Asia and, 94–95; borderless world and, 101–111; conflicts and, 134–135; Das on, 309–319; developing countries and, 324–349; discrepancy and, 324–328; e-lance and, 289–299; electronic cash and, 300–308; environment and, 377–382; genetics and, 369; globalization and, 127, 448–450; government and, 96–99; IMF and, 15; integration and, 102–104; liberalization and, 128; Marxism-Leninism and, 170; materialism and, 165–166; modernization and, 6; national savings and, 328; nation state and, 93; privatization and, 188; regionalism and, 7, 93–100; shortcomings and, 74–76; Thailand and, 126; U.S. and Japan, 11–12; war and, 144–145; zones and, 93–94
Economist, The (magazine), 418, 454–460
ECO-OK, 380
Ecumenism, 420
Education, 328; Africa and, 342–343; Egypt and, 337; English and, 433–434; females and, 378; forecast of, 359–361; Latin America and, 334; labor and, 327
Egypt, 58, 336; education and, 337; modernization and, 65; population and, 345; trends of, 344
Ehrlich, Paul, 387, 391, 399
Ekagrata, 312
El Niño, 398
El Salvador, 380, 400
E-lancing: business and, 290–293; future and, 297–298; Linux and, 289–290; management and, 295–297; the temporary company and, 293–295
Electronic cash, 300–302, 307–308; geography and, 305–306; governance and, 303–305
Elitism, 146–147
Elliot, Jonathan, 284
Ellis, Stephen, 144
Employment. *See* Economic factors
Empress Elizabeth, 149
Encryption, 304, 307
End of Nature, The (McKibben), 394
Engels, Friedrich, 387
England. *See* Britain
English, 448; future and, 440–442; globalization and, 448–449; imperialism and, 426–427; influence of, 428–436
English as a Global Language (Crystal), 429
Enlargement policy, 114
Entertainment industry, U.S., 26, 454–457; finances of, 98
Environment, 72; decline of, 137–138; developing countries and, 345–347;

earth2 and, 391–395; economic factors and, 75, 377–382; food and, 387–391; forecasts and, 361, 363; global warming, 397; growth and, 377–382; as hostile power, 42–45; Last Map and, 57–58; new world order and, 113; population and, 384–385, 388, 399–405; population limits and, 388–391; progressivism and, 77; rainforests, 37, 137; resource use and, 385–387, 400; transformation of, 391–395; urban areas and, 406–415; weather and, 395–399

Environmental Protection Agency, 394
Enzensberger, Hans Magnus, 146
Epstein, Paul, 409
Ethiopia, 328
Ethnic conflicts. *See* Conflicts
EU. *See* European Union
Europe, 18, 21; Bosnia and, 13–14; Court of Justice of, 116; democracy and, 182, 185; economic factors and, 72, 325, 449; English and, 429, 436; environment and, 400; fault lines and, 131; internationalism and, 175–176; liberal democracy and, 184; Maastricht and, 32; nationalism and, 174, 176; privatization and, 188; religious differences and, 8–9; rock music and, 457–458; single market and, 94; trade and, 329
European Commission, 112
European Community, 7, 16
European Union (EU), 113, 119, 420; courts and, 116; European Commission and, 117
Evangelical Protestantism, 425–427. *See also* Religion
Expansionism, 176–177
Exxon Corporation, 291
Eyadema, Etienne, 30

Faculty club structure, 422–423
Fairbanks Daily News-Miner (newspaper), 397
Famine–1975! (Paddock and Paddock), 387
Fascism, 161, 176, 179
Fatwa (ruling opinion), 68
Fault lines, 131
Federalist, The (Madison), 186
First Man, 44
Fishman, Joshua A., 417
Food, 387, 423; population and, 388–391, 414–415
Forecast Project, 355–367
Foreign Affairs (magazine), 42, 45–46, 72, 112, 132
Foreign investment, 97–98
Foreign policy: judicial, 114–116; liberalism and, 192–193; new world order and, 113–114
Forster, E. M., 182
Fortress lobbies, 141
Foucault, Michel, 142

Fox network, 456
France, 176; centralization and, 187; courts and, 115; culture and, 446, 454–455, 459–460; English and, 431–433, 437–438; music and, 457
Freedom in the World (Freedom House), 182
Free markets, 166
Freeman, Alan, 417
French Revolution, 4, 163
Friedman, Milton, 171
Führerprinzip, 31
Fujimori, Alberto, 186, 188, 282
Fukuyama, Francis, 43, 71, 159
Fundamental Orders of Connecticut, 184
Future shock, 155–157
Futurists, 355–367, 368–374

Gabon, 342
Gammon, Richard, 397
Gandhi, Rajiv, 151
Gastarbeiter, 336
Gates, Bill, 446
Gaullism, 176–177
GDP. *See* Gross Domestic Product
Gecekondus (built in a night), 49
General Motors, 294
Genetics, 368; economy and, 369; engineering, 358, 361; globalization and, 372–373; humans and, 373–374; industry and, 370–372; species management and, 369–370
Geographic proximity, 105
Geography and the Human Spirit (Buttimer), 57
George Washington University, 135, 355–367
Germany, 13, 17, 30, 46; centralized states and, 187; conflicts and, 132; courts and, 115; education and, 328; English and, 438; imperialism and, 175–176; internationalism and, 175; music and, 457–458; nationalism and, 174; terrorism and, 151
Ghana, 324
Glasnost, 26, 30, 170, 177
Glenn, Jerome C., 367
Glenny, Misha, 80
Global Information Infrastructure, 449–450, 452
Globalization: anarchy and, 34–60; bipartisan, 118–119; borders and, 101–111; business and, 289–319; civilization and, 63–70; conflicts and, 3–22, 79–89; culture and, 419–427, 443–460; democracy and, 161–214; developing countries and, 323–354; economic factors and, 74–76, 217–319; English and, 426–442; environment and, 377–418; future trends and, 323–374; genetics and, 368–374; governance and, 113; integration and, 102–104; Jihad vs. McWorld and, 23–33; liberalism and, 282–286; new world order and, 112–122, 140–148; politics and, 125–130; progres-

sivism and, 71–78; region state and, 93–100; schisms and, 131–139; security and, 131–139; terrorism and, 149–159
GNP. *See* Gross National Product
Goddard Institute for Space Studies, 396
Goebbels, Joseph, 445
Goehlert, Robert, 461
Gog and Magog, 155
Golden Mountain, 47–50
Gondama, 36
Gorbachev, Mikhail, 170–173, 177
Gordon, Theodore J., 367
Gore, Al, 118
Government: digital world and, 303–305; living standards and, 99–100; region states and, 96–99
Great Lakes region state, 98
Green Revolution, 387, 389, 415
Greene, Graham, 37
Greenhouse warming, 137
Greenpeace, 24, 392, 404
Greenway, H. D. S., 12
Gross Domestic Product (GDP): Africa and, 341; Germany and, 108; Latin America and, 331–332; open economy and, 103; Pakistan and, 407; United States and, 104; widening gap and, 134
Gross National Product (GNP), 99, 324; developing countries and, 325–327; liberal democracy and, 184
Group of Seven, 73, 117, 149
Growth triangle, 94
Guehenno, Jean-Marie, 73
Guerrillas, 151
Gulag, 142
Gulf War, 12, 16, 19, 68
Gurr, Ted, 86

Habyarimana, Juvenal, 83
Halal, William E., 321
Hamas, 150–151
Harvard Business Review, 298
Harvard School of Public Health, 409
Heart of the Matter, The (Greene), 37
Hegel, Georg Wilhelm Friedrich, 162–166, 168
Heilbroner, Robert L., 71
Helmer, Olaf, 356, 367
Helms, Christine M., 53
Helms, Jesse, 114
Hervieu-Léger, Danièle, 420
Hezbollah, 151
Hinduism: conflicts and, 444; modernization and, 64; terrorism and, 152. *See also* Religion
Hines, Andy, 321
History: Hegel and, 161–164; ideological change and, 161–162; internationalism and, 174–178; liberalism and, 167–171; materialism and, 164–166; religion and, 173–174; Russia and, 171–173

History of Warfare, A (Keegan), 56
Hitachi Corporation, 169
Hitler, Adolf, 176, 445
HIV, 40, 339
Ho Chi Minh City, 94
Hobbes, Thomas, 183
Holbrooke, Richard, 181
Hollywood, 98, 293, 455–457, 459
Homer-Dixon, Thomas Fraser, 43–45, 47, 58, 138, 415
Hong Kong, 115; culture and, 455; democracy and, 185–186, 328; economic factors and, 94, 326, 330; region states and, 100; trade and, 329
Horizontal usurpation, 186
Horowitz, Donald, 6, 87, 189–190
Houphouët-Boigny, Félix, 38
How Many People Can the Earth Support? (Cohen), 387, 391
Hower, Wendy, 397
Huntington, Samuel P., 1, 183, 420–421, 444; Ajami on, 46, 63–70; on civilization clashes, 3–22; Kaplan on, 45–46; Klare on, 132–133; Sakakibara on, 71–72; Slaughter on, 114
Hussein, Saddam, 10, 12, 29–30, 68
Hutus, 81–84, 146
Hypercards, 300–301

Ibiza, 457
IBM, 291; Linux and, 289
Identity (ethnic, linguistic), 439–440
Ideology, 6; Cold War and, 42–43; conflicts and, 3–4; democracy and, 161; Hegel on, 164–165; information technology imperative and, 26; internationalism and, 174–178; liberalism and, 167–171; materialism and, 166–167; new world order and, 120–122; progressivism and, 71–78; religion and, 8–12, 173–174; Russia and, 171–173, 176; states and, 8
Imagined Communities (Anderson), 51
IMF. *See* International Monetary Fund
Impannatori, 294
Imperialism, 175–176; cultural, 423, 426, 443–453; globalization and, 284; labor and, 284–286
In the Forests of the Night (Simpson), 145
India: Congress Party and, 151; culture and, 455; Das memoirs and, 309–319; environment and, 400; ethnic factors and, 95, 136; Last Map and, 58; modernization and, 64; population and, 399, 407; usurpation and, 186–187
India: A Wounded Civilization (Naipaul), 49
Indonesia, 414; economic factors and, 94, 326, 330; ethnic factors and, 95; investment and, 97; national savings and, 328
Information technology, 24–27, 113, 356–359, 446

Institute of Global Cultural Studies, 39
Insurance industry, 117, 392
Intellectual property, 119
Inter-American Development Bank, 334
International banks. *See* Banks
International corporations. *See* Business;
    Corporations
International courts, 114–116
International Food Policy Research Institute,
    414–415
International Institute for Environment and
    Development, 408
International law, 118
International Monetary Fund (IMF), 15, 117,
    119, 452; labor and, 286; Latin America
    and, 333; poverty and, 282–283;
    privatization and, 188; Statements of
    Intentions and, 283
International Organization of Securities
    Commissioners, 117
International Red Cross, 27
International Security (journal), 43, 132
Internationalism, 112–114, 118–119; end of
    history and, 174–177
Internet, 307, 362, 364–365, 462–463; business
    and, 289–299; English and, 435; Linux
    and, 289; web sites, 175–482; Web TV
    and, 358
Intrapreneurs, 290
IRA. *See* Irish Republican Army
Iran, 46, 65, 336; conflicts and, 133; education
    and, 328; map borders and, 52; military
    build-up of, 19–20; terrorism and, 151.
    See also Arab world
Iraq, 336; conflicts and, 133; military build-up
    of, 19–20; population and, 345. *See also*
    Arab world; Gulf War
Ireland: nationalism and, 174
Irish Republican Army (IRA), 150, 157
Iron Curtain, 8, 9, 131–132
Iron Guard, 154
Islam, 65, 67, 154, 335–338, 425; Abbasid
    empire and, 76–77; Christianity and, 10–
    11, 46–47; conflicts and, 132, 142;
    Confucian Connection and, 18–21;
    fundamentalism and, 140, 154; militancy
    of, 50; superficial, 35; Western world and,
    9–10, 78. *See also* Religion
Islamic Salvation Front, 134
Israel, 52–53, 115
Italy, 94, 293–294; economic factors and, 93;
    English and, 431
Itoh, 98
Ivory Coast, 36–38

Jacob, Giles, 454
Jakarta, 95, 97
James, Henry, 149
Japan, 12, 15, 18, 21, 114; conflicts and, 132;
    economic factors and, 72, 325, 327, 330,

449; education and, 327; English and,
    431; environment and, 379–380, 400;
    Hollywood and, 98; liberalism and, 169;
    multinational corporations and, 96; music
    and, 457; NAFTA and, 94; national
    savings and, 328; as NIE model, 329;
    region states and, 100; religion and, 425;
    Silicon Island and, 98; terrorism and,
    151; United States and, 97–98
Java, 86
Jews: apocalyptic beliefs and, 155; conflicts
    and, 444; fundamentalism and, 173
Jihad, 23–24; confederal option and, 31–33;
    democracy and, 29–31; Lebanonization
    and, 27–29; McWorld and, 23–33
Jihad vs. McWorld (Barber), 420
Jordan, 336, 346
Judicial foreign policy, 114–116
Juju, 35–36, 45–47

Kabila, Laurent, 429
Kabul, Indiang, 411
Kagian, Jules, 284
Kansai region, 96
Kant, Immanuel, 190
Kaplan, Robert D., 1, 140–141, 159
Karachi, 407, 410
Karl, Thomas, 395
Karma, 319
Kautsky, Karl, 172
Kazakstan, 185, 191; democracy and, 187
Keegan, John, 36
Keen, David, 123
Kelling, Charles, 396
Kennan, George F., 42
Kennedy, Paul M., 163, 321
Kennedy, Ted, 114
Kenya, 339, 342–343; genetics and, 372
Keohane, Robert, 113
Kepel, Gilles, 6
Keynes, John Maynard, 164
Khartoum, 151
Khmer Rouge, 145, 177
Kigali, 410
Kin-country syndrome, 12–14
King Hussein, 12
Kinshasa, 410–411, 415; English and, 428–429
Klare, Michael T., 123
Kobe, 96
Kobrin, Stephen J., 287
Kojève, Alexandre, 163–164, 166, 168
Komsomol functionaries, 423–424
Koranko ethnic group, 37
Korea, 19–20; conflicts and, 133; democracy
    and, 328; economic factors and, 325–327,
    330; education and, 328; English and,
    431; fault lines and, 131; GNP and, 324;
    liberalism and, 169; national savings and,
    328; Silicon Peninsula and, 98; trade and,
    329

Krauthammer, Charles, 19, 175
Kuala Lumpur, 97
Kull, Michael D., 321
Kurdish Workers Party, 157
Kurds, 52–53, 150, 336
Kurth, James, 59
Kuwait, 336
Kyrgyzstan, 185–186
Kyushu, 98

Labor, 107; capitalism and, 284–286; cities
    and, 409; education and, 327; e-lancing
    and, 289–299; globalization and, 443
Lake, Anthony, 132–133
Lang, Jack, 189
Language: future of, 440–442; identity and,
    439–440; imperialism and, 426–427;
    influence of English, 428–436; national
    language question, 98; regional, 436–440;
    translation by computer, 357
Laos, 94
Laqueur, Walter, 123, 149–157, 485
Last Man, 44
Last Map, 57–60
Latin America, 17–18; conflicts and, 132;
    democracy and, 182, 185; economic
    factors and, 134, 325, 331–335;
    environment and, 379–380; music and,
    457; population and, 346, 399; poverty
    and, 282–283; religion and, 425–426;
    Statements of Intentions and, 283;
    terrorism and, 150; trends of, 344;
    usurpation and, 187
Laubacher, Robert J., 287
Law of the Sea Treaty, 119
Lebanonization, 27–29
Lee Kuan Yew, 450
Leffmann, Ann, 321
Leninism, 24, 172–173
Leopold, Aldo, 390
Lerner, Jaime, 413
Lesotho, 342
Less-developed countries (LDCs), 136
Lewis, Bernard, 10
Liberal Democratic Party, 169
Liberalism, 128; constitutional, 184; democ-
    racy and, 181–194; end of history and,
    167–171; globalization and, 282–286;
    ideological change and, 161–162;
    internationalism and, 112–114, 118–119;
    nationalism and, 174; non-liberalism and,
    283–284; Russia and, 171–173
Liberia, 144
Liberty, 182–184
Libya: conflicts and, 133; military build-up of,
    19–20; population and, 345; terrorism
    and, 151
Limits of Social Cohesion, The (Berger), 420
Lind, William, 4, 72

Linden, Eugene, 375
Linguistics. See Language
Linstone, Harold A., 367
Linux, 289–290
Linz, Juan, 187
Living standards, 99–100, 388; China and,
    386; comparison of, 330; developing
    countries and, 323–349; globalization
    and, 101–102
Locke, John, 183, 419
London Observer, The, 39
London School of Hygiene and Tropical
    Medicine, 409
Loral Space & Communications, 446
Ludwig, Eugene, 301
Luxembourg, Rosa, 172
Luzhkov, Yuri, 432

Macintosh, Cameron, 458
McCaw, Craig, 446
McCurdy, Dave, 20
McKibben, Bill, 375
McKinley, William, 149
McKinsey & Company, 297
McMurdo Sound, 397
McWorld, 422; confederal option and, 31–33;
    culture and, 423–425; democracy and,
    29–31; Jihad and, 23–33; political
    globalization and, 24–27
Madison, James, 186, 192–193
Magna Carta, 184
Mahabharata, 310
Mahaffie, John B., 321
Mahbubani, Kishore, 16
Malaria, 40–41, 409
Malawi, 342
Malaysia: economic factors and, 94, 326, 330;
    investment and, 97; national savings and,
    328
Malone, Thomas W., 287
Malraux, André, 54
Malthus, Thomas, 37, 387–388, 393
Man For All Seasons, A (Bolt), 188
Mandelbaum, Michael, 42
Mann, Charles C., 390–391
Manpower Incorporated, 291
Man's Fate (Malraux), 54
"Man's Role in Changing the Face of the
    Earth" (symposium), 392
Mansfield, Edward, 190–191
Mao Zedong, 387
Maoism, 170
Maps, 57–60; lies and, 51–53; new cartography
    and, 138–139
Markets, 24–25, 300, 306–308; American
    model and, 450–452; borders and, 101–
    111; conflicts and, 127–128; cyberspace
    and, 305–306; developing countries and,
    348; digital governance and, 303–305; e-

lancing and, 289–299; electronic cash
and, 301–302; free, 166; globalization
and, 448–449; imperialism and, 284–286;
products and, 102–104; tariffs and, 106;
United States and, 284. *See also*
Economic factors
Marshall Islands, 398
Marshall Plan, 284
Martin, David, 425
Martino, Joseph P., 367
Marx, Karl, 147; end of history and, 162;
liberalism and, 168; superstructure and,
165
Marxism, 24, 161, 163, 173, 423, 426
Marxism-Leninism, 18, 170–173, 176, 177;
internationalism and, 174–175
Massachusetts Institute of Technology, 295,
298
Materialism, 162, 165, 166
Matsushita, 98
Matthews, Jessica T., 112–113, 120
Mazrui, Ali A., 39
MCA, 98
MCI, 291
Medievalism, 112–113, 120
Menem, Carlos, 182, 188
Menichetti Massimo, 293
Mercosur, 8
Mexico, 17; NAFTA and, 94; population and,
407–408; regional integration and, 103;
religion and, 425; United States and, 97;
urbanization and, 412; violence and, 283
MGM, 293
Microelectronics industry, 98
Microsoft, 113, 446; Linux and, 289
Middle East, 335–338; population and, 346;
trends of, 344
Mill, John Stuart, 183, 186
Millenarians, 154–155
Milosevic, Slobodan, 67 60, 81, 84–85, 189
Milton, John, 183
Miramax, 459
Mobil Oil Corporation, 403
Modernization, 6; of Africa, 10–11; armed
forces and, 19; developing countries and,
346–349; ecological imperative and, 27;
economic factors and, 45–47, 74–76;
Islam and, 50; neoclassical paradigm and,
73–74; power of, 64–66
Mogadishu, 410, 415
Mohamad, Mahathir bin-, 450
Molière, 176
Moment on the Earth, A (Easterbrook), 405
Mondex, 301
Monrovia, 410, 415
Montesquieu, Baron de, 183
Moore, Caroline, 429, 432
Moreau, Jeanne, 459
Mosley-Thompson, Ellen, 397

Mosquitoes, 409
Motorola, 446
Mount Kenya, 397
Mr. President, 457
MRTA. *See* Tupac Amaru Revolutionary
Movement
MTV, 457
Multinational corporations, 96, 98. *See also*
Corporations
Mumford, Lewis, 412
Murdoch, Rupert, 98
Musa, Solomon Anthony Joseph, 34
Muslim Brotherhood, 150, 345
Muslims, 46, 67, 335–338, 425; apocalyptic
beliefs and, 154–155; conflicts and, 444;
English and, 437–438; fundamentalism
and, 173; Middle East and, 335–338;
states and, 344; Western world and, 10;
Yugoslavia and, 85. *See also* Religion
Myanmar, 327
Myneni, R. B., 396

NAFTA. *See* North American Free Trade
Agreement
Nagoya City, 96
Naipaul, V. O., 17, 44 160
Namibia, 342
Napoleon, 163
NASA, 396
Nation state, 93–97
National Academy of Sciences, 43, 58
National Center for Atmospheric Research, 395
National Endowment for Democracy, 192
National Interest, The, 59
National Oceanic and Atmospheric Administra-
tion, 395
National Research Council, 304
National saving, 328
National Socialism, 174
Nationalism, 28, 127, 188; corporations and,
291; cultural imperialism and, 443–453;
Europe and, 176; forecasts of, 362;
liberalism and, 174; markets and, 300–
308
NATO, 10, 16, 17, 131, 138
Nature (magazine), 396
Neoclassical paradigm, 73–74
Neo-liberal model, 283
Neo-realist theory, 176
Nestlé, 96
Netherlands, 433
Neues Forum, 30
New medievalism, 112, 113, 120
New moral panic, 141
New Sovereignty, The (Chayes and Chayes),
121
New Transatlantic Agenda, 119
New World of the Gothic Fox, The (Veliz), 426
New world order: bipartisan globalization and,

118–119; democratization and, 119–120; foreign policy and, 114–116; idealism and, 120–122; organized chaos and, 140–148; regulatory web and, 116–118; vs. the state, 112–114
New York Times, The, 396, 404
New Zealand, 176
Newly industrialized economies (NIEs), 326–327; Latin America and, 331–332; markets and, 349; technology and, 347; trade and, 329
Newly industrializing countries (NICs), 169
News Corporation, 456
NICs. *See* Newly industrializing countries
Nigeria, 39–40, 87
Nokia, 293
Nongovernmental organizations (NGOs), 27, 113, 120
Nontariff barriers, 106–107
North American Free Trade Agreement (NAFTA), 7, 17, 94, 98, 103, 105
North American Media Experts, 432
Norway, 403
Nostradamus, 155
Nuclear weapons, 19, 152–154, 156
Nye, Joseph, 113

O'Connor, Sandra Day, 115
OCSA. *See* Organization of Supreme Courts of the Americas
OECD. *See* Organization of Economic Cooperation and Development
Ohmae, Kenichi, 91
Oklahoma City bombing, 156
Olin Institute for Strategic Studies, 45
On Liberty (Mill), 186
Ong, Aihwa, 215–216
Ontario, 105; domestic protection and, 107
OPEC, 24, 27
Open economy, 102–103
Organization of Economic Cooperation and Development (OECD), 97, 176
Organization of Supreme Courts of the Americas (OCSA), 116, 119
Ortega y Gasset, 28, 31
Osaka, 96
Out of the Blue (Petersen), 367
Ozal, Turgut, 13, 17
Ozone layer, 137

Paddock, Paul, 387
Paddock, William, and Paul Paddock, 387
Pakistan, 407; Last Map and, 57–58; military build-up and, 20
Palestine, 336; map borders and, 52–53; terrorism and, 150–152
Palestinian Hamas, 150
Palmer, R. R., 4
Panorama, 140

Patagonia, 397
Pax Americana, 452
Peace and Conflict Studies Program, 43, 415
Peace of Westphalia, 3, 36
Pentecostalism, 425
Peral River Delta, 94
Perestroika, 30, 170, 173
Peru, 409–410; economic factors and, 134; Statements of Intentions and, 283
Petersen, John L., 367
Phenomenology of Mind (Hegel), 163
Philips Corporation, 291
Philips, Kevin, 73
Pimentel, David, 389–390
Politics: economic factors and, 98; ethnic conflicts and, 79–89; future conflicts and, 3–8; globalization and, 125–130, 448; GNP and, 99; importance of choice and, 87–88; kin-country syndrome and, 12; Marxism and, 165; rightist, 141; usurpation and, 186–187; violence and, 189
Pollution, 393–394, 396, 401–404; cities and, 409–410. *See also* Environment
Polygamy, 35
Pop music industry, 457–458
Pope John Paul II, 11
Population, 75, 136–137; Africa and, 339–340; Asia and, 346; cities and, 406–415; environment and, 384–388; food and, 387–391; growth of, 384–385, 399–405; Latin America and, 346; limits of, 388–391; mortality rates and, 345; Muslim states and, 344–345; Western world and, 384
Population Bomb, The (Ehrlich), 387, 399
Portugal, 431
Postel, Sandra, 389
Post-historical realm, 43
Poverty, 282–283
Power, 1, 141–142
"Power Shift" (Matthews), 112–113
Prato, Italy, 293–294
President's Council on Sustainable Development, 403
Privatization, 188; labor and, 284–286
Procter & Gamble, 96, 309, 311
Profit, 141–142
Progressivism, 71; alternatives and, 76–77; capitalism and, 72–73; neoclassical paradigm and, 73–74; shortcomings and, 74–76; success and, 77–78
Protectionism, 98–99, 107; culture and, 454–460; English and, 426–436
Protestant Ethic and the Spirit of Capitalism, The (Weber), 165
Protestantism, 165–166, 425–427, 444. *See also* Religion
Prussia, 187
Pye, Lucian, 5

Quebec, 59–60; economic factors and, 98;
    English and, 427, 429, 432; National
    Assembly and, 117
Quelccaya ice cap, 397

Rabelais, 175
Rabin, Yitzhak, 151–152, 155
Race to the bottom, 114
Racial stereotypes, 59
Rafsanjani, Ali Akbar Hashemi, 152
Rain forests, 37, 137
Random House, 458
Red Army, 150
Reformism, 285
Region state, 93–94; composition of, 95;
    government challenges and, 96–99; living
    standards and, 99–100; multinational
    corporations and, 96
Regionalism, 7, 102–104
Regulatory web, 116–118, 120
Reich, Robert, 74
Relativism, 162
Religion, 6–7, 424, 451; Bosnia and, 13–14;
    conflicts and, 8–12, 46, 80, 85, 135, 285,
    444–445; Confucian-Islamic Connection
    and, 18–20; end of history and, 170–171,
    environment and, 77; Evangelical
    Protestantism and, 425–427; fundamen-
    talism and, 173; identity and, 6; Jihad
    and, 29; juju and, 35–36; liberalism and,
    173–174; market imperative and, 24;
    superficial, 35–36; terrorism and, 152;
    Weber and, 163
Re-primitivized man, 56
Resnick, Mitch, 298
Resource imperative, 24–25
Resources. See Environment
Revelation, Book of, 155
Revolt of the Masses, The (Ortega), 28
Ricardo, David, 283
Rise and Fall of the Great Powers, The
    (Kennedy), 165
Ritter, Carl, 57
Road to 2015, The (Petersen), 367
Rock music, 423–424, 457–458
Rodrik, Dani, 215
Roman Catholic Church, 113
Rome, 409
Roosevelt, Archie, 10–11
Roosevelt, Franklin Delano, 130
Rosenau, James, 135
Rosenzweig, Cynthia, 396
Roth, Rhys, 396
Rothkopf, David, 417–418, 443–453
Runnymede, 183
Russia, 4, 17–18, 21, 188; Bosnia and, 13–14;
    centralized states and, 187; courts and,
    115; democracy and, 73; economic
    factors and, 134, 325; end of history and,

171–173; English and, 420, 430, 432–
    433; expansionism and, 176–177;
    ideology and, 176; internationalism and,
    174–175; liberalism and, 171–173;
    military reduction and, 19; religious
    conflicts and, 13
Russian Revolution, 4
Ruwenzori range, 397
Rwanda, 81–86, 126; civil defense and, 146;
    conflicts and, 143; population and, 385,
    400
Rypinski, Arthur, 402–403

Sachs, Jeffrey, 215
Saigon, 94
Sakakibara, Eisuke, 61
Salinas de Gortari, Carlos, 17
Samizdat circles, 26
São Paulo, 97, 410
Sarajevo, 152
Satterthwaite, David, 408
Saudi Arabia, 114
Savignat, Didier, 433
Schisms: demographic, 136–137; economic
    factors and, 134–135; ethnic strife and,
    135–136; future battle lines and, 131–
    133; threat from within and, 133–134.
    See also Conflicts
Schmitter, Philippe, 181
Schroeder, Gerhard, 436
Schumpeter, Joseph, 183
Schwarzenegger, Arnold, 432
Science (magazine), 390, 393
Scotland, 434
Scripps Institution of Oceanography, 396
Sears, 291
Security: demographic schisms and, 136–137;
    economic factors and, 134–135;
    environment and, 137–138; ethnic strife
    and, 135–136; future battle lines and,
    131–133; new cartography and, 138–139;
    threat from within and, 133–134
Seko, Mobutu Sese, 410–411, 429
Sen, Amartya, 387, 399
"Sepzone," 94
Serbs, 80–81, 84–85
Shanghai, 94
Shariah, 169
Shell Corporation, 291
Shenzhen, 94
Shi'ite Muslims, 46
Shining Path, 134, 145
Shoko Asahara, 155
Siberia, 330
Sierra Leone, 34–36, 39; civil defense and,
    145–146; conflicts and, 143–144, 147
Silicon: Island, 98; Peninsula, 98; Valley, 98
Simon, Julian, 388, 390, 392, 398
Simpson, John, 145

Singapore: culture and, 446–447; democracy and, 328; economic factors and, 325–326; ethnic factors and, 95; investment and, 97; region states and, 100
SIPRI. *See* Stockholm International Peace Research Institute
Skinhead cossacks, 45–47
Slaughter, Anne-Marie, 91, 112–122, 486
Smart cards, 301, 307
Smil, Vaclav, 45
Smith, Adam, 183, 283
Snow Crash (Stephenson), 300
Snyder, Gary, 52
Snyder, Jack, 190
Somalia, 283
Sony Corporation, 98, 169, 291, 456, 459
Sovereignty, 186–189
Sovereignty at Bay (Vernon), 300
Soviet Union: conflicts and, 135, 142; environment and, 390; fault lines and, 131; as Red Devil, 140; terrorism and, 150–151. *See also* Russia
Spain, 188, 431
Speedy Line, 413
Speth, James Gustave, 408
Spiro, David, 190
SPLA. *See* Sudanese People's Liberation Army
Sri Lanka, 82, 152
Stalinism, 171–173
Stamatoplos, Anthony, 461
Stankevich, Sergei, 17–18
Statements of Intentions, 283
States, 1; battles against, 146–147; borderless world and, 101–111; centralized, 187; civil defense and, 145–146; conflict and, 55; decline of, 3; government challenges and, 96–99; ideology and, 8; imagined boundaries of, 51–53; Last Map and, 57–60; living standards and, 99–100; modernization and, 64–66; multinational corporations and, 96; nation, 93–95; new world order and, 112–122; Peace of Westphalia and, 36; political choice and, 87–88; progressivism and, 71–78; region type, 93–100; security and, 131–139; terrorism and, 151; tradition and, 66–69; welfare, 285; writ of, 69
Stephens, Carolyn, 409–410
Stephenson, Neal, 300
Stevens, William K., 404
Stockholm International Peace Research Institute (SIPRI), 135
Strasser, Valentine, 36, 56
Study in History, A (Toynbee), 5
Sudan, 142–144, 336; conflicts and, 133; population and, 400; terrorism and, 151
Sudan People's Liberation Army (SPLA), 142–144

Summers, Lawrence, 391
Sweden, 187; education and, 328, 342; music and, 457
Swiss Re Corporation, 392
Switzerland: banking and, 113, 117, 121, 308; musicals and, 458
Syria, 133

Taiwan: democracy and, 328; economic factors and, 325–326, 330; national savings and, 328; trade and, 329
Talbott, Strobe, 118
Tales From the Garbage Hills (Tekin), 49
Tamil Tigers, 150, 152, 157; apocalyptic beliefs and, 154
Tariffs, 106
Tashkent, 17
Taxation, 304–306, 328
Teachout, Terry, 456
Technological Forecasting and Social Change (journal), 367
Technology: culture and, 446, 448; developing countries and, 346–349; emerging, 355–367; environment and, 402; Forecast's future and, 362–367; genetics and, 368–374; information, 356–357; survey of, 357–359; 21st century and, 323–354; 2001–2010 decade and, 359–361; 2011–2020 decade and, 361; 2021–2030 decade and, 361–362; urbanization and, 413. *See also* Modernization
Tekin, Latife, 49
Teledesic, 446
Television, 95, 458
Tenth Central Committee, 170
Terrorism, 113, 176; apocalypse and, 154–155; future shock and, 155–157; new rules of, 149–151; opportunities in, 151–153; weapons use and, 153–154
Textile industry, 294
Thailand: economic factors and, 94, 126, 326, 330; investment and, 97; multinational corporations and, 96
Third Wave, The (Huntington), 183
Thomas, Vinod, 375
Thurow, Lester C., 215
Time-Warner, 98
Tocqueville, Alexis de, 183, 186, 419
Tokyo, 96
Tongues of Fire (Martin), 425
Topsy Tail, 293
Toronto, 105
Torvalds, Linus, 289
Toshiba Corporation, 98
Toynbee, Arnold, 5
Trade: conflicts and, 127–128; developing countries and, 329; GATT and, 455; United States and, 284. *See also* Markets

Tradition, 66–69
Transformation of War, The (Van Creveld), 54, 141
Transgovernmentalism, 113; bipartisan globalization and, 119; democratization and, 119–120; new world order and, 120–122; regulation and, 116–118; virtues of, 114. *See also* World government
Transplant factories, 98
Transportation, 413
Treaty of Rome, 116
Trenberth, Kevin, 395–396
Tribalism. *See* Conflicts
Tripartite Group, 117
Tuchman, Barbara, 145
Tudjman, Franjo, 67–68, 81, 85
Tupac Amaru Revolutionary Movement (MRTA), 215
Turkey, 13, 16, 18, 46–47; map borders and, 51–53; modernization and, 65–66; population and, 385; slums and, 47–51
Tutsis, 81–84
20th Century Fox, 98

Ulama (men of religion), 68
Ultimate Resource, The (Simon), 390
Umberto I, 149
United Nations, 27, 52, 136, 343, 401, 452; Committee on Human Rights and, 113; Development Program and, 408; English and, 434; globalization and, 130; Intergovernmental Panel on Climate Change and, 395, 399; new world order and, 112–114; pollution and, 402, 404; population and, 407; Security Council, 15; supranational authority and, 121, UNESCO and, 348; U.S. military and, 119
United States, 17; Bosnia and, 13–14; Canada and, 98–99, 104–109; capitalism and, 72–74; conflicts and, 132–133; Constitution and, 184; culture and, 446–447, 450–460; democracy and, 191–192; Department of Energy and, 402; Department of Justice and, 117; economic factors and, 72, 325; English and, 448–449; environment and, 403; globalization and, 101–102; Japan and, 97–98; Last Map and, 58–59; Latin America and, 335; liberalism and, 168; living standards and, 101; migration and, 335; multinational corporations and, 96; NAFTA and, 94; national savings and, 328; new threats to, 140; nuclear power and, 19; population and, 400; product markets and, 102–104; religion and, 425; rock music and, 457; State Department, 402, 411; Supreme Court, 115–116; Treasury, 305; trade and, 284, 329

Universal civilization, 15–16
University College, 414
University of California, 132
University of Helsinki, 289
UNIX, 289
UPS, 291
US Airways, 291
Ustashe (Uprising), 80–81, 84–85
Usurpation, 186–187

Van Creveld, Martin, 54–56, 140–141
Van Mierlo, Hans, 428
Vancouver, 98
Veliz, Claudio, 426
Velvet Curtain, 9
Venezuela, 283, 380
Vernon, Raymond, 300
Verschave, François-Xavier, 430
Vertical relationships, 98
Vertical usurpation, 186–187
Vicks Company, 309, 311–314, 316–318
Vietnam, 94; economic factors and, 327; education and, 328
Violence. *See* Conflicts
Vitousek, Peter, 388–389
Vlahos, Michael, 17, 56

wa Dondo, Kengo, 411
Wales, 94
Wallace, William, 8
Wal-Mart Corporation, 291
Waltz, Kenneth, 132
War: culture and, 454–460; cyber, 156–157; ethnic conflicts and, 189–191; privatization of, 144–145; religion and 8–12, 46, 80, 85, 135, 285, 444–445. *See also* Conflicts
Warner Brothers, 459
Warsaw Pact, 138, 430
Warsaw Treaty Organization, 131
Water, 389–390, 397
Ways of War and Peace (Doyle), 190
Weapons: chemical, 152–154, 157; nuclear, 19, 152–154, 156
Webber, Andrew Lloyd, 458
Weber, Max, 165, 425
Web-TV, 358
Weidenbaum, Murray, 7
Welfare statism, 285
Wellstone, Paul, 114
Western world, 4, 6, 426; capitalism and, 72; conflicts and, 9–10, 132; environment and, 400; implications for, 20–21; internationalism and, 174; Islam and, 9–10, 78; kin-country syndrome and, 13; liberal democracy and, 184–186; military reduction and, 19; nuclear weapons and, 19; population and, 384; progressivism

and, 71–78; religion and, 426; success of, 161–162; transgovernmentalism and, 114; vs. rest of world, 15–16

Wigel, George, 6

Wired (magazine), 290

Wisniewski, Grzegorz, 430

World Bank, 27, 113, 117, 119, 391, 452; cities and, 408; labor and, 286; Latin America and, 333; population and, 415; poverty and, 282–283

World Bibliographic Series, 462

World Development Report, 349

World government: bipartisan globalization and, 118–119; democratization and, 119–120; foreign policy and, 114–116; idealism and, 120–122; regulatory web and, 116–118; state and, 112–114

World Health Organization, 423

World Trade Organization (WTO), 112, 114, 118–119

World War I, 4

World War II, 9; capital and, 284–285; ethnic conflicts and, 81; Last Map and, 59;

liberal democracy and, 184; nationalism and, 176; neoclassical paradigm and, 73–74; population and, 384

World Wide Web. *See* Internet

WorldCom, 291

Worldwatch Institute, 134

WTO. *See* World Trade Organization

Yeltsin, Boris, 13, 17, 18, 182, 188, 432

Yoga, 312

Youth (Conrad), 63

Yugoslavia, 81, 86; civil defense and, 146; democracy and, 181; ethnic strife and, 13–14, 80, 132, 135. *See also* Balkans, crisis in; Bosnia; Croats; Serbs

Yunnan, 94

Zaire, 342, 410–411

Zakaria, Fareed, 159

Zambia, 342

Zimbabwe, 114

Zimmerman, Warren, 85

Zyuganov, Gennadi, 134